The Complete Guide
to Medications During
Pregnancy and
Breast-feeding

WITHDRAWN

7/3/2013

ALSO BY CARL WEINER

Drugs for Pregnant and Lactating Women
High Risk Pregnancy – Management Options
When to Screen in Obstetrics and Gynecology
Normal Values in Pregnancy
Anesthesia and the Fetus

The Complete Guide
to Medications During
Pregnancy and
Breast-feeding

Everything You Need to Know to Make
the Best Choices for You and Your Baby

CARL P. WEINER, M.D., AND KATE ROPE

St. Martin's Griffin
New York

The views expressed by the authors of this book are not intended as a substitute for medical advice, diagnosis, or treatment provided by the reader's personal physicians.

Contents

Authors' Note

W e're glad you picked up this book and are doing the research necessary to make the best medical choices you can for you and your developing or breast-feeding baby. Those decisions are yours to make after thorough consultation with your health-care provider. This book provides valuable information to help you make those informed decisions with your doctor, midwife, or pediatrician. Before you dive in, we'd like to explain a few things about the information you will read in these pages.

First and foremost, this book is not a substitute for current medical advice from your health-care provider. All decisions about whether to take (or to stop taking) a prescription or over-the-counter medication, how much of a medication to take, and whether it can be taken in conjunction with other medications are the responsibility of the trained medical professional providing your health care.

The conclusions of Dr. Carl Weiner, a medical expert and author of this book, are based on the most current information available at the time his research was done, and so it may have been superseded by subsequent science. This field is constantly changing as new findings are made available, and your health-care provider should consult the latest information to make sure your choices are based on the most recent and reliable studies. In addition, Dr. Weiner's conclusions about safety, lack of safety, or lack of information to make a conclusion about safety are based solely on the medication when used as directed by your health-care provider for conditions for which the medication is proven to be effective and not otherwise (such as recreationally or at inappropriate doses).

You will notice as you read this book that there are times when the Food and Drug Administration's (FDA) category rating about use of a medication in pregnancy suggests that a medication is likely safe, while Dr. Weiner is concerned that it is not, and vice versa. The FDA's classification system is typically based on what was known about the drug at the time that it first went to market—which is often many years ago—and it is infrequently updated. As a result, the information the FDA provides is often not helpful to a prescribing physician today. The FDA is well aware of the limitations of the system (which are discussed in more detail in the Introduction) and is currently creating a new way of labeling drugs according to safety during pregnancy.

Note that the section outlining drug interactions usually does not cover every potential interaction, as new interactions are frequently discovered—which is why your physician and pharmacist should always know all medications (prescription *and* over-the-counter) you are taking before you add another.

Throughout the text we mention the results of animal studies. It's important to know that animal studies are not a perfect indicator of how a drug will behave in humans. In fact, some substances have been proved to cause birth defects in humans, but did not do so in animal studies, and vice versa (again, this is discussed in more detail in the Introduction). Doctors use information from animal studies to make educated guesses about the safety of medications.

Finally, keep in mind that you are never alone in facing these decisions. We will explain how to find the expert medical care you need to guide you through this time of your life, and it is our hope that this book will provide a foundation on which to build a safe plan for a healthy pregnancy. We wish you well.

The Complete Guide
to Medications During
Pregnancy and
Breast-feeding

Introduction

WHY WE CREATED THIS BOOK

Since you've picked up this book, you want to make the best decisions possible about the use of medication during pregnancy and/or while breast-feeding—whether it's pain relief for an occasional headache or a prescription medication for a sudden, serious, or long-term problem. You are not alone. Every day, thousands of pregnant or breast-feeding women take one or more medications. Almost all women take at least one medication during pregnancy, and nearly two-thirds of them use four to five different drugs sometime between conception and delivery.

But taking any medication can be scary, especially when your choices could impact your developing or growing baby now or in the future. The safest choice might seem to be avoiding medications altogether, but as a doctor and expert in maternal-fetal medicine, and a health journalist who had to take medication during her own difficult pregnancy and while breast-feeding, we emphasize that taking care of yourself is the best thing you can do to take care of your baby. And sometimes taking care of yourself and your baby means taking medication. It also means finding the best medical care, communicating honestly with your doctor, and being informed, so that you can be a part of the decision-making process. That is exactly why we created this easy-to-use guide—to provide the information you need to make an informed decision with your doctor and to feel good about it.

WHAT DOCTORS KNOW ABOUT TAKING MEDICATION DURING PREGNANCY

The short answer is: not enough. The study of medication use during pregnancy and breast-feeding is one of the least explored and most neglected areas of drug research. In fact, until 1993, no drugs were tested on any women of childbearing age out of concern that they might harm a developing fetus. Although that ban has been lifted, pharmaceutical companies are so concerned about liability that they rarely test new products on pregnant women. But the fact is that pregnant women often need medication for their own health and the health of their baby.

For instance, women with health conditions such as asthma, diabetes, hypertension, and epilepsy usually need to continue medically required treatment during pregnancy both for their own health and the health of their babies. Many women develop pregnancy complications such as gestational diabetes and high blood pressure that necessitate the use of drugs. More and more women are facing these decisions as they choose to have children later in life and are more likely to enter pregnancy with a health condition or to develop a pregnancy complication. In the past two decades, the number of women having children between the ages of 35 and 39 has risen by 50 percent and the number of women getting pregnant between the ages of 40 and 44 has shot up by 70 percent. Finally, some women inadvertently take medications before they discover they are pregnant, because less than half of the births in the United States are planned.

Breast-feeding rates are also on the rise. Nearly 80 percent of moms begin breast-feeding, almost 50 percent are still breast-feeding at 6 months, but only 25 percent are doing so at one year. For women who start and then stop breast-feeding, medication often plays a role. Knowing how to safely take medication during breast-feeding will help many women breast-feed for as long as they would like to. All these statistics mean two things: the number of women facing the choice of taking medication during pregnancy and breast-feeding and the number of women actually taking medication is growing exponentially.

Even though very few drugs are tested in pregnant women, the thousands who take medications provide valuable information about how those medications can affect a developing or breast-feeding baby and a pregnant woman. From their experiences, we learn what drugs are likely safe and which can or may cause harm. Armed with that information, and what scientists learn by studying the drug in the laboratory and in animals, health-care providers can make an educated decision about whether a medication is relatively safe for you to take when you are expecting or breast-feeding a child. Most experts in the field agree that there are only a handful of medications known to cause birth defects, but others can cause adverse effects in a growing fetus, a pregnant woman, or a breast-feeding baby.

But since few medications are tested during pregnancy and many doctors aren't comfortable prescribing them, making the right choice can be complicated. We wrote this book to give you the tools and up-to-date information you need to make a good decision with your doctor.

WHY SOME DOCTORS ARE CONFUSED

Many pregnant and breast-feeding women receive conflicting information on what medications are safe for them to take. Your primary care doctor may have one opinion, while your OB, midwife, or pediatrician has another—and that makes following the advice of any one of them seem risky. It is not that they don't care— it's that there is very little clear information readily available to *them*.

Most of the time when doctors prescribe medication during pregnancy, they follow the guidelines provided by the Food and Drug Administration, but the FDA system to help doctors understand the safety of medications during pregnancy is flawed. Here's a little history to explain why.

A lot of the fear surrounding prescribing medication during pregnancy arose from the Thalidomide scare of the 1960s. Thalidomide, a sleeping aid prescribed to pregnant women in Canada, Europe, and Africa (but not the United States), resulted in babies being born with severely deformed limbs. It had not shown any problems in the animals studied before being released on the market. In the wake of the tragedy, the FDA introduced a letter grading system to help doctors make decisions about prescribing drugs to pregnant women (see Appendix). Drugs receive a rating of A, B, C, D, or X, depending upon whether they have been studied in pregnancy and whether laboratory or animal tests indicate that there could be a risk to a developing fetus. A is generally considered safest and X very dangerous. But the system does not explain how likely those risks are or how good the research is that found them. Even the FDA agrees the system actually causes more confusion than it settles and is currently creating a new one that they hope will be more helpful to doctors and women.

Far too often, health-care providers and patients check only the FDA Pregnancy Category before making a decision to prescribe or discontinue a medication, and they do so without understanding the limitations of the FDA system. Two-thirds of all drugs sold in the United States are classified Category C, which means there is a lack of adequate human data to say whether they may harm a developing fetus. Yet many Category C medicines are routinely prescribed to pregnant women. Category C includes drugs that have been later found (after use in pregnant women) to harm a fetus, yet they frequently continue to be classified as Category C. Less than 1 percent of the drugs sold in the United States are placed into Category A (considered safe for use in pregnancy), and even some Category X drugs (considered the most potentially harmful) are routinely used during pregnancy (e.g. oxytocin, which is used to induce labor). So it's easy to see why doctors can be as confused as you are.

The ambiguity of this system was brought home by a study that compared how agencies in the United States, Australia, and Sweden categorized drugs. Though they use similar guidelines only 25 percent of the 236 drugs common to all three systems were placed into the same risk-factor category. The FDA is well aware of these limitations and is transitioning to a new system, but it will take years to implement. That's why you need good information now.

This A-to-Z guide is based on author Dr. Carl Weiner's *Drugs for Pregnant and Lactating Women,* a textbook for doctors to help them prescribe medication to their pregnant and breast-feeding patients. Medicine is a constantly changing field, and there are many gaps in our knowledge of the impact of drugs on pregnancy, on breast-feeding, or on other medications. Dr. Weiner spent more than five years reviewing, analyzing, and interpreting thousands of scientific studies to create his medical textbook. We have taken that information, updated and translated it into easy-to-understand language for you and your doctor to read together. Even though the information was up to date when Dr. Weiner's research was completed, new information is constantly being published, so be sure to ask your doctor for the most current research.

How Medications Work in Pregnancy and Breast-feeding

To understand how a medication may affect you or your developing or breast-feeding baby, it's important to understand how pregnancy changes your body, how an embryo and a fetus develop, how substances can cause birth defects or other medical problems, and how medications can or cannot pass into breast milk and affect a breast-feeding baby.

HOW PREGNANCY CHANGES YOU AND YOUR RESPONSE TO DRUGS

During pregnancy, a woman's body goes through physiological adaptations that alter how medications are absorbed, distributed, and eliminated by her body. For example, a pregnant woman's stomach empties more slowly and food and medications spend a longer time in the bowel, which changes the rate of absorption of drugs taken by mouth. Blood flow to the lungs increases, and breathing is faster and deeper, which increases the absorption of inhaled drugs (such as asthma medications). And a pregnant woman's blood volume increases by half, which reduces the concentrations of proteins in the blood that help bind and regulate drug distribution and elimination.

All of these changes mean that doses of medications appropriate for nonpregnant women are frequently too low to produce the intended therapeutic effect in pregnancy, or are too high, raising the risk of side effects. Doctors often prescribe lower doses than normal to pregnant women in the mistaken belief this will eliminate any possibility of side effects, but this increases the chance the patient will not get the full benefit of the medication.

HOW MEDICATION CAN AFFECT A DEVELOPING EMBRYO OR FETUS

The possibility of birth defects

A birth defect is a general term for a recognizable anatomical problem in a baby that is present at birth. It may be the result of abnormal development or damage to a structure or organ after it has developed. Nobody likes to talk about it, but in any pregnancy, an average, healthy woman has a 2 to 3 percent chance of delivering a baby who has a major birth defect. That's the everyday risk of bringing a child into this world, and it is beyond anyone's control. For women who have a history of genetic defects or who are living with particular chronic health conditions, that risk can be increased, and taking certain substances, including some medications, can also increase the likelihood of having a baby with a birth defect.

Environmental exposures

The scientific name for a substance (such as a medication) that causes birth defects is teratogen. There is a wide range of known teratogens, including prescription and over-the-counter medications, recreational drugs and alcohol, chemicals, physical agents (such as radiation), and maternal diseases. It is estimated at least 10 percent of major birth defects are due to environmental exposures (such as medications and chemicals or nutritional shortages) and therefore they are, to some extent, preventable. In addition, there are substances that are not known to cause birth defects but may increase the risk of adverse outcomes such as miscarriage, stillbirth, preterm delivery (delivery before 37 weeks), low birth weight, and behavioral or mental deficits.

Obviously, this is one of the reasons doctors are so careful about what medications they prescribe during a pregnancy. The purpose of this book is to give you information on the possible effect drugs may have on a developing embryo or fetus. The purpose of this chapter is to help explain how substances can do that, what time periods of development are more sensitive than others, how the dose of a medication can change its effect, and other factors that play a role in deciding if a medication can be taken with relative safety during pregnancy.

Six factors that influence whether a substance will cause a birth defect

1. Whether it crosses the placenta
The first line of defense for a developing embryo and fetus is the placenta. The placenta provides the baby with oxygen, nutrients, and hormones. Some drugs cross the placenta and reach the developing fetus and some do not. If a drug does not cross the placenta, it cannot have a direct effect on the fetus. Drugs that cross the placenta poorly will typically have less of an effect than those that pass efficiently.

2. Genetic susceptibility and other exposures
Environmental exposures (such as medications, chemicals, nutritional deficits, and viruses) can affect different species and even different members of one species in different ways. That is why a drug that causes birth defects in animals may not cause them in humans, and vice versa, and why one human embryo might be affected by a substance when another one isn't. This is why animal studies are not necessarily accurate indicators

of how a drug will behave in humans. It can also explain in great part why medications that are known to cause birth defects, such as thalidomide and isotretinoin (Accutane), affect less than half of the embryos and fetuses exposed to them. The chance that a substance will cause a birth defect can be increased when it is combined with another substance and it can be decreased if a mother takes other medicines (such as certain vitamins). As a result of all of these variables, there are few hard-and-fast rules about whether something will definitely cause a birth defect.

3. Timing

Whether something can cause an anatomical defect in a developing embryo also depends on when in pregnancy the exposure occurs. In order for a teratogen (again, a substance that is known to cause birth defects) to affect a developing embryo or fetus it has to be taken at the time when the particular structure it can affect is developing. For instance, the antiseizure medication carbamazepine is known to increase the risk of neural tube defects such as spina bifida. Since the closure of the spine occurs around three weeks after conception (or three to five weeks after the last menstrual period), the medication cannot cause that defect if it is taken after that period of time. This is why certain medications may be safe to take at certain times in a pregnancy and not at others. In addition, some medications can affect multiple areas of an embryo or fetus depending on when they are taken. For example, certain blood thinners (coumarin-derivative anticoagulants such as warfarin) taken in the first trimester, can cause a group of birth defects known as fetal warfarin syndrome, which includes abnormalities in the skeleton, an underdeveloped spine and thigh and heel bones, low birth weight, and developmental difficulties. Second- and third-trimester use can cause central nervous system disorders such as spasticity and seizures due to fetal bleeding. For that reason, it is never considered safe to take these kinds of medications during pregnancy, although some medical conditions require their use.

It is generally agreed that exposure to substances during the first two weeks after conception poses very little risk of birth defects in part because the placenta (which is how substances reach the embryo) is not yet developed, and in part because at that point the embryo is primarily made up of stem cells, which have the ability to develop into many different kinds of cells (for instance they could become bone, blood, nerves, or connective tissue). So if some are damaged for any reason, other cells may be able to assume their roles and enable development to continue normally. Or if the damage is too great, the result may be a miscarriage, which can happen before a woman even knows she is pregnant. This is why the first two weeks after conception are called the "all-or-nothing" period of development.

Virtually all of a fetus's physical structures, with the exception of the brain, develop in the first ten weeks after the last normal menstrual period, and most birth defects, if they are going to occur, happen during that time. Brain development continues throughout pregnancy and after birth, which means that the brain is susceptible to environmental exposures throughout pregnancy. Some birth defects can happen after a fetus's structural development is complete because of events such as fetal blood clots, abnormal bleeding or heart rates, low blood pressure, and viral infections. In addition, exposure to certain substances at any time in pregnancy can increase the rate for other adverse outcomes such as low birth weight or preterm delivery (before 37 weeks).

4. Dose

Some substances that cause birth defects will do so only if the dose is high enough, or they will cause more severe birth defects with higher doses. For instance, the anticonvulsant valproic acid increases the risk of neural tube defects such as spina bifida when it is taken around three weeks after conception (or five weeks after the last normal menstrual period), but this birth defect has been seen when women took very high doses of the medication. Women taking significantly lower doses at the same period of time typically delivered normal, healthy babies.

5. How the medicine is taken

Whether a medication is taken by mouth, through an IV, or applied topically affects how much of it enters a pregnant woman's bloodstream and therefore how much can reach the placenta. For example, retinoid medications (often used to treat severe acne) have been proved to be teratogens. One of them, isotretinoin (Accutane), is a very powerful teratogen when it is taken by mouth (which is why women taking Accutane should use effective birth control and receive monthly pregnancy tests), while topical retinoids (such as Retin-A) when used sparingly are not associated with an increase in the same birth defects. This does not rule out the possibility that topical retinoids could cause birth defects (and so they are not recommended during pregnancy), but it suggests that the amount of topical medication that typically reaches the bloodstream of a pregnant woman is too low to increase the rate of birth defects in a way that is detectable by scientific study.

6. Spectrum of outcomes

"Spectrum of outcomes" is a scientific term for the idea that certain substances, such as alcohol, can cause a range of adverse outcomes in a pregnancy depending on both how much of the substance is taken, how often, and when. Those outcomes can include miscarriage, stillbirth, birth defects, slowed growth (also called growth restriction), low birth weight, preterm delivery (before 37 weeks), and mental deficits or learning disabilities. In the case of alcohol, moderate to heavy use during pregnancy, particularly if it's consumed in a binge pattern, increases the risk for miscarriage, stillbirth, and fetal alcohol syndrome—a characteristic pattern of minor face and skull abnormalities, heart defects, cleft mouth and palate, growth deficiency, and deficits in IQ and learning disabilities. Animal and human studies have shown that these outcomes are not all found in any one pregnancy and that they depend on how much a woman drinks and the pattern of her drinking. The risk is also affected by genetic susceptibility and other factors such as the pregnant woman's nutritional status.

Your doctor should use all of these factors as well as the latest research on medications to determine whether taking a particular medication could present a risk to your health or the health of your developing baby and to decide which medication is the best choice for both of you.

HOW MEDICATIONS CAN AFFECT A BREAST-FEEDING CHILD

It is much easier to study how drugs pass into breast milk than to study them during pregnancy, and most experts in the field agree that most medications are compatible with breast-feeding. That said, a lot of physicians are still not comfortable prescribing medications you need while you are breast-feeding. Here's what you need to know.

Similar to the developing fetus, the amount of a medication that a breast-feeding baby is exposed to varies. In order for a drug you take to affect your breast-feeding baby, it has to be absorbed into your bloodstream in large enough amounts to then be transmitted into your breast milk. If it does reach your milk, it then goes into your baby's stomach and, in order to be absorbed into your baby's bloodstream, it has to not be destroyed by the baby's stomach acid and be easily absorbed out of the gut. Assuming it passes all those hurdles, the resulting amount in your baby must be high enough relative to his or her weight to have an effect. In addition, it is possible to lower the amount of a medication your baby receives in your milk by feeding him or her when the medication is at its lowest concentration in your system. All of these factors mean that many medications can be safely taken by a breast-feeding mom without causing any harm to or side effects in her baby.

More often than not, if you are taking a medication that is necessary and beneficial to your health, there will be a way for you to safely take it while you are breast-feeding, or there will be another medication you can switch to during that time. It is important that you talk with your pediatrician *rather than* your general physician (who may not be experienced with how medications affect a breast-feeding baby), ask him or her to consult the most recent information, and then make an informed choice together.

Taking Care of You and Your Baby

Because there is so little good information about how medications affect a pregnant woman and her developing embryo or fetus, even the best doctors can become confused about how to treat medical conditions in pregnancy. If you are living with a chronic condition, develop a medical complication during pregnancy, or have experienced complications in a previous pregnancy, it's important that you have access to a maternal-fetal medicine (MFM) expert—a doctor who, like Dr. Weiner, specializes in high-risk conditions during pregnancy and in managing the health of a pregnant woman as well as the health of her baby. He or she will have access to the latest information on how to treat your condition and how to prescribe medication during pregnancy if necessary.

PLANNING AHEAD

It's always a good idea if you are planning a pregnancy to talk with your obstetrician or midwife before you become pregnant. Your provider can run down a checklist of items to do before trying to conceive, such as seeing if your immunizations are current, testing for HIV, hepatitis B, and whether you are a carrier of any genetic conditions that may affect your future child. "It's a lot easier for people to listen and absorb this information before they are pregnant, when the stakes are lower," says M. Kathryn Menard, MD, president of the Society for Maternal-Fetal Medicine and director of the Center for Maternal and Infant Health at the University of North Carolina School of Medicine. Your provider should also take a thorough medical history to find out if you have any conditions that need to be brought under control before pregnancy or may require special attention during pregnancy.

If you are living with a chronic medical condition such as asthma, epilepsy, high blood pressure, an autoimmune condition, or diabetes, there are many things you can do before conceiving to improve your health and lower the risks to you and your future baby. For instance, getting good control of your blood sugar if you are diabetic will significantly improve your health during pregnancy and lower your child's chance of having a birth defect due to poorly controlled blood sugar. If you are on medication for a seizure disorder or a psychiatric condition, some medications are considered safer than others to take during pregnancy, so preconception counseling will enable you to switch to the best choice before becoming pregnant.

But since more than half of pregnancies are unplanned, prepregnancy preparation isn't always possible. If you discover you are pregnant while taking a medication that is critical to your health (mental or physical), *do not* stop the medication on your own. Instead, see your treating physician and an obstetrician/maternal-fetal medicine expert right away to discuss the medication, its benefits for you, and its potential effect on your pregnancy. It is important that you find a specialist who is comfortable treating your specific condition during pregnancy and is knowledgeable about medications during pregnancy.

FINDING THE RIGHT MEDICAL CARE

If you are not living with a chronic condition and have no history of pregnancy complications, a general obstetrician or midwife can conduct your preconception screening. But if you are being treated for a medical condition, have a history of complications, or develop them during pregnancy, it is best if you (or your obstetrician) have access to a board-certified maternal-fetal medicine expert.

A maternal-fetal medicine expert has not only completed training in obstetrics but also has done a three-year fellowship in advanced care of obstetrical complications, prenatal diagnosis of medical problems, genetics, and fetal therapy. These doctors are also sometimes called perinatologists or high-risk OBs (note, however, that some generalist obstetricians call themselves high-risk OBs without being specifically certified in maternal-fetal medicine by the American Board of Obstetrics and Gynecology). Their training and their clinical experience mean they are more likely to be able to manage medical conditions in pregnancy, are familiar with the latest information on what medications are best to use, are more likely skilled at using ultrasound to look for problems in an embryo or fetus as it develops, and can even treat certain conditions in a fetus before delivery.

"A lot of women get scared away from pregnancy because there are internists who aren't comfortable with managing medical conditions in pregnancy. That's where a maternal-fetal medicine specialist comes in," says Dr. Menard. "It happens over and over again that someone goes to a cardiologist who says, 'Don't get pregnant with your condition.' If they come to a maternal-fetal medicine specialist, we will say, 'These are the risks of your condition, this is what we know, this is what could happen, and this is how we will manage you in pregnancy.'"

How to find a maternal-fetal medicine specialist

The first place to start is with your physician if you see a specialist for a chronic condition such as high blood pressure, or your obstetrician. Ask if they have experience treating pregnant women with your condition and, if not, if they can recommend a colleague who does and if there is a maternal-fetal medicine expert in the area that they recommend you see. Often, in areas where there are not many maternal-fetal medicine experts, obstetricians have someone they consult with when they are treating women with medical conditions or complications. "You don't need to be shy about bringing this up," says Dr. Menard. "Just tell them you would like to see a maternal-fetal medicine expert and ask if they can recommend someone with whom they have a good relationship. That tells your doctor you value your relationship with them and ties them into the care team."

If your doctor is unable to recommend an MFM specialist, most hospitals and academic medical centers have one or more on staff and you can search for them on the institution's Web site. You can also visit the Web site of the Society for Maternal-Fetal Medicine (www.smfm.org), which has a physician locator tool that enables you to search for specialists near your zip code and even lists the particular medical conditions they focus on (although any MFM specialist should be able to address a wide range of conditions).

HOW TO USE THIS BOOK

This book is intended to be a resource for you to understand the potential consequences to your health and the health of a developing embryo or fetus or breast-feeding baby of taking (or not taking) certain medications. You should bring it to your doctor and discuss the pros and cons of taking (or stopping) a particular medication. All decisions about whether to take (or stop taking) a prescription or over-the-counter medication, how much of a medication to take, and whether it can be taken in conjunction with other medications are the responsibility of the trained medical professional providing your health care. And since information surrounding medication use during pregnancy is constantly changing, it is important to ask your doctor also to consult the most recent information available so that together you can come up with the best possible treatment plan for you and your baby.

The A-to-Z Drug Directory is divided into thirteen sections:

- **Brand name(s)** lists the common or generic name of the medication, followed by some of the trade or brand names used for it. Many drugs have many different names but are otherwise clinically identical, and because names change frequently, this list may not include all brands on the market at a given time.

- **Drug class** explains what type of drug it is, such as an antibiotic, nonsteroidal anti inflammatory drug (NSAID), anticonvulsant, antihypertensive, etc. Knowing a drug's class makes it easier for doctors to compare drugs that have a similar treatment effect and switch a patient to a safer medication if necessary.

- **Indications (what it is used for)** outlines the conditions for which the medication is typically prescribed and for which the FDA has approved it.

- **How it works** explains how the drug produces its intended effect. Doctors call this the "mechanism of action." Understanding a drug's mechanism of action is important in helping doctors predict whether the drug can cause problems for an expecting mother, embryo, fetus, or breast-feeding baby, and whether other drugs might be safer treatment options.

- **Contraindications (reasons you shouldn't use it)** includes the reasons the medication should not be used for a particular woman, such as an allergy to it or an existing medical condition. This section covers the primary contraindications listed by the manufacturer, which may include pregnancy even if the medication is sometimes used during pregnancy. It also may not be a complete list, as contraindications change when new information becomes available.

- **Possible side effects and warnings** covers the serious and not-so-serious complications that can arise from taking the medication as well as medical conditions that might be worsened by the medication and for which prescribing physicians need to exercise caution. Because this is a book for women, this section does not mention male-only problems such as impotence or prostate issues. It also omits any corporate liability comments pharmaceutical companies make related to pregnancy that have not been confirmed by either animal or human experience. Again this information is constantly changing as new research becomes available, so your doctor should consult the most recent information.

- **How it can affect pregnant women** explains how much (if any) research has been done into the use of the medication during pregnancy and what is known about how the drug impacts pregnancy and how pregnancy can change the effectiveness of the medication, highlighting any known problems for the health of an expecting mother. Most medications prescribed during pregnancy are used "off-label." Off-label uses are those not approved by the FDA but are generally accepted to be useful in clinical practice. This does not mean the drug is not effective for that off-label indication. Rather, it means the manufacturer did not want to study pregnant women and seek FDA approval for that specific indication during pregnancy. Off-label uses in pregnancy are discussed in this section. It also comments on conditions for which the medication has been proved ineffective and should no longer be used.

- **How it can affect a developing embryo or fetus** explains how much (if any) research has been conducted on the use of the medication during pregnancy. It covers what is known about the impact of the medication on a developing embryo or fetus, including information on how the drug passes (or does not pass) through the placenta, and whether there are any known or suspected adverse effects (including birth defects) on a developing embryo or fetus. Information from animal studies is presented where relevant, but it's important to know that animal studies are not perfect indicators of how a drug will behave in humans. In fact, some substances have been proved to cause birth defects in humans but they did not do so in animal studies (for example, thalidomide), and vice versa.

- **Breast-feeding** includes information on whether the drug enters breast milk and, if known, how much of it enters, as well as whether it has been shown to harm a growing baby. When possible, Dr. Weiner makes specific evidence-based recommendations such as noting when drugs are best used for only a limited period or even one-time use. Your obstetrician or pediatrician should check for the most current information.

- **Potential drug interactions** identifies other medications that should not be used (or should be used with caution) with the medication because of the potential for a dangerous or even lethal interaction. This section may not cover every potential interaction, as new interactions are frequently discovered. Anytime you are considering adding a medication (prescription or over-the-counter) to ones you are already taking, you should consult your physician and pharmacist.

- **What the FDA says about use in pregnancy** is the letter category the FDA assigns to the medication related to what research has been done on the medication. See Appendix for a full explanation of the FDA categories. Note, sometimes a medication receives one category rating in one trimester and a different one for another. When this happens the trimester designations appear after the letter category. You will also find that there are times when the FDA's category rating about the use of a medication in pregnancy suggests that a medication is likely safe, while Dr. Weiner is concerned that it is not, and vice versa. The FDA's classification system is based on what was known about the drug at the time that it first went to market, and it is infrequently updated. As a result, the information the FDA provides is often not helpful to a prescribing physician. The FDA is well aware of the limitations of the system (which are discussed in more detail in the Introduction) and is currently creating a new way of labeling drugs according to safety during pregnancy.

- **What the available evidence suggests about breast-feeding safety** includes Dr. Weiner's assessment, based on the available research, of whether a medication may be used with relative safety during breast-feeding.

- **The bottom line for you** is a bulleted list of Dr. Weiner's conclusions about the safety, lack of safety, or lack of information to make a conclusion about use of the medication during pregnancy and breast-feeding. If there is a concern about a medication, this section often contains alternatives that are considered safer. Dr. Weiner's conclusions are based solely on the medication when used as directed by your health-care provider and not otherwise (such as recreationally or at inappropriate doses).

THIS BOOK IS FOR YOU

This book is your go-to resource. The information will help you understand more about how taking a particular medication may impact you and your developing or breast-feeding baby and help you feel comfortable with the decisions that you and your doctor make during this new, exciting, and, yes, sometimes scary time of your life. Bring it to your doctors' visits, take it down from the shelf when you feel anxious about your or your baby's health, share it with friends and family so they can understand what the research says and why your health is paramount. Our goal is to give you information to make the best choices possible for you and your baby.

A-to-Z Drug Directory

ACARBOSE

Brand name: Precose
Drug classes: A-glucosidase inhibitor; Antidiabetic agent; Oral hypoglycemic
Indications (what it is used for): Type II diabetes.
How it works: Slows the rise in blood sugar after eating by reducing carbohydrate absorption in the bowel.
Contraindications (reasons you shouldn't take it): Hypersensitivity to drug or class, history of diabetic ketoacidosis (lack of insulin prevents body using sugar as a fuel), cirrhosis, intestinal obstruction, malabsorption syndrome (small intestine cannot absorb nutrients from food).
Possible side effects and warnings: Can cause intestinal discomfort and pain, diarrhea, flatulence, elevated liver enzymes, and jaundice. Should be used with caution in women with kidney damage.
How it can affect pregnant women: Acarbose can reduce or delay the onset of type II diabetes in people who have impaired glucose tolerance. There are no adequate reports or well-controlled studies in pregnant women. There are now several reports of pregnant women treated with acarbose. They show success in women whose blood sugars were still high after using metformin and glyburide and this author has had similar success.
How it can affect a developing embryo or fetus: There are no adequate reports or well-controlled studies in human fetuses. Less than 2% of acarbose ends up circulating in the bloodstream, which means that little can reach the fetus. Rodent studies using doses 10 times higher than those used clinically found no evidence that acarbose causes birth defects or low birth weight. However, animal studies are not necessarily good indicators of how a drug will behave in humans.
Breast-feeding: There is no published data in nursing women. It is unknown whether acarbose enters human breast milk. But considering the low level that is absorbed by the mother, it is unlikely that a significant amount of the drug would reach the milk and/or be absorbed by a breast-feeding baby. One study suggested that acarbose might alter breast milk composition by inhibiting fat synthesis.
Potential drug interactions: Interaction between the following medications and acarbose has the potential to impact the effect of one or more of the

drugs. In some instances the interaction can be dangerous or life-threatening and must be avoided: thiazides, corticosteroids, phenothiazines, thyroid products, estrogens, oral contraceptives, phenytoin, nicotinic acid, sympathomimetics, calcium channel blockers, isoniazid, digoxin, charcoal, digestive enzymes.

What the FDA says about use in pregnancy: Category B (see Appendix).

What the available evidence suggests about breast-feeding safety: Likely safe.

The bottom line for you:
- There is a growing interest in the use of acarbose during pregnancy because so little of the drug is absorbed out of the mother's gastrointestinal tract.
- However, oral hypoglycemics such as metformin and glyburide, insulin, and diet regulation remain standard treatments for glucose intolerance during pregnancy and while breast-feeding.

ACETAMINOPHEN

Brand names: Acephen, Aceta, Acetaminophen Uniserts, Anapark, Apacet, APAP, Asidon, Calip, Dapacin, Ed-Apap, Feverall, Genapap, Genebs, Mapap, Maranox, Neopap, Oraphen-PD, Panadol, Redutemp, Ridenol, Silapap, Tapanol, Tempra, Tylenol, Uni-Ace. (NOTE: Acetaminophen is sold in combination with many different drugs, including antihistamines and all-in-one cold medicines such as NyQuil and TheraFlu. Always check all-in-one medicines for the inclusion of acetaminophen.)

Drug classes: Analgesic, nonnarcotic; Antipyretic; Nonsteroidal anti-inflammatory

Indications (what it is used for): Mild pain, fever, menstrual cramps, osteoarthritis, tension headache.

How it works: Inhibits the production of some prostaglandins, natural substances that cause muscle cramps; decreases inflammation.

Contraindications (reasons you shouldn't take it): Hypersensitivity to the drug or class.

Possible side effects and warnings: Can cause liver or kidney damage (especially in people with alcoholism or after excessive alcohol use, and in women with certain inherited diseases such as G6PD deficiency and phenylketonuria), blood disorders such as anemia, low platelet and/or white blood cell counts, skin rash, and inflammation of the pancreas. Acetaminophen does not cause stomach irritation or damage when taken as recommended. Overuse of acetaminophen is the leading cause of liver toxicity that results in liver failure.

How it can affect pregnant women: Up to two-thirds of pregnant women take acetaminophen at some time during pregnancy. At least during early pregnancy, the drug is cleared from the body faster, and its effect may not last as long as it does in women who are not pregnant. Acetaminophen plus a codeine-like drug is better than morphine to control pain after cesarean delivery. Chronic abuse and overdose are the most typical problems, and acetaminophen poisoning is one the most common causes of liver failure and liver transplantation. In one study of pregnant women using this group of drugs in the first trimester, the prenatal use of other painkillers—ibuprofen, naproxen, and aspirin—increased the risk of miscarriage by 80%, while acetaminophen did not.

How it can affect a developing embryo or fetus: Acetaminophen does cross the placenta. Studies of animal fetuses find that the level of acetaminophen is about 10% of the mother's. Several studies have found that taking acetaminophen in the first trimester may increase (by a small amount) the risk of a weakening in the fetus's abdominal wall, which can lead to gastroschisis (the bowel protruding through the abdomen) and requires surgical repair after birth. The risk of a bowel abnormality is further increased (as much as 4 to 5 times) when combined with pseudoephedrine. However, one recent report concluded that if taken alone in the first trimester for fever, acetaminophen may actually help prevent neural tube defects (another type of birth defect). Acetaminophen is used during labor to treat fever that otherwise would increase the fetal need for oxygen. Unlike aspirin, acetaminophen does not increase the risk of bleeding in the fetus.

Breast-feeding: Acetaminophen is excreted in low concentrations (estimated to be about 0.04–0.23% of the mother's dose) into breast milk and is generally considered compatible with breast-feeding.

Potential drug interactions: Tramadol may increase the risk of acetaminophen toxicity. Pseudoephedrine may increase the risk of gastroschisis in the fetus.

What the FDA says about use in pregnancy: No assigned category (see Appendix).

What the available studies suggest about breast-feeding: Safe.

The bottom line for you:

- Taking too much acetaminophen is a leading cause of maternal liver toxicity.
- Many obstetricians and gynecologists consider acetaminophen safe to take during pregnancy to reduce fever and for pain relief.
- Single-ingredient acetaminophen use during the first trimester does not appear to increase the risk of major birth defects. It may decrease the risk of selected defects when used for an illness involving a fever. As such, acetaminophen is the fever-reducing agent and pain reliever of choice in the first trimester if one must be used.
- Limited use of other nonsteroidal agents such as ibuprofen are considered safer after the first trimester and are usually preferred because of their lower risk of maternal toxicity. After 32 weeks, there is a very small risk that prolonged use of ibuprofen or related drugs could cause a fetal cardiovascular problem, and acetaminophen is preferred after this time for pain relief.
- Acetaminophen is considered safe while breast-feeding.

ACETAZOLAMIDE

Brand names: Acetadiazol, Acetamide, Azomid, Dehydratin, Diamox, Ederen, Glauconox, Inidrase, Nephramid, Oratrol

Drug classes: Carbonic anhydrase inhibitor; Diuretic

Indications (what it is used for): Glaucoma, altitude sickness, epilepsy, increased pressure in the brain, heart failure, drug-induced edema (swelling), urinary alkalinization.

How it works: Suppresses the enzyme carbonic anhydrase.

Contraindications (reasons you shouldn't take it): Hypersensitivity to drug or class, low sodium or potassium levels, high chloride levels leading to a buildup of acid, reduced lung function, cirrhosis, adrenocortical insufficiency (inadequate production of one or more adrenal hormones; also called Addison's disease).

Possible side effects and warnings: Can cause aplastic anemia, Stevens-Johnson syndrome and toxic epidermal necrolysis (rare but serious skin disorders), sudden liver failure, pins and needles, loss of appetite, taste changes, indigestion, and increased urine production. Should be used with caution in women with liver or kidney disease.

How it can affect pregnant women: There are no adequate reports or well-controlled studies in pregnant women. However, long years of clinical experience in pregnant women suggest relative safety.

How it can affect a developing embryo or fetus: Acetazolamide crosses the human placenta, There are no reports of birth defects despite years of use during pregnancy. A single case report documents an infant who was born preterm (before 37 weeks) with a rare form of kidney disease (renal tubular acidosis) to a mother who had been treated with acetazolamide throughout pregnancy for glaucoma. In some rodents, acetazolamide caused skeletal abnormalities in rats and urinary malformations in mice when combined with amiloride and/or ibuprofen. However, animal studies are not necessarily good indicators of how a drug will behave in humans.

Breast-feeding: A breast-feeding baby is exposed to less than 0.5% of the mother's dose. Acetazolamide is generally considered compatible with breast-feeding.

Potential drug interactions: Interaction between

the following medications and acetazolamide has the potential to impact the effect of one or more of the drugs. In some instances the interaction can be dangerous or life-threatening and must be avoided: phenytoin, primidone, quinidine, lithium, cyclosporine.

What the FDA says about use in pregnancy: Category C (see Appendix).

What the available evidence suggests about breast-feeding safety: Safe.

The bottom line for you:

- In light of its reasonable safety profile, acetazolamide may be used during pregnancy and while breast-feeding when indicated.

ACETOHEXAMIDE

Brand names: Dimelin, Dimelor, Dymelor, Gamadiabet, Ordimel, Toyobexin

Drug classes: Carbonic anhydrase inhibitor; Oral hypoglycemic; Sulfonylurea

Indications (what it is used for): Type II diabetes.

How it works: Stimulates the release of insulin.

Contraindications (reasons you shouldn't take it): Hypersensitivity to drug or class, diabetic ketoacidosis (lack of insulin prevents body using sugar as a fuel), type I diabetes.

Possible side effects and warnings: Can cause low blood sugar, jaundice, stomach upset, allergic skin reactions, disordered pituitary function, hemolytic anemia, various cytopenias (reduced blood cells), and hepatic porphyria (enzyme disorder of the liver). Should not be used during pregnancy (see "How it can affect a developing embryo or fetus" below).

How it can affect pregnant women: There are no adequate reports or well-controlled studies of acetohexamide in pregnant women. Some oral hypoglycemic drugs are associated with an increased risk of cardiac death (in the general population) compared to patients using only diet and insulin.

How it can affect a developing embryo or fetus: There are no adequate reports or well-controlled studies in human fetuses. Acetohexamide does cross the placenta, and prolonged low blood sugar levels are reported in newborns of mothers being treated with it. There are no reports of it causing birth defects in humans.

Breast-feeding: There is no published data in nursing women. It is unknown whether acetohexamide enters human breast milk but other sulfonylureas do.

Potential drug interactions: Interaction between the following medications and acetohexamide has the potential to impact the effect of one or more of the drugs. In some instances the interaction can be dangerous or life-threatening and must be avoided: thiazide diuretics, corticosteroids, phenothiazines, thyroid products, estrogens, oral contraceptives, phenytoin, nicotinic acid, sympathomimetics, calcium channel blockers, isoniazid, oral miconazole, oral hypoglycemic agents, nonsteroidal anti-inflammatory drugs (NSAIDs), salicylates, sulfonamides, chloramphenicol, probenecid, coumarins, monoamine oxidase inhibitors (MAOIs), beta-blockers.

What the FDA says about use in pregnancy: Category C (see Appendix).

What the available evidence suggests about breast-feeding safety: Unknown.

The bottom line for you:

- There is growing interest in the use of oral hypoglycemic agents for type II diabetes during pregnancy, but acetohexamide is a poor choice because of how much crosses the placenta and the possible resulting low blood sugars in the fetus and newborn.

- There are better choices for use while breast-feeding.

ACETYLCYSTEINE

Brand names: Acetyst, Alveolux, Bromuc, Mucomyst, Mucosil, Mucosol, Mukosil, Respaire

Drug classes: Antidote; Antioxidant; Mucolytic

Indications (what it is used for): Treatment of acetaminophen or amanita mushroom toxicity, mucolytic (mucus-dissolving agent) in patients with cystic fibrosis (life-threatening lung disease). It is being studied for its potential to treat the effects of low blood oxygen levels in the fetus.

How it works: An antioxidant; restores oxidative balance.

Contraindications (reasons you shouldn't take it): Hypersensitivity to drug or class.

Possible side effects and warnings: Can cause severe respiratory failure, asthma, life-threatening allergic reaction, nausea and vomiting, stomatitis (inflammation of the mucous linings of the mouth), runny nose, hives, and rash.

How it can affect pregnant women: N-acetylcysteine is an antioxidant used during pregnancy for the treatment of maternal drug toxicity (such as an overdose of acetaminophen). There are no adequate reports or well-controlled studies in pregnant women, although clinical experience during pregnancy does not reveal any problems. In the future, N-acetylcysteine may have a role in the treatment of several disorders associated with excess oxygen free radical generation, including fetal growth restriction, and preeclampsia (high blood pressure and protein in the urine during pregnancy and complications associated with it).

How it can affect a developing embryo or fetus: N-acetylcysteine crosses the placenta and achieves levels in the fetus equal to those in the mother. In laboratory studies, it reduced damage to the embryo associated with high blood sugar, hypoxia (inadequate oxygen supply), and sepsis (chemicals released into the bloodstream to fight infection trigger inflammation throughout the body). In other studies, it reduced the adverse effects of maternal inflammation on the fetus by blocking the release of certain proteins. It also has been shown to prevent brain damage in guinea pig fetuses that have been chronically deprived of oxygen.

Breast-feeding: There is no published data in nursing women. It is unknown whether N-acetylcysteine enters human breast milk.

Potential drug interactions: N-acetylcysteine should not be mixed in solution with tetracyclines or erythromycin.

What the FDA says about use in pregnancy: Category B (see Appendix).

What the available evidence suggests about use in breast-feeding: Likely safe.

The bottom line for you:

- N-acetylcysteine is a drug of choice during pregnancy for the treatment of acetaminophen overdose and cystic fibrosis.
- N-acetylcysteine is considered safe while breast-feeding.

ACYCLOVIR

Brand names: Acivir Cream, Acivir Eye, Avirax, Avorax, Clovicin, Clovix, Entir, Supra-Vir, Zovirax

Drug class: Antiviral

Indications (what it is used for): First-time or recurrent herpes infection/suppression, treatment or prevention of varicella pneumonia.

How it works: Stops the virus from replicating itself.

Contraindications (reasons you shouldn't take it): Hypersensitivity to drug or class.

Possible side effects and warnings: Can cause seizures, coma, a decrease in white blood cells, low platelet levels, kidney dysfunction, nausea and vomiting, diarrhea, headache, dizziness, lethargy, rash, confusion.

How it can affect pregnant women: Acyclovir has been used for many years to suppress the herpes virus in pregnant women without significant adverse effects to the mother. Treatment doesn't eliminate the herpes virus but reduces the duration of symptoms and viral shedding (the ability to pass the virus to others or the baby through contact). Prophylactic acyclovir beginning at 36 weeks reduces the risk of active genital herpes at delivery, which would require a cesarean delivery to avoid transmission to the newborn. Because acyclovir is excreted via the kidneys, its clearance from the mother's bloodstream may be increased during pregnancy.

How it can affect a developing embryo or fetus: There are no adequate reports or well-controlled

studies in human fetuses, and it is unknown whether acyclovir crosses the human placenta. Although acyclovir lessens the risk of having an outbreak during delivery, it is not clear whether treating the mother with acyclovir actually reduces the chance of a newborn contracting herpes. Surveillance of 756 pregnancies by the medication's manufacturer has not revealed any increase in, or pattern of, birth defects after acyclovir exposure during the first trimester. A study from Denmark that included 90 women who took the drug orally and 995 women who used it topically also failed to show any increase in birth defects. Rodent studies also show no evidence of fetal damage despite the use of doses higher than those used clinically. However, animal studies are not necessarily good indicators of how a drug will behave in humans.

Breast-feeding: Although acyclovir achieves concentrations in breast milk that are actually higher than those in the blood of the breast-feeding mother, the drug is used to treat herpes in newborns and is generally considered safe when breast-feeding.

Potential drug interactions: Interaction between the following medications and acyclovir has the potential to impact the effect of one or more of the drugs. In some instances the interaction can be dangerous or life-threatening and must be avoided: probenecid.

What the FDA says about use in pregnancy: Category B (see Appendix).

What the available evidence suggests about breast-feeding safety: Safe.

The bottom line for you:
- Acyclovir significantly reduces the duration of shedding and the number of recurrent HSV outbreaks during pregnancy.
- Treatment should be initiated at 36 weeks in women with herpes infection to prevent recurrence and reduce the need for cesarean delivery.
- Acyclovir is considered safe while breast-feeding.

ADAPALENE

Brand names: Differin, Differine
Drug classes: Dermatologic; Retinoid
Indications (what it is used for): Acne.
How it works: Interferes with keratin formation and inflammation.
Possible side effects and warnings: Can cause skin redness, dryness, burning, scaling, and sun sensitivity.
How it can affect pregnant women: There are no adequate reports or well-controlled studies of adapalene in pregnant women. Absorption of adapalene through the skin is low—none was detected in the blood of 6 patients who were treated over 5 days for acne.
How it can affect a developing embryo or fetus: There are no adequate studies of adapalene in human pregnancy. It is unknown whether adapalene crosses the human placenta. Although some retinoids have proved to cause birth defects, the absence of a detectable blood level of adapalene in the mother means that the risks to the fetus are minimal. Although several reports associate adapalene with fetal malformation after topical exposure, the available information is insufficient to conclude that the birth defects were caused by the medication. There was an increase in birth defects when rodents were given more than 100 times the recommended clinical dose, but no abnormalities were seen when the animals were exposed to lower concentrations. However, animal studies are not necessarily good indicators of how a drug will behave in humans.
Breast-feeding: There is no published data in nursing women. It is unknown whether adapalene enters human breast milk. But considering the dose and the fact that it is applied topically, it is unlikely to pose a significant risk to a breast-feeding baby.
Drug interactions: Since adapalene can cause local irritation, use of other topical agents such as medicated or abrasive soaps and cleansers, soaps and cosmetics with a strong drying effect, and products

with high concentrations of alcohol should be avoided. Care is also recommended in using preparations containing sulfur, resorcinol, or salicylic acid in combination with adapalene.

What the FDA says about use in pregnancy: Category C (see Appendix).

What the available evidence suggests about breast-feeding safety: Unknown but likely safe.

The bottom line for you:

- Women of childbearing age are advised to use contraception while being treated with oral adapalene.
- It is best to avoid oral and topical retinoids such as adapalene, especially in early pregnancy, since acne rarely poses a significant health risk and isn't worth any potential risk to the embryo or fetus.
- There are alternative medications for the treatment of severe acne with which there is more experience during pregnancy and breast-feeding.

ALBUTEROL

Brand names: Airet, Albuterol Sulfate, Asmalin, Asmanil, Asmavent, Butamol, Buventol, Proventil, Salbusian, Salbutamol, Theosal, Ventolin; Ventolin Rotacaps, Volmax

Drug classes: Adrenergic agonist; Bronchodilator

Indications (what it is used for): Bronchospasm/asthma.

How it works: Dilates the bronchioles by selectively activating the beta-2 adrenoceptors.

Contraindications (reasons you shouldn't take it): Hypersensitivity to drug or class.

Possible side effects and warnings: May worsen asthma when given through an inhaler. Can cause tremor, nervousness, rapid heart rate, dizziness, headache, high blood pressure, nausea, hyperactivity, low potassium, and high blood sugar. Should be used with caution in women with overactive thyroid, cardiovascular disease, diabetes, or a seizure disorder.

How it can affect pregnant women: Asthma is a common disease in life and in pregnancy. Approximately one-third of pregnant women with asthma get worse during pregnancy, one-third get better, and one-third remain clinically unchanged. When asthma is well controlled it does not affect pregnancy, but poorly controlled asthma may increase the risk of preterm birth (before 37 weeks) or low birthweight. Inhaled corticosteroids are considered the preventative medication of choice for pregnant women with persistent asthma unless their condition is well controlled by cromolyn or nedocromil. Although albuterol has been used to stop or slow preterm labor (before 37 weeks), there is no evidence that it prevents delivery. At most, it can delay delivery up to 48 hours, enough time to give corticosteroids to promote fetal lung development. Its use to stop labor has been shown to increase the risk of fluid in the mother's lungs, especially in women with twins or triplets, and in women also receiving corticosteroids to hasten fetal lung maturation, or who have an infection.

How it can affect a developing embryo or fetus: There are no adequate reports or well-controlled studies in human fetuses. Albuterol appears to cross the human placenta, although how much passes through is unclear. Less than 10% is absorbed by the mother when given by inhalation. There is no convincing evidence of an increased risk of birth defects when given in the first trimester. Albuterol, like other b-adrenoceptor agonists, is associated with a reduction in the incidence of newborn breathing problems. Although albuterol can cause birth defects in mice at lower doses than those used clinically, this appears to be an example of how animal studies are not necessarily good indicators of how a drug will behave in humans.

Breast-feeding: There is no published data in nursing women. It is unknown whether albuterol enters human breast milk. However, since only 10% or less of albuterol reaches the mother's bloodstream when inhaled, little is likely to enter the breast milk.

Potential drug interactions: Interaction between

the following medications and albuterol has the potential to impact the effect of one or more of the drugs. In some instances the interaction can be dangerous or life-threatening and must be avoided: monamine oxidase inhibitors (MAOIs), tricyclic antidepressants (TCAs), beta-receptor blockers.

What the FDA says about use in pregnancy: Category C (see Appendix).

What the available evidence suggests about breast-feeding safety: Likely safe.

The bottom line for you:

- Albuterol may be used during pregnancy for the treatment of asthma.
- Albuterol is not effective in stopping preterm labor.
- As a drug to delay delivery, albuterol has no advantage over any other b-adrenoceptor agonist, since it prolongs pregnancy an average of only 48 hours.
- Adrenoceptor agonists should be avoided in diabetic women if possible, as it may increase their blood sugar levels.
- Although there is no information on the use of albuterol while breast-feeding, data from a related drug, terbutaline, indicates that very little is expected to be excreted into breast milk. It is generally agreed that use of inhaled bronchodilators is acceptable during breast-feeding.

ALFENTANIL

Brand names: Alfenta, Alfentanyl, Rapifen

Drug class: Analgesic, narcotic

Indications (what it is used for): Labor or surgical pain.

How it works: A short-acting lipophilic opioid (fat-soluble narcotic painkiller).

Contraindications (reasons you shouldn't take it): Hypersensitivity to drug or class.

Possible side effects and warnings: Can cause respiratory arrest or depression, irregular heartbeat, seizure, coma, abuse or dependency, muscle rigidity, nausea and vomiting, dizziness, high or low blood pressure, fast or slow heart rate, confusion, sweating, dry mouth, constipation, urinary retention. Should be used with caution in women with chest wall rigidity; liver, kidney, or lung dysfunction; head injury; or bowel obstruction.

How it can affect pregnant women: Alfentanil is a narcotic that works quickly and does not last long. It reduces the total amount of local anesthetic needed to provide comfort with an epidural. Alfentanil is also given just prior to inserting a breathing tube for general anesthesia to reduce the risk of increased blood pressure in women with preeclampsia (high blood pressure and protein in the urine during pregnancy and complications associated with it).

How it can affect a developing embryo or fetus: Alfentanil crosses the placenta if given intravenously, although its transfer rate is slower and lower than that of fentanyl (a similar narcotic). Neither damage to human embryos nor birth defects have been reported with its use, although there is little data on use during the first trimester (the most sensitive period of embryonic and fetal development). There are no reported effects on fetuses or newborns after use during labor. A short-term decrease in muscle tone may be seen in human newborns when given to the mother just prior to delivery and may require treatment with a narcotic blocker. Animal studies have found evidence that alfentanil can damage an embryo and cause newborn cognitive development when used at high doses over a long period of time. However, animal studies are not necessarily good indicators of how a drug will behave in humans.

Breast-feeding: Alfentanil is excreted into human breast milk, but the amount is too small to have any significant effect on a breast-feeding baby.

Potential drug interactions: Interaction between the following medications and alfentanil has the potential to impact the effect of one or more of the drugs. In some instances the interaction can be dangerous or life-threatening and must be avoided: other central nervous system (CNS) depressants such as barbiturates, tranquilizers, opioids, or general anesthetics given through inhalation; erythromycin; cimetidine.

What the FDA says about use in pregnancy: Category C (see Appendix).

What the available evidence suggests about breast-feeding safety: Safe.

The bottom line for you:

- Alfentanil is probably safe when used as a short-term analgesic during pregnancy and while breast-feeding.

ALLOPURINOL

Brand names: Aipico, Alloremed, Alloscan, Alonol, Aloral, Aluline, Aluprin, Apurol, Isanol, Lopurin, Lysuron, Unizuric, Uricemil, Uriconorm-E, Zyloprim, Zyroric

Drug classes: Antigout; Antioxidant; Purine analog

Indications (what it is used for): Gout, kidney stones due to urate or calcium; it is being studied for its potential to treat low blood oxygen levels in the fetus.

How it works: Interferes with the conversion of the protein building blocks xanthine and hypoxanthine into uric acid.

Contraindications (reasons you shouldn't take it): Hypersensitivity to drug or class.

Possible side effects and warnings: Can cause very low white and/or red blood cell counts, low platelet counts, liver dysfunction, hives, Stevens-Johnson syndrome and toxic epidermal necrolysis (rare but serious skin disorders), rash, diarrhea, itching, nausea. Should be used with caution in women with kidney dysfunction.

How it can affect pregnant women: There are no adequate reports or well-controlled studies of allopurinol in pregnant women. Gout is unusual in young women, so it is rarely prescribed for pregnant or breast-feeding women. There is a single report of a woman treated with allopurinol during pregnancy for primary gout; she delivered a healthy child. More often, allopurinol is used during pregnancy for women undergoing treatment of acute leukemia. Allopurinol was used unsuccessfully in one trial for the treatment of preeclampsia (high blood pressure and protein in the urine during pregnancy and complications associated with it).

How it can affect a developing embryo or fetus: There are no adequate reports or well-controlled studies in human fetuses, but clinical use has not yet yielded any evidence that allopurinol causes birth defects in humans. We do know that allopurinol readily crosses the sheep placenta, reaching the same level in the fetus as it does in the mother. In more recent animal studies, allopurinol reduced toxic oxygen free radical generation in the brains of fetuses whose umbilical cord was blocked intermittently, as can occur during labor. Cleft palate and skeletal defects have been reported in some rodent studies. However, animal studies are not necessarily good indicators of how a drug will behave in humans.

Breast-feeding: A small amount of allopurinol and its breakdown product, oxypurinol, are excreted into breast milk. It is considered compatible with breast-feeding.

Potential drug interactions: Interaction between the following medications and allopurinol has the potential to impact the effect of one or more of the drugs. In some instances the interaction can be dangerous or life-threatening and must be avoided: mercaptopurine, azathioprine, dicumarol, chlorpropamide.

What the FDA says about use in pregnancy: Category C (see Appendix).

What the available evidence suggests about breast-feeding safety: Safe.

The bottom line for you:

- Allopurinol is rarely indicated in pregnancy, but when needed, the benefits to the woman likely outweigh any theoretical risk to the fetus or newborn.

- Allopurinol is considered compatible with breast-feeding.

ALMOTRIPTAN

Brand name: Axert

Drug class: Serotonin receptor agonist

Indications (what it is used for): Migraine headache.

How it works: Constricts blood vessels by binding brain receptors that are involved in brain vessel dilation.

Contraindications (reasons you shouldn't take it): Hypersensitivity to drug or class, uncontrolled high blood pressure, heart disease and spasm of the blood vessels supplying the heart, migraine with aura or neurological symptoms such as numbness, having taken another 5-HT1 agonist or an ergot-related compound within 24 hours.

Possible side effects and warnings: Can cause hypertensive crisis (sudden, severe high blood pressure); heart attack; irregular heart rate; stroke; reduced blood flow to limbs and/or bowels; nausea and vomiting; sleepiness; headache; numbness and tingling; chest, jaw, or neck pain. Should be used with extreme caution in women with preexisting blockage of either brain or limb blood vessels or cardiac risk factors such as obesity, cigarette use; or with a prior heart attack or liver or kidney dysfunction.

How it can affect pregnant women: Fifty to 90% of women who suffer migraines experience improvement during pregnancy, mainly during the second and third trimesters. A higher percentage of women who have menstrual migraine experience this improvement compared to women with other types of migraines. There is no published data on almotriptan during pregnancy. Clinically, it is similar to sumatriptan, for which the best study available included 1,394 women who used either an ergot or triptanlike drug after the first trimester. Women using drugs for migraine were older and more likely to be overweight and hence at greater risk for pregnancy complications to begin with. A 40% increased risk for preeclampsia (high blood pressure and protein in the urine during pregnancy and complications associated with it), and a 50% increased risk for preterm birth (delivery before 37 weeks) was seen after the drugs were used to treat migraine later in pregnancy. There was no increased risk for stillbirth or early newborn death.

How it can affect a developing embryo or fetus: There are no adequate reports or well-controlled studies in human fetuses, and it is unknown whether almotriptan crosses the human placenta. Rodent studies showed no evidence it causes birth defects or restricts fetal growth even at doses higher than those used clinically. However, the embryos did not survive when a dose 1,000 times the maximum recommended clinical dose was used, and pregnancy was prolonged when 160 times the maximum recommended clinical dose was used. However, animal studies are not necessarily good indicators of how a drug will behave in humans.

Breast-feeding: There is no published data in nursing women, and it is unknown whether almotriptan enters human breast milk.

Potential drug interactions: Interaction between the following medications and almotriptan has the potential to impact the effect of one or more of the drugs. In some instances the interaction can be dangerous or life-threatening and must be avoided: selective serotonin reuptake inhibitors (SSRIs; e.g., fluoxetine, fluvoxamine, paroxetine, sertraline); ketoconazole and other potent inhibitors of metabolic enzymes, such as cytochrome P450s (e.g., itraconazole, ritonavir, erythromycin).

What the FDA says about use in pregnancy: Category C (see Appendix).

What the available evidence suggests about breast-feeding safety: Unknown.

The bottom line for you:

- Almotriptan should be used during pregnancy and breast-feeding only if the benefit to the woman justifies the potential risk to the fetus or newborn.

- Triptans, as a group, may be associated with preeclampsia and preterm birth and are best avoided at the extremes of prematurity (before 28 weeks) until more data is available.

- Because there is so little experience with almotriptan, it is best to try alternative medications first.

ALOE VERA

Brand names: Cape, Socotrine, Zanzibar
Drug class: Dermatologic
Indications (what it is used for): Wound healing.
How it works: Exact mechanism unknown; may promote proliferation of, and better communication between, skin cells.
Contraindications (reasons you shouldn't take it): Hypersensitivity to drug or class.
Possible side effects and warnings: Can cause severe gastric cramping and diarrhea if taken internally, so it should never be ingested.
How it can affect pregnant women: Aloe vera gel comes from the inner part of the leaf of the aloe vera plant and contains many different compounds. There are no adequate reports or well-controlled studies in pregnant women.
How it can affect a developing embryo or fetus: There are no adequate reports or well-controlled studies in human fetuses. Though the active compound(s) are unknown, it is unlikely that the maternal blood level achieved after topical application is high.
Breast-feeding: There is no published data during breast-feeding. However, considering that aloe vera is used topically, it is unlikely that a breast-fed infant would ingest clinically relevant amounts of the active compounds.
Drug interactions: No drug-drug interaction studies in human subjects have been conducted.
What the FDA says about use in pregnancy: No assigned category (see Appendix).
What the available evidence suggests about breast-feeding safety: Likely safe.
The bottom line for you:
- Topically applied aloe vera during pregnancy or while breast-feeding is unlikely to pose a significant risk to mother, fetus, or newborn.

ALOSETRON

Brand name: Lotronex
Drug classes: Antidiarrheal; Gastrointestinal; Serotonin receptor antagonist
Indications (what it is used for): Severe diarrhea-dominant irritable bowel syndrome.
How it works: A selective and potent blocker of the serotonin 5-HT3 receptor, which stimulates bowel motility.
Contraindications (reasons you shouldn't take it): Hypersensitivity to drug or class, constipation.
Possible side effects and warnings: Can cause poor circulation to the colon, constipation, high blood pressure, allergic runny nose, indigestion, depression.
How it can affect pregnant women: There are no published reports of alosetron use during pregnancy.
How it can affect a developing embryo or fetus: There are no adequate reports or well-controlled studies in human fetuses. It is unknown whether alosetron crosses the human placenta. Rodent studies reveal no evidence that maternal use of alosetron causes birth defects or restricts fetal growth despite the use of doses higher than those used clinically. However, animal studies are not necessarily good indicators of how a drug will behave in humans.
Breast-feeding: There is no published data in nursing women. It is unknown whether alosetron enters human breast milk; it is excreted into the milk of lactating rats.
Potential drug interactions: Interaction between the following medications and alosetron has the potential to impact the effect of one or more of the drugs. In some instances the interaction can be dangerous or life-threatening and must be avoided: fluvoxamine, quinolone antibiotics, cimetidine, ketoconazole, clarithromycin, telithromycin, protease inhibitors, voriconazole, itraconazole.
What the FDA says about use in pregnancy: Category B (see Appendix).
What the available studies suggest about breast-feeding safety: Unknown.

The bottom line for you:
- Alosetron should be reserved for pregnant or breast-feeding women with severe diarrhea due to irritable bowel syndrome that has proved resistant to other, more commonly used, medications.

ALPRAZOLAM

Brand names: Alpralid, Alprazolam Intensol, Altraxic, Apo-Alpraz, Xanax; Xanax TS, Xanolam, Zoldac, Zolam, Zopax

Drug classes: Anxiolytic; Benzodiazepine; Sedative

Indications (what it is used for): Acute anxiety.

How it works: A short-acting benzodiazepine that reduces anxiety by enhancing the effects of the neurotransmitter GABA.

Contraindications (reasons you shouldn't take it): Hypersensitivity to drug or class, glaucoma, pregnancy, central nervous system depression.

Possible side effects and warnings: Can cause physical dependence, light-headedness, fainting, rapid heart rate, seizures, respiratory depression, coma, drowsiness, dry mouth, depression, headache, constipation, diarrhea, nausea and vomiting, insomnia, blurred vision, low blood pressure, increased salivation, skin inflammation. Should be used with caution in women with liver or kidney damage.

How it can affect pregnant women: There are few published reports of alprazolam use during pregnancy. Stopping alprazolam treatment abruptly is associated with a sudden onset of problems that include neuropsychiatric, bowel, skin, heart, and visual symptoms.

How it can affect a developing embryo or fetus: There are no adequate reports or well-controlled studies in human fetuses. Although there is no evidence from case reports and manufacturer surveillance that alprazolam causes birth defects in humans, diazepam (which is related to alprazolam) has been associated with fetal malformations. There is also concern, based on studies of other benzodiazepines, that newborn behavior can be altered by exposure in the womb, and newborn withdrawal syndrome has been reported. Mice exposed to alprazolam in utero showed an inclination toward more individual (rather than group) activities, avoided open areas, and the males were more aggressive. However, animal studies are not necessarily good indicators of how a drug will behave in humans.

Breast-feeding: Alprazolam enters breast milk, with the newborn ingesting about 3% of the maternal dose. This is not likely to result in a significant blood level in a breast-fed baby.

Potential drug interactions: Interaction between the following medications or substances and alprazolam has the potential to impact the effect of one or more of the drugs. In some instances the interaction can be dangerous or life-threatening and must be avoided: other psychotropic medications, anticonvulsants, antihistamines, ethanol, and drugs that produce central nervous system depression; drugs that cause dry mouth or raise stomach pH; drugs that inhibit certain liver-metabolizing enzymes (e.g., fluoxetine, propoxyphene, oral contraceptives); diltiazem; isoniazid; macrolide antibiotics such as erythromycin and clarithromycin; carbamazepine; grapefruit and grapefruit juice.

What the FDA says about use in pregnancy: Category D (see Appendix).

What the available studies suggest about breast-feeding: Likely safe.

The bottom line for you:
- In contrast to depression, anxiety is rarely a debilitating or life-threatening problem, suggesting that medication can often be avoided during pregnancy.
- There are antianxietal agents with which there is more experience in pregnancy. However, most are in the same drug class and have similar risks.
- Stopping alprazolam treatment abruptly may be associated with a sudden onset of problems that include neuropsychiatric, bowel, skin, heart, and visual symptoms. Consult your physician before choosing to discontinue the medication.

- Although the risk is reasonably small, alprazolam is best avoided during pregnancy and breast-feeding because of the potential to alter neuro-development and the potential risks of fetal withdrawal.

AMIKACIN
Brand name: Amikin
Drug classes: Aminoglycoside; Antibiotic
Indications (what it is used for): Short-term treatment of serious bacterial infections.
How it works: Inhibits protein synthesis necessary for the bacteria to live.
Contraindications (reasons you shouldn't take it): Hypersensitivity to drug or class.
Possible side effects and warnings: Can cause weakness, paralysis, kidney damage, loss of hearing, rash, fever, headache, numbness and tingling, vomiting, anemia, low blood pressure, joint pain. Should be used with caution in women with kidney damage.
How it can affect pregnant women: There are no adequate reports or well-controlled studies of amikacin during pregnancy. Pregnancy increases the rate of removal of drugs such as amikacin from the body, so women with normal kidney function are likely to need an increased dose to achieve the desired blood levels.
How it can affect a developing embryo or fetus: There are no adequate reports or well-controlled studies in human fetuses. Amikacin crosses the placenta, although the levels achieved in the fetus are lower than those of the mother. Amikacin may damage the fetal kidneys, as irreversible failure has been reported in fetuses after exposure to some aminoglycosides, but not amikacin. There is no evidence thus far that amikacin causes birth defects in either humans or animals.
Breast-feeding: Amikacin is excreted into breast milk but at low concentrations. Little of the drug in breast milk is absorbed by the breast-fed baby, suggesting that there is little risk to the baby.

Potential drug interactions: Interaction between the following medications and amikacin has the potential to impact the effect of one or more of the drugs. In some instances the interaction can be dangerous or life-threatening and must be avoided: paralyzing agents such as tubocurarine and succinylcholine; systemic, oral, or topical nerve or kidney toxic agents, particularly bacitracin, cisplatin, amphotericin B, cephaloridine, polymyxin B, colistin, vancomycin, and other aminoglycosides; potent diuretics such as ethacrynic acid and furosemide.
What the FDA says about use in pregnancy: Category D (see Appendix).
What the available evidence suggests about breast-feeding safety: Safe.
The bottom line for you:
- Aminoglycosides such as amikacin are indicated during pregnancy only for the treatment of serious bacterial infections.
- There are aminoglycosides, such as gentamicin, with which we have more experience during pregnancy and therefore are preferred choices.
- The amount of amikacin excreted into breast milk appears to be clinically insignificant.

AMILORIDE
Brand names: Amilospare, Arumil, Midamor, Moduretic 5–50
Drug classes: Antihypertensive; Diuretic, potassium sparing
Indications (what it is used for): High blood pressure or heart failure.
How it works: Prevents the kidneys from reabsorbing sodium.
Contraindications (reasons you shouldn't take it): Hypersensitivity to drug or class, high potassium, poor kidney function, no urine production, potassium-sparing diuretic use, and nerve damage due to diabetes.
Possible side effects and warnings: Can cause aplastic anemia, loss of white blood cells, high

potassium, headache, nausea and vomiting, diarrhea, muscle cramps, weakness, cough. Should be used with caution in women with diabetes.

How it can affect pregnant women: There are no adequate reports or well-controlled studies of amiloride in pregnant women. The published data is limited to an occasional case report.

How it can affect a developing embryo or fetus: There are no adequate reports or well-controlled studies in human fetuses. Amiloride crosses the placenta in modest amounts. Rodent studies are reassuring, even when the drug is used at a dose 20 times the recommended clinical dose. However, animal studies are not necessarily good indicators of how a drug will behave in humans.

Breast-feeding: Amiloride is concentrated in breast milk and should probably be avoided while breast-feeding.

Potential drug interactions: Interaction between the following medications and amiloride has the potential to impact the effect of one or more of the drugs. In some instances the interaction can be dangerous or life-threatening and must be avoided: ACE inhibitors, cyclosporine, tacrolimus, alcohol, barbiturates, narcotics, oral blood-sugar-lowering medications, insulin, other blood-pressure-lowering medications, corticosteroids, adrenocorticotropic hormone, skeletal muscle relaxants, paralyzers such as tubocurarine, lithium.

What the FDA says about use in pregnancy: Category B (see Appendix).

What the available studies suggest about breast-feeding: Possibly unsafe.

The bottom line for you:

- Amiloride is rarely required in pregnancy but is likely low risk if needed.
- There are other diuretic agents with which there is more experience during pregnancy and while breast-feeding that may be used in its place.
- Probably best to avoid during breast-feeding.

AMINOCAPROIC ACID
Brand names: Amicar, Capracid, Epsikapron
Drug class: Hemostatic
Indications (what it is used for): Hemorrhage associated with excess breakdown of fibrinogen/fibrin, for example, the placenta separating from the wall of the uterus or a fetus that has died in utero, heart surgery, cirrhosis, increased consumption of platelets, hemorrhagic telangiectasia (a problem with blood vessel formation).

How it works: Blocks the breakdown of fibrin or its chemical precursor.

Contraindications (reasons you shouldn't take it): Hypersensitivity to drug or class, disseminated intravascular coagulation, any hemorrhage of unknown cause.

Possible side effects and warnings: Can cause seizures, sudden kidney failure, irregular heart rate, dizziness, muscle problems, confusion, and clotting disorders. Should be used with caution in women with kidney or liver damage or coronary artery disease.

How it can affect pregnant women: There are no adequate reports or well-controlled studies of aminocaproic acid during pregnancy. The literature consists mostly of case reports, where it has been used in a variety of life-threatening pregnancy-related bleeding problems.

How it can affect a developing embryo or fetus: There are no adequate reports or well-controlled studies in human fetuses, and it is unknown whether aminocaproic acid crosses the human placenta. Aminocaproic acid decreases egg implantation in several animals. However, animal studies are not necessarily good indicators of how a drug will behave in humans.

Breast-feeding: There are no adequate reports or well-controlled studies in nursing women, and it is unknown whether aminocaproic acid enters human breast milk.

Drug interactions: No drug-drug interaction studies in human subjects have been conducted.

What the FDA says about use in pregnancy: Category C (see Appendix).

What the available studies say about breast-feeding: Unknown.

The bottom line for you:

- Aminocaproic acid is indicated in rare instances for the treatment of pregnancy-related life-threatening hemorrhage where alternative therapies have failed.
- Although there are no reports of aminocaproic acid use while breast-feeding, its short-term use around delivery should not pose significant risk for breast-feeding.

AMINOPHYLLINE

Brand names: Aminophylline, Drafilyn "Z", Inophyline, Norphyl, Novphyllin, Somophylin, Synthophyllin, Theourin, Truphylline

Drug classes: Antiasthmatic; Bronchodilator; Xanthine derivative

Indications (what it is used for): Relief and prevention of symptoms of asthma and/or reversible bronchospasm.

How it works: Unknown.

Contraindications (reasons you shouldn't take it): Hypersensitivity to drug or class, seizure disorder, peptic ulcer disease, irregular heart rate.

Possible side effects: Can cause seizures, respiratory arrest, irregular heart rate, nausea and vomiting, insomnia, headache, fever, agitation, tremor, and tachycardia. Should be used with caution in women with kidney or liver damage or heart failure.

How it can affect pregnant women: Asthma is a common disease in life and in pregnancy. Approximately one-third of pregnant women with asthma have increased symptoms during pregnancy, one-third get better, and one-third remain clinically unchanged. Well-controlled asthma does not adversely affect pregnancy outcome, but poorly controlled asthma may increase the risk of preterm birth or low birth weight. Aminophylline is used for long-term control of asthma (as opposed to rescue therapies used during an attack). Although there are no adequate reports or well-controlled studies of aminophylline in pregnant women, the long clinical experience suggests that it is as effective during pregnancy as it is in nonpregnant women. It does not appear to affect uterine blood flow. Patients using aminophylline during pregnancy should have their blood levels periodically monitored because drug clearance (how fast the drug is processed by the body) changes during pregnancy. Certain medications used during labor and delivery have the potential to worsen asthma, including nonselective beta-blockers, some prostaglandins (used to induce labor), and ergonovine (used to control blood loss after delivery).

How it can affect a developing embryo or fetus: There are no adequate reports or well-controlled studies in human fetuses. Aminophylline rapidly crosses the human placenta, reaching a level in the fetus similar to the mother's. Although there is no strong evidence that aminophylline causes birth defects in humans, studies in rodents noted an increase in birth defects and damage to embryos at doses that exceed the maximum recommended clinical dose by more than 20 times. However, animal studies are not necessarily good indicators of how a drug will behave in humans.

Breast-feeding: Aminophylline is excreted into breast milk and may cause irritability or other signs of toxicity in nursing newborns. However, it is generally considered safe for use while breast-feeding when the child is monitored by a pediatrician.

Potential drug interactions: Interaction between the following medications and aminophylline has the potential to impact the effect of one or more of the drugs. In some instances the interaction can be dangerous or life-threatening and must be avoided: allopurinol, cimetidine, ciprofloxacin, erythromycin, oral contraceptives, propranolol, a combination of theophylline and phenytoin, rifampin, lithium.

What the FDA says about use in pregnancy: Category C (see Appendix).

What the available studies say about breast-feeding: Probably safe.

The bottom line for you:

- Aminophylline can be used during pregnancy and while breast-feeding when required to control severe asthma. Mild to moderate asthma is best managed during pregnancy with inhaled steroids and/or beta-2 agonists.
- Be sure your pediatrician is aware that you are taking aminophylline if you choose to breast-feed.

AMITRIPTYLINE

Brand names: Amicen, Amilent, Amyzol, Elavil, Larozyl, Pinsanu, Vanatrip

Drug class: Antidepressant, tricyclic

Indications (what it is used for): Depression, chronic pain, headache (rarely). Uses not approved by the FDA include bulimia, bed-wetting, migraine, panic disorder, and postherpetic neuralgia.

How it works: Unknown; increases brain levels of the neurotransmitters serotonin and norepinephrine, which are involved in mood.

Contraindications (reasons you shouldn't take it): Hypersensitivity to drug or class, use of a monoamine oxidase inhibitor (MAOI) within 14 days.

Possible side effects and warnings: Can cause heart attack, seizures, stroke, low white blood cell or low platelet count, dry mouth, drowsiness, constipation, urinary retention, blurred vision, increased appetite, and confusion. Should be used with caution in women with a history of urinary retention, glaucoma, seizures, thyroid disease, liver damage, or suicidal thoughts.

How it can affect pregnant women: Depression is common during and after pregnancy but often goes unrecognized and untreated. Depression can be made worse by pregnancy or delivery, and suicide is a not uncommon cause of maternal death. Pregnancy is not a reason to discontinue antidepressant drugs if the medication is effective and needed. A woman being treated for depression who becomes pregnant should not discontinue medication abruptly on her own but rather discuss her treatment and condition with her medical provider. Despite the fact that pregnant women often use tricyclic antidepressants (TCAs), there are no well-controlled studies of amitriptyline during pregnancy. Recent population-based studies have revealed the use of tricyclic antidepressants may significantly increase the risk of preeclampsia by 2–3 times. The drug is metabolized by a specific liver enzyme that is reduced in some Caucasians (about 7–10% of Caucasians are so-called poor metabolizers); the prevalence of poor metabolizers among Asian, black, and other populations is unclear. Poor metabolizers have higher than expected levels of amitriptyline when given usual doses, so their levels should be measured during pregnancy. Although amitriptyline had no effect on placental blood flow in sheep, there is potential for a negative impact on placental blood flow if high blood pressure or preeclampsia (high blood pressure and protein in the urine during pregnancy and complications associated with it) complicates the pregnancy.

How it can affect a developing embryo or fetus: There are no controlled studies of the effect of amitriptyline on the human fetus. Both amitriptyline and its sibling, nortriptyline, cross the human placenta. Case reports of limited value suggest that there is a potential for central nervous system/limb abnormalities and developmental delay. However, a severely depressed mother is a risk to both fetus and newborn, and any adverse effect of amitriptyline is likely small considering the scarcity of such reports after years of experience with pregnant women. Rodent studies showed no adverse effects at doses up to 10 times the maximum recommended clinical dose. However, animal studies are not necessarily good indicators of how a drug will behave in humans.

Breast-feeding: Only low concentrations of amitriptyline are excreted into breast milk, and the resulting concentrations in the newborn are extremely low.

Potential drug interactions: Interaction between the following medications and amitriptyline has the potential to impact the effect of one or more of the drugs. In some instances the interaction can be dangerous or life-threatening and must be avoided: drugs that inhibit the liver enzyme CYP2D6, including quinidine, cimetidine, many other antidepressants, phenothiazines, certain antiarrhythmics such as propafenone and flecainide, and selective serotonin reuptake inhibitors (SSRIs) such as sertraline.

What the FDA says about use in pregnancy: Category D (see Appendix).

What the available studies say about breast-feeding: Likely safe.

The bottom line for you:

- Clinically significant depression should not be ignored during pregnancy.
- Amitriptyline may be used during pregnancy when a TCA is indicated for the treatment of significant depression.
- Women who become pregnant while taking and responding to a TCA should not discontinue their medication without consulting their physician and obstetrician.
- As for most psychotropic drugs, using amitriptyline alone and at the lowest effective quantity in divided doses to minimize the peaks and valleys of the drug in the maternal bloodstream may reduce any potential risks to the developing embryo or fetus.
- Amitriptyline is likely a drug of choice for breast-feeding women with depression in need of drug therapy.

AMLODIPINE

Brand name: Norvasc
Drug class: Calcium channel blocker

Indications (what it is used for): Chronic high blood pressure, angina (chest pain).

How it works: Calcium is necessary for muscle contraction. These agents work by blocking the flow of calcium into the muscle in blood vessels and the heart.

Contraindications (reasons you shouldn't take it): Hypersensitivity to drug or class.

Possible side effects and warnings: Can cause irregular heart rate, headache, dizziness, fatigue, nausea, palpitations, abdominal pain, muscle cramps, and loss of consciousness.

How it can affect pregnant women: There are no well-controlled studies of amlodipine in pregnant women. Other calcium channel antagonists are used to slow or stop preterm labor, and although amlodipine has similar properties, it has not been tested for effectiveness.

How it can affect a developing embryo or fetus: There are no adequate reports or well-controlled studies in human fetuses, and it is unknown whether amlodipine crosses the human placenta. Rodent studies are reassuring despite using doses more than 20 times the maximum recommended clinical dose. However, animal studies are not necessarily good indicators of how a drug will behave in humans.

Breast-feeding: There is no published data in nursing women. It is unknown whether amlodipine enters human breast milk.

Potential drug interactions: No drug-drug interaction studies in human subjects have apparently been conducted.

What the FDA says about use in pregnancy: Category C (see Appendix).

What the available studies suggest about breast-feeding: Unknown.

The bottom line for you:

- Amlodipine is a reasonable choice for the treatment of chronic high blood pressure in pregnancy if first-line agents such as labetalol fail.

- There are no published studies during breast-feeding. The children of women who breast-feed should be monitored for adverse effects.

AMOBARBITAL

Brand names: Amybal, Amycal, Amytal Sodium, Isobec, Placidyl, Sumital

Drug classes: Anxiolytic; Barbiturate; Sedative-hypnotic

Indications (what it is used for): Anxiety, sedative, hypnotic.

How it works: Depresses the central nervous system.

Contraindications (reasons you shouldn't take it): Hypersensitivity to drug or class, history of liver damage, porphyria (a rare group of blood disorders).

Possible side effects and warnings: Can cause respiratory depression or arrest, shortness of breath, liver toxicity, nausea and vomiting, drowsiness, agitation, confusion, loss of muscle control, nervousness, hallucinations, nightmares, constipation, central nervous system depression, and insomnia. Should be used with caution in women with kidney or lung disease.

How it can affect pregnant women: There are no adequate reports or well-controlled studies of amobarbital in pregnant women.

How it can affect a developing embryo or fetus: There are no adequate reports or well-controlled studies in human fetuses. Amobarbital crosses the human placenta, achieving fetal levels similar to those in the mother. There is no substantive evidence that amobarbital causes birth defects.

Breast-feeding: There is no published data in nursing women. It is unknown whether amobarbital enters human breast milk, although similar medications do.

Potential drug interactions: Interaction between the following medications and amobarbital has the potential to impact the effect of one or more of the drugs. In some instances the interaction can be dangerous or life-threatening and must be avoided: blood thinners; corticosteroids; griseofulvin; doxycycline; phenytoin; valproate and valproic acid, other central nervous system depressants, including sedatives or hypnotics, antihistamines, tranquilizers, or alcohol; monamine oxidase inhibitors (MAOIs) such as amitriptyline. May decrease the effect of estradiol in oral contraceptives, and there are reports of women treated with a similar drug, phenobarbital, becoming pregnant while taking oral contraceptives.

What the FDA says about use in pregnancy: Category D (see Appendix).

What the available studies suggest about breast-feeding: Unknown.

The bottom line for you:

- There are better alternatives to aid sleep during pregnancy and while breast-feeding, such as zolpidem or eszopiclone.

AMOXICILLIN

Brand names: Amoflux, Amoxiden, Amoxil, Amoxin, Amoxipenil, Amoxycillin, Anemol, Apitart, Aspenil, Audumic, Biomox, Bridopen, Excillin, Gemox, Imoxil, Jerramcil, Larotid, Limox, Pensyn, Polymox, Protexillin, Reloxyl, Ronemox, Samosillin, Samthongcillin, Senox, Sigmopen, Suprapen, Trilaxin, Trimox, Twicyl, Unicillin, Virgoxillin, Wymox, Yisulon, Zamocillin

Drug classes: Antibiotic; Penicillin

Indications (what it is used for): Bacterial infections, including chlamydia; preterm premature rupture of membranes (PPROM, water breaking before 37 weeks).

How it works: Kills bacteria by inhibiting maintenance of the bacterial cell wall.

Contraindications (reasons you shouldn't take it): Hypersensitivity to drug or class.

Possible side effects and warnings: Can cause low platelet and/or white blood cell count, life-threatening allergic reaction, anemia, Stevens-Johnson syndrome (a rare but serious skin reaction to medication), seizures, liver damage, nausea and vomiting, diarrhea, rash, hives, and eosinophilia (elevated level of one type of white blood cell). People with cytomegalovirus, Epstein-Barr virus (a virus of the herpes family), kidney damage, phenylketonuria (PKU), or an allergy to cephalosporin may be especially susceptible to adverse reactions to amoxicillin.

How it can affect pregnant women: Like ampicillin, amoxicillin is generally considered safe during pregnancy. It provides a greater than 90% cure rate for chlamydia.

How it can affect a developing embryo or fetus: Amoxicillin crosses the placenta and reaches therapeutic levels in the fetus and amniotic fluid. There are no reports of associated defects despite common use in pregnancy. It is generally considered safe for the fetus.

Breast-feeding: Amoxicillin is excreted into the breast milk in low concentrations and is considered safe during breast-feeding.

Potential drug interactions: Interaction between the following medications and amoxicillin has the potential to impact the effect of one or more of the drugs. In some instances the interaction can be dangerous or life-threatening and must be avoided: probenecid, chloramphenicol, macrolides, sulfonamides, tetracyclines. All broad-spectrum antibiotics such as amoxicillin may reduce the efficacy of oral contraceptives, so alternative methods of contraception are recommended during treatment.

What the FDA says about use in pregnancy: Category B (see Appendix).

What the available evidence suggests about breast-feeding safety: Safe.

The bottom line for you:

- Amoxicillin can be used to safely treat bacterial infections during pregnancy and while breast-feeding.

AMOXICILLIN-CLAVULANATE POTASSIUM

Brand names: Amoclan, Amoclav, Augmentin
Drug classes: Antibiotic; Beta-lactamase inhibitor; Penicillin

Indications (what it is used for): Killing bacteria that may be resistant to amoxicillin.

How it works: Clavulanate extends the antibiotic spectrum of amoxicillin to include bacteria normally resistant to amoxicillin.

Contraindications (reasons you shouldn't take it): Hypersensitivity to drug or class, augmentin-associated liver damage.

Possible side effects and warnings: See amoxicillin.

How it can affect pregnant women: Amoxicillin-clavulanate can prolong the time between preterm premature rupture of membranes (PPROM, water breaking before 37 weeks) and delivery by decreasing the chance of bacterial infection. However, there is an increased risk of bowel damage in a newborn, so erythromycin is the preferred antibiotic to prolong pregnancy after PPROM. Amoxicillin-clavulanate does not stop preterm labor with intact membranes (when water hasn't broken). Amoxicillin-clavulanate during pregnancy has been used safely and successfully as part of a multidrug regimen to treat drug-resistant tuberculosis.

How it can affect a developing embryo or fetus: Amoxicillin-clavulanate does not cause birth defects in animal or human studies. However, it does increase the risk of bowel damage in the newborn when used to treat women with PPROM.

Breast-feeding: Amoxicillin-clavulanate is excreted in breast milk, but no adverse effects in breast-feeding babies have been reported. It is generally considered safe.

Potential drug interactions: See amoxicillin

What the FDA says about use in pregnancy: Category B (see Appendix).

What the available studies suggest about breast-feeding: Safe.

The bottom line for you:

- Amoxicillin-clavulanate can be used with relative safely to treat bacterial infections during pregnancy and while breast-feeding.
- Because amoxicillin-clavulanate increases the risk of newborn bowel damage when used to

treat preterm premature rupture of membranes, erythromycin is the preferred medication.

- Amoxicillin-clavulanate does not prolong pregnancy in women who have preterm labor and intact membranes (water has not broken).

AMPHETAMINE-DEXTROAMPHETAMINE

Brand name: Adderall

Drug classes: Adrenergic agonist; Amphetamine; Anorexiant; Central nervous system stimulant

Indications (what it is used for): Attention deficit disorder, narcolepsy.

How it works: Unknown.

Contraindications (reasons you shouldn't take it): Hypersensitivity to drug or class, moderate to severe high blood pressure, overactive thyroid, substance abuse, glaucoma, use of a monoamine oxidase inhibitor (MAOI) within 14 days, symptomatic athersclerotic heart disease.

Possible side effects and warnings: Can cause poorly functioning heart muscle, rapid heart rate, tremor, psychosis, dependency, headache, high blood pressure, dizziness, dry mouth, heartburn, constipation, abdominal pain, anorexia, weight loss, mood swings, weakness, diarrhea, and hives. Should be used with caution in patients with a history of psychosis, high blood pressure, or tics.

How it can affect pregnant women: There are no adequate reports or well-controlled studies of amphetamine-dextroamphetamine in pregnancy. Methamphetamine is metabolized to amphetamine, and dependency on amphetamine (legal or street) is associated with preterm delivery (before 37 weeks). With the exception of narcolepsy, amphetamines are rarely indicated in pregnancy.

How it can affect a developing embryo or fetus: There are no adequate reports or well-controlled studies in human fetuses. There are scattered reports from individual women of various birth defects occurring after first-trimester use, but no pattern of birth defects has been detected. Infants born to amphetamine-dependent women show signs of withdrawal, indicating that amphetamine crosses the placenta and reaches the fetus. Amphetamine use is associated with an increased risk of fetuses who do not grow normally in the womb and may have been oxygen deprived. Exposure to amphetamine in the womb is associated with aggressive behavior and delayed development in offspring.

Breast-feeding: Amphetamine is concentrated in breast milk and is generally considered incompatible with breast-feeding.

Potential drug interactions: Many drugs can interact badly with amphetamines. Interaction between the following medications or substances and amphetamine has the potential to impact the effect of one or more of the drugs. In some instances the interaction can be dangerous or life-threatening and must be avoided: medicines and foods that increase gastrointestinal activity, including guanethidine, reserpine, ascorbic acid, and fruit juices; drugs that increase acid in the urine, such as ammonium chloride; drugs to make urine more alkaline, such as acetazolamide; thiazides. Before prescribing an amphetamine, it is important for the doctor to know every medication (prescription and over-the-counter) the woman is currently taking.

What the FDA says about use in pregnancy: Category C (see Appendix).

What the available evidence suggests about breast-feeding safety: Generally considered unsafe.

The bottom line for you:

- Amphetamine is rarely a necessary treatment in women of reproductive age and should be avoided in pregnant and breast-feeding women.
- Women who are dependent on amphetamine should be counseled and enrolled in a detoxification program before conception when possible.

AMPHOTERICIN B

Brand names: Abelcet, AmBisome, Amphocin, Amphotec, Fungilin, Fungizone IV, Fungizone Topical

Drug class: Antifungal

Indications (what it is used for): Systemic fungal infection.

How it works: Weakens the cell wall of the fungus so it cannot reproduce.

Contraindications (reasons you shouldn't take it): Hypersensitivity to drug or class.

Possible side effects and warnings: Can cause seizures, abnormal heart rate, cardiac arrest, bleeding from the bowel, kidney failure, low platelet and/or white blood cell counts, liver dysfunction, chills, fever, high blood pressure, nausea and vomiting, headache, loss of appetite, diarrhea, and rash. Should be used with caution in women with kidney dysfunction.

How it can affect pregnant women: There are no adequate reports or well-controlled studies of amphotericin in pregnant women. It is the drug of choice for widespread, invasive fungal infections, whether life-threatening or less severe. Amphotericin has been used extensively during pregnancy without increased risk of complications.

How it can affect a developing embryo or fetus: There are no adequate reports or well-controlled studies in human fetuses. Amphotericin crosses the human placenta and is deposited in fetal tissues, where it can remain at significant levels weeks after the mother has discontinued the medication or given birth. There are no reports of birth defects in either humans or rodents.

Breast-feeding: There is no published data in nursing women. It is unknown whether amphotericin enters human breast milk.

Potential drug interactions: Interaction between the following medications and amphotericin has the potential to impact the effect of one or more of the drugs. In some instances the interaction can be dangerous or life-threatening and must be avoided: corticosteroids; digoxin; imidazoles such as ketoconazole, miconazole, clotrimazole, fluconazole.

What the FDA says about use in pregnancy: Category B (see Appendix).

What the available evidence suggests about breast-feeding safety: Unknown.

The bottom line for you:
- Amphotericin B remains the drug of choice during pregnancy for systemic, invasive fungal infections, whether life-threatening or less severe.
- There are no identified studies of amphotericin B while breast-feeding. The safest approach is to avoid it.

AMPICILLIN

Brand names: Adumic, Amblosin, Ampen, Ampesid, Ampibel, Ampicillin, Ampiclox, Ampikel, Ampil, Ampisol, Austrapen, Bionacillin, Cinpillin, Copharcilin, Cryocil, Doktacillin, Fortapen, Herpen, Ingacillin, Isocillin, Marcillin, Nelpicil, Pentrex, Pfizerpen, Principen, Protexillin, Resan, Statcillin, Tampicillin, Tokiocillin, Totacillin, Trilaxan, Ukapen, Vialicina

Drug classes: Antibiotic; Penicillin

Indications (what it is used for): Group B streptococcal infection (widespread), prevention of endocarditis (inflammation of the lining of the heart), bacterial infections.

How it works: Kills bacteria by destroying the cell wall.

Contraindications (reasons you shouldn't take it): Hypersensitivity to drug or class, pseudomembranous colitis (bacterial infection of the colon).

Possible side effects and warnings: Can cause seizures, low platelet and/or white blood cell counts, Stevens-Johnson syndrome (a rare but serious skin reaction to medication), interstitial nephritis (inflammation in the kidneys), hemolytic anemia, nausea and vomiting, diarrhea, headache, confusion, and rash. Should be used with caution in women with Epstein-Barr virus (a virus of the herpes family), cytomegalovirus, penicillin or cephalosporin allergy, or kidney dysfunction.

How it can affect pregnant women: Ampicillin is one of the most commonly used antibiotics during pregnancy. It reduces the risk of postoperative fever in women undergoing cesarean delivery. Pregnancy significantly increases the rate at which ampicillin is cleared from the body, so the dose during pregnancy should be increased and the interval between doses decreased. When combined with sulbactam, ampicillin significantly prolongs the period from membrane rupture (water breaking) to delivery in women with preterm premature rupture of membranes (PPROM), water breaking before 37 weeks. Ampicillin alone is less effective. Ampicillin has been unsuccessful in delaying or avoiding preterm delivery (before 37 weeks) in women without PPROM.

How it can affect an embryo or fetus: There is a long clinical experience with ampicillin during pregnancy. There is no evidence that it causes birth defects in either humans or rodents.

Breast-feeding: Minimal amounts of ampicillin are excreted in breast milk. It is generally considered compatible with breast-feeding.

Potential drug interactions: Interaction between the following medications and ampicillin has the potential to impact the effect of one or more of the drugs. In some instances the interaction can be dangerous or life-threatening and must be avoided: probenecid, chloramphenicol, macrolides, sulfonamides, tetracyclines.

What the FDA says about use in pregnancy: Category B (see Appendix).

What the available evidence suggests about breast-feeding safety: Safe.

The bottom line for you:

- Ampicillin appears safe and effective for the treatment of susceptible bacterial infections during pregnancy and while breast-feeding.

AMPICILLIN-SULBACTAM SODIUM

Brand names: Ubacillin, Unasyn
Drug classes: Antibiotic; Penicillin
Indications (what it is used for): Bacterial infections that are resistant to ampicillin alone.
How it works: Kills bacteria by destroying the cell wall, with the added ability to kill bacteria that destroy penicillin agents.

Contraindications (reasons you shouldn't take it): Hypersensitivity to drug or class.

Possible side effects: Can cause vaginitis, seizures, low platelet and/or low white blood cell counts, anemia, Stevens-Johnson syndrome and toxic epidermal necrosis (rare but serious skin disorders), kidney inflammation, hemolytic anemia, nausea and vomiting, diarrhea, headache, confusion, and rash. Should be used with caution in women who have Epstein-Barr virus (a virus of the herpes family), cytomegalovirus, penicillin or cephalosporin allergy, or kidney dysfunction.

How it can affect pregnant women: Unlike ampicillin alone, ampicillin-sulbactam can prolong the time between preterm premature rupture of membranes (PPROM, water breaking before 37 weeks) and delivery. See ampicillin for other possible effects.

How it can affect a developing embryo or fetus: Ampicillin-sulbactam delays delivery after PPROM and reduces newborn infections after delivery. However, it is no more effective for that purpose than erythromycin, which is the current drug of choice. There is no substantive evidence that ampicillin-sulbactam causes birth defects in either humans or rodents.

Breast-feeding safety: Minimal amounts of ampicillin-sulbactam are excreted in breast milk. It is generally considered compatible with breast-feeding.

Potential drug interactions: See ampicillin.

What the FDA says about use in pregnancy: Category B (see Appendix).

What the available studies say about use in breast-feeding: Safe.

The bottom line for you:

- Ampicillin-sulbactam appears safe and effective for use during pregnancy and while breast-feeding.

ANTHRALIN

Brand names A-Fil, Amitase, Anthraderm, Anthra-Derm, Anthraforte, Anthra-Tex, Dithranol, Drithocreme, Dritho-Scalp, Lasan, Micanol, Psoriate

Drug classes: Dermatologic; Psoriasis

Indications (what it is used for): Pustular psoriasis.

How it works: Appears to block the DNA synthesis needed for skin cell growth as well as decrease the ability of skin cells to stick together.

Contraindications (reasons you shouldn't take it): Hypersensitivity to drug or class, lesions on the face or genitals.

Possible side effects: Can cause skin irritation, contact dermatitis, hair and nail discoloration, and red skin. Should be used with caution in women with kidney dysfunction or aspirin allergy.

How it can affect pregnant women: Psoriasis is a chronically recurring inflammatory disease that affects the skin, scalp, and joints. Pregnancy may trigger pustular psoriasis. Although anthralin is generally considered safe for use during pregnancy when applied to the skin, there are no adequate reports or well-controlled studies of it in pregnant women.

How it can affect a developing embryo or fetus: There are no adequate reports or well-controlled studies in human or rodent fetuses.

Breast-feeding: There is no published data in nursing women. It is unknown whether anthralin enters human breast milk. However, since it is applied topically, it is unlikely that a breast-feeding baby would ingest a clinically significant amount.

Potential drug interactions: No drug-drug interaction studies in human subjects have been conducted.

What the FDA says about use in pregnancy: Category C (see Appendix).

What the available evidence suggests about breast-feeding safety: Likely safe.

The bottom line for you:

- Anthralin should be used during pregnancy and while breast-feeding only if the benefit to the woman justifies the potential risk to the embryo or fetus. If possible, use should be confined to the second and third trimesters.
- Probably safe for use while breast-feeding.

ANTIHEMOPHILIC FACTOR

Brand names: Alphanate, Bioclate, Factor VIII, Green Eight, Haemoctin SDH, Helixate, Hemofil-M, Humate-P, Hyate:C, Koate, Koate-HP, Kogenate, Melate, Nybcen, Omrixate, Profilate

Drug classes: Antihemophilic; Blood-clotting factor

Indications (what it is used for): Hereditary factor VIII deficiency (a rare blood-clotting disorder).

How it works: Replaces the missing factor necessary for clot formation.

Contraindications (reasons you shouldn't take it): Hypersensitivity to drug or class.

Possible side effects: Can cause life-threatening allergic reaction, HIV, hepatitis, hives, wheezing, nausea, fever, chills, and chest tightness. Should be used with caution in women with liver dysfunction.

How it can affect pregnant women: There are no adequate reports or well-controlled studies of antihemophilic factor in pregnancy since the factor VIII deficiency is linked to the X chromosome and therefore occurs almost exclusively in males (though there are rare cases involving women). Replacement does not work in women with an acquired inhibitor of factor VIII.

How it can affect a developing embryo or fetus: There are no adequate reports or well-controlled studies in human fetuses and no studies at all in animals. However, factor VIII is a large protein that is not likely to cross the placenta.

Breast-feeding: There are no adequate reports or well-controlled studies in nursing women. However, the digestive process destroys factor VIII, which means that a breast-feeding baby would not absorb the active medication.

Potential drug interactions: No drug-drug interaction studies in human subjects have been reported.

What the FDA says about use in pregnancy: Category C (see Appendix).

What the available evidence suggests about breast-feeding safety: Likely safe.

The bottom line for you:
- Antihemophilic factor is safe for use during pregnancy and while breast-feeding.

ANTITHROMBIN III CONCENTRATE

Brand names: ATnativ, Thrombate III

Drug classes: Anticoagulant; Blood-clotting factor

Indications (what it is used for): ATIII deficiency, hereditary or acquired.

How it works: Replaces an important anticoagulation substance that is missing.

Contraindications (reasons you shouldn't take it): Hypersensitivity to drug or class.

Possible side effects and warnings: Can cause dizziness, nausea, bitter taste, cramps, and chest tightness.

How it can affect pregnant women: Antithrombin III is an important naturally occurring substance that prevents the development of blood clots. There are no adequate studies of antithrombin III concentrate in pregnant women. However, ATIII production and consumption increases during normal pregnancy, and pregnant women with a hereditary deficiency have a dramatically increased risk of developing blood clots. In these women, heparin, the drug of choice for preventing blood clots in pregnancy, may be ineffective, in which case, ATIII replacement will be necessary to prevent or treat clots. It is used on an ongoing basis throughout pregnancy when indicated. Also, several studies suggest that ATIII replacement may help women with preeclampsia (high blood pressure and protein in the urine during pregnancy and complications associated with it) since preeclampsia causes an ATIII deficiency.

How it can affect a developing embryo or fetus: There are no adequate reports or well-controlled studies in human fetuses. There are no reports of adverse fetal effects, and because the ATIII molecule is likely too large to pass through the placenta, it is unlikely to have any adverse effects on the fetus.

Breast-feeding: There are no adequate reports or well-controlled studies in nursing women, and it is unknown whether antithrombin III concentrate enters human breast milk. However, the digestive process destroys antithrombin III, which means that a breast-feeding baby would not absorb the active medication.

Potential drug interactions: No drug-drug interactions in human subjects have been reported.

What the FDA says about use in pregnancy: Category C (see Appendix).

What the available evidence suggests about breast-feeding safety: Likely safe.

The bottom line for you:
- Antithrombin III concentrate is safe for use during pregnancy and while breast-feeding.

ARDEPARIN SODIUM

Brand name: Normiflo

Drug classes: Anticoagulant; Low-molecular-weight heparin

Indications (what it is used for): Prevention of blood clots after joint replacement.

How it works: Binds to and accelerates the activity of ATIII (an important naturally occurring substance that prevents the development of blood clots); also binds heparin cofactor II.

Contraindications (reasons you shouldn't take it): Hypersensitivity to drug, class, or pork products; bleeding; low platelet count.

Possible side effects and warnings: Can cause hemorrhage, bruising at injection site and elsewhere, fever, nausea and vomiting, joint or chest pain. Injections (intramuscular, intravenous, spinal, or epidural) may be contraindicated during treatment with ardeparin sodium.

How it can affect pregnant women: There is no published data with ardeparin during pregnancy. This class of drugs is being used with increasing frequency during pregnancy for the treatment of a variety of clotting abnormalities; however, there are medications with which there is more experience during pregnancy.

How it can affect a developing embryo or fetus: There are no adequate reports or well-controlled studies in human fetuses, but the molecular weight of ardeparin suggests that it cannot cross the placenta. Rodent studies do not show any adverse effects at up to 3 times the maximum recommended clinical dose. However, animal studies are not necessarily good indicators of how a drug will behave in humans.

Breast-feeding: There are no adequate reports or well-controlled studies in nursing women. It is unknown whether ardeparin enters human breast milk. However, the digestive process destroys ardeparin, which means that a breast-feeding baby would not absorb the active medication.

Potential drug interactions: Ardeparin may increase the effects of other anticoagulant agents.

What the FDA says about use in pregnancy: Category C (see Appendix).

What the available evidence suggests about breast-feeding safety: Likely safe.

The bottom line for you:

- There are alternative agents for the prevention of blood clots, such as unfractionated heparin and enoxaparin, with which there is more experience during pregnancy and while breast-feeding.

ASCORBIC ACID

Brand names: Ascor L 500, Cee-500, Cenolate, Mega-C/A Plus, vitamin C

Drug class: Vitamin, nutritional

Indications (what it is used for): Vitamin deficiency, vitamin supplementation during pregnancy, scurvy.

How it works: Plays an essential in the production of new cells.

Contraindications (reasons you shouldn't take it): Hypersensitivity to drug or class, undiagnosed anemia.

Possible side effects and warnings: Can cause loss of appetite, nausea and vomiting, abdominal pain, gas, altered sleep patterns, irritability, hyperactivity, red skin, rash, itching.

How it can affect pregnant women: Ascorbic acid is an essential vitamin contained in most prenatal vitamins. The recommended daily dietary allowance (RDA) is 80–85 mg during pregnancy. And although it is necessary for collagen formation, tissue repair, synthesis of lipids and proteins, metabolism of iron and folic acid, resistance to infection, and preservation of blood vessel integrity, excess ascorbic acid does not reduce the risk of pregnancy complications. Prolonged deficiency leads to a disease called scurvy.

How it can affect a developing embryo or fetus: There are no adequate and well-controlled studies in human fetuses. Ascorbic acid crosses the placenta and is concentrated in the fetus. Rodent studies using doses higher than those recommended in humans have not found adverse effects. In diabetic rats, ascorbic acid reduced the rate of birth defects. However, animal studies are not necessarily good indicators of how a drug will behave in humans.

Breast-feeding: There are no adequate reports or well-controlled studies in nursing women. Ascorbic acid is excreted in breast milk; the RDA for breast-feeding women is 120 mg. The level of ascorbic acid in refrigerated breast milk declines by a third within 24 hours.

Potential drug interactions: No drug-drug interactions in humans have been reported.

What the FDA says about use in pregnancy: Category A (which changes to C if maternal intake exceeds the RDA) (see Appendix).

What the available evidence suggests about breast-feeding safety: Safe.

The bottom line for you:

- Ascorbic acid is an essential vitamin contained in most prenatal vitamins.
- The recommended daily allowance for pregnant women is 80–85 mg.

- The recommended daily allowance for breast-feeding women is 120 mg.

ASPIRIN

Brand names: Aspergum, Bufferin, Easprin, Ecotrin, Empirin, Fasprin, Genacote, Halfprin, Zorprin

Drug classes: Analgesic, nonnarcotic; Antipyretic; NSAID; Platelet inhibitor; Salicylate

Indications (what it is used for): Fever, mild pain, small brain strokes, heart attack, arthritis, rheumatic fever.

How it works: Aspirin has multiple actions including inhibition of the synthesis and release of prostaglandins (substances related to muscle cramps and inflammation); its painkilling properties also appear to reflect its effect on the peripheral and central nervous systems.

Contraindications (reasons you shouldn't take it): Hypersensitivity to drug or class, G6PD deficiency, bleeding disorder.

Possible side effects and warnings: Can cause bleeding from the bowel, low platelet count, life-threatening allergic reaction, swelling underneath the skin, Reye's syndrome (swelling in the liver and brain), liver damage, heartburn, ringing in the ears, rash, bruising, and bleeding. Should be used with caution in women with gastrointestinal lesions, kidney or liver damage, thrombotic thrombocytopenic purpura (a serious clotting disorder), or low levels of blood-clotting factors.

How it can affect pregnant women: Aspirin is a potent drug found in many over-the-counter medications. A daily dose of aspirin (81 mg) is recommended by the American Heart Association for women with at least a 10% risk of developing coronary heart disease within the next 10 years, and by the U.S. Preventive Services Task Force for a risk 3% or higher within 5 years.

Aspirin is as effective as warfarin for preventing recurrent stroke in nonpregnant women with a single positive antiphospholipid antibody test result and a history of stroke. Low-dose aspirin plus heparin is an effective treatment for antiphospholipid syndrome in pregnancy, which is characterized by recurrent miscarriages associated with laboratory abnormalities and the development of blood clots. It is not effective for unexplained miscarriage. There are numerous studies of the effect of aspirin in healthy women and women with recurrent miscarriage. These trials have reached conflicting conclusions, and the safest course is to avoid aspirin in the first trimester.

Several studies find that low-dose aspirin can have beneficial effects on the rates of preeclampsia or reduced fetal growth based on the time in pregnancy when it is started. For the maximum benefit, it should be started before 16 weeks. There is little benefit if begun after 20 weeks. Pregnant women ingesting large quantities of aspirin are at risk for complications such as prolonged pregnancy, bleeding after delivery, decreased birth weight, and stillbirth. It is generally recommended that high doses of aspirin be avoided during the third trimester.

How it can affect a developing embryo or fetus: Aspirin crosses the human placenta, and maternal aspirin use has been linked to bowel defects in the newborn. It is probably best avoided during the first 12 weeks of pregnancy while the fetus's organs are forming. No negative effects have been shown after the first trimester with 81 mg or less of aspirin daily, despite the fact it reduces fetal prostaglandin levels. Low-dose aspirin, less than 160 mg per day, does not increase the risk of fetal bleeding; however, high doses of aspirin have been associated with an increase in fetal or newborn bleeding and should be avoided certainly in the third trimester.

Breast-feeding: Single doses of aspirin should not pose any risk to the breast-feeding newborn. However, for women on high doses of aspirin to treat, for example, arthritis or rheumatic fever, breast-feeding can result in newborn levels as high as if the babies themselves were being treated. In those instances, the aspirin should either be temporarily discontinued or the infant only partially breast-fed to minimize exposure.

Potential drug interactions: Interaction between the following medications and aspirin has the potential to impact the effect of one or more of the drugs. In some instances the interaction can be dangerous or life-threatening and must be avoided: probenecid; sulfinpyrazone; alcohol; corticosteroids; pyrazolone derivatives such as phenylbutazone, oxyphenbutazone, and dipyrone; phenobarbital and urinary alkalinizers; phenytoin; propranolol.

What the FDA says about use in pregnancy: No assigned category. Should be avoided in the third trimester. (see Appendix).

What the available evidence suggests about breast-feeding safety: Likely safe.

The bottom line for you:

- Aspirin may be associated with adverse pregnancy outcomes when taken in the first trimester. It is best to avoid aspirin in the first trimester.
- Low dose aspirin improves pregnancy outcome when initiated between 12 and 16 weeks gestation.
- It is generally recommended that high doses of aspirin be avoided during the third trimester.
- Taking up to 2 adult aspirin every 6 hours is safe while breast-feeding. Higher doses may also be safe, but it is essential that you speak with your pediatrician about higher dose regimens.

ATENOLOL

Brand names: Alinor, Atolmin, Blotex, B-Vasc, Seles, Tenolin, Tenormin, Tensig

Drug classes: Antiadrenergic; Beta-blocker

Indications (what it is used for): High blood pressure, heart attack, angina (chest pain).

How it works: Relaxes blood vessels and slows the heart rate to decrease blood pressure and lower oxygen consumption.

Contraindications (reasons you shouldn't take it): Hypersensitivity to drug or class, second- or third-degree heart block, slow heart rate, poor heart function.

Possible side effects and warnings: Can cause congestive heart failure, bronchospasm, slow heart rate, cold extremities, fatigue, nausea, rash, and low blood pressure. Should be used with caution in women with kidney disease.

How it can affect pregnant women: High blood pressure complicates 5–10% of pregnancies and is a leading cause of maternal disease and death both during pregnancy and after delivery. Severe high blood pressure (systolic equal to or greater than 160 and diastolic equal to or greater than 110) should be treated immediately. Mild chronic high blood pressure is associated with increased maternal and fetal risks, but there is no consensus as to whether mild to moderate high blood pressure should be treated during pregnancy. The choice involves balancing the risk that mild chronic high blood pressure could progress to severe high blood pressure and preterm birth (before 37 weeks) with potential risks from the medications used to treat high blood pressure. In one small trial, atenolol reduced the frequency of preeclampsia (high blood pressure and protein in the urine during pregnancy and complications associated with it) in women who were pumping more blood than is average for pregnancy.

How it can affect a developing embryo or fetus: There are no adequate reports or well-controlled studies in human fetuses. Atenolol crosses the placenta. There is no reasonable evidence that it causes birth defects. As a group, beta-blockers are associated with a fetus that does not grow as well as it should, though controversy continues as to whether this is caused by the medication itself or the disease the medication is used to treat. Atenolol reduces maternal cardiac output, which means that less blood is available to the fetus. If the dose is not adjusted to account for this possibility, there is a risk that the decreased output will result in restricted growth of the fetus.

Breast-feeding: Atenolol is concentrated in breast milk, and a significantly slowed heart rate may occur in newborns nursed by women on atenolol. It should probably be avoided.

Potential drug interactions: Interaction between the following medications and atenolol has the potential to impact the effect of one or more of the drugs. In some instances the interaction can be dangerous or life-threatening and must be avoided: calcium channel blockers (e.g., nifedipine), catecholamine-depleting drugs (e.g., reserpine), clonidine (withdrawal), prostaglandin synthase–inhibiting drugs, such as indomethacin.

What the FDA says about use in pregnancy: Category D (see Appendix).

What the available evidence suggests about breast-feeding safety: Not safe.

The bottom line for you:

- Atenolol use is associated with fetuses that do not grow normally unless the mother's cardiac output is monitored. There are alternative drugs for the treatment of chronic high blood pressure (e.g., labetalol) with a greater margin of safety during pregnancy.
- Atenolol should be avoided while breast-feeding.

ATORVASTATIN

Brand name: Lipitor

Drug classes: Antihyperlipidemic; HMG-CoA reductase inhibitor; Statin

Indications (what it is used for): Hypercholesterolemia and familial hypercholesterolemia, hypertriglyceridemia, dysbetalipoproteinemia (all disorders in which there are too many fatty substances such as triglycerides and lipids in the blood).

How it works: Inhibits an enzyme involved in the production of cholesterol.

Contraindications (reasons you shouldn't take it): Hypersensitivity to drug or class, active liver disease, unexplained elevated liver function tests, pregnancy, breast-feeding.

Possible side effects and warnings: Can cause muscle breakdown, liver damage, heartburn, constipation, diarrhea, rash, muscle aches, and elevated liver function tests or creatinine phosphokinase (CPK). Should be used with caution in women with a history of liver disease or alcohol abuse.

How it can affect pregnant women: Only several hundred women who took atorvastatin during pregnancy have been documented. There is evidence to suggested an increase in adverse outcomes.

How it can affect a developing embryo or fetus: Cholesterol and related substances are building blocks for the placenta and fetus, which is why there is concern about using drugs to block their production during pregnancy. There are no adequate reports or well-controlled studies of atorvastatin in human fetuses. Atorvastatin inhibits a placental transport protein that usually acts to protect the fetus from maternal toxins. It is unknown whether atorvastatin crosses the human placenta; it does cross the rodent placenta. Case reports raise the possibility that atorvastatin can have an adverse effect on a fetus. However, in a prospective study (a study that follows a group of individuals for a period of time, which has a lower risk of false conclusions) there was no increase in birth defects, although the women treated with statins did deliver earlier. No realistic conclusion is possible without additional study.

Breast-feeding: There are no adequate reports or well-controlled studies in nursing women. It is unknown whether atorvastatin enters human breast milk, although it is excreted in the breast milk of rats. Because it is not well absorbed orally and has a high degree of protein binding, it is unlikely that clinically relevant amounts of the medication would be found in breast-fed infants.

Potential drug interactions: Interaction between the following medications or substances and atorvastatin has the potential to impact the effect of one or more of the drugs. In some instances the interaction can be dangerous or life-threatening and must be avoided: digoxin, erythromycin, grapefruit and grapefruit juice. Atorvastatin increases the level of two components of oral contraceptives—norethindrone and ethinyl estradiol—so a lower dose oral contraceptive is preferred for women being treated with atorvastatin.

What the FDA says about use in pregnancy: Category X (see Appendix).

What the available evidence suggests about breast-feeding safety: Unknown; may be safe.

The bottom line for you:

- For most women with high cholesterol and triglycerides, stopping statin therapy during pregnancy should not significantly impact their long-term health.
- Atorvastatin should be used during the first trimester and breast-feeding only if the benefit to the woman justifies the potential risk to the embryo, fetus, or newborn.

ATOVAQUONE

Brand name: Mepron

Drug classes: Antiprotozoal; Antifungal

Indications (what it is used for): Malaria, *Pneumocystis* pneumonia (PCP) in patients who can't tolerate trimethoprim sulfamethoxazole.

How it works: Blocks energy generation (stops the growth) in the parasite that causes PCP.

Contraindications (reasons you shouldn't take it): Hypersensitivity to drug or class.

Possible side effects and warnings: Can cause rash, fever, nausea, diarrhea, headache, insomnia, hyperglycemia, and elevated amylase.

How it can affect pregnant women: There are no adequate reports or well-controlled studies of atovaquone during pregnancy. Pregnant women have a higher risk of sickness and death from malaria. Several studies suggest that the combination of atovaquone and proguanil is effective for the prevention of malaria during pregnancy. Recent reports on the use of atovaquone in combination with other antimalarials (artesunate and proguanil) to treat pregnant women with multidrug-resistant tuberculosis during their second and third trimesters found the combination was well tolerated and effective. The research suggested that the dose of atovaquone may need to be increased during pregnancy to en-

sure effectiveness and minimize the risk of developing drug tolerance.

How it can affect a developing embryo or fetus: There are no adequate reports or well-controlled studies in human fetuses. It is unknown whether atovaquone crosses the human placenta. The malaria treatment trials conducted thus far have found no unexplained adverse outcomes in the newborn. Atovaquone crosses the rodent placenta poorly, achieving a level only 30% of the maternal level, and there is no evidence in rodent studies of birth defects or low birth weight despite the use of doses higher than those used clinically. However, animal studies are not necessarily good indicators of how a drug will behave in humans.

Breast-feeding: There are no adequate reports or well-controlled studies in nursing women. If a nursing mother has malaria, having a high level of drug in the breast milk would actually be desirable. It is unknown whether atovaquone enters human breast milk. In rats, the milk achieves a level approximately one-third of the drug level in the mother. The Centers for Disease Control and Prevention recommend that women breast-feeding infants under 25 pounds use mefloquine instead if they need to be on medication to prevent malaria.

Potential drug interactions: Interaction between the following medications and atovaquone has the potential to impact the effect of one or more of the drugs. In some instances the interaction can be dangerous or life-threatening and must be avoided: other plasma protein–bound drugs, such as rifampin.

What the FDA says about use in pregnancy: Category C (see Appendix).

What the available evidence suggests about breast-feeding safety: Unknown.

The bottom line for you:

- The risk of malaria or PCP to mother and fetus is greater than the risk of atovaquone.
- The CDC recommends that breast-feeding women with infants weighing under 25 pounds use mefloquine for malaria prevention.

ATOVAQUONE-PROGUANIL

Brand name: Malarone

Drug classes: Antimalarial; Antiprotozoal

Indications (what it is used for): Treatment and prevention of malaria.

How it works: Atovaquone blocks energy generation in the parasite that causes malaria. The addition of proguanil inhibits an enzyme that helps cells proliferate.

Contraindications (reasons you shouldn't take it): Hypersensitivity to drug or class, poor kidney function.

Possible side effects and warnings: Can cause a failure to make blood cells, low platelet and/or white blood cell count, light sensitivity, abdominal pain, nausea and vomiting, diarrhea, dizziness, itching, rash, ringing in the ears, mouth ulcerations, and liver abnormalities. Should be used with caution in women with poor kidney function, nausea and vomiting, diarrhea, dizziness, itching, rash, ringing in the ears, mouth ulcerations, or liver abnormalities.

How it can affect pregnant women: Pregnant women have a higher risk of sickness and death from malaria. There are no adequate reports or well-controlled studies of atovaquone-proguanil in pregnant women. This is a combination pill, and both drugs appear to be eliminated more rapidly during pregnancy, suggesting that the dose may need to be increased during pregnancy to ensure effectiveness and minimize the risk of drug resistance.

How it can affect a developing embryo or fetus: There are no adequate reports or well-controlled studies in human fetuses. It is unknown whether atovaquone-proguanil crosses the human placenta. The malaria studies did not find an increase in adverse outcomes for newborns. Atovaquone crosses the rodent placenta poorly, achieving a level only 30% of the maternal level. Though maternal and placental parasitemia (parasites in the blood) is reduced by treatment, it has not resulted in a detectable reduction in the newborn death rate from parasitemia.

Breast-feeding: See atovaquone. Only trace amounts of proguanil are found in human breast milk. The CDC recommends that women breast-feeding infants under 25 pounds use mefloquine instead if they need to be on medication to prevent malaria.

Drug interactions: See atovaquone. Reduced absorption of cloxacillin has been reported when given with proguanil.

What the FDA says about use in pregnancy: Category C (see Appendix).

What the available evidence suggests about breast-feeding safety: Safe.

The bottom line for you:

- Atovaquone-proguanil may be used to treat malaria during pregnancy and while breast-feeding when indicated, since the risk of harm to the newborn from treatment is likely lower than the risk of untreated malaria.
- The CDC recommends that breast-feeding women with infants under 25 pounds use mefloquine instead for malaria prevention.

ATRACURIUM

Brand name: Tracrium

Drug classes: Anesthesia, adjunct; Musculoskeletal agent; Neuromuscular blocker, nondepolarizing

Indications (what it is used for): Muscle relaxation during surgery.

How it works: Prevents nerve messages from triggering muscle contraction.

Contraindications (reasons you shouldn't take it): Hypersensitivity to drug or class.

Possible side effects and warnings: Can cause cardiovascular collapse, rapid heart rate, low blood pressure, rash, flushing, and hives. Should be administered with caution to women with liver or kidney dysfunction, low blood pressure, cardiovascular disease, or electrolyte abnormalities.

How it can affect pregnant women: There are no adequate reports or well-controlled studies of atracurium in pregnant women. Pregnancy does not alter the way atracurium is processed in the body.

How it can affect a developing embryo or fetus: There are no adequate reports or well-controlled

studies in human fetuses. Although small amounts are shown to cross the human placenta, its use during cesarean section is not associated with harmful effects on the newborn. Atracurium has been administered to fetuses to immobilize them during fetal surgery.

Breast-feeding: There are no adequate reports or well-controlled studies in nursing women. It is unknown whether atracurium enters human breast milk. Considering its short-term use at delivery, atracurium is unlikely to affect a breast-feeding newborn.

Potential drug interactions: Drugs that block nerve impulses to muscles may increase the effect of atracurium, including enflurane, isoflurane, and halothane; certain antibiotics, especially the aminoglycosides and polymyxins; lithium; magnesium salts; procainamide; quinidine.

What the FDA says about use in pregnancy: Category C (see Appendix).

What the available evidence suggests about breast-feeding safety: Likely safe.

The bottom line for you:

- Atracurium can be used for surgery during pregnancy and while breast-feeding.

ATROPINE

Brand names: Atro Ofteno, Atropair, Atropen, Atropinol, Atropisol, Borotropin, Dosatropine, Isopto Atropine, Isotic Cycloma, I-Tropine, Liotropina, Minims-Atropine, Ocu-Tropine, Sal-Tropine, Spectro-Atropine

Drug classes: Anesthesia, adjunct; Antiarrhythmics; Antidote; Cycloplegic; Mydriatic; Ophthalmic.

Indications (what it is used for): Symptomatic slow heart rate, organophosphate poisoning, with general anesthesia to reduce oral secretions.

How it works: Reduces nerve transmission by blocking a nerve receptor.

Contraindications (reasons you shouldn't take it): Hypersensitivity to drug or class, narrow-angle glaucoma, paralytic ileus (bowel obstruction),

asthma, myasthenia gravis (an autoimmune disease causing muscle weakness).

Possible side effects and warnings: Can cause slow or rapid heart rate; palpitations; blurred vision; headache; nausea and vomiting; dizziness; dry mouth; restlessness; delirium; tremor; hot, dry skin.

How it can affect pregnant women: There are no adequate reports or well-controlled studies of atropine in pregnant women. However, it has been used with apparent safety during pregnancy for more than 50 years.

How it can affect a developing embryo or fetus: There are no adequate reports or well-controlled studies in human fetuses. Atropine rapidly crosses the human placenta, and the fetus responds to the direct administration of atropine with an increase in heart rate.

Breast-feeding: There are no adequate reports or well-controlled studies in nursing women. It is unknown whether atropine enters human breast milk. Considering its brief use, atropine is unlikely to have an effect on a breast-feeding newborn.

Potential drug interactions: The signs of atropine's effect (flushing, excessive dilation of the pupil, rapid heart rate, dryness of the mouth and nose) may occur earlier than expected when used with pralidoxime.

What the FDA says about use in pregnancy: Category C (see Appendix).

What the available evidence suggests about breast-feeding safety: Unknown; probably safe when used in a limited fashion as described.

The bottom line for you:

- Atropine may be safely used in surgery during pregnancy and while breast-feeding.

ATTAPULGITE
Not available in the U.S.

Brand names: Diar-Aid, Diarrest, Diasorb, Diatrol, Donnagel, Kaopectate K-Pek, Parepectolin, Rheaban

Drug class: Antidiarrheal

Indications (what it is used for): Diarrhea.

How it works: Unknown; it is believed to absorb the bacteria that may be causing diarrhea.

Contraindications (reasons you shouldn't take it): Hypersensitivity to drug or class, bowel obstruction.

Possible side effects and warnings: Can cause constipation, heartburn, flatulence, and nausea and vomiting. Should be used with caution in women experiencing fever or dehydration.

How it can affect pregnant women: Attapulgite is an ingredient in many over-the-counter products to treat diarrhea. There are no adequate reports or well-controlled studies of attapulgite in pregnant women.

How it can affect a developing embryo or fetus: There are no adequate reports or well-controlled studies in human fetuses. It is unlikely that any attapulgite would reach the fetal bloodstream.

Breast-feeding: There is no published data in nursing women. It is unknown whether attapulgite alters breast milk. Considering that little, if any, is absorbed into the mother's bloodstream, it should be safe.

Potential drug interactions: Attapulgite may alter absorption of a wide variety of drugs if taken together.

What the FDA says about use in pregnancy: No assigned category. (see Appendix).

What the available evidence suggests about breast-feeding safety: Probably safe.

The bottom line for you:
- There is no published data in pregnant women, but a long clinical experience supports the safety of attapulgite when used occasionally during pregnancy.
- Attapulgite is safe to use while breast-feeding.

AURANOFIN

Brand name: Ridaura

Drug classes: Antiarthritic; Gold compound

Indications (what it is used for): Rheumatoid arthritis.

How it works: Unknown.

Contraindications (reasons you shouldn't take it): Hypersensitivity to drug or class, gold toxicity, pulmonary fibrosis (inflammation and/or scarring of the lungs), dermatitis, bone marrow failure, necrotizing enterocolitis (death of intestinal tissue).

Possible side effects and warnings: Can cause seizures, nephritic syndrome (a collection of conditions affecting the kidneys), kidney failure, low platelet count, ulcerative colitis, aplastic anemia, inflammation and/or scarring of the lungs, diarrhea, rash, itching, nausea, abdominal pain, conjunctivitis, blood in the urine, anemia, and loss of appetite. Should be used with caution in women with liver or kidney dysfunction.

How it can affect pregnant women: There is no published data with auranofin during pregnancy.

How it can affect a developing embryo or fetus: There are no adequate reports or well-controlled studies in human fetuses. It is unknown whether auranofin crosses the human placenta. Rodent studies reveal an increased risk of damage to the embryo or fetus, abdominal wall defects in the fetus, and umbilical hernia. However, animal studies are not necessarily good indicators of how a drug will behave in humans.

Breast-feeding: There are no adequate reports or well-controlled studies in nursing women. It is unknown whether auranofin enters human breast milk, but gold is excreted into rodent milk.

Drug interactions: A single case report suggests that auranofin may increase phenytoin blood levels.

What the FDA says about use in pregnancy: Category C (see Appendix).

What the available evidence suggests about breast-feeding safety: Unknown.

The bottom line for you:
- Auranofin should be used during pregnancy and breast-feeding only if the benefit to the woman justifies the potential risk to the embryo, fetus, or newborn. There are alternative agents with which there is more experience during pregnancy and breast-feeding that should be used first.

AZATADINE

Brand name: Optimine
Drug class: Antihistamine, H1
Indications (what it is used for): Allergic rhinitis, hives.
How it works: Blocks a histamine receptor.
Contraindications (reasons you shouldn't take it): Hypersensitivity to drug or class, use of a monamine oxidase inhibitor (MAOI) within 14 days, inability to urinate.
Possible side effects and warnings: Can cause low white blood cells and/or platelets, life-threatening allergic reaction, dry mouth, nausea, abdominal pain, inability to urinate, headache, constipation, and weight gain. Should be used with caution in women with asthma or glaucoma.
How it can affect pregnant women: There is no published data during pregnancy.
How it can affect a developing embryo or fetus: There are no adequate reports or well-controlled studies of azatadine in human fetuses. Rodent studies reveal no evidence of birth defects or abnormal growth despite the use of doses higher than those used clinically. However, animal studies are not necessarily good indicators of how a drug will behave in humans.
Breast-feeding: There are no adequate reports or well-controlled studies in nursing women. It is unknown whether azatadine enters human breast milk.
Potential drug interactions: Monoamine oxidase inhibitors (MAOIs) prolong and intensify the effects of antihistamines. Using an antihistamine at the same time as a tricyclic antidepressant could increase the effects of both.
What the FDA says about use in pregnancy: Category B (see Appendix).
What the available evidence suggests about breast-feeding safety: Unknown.
The bottom line for you:
● Like similar over-the-counter antihistamines, azatadine is likely safe to use during pregnancy and while breast-feeding, although there are alternative medications with which there is more experience during pregnancy and breast-feeding.

AZATHIOPRINE

Brand name: Imuran
Drug class: Immunosuppressant
Indications (what it is used for): Prevention of transplant rejection; immune disorders such as systemic lupus erythematosus (a chronic inflammatory disease in which the immune system attacks the body's own tissues and organs), inflammatory bowel disease, and rheumatoid arthritis.
How it works: Inhibits the activity of the immune T cells.
Contraindications (reasons you shouldn't take it): Hypersensitivity to drug or class.
Possible side effects and warnings: Can cause pancreatitis, fever, low white blood cell count, bone marrow suppression, suppressed immunity, liver toxicity, abnormal growth of tissue, nausea and vomiting, diarrhea, abdominal pain, rash, liver abnormalities, muscle aches, and joint pain. Should be used with caution during pregnancy and breast-feeding.
How it can affect pregnant women: There are no adequate reports or well-controlled studies of azathioprine in pregnant women. Immune-related disorders are fairly common in reproductive-age women and are therefore common during pregnancy. Women with inactive inflammatory bowel disease are likely to have an uncomplicated pregnancy, whereas women with active disease are more likely to have complications such as miscarriage, stillbirth, and exacerbation of their disease. Most pregnancies treated with azathioprine end successfully, even in transplant patients. It has been used successfully for the treatment of autoimmune hepatitis during pregnancy.
How it can affect a developing embryo or fetus: There are no adequate reports or well-controlled studies in human fetuses. Azathioprine crosses the human placenta, appearing to reach the same level

in the fetus as in the mother. Studies in humans (approximately 6 studies) have not detected a clear pattern of malformation in the large number of pregnant women who have been exposed to azathioprine during pregnancy. There are reports of newborns with reduced levels of certain antibodies and low white blood cell counts and low birth weight. But it is unclear if the low birth weight resulted from the medication or the disease it was being used to treat. There is one report of a woman whose mother had been treated with azathioprine during pregnancy who went on to have heightened immune responses in her own pregnancy much later in life. However, that pregnancy ended successfully.

Breast-feeding: Azathioprine is excreted into breast milk, but it appears that a newborn would ingest less than 0.5% of the mother's dose. There are no well-documented instances of a breast-fed baby being negatively affected.

Potential drug interactions: Women using both azathioprine and allopurinol should have their dose of azathioprine reduced by one-third to one-fourth of the usual dose. Drugs that may affect leukocyte production, including cotrimoxazole, may lead to exaggerated low white blood cell counts in women taking azathioprine. This is especially true in kidney transplant patients.

What the FDA says about use in pregnancy: Category D (see Appendix).

What the available evidence suggests about breast-feeding safety: Likely safe.

The bottom line for you:

- Azathioprine should not be withheld if it is clinically indicated, since the effects of not treating the relevant conditions can be life-threatening.
- However, consideration should be given to switching to a different medication with a more researched safety profile, or reducing the dose to the minimum required for the control of symptoms.

AZITHROMYCIN

Brand names: Aruzilina, Zithromax
Drug classes: Antibiotic; Macrolide
Indications (what it is used for): Infection of the fallopian tubes, chlamydia, chancroid, uncomplicated gonorrhea, community-acquired pneumonia.
How it works: Blocks the bacteria from synthesizing new proteins necessary for survival.
Contraindications (reasons you shouldn't take it): Hypersensitivity to drug or class.
Possible side effects and warnings: Can cause widespread swelling of the skin, life-threatening allergic reaction, cholestatic jaundice, Stevens-Johnson syndrome (a rare but serious skin reaction to medication), infection of the colon, diarrhea, nausea, vaginitis, rash, anorexia, and itching. Should be used with caution in women with liver dysfunction or who are taking astemizole or terfenadine.
How it can affect pregnant women: Pregnancy does not alter the effectiveness of azithromycin. When combined with doxycycline, azithromycin reduces the risk of postcesarean uterine infection. Azithromycin is probably the treatment of choice for chlamydia during pregnancy. Single-dose azithromycin may be as effective as penicillin G for the treatment of early syphilis. Azithromycin has been used in combination with artesunate to prevent malaria. Azithromycin also improves lung function in women with cystic fibrosis (a life-threatening lung disease).
How it can affect a developing embryo or fetus: There are no adequate reports or well-controlled studies in human fetuses. Less than 3% of azithromycin crosses the placenta, and there have been no adverse effects reported in humans.
Breast-feeding: Azithromycin is excreted in breast milk, but the level achieved is too small to have an effect.
Potential drug interactions: Interaction between the following medications and azithromycin has the potential to impact the effect of one or more of the drugs. In some instances the interaction can be dan-

gerous or life-threatening and must be avoided: aluminum- and magnesium-containing antacids, coumarin, digoxin, carbamazepine, terfenadine, cyclosporine, hexobarbital, phenytoin.

What the FDA says about use in pregnancy: Category B (see Appendix).

What the available evidence suggests about breast-feeding safety: Safe.

The bottom line for you:

- Azithromycin is an effective and safe antimicrobial agent for a variety of disorders complicating pregnancy.
- Azithromycin is considered safe to use while breast-feeding.

AZTREONAM

Brand name: Azactam

Drug classes: Antibiotic; Monobactam

Indications (what it is used for): Susceptible bacterial infections including gonorrhea.

How it works: Inhibits bacterial cell wall synthesis, causing the bacteria to die.

Contraindications (reasons you shouldn't take it): Hypersensitivity to drug or class.

Possible side effects and warnings: Can cause seizures, life-threatening allergic reaction, infection of the colon, phlebitis (inflammation of the veins), diarrhea, nausea, rash, and liver abnormalities. Should be used with caution in women with kidney dysfunction.

How it can affect pregnant women: There are no adequate reports or well-controlled studies of aztreonam in pregnant women. Aztreonam is as effective as gentamicin plus clindamycin for the treatment of postpartum uterine infection.

How it can affect a developing embryo or fetus: There are no adequate reports or well-controlled studies in human fetuses. Aztreonam crosses the human placenta in therapeutic concentrations, suggesting that it might be useful for treating an intrauterine infection before birth. Rodent studies reveal

no increase in either birth defects or low birth weight despite the use of doses higher than those used clinically. However, animal studies are not necessarily good indicators of how a drug will behave in humans.

Breast-feeding: There are no adequate reports or well-controlled studies during breast-feeding. Aztreonam is excreted into the breast milk at trace levels.

Potential drug interactions: None reported in humans.

What the FDA says about use in pregnancy: Category B (see Appendix).

What the available evidence suggests about breast-feeding safety: Safe.

The bottom line for you:

- Aztreonam is safe for use during pregnancy and while breast-feeding.

BACITRACIN

Brand names: Ak-Tracin, Baci-IM, Baci-Rx, Bacticin, Ocutricin, Spectro-Bacitracin

Drug class: Antibiotic, miscellaneous ophthalmic and dermatologic use

Indications (what it is used for): Bacterial infections.

How it works: Kills bacteria by damaging their outer wall.

Contraindications (reasons you shouldn't take it): Hypersensitivity to drug or class.

Possible side effects and warnings: Can cause contact dermatitis (skin inflammation). Should be used with caution in people with myasthenia gravis (an autoimmune disease causing muscle weakness).

How it can affect pregnant women: There is no published data during pregnancy, but the long clinical experience with topical use raises no concerns.

How it can affect a developing embryo or fetus: There are no adequate reports or well-controlled studies in human fetuses. It is unknown whether

bacitracin crosses the human placenta. Considering the typical dose and topical application, it is unlikely that the mother's blood level would reach a level that could jeopardize the fetus.

Breast-feeding: There are no adequate reports or well-controlled studies in nursing women. It is unknown whether bacitracin enters human breast milk. However, considering the typical dose and topical application, it is unlikely that a breast-feeding baby would ingest relevant amounts.

Potential drug interactions: None currently identified.

What the FDA says about use in pregnancy: Category C (see Appendix).

What the available evidence suggests about breast-feeding safety: Safe.

The bottom line for you:

- Bacitracin promotes wound healing and reduces scarring. The long clinical experience with topical administration suggests that it is safe for use during pregnancy and while breast-feeding.

BACLOFEN

Brand name: Lioresal

Drug class: Muscle relaxant

Indications (what it is used for): Controls muscle spasm associated with multiple sclerosis (MS) and other spinal cord diseases.

How it works: Blocks GABA(B) receptors in the autonomic nervous system.

Contraindications (reasons you shouldn't take it): Hypersensitivity to drug or class.

Possible side effects and warnings: Can cause depression, seizures, cardiovascular collapse, drowsiness, headache, dizziness, blurred vision and slurred speech, constipation, itching, urinary frequency, and rash. Should be used with caution in women with kidney disease or a seizure disorder.

How it can affect pregnant women: There are no adequate reports or well-controlled studies of baclofen in pregnant women. The published data is mostly limited to case reports of spinal cord injections of baclofen used to treat women with MS. There is one report of the successful use of baclofen to treat severe tetanus in pregnancy and another for the long-term treatment of muscle spasm after a spinal fracture. Baclofen has been used to treat pain associated with pregnancy termination.

How it can affect a developing embryo or fetus: There are no adequate reports or well-controlled studies in human fetuses. It is unknown whether baclofen crosses the human placenta. There is a single case report of a newborn whose mother had taken baclofen during pregnancy experiencing convulsions 7 days after delivery. Rodent studies revealed an increased prevalence of several birth defects including umbilical hernia (a bulging of the abdominal lining or organs through the belly button, which is treatable or resolves on its own), incomplete formation of the sternum, spine deformities, and neural tube defects (birth defects of the brain and/or spinal cord, such as spina bifida) when given at 10 times the maximum recommended human dose. However, animal studies are not necessarily good indicators of how a drug will behave in humans.

Breast-feeding: There are no adequate reports or well-controlled studies in nursing women. Only about 0.1% of the maternal dose is excreted into human breast milk, so it is generally considered safe.

Potential drug interactions: None currently identified.

What the FDA says about use in pregnancy: Category C (see Appendix).

What the available evidence suggests about breast-feeding safety: Safe.

The bottom line for you:

- Baclofen is rarely necessary during pregnancy and should be given only to relieve debilitating muscle spasms associated with spinal fracture or chronic diseases such as multiple sclerosis.
- The amount of baclofen a breast-feeding baby ingests is likely clinically insignificant, and it is generally considered safe.

BALSALAZIDE

Brand name: Colazal

Drug classes: Gastrointestinal; Salicylate

Indications (what it is used for): Acute ulcerative colitis.

How it works: Unclear; appears to act centrally to relax the bowel.

Contraindications (reasons you shouldn't take it): Hypersensitivity to drug or class.

Possible side effects and warnings: Can cause swelling beneath the skin, slow heart rate, bronchospasm, inflammation of the large intestine, nausea, vomiting, diarrhea, abdominal pain, anemia, nosebleed, anxiety, depression, kidney inflammation, joint aches, hair loss, and skin inflammation. Should be used with caution in women with reduced kidney function, seizure disorder, or pyloric stenosis (narrowing of the opening between stomach and small intestine), or who are being treated with antibiotics.

How it can affect pregnant women: Although considered safe based on long experience treating pregnant women, there are no adequate reports or well-controlled studies.

How it can affect a developing embryo or fetus: There are no adequate reports or well-controlled studies in human fetuses. It is unknown whether balsalazide crosses the human placenta. Rodent studies have not found any significant adverse effects despite the use of doses higher than those used in humans. However, animal studies are not necessarily good indicators of how a drug will behave in humans.

Breast-feeding: There is no published data in nursing women. It is unknown whether balsalazide enters human breast milk.

Potential drug interactions: None currently identified.

What the FDA says about use in pregnancy: Category B (see Appendix).

What the available evidence suggests about breast-feeding safety: Unknown.

The bottom line for you:

- Balsalazide may be used during pregnancy and while breast-feeding if the activity level of ulcerative colitis is high and unresponsive to other, better-studied drugs.

BASILIXIMAB

Brand name: Simulect

Drug classes: Immunosuppressant; Monoclonal antibody

Indications (what it is used for): To prevent rejection of a transplanted kidney.

How it works: IL-2 receptor antagonist.

Contraindications (reasons you shouldn't take it): Hypersensitivity to drug or class.

Possible side effects: Can cause constipation, diarrhea, nausea, high or low potassium levels, acne, insomnia, angina, headache, tremor, high blood pressure, burning during urination, swelling, fever, weakness, and high cholesterol.

How it can affect pregnant women: There are only case reports of basiliximab use during pregnancy.

How it can affect a developing embryo or fetus: There are no adequate reports or well-controlled studies in human fetuses. It is unknown whether basiliximab crosses the human placenta. Rodent studies are reassuring despite using doses higher than those used in humans. However, animal studies are not necessarily good indicators of how a drug will behave in humans.

Breast-feeding: There is no published data in nursing women. It is unknown whether basiliximab enters human breast milk.

Potential drug interactions: It is best to avoid live vaccines.

What the FDA says about use in pregnancy: Category B (see Appendix).

What the available evidence suggests about breast-feeding safety: Unknown.

The bottom line for you:

- Considering that basiliximab is used to prevent life-threatening organ rejection, its benefit during pregnancy outweighs the potential risks.

- There is no information on basiliximab while breast-feeding, and it would be prudent to discontinue breast-feeding if the drug is necessary.

BECLOMETHASONE

Brand names: Beclovent, Beconase, Vanceril, Vanceril DS

Drug class: Corticosteroid

Indications (what it is used for): Treatment of asthma and runny nose, prevention of nasal polyps.

How it works: Anti-inflammatory mechanism unknown.

Contraindications (reasons you shouldn't take it): Hypersensitivity to drug or class.

Possible side effects and warnings: Can cause irritation of nasal mucous membranes, allergic skin reactions such as welts, swelling, bronchospasm, headache, and nausea. Because of its immunosuppressive action, beclomethasone should be used with caution in women who have a bacterial infection.

How it can affect pregnant women: Asthma is a common disease in life and in pregnancy. Approximately one-third of pregnant women with asthma get worse during pregnancy, one-third get better, and one-third remain clinically unchanged. Well-controlled asthma does not affect pregnancy outcome, but poorly controlled asthma may increase the risk of preterm birth (before 37 weeks) or low birth weight. Beclomethasone is considered a first-line treatment during pregnancy along with budesonide. Inhaled corticosteroids are generally considered the preventative treatment of choice when used regularly in pregnant women with persistent asthma, unless the asthma is well controlled by cromolyn or nedocromil. Certain medications used during labor and delivery have the potential to worsen asthma, including nonselective beta-blockers, some prostaglandins (used to induce labor), and ergonovine (used to control blood loss after delivery).

How it can affect a developing embryo or fetus: Severe uncontrolled asthma increases the risk of preterm birth and poor fetal growth. It is unknown whether beclomethasone specifically crosses the human placenta. However, steroid production may be suppressed in newborns of women who used beclomethasone during pregnancy, suggesting that it does cross the placenta. Rodent studies using up to 10 times the maximum recommended human dose resulted in an increased prevalence of certain birth defects. However, animal studies are not necessarily good indicators of how a drug will behave in humans; a similar pattern of defects is not seen in humans, and beclomethasone is generally considered safe.

Breast-feeding: There are no adequate reports or well-controlled studies in nursing women. It is unknown whether beclomethasone enters human breast milk. Other steroids are excreted in low amounts. Given that, and the small dosage used, breast-feeding is probably safe.

Potential drug interactions: None currently identified.

What the FDA says about use in pregnancy: Category C (see Appendix).

What the available evidence suggests about breast-feeding safety: Probably safe.

The bottom line for you:

- Beclomethasone is a first-line drug for the prevention of asthma attacks during pregnancy. Notify your pediatrician if you have taken beclomethasone during pregnancy or are taking it while breast-feeding, because of the occasional reports of lowered steroid production in exposed fetuses.

BELLADONNA

Brand names: Atropine Sulfate, Donnatal, Lomotil

Drug classes: Analgesic, narcotic; Parasympatholytic

Indications (what it is used for): Secondary therapy for irritable bowel syndrome, acute enterocolitis (digestive tract infection), duodenal ulcer; before surgery to reduce the production of saliva; increasing a slow fetal heart rate.

How it works: See atropine (which is the active agent).

Contraindications (reasons you shouldn't take it): Hypersensitivity to drug or class.

Possible side effects and warnings: Can cause dry mouth, taste changes, blurred vision, slow heart rate, palpitations, drowsiness, headache, and life-threatening allergic reaction. Should be used with caution in women with neuropathy (nerve damage), glaucoma, liver disease, an overactive thyroid, coronary heart disease, or chronic lung disease.

How it can affect pregnant women: Belladonna, or deadly nightshade, is a plant whose foliage and berries contain scopolamine, atropine, and hyoscyamine. It is extremely toxic if too much is ingested, with the potential to cause delirium and hallucinations. There are no well-controlled studies of belladonna in pregnant women.

How it can affect a developing embryo or fetus: There are no adequate reports or well-controlled studies in human fetuses. The toxins found in belladonna rapidly cross the placenta, causing a fast fetal heart rate and decreased fetal breathing. However, no adverse acute or chronic fetal effects have been documented in women taking atropine (one of the compounds in belladonna). Nor is there an association with birth defects.

Breast-feeding: It is generally considered safe for breast-feeding.

Potential drug interactions: Belladonna-butabarbital may decrease the systemic effects of corticosteroids. Use with other central nervous system depressants, such as sedatives or hypnotics, antihistamines, tranquilizers, or alcohol, may increase the sedative and nervous system depressant effects.

What the FDA says about use in pregnancy: Category C (see Appendix).

What the available evidence suggests about breast-feeding safety: Likely safe.

The bottom line for you:
- Belladonna extract is useful and safe as a secondary therapy for irritable bowel syndrome, acute enterocolitis, and duodenal ulcer during pregnancy.
- There is no information on belladonna and breast-feeding. Other chemically related substances (e.g., atropine) are considered compatible with breast-feeding.

BENAZEPRIL

Brand name: Lotensin

Drug classes: ACEI/A2R-antagonist; Antihypertensive

Indications (what it is used for): High blood pressure, congestive heart failure.

How it works: Inhibits an enzyme that leads to blood vessel constriction.

Contraindications (reasons you shouldn't take it): Hypersensitivity to drug or class, pregnancy, narrowing of the arteries in the kidneys.

Possible side effects and warnings: Can cause swelling under the skin; low blood pressure; kidney failure; high potassium, urea, and creatinine levels; inflammation of the pancreas; liver damage; low white blood cell count; dizziness; headache; heartburn; cough; rash; allergic skin reactions such as welts; fatigue; muscle aches; diarrhea; and taste changes. Should be used with caution in women with kidney disease, low blood volume, dehydration, collagen vascular disease, or severe heart failure.

How it can affect pregnant women: The published data during pregnancy consists of case reports only. However, this class of drugs is associated with severe fetal kidney damage when taken in any trimester and should not be taken during pregnancy.

How it can affect an embryo or fetus: Benazepril can cause embryonic, fetal, and newborn illness and death. Benazepril use in humans is associated with low amniotic fluid levels, which may reverse if the drug is discontinued in time. Similar drugs can cause low fetal blood pressure, poor skull development, and kidney failure. Women who have used benazepril during pregnancy should seek the advice of a skilled perinatologist. Although it is not known whether all ACE inhibitors have the same degree of risk, it is better to err on the side of caution and avoid them during pregnancy.

Breast-feeding: There is no published data in nursing women. Minimal amounts of benazepril enter breast milk.

Potential drug interactions: Interaction between the following medications and benazepril has the potential to impact the effect of one or more of the drugs. In some instances the interaction can be dangerous or life-threatening and must be avoided: diuretics, thiazide diuretics, potassium-sparing diuretics (e.g., spironolactone, amiloride, triamterene), potassium supplements, lithium.

What the FDA says about use in pregnancy: Category D (see Appendix).

What the available evidence suggests about breast-feeding safety: Likely safe.

The bottom line for you:

- Benazepril is known to cause birth defects or fetal damage at all times during pregnancy and should not be used. There are other drugs with a higher safety profile with which there is more experience during pregnancy and while breast-feeding.
- Women who have used benazepril during pregnancy should seek the advice of a skilled perinatologist.

BENZOCAINE

Brand names: Americaine, Anacaine, Otocain

Drug class: Anesthetic, local

Indications (what it is used for): Topical anesthetic, lubricant, relief of pain due to ear infection, swimmer's ear, to anesthetize a mucous membrane.

How it works: Decreases the transmission of nerve impulses to block the sensation of pain.

Contraindications (reasons you shouldn't take it): Hypersensitivity to drug or class, perforated tympanic membrane (burst eardrum).

Possible side effects and warnings: Can cause skin burning and itching.

How it can affect pregnant women: There are no well-controlled studies of benzocaine during pregnancy. It provides relief from episiotomy (a surgical incision to aid vaginal childbirth) pain, especially when given with a corticosteroid. Some practitioners use it as an alternative to lidocaine for relieving the pain and itching of vaginal herpes during pregnancy.

How it can affect a developing embryo or fetus: There are no well-controlled studies of benzocaine in human fetuses. It is unknown whether benzocaine crosses the human placenta. Considering the typical dose and topical application, it is unlikely that the level in the mother will affect the fetus.

Breast-feeding: There is no published data in nursing women. However, considering the typical dose and topical application, it is unlikely that a breast-feeding baby would ingest relevant amounts of the medication.

Potential drug interactions: None currently identified.

What the FDA says about use in pregnancy: Category C (see Appendix).

What the available evidence suggests about breast-feeding safety: Unknown but likely safe.

The bottom line for you:

- Benzocaine is used to safely and effectively treat pain from genital herpes during pregnancy or after delivery to reduce the pain from an episiotomy.
- Benzocaine is likely safe for use while breast-feeding.

BENZOYL PEROXIDE

Brand names: Benzac, Brevoxyl, Desquam-E, Desquam-X 5, Desquam-X 10

Drug classes: Anti-infective, topical; Dermatologic

Indications (what it is used for): Acne.

How it works: Drying agent.

Contraindications (reasons you shouldn't take it): Hypersensitivity to drug or class.

Possible side effects and warnings: Can cause skin dryness, irritation, and itching.

How it can affect pregnant women: Acne frequently worsens during pregnancy. Benzoyl peroxide is for external use only and has been used for the treatment of acne (during pregnancy and otherwise) since the 1930s. There are no well-controlled studies in pregnant women.

How it can affect a developing embryo or fetus: There are no adequate reports or well-controlled studies in human fetuses. It is unknown whether benzoyl peroxide crosses the human placenta. Animal studies have apparently not been conducted for birth defects. Considering the typical dose and topical application, it is unlikely that the maternal systemic level will have an effect on the fetus.

Breast-feeding: There is no published data in nursing women. It is unknown whether benzoyl peroxide enters human breast milk. Considering the typical dose and topical application, it is unlikely that breast milk will contain a relevant level of medication.

Potential drug interactions: None currently identified.

What the FDA says about use in pregnancy: Category C (see Appendix).

What the available evidence suggests about breast-feeding safety: Likely safe.

The bottom line for you:
- It is unlikely that topically applied benzoyl peroxide presents any risk to the embryo, fetus, or breast-feeding baby.

BETA-CAROTENE
Brand name: Vitamin A
Drug class: Vitamins/minerals
Indications (what it is used for): Nutritional supplementation.
How it works: Antioxidant.
Contraindications (reasons you shouldn't take it): Malabsorption syndrome (small intestine cannot absorb nutrients from food).
Possible side effects and warnings: Overdose may cause fatigue, malaise, lethargy, abdominal pain, skeletal malformations in exposed fetuses, joint pain, hair loss, and cracked lips.

How it can affect pregnant women: Beta-carotene is an antioxidant contained in most prenatal vitamins, and consuming foods rich in b-carotene may offer protection from oxygen free radical damage. Some studies suggest that high dietary intake of b-carotene may reduce the risk of heart disease and cancer in the general population. There are no adequate reports or well-controlled studies in pregnant women. It has been suggested that millions of pregnant women annually experience night blindness because of a deficiency. The recommended daily allowance during pregnancy is about 2,500 IU. The safety of doses exceeding 6,000 IU during pregnancy is not established.

How it can affect a developing embryo or fetus: There are no adequate reports or well-controlled studies in human fetuses. Doses greater than 25,000 IU per day of b-carotene are associated with defects in fetal heart development and bone formation. There is no evidence of an increased risk of birth defects in women consuming 8,000–25,000 IU per day.

Breast-feeding: There is no published data in nursing women. Beta-carotene raises the level in human breast milk. There is no evidence of risk when the breast-feeding mother ingests the recommended daily dose.

Potential drug interactions: None identified currently.

What the FDA says about use in pregnancy: Category C (see Appendix).

What the available evidence suggests about breast-feeding safety: Likely safe.

The bottom line for you:
- Beta-carotene supplementation is likely safe during pregnancy and while breast-feeding.
- Most prenatal vitamins contain the recommended daily level of b-carotene.
- Physicians should consider additional b-carotene supplementation during pregnancy when deficiency is likely or night blindness is an issue.

BETAMETHASONE

Brand names: Benoson, Betaderm, Betason, Celestone, Rinderon, Unicort

Drug class: Corticosteroid

Indications (what it is used for): Improving lung function in preterm infants, joint inflammation, arthritis.

How it works: Speeds maturation of lung cells that produce surfactant (a substance that prevents the air sacs in the lungs from collapsing), anti-inflammatory.

Contraindications (reasons you shouldn't take it): Hypersensitivity to drug or class, sepsis, uncontrolled diabetes.

Possible side effects and warnings: Can cause adrenal insufficiency (inadequate production of steroids by the adrenal glands), glucose intolerance, and fluid in the lungs. Should be used with caution in women with diabetes or who are taking a medication to inhibit preterm labor.

How it can affect pregnant women: Betamethasone may increase (by a very small amount) the risk of infection in women with preterm premature rupture of the membranes (PPROM, water breaking before 37 weeks). It may cause an abnormal diabetes test or worsen existing diabetes, and is associated with pulmonary edema (fluid in the lungs), especially when given with a tocolytic agent (a medication used to stop preterm labor) when there is an existing underlying infection.

How it can affect a developing embryo or fetus: Betamethasone crosses the human placenta and improves newborn survival rates after preterm birth (before 37 weeks) by lowering the rate and severity of respiratory distress syndrome (acute lung dysfunction), bowel damage, and bleeding into the brain. Betamethasone treatment is typically given twice, 24 hours apart. Two courses of 2 shots, if given more than a week apart, improve outcomes compared to a single course. However, more than 2 courses of betamethasone are not recommended because animal and human studies have found an increased risk of adverse newborn effects after repeated courses.

Even though steroids work by suppressing the immune system, betamethasone does not increase the risk of infection in a newborn. Betamethasone does affect a range of fetal activities (such as heart rate, breathing, and sleep-wake cycles); however, long-term studies have not shown any effect on intellectual and motor development or school achievement.

The best evidence is that corticosteroids are weak teratogens (substances that cause birth defects) when taken in the first trimester. Although there is no increase in major birth defects, the rates of both cleft lip and cleft palate are increased. There is no increase in risk of anomalies when steroids are begun after organ formation (after 11 weeks) or if given only topically. A few small studies suggested a possible relationship between long-term steroid use during pregnancy and poor fetal growth; however, it is hard to tell if that was the result of the medication or the disease it was being used to treat.

Breast-feeding: There are no adequate reports or well-controlled studies in breast-feeding women. Cortisone is naturally present in human milk, and it is unclear whether maternal treatment with betamethasone increases that concentration. Considering the limited duration of use of betamethasone, it is unlikely to have any clinically significant effect on a breast-fed newborn.

Potential drug interactions: None currently identified.

What the FDA says about use in pregnancy: Category C (see Appendix).

What the available evidence suggests about breast-feeding safety: Likely safe.

The bottom line for you:

- Betamethasone improves lung function in preterm infants and reduces the incidence of respiratory distress syndrome, bleeding in the brain, and death in newborns that are born preterm.

- There is no convincing scientific evidence that betamethasone increases the incidence of maternal or newborn infection, and when it is used after the first trimester, it does not cause birth defects.

- Betamethasone used as directed has no impact on breast-feeding.

BETHANECHOL

Brand names: Duvoid, Myocholine, Myotonachol, Myotonine, Urecholine

Drug classes: Cholinergic; Genitourinary

Indications (what it is used for): Postoperative or postpartum urinary retention that is not due to a physical blockage.

How it works: Increases tone and contractility of bladder muscle by stimulating nerve receptors.

Contraindications (reasons you shouldn't take it): Hypersensitivity to drug or class, bladder inflammation, physical blockage, overactive thyroid, peptic ulcer disease, asthma, Parkinson's disease (disorder of the brain that affects movement and coordination), seizures.

Possible side effects and warnings: Can cause bronchospasm, chest pain, diarrhea, headache, flushing, nausea, vomiting, low blood pressure, a sense of needing to urinate, rapid heart rate, sweating, and constricted pupils.

How it can affect pregnant women: There are no adequate reports or well-controlled studies of bethanechol during pregnancy. It has been used for decades for the treatment of postpartum urinary retention.

How it can affect a developing embryo or fetus: There are no adequate reports or well-controlled studies in human fetuses. It is unknown whether bethanechol crosses the human placenta.

Breast-feeding: There is no published data in nursing women. It is unknown whether bethanechol enters human breast milk.

Potential drug interactions: Bethanechol may cause low blood pressure if given with a ganglion-blocking compound.

What the FDA says about use in pregnancy: Category C (see Appendix).

What the available evidence suggests about breast-feeding safety: Unknown.

The bottom line for you:

- Bethanechol is rarely needed during pregnancy.
- Its postpartum use for urinary retention is short term and should have no impact on breast-feeding.

BISMUTH SUBSALICYLATE

Brand name: Pepto-Bismol

Drug class: Antidiarrheal

Indications (what it is used for): Diarrhea, heartburn, nausea.

How it works: Works on the lining of the stomach to prevent acid secretion, bind bacterial toxins, and inhibit bacterial growth.

Contraindications (reasons you shouldn't take it): Hypersensitivity to drug or class.

Possible side effects and warnings: Can cause anxiety, loss of hearing, confusion, severe constipation, diarrhea, difficulty speaking or slurred speech, dizziness or light-headedness, drowsiness, and fast or deep breathing. Should be used with caution in women with liver or kidney problems, or who are taking oral anticoagulants or hypoglycemic agents.

How it can affect pregnant women: There are no adequate reports or well-controlled studies of bismuth subsalicylate in pregnant women. The long clinical experience with this over-the-counter medication has not revealed any adverse effects. Bismuth subsalicylate use may cause stool darkening, which should not be confused with blood in the stool.

How it can affect a developing embryo or fetus: Only small amounts of bismuth subsalicylate are absorbed from the stomach, and the bismuth is not transported across the placenta, so there is little likelihood of any fetal harm.

Breast-feeding: Bismuth ion is not excreted into breast milk to any significant degree.

Potential drug interactions: Bismuth may worsen low sugar levels in women taking salicylates or aspirin, probenecid, or sulfinpyrazone. Tetracycline absorption may be reduced.

What the FDA says about use in pregnancy: No assigned category (see Appendix).

What the available evidence suggests about breast-feeding safety: Likely safe.

The bottom line for you:
- Bismuth subsalicylate is safe for use during pregnancy and while breast-feeding.

BLEOMYCIN

Brand name: Blenoxane

Drug classes: Antibiotic; Antineoplastic

Indications (what it is used for): A noncurative treatment for squamous cell carcinoma of the neck, tongue, cervix, or vulva; lymphoma; and the associated fluid buildup around the lungs.

How it works: Inhibits synthesis of DNA, RNA, and proteins.

Contraindications (reasons you shouldn't take it): Hypersensitivity to drug or class.

Possible side effects and warnings: Can cause pulmonary fibrosis (inflammation and/or scarring of the lungs), rash, allergic skin reactions such as welts, hair loss, and stomatitis (inflammation of the mucous linings of the mouth). Should be used with caution in women with kidney or liver conditions.

How it can affect pregnant women: There are no adequate reports or well-controlled studies in pregnant women. Several studies conclude that subsequent fertility is unaffected by treatment, but those studies are inadequate to be considered conclusive.

How it can affect a developing embryo or fetus: There are no adequate reports or well-controlled studies in the human fetus. It is unknown whether bleomycin crosses the human placenta. Low white blood cell counts have been reported in newborns whose mothers took bleomycin during preg-

nancy, suggesting it does cross. No birth defects have been reported in humans. Bleomycin does cause birth defects in rodents. However, animal studies are not necessarily good indicators of how a drug will behave in humans.

Breast-feeding: There is no published data in nursing women. It is unknown whether bleomycin enters human breast milk. It is usually recommended that the drug be discontinued in women who are breast-feeding.

Potential drug interactions: None identified currently.

What the FDA says about use in pregnancy: Category D (see Appendix).

What the available evidence suggests about breast-feeding safety: Unknown.

The bottom line for you:
- Bleomycin may be used during pregnancy when needed to treat a life-threatening disease. Although no associated birth defects have been reported in humans, it is best to avoid bleomycin in the first trimester.
- It is usually recommended that the drug be discontinued in women who are breast-feeding.

BUDESONIDE

Brand names: Budecort, Budeflam, Pulmicort, Rhinocort, Rhinocort Aqua

Drug classes: Corticosteroid; Corticosteroid, inhalation

Indications (what it is used for): Asthma, rhinitis.

How it works: Acts as an anti-inflammatory.

Contraindications (reasons you shouldn't take it): Hypersensitivity to drug or class; should not be used to treat status asthmaticus (severe and potentially life-threatening asthma attack).

Possible side effects and warnings: Can cause allergic reaction, airway obstruction, eczema, red blotches caused by bleeding under the skin, back pain, fracture, and muscle aches. Should be used with caution in women who have a current infection or who are taking systemic steroids.

How it can affect pregnant women: Asthma is a common disease in life and in pregnancy. Approximately one-third of pregnant women with asthma get worse during pregnancy, one-third get better, and one-third remain clinically unchanged. Well-controlled asthma does not affect pregnancy outcome, but poorly controlled asthma may increase the risk of preterm birth (before 37 weeks) or low birth weight. Inhaled corticosteroids are considered the preventative medication of choice for pregnant women with persistent asthma unless their condition is well controlled by cromolyn or nedocromil. Budesonide and beclomethasone are considered the first-line treatments. Certain medications used during labor and delivery have the potential to worsen asthma, including nonselective beta-blockers, some prostaglandins (used to induce labor), and ergonovine (used to control blood loss after delivery).

How it can affect a developing embryo or fetus: There are no adequate reports or well-controlled studies of budesonide in human fetuses. It is unknown whether budesonide crosses the human placenta. The large clinical experience suggests that it does not cause birth defects.

Breast-feeding: There is no published data in nursing women. It is unknown whether budesonide enters human breast milk. Considering that less than 20% of the inhaled dose reaches the mother's blood, it is unlikely that relevant amounts enter the breast milk and are absorbed by a breast-feeding baby.

Potential drug interactions: Interaction between the following medications or substances and budesonide has the potential to impact the effect of one or more of the drugs. In some instances the interaction can be dangerous or life-threatening and must be avoided: CYP3A4 inhibitors such as ketoconazole, intraconazole, ritonavir, indinavir, saquinavir, erythromycin, itraconazole, and clarithromycin. Avoid grapefruit and grapefruit juice.

What the FDA says about use in pregnancy: Category B for inhalation; C for oral use (see Appendix).

What the available evidence suggests about breast-feeding safety: Likely safe.

The bottom line for you:
- Budesonide may be used during pregnancy and while breast-feeding with little risk.

BUPIVACAINE

Brand names: Bupivacaine HCl, Marcaine, Sensorcaine

Drug class: Anesthetic, local

Indications (what it is used for): Conduction (e.g., spinal block, saddle block, epidural) and local anesthesia.

How it works: Blocks nerve impulses that transmit pain.

Contraindications (reasons you shouldn't take it): Hypersensitivity to drug or class.

Possible side effects and warnings: Can cause nerve toxicity, poor heart function, slow or irregular heart rate, cardiac arrest, convulsions, respiratory arrest, unconsciousness, low blood pressure, nausea, vomiting, numbness or tingling, fever, chills, itching, dizziness, restlessness, anxiety, and tremor. Should be used with caution in women who are acutely ill (such as with preeclampsia, chronic hepatitis, or liver cancer) or who have liver or kidney dysfunction, heart block, low blood volume, or low blood pressure.

How it can affect pregnant women: Bupivacaine is a very popular and, when used as instructed, safe agent for epidural or spinal anesthesia during labor and delivery, alone or in combination with other local anesthetic or narcotic agents.

How it can affect a developing embryo or fetus: There are no adequate reports or well-controlled studies in human fetuses. Only trace amounts of bupivacaine cross the human placenta, too small to have a clinically significant effect on the fetus.

Breast-feeding: Bupivacaine and/or the main component it is broken down into are found in breast milk after an epidural has been administered during labor, but not at a clinically relevant level. Although it has not been studied after its use as a local anesthetic injected under the skin, one-time use is unlikely to pose a significant risk to a breast-feeding baby.

Potential drug interactions: Interaction between the following medications and bupivacaine has the potential to impact the effect of one or more of the drugs. In some instances the interaction can be dangerous or life-threatening and must be avoided: local anesthetic agents containing epinephrine or norepinephrine, monoamine oxidase inhibitors (MAOIs), tricyclic antidepressants (TCAs), vasopressor or ergot-type oxytocic drugs, methergine.

What the FDA says about use in pregnancy: Category C (see Appendix).

What the available evidence suggests about breast-feeding safety: Safe.

The bottom line for you:

- Bupivacaine is a popular and safe drug for epidural or spinal anesthesia during labor and delivery, alone or in combination with other local anesthetic or narcotic agents.
- Considered safe for limited use as a local anesthetic while breast-feeding.

BUPRENORPHINE

Brand names: Buprenex, Subutex
Drug class: Analgesic, narcotic
Indications (what it is used for): Moderate to severe pain, addiction management.
How it works: Blocks the opiate/narcotic receptors.
Contraindications (reasons you shouldn't take it): Hypersensitivity to drug or class.
Possible side effects and warnings: Can cause respiratory depression (difficulty breathing) and/or arrest, low blood pressure, slow heart rate, nausea, vomiting, sedation, constriction of the pupils, blurred vision, euphoria, hallucinations, an unpleasant mood, dry mouth, itching, sweating, and constipation. Should be used with caution in women with impaired liver function.
How it can affect pregnant women: Buprenorphine, methadone, and morphine have all been used successfully to treat pregnant women recovering

from narcotic addiction, although there are fetal reasons to prefer buprenorphine.

How it can affect a developing embryo or fetus: The majority of babies born to women who use narcotics experience withdrawal. Narcotic withdrawal is difficult for the fetus or newborn. There are no adequate reports or well-controlled studies in human fetuses. Less buprenorphine crosses the placenta to reach the fetus compared to either morphine or methadone, so buprenorphine is used as a substitute narcotic to lower the risk of newborn withdrawal. Buprenorphine does not appear to cause birth defects, although short-term movement abnormalities have been reported in some exposed children.

Breast-feeding: There are no adequate reports or well-controlled studies in nursing women. In one case study, the daily amount ingested by a newborn whose mother was taking buprenorphine was too low to have any effect on the baby, and no withdrawal signs were noted when the mother abruptly stopped breast-feeding.

Potential drug interactions: Interaction between the following medications and buprenorphine has the potential to impact the effect of one or more of the drugs. In some instances the interaction can be dangerous or life-threatening and must be avoided: other central nervous system depressants; monamine oxidase inhibitors (MAOIs); benzodiazepines; phenprocoumon; CYP3A4 inhibitors, such as macrolide antibiotics (e.g., erythromycin), azole antifungal agents (e.g., ketoconazole), and protease inhibitors (e.g., ritanovir); CYP3A4 inducers, such as rifampin, carbamazepine, and phenytoin.

What the FDA says about use in pregnancy: Category C (see Appendix).

What the available evidence suggests about breast-feeding safety: Likely safe.

The bottom line for you:

- Buprenorphine is effective and comparatively safe for the treatment of narcotic addiction or pain during pregnancy and may offer some advantage over methadone and morphine for pregnant or breast-feeding women seeking recovery.

BUPROPION

Brand names: Aplenzin, Buproban, Wellbutrin, Zyban
Drug classes: Antidepressant
Indications (what it is used for): Smoking cessation, treatment of depression.
How it works: May increase the blood levels of serotonin, a neurotransmitter involved in mood.
Contraindications (reasons you shouldn't take it): Hypersensitivity to drug or class, seizure disorder, use of monoamine oxidase inhibitors (MAOIs) within 14 days, bulimia, anorexia nervosa.
Possible side effects and warnings: Can cause abnormal heart rate, Stevens-Johnson syndrome (a rare but serious skin reaction to medication), depression, rash, muscle breakdown, difficulty swallowing, vaginal irritation, mania/hypomania, nausea, vomiting, loss of appetite, sedation, constipation, and confusion. Should be used with caution in women experiencing agitation, insomnia, psychosis, confusion, altered appetite, or weight change.
How it can affect pregnant women: Depression is common during and after pregnancy but often goes unrecognized and untreated. Depression can be made worse by pregnancy or delivery, and suicide is a not uncommon cause of maternal death. Pregnancy is not a reason to discontinue antidepressant drugs if the medication is effective and needed. A woman being treated for depression who becomes pregnant should not discontinue medication abruptly on her own but rather discuss her treatment and condition with her medical provider. Pregnancy may increase the dose needed to be effective, and women with a history of depression have a higher rate of recurrence after delivery.

There are no adequate reports or well-controlled studies in pregnant women. Bupropion appears effective for some women with postpartum depression. It also is an effective medication to help stop smoking and may even work better than the nicotine patch. Using bupropion to stop smoking during pregnancy is safer than either continuing to smoke or using the nicotine patch or gum. The manufacturer of Wellbutrin, GlaxoSmithKline, maintained an international registry to follow women treated during pregnancy, and health-care practitioners were encouraged to register treated patients through 2008. The population exposed was adequate to conclude bupropion is not a major source of birth defects.
How it can affect a developing embryo or fetus: There are no adequate reports or well-controlled studies in human fetuses. Bupropion crosses the human placenta and reaches levels in the fetus that are similar to the mother's level. One study looked at 1,200 first-trimester exposures and concluded that there was no increase in birth defects. A much smaller study, of 136 pregnant women taking bupropion and then followed for up to a year after delivery, noted an increased rate of first-trimester miscarriage. Rodent studies are reassuring despite the use of doses higher than those used in humans. However, animal studies are not necessarily good indicators of how a drug will behave in humans.
Breast-feeding: Bupropion is concentrated in human breast milk. However, an analysis of 3 newborns who were breast-fed while their mothers took bupropion found no detectable level of the drug in the babies.
Potential drug interactions: Interaction between the following medications and bupropion has the potential to impact the effect of one or more of the drugs. In some instances the interaction can be dangerous or life-threatening and must be avoided: drugs that affect CYP2B6 (e.g., orphenadrine, cyclophosphamide), drugs metabolized by CYP2D6 (e.g., SSRIs and many TCAs, including nortriptyline, imipramine, desipramine, paroxetine, fluoxetine, sertraline), beta-blockers (e.g., metoprolol), type 1C antiarrhythmics (e.g., propafenone, flecainide), antipsychotics (e.g., haloperidol, risperidone, thioridazine), carbamazepine, phenobarbital, phenytoin, levodopa, amantadine, agents that lower

seizure threshold (e.g., antipsychotics, other anti-depressants, theophylline, systemic steroids). Alcohol consumption should be avoided during treatment.

What the FDA says about use in pregnancy: Category C (see Appendix).

What the available evidence suggests about breast-feeding safety: Likely safe.

The bottom line for you:

- Depression is dangerous to both a mother and her embryo or fetus, and bupropion can be effective therapy.
- Women already taking bupropion when they conceive should consult with their physician and obstetrician before discontinuing their medication.
- Bupropion is a safe and useful aid to smoking cessation and is preferred to continued smoking during pregnancy.
- Bupropion is excreted into breast milk and its effect on a nursing newborn is unknown. The manufacturer suggests that the decision to discontinue breast-feeding or discontinue bupropion therapy should be based on the woman's need of the drug.

BUSPIRONE

Brand names: Ansiced, BuSpar

Drug class: Sedative

Indications (what it is used for): Anxiety.

How it works: Not well understood.

Contraindications (reasons you shouldn't take it): Hypersensitivity to drug or class.

Possible side effects and warnings: Can cause dizziness, nausea, vomiting, insomnia, rash, headache, fatigue, dry mouth, diarrhea, decreased concentration, hostility, depression, blurred vision, abdominal pain, numbness, and weakness. Should be used with caution in women who are taking a monoamine oxidase inhibitor (MAOI) or who have liver or kidney dysfunction.

How it can affect pregnant women: There is no published data with buspirone during pregnancy. Buspirone interacts with numerous other drugs, increasing the risk of an adverse side effect.

How it can affect a developing embryo or fetus: There are no adequate reports or well-controlled studies in human fetuses. It is unknown whether buspirone crosses the human placenta. Rodent studies are reassuring despite the use of doses higher than those used in humans. Some rodent studies suggest that maternal treatment with buspirone may protect the fetus from alcohol-induced brain damage. However, animal studies are not necessarily good indicators of how a drug will behave in humans.

Breast-feeding: There is no published data in nursing women. It is unknown whether buspirone enters human breast milk. Buspirone is excreted into rodent breast milk.

Potential drug interactions: Interaction between the following medications or substances and buspirone has the potential to impact the effect of one or more of the drugs. In some instances the interaction can be dangerous or life-threatening and must be avoided: monoamine oxidase inhibitors (MAOIs), diazepam, diltiazem, verapamil, erythromycin, itraconazole, nefazodone, rifampin, grapefruit and grapefruit juice.

What the FDA says about use in pregnancy: Category B (see Appendix).

What the available evidence suggests about breast-feeding safety: Unknown.

The bottom line for you:

- Although little evidence suggests that buspirone causes birth defects, there are other drugs in the class with which there is more experience during pregnancy and that have less potential to interact with other medications.
- Limited experience suggests that the amount of buspirone excreted into breast milk is clinically insignificant. However, there are alternative agents with which there is more experience while breast-feeding.

BUSULFAN

Brand names: Citosulfan, Leukosulfan, Misulban, Myleran

Drug classes: Alkylating agent; Antineoplastic

Indications (what it is used for): Leukemia, myelofibrosis (a bone marrow disorder).

How it works: Prevents the translation of DNA that is needed for the cells to operate.

Contraindications (reasons you shouldn't take it): Hypersensitivity to drug or class, resistance to prior treatment, blast crisis (the terminal stage of the disease), acute lymphocytic leukemia.

Possible side effects and warnings: Can cause low white blood cell count, scarring in the lungs, scarring in the pericardium (the sac that protects the heart), seizures, and increased pigmentation. Should be used with caution in women with bone marrow suppression or a history of seizures.

How it can affect pregnant women: There are no adequate reports or well-controlled studies in pregnant women. Busulfan has been used successfully to treat leukemia and essential polycythemia (too many blood cells) during pregnancy.

How it can affect a developing embryo or fetus: There are no adequate reports or well-controlled studies in human fetuses. It is unknown whether busulfan crosses the human placenta. No pattern of anomalies has been identified in children exposed during pregnancy, which indicates that busulfan is not a major cause of birth defects. There are reports of babies being born underweight when their mothers were treated with busulfan during pregnancy. However, it is unclear whether the low birth weight was a result of the medication or the disease it was used to treat.

Breast-feeding: There is no published data in nursing women. It is unknown whether busulfan enters human breast milk.

Potential drug interactions: Interaction between the following medications and busulfan has the potential to impact the effect of one or more of the drugs. In some instances the interaction can be dangerous or life-threatening and must be avoided: itraconazole, acetaminophen, other marrow-suppressing drugs, metronidazole.

What the FDA says about use in pregnancy: Category D (see Appendix).

What the available evidence suggests about breast-feeding safety: Unknown; safest to assume not safe.

The bottom line for you:

- Busulfan may be used for the treatment of life-threatening maternal disease during pregnancy with an apparently low risk to the fetus. Delaying treatment out of concern for the safety of the fetus is not a wise choice.
- Busulfan should not be used while breast-feeding

BUTALBITAL

Brand names: Butal compound, Farbital, Fioricet, Fiorinal, Fiormor, Fiortal, Fortabs, Idenal, Isollyl, Laniroif, Lanorinal, Tecnal, Trianal

Drug classes: Barbiturate; Sedative/hypnotic

Indications (what it is used for): Sedation, insomnia, preoperative sedation, tension headache.

How it works: Alters the brain's sensory and motor centers.

Contraindications (reasons you shouldn't take it): Hypersensitivity to drug or class, porphyria polycythemia (bone marrow makes too many red blood cells), pneumonia, pulmonary insufficiency.

Possible side effects and warnings: Can cause low platelet counts, Stevens-Johnson syndrome (a rare but serious skin reaction to medication), drowsiness, sedation, constipation, heartburn, nausea, vomiting, shortness of breath, and abdominal pain. Should be used with caution in women with poor kidney or liver function, or who have a history of drug abuse.

How it can affect pregnant women: There are no adequate reports or well-controlled studies of butalbital in pregnant women.

How it can affect a developing embryo or fetus: There are no adequate reports or well-controlled studies in animal or human fetuses. It is unknown whether butalbital crosses the human placenta. Withdrawal seizures have been reported in newborns whose mothers used butalbital chronically during pregnancy, which suggests that the drug does reach the fetus.

Breast-feeding: There is no published data in nursing women. It is unknown whether butalbital enters human breast milk as other barbiturates do.

Potential drug interactions: See phenobarbital.

What the FDA says about use in pregnancy: Category C (see Appendix).

What the available evidence suggests about breast-feeding safety: Unknown.

The bottom line for you:

- There is little experience with butalbital during pregnancy. There are superior agents with which there is more experience during pregnancy and while breast-feeding.

BUTORPHANOL

Brand name: Stadol

Drug class: Analgesic, narcotic agonist-antagonist

Indications (what it is used for): Labor pain management, anesthesia.

How it works: Binds to opiate receptors.

Contraindications (reasons you shouldn't take it): Hypersensitivity to drug or class, history of heart attack or coronary insufficiency (impaired heart function)

Possible side effects and warnings: Can cause drowsiness, low blood pressure, respiratory depression, sedation, dizziness, nausea, vomiting, sweating, headache, euphoria, confusion, nervousness, anorexia, and constipation. Should be used with caution in women with liver or kidney dysfunction, central nervous system depression, impaired lung function, head injury, prior gallbladder surgery, or a history of substance abuse.

How it can affect pregnant women: There are no adequate reports or well-controlled studies in pregnant women prior to 37 weeks since it is used for the most part during labor. Butorphanol provides better initial analgesia than fentanyl during labor with fewer patients requesting more medication or epidural analgesia. In one well-designed study, butorphanol was less effective than meperidine for the relief of pain during labor. Some women feel a sense of euphoria; psychosis has been reported rarely.

How it can affect a developing embryo or fetus: There are no adequate reports or well-controlled studies in human fetuses. Butorphanol rapidly crosses the human placenta, achieving the same level in the fetus as it does in the mother. Its use during labor is associated with a unique but short-term ($1\frac{1}{2}$ to 2 hours) fetal heart rhythm pattern. The addition of butorphanol, fentanyl, or sufentanil to epidural bupivacaine does not alter the fetal heart rhythm. Newborns may experience short-term respiratory depression (difficulty breathing) after their mothers have been treated with butorphanol shortly before delivery. Rodent studies are reassuring.

Breast-feeding: There are no adequate reports or well-controlled studies in nursing women. Butorphanol is excreted into human breast milk, but it is estimated that even an exclusively breast-fed newborn would ingest a clinically insignificant amount.

Potential drug interactions: Use with other central nervous system depressants (e.g., alcohol, barbiturates, tranquilizers, antihistamines) may increase the sedative effect of butorphanol. The pain-relieving effect of butorphanol may be diminished if given shortly after sumatriptan nasal spray.

What the FDA says about use in pregnancy: Category C (see Appendix).

What the available evidence suggests about breast-feeding safety: Likely safe.

The bottom line for you:

- Butorphanol is a popular and safe agent for managing labor pain given either by injection or as part of an epidural or caudal block.

- Breast-feeding is unaffected by the use of butorphanol during labor.

CAFFEINE

Brand names: Numerous products contain caffeine.

Drug classes: Analeptic; CNS stimulant; Xanthine

Indications (what it is used for): Migraine, tension, or cluster headaches.

How it works: Primarily blocks the actions of the adenosine receptors.

Contraindications (reasons you shouldn't take it): Hypersensitivity to drug or class, peptic ulcer disease, porphyria.

Possible side effects and warnings: Can cause rapid heart rate and anxiety. In combination with other drugs, caffeine can cause a life-threatening allergic reaction, toxic epidermal necrolysis and Stevens-Johnson syndrome (rare but serious skin disorders), bone marrow suppression, and bleeding in the gastrointestinal tract. Should be used with caution in women with a history of caffeine abuse.

How it can affect pregnant women: Caffeine is widely used either as a medication or in food products (coffee, tea, chocolate). There is no clear evidence that modest amounts of caffeine have an adverse effect on pregnancy. Toxicity occurs only in very high doses (more than about 17 eight-ounce cups a day).

How it can affect a developing embryo or fetus: Caffeine crosses the placenta, achieving the same level found in the mother. An irregular fetal heart rate is associated with maternal caffeine use in excess of 500 mg per day (e.g., 3 NoDoz or Vivarin, 2½ to 5 eight-ounce cups of regular coffee, 6 Red Bulls, or 10–15 twelve-ounce sodas). There is no substantive evidence that caffeine causes birth defects or restricts fetal growth. Several epidemiologic studies suggest a connection between maternal caffeine intake and the risk of miscarriage. However, these studies rely on people's estimates of caffeine use, which are subject to error.

Breast-feeding: Although small amounts enter human breast milk, caffeine is generally considered safe for breast-feeding women.

Potential drug interactions: Interaction between the following medications and caffeine has the potential to impact the effect of one or more of the drugs. In some instances the interaction can be dangerous or life-threatening and must be avoided: propanolol, sympathomimetics, nicotine.

What the FDA says about use in pregnancy: Category C (see Appendix).

What the available evidence suggests about breast-feeding safety: Safe.

The bottom line for you:
- Caffeine is often used in combination with products containing aspirin, acetaminophen, and codeine.
- Caffeine is in many common food substances. If a risk exists, it may be for excess consumption in the first trimester. It has not been shown to cause birth defects in humans.
- If you are a caffeine drinker, talk with your health-care provider about the amount he or she is comfortable with you drinking daily while you are pregnant or breast-feeding.

CAFFEINE PLUS ERGOTAMINE

Brand names: Cafatine, Cafergot, Cafermine, Cafetrate, Ercaf, Ercatab, Ergo-Caff, Gotamine, Micomp-Pb, Migergot, Secadol, Wigraine

Drug classes: Adrenergic antagonist; CNS stimulant; Ergot alkaloid; Xanthine

Indications (what it is used for): Migraine, tension, or cluster headaches.

How it works: Combination drug; see entries for caffeine and ergotamine.

Contraindications (reasons you shouldn't take it): Hypersensitivity to drug or class, pregnancy, peptic ulcer disease, porphyria (a rare group of blood disorders).

Possible side effects and warnings: See individual entries for caffeine and ergotamine.

How it can affect pregnant women: This combination is contraindicated (should not be taken) during pregnancy because ergotamine can cause strong uterine contractions. There are only scattered case reports of use during pregnancy, but they suggest that the medication may be associated with miscarriage. Also see individual entries for caffeine and ergotamine.

How it can affect a developing embryo or fetus: There is a report of one woman who took caffeine plus ergotamine in five consecutive pregnancies. Four pregnancies ended in miscarriage, and one child was born with bowel damage. Also see individual entries for caffeine and ergotamine.

Breast-feeding: There is no published data in nursing women. See individual entries for caffeine and ergotamine.

Potential drug interactions: Interaction between the following medications and caffeine-ergotamine has the potential to impact the effect of one or more of the drugs. In some instances the interaction can be dangerous or life-threatening and must be avoided: propranolol, sympathomimetics, nicotine, macrolide antibiotics.

What the FDA says about use in pregnancy: Category X (see Appendix).

What the available evidence suggests about breast-feeding safety: Not safe.

The bottom line for you:

- Caffeine plus ergotamine should not be taken during pregnancy because of its potential to cause strong uterine contractions.
- Ergotamine is excreted in breast milk and can cause vomiting, diarrhea, weak pulse, and unstable blood pressure in nursing infants. It is not safe while breast-feeding.

CALCIFEDIOL (VITAMIN D)

Brand names: Dical-D, Calcijex
Drug class: Vitamin/mineral
Indications (what it is used for): Vitamin D deficiency, hypoparathyroidism (abnormally low levels of parathyroid hormone), osteoporosis, hypocalcemia (calcium deficiency).

How it works: Stimulates bowel absorption of calcium and phosphorus.

Contraindications (reasons you shouldn't take it): High calcium or vitamin D levels.

Possible side effects and warnings: Can cause high calcium levels, elevated creatinine, excess fluid intake, nausea, and convulsion. Should be used with caution in women with kidney disease or a high phosphate level.

How it can affect pregnant women: Vitamin D supplementation is recommended during pregnancy, although the amount is still debated. There are no adequate reports or well-controlled studies in pregnant women. Veiled or dark-skinned pregnant women have an increased risk of deficiency, since exposure to sunlight helps the body manufacture vitamin D. The RDA during pregnancy is 400–600 IU. In one study, women who took 4,000 IU daily in their second and third trimesters experienced a lower rate of pregnancy-related complications compared to women who took 400 IU every day.

How it can affect a developing embryo or fetus: There are no adequate reports or well-controlled studies in human fetuses. Though causality has not been proved, low levels of vitamin D have been linked to lower birth weight. It is unknown whether calcifediol crosses the human placenta, though the placenta makes the active form of vitamin D. Calcifediol reportedly caused birth defects in some rodents. However, animal studies are not necessarily good indicators of how a drug will behave in humans.

Breast-feeding: There is no published data in nursing women. It is unknown whether calcifediol enters human breast milk, but supplementation has little effect on the levels of vitamin D in milk.

Potential drug interactions: No interactions have been reported.

What the FDA says about use in pregnancy: Category B (see Appendix).

What the available evidence suggests about breast-feeding safety: Safe.

The bottom line for you:

- Vitamin D supplementation is recommended during pregnancy. Most multivitamin supplements (prenatal or otherwise) as well as calcium supplements contain vitamin D in one form or another. Speak with your health-care provider before deciding to take an additional amount.

CALCITONIN

Brand names: Calcimar, Miacalcin

Drug class: Hormone

Indications (what it is used for): Osteoporosis, Paget's disease (breakdown of bone tissue), lowering high calcium levels.

How it works: Unknown.

Contraindications (reasons you shouldn't take it): Hypersensitivity to drug or class.

Possible side effects and warnings: Can cause stuffy nose, back pain, nosebleeds, and headache. Should be used with caution in women with kidney disease, kidney stones, or a high phosphate level.

How it can affect pregnant women: Calcitonin regulates calcium levels, which are important for most body functions, including bone strength and muscle contraction. There are no adequate reports or well-controlled studies in pregnant women.

How it can affect a developing embryo or fetus: Calcitonin does not cross the placenta. There are no adequate reports or well-controlled studies in pregnant women.

Breast-feeding: Procalcitonin is a natural substance that is a normal part of human breast milk, where it is concentrated to 40 times the level in the mother's blood. There is no published data on supplemental calcitonin in nursing women, and it is unknown whether it enters human breast milk. The large size of the molecule suggests that it can't, and any calcitonin that might end up in the milk would be destroyed by the baby's stomach acid.

Potential drug interactions: Diphosphonate appears to decrease the response to calcitonin in people with Paget's disease.

What the FDA says about use in pregnancy: Category C (see Appendix).

What the available evidence suggests about breast-feeding safety: Likely safe.

The bottom line for you:

- There are only rare indications for the use of calcitonin during pregnancy. It is likely safe for use.
- Calcitonin is likely safe for use while breast-feeding, although direct measurements of its level in the breast-feeding newborn have not been made.

CALCITRIOL

Brand name: Rocaltrol

Drug class: Vitamin/mineral

Indications (what it is used for): Hypoparathyroidism (abnormally low levels of parathyroid hormone), calcium supplementation during pregnancy, low calcium, osteoporosis.

How it works: Active form of vitamin D; stimulates bowel absorption of calcium and phosphorus.

Contraindications (reasons you shouldn't take it): Hypersensitivity to drug or class, high calcium or vitamin D levels.

Possible side effects and warnings: Can cause nausea, vomiting, loss of appetite, convulsion, dry mouth, bone pain, excess fluid intake, irritability, weight loss, liver abnormalities, and conjunctivitis. Should be used with caution in women with kidney disease or stones or a high phosphate level.

How it can affect pregnant women: Calcitriol is the active form of vitamin D. There are no adequate reports or well-controlled studies in pregnant women. Vitamin D supplementation is recommended during pregnancy. Veiled or dark-skinned pregnant women have an increased risk of vitamin D deficiency, since exposure to sunlight helps the body manufacture vitamin D. The RDA during pregnancy is 400–600 IU. In one study, women who took 4,000 IU daily in their second and third trimesters experienced a lower rate of pregnancy-related complications compared to women who took 400 IU every day.

How it can affect a developing embryo or fetus: There are no adequate reports or well-controlled studies of the effect of calcitriol in human fetuses. It is unknown whether calcitriol crosses the human placenta, though it is known to make the active form of vitamin D.

Breast-feeding: There are no adequate reports or well-controlled studies in nursing women. It is unknown whether calcitriol enters human breast milk, but supplementation has little effect on the levels of vitamin D in milk.

Potential drug interactions: Interaction between the following medications and calcitriol has the potential to impact the effect of one or more of the drugs. In some instances the interaction can be dangerous or life-threatening and must be avoided: cholestyramine, phenytoin/phenobarbital, thiazide diuretics, phosphate-binding agents.

What the FDA says about use in pregnancy: Category C (see Appendix).

What the available evidence suggests about breast-feeding safety: Unknown.

The bottom line for you:
- Calcitriol should be used during pregnancy and while breast-feeding only if the woman's deficiency is too great for normal over-the-counter vitamin D supplements or prenatal vitamins.

CALCIUM CHLORIDE

Brand name: None
Drug classes: Electrolyte replacement; Mineral
Indications (what it is used for): Low calcium level, high magnesium level.
How it works: Regulates cellular events (e.g., contraction, signaling).
Contraindications (reasons you shouldn't take

it): Ventricular fibrillation, high calcium level, digitalis toxicity, liver dysfunction.

Possible side effects and warnings: Can cause tissue damage and heart rate disturbances related to high potassium. Should be used with caution in women with cardiovascular defects, impaired breathing, or acidosis.

How it can affect pregnant women: Calcium chloride is a lifesaving treatment for toxic magnesium levels, most often in women experiencing preeclampsia (high blood pressure and protein in the urine during pregnancy and complications associated with it) or preterm labor (before 37 weeks).

How it can affect a developing embryo or fetus: Calcium chloride has been shown to decrease aspirin toxicity in pregnant rats. It is unlikely that treating a pregnant woman with calcium increases the fetal calcium level.

Breast-feeding: It is unknown whether calcium chloride supplementation increases calcium concentration in breast milk.

Potential drug interactions: Women receiving digoxin should not be given intravenous calcium compounds unless the condition is life-threatening.

What the FDA says about use in pregnancy: Category C (see Appendix).

What the available evidence suggests about breast-feeding safety: Unknown.

The bottom line for you:
- Women who experience preeclampsia or preterm labor are sometimes treated with magnesium sulfate (see individual entry). Calcium may be lifesaving in the event the magnesium levels get too high.

CAMPHOR

Brand names: Found in Absorbine Arthritic Pain Lotion 10%, Act-On Rub Lotion 1.5%, Anabalm Lotion 3%, Avalgesic, Aveeno Anti-Itch Concentrated Lotion 0.3%, Banalg Muscle Pain Reliever 2%, Bengay Children's Vaporizing Rub 5%, Campho-Phenique Pain Relieving Antiseptic Gel 10.8%, Vicks VapoRub

Drug classes: Anesthetic, local; Itching relief
Indications (what it is used for): Cold relief symptoms, muscle strain.
How it works: Unknown.
Contraindications (reasons you shouldn't take it): Hypersensitivity to drug or class.
Possible side effects and warnings: Can cause local irritation and burning sensation. Should be used with caution in women with a history of seizures.
How it can affect pregnant women: There are no adequate reports or well-controlled studies in pregnant women. The FDA states that over-the-counter drug products containing camphor may not exceed concentrations of 11%. Long experience with the use of topical preparations (such as Vick's) during pregnancy suggests safety.
How it can affect a developing embryo or fetus: There are no adequate reports or well-controlled studies in human fetuses. Camphor crosses the placenta, but there is no evidence that it causes birth defects or harm to the embryo or fetus.
Breast-feeding: There is no published data, and it is unknown whether camphor enters human breast milk. Considering the typical dose and that it is applied topically, it is unlikely that a breast-feeding baby would ingest a significant amount.
Potential drug interactions: None have been reported after topical use.
What the FDA says about use in pregnancy: Category C (see Appendix).
What the available evidence suggests about breast-feeding safety: Safe.
The bottom line for you:
- Topical camphor should be safe to use during pregnancy and while breast-feeding.

CANDESARTAN
Brand name: Atacand
Drug classes: Angiotensin-converting enzyme inhibitor/angiotensin receptor-antagonist; Antihypertensive

Indications (what it is used for): High blood pressure.
How it works: Blocks the receptor for angiotensin.
Contraindications (reasons you shouldn't take it): Hypersensitivity to drug or class, history of angioedema (swelling underneath the skin).
Possible side effects and warnings: Can cause fetal and newborn illness and death, low blood volume, weakness, fever, tingling, dizziness, heartburn, stomach upset, rapid heart rate, liver damage, low white blood cell count, high potassium levels, swelling, diarrhea, chest pain, cough, liver abnormalities, itching, and rash. Should be used with caution in women with narrowing of the kidney artery, liver or kidney dysfunction, low sodium levels, or heart failure.
How it can affect pregnant women: The few published reports during pregnancy suggest that the effects of candesartan are similar to other ACE inhibitors (see "How it can affect a developing embryo or fetus"). Therefore, candesartan should be avoided throughout pregnancy unless there is no other option to treat life-threatening high blood pressure in the mother. In that instance, the lowest effective dose should be used.
How it can affect a developing embryo or fetus: There are no adequate reports or well-controlled studies in human fetuses. Candesartan presumably crosses the human placenta as other ACE inhibitors do because damage to the fetal kidney has been shown. ACE inhibitors are a cause of both birth defects and fetal toxicity. All agents in this class of drugs are contraindicated (should not be taken) throughout pregnancy because they can cause underdevelopment of the skull, reversible or irreversible kidney failure, low amniotic fluid, prematurity, growth restriction, and fetal death.
Breast-feeding: There is no published data in nursing women. It is unknown whether candesartan enters human breast milk.
Potential drug interactions: Candesartan can increase the level of lithium in the blood to dangerously high, and even toxic, levels.

What the FDA says about use in pregnancy: Category D (see Appendix).

What the available evidence suggests about breast-feeding safety: Unknown.

The bottom line for you:

- Candesartan causes birth defects and should not be used during pregnancy unless there is no other option.
- When the mother's disease requires treatment with candesartan, the lowest dose should be used followed by close monitoring of the fetus with ultrasound.
- There is not enough information available to reach a conclusion on the safety of candesartan while breast-feeding.

CAPTOPRIL

Brand names: Capoten, Tenofax

Drug classes: Angiotensin-converting enzyme inhibitor/angiotensin receptor-antagonist; Antihypertensive

Indications (what it is used for): High blood pressure, congestive heart failure, diabetes, recent heart attack.

How it works: Blocks the conversion of an inactive protein to the active angiotensin.

Contraindications (reasons you shouldn't take it): Hypersensitivity to drug or class, narrowing of the artery going to the kidney.

Possible side effects and warnings: Can cause swelling under the skin, low blood pressure, kidney failure, liver toxicity, pancreatitis, protein in the urine, low white blood cell count, rash, itching, cough, abdominal pain, nausea, vomiting, diarrhea, loss of appetite, constipation, peptic ulcer, dizziness, headache, malaise, fatigue, inability to sleep, dry mouth, shortness of breath, hair loss, and tingling. Should be used with caution in women with collagen vascular diseases (diseases of the connective tissue), congestive heart failure, narrowing of the renal artery, liver or kidney dysfunction, or low sodium levels.

How it can affect pregnant women: There are no adequate reports or well-controlled studies of captopril in pregnant women. All ACE inhibitors are contraindicated (should not be used) during pregnancy unless there is no other option for the mother (see "How it can affect a developing embryo or fetus"). When required, the lowest effective dose should be used, and amniotic fluids and the fetus should be closely monitored with ultrasound.

How it can affect a developing embryo or fetus: There are no adequate reports or well-controlled studies in human fetuses. Captopril apparently crosses the human placenta and causes birth defects and fetal toxicity. Captopril and all other ACE inhibitors should not be used at any time during pregnancy. Problems include poor skull development, reversible or irreversible kidney failure, low amniotic fluid, prematurity, growth restriction, and fetal death. Captopril causes embryo death and stillbirths in a variety of animals, including sheep, rabbits, and rats.

Breast-feeding: Captopril is excreted in breast milk at a very low concentration and is generally considered compatible with breast-feeding.

Potential drug interactions: Interaction between the following medications or procedures and captopril has the potential to impact the effect of one or more of the drugs. In some instances the interaction can be dangerous or life-threatening and must be avoided: severe dietary salt restriction or dialysis; diuretics; nitroglycerin or other nitrates or drugs that dilate blood vessels; salt substitutes containing potassium, indomethacin, lithium.

What the FDA says about use in pregnancy: Category D (see Appendix).

What the available evidence suggests about breast-feeding safety: Safe.

The bottom line for you:

- Captopril and all other ACE inhibitors cause birth defects and fetal toxicity; they should be avoided throughout pregnancy.
- When the mother's disease requires treatment with captopril, the lowest dose should be used

followed by close monitoring of the fetus with ultrasound.

CARBAMAZEPINE

Brand names: Atretol, Convuline, Epitol, Macrepan, Tegretol

Drug class: Anticonvulsant

Indications (what it is used for): Seizure disorder, trigeminal neuralgia (a nerve disorder involving tics or muscle spasms in the face).

How it works: Unknown.

Contraindications (reasons you shouldn't take it): Hypersensitivity, use of monoamine oxidase inhibitors (MAOIs) within 14 days.

Possible side effects and warnings: Can cause seizures, Stevens-Johnson syndrome (a rare but serious skin reaction to medication), irregular heart rate, bone marrow suppression, low platelet count, and hepatitis. Should be used with caution in women with liver or kidney failure or bone marrow depression.

How it can affect pregnant women: Women on medication for a seizure disorder should (when possible) plan their pregnancies, discuss the optimal medication with their neurologist, and begin appropriate supplemental folate therapy before conception (4 mg per day) to minimize the risk of birth defects. The risks of birth defects associated with antiseizure medications must be weighed against the risks of continued seizures to both the mother and fetus.

There are no adequate reports or well-controlled studies of carbamazepine in pregnant women. Anticonvulsant drugs should not be discontinued abruptly during pregnancy when used to prevent seizures since there is a significant chance that stopping the medication will bring on a seizure, which can have serious negative effects on both mother and embryo or fetus. Instead, women who become pregnant while on carbamazepine should immediately consult their health-care provider to see whether another medication with a better safety profile may be substituted during pregnancy or to adjust the dose to the lowest amount required for seizure control. Women considering pregnancy while on carbamazepine should also consult their providers to discuss switching medications or lowering dosage in advance.

How it can affect a developing embryo or fetus: There are no adequate reports or well-controlled studies in human fetuses. Carbamazepine rapidly crosses the placenta and accumulates in fetal organs, including the brain. The most recent studies conclude that carbamazepine is a modest teratogen (a substance that can cause birth defects)—less than phenytoin but more than other anticonvulsant medications. It is associated with birth defects that include facial dysmorphism (disfigurement), spina bifida (an opening in the spine), underdevelopment of the fingers, and developmental delay. In a study of 1,255 pregnancies, carbamazepine was also associated with increased rates of cardiovascular, urinary tract, and cleft palate anomalies. The use of carbamazepine with other antiepileptic drugs increases the rate of birth defects. There is also concern that carbamazepine exposure increases the risk of bleeding in the brain of newborns after birth. It is imperative that women who are being treated with carbamazepine during pregnancy receive an early, detailed ultrasound by a skilled perinatal sonographer and another around 20 to 22 weeks. Vitamin K has been recommended during the last month of pregnancy in women taking some enzyme-inducing agents such as oxcarbazepine, carbamazepine, phenobarbital, phenytoin, and topiramate under the theory it will reduce the risk of newborn bleeding. However, there is not good evidence that the risk is increased and the incidence of newborn bleeding does not appear to be decreased by maternal treatment with vitamin K.

Breast-feeding: Carbamazepine is excreted in human breast milk. Although it is generally considered safe for breast-feeding women, there are some reports of problems, including cholestatic hepatitis.

The drug should be given at the lowest effective dose to prevent seizures and breast-feeding avoided at times of peak drug levels. The infant should be monitored for possible adverse effects.

Potential drug interactions: Interaction between the following medications or substances and carbamazepine has the potential to impact the effect of one or more of the drugs. In some instances the interaction can be dangerous or life-threatening and must be avoided: other anticonvulsants, CYP3A4 inhibitors, acetaminophen, acetazolamide, alprazolam, amitriptyline, bupropion, buspirone, cisplatin, citalopram, cimetidine, clarithromycin, clobazam, clomipramine, clonazepam, clozapine, cyclosporine, dalfopristin, danazol, delavirdine, desipramine, diazepam, dicumarol, diltiazem, doxorubicin, doxycycline, erythromycin, ethosuximide, felbamate, fluoxetine, grapefruit and grapefruit juice, haloperidol, isoniazid, itraconazole, ketoconazole, lamotrigine, levothyroxine, loratadine, lorazepam, macrolides, methadone, methsuximide, midazolam, mirtazapine, niacinamide, nicotinamide, nortriptyline, olanzapine, oral contraceptives, phenobarbital, phensuximide, phenytoin, primidone, propoxyphene, quinine, rifampin, terfenadine, theophylline, tiagabine, topiramate, troleandomycin, valproate, verapamil, warfarin, lithium.

What the FDA says about use in pregnancy: Category D (see Appendix).

What the available evidence suggests about breast-feeding safety: Likely safe.

The bottom line for you:
- Women taking carbamazepine for seizure control who become pregnant should not abruptly discontinue therapy on their own but consult with their health-care practitioner immediately.
- Carbamazepine is a cause of birth defects; other anticonvulsants are preferable, if effective.
- If carbamazepine is the only effective therapy, it should be given at the lowest possible dose in divided doses to minimize drug peaks and without the addition of other medications. The fetus should be monitored closely by ultrasound.
- Carbamazepine is generally considered safe for use while breast-feeding. The highest breast milk levels typically occur 1 to 1½ hours after the maternal dose. Scheduling feedings to avoid this time may further lower newborn exposure.

CARBENICILLIN

Brand name: Geocillin
Drug classes: Antibiotic; Penicillin
Indications (what it is used for): Treatment of infections of the upper and lower urinary tract.
How it works: Inhibits cell wall synthesis.
Contraindications (reasons you shouldn't take it): Hypersensitivity to drug or class.
Possible side effects and warnings: Can cause seizures, life-threatening allergic reaction, Stevens-Johnson syndrome (a rare but serious skin reaction to medication), hemolytic anemia, low white blood cell count, nausea, hives, rash, diarrhea, and fever. Should be used with caution in women with a cephalosporin allergy, seizure disorder, or kidney dysfunction.
How it can affect pregnant women: There are no adequate reports or well-controlled studies in pregnant women.
How it can affect a developing embryo or fetus: There are no adequate reports or well-controlled studies in human fetuses. It is unknown whether carbenicillin crosses the human placenta, although other penicillins do to varying degrees. Rodent studies found no evidence of birth defects or poor fetal growth. However, animal studies are not necessarily good indicators of how a medication will behave in humans.
Breast-feeding: There is no published data in nursing women. Carbenicillin is excreted into breast milk in low concentrations but is generally considered safe during breast-feeding.
Potential drug interactions: Carbenicillin blood levels may increase when used with probenecid.

What the FDA says about use in pregnancy: Category B (see Appendix).
What the available evidence suggests about breast-feeding safety: Safe.
The bottom line for you:
- There is a long experience using drugs from the penicillin class during pregnancy and while breast-feeding, and they are generally considered safe.

CARBINOXAMINE

Brand name: Rondec (includes carbinoxamine/dextromethorphan/pseudoephedrine)
Drug class: Antihistamine
Indications (what it is used for): Cold symptoms.
How it works: Blocks central and peripheral histamine receptors.
Contraindications (reasons you shouldn't take it): Hypersensitivity to drug or class, use of monoamine oxidase inhibitors (MAOIs).
Possible side effects and warnings: Can cause irregular heart rate, high blood pressure, coronary vasospasm, drowsiness, thickened secretions, and dry mouth. Should be used with caution in women with glaucoma, high blood pressure, diabetes, asthma, or lung disease.
How it can affect pregnant women: There is no published data with carbinoxamine during pregnancy.
How it can affect a developing embryo or fetus: There are no adequate reports or well-controlled studies in human fetuses. It is unknown whether carbinoxamine crosses the human placenta.
Breast-feeding: There is no published data in nursing women. It is unknown whether carbinoxamine enters human breast milk.
Potential drug interactions: Antihistamines such as carbinoxamine may increase the effects of tricyclic antidepressants, barbiturates, alcohol, and other central nervous system depressants. Monoamine

oxidase inhibitors (MAOIs) prolong and intensify the drying effects of antihistamines.
What the FDA says about use in pregnancy: Category C (see Appendix).
What the available evidence suggests about breast-feeding safety: Unknown.
The bottom line for you:
- There are alternative antihistamines with which there is more experience during pregnancy and breast-feeding.
- Carbinoxamine may be used during pregnancy and breast-feeding when those other medications are contraindicated (should not be used).

CARBOPROST

Brand name: Hemabate
Drug classes: Abortifacient; Oxytocic; Prostaglandin
Indications (what it is used for): Pregnancy termination, uterine atony (lack of uterine contractions).
How it works: Stimulates prostaglandin receptors.
Contraindications (reasons you shouldn't take it): Hypersensitivity to drug or class; fallopian tube infection; acute kidney, liver, or pulmonary disease; coronary artery disease; pregnancy.
Possible side effects and warnings: Can cause fluid in the lungs, respiratory distress, bronchospasm, vomiting of blood, uterine rupture, diarrhea, nausea, vomiting, fever, flushing, high blood pressure, cough, headache, and pain. Should be used with caution in women with high blood pressure, diabetes, asthma, liver or kidney disease, anemia, seizure disorder, uterine scarring, or chorioamnionitis (infection of fetal membranes).
How it can affect pregnant women: Carboprost should not be used during pregnancy because it causes powerful and sustained uterine contractions. It is a second-line agent for the treatment of postpartum hemorrhage (excessive bleeding after delivery) caused when the uterus fails to contract and after the typical treatments such as oxytocin and

methergine/ergotrate fail. Those treatments are generally preferred because carboprost is more expensive and has a much higher chance of causing gastrointestinal problems. Carboprost has been used for pregnancy termination, although both misoprostil and PGE2 are superior. Although carboprost can speed the ripening of the cervix before surgery, it is harder to control than misoprostil, which is the preferred medication for that purpose.

How it can affect a developing embryo or fetus: There are no adequate reports or well-controlled studies in human fetuses. The only reason to use it before delivery is for pregnancy termination. It is unknown whether carboprost crosses the human placenta, but it can put the fetus at great risk by causing prolonged and severe contractions that deprive the fetus of oxygen.

Breast-feeding: There is no published data in nursing women. It is unknown whether carboprost enters human breast milk. Limited use for postpartum hemorrhage should have little impact on breast-feeding.

Potential drug interactions: Because other oxytocic agents have the potential to interact in a dangerous way with carboprost, they should not be used together.

What the FDA says about use in pregnancy: Category C (see Appendix).

What the available evidence suggests about breast-feeding safety: Unknown.

The bottom line for you:
- Carboprost should not be taken during pregnancy unless the intent is pregnancy termination.
- Carboprost is generally reserved for the treatment of postpartum uterine hemorrhage that is unresponsive to first-line drugs.
- When used for postpartum hemorrhage, carboprost should have little impact on breast-feeding.

CARISOPRODOL

Brand names: Caridolin, Chinchen, Flexartal, Mus-Lax, Neotica, Rela, Rotalin, Scutamil-C, Soma

Drug class: Muscle relaxant

Indications (what it is used for): Muscle spasm.

How it works: Blocks nerve traffic from the spinal cord.

Contraindications (reasons you shouldn't take it): Hypersensitivity to drug or class, porphyria (a rare group of blood disorders).

Possible side effects and warnings: Can cause life-threatening allergic reaction, erythema multiforme (a skin disorder), drowsiness, positional low blood pressure, dizziness, lack of gross-muscle control, vomiting, tremor, rash, swelling underneath the skin, and headache. Should be used with caution in women with liver or kidney disease.

How it can affect pregnant women: There are no adequate reports or well-controlled studies in pregnant women.

How it can affect a developing embryo or fetus: There are no adequate reports or well-controlled studies in human fetuses. Carisoprodol crosses the human placenta. Three hundred and twenty-six pregnant women took carisoprodol in the first trimester in Michigan in a study between 1985 and 1992. There was no evidence of an increased risk of birth defects.

Breast-feeding: Carisoprodol is concentrated in breast milk. However, the absolute dose ingested and absorbed by an exclusively breast-fed infant is small and no adverse effects have been reported.

Potential drug interactions: Interaction between the following medications and carisoprodol has the potential to impact the effect of one or more of the drugs. In some instances the interaction can be dangerous or life-threatening and must be avoided: azelastine nasal, dexmedetomidine.

What the FDA says about use in pregnancy: Category C (see Appendix).

What the available evidence suggests about breast-feeding safety: Probably safe.

The bottom line for you:
- Carisoprodol is probably safe for use during pregnancy, although the data is incomplete.

- It should be used during pregnancy and while breast-feeding only when the benefit to the woman justifies the potential risk to the embryo, fetus, or baby.

CASANTHRANOL

Brand names: Peri-Colace (casanthranol/docusate sodium)

Drug classes: Anthraquinone; Purgative

Indications (what it is used for): Constipation.

How it works: Keeps the stool soft and stimulates bowel motility.

Contraindications (reasons you shouldn't take it): Hypersensitivity to drug or class, constipation, appendicitis, abdominal pain, taking mineral oil.

Possible side effects and warnings: Can cause bowel obstruction, abdominal cramps, rash, and electrolyte disorders. Should be used with caution in women who are experiencing nausea or vomiting.

How it can affect pregnant women: There are no adequate reports or well-controlled studies of casanthranol in pregnant women.

How it can affect a developing embryo or fetus: There are no adequate reports or well-controlled studies in human fetuses. It is unknown whether casanthranol crosses the human placenta. It has not been associated with an increased incidence of birth defects.

Breast-feeding: There is no published data during pregnancy. It is unknown whether casanthranol enters human breast milk. However, it is generally considered safe during breast-feeding. Anthraquinone, one of the compounds that casanthranol is broken down into by the body, is excreted into breast milk and may increase diarrhea in nursing infants.

Potential drug interactions: Casanthranol and mineral oil should not be taken at the same time.

What the FDA says about use in pregnancy: Category C (see Appendix).

What the available evidence suggests about breast-feeding safety: Probably safe.

The bottom line for you:

- Because there is so little information on casanthranol during pregnancy, milk of magnesia or a stool softener are preferable treatments for constipation.
- Casanthranol is generally considered safe for use while breast-feeding.

CEFACLOR

Brand names: Ceclor, Ceclor CD, Cefaclor

Drug classes: Antibiotic; Cephalosporin

Indications (what it is used for): Bacterial infection.

How it works: Kills bacteria by inhibiting the synthesis of the cell wall.

Contraindications (reasons you shouldn't take it): Hypersensitivity to drug or class.

Possible side effects and warnings: Can cause life-threatening allergic reaction, seizures, infection of the colon, kidney damage, low white blood cell and/or low platelet counts, erythema multiforme or exfoliative dermatitis (skin disorders), and cholestatic jaundice. Should be used with caution in women with penicillin allergy, kidney dysfunction, antibiotic-associated colitis, or seizure disorder, or who are taking drugs toxic to the kidneys.

How it can affect pregnant women: Cefaclor is used to treat acute bronchitis, pharyngitis, and skin infections. Although there are no adequate reports or well-controlled studies in pregnant women, cephalosporins are usually considered safe for use during pregnancy based on years of clinical experience.

How it can affect a developing embryo or fetus: There are no adequate reports or well-controlled studies in human fetuses. It is unknown whether cefaclor crosses the human placenta, although other cephalosporins do cross. Rodent studies showed no evidence of birth defects or low birth weight despite the use of doses higher than those used in humans. However, animal studies are not necessarily good indicators of how a drug will behave in humans.

Breast-feeding: Most cephalosporins are excreted into breast milk. Although there are no adequate reports or well-controlled studies in nursing women, cefaclor is generally considered compatible with breast-feeding.

Potential drug interactions: Interaction between the following medications and cephalosporins has the potential to impact the effect of one or more of the drugs. In some instances the interaction can be dangerous or life-threatening and must be avoided: aminoglycosides, probenecid.

What the FDA says about use in pregnancy: Category B (see Appendix).

What the available evidence suggests about breast-feeding safety: Safe.

The bottom line for you:

- Cefaclor is considered safe and effective during pregnancy and while breast-feeding for the treatment of acute bronchitis, pharyngitis, and skin infection.

CEFADROXIL

Brand names: Cedroxim, Droxicef, Duricef, Kefroxil, Nor-Dacef, Ultracef, Wincef

Drug classes: Antibiotics; Cephalosporins, first-generation

Indications (what it is used for): Bacterial infections.

How it works: Kills bacteria by inhibiting the synthesis of cell walls.

Contraindications (reasons you shouldn't take it): Hypersensitivity to drug or class.

Possible side effects and warnings: Can cause life-threatening allergic reaction, seizures, infection of the colon, damage to the kidneys, low white blood cell and/or platelet counts, erythema multiforme and exfoliative dermatitis (skin disorders), cholestatic jaundice, diarrhea, nausea, heartburn, hives, itching, and vaginal yeast infection. It should be used with caution in women with penicillin allergy, kidney dysfunction, antibiotic-associated colitis, or seizure disorder, or who are taking drugs toxic to the kidneys.

How it can affect pregnant women: Cefadroxil is used to treat urinary tract infections and pharyngitis. Although there are no adequate reports or well-controlled studies in pregnant women, cephalosporins are generally considered safe for use during pregnancy based on years of clinical experience.

How it can affect a developing embryo or fetus: There are no adequate reports or well-controlled studies in human fetuses. It is unknown whether cefadroxil crosses the human placenta, although other cephalosporins do; as a group, they are generally considered safe. Rodent studies revealed no evidence of birth defects or fetal harm despite the use of doses higher than those used in humans. However, animal studies are not necessarily good indicators of how a drug will behave in humans.

Breast-feeding: Cefadroxil is excreted into breast milk in low concentrations; it is generally considered compatible with breast-feeding.

Potential drug interactions: Interaction between the following medications and cephalosporins has the potential to impact the effect of one or more of the drugs. In some instances the interaction can be dangerous or life-threatening and must be avoided: aminoglycosides, probenecid.

What the FDA says about use in pregnancy: Category B (see Appendix).

What the available evidence suggests about breast-feeding safety: Safe.

The bottom line for you:

- Cefadroxil is considered safe for use during pregnancy and while breast-feeding.

CEFAMANDOLE

Not available in the U.S.

Brand name: Mandol

Drug classes: Antibiotic; Cephalosporin, second generation

Indications (what it is used for): Bacterial infections.

How it works: Kills bacteria by inhibiting the synthesis of cell walls.

Contraindications (reasons you shouldn't take it): Hypersensitivity to drug or class.

Possible side effects and warnings: Can cause life-threatening allergic reaction, seizures, infection of the colon, damage to the kidneys, low white blood cell and/or platelet counts, erythema multiforme and exfoliative dermatitis (skin disorders), and cholestatic jaundice. Should be used with caution in women with penicillin allergy, kidney dysfunction, antibiotic-associated colitis, or seizure disorder, or who are taking drugs toxic to the kidneys.

How it can affect pregnant women: Cefamandole is used to treat lower respiratory tract infections, urinary tract infections, peritonitis (infection of the abdominal lining), and septicemia (bacteria in the blood), and to prevent infection after cesarean section. Although also used to treat group B streptococcus infection, the bacteria are becoming resistant to this treatment; penicillin is preferred. Cephalosporins are usually considered safe for use during pregnancy based on years of clinical use.

How it can affect a developing embryo or fetus: There are no adequate reports or well-controlled studies in human fetuses. It is unknown whether cefamandole crosses the human placenta. Animal studies reveal no evidence of birth defects or low birth weight despite the use of doses higher than those used in humans. However, animal studies are not necessarily good indicators of how a drug will behave in humans.

Breast-feeding: Cefamandole is excreted into breast milk in low concentrations; it is generally considered safe for use during breast-feeding.

Potential drug interactions: Interaction between the following medications and cephalosporins has the potential to impact the effect of one or more of the drugs. In some instances the interaction can be dangerous or life-threatening and must be avoided: aminoglycosides, probenecid.

What the FDA says about use in pregnancy: Category B (see Appendix).

What the available evidence suggests about breast-feeding safety: Safe.

The bottom line for you:
- Cefamandole is considered safe during pregnancy and while breast-feeding.

CEFAZOLIN

Brand names: Ancef, Cefazolin, Kefzol, Zolicef

Drug classes: Antibiotic; Cephalosporin, first generation

Indications (what it is used for): Bacterial infections.

How it works: Kills bacteria by inhibiting the synthesis of cell walls.

Contraindications (reasons you shouldn't take it): Hypersensitivity to drug or class.

Possible side effects and warnings: Can cause seizures, infection of the colon, damage to the kidneys, low white blood cell and/or platelet counts, erythema multiforme and Stevens-Johnson syndrome (skin disorders). Should be used with caution in women with penicillin allergy, kidney dysfunction, antibiotic-associated colitis, or seizure disorder, or who are taking drugs toxic to the kidneys.

How it can affect pregnant women: Cefazolin is used to treat lower respiratory tract infections, genitourinary tract infections, skin infections, peritonitis (infection of the peritoneum), septicemia (bacteria in the blood), and endocarditis (inflammation of the lining of infection in the heart); to prevent infection after cesarean section; and during delivery to prevent the transmission of group B streptococcus from mother to newborn. In penicillin-allergic women who do not have a serious allergy, cefazolin is a treatment of choice for group B streptococcus. Cephalosporins are usually considered safe during pregnancy based on years of clinical use.

How it can affect a developing embryo or fetus: There are no adequate reports or well-controlled studies in human fetuses. Cefazolin rapidly crosses the human placenta and reaches levels high enough to kill group B streptococcus in the fetus. Rodent studies have found no evidence of birth defects or low birth weight despite the use of doses higher than those used in humans. However, animal studies are not necessarily good indicators of how a drug will behave in humans.

Breast-feeding: Although there are no adequate reports or well-controlled studies in nursing women, cefazolin is apparently excreted into human breast milk. It is generally considered compatible with breast-feeding.

Potential drug interactions: Interaction between the following medications and cephalosporins has the potential to impact the effect of one or more of the drugs. In some instances the interaction can be dangerous or life-threatening and must be avoided: aminoglycosides, probenecid.

What the FDA says about use in pregnancy: Category B (see Appendix).

What the available evidence suggests about breast-feeding safety: Safe.

The bottom line for you:

- Cephalosporins are generally considered safe during pregnancy and while breast-feeding.
- Cefazolin is a treatment of choice for group B streptococcus in women allergic to penicillin if the allergy is not severe.

CEFDINIR

Brand name: Omnicef

Drug classes: Antibiotic; Cephalosporin, first generation

Indications (what it is used for): Bacterial infections.

How it works: Kills bacteria by inhibiting the synthesis of cell walls.

Contraindications (reasons you shouldn't take it): Hypersensitivity to drug or class.

Possible side effects and warnings: Can cause diarrhea, vaginal yeast infection, vaginitis, rash, nausea, vomiting, headache, abdominal pain, heartburn, flatulence, loss of appetite, constipation, abnormal stools, weakness, dizziness, inability to sleep, vaginal discharge, itching, and sleepiness. Should be used with caution in women with penicillin allergy, kidney dysfunction, antibiotic associated colitis, or seizure disorder, or who are taking drugs toxic to the kidneys.

How it can affect pregnant women: There are no adequate reports or well-controlled studies of cefdinir in pregnant women. Although cefdinir appears effective and safe during pregnancy for the treatment of acute infections, it has no unique advantage over other cephalosporins for most indications.

How it can affect a developing embryo or fetus: There are no adequate reports or well-controlled studies in human fetuses. Although cephalosporins are generally considered safe during pregnancy, it is unknown whether cefdinir crosses the human placenta; other cephalosporins do. Rodent studies have found no evidence of birth defects or low birth weight despite the use of doses higher than those used in humans. However, animal studies are not necessarily good indicators of how a drug will behave in humans.

Breast-feeding: Most cephalosporins are excreted into breast milk. Although there is no published data in nursing women, cefdinir is generally considered compatible with breast-feeding.

Potential drug interactions: Interaction between the following medications and cefdinir has the potential to impact the effect of one or more of the drugs. In some instances the interaction can be dangerous or life-threatening and must be avoided: Maalox TC suspension, probenecid, iron supplement.

What the FDA says about use in pregnancy: Category B (see Appendix).

What the available evidence suggests about breast-feeding safety: Safe.

The bottom line for you:

- Although cephalosporins are generally considered safe for use during pregnancy and while breast-feeding, there are other drugs in this class with which there is more experience.

CEFEPIME

Brand name: Maxipime

Drug classes: Antibiotic; Cephalosporin, fourth generation

Indications (what it is used for): Bacterial infections.

How it works: Kills bacteria by inhibiting the synthesis of cell walls.

Contraindications (reasons you shouldn't take it): Hypersensitivity to drug or class.

Possible side effects and warnings: Can cause life-threatening allergic reaction, seizures, infection of the colon, kidney damage, low white blood cell and/or platelet counts, erythema multiforme and exfoliative dermatitis or Stevens-Johnson syndrome (skin disorders), and cholestatic jaundice. Should be used with caution in women with penicillin allergy, kidney dysfunction, antibiotic-associated colitis, or seizure disorder, or who are taking drugs toxic to the kidneys.

How it can affect pregnant women: Cephalosporins are usually considered safe during pregnancy. Cefepime is used to treat lower respiratory tract infections, genitourinary tract infections, and skin infections, and those with low white blood cell counts. Fourth-generation cephalosporin drugs are not usually recommended solely for the prevention of infections since there are cheaper, equally effective options.

How it can affect a developing embryo or fetus: There are no adequate reports or well-controlled studies in human fetuses. Cephalosporins are generally considered safe during pregnancy. It is unknown whether cefepime crosses the human placenta, though other cephalosporins do so. Rodent studies have found no evidence of birth defects or low birth weight despite the use of doses higher than those used in humans. However, animal studies are not necessarily good indicators of how a drug will behave in humans.

Breast-feeding: Most cephalosporins are excreted into breast milk. Although there is no published data in nursing women, cefepime is generally considered compatible with breast-feeding.

Potential drug interactions: Interaction between the following medications and cefepime has the potential to impact the effect of one or more of the drugs. In some instances the interaction can be dangerous or life-threatening and must be avoided: aminoglycosides, probenecid, potent diuretics such as furosemide.

What the FDA says about use in pregnancy: Category B (see Appendix).

What the available evidence suggests about breast-feeding safety: Safe.

The bottom line for you:

- Although cefepime is generally considered safe, there are alternative agents with which there is more experience during pregnancy and while breast-feeding.
- Third- and fourth-generation cephalosporins such as cefepime are generally not recommended solely to prevent surgical infection, including during cesarean sections.

CEFMETAZOLE

Brand name: Zefazone

Drug classes: Antibiotic; Cephalosporin, second generation

Indications (what it is used for): Bacterial infection.

How it works: Kills bacteria by inhibiting the synthesis of cell walls.

Contraindications (reasons you shouldn't take it): Hypersensitivity to drug or class.

Possible side effects and warnings: Can cause life-threatening allergic reaction, Stevens-Johnson syndrome (a rare but serious skin reaction to medication), kidney failure, diarrhea, headache, low blood pressure, nausea, rash, itching, fever, epigastric pain (pain in the upper abdomen), vaginitis, pleural effusion (fluid in the lining of the lungs), shortness of breath, and skin redness. Should be used with caution in women with penicillin allergy, kidney dysfunction, antibiotic-associated colitis, or seizure disorder, or who are taking drugs toxic to the kidneys.

How it can affect pregnant women: There are no adequate reports or well-controlled studies in pregnant women. Cephalosporins are usually considered safe during pregnancy. Cefmetazole is highly effective against most causes of bacterial vaginitis during pregnancy. Cefmetazole is as effective as cefoxitin in reducing post–cesarean section endometritis (inflammation of the lining of the uterus).

How it can affect a developing embryo or fetus: There are no adequate reports or well-controlled studies in human fetuses. Cephalosporins are usually considered safe during pregnancy. Cefmetazole rapidly crosses the human placenta, reaching therapeutic levels needed to kill bacteria in the fetus. Rodent studies have found no evidence of birth defects or low birth weight, despite the use of doses higher than those used in humans. However, animal studies are not necessarily good indicators of how a drug will behave in humans.

Breast-feeding: Only a scant amount of cefmetazole is excreted into human breast milk, and it is generally considered compatible with breast-feeding.

Potential drug interactions: Interaction between the following medications and cephalosporins has the potential to impact the effect of one or more of the drugs. In some instances the interaction can be dangerous or life-threatening and must be avoided: aminoglycosides, probenecid.

What the FDA says about use in pregnancy: Category B (see Appendix).

What the available evidence suggests about breast-feeding safety: Safe.

The bottom line for you:

- Cephalosporins are usually considered safe during pregnancy and while breast-feeding.
- Cefmetazole is an effective treatment for bacterial vaginitis during pregnancy and for postpartum endometritis. However, there are cheaper agents with which we have more experience.

CEFONICID

Brand name: Monocid

Drug classes: Antibiotic; Cephalosporin, second generation

Indications (what it is used for): Bacterial infections.

How it works: Kills bacteria by inhibiting the synthesis of cell walls.

Contraindications (reasons you shouldn't take it): Hypersensitivity to drug or class.

Possible side effects and warnings: Can cause life-threatening allergic reaction, seizures, low white blood cell and/or platelet counts, infection of the colon, erythema multiforme or exfoliative dermatitis (skin disorders), cholestatic jaundice, and positive Coombs' test (presence of antibodies that can destroy red blood cells). Should be used with caution in women with penicillin allergy, kidney dysfunction, antibiotic-associated colitis, or seizure disorder, or who are taking drugs toxic to the kidneys.

How it can affect pregnant women: Cephalosporins are usually considered safe during pregnancy. Cefonicid appears effective and safe during pregnancy and is used to treat lower respiratory tract infections, genitourinary tract infections, skin infections, and septicemia (bacteria in the blood), and to prevent infection after surgery.

How it can affect a developing embryo or fetus: There are no adequate reports or well-controlled studies in human fetuses. Cephalosporins are usually considered safe during pregnancy. It is unknown whether cefonicid crosses the human placenta, although other cephalosporins do. Rodent studies have found no evidence of birth defects or low birth weight despite the use of doses higher than those used in humans. However, animal studies are not necessarily good indicators of how a drug will behave in humans.

Breast-feeding: Cefonicid is excreted at low concentrations into human breast milk and is generally considered compatible with breast-feeding.

Potential drug interactions: Interaction between the following medications and cephalosporins has the potential to impact the effect of one or more of the drugs. In some instances the interaction can be dangerous or life-threatening and must be avoided: aminoglycosides, probenecid.

What the FDA says about use in pregnancy: Category B (see Appendix).

What the available evidence suggests about breast-feeding safety: Safe.

The bottom line for you:

- Cephalosporins are usually considered safe during pregnancy and while breast-feeding.
- Cefonicid specifically is considered safe during pregnancy for the treatment of acute infection and to prevent infection after surgery.

CEFOPERAZONE

Brand name: Cefobid

Drug classes: Antibiotic; Cephalosporin, third generation

Indications (what it is used for): Bacterial infections.

How it works: Kills bacteria by inhibiting the synthesis of cell walls.

Contraindications (reasons you shouldn't take it): Hypersensitivity to drug or class.

Possible side effects and warnings: Can cause life-threatening allergic reaction, serum sickness (a reaction to proteins in antiserum derived from an animal source), infection of the colon, low white blood cell and/or platelet counts, rash, hives, and nausea. Should be used with caution in women with penicillin allergy, kidney dysfunction, antibiotic-associated colitis, seizure disorder, or altered liver function, or who are taking drugs toxic to the kidneys.

How it can affect pregnant women: Cefoperazone appears effective and safe during pregnancy for the treatment of acute lower respiratory tract infections, genitourinary tract infections, skin infections, and septicemia (bacteria in the blood). Third- and fourth-generation cephalosporins (e.g., cefotaxime, cefoperazone, ceftriaxone, ceftazidime, ceftizoxime) are generally not recommended for preventing infection after surgery, as there are less expensive but equally effective agents available.

How it can affect a developing embryo or fetus: There are no adequate reports or well-controlled studies in human fetuses. Cephalosporins are usually considered safe during pregnancy. Cefoperazone crosses the human placenta but to a lower degree than ceftizoxime. Rodent studies have found no evidence of birth defects or low birth weight despite the use of doses higher than those used in humans. However, animal studies are not necessarily good indicators of how a drug will behave in humans.

Breast-feeding: Cefoperazone is excreted in small amounts into human breast milk and is generally considered compatible with breast-feeding.

Potential drug interactions: Interaction between the following medications and cephalosporins has the potential to impact the effect of one or more of the drugs. In some instances the interaction can be dangerous or life-threatening and must be avoided: aminoglycosides, probenecid.

What the FDA says about use in pregnancy: Category B (see Appendix).

What the available evidence suggests about breast-feeding safety: Safe.

The bottom line for you:

- Cephalosporins are usually considered safe during pregnancy and while breast-feeding.
- Cefoperazone appears effective and safe for the treatment of acute obstetric infection.
- Third- and fourth-generation cephalosporins are generally not recommended for surgical prophylaxis because there are cheaper, equally effective options.

CEFOTAXIME

Brand names: Claforan, Zetaxim

Drug classes: Antibiotic; Cephalosporin, third generation

Indications (what it is used for): Bacterial infections.

How it works: Kills bacteria by inhibiting the synthesis of cell walls.

Contraindications (reasons you shouldn't take it): Hypersensitivity to drug or class.

Possible side effects and warnings: Can cause life-threatening allergic reaction, serum sickness (a reaction to proteins in antiserum derived from an animal source), infection of the colon, diarrhea, nausea, vomiting, constipation, headache, fever, low white blood cell and/or platelet counts, rash, and hives. Should be used with caution in women with penicillin allergy, kidney dysfunction, antibiotic-associated colitis, or seizure disorder, or who are taking drugs toxic to the kidneys.

How it can affect pregnant women: Cephalosporins are usually considered safe during pregnancy. Cefotaxime is used during pregnancy to treat infection in the lower respiratory tract, gastrointestinal tract, skin, and blood. It is also used for the prevention of infection after surgery. Third- and fourth-generation cephalosporins (e.g., cefotaxime, cefoperazone, ceftriaxone, ceftazidime, ceftizoxime) are generally not recommended for preventing infection after surgery because there are cheaper but equally effective drugs.

How it can affect a developing embryo or fetus: There are no adequate reports or well-controlled studies in human fetuses. Cephalosporins are usually considered safe during pregnancy. Cefotaxime crosses the human placenta, reaching levels in the amniotic fluid that will kill most sensitive bacteria, suggesting that it would be good for the treatment of chorioamnionitis (inflammation of the fetal membranes). Rodent studies have found no evidence of birth defects or low birth weight despite the use of doses higher than those used in humans. However, animal studies are not necessarily good indicators of how a drug will behave in humans.

Breast-feeding: Only scant quantities of cefotaxime are excreted into human breast milk, and it is generally considered compatible with breast-feeding.

Potential drug interactions: Interaction between the following medications and cephalosporins has the potential to impact the effect of one or more of the drugs. In some instances the interaction can be dangerous or life-threatening and must be avoided: aminoglycosides, probenecid.

What the FDA says about use in pregnancy: Category B (see Appendix).

What the available evidence suggests about breast-feeding safety: Safe.

The bottom line for you:

- Cephalosporins are usually considered safe during pregnancy and while breast-feeding.
- Cefotaxime appears effective and safe during pregnancy for the treatment of acute obstetric infection and the prevention of infection during and after surgery.
- However, third- and fourth-generation cephalosporins are generally not recommended for the prevention of infection after surgery because there are cheaper, equally effective options.

CEFOTETAN

Brand names: Apatef, Cefotan

Drug classes: Antibiotic; Cephalosporin, second generation

Indications (what it is used for): Bacterial infections.

How it works: Kills bacteria by inhibiting the synthesis of cell walls.

Contraindications (reasons you shouldn't take it): Hypersensitivity to drug or class.

Possible side effects and warnings: Can cause life-threatening allergic reaction, bone marrow suppression, prolonged bleeding, infection of the colon, low white blood cell and/or platelet counts, rash, hives, hemolysis (breakdown of red blood cells), and hemolytic anemia. Should be used with caution in women with penicillin allergy, kidney dysfunction, antibiotic-associated colitis, or seizure disorder, or who are taking drugs toxic to the kidneys.

How it can affect pregnant women: Cefotetan appears effective and safe during pregnancy for the treatment of acute infections of the lower respiratory and genitourinary tracts, and septicemia (bacteria in the blood), and to prevent infection after surgery such as cesarean section. There are rare reports of severe maternal red blood cell breakdown when cefotetan was used to prevent infection after C-section.

How it can affect a developing embryo or fetus: There are no adequate reports or well-controlled studies in human fetuses. Cephalosporins are usually considered safe during pregnancy. Cefotetan crosses both rodent and human placentas. Rodent studies have found no evidence of birth defects or low birth weight despite the use of doses higher than those used in humans. However, animal studies are not necessarily good indicators of how a drug will behave in humans.

Breast-feeding: Although there are no adequate reports or well-controlled studies in nursing women, cefotetan is excreted in scant quantities into human breast milk and is generally considered compatible with breast-feeding.

Potential drug interactions: Interaction between the following medications and cephalosporins has the potential to impact the effect of one or more of the drugs. In some instances the interaction can be dangerous or life-threatening and must be avoided: aminoglycosides, probenecid.

What the FDA says about use in pregnancy: Category B (see Appendix).

What the available evidence suggests about breast-feeding safety: Safe.

The bottom line for you:

- Cefotetan appears effective and safe during pregnancy for the treatment of acute infection and for preventing infection after surgery. Complications are rare and typically related to an allergy.
- Cefotetan is generally considered safe for use while breast-feeding.

CEFOXITIN

Brand names: Cefxitin, Mefoxin

Drug classes: Antibiotic; Cephalosporin, second generation

Indications (what it is used for): Bacterial infections.

How it works: Kills bacteria by inhibiting cell wall synthesis.

Contraindications (reasons you shouldn't take it): Hypersensitivity to drug or class.

Possible side effects and warnings: Can cause life-threatening allergic reaction, bone marrow suppression, serum sickness (a reaction to proteins in antiserum derived from an animal source), infection of the colon, low white blood cell and/or platelet counts, kidney failure, and hemolytic anemia. Should be used with caution in women with penicillin allergy, kidney dysfunction, antibiotic-associated colitis, or seizure disorder, or who are taking drugs toxic to the kidneys.

How it can affect pregnant women: Cefoxitin appears effective and safe during pregnancy for the treatment of acute infection, though it does not prevent infection after elective cesarean section. Cefoxitin is used to treat infections of the lower respiratory tract, genitourinary tract, and skin, and septicemia (bacteria in the blood), and to prevent infection after nonelective cesarean delivery following either labor or ruptured membranes (water breaking).

How it can affect a developing embryo or fetus: Cephalosporins are usually considered safe during pregnancy. There are no adequate reports or well-controlled studies in human fetuses. Cefoxitin crosses the human placenta, achieving levels in the fetus that are about half of the mother's level, too low to be sure bacteria in the fetal blood will be killed.

Breast-feeding: There is little detectable cefoxitin in human breast milk after it has been used to prevent infection after C-section. It is generally considered compatible with breast-feeding.

Potential drug interactions: Interaction between the following medications and cephalosporins has the potential to impact the effect of one or more of the drugs. In some instances the interaction can be dangerous or life-threatening and must be avoided: aminoglycosides, probenecid.

What the FDA says about use in pregnancy: Category B (see Appendix).

What the available evidence suggests about breast-feeding safety: Safe.

The bottom line for you:

- Cefoxitin appears effective and safe during pregnancy and while breast-feeding for the treatment of acute infection.
- There are superior cephalosporins to treat intra-amniotic infections.

CEFTAZIDIME

Brand names: Ceptaz, Fortaz, Tazicef, Tazidime

Drug classes: Antibiotic; Cephalosporin, third generation

Indications (what it is used for): Bacterial infections.

How it works: Kills bacteria by inhibiting the synthesis of cell walls.

Contraindications (reasons you shouldn't take it): Hypersensitivity to drug or class.

Possible side effects and warnings: Can cause seizures, bone marrow suppression, low platelet count, and life-threatening allergic reaction. Should be used with caution in women with penicillin allergy, impaired kidney function, antibiotic-associated colitis, or seizure disorder, or who are taking drugs toxic to the kidneys.

How it can affect pregnant women: Ceftazidime is a third-generation cephalosporin. There are no adequate reports or well-controlled studies of ceftazidime in pregnant women. Cephalosporins are usually considered safe during pregnancy. Ceftazidime-containing regimens are important for the treatment of women with fever and low white blood cell counts. Elimination of ceftazidime by the kidneys is increased during pregnancy, and the dose may need to be increased. Third- and fourth-generation cephalosporins are generally not recommended to prevent infection after surgery because there are equally effective but cheaper alternatives.

How it can affect a developing embryo or fetus: There are no adequate reports or well-controlled studies in human fetuses. Cephalosporins are usually considered safe during pregnancy. Ceftazidime crosses the human placenta, achieving a fetal level one-sixth of that in the mother, too low to reliably kill bacteria in the fetal blood. Rodent studies are reassuring, revealing no evidence of birth defects or low birth weight despite the use of doses higher than those used clinically. However, animal studies are not necessarily good indicators of how a drug will behave in humans.

Breast-feeding: Ceftazidime is excreted into human breast milk in very small quantities. It is generally considered compatible with breast-feeding.

Potential drug interactions: Interaction between the following medications and ceftazidime has the potential to impact the effect of one or more of the drugs. In some instances the interaction can be dangerous or life-threatening and must be avoided: aminoglycosides, chloramphenicol, probenicid.

What the FDA says about use in pregnancy: Category B (see Appendix).

What the available evidence suggests about breast-feeding safety: Safe.

The bottom line for you:

- Cephalosporins are usually considered safe during pregnancy and while breast-feeding.
- Third- and fourth-generation cephalosporins such as ceftazidime are generally not recommended for preventing infection after C-section; they are usually reserved for very specific indications.
- There are superior cephalosporins to treat intra-amniotic infections.

CEFTIBUTEN

Brand name: Cedax

Drug classes: Antibiotic; Cephalosporin, third generation

Indications (what it is used for): Bacterial infections.

How it works: Kills bacteria by inhibiting the synthesis of cell walls.

Contraindications (reasons you shouldn't take it): Hypersensitivity to drug or class.

Possible side effects and warnings: Can cause seizures, bone marrow suppression, low platelet count, and life-threatening allergic reaction. Should be used with caution in women with penicillin allergy, antibiotic-associated colitis, seizure disorder, or kidney dysfunction, or who are taking drugs toxic to the kidneys.

How it can affect pregnant women: Ceftibuten is an effective treatment for acute urinary tract infection during pregnancy. There is little data during pregnancy with other conditions. Cephalosporins are usually considered safe during pregnancy. Third- and fourth-generation cephalosporins such as ceftibuten are not generally recommended for the prevention of infection after C-section or other surgery.

How it can affect a developing embryo or fetus: There are no adequate reports or well-controlled studies in human fetuses. It is unknown whether ceftibuten crosses the human placenta. Cephalosporins are usually considered safe during pregnancy. Rodent studies are reassuring, revealing no evidence of birth defects or low birth weight despite the use of doses higher than those used clinically. However, animal studies are not necessarily good indicators of how a drug will behave in humans.

Breast-feeding: The concentration of ceftibuten in breast milk is minimal, and it is considered compatible with breast-feeding.

Potential drug interactions: Interaction between the following medications and cephalosporins has the potential to impact the effect of one or more of the drugs. In some instances the interaction can be dangerous or life-threatening and must be avoided: aminoglycosides, probenecid.

What the FDA says about use in pregnancy: Category B (see Appendix).

What the available evidence suggests about breast-feeding safety: Safe.

The bottom line for you:
- Ceftibuten is an effective treatment for acute urinary tract infection during pregnancy.
- Third- and fourth-generation cephalosporins are generally not recommended for the prevention of infection after C-section as there are equally effective but less expensive alternatives.

CEFTIZOXIME

Brand name: Cefizox

Drug classes: Antibiotic; Cephalosporin, third generation

Indications (what it is used for): Bacterial infections.

How it works: Kills bacteria by inhibiting the synthesis of cell walls.

Contraindications (reasons you shouldn't take it): Hypersensitivity to drug or class.

Possible side effects and warnings: May cause rash, life-threatening allergic reaction, itching, eosinophilia (elevated level of one type of white blood cell), and liver damage. Should be used with caution in women with penicillin allergy, antibiotic-associated colitis, seizure disorder, or kidney dysfunction, or who are taking drugs toxic to the kidneys.

How it can affect pregnant women: Ceftizoxime appears effective and safe for the treatment of acute infections during pregnancy. Third- and fourth-generation cephalosporins are not generally recommended for preventing infection after C-section as there are cheaper alternatives.

How it can affect a developing embryo or fetus: There are no adequate reports or well-controlled studies in human fetuses. Cephalosporins are usually considered safe during pregnancy. Ceftizoxime concentrations are higher in the fetus than in the mother. It is one of the few antibiotics known to have such high transfer, making it an excellent choice for the treatment of chorioamnionitis (infection of fetal membranes) before or during labor.

Rodent studies are reassuring, revealing no evidence of birth defects or low birth weight despite the use of doses higher than those used in humans. However, animal studies are not necessarily good indicators of how a drug will behave in humans.

Breast-feeding: The amount of ceftizoxime excreted is minimal and it is generally considered compatible with breast-feeding.

Potential drug interactions: Interaction between the following medications and cephalosporins has the potential to impact the effect of one or more of the drugs. In some instances the interaction can be dangerous or life-threatening and must be avoided: aminoglycosides, probenecid.

What the FDA says about use in pregnancy: Category B (see Appendix).

What the available evidence suggests about breast-feeding safety: Safe.

The bottom line for you:
- Cephalosporins are usually considered safe during pregnancy and while breast-feeding.
- Ceftizoxime may be advantageous for the treatment of chorioamnionitis prior to delivery.
- Third- and fourth-generation cephalosporins are generally not recommended for preventing infection after C-section as there are equally effective but less expensive options.

CEFTRIAXONE

Brand names: Cef-3, Rocephin, Rowecef
Drug classes: Antibiotic; Cephalosporin, third generation
Indications (what it is used for): Bacterial infections.
How it works: Kills bacteria by inhibiting the synthesis of cell walls.
Contraindications (reasons you shouldn't take it): Hypersensitivity to drug or class.
Possible side effects and warnings: Can cause life-threatening allergic reaction, eosinophilia (elevated level of one type of white blood cell), low platelet count, diarrhea, infection of the colon, and vomiting. Should be used with caution in women with penicillin allergy, kidney dysfunction, antibiotic-associated colitis, or seizure disorder, or those taking drugs toxic to the kidneys.

How it can affect pregnant women: Ceftriaxone appears effective and safe during pregnancy for the treatment of acute infections. It is a drug of choice for the treatment of gonorrhea in pregnancy. Third- and fourth-generation cephalosporins are not generally recommended for preventing infection after C-section as there are equally effective but cheaper options.

How it can affect a developing embryo or fetus: Cephalosporins are generally considered safe during pregnancy. There are no adequate reports or well-controlled studies in human fetuses. Ceftriaxone rapidly crosses the human placenta, reaching concentrations in the fetus high enough to treat fetal infections. Some studies suggest that treating a mother with ceftriaxone during labor and delivery beneficially reduces bacterial colonization and early onset infection in newborns. Rodent studies have found no evidence of birth defects or low birth weight despite the use of doses higher than those used clinically. However, extremely high levels block kidney development in rodent fetuses. Animal studies are not necessarily good indicators of how a drug will behave in humans.

Breast-feeding: The amount of ceftriaxone excreted into breast milk is very low. It is generally considered compatible with breast-feeding.

Potential drug interactions: Interaction between the following medications and cephalosporins has the potential to impact the effect of one or more of the drugs. In some instances the interaction can be dangerous or life-threatening and must be avoided: aminoglycosides, probenecid.

What the FDA says about use in pregnancy: Category B (see Appendix).

What the available evidence suggests about breast-feeding safety: Safe.

The bottom line for you:
- Cephalosporins are usually considered safe during pregnancy and while breast-feeding.

- Ceftriaxone appears effective and safe during pregnancy for the treatment of acute obstetric infections.
- Third- and fourth-generation cephalosporins such as ceftriaxone are generally not recommended for preventing infection after C-section as there are equally effective but cheaper options.

CELECOXIB

Brand name: Celebrex

Drug classes: COX-2 inhibitor; Nonsteroidal anti-inflammatory drug (NSAID)

Indications (what it is used for): Osteoarthritis, rheumatoid arthritis, familial adenomatous polyposis (inherited polyps in the colon), acute pain.

How it works: Inhibits the action of the enzyme COX-2, which is responsible for inflammation and pain.

Contraindications (reasons you shouldn't take it): Hypersensitivity to drug or class, nonsteroidal drug–induced asthma or hives, aspirin triad (aspirin allergy, asthma, and nasal polyps), liver or kidney failure.

Possible side effects and warnings: Can cause bleeding and ulcers in the stomach or intestinal tract, inflammation of the esophagus, hypersensitivity reaction, bronchospasm, heart failure, liver and/or kidney damage, diarrhea, abdominal pain, flatulence, dizziness, and pharyngitis. Should be used with caution in women with nasal polyps, intestinal bleeding, kidney or liver dysfunction, congestive heart failure, high blood pressure, dehydration, fluid retention, or asthma.

How it can affect pregnant women: There are no adequate reports or well-controlled studies in pregnant women. In two small trials, celecoxib was used as a tocolytic agent (medication to delay or stop preterm labor) but had only modest effect. It does relieve episiotomy pain. However, COX-2 inhibition has been associated with an increase in death from cardiovascular causes such as heart attack, stroke, or heart failure. In light of these reports, celecoxib should not be used during pregnancy, as there are numerous other medications that have been better studied and with which there is more experience.

How it can affect a developing embryo or fetus: There are no adequate reports or well-controlled studies in human fetuses. Celecoxib crosses the human placenta, as do other NSAIDs, and may adversely affect the fetal cardiovascular system.

Breast-feeding: There are no adequate reports or well-controlled studies of celecoxib in nursing women. A small study of patients suggests that the amount of celecoxib ingested by a breast-feeding newborn is not clinically significant.

Potential drug interactions: Interaction between the following medications and celecoxib has the potential to impact the effect of one or more of the drugs. In some instances the interaction can be dangerous or life-threatening and must be avoided: aspirin, drugs that inhibit the enzyme CYP2C9, other NSAIDs, ACE inhibitors, fluconazole, furosemide, lithium, thiazide, warfarin.

What the FDA says about use in pregnancy: Category C before 30 weeks gestation; Category D, 30 weeks and after (see Appendix).

What the available evidence suggests about breast-feeding safety: Possibly safe.

The bottom line for you:

- Celecoxib and other COX-2 inhibitors may be associated with increased rate of complications in mother and fetus. It should not be used during pregnancy until there is new evidence of safety.
- Based on limited information, celecoxib is likely relatively safe for use while breast-feeding.

CEPHALEXIN

Brand names: Alsporin, Biocef, Carnosporin, Cefaseptin, Cephin, Ceporexin-E, Ed A-Ceph, Keflet, Keflex, Lopilexin, Mamlexin, Synecl, Winlex

Drug classes: Antibiotic; Cephalosporin, first generation

Indications (what it is used for): Bacterial infections.

How it works: Kills bacteria by inhibiting the synthesis of cell walls.

Contraindications (reasons you shouldn't take it): Hypersensitivity to drug or class.

Possible side effects and warnings: Can cause low white blood cell and/or platelet counts, life-threatening allergic reaction, infection of the colon, diarrhea, nausea, and liver damage. Should be used with caution in women with penicillin allergy, kidney dysfunction, or antibiotic-associated colitis.

How it can affect pregnant women: Cephalexin appears effective and safe during pregnancy for the treatment of urinary tract infections, acute obstetric infections, and pharyngitis.

How it can affect a developing embryo or fetus: There are no adequate reports or well-controlled studies in human fetuses. Cephalosporins are usually considered safe during pregnancy. Cephalexin crosses the human placenta, and the resulting level in the fetus will kill most sensitive bacteria, suggesting that it is useful in women with chorioamnionitis (infection of fetal membranes). There is no evidence that it causes birth defects in humans despite extensive clinical experience. Rodent studies are also reassuring, finding no evidence of birth defects or low birth weight despite the use of doses higher than those used clinically. However, animal studies are not necessarily good indicators of how a drug will behave in humans.

Breast-feeding: The amount of cephalexin excreted into breast milk is small, and it is generally considered compatible with breast-feeding.

Potential drug interactions: Interaction between the following medications and cephalosporins has the potential to impact the effect of one or more of the drugs. In some instances the interaction can be dangerous or life-threatening and must be avoided: aminoglycosides, probenecid.

What the FDA says about use in pregnancy: Category B (see Appendix).

What the available evidence suggests about breast-feeding safety: Safe.

The bottom line for you:

- Cephalexin is a popular cephalosporin for which there is broad and reassuring experience during pregnancy and while breast-feeding.

CEPHRADINE

Brand names: Anspor, Cefamid, Cefradina, Eskefrin, Nobitina, Velosef

Drug classes: Antibiotic; Cephalosporin, first generation

Indications (what it is used for): Bacterial infections.

How it works: Kills bacteria by inhibiting cell wall synthesis.

Contraindications (reasons you shouldn't take it): Hypersensitivity to drug or class.

Possible side effects and warnings: Can cause anemia, low platelet count, life-threatening allergic reaction, infection of the colon, diarrhea, nausea, and elevated liver enzymes. Should be used with caution in women with penicillin allergy, kidney dysfunction, antibiotic-associated colitis, or seizure disorder, or who are taking drugs toxic to the kidneys.

How it can affect pregnant women: Cephradine has been used safely and effectively during pregnancy for the treatment of urinary tract infection and pharyngitis.

How it can affect a developing embryo or fetus: There are no adequate reports or well-controlled studies in human fetuses. Cephalosporins are usually considered safe during pregnancy. Cephradine rapidly crosses the human placenta. Rodent studies are reassuring, revealing no evidence of birth defects or low birth weight despite the use of doses higher than those used clinically. However, animal studies are not necessarily good indicators of how a drug will behave in humans.

Breast-feeding: Cephradine is excreted at low concentrations into human breast milk and is compatible with breast-feeding.

Potential drug interactions: Interaction between the following medications and cephradine has the potential to impact the effect of one or more of the drugs. In some instances the interaction can be dangerous or life-threatening and must be avoided: bacteriostatic agents, aminoglycosides, colistin, polymyxins, vancomycin, furosemide, ethacrynic acid, probenecid.

What the FDA says about use in pregnancy: Category B (see Appendix).

What the available evidence suggests about breast-feeding safety: Safe.

The bottom line for you:

- Extensive clinical experience indicates that cephradine is safe and effective during pregnancy and while breast-feeding for the treatment of urinary tract infections and pharyngitis.

CETIRIZINE

Brand names: Alltec, Zyrtec

Drug classes: Allergy; Antihistamine

Indications (what it is used for): Allergic rhinitis, hives.

How it works: Inhibition of peripheral H1 receptors, which are involved in the production of allergic symptoms.

Contraindications (reasons you shouldn't take it): Hypersensitivity to drug or class.

Possible side effects and warnings: Can cause bronchospasm, hepatitis, hypersensitivity (excess reaction), sleepiness, fatigue, dry mouth, pharyngitis, dizziness, abdominal pain, and diarrhea. Should be used with caution in women with liver or kidney dysfunction, or who are taking a central nervous system depressant.

How it can affect pregnant women: There are no adequate reports or well-controlled studies of cetirizine in pregnant women. Because of longer clinical experience, treatment of allergic rhinitis during pregnancy should begin with the first-generation antihistamines such as chlorpheniramine and tripel-

ennamine. Pregnant women who cannot tolerate first-generation antihistamines may be offered a second-generation medication such as loratadine or cetirizine.

How it can affect a developing embryo or fetus: There are no adequate reports or well-controlled studies in human fetuses. It is unknown whether cetirizine crosses the human placenta. Neither first- (e.g., chlorpheniramine) nor second-generation (e.g., cetirizine) antihistamines appear to cause birth defects in humans, contrary to warnings in the product labels.

Breast-feeding: There are no adequate reports or well-controlled studies in nursing women. Cetirizine enters human breast milk.

Potential drug interactions: None significant.

What the FDA says about use in pregnancy: Category B (see Appendix).

What the available evidence suggests about breast-feeding safety: Unknown.

The bottom line for you:

- Cetirizine is a reasonable choice for the listed indications, although there are alternative agents with which there is more experience during pregnancy and while breast-feeding.

CHENODIOL

Brand names: Chebil, Chelobil, Chendal, Chenix, Chenocol, Chenodex, Chino, Solusto

Drug class: Gallstone solubilizer

Indications (what it is used for): Gallstones.

How it works: Reduces liver synthesis of cholesterol.

Contraindications (reasons you shouldn't take it): Hypersensitivity to drug or class, acute cholecystitis (sudden inflammation of the gallbladder), cholangitis (infection of the bile duct connecting the liver to the gallbladder), gallstone pancreatitis (gallstones lodge in the duct shared with the pancreas, causing inflammation), intrahepatic cholestasis (slow or blocked flow of bile from the liver), primary biliary cirrhosis (replacement of liver tissue by fibrous scar tissue), or sclerosing cholangitis (scarring and hardening of the bile ducts).

Possible side effects and warnings: Can cause diarrhea, heartburn, nausea, vomiting, constipation, and dizziness. Should be used with caution in women with gallstones.

How it can affect pregnant women: There are no adequate reports or well-controlled studies of chenodiol during pregnancy. Chenodiol should not be used by women who are or may become pregnant. Gallstones are relatively common during pregnancy, but chenodiol is not appropriate treatment because of the potential for liver damage and the increased rates of gallbladder removal in treated patients.

How it can affect a developing embryo or fetus: There are no adequate reports or well-controlled studies in human fetuses. It is unknown if chenodiol crosses the human placenta. When chenodiol was given to rhesus monkeys early in pregnancy at 4 times the human dose, the fetuses suffered serious liver and kidney damage. Liver damage was also found in newborn baboons whose mothers received 1 to 2 times the maximum recommended human dose throughout pregnancy. No birth defects were recorded. However, animal studies are not necessarily good indicators of how a drug will behave in humans.

Breast-feeding: There are no adequate reports or well-controlled studies in nursing women. It is unknown whether chenodiol enters human breast milk.

Potential drug interactions: None significant.

What the FDA says about use in pregnancy: Category X (see Appendix).

What the available evidence suggests about breast-feeding safety: Unknown.

The bottom line for you:
- Chenodiol should not be used by women who are or may become pregnant.
- There is not enough information to reach a con-

clusion on the safety of chenodiol while breast-feeding.

CHICKENPOX VACCINE, SEE VARICELLA VACCINE

CHLORAL HYDRATE

Brand names: Aquachloral, Chloralhydrat, Chloralix, Dormel, Kloral, Noctec

Drug classes: Hypnotic; Sedative

Indications (what it is used for): Inability to sleep, anxiety, alcohol withdrawal.

How it works: Unknown.

Contraindications (reasons you shouldn't take it): Hypersensitivity to drug or class, heart disease, liver failure.

Possible side effects and warnings: Can cause hypersensitivity to the drug, dependence, respiratory depression, low white blood cell count, hyperbilirubinemia (too much bilirubin in the blood), and swelling under the skin. Should be used with caution in women with depression, drug abuse, or porphyria (a rare group of blood disorders).

How it can affect pregnant women: There are no adequate reports or well-controlled studies in pregnant women. There is a case report of successful hemodialysis during pregnancy for the treatment of a chloral hydrate overdose.

How it can affect a developing embryo or fetus: There are no adequate reports or well-controlled studies in human fetuses. Chronic use during pregnancy may result in newborn withdrawal, suggesting that chloral hydrate does cross the placenta. Rodent studies have apparently not been performed for birth defects. Studies in horses suggest a higher frequency of miscarriage after taking chloral hydrate. However, animal studies are not necessarily good indicators of how a drug will behave in humans.

Breast-feeding: There are no adequate reports or

well-controlled studies in nursing women. Chloral hydrate is excreted into human breast milk and may cause sedation in a breast-feeding newborn.

Potential drug interactions: Alcohol and furosemide increase the potency of chloral hydrate.

What the FDA says about use in pregnancy: Category C (see Appendix).

What the available evidence suggests about breast-feeding safety: Not safe.

The bottom line for you:

- There are superior drugs for the treatment of severe insomnia during pregnancy and while breast-feeding (e.g., zolpidem, eszopiclone).

CHLORAMBUCIL

Brand names: Leukeran, Linfolysin

Drug class: Antineoplastic, alkylating agent

Indications (what it is used for): Palliative therapy for a variety of cancers, including leukemia, lymphoma, and trophoblastic disease (tumors in the uterus).

How it works: Slows or halts the growth of cancer cells by interfering with the reading and translation of DNA.

Contraindications (reasons you shouldn't take it): Hypersensitivity to drug or class, resistance to drug.

Possible side effects and warnings: Can cause bone marrow suppression, nausea, vomiting, confusion, anxiety, seizures, skin hypersensitivity, and pulmonary fibrosis (inflammation and/or scarring of the lungs). Should be used with caution in women with low white blood cell and/or platelet counts, seizures, fever, liver damage, or epilepsy.

How it can affect pregnant women: Chlorambucil is used to treat a number of life-threatening malignant diseases, including trophoblastic disease and ovarian cancer. There are no adequate reports or well-controlled studies in pregnant women. There are many case reports of successful outcomes in women treated throughout pregnancy with chlorambucil.

How it can affect a developing embryo or fetus: There are no adequate reports or well-controlled studies in animal and human fetuses. It is unknown whether chlorambucil crosses the human placenta. There is one report of a twin born to a mother who was treated with chlorambucil who failed to develop kidneys properly; the other twin was normal. The lack of reports suggests that chlorambucil is not a significant cause of birth defects in humans and that fetal tolerance to the drug late in pregnancy is quite high. Chlorambucil does cause brain and skeletal abnormalities in rodents. However, animal studies are not necessarily good indicators of how a drug will behave in humans.

Breast-feeding: There are no adequate reports or well-controlled studies in nursing women. It is unknown whether chlorambucil enters human breast milk.

Potential drug interactions: Interaction between the following medications and chlorambucil has the potential to impact the effect of one or more of the drugs. In some instances the interaction can be dangerous or life-threatening and must be avoided: alefacept, allopurinol, azathioprine, dasatinib, flucytosine, ganciclovir, hydroxyurea, ibritumomab, natalizumab, palifermin, primaquine, pyrimethamine, trimetrexate, zidovudine.

What the FDA says about use in pregnancy: Category D (see Appendix).

What the available evidence suggests about breast-feeding safety: Unknown.

The bottom line for you:

- Chlorambucil is a reasonable choice during pregnancy and while breast-feeding to treat a life-threatening maternal malignancy.

CHLORAMPHENICOL

Brand names: Amphicol, Archifen, Aromycetin, Biomycetin, Chlomin, Chlornitromycin, Chlorofair, Chloromycetin, Chloromyxin, Chloronitrin, Chloroptic, Cloramfeni, Cloramplast, Cloromicetin,

Danmycetin, Denicol, Econochlor, Heminevrin, I-Chlor, Infa-Chlor, Isopto, Kemicetina, Leukomycin, Mychel, Newlolly, Ocu-Chlor, Ophthochlor, Optomycin, Spectro-Chlor, Sunchlormycin, Troymycetin, Vernacetin

Drug classes: Antibiotic; Ophthalmic; Otic

Indications (what it is used for): Severe, potentially life-threatening bacterial infections.

How it works: Limits the growth of bacteria by inhibiting protein synthesis.

Contraindications (reasons you shouldn't take it): Hypersensitivity to drug or class, pregnancy, minor infections. Should not be used by children under 2 years of age.

Possible side effects and warnings: Can cause nausea, vomiting, fever, rash, hives, itching, nerve damage, optic neuritis (inflammation of the optic nerve), blurred vision, headache, mental confusion, gray baby syndrome (a serious reaction in the liver to chloramphenicol), bone marrow suppression, low platelet count, aplastic anemia, and infection of the colon. Should be used with caution in women with liver failure, G6PD deficiency, or bone marrow suppression.

How it can affect pregnant women: There are no adequate reports or well-controlled studies of chloramphenicol in pregnant women. It has been used for the treatment of scrub typhus, a disease largely found in Asia and Russia.

How it can affect a developing embryo or fetus: There are no adequate reports or well-controlled studies in human fetuses. It is unknown whether chloramphenicol crosses the human placenta. A similar drug, thiamphenicol, does cross the rodent placenta. Chloramphenicol has not been shown to cause birth defects in either humans or rodents. However, it does cause gray baby syndrome (see "Possible side effects and warnings" above). Chloramphenicol is used on occasion to treat infectious diseases in the newborn.

Breast-feeding: There are no adequate reports or well-controlled studies in nursing women. Chloramphenicol enters human breast milk at low to modest levels. Caution is advised in nursing mothers treated systemically due to the danger of gray baby syndrome.

Potential drug interactions: Interaction between the following medications and chloramphenicol has the potential to impact the effect of one or more of the drugs. In some instances the interaction can be dangerous or life-threatening and must be avoided: bosentan, entacapone, mycophenolate mofetil, oral anticoagulants, phenytoin, sulfonylureas, tacrolimus, variconazole.

What the FDA says about use in pregnancy: Category C (see Appendix).

What the available evidence suggests about breast-feeding safety: Possibly unsafe.

The bottom line for you:

- Chloramphenicol use during pregnancy and while breast-feeding is reserved for women with life-threatening infections.
- Gray baby syndrome is a rare but serious risk of the systemic use of chloramphenicol during pregnancy or while breast-feeding.

CHLORDIAZEPOXIDE

Brand names: Benzodiapin, Chlordiazachel, Chuichin, Kalbrium, Karmoplex, Libnum, Libritabs, Librium, Medilium, Poxi, Reposans, Restocalm, Ripolin, Vapine, Zenecin

Drug classes: Anxiolytic; Benzodiazepine

Indications (what it is used for): Anxiety, severe alcohol dependence.

How it works: Enhances the effects of the neurotransmitter GABA and acts through benzodiazepine receptors.

Contraindications (reasons you shouldn't take it): Hypersensitivity to drug or class.

Possible side effects and warnings: Can cause bone marrow suppression, drowsiness, loss of muscle coordination, confusion, rash, swelling, menstrual irregularities, decreased libido, and loss of motor coordination. Should be used with caution in women who drink alcohol or have liver or kidney failure.

How it can affect pregnant women: There are no adequate reports or well-controlled studies of chlordiazepoxide during pregnancy. The available information is not sufficient to determine whether the potential benefits of benzodiazepines to the mother outweigh the risks to the fetus. If chlordiazepoxide is prescribed during pregnancy, peak concentrations can be avoided by giving one dose every eight hours.

How it can affect a developing embryo or fetus: Benzodiazepines rapidly cross the placenta during early and late pregnancy, and first-trimester exposure to this group of drugs has been linked to an increased risk of problems in the fetus. Some infants exposed in the third trimester exhibit floppy infant syndrome (a laxness to muscles when lying down) or withdrawal symptoms such as mild sedation, low muscle tone, reluctance to suck, cessation of breathing, cyanosis (a blue tinge to the skin indicating poor oxygen supply), and impaired heat generation in response to cold stress. Long term, the overall experience is reassuring. In 550 children whose mothers took chlordiazepoxide during pregnancy and who were then followed for 4 years, there was no increase in either malformations or adverse neurobehavioral development and IQ.

Breast-feeding: There are no adequate reports or well-controlled studies of chlordiazepoxide in nursing women. The drug enters human breast milk in low concentrations, so it would likely take a high clinical dose in a breast-feeding mother to have an effect on a nursing newborn.

Potential drug interactions: None currently reported.

What the FDA says about use in pregnancy: Category D (see Appendix).

What the available evidence suggests about breast-feeding safety: Likely safe.

The bottom line for you:

- Chlordiazepoxide should be used during pregnancy and while breast-feeding only if the benefit to the woman justifies the potential risk to the fetus and newborn.

- If there is no alternative, chlordiazepoxide should be used alone at the lowest effective dose for the shortest possible duration to minimize the potential for adverse events.

CHLORHEXIDINE

Brand names: Peridex, PerioGard, Plakicide, Savacol

Drug class: Anti-infective, topical

Indications (what it is used for): Gingivitis (gum inflammation), cleansing of the birth canal prior to delivery to prevent infection.

How it works: Antibacterial.

Contraindications (reasons you shouldn't take it): Hypersensitivity to drug or class.

Possible side effects and warnings: Can cause staining of teeth, taste changes, and salivary gland inflammation.

How it can affect pregnant women: Although there are no adequate reports or well-controlled studies in pregnant women, chlorhexidine is considered safe for cleansing the birth canal just before delivery and may be as effective as ampicillin in preventing neonatal group B streptococcus transmission from a mother (who is positive for the bacteria) to her baby. Some studies suggest that its use during labor may also decrease HIV transmission.

How it can affect a developing embryo or fetus: There are no adequate reports or well-controlled studies in human fetuses. It is unknown whether chlorhexidine crosses the human placenta. Since it is applied topically, the mother's systemic absorption and, therefore, the risk to the fetus, will be low. Exposure to chlorhexidine during birth is not associated with any increase in newborn mortality.

Breast-feeding: It is not known whether chlorhexidine enters human breast milk. Although there are no adequate reports or well-controlled studies in nursing women, the quantity of drug absorbed systemically during a brief exposure from topical use is likely minimal.

Potential drug interactions: None significant currently identified.

What the FDA says about use in pregnancy: Category B (see Appendix).

What the available evidence suggests about breast-feeding safety: Likely safe.

The bottom line for you:

- Chlorhexidine is safe to use for cleansing of the birth canal before delivery; its use may decrease group B streptococcus and HIV transmission from mother to newborn.

CHLOROQUINE

Brand names: Aralen, Aralen Injection, Chlorofoz, Dichinalex, Lariago, Quinalan

Drug class: Antiprotozoal

Indications (what it is used for): Malaria prevention and treatment, amebiasis (a parasitic intestinal infection).

How it works: Unknown.

Contraindications (reasons you shouldn't take it): Hypersensitivity to drug or class, porphyria (a rare group of blood disorders), retinal field changes.

Possible side effects and warnings: Can cause bone marrow suppression, low platelet count, aplastic anemia, dermatitis, ototoxicity (damage to the ears), vomiting, dizziness, diarrhea, and itching. Should be used with caution in women with gastrointestinal disorders, neurologic disease, or liver failure.

How it can affect pregnant women: Chloroquine is closely related to hydroxychloroquine and has similar uses. Clinical experience suggests that chloroquine is safe during pregnancy and improves the outcome in women with parasitic infection. Chloroquine is also used to treat lupus erythemastosus (a chronic inflammatory disease in which the immune system attacks the body's own tissues and organs) in pregnant women who have failed to respond to first-line treatments. Recent studies suggest that it may have a role in the treatment of HIV and may be useful for HIV-infected breast-feeding women (generally breast-feeding is not recommended in HIV-positive women when infant formula is available, because breast milk can transmit HIV). There is a risk of pigmentary retinopathy (loss of vision caused by pigment deposits in the retina) from prolonged treatment with quinine-type drugs, but pregnancy does not increase that risk, and health professionals can monitor the woman to stop treatment if this becomes an issue.

How it can affect a developing embryo or fetus: Chloroquine crosses the placenta, achieving levels in the fetus that are about 80% of the mother's level. No increase in miscarriage or major birth defects has been reported in humans.

Breast-feeding: Chloroquine enters human breast milk but is generally considered compatible with breast-feeding.

Potential drug interactions: Interaction between the following medications and chloroquine has the potential to impact the effect of one or more of the drugs. In some instances the interaction can be dangerous or life-threatening and must be avoided: ampicillin, cimetidine, cyclosporine. Antacids and kaolin may reduce absorption of chloroquine, so chloroquine should not be taken within 4 hours of these treatments.

What the FDA says about use in pregnancy: No assigned category (see Appendix).

What the available evidence suggests about breast-feeding safety: Safe.

The bottom line for you:

- Chloroquine may be used safely during pregnancy and while breast-feeding when the benefit to the mother outweighs any potential risk to the fetus or newborn.

CHLOROTHIAZIDE

Brand names: Azide, Chlothin, Diurazide, Diuret, Diuril, Saluretil

Drug classes: Diuretic; Thiazide

Indications (what it is used for): High blood pressure, swelling of the legs and feet, heart failure.

How it works: Inhibits reabsorption of sodium and chloride.

Contraindications (reasons you shouldn't take it): Hypersensitivity to drug or class, electrolyte imbalances.

Possible side effects and warnings: Can cause kidney failure; low sodium, chloride, or magnesium levels; diabetes; hyperlipidemia (elevated lipid levels in the blood); and sensitivity to sunlight.

How it can affect pregnant women: Although chlorothiazide was popular with obstetricians for the treatment of swelling and weight gain in the 1970s, there are no adequate reports or well-controlled studies of it in pregnant women. Normal swelling during pregnancy does not need to be treated. Thiazide diuretics increase a pregnant woman's likelihood of developing gestational diabetes, and severe electrolyte imbalances have been reported. Hemorrhagic pancreatitis (sudden, acute inflammation of the pancreas) is another risk of thiazide exposure during pregnancy.

How it can affect a developing embryo or fetus: There are no adequate reports or well-controlled studies in human fetuses. Thiazide diuretics readily cross the placenta. There is no clear evidence chlorothiazide increases the risk of birth defects. However, older studies suggest that thiazide diuretics may reduce placental blood flow and increase the risk of growth restriction in fetuses. Further, exposed fetuses are at risk for dangerously low platelet count and blood glucose levels, and newborns have been observed with electrolyte abnormalities.

Breast-feeding: Thiazide diuretics enter human breast milk in low concentrations; they are generally considered compatible with breast-feeding.

Potential drug interactions: Interaction between the following medications and thiazide diuretics has the potential to impact the effect of one or more of the drugs. In some instances the interaction can be dangerous or life-threatening and must be avoided: ACTH, alcohol, barbiturates, cholestyramine, colestipol, corticosteroids, insulin, muscle relaxants, narcotics, nonsteroidal anti-inflammatory drugs (NSAIDs), oral hypoglycemic agents, turbocurarine.

What the FDA says about use in pregnancy: Category C (see Appendix).

What the available evidence suggests about breast-feeding safety: Safe.

The bottom line for you:

- Chlorothiazide, like other thiazide diuretics, may pose a risk to the fetus and generally should not be taken during pregnancy except for the treatment of chronic congestive heart failure.
- Chlorothiazide is generally considered safe for use while breast-feeding.

CHLORPHENIRAMINE

Brand names: Allerkyn, Chlor-Trimeton, Cloroetano, Clorten, Comin, Cophene-B, Corometon, Evenin, Histacort, Histex, Kelargine, Methyrit, Polaramine, Polaronil

Drug classes: Allergy; Antihistamine, first generation

Indications (what it is used for): Allergic rhinitis, anaphylaxis.

How it works: Blocks the histamine receptors (H1), the activation of which is responsible for many allergy and cold symptoms.

Contraindications (reasons you shouldn't take it): Hypersensitivity to drug or class.

Possible side effects and warnings: Can cause low blood pressure, dry mouth, nausea, vomiting, and constipation. Should be used with caution in women with a bowel obstruction or who are taking sedative medications.

How it can affect pregnant women: There are no adequate reports or well-controlled studies of chlorpheniramine in pregnant women. However, it is widely available in many over-the-counter preparations and has to date not been connected to adverse outcomes during pregnancy. In general, first-generation antihistamines such as chlorpheniramine are preferred to later generations because there is a longer clinical history of use during pregnancy.

How it can affect a developing embryo or fetus: There are no adequate reports or well-controlled studies in human fetuses, and it is unknown whether chlorpheniramine crosses the human placenta. However, large follow-up studies of women who have taken chlorpheniramine suggest that it does not cause birth defects. Because newborns (both preterm and full term) can have adverse reactions to antihistamines, chlorpheniramine should probably be avoided in the third trimester. Rodent studies are generally reassuring despite the use of doses higher than those used clinically. However, animal studies are not necessarily good indicators of how a drug will behave in humans.

Breast-feeding: There is no published data with chlorpheniramine in nursing women.

Potential drug interactions: Interaction between the following medications and chlorpheniramine has the potential to impact the effect of one or more of the drugs. In some instances the interaction can be dangerous or life-threatening and must be avoided: azelastine, dexmedetomidine, pramlintide.

What the FDA says about use in pregnancy: Category B (see Appendix).

What the available evidence suggests about breast-feeding safety: Probably unsafe; observe for sedation.

The bottom line for you:

- Chlorpheniramine may be used during pregnancy but is probably best avoided in the third trimester.
- Small, occasional doses of chlorpheniramine are not likely to cause any adverse effects in breast-fed infants. Larger doses or more prolonged use might cause adverse reactions in the infant or decrease the milk supply, particularly in combination with pseudoephedrine or before breast-feeding is well established. A single bedtime dose after the last feeding may be adequate for many and minimize any effects of the drug.
- Chlorpheniramine is often found in all-in-one medications that may include medications that

have been associated with birth defects, such as pseudophedrine and some nonsteroidal anti-inflammatory drugs (NSAIDs), so, if needed, it should be taken alone.

CHLORPROMAZINE

Brand names: Artomin, Fenactil, Klorazin, Megaphen, Promacid, Protran, Romazine, Sonazine, Thorazine

Drug classes: Antiemetic/antidizziness agent; Antipsychotic; Phenothiazine; Tranquilizer

Indications (what it is used for): Psychosis, nausea, vomiting, hiccups, tetanus, acute porphyria (a rare group of blood disorders).

How it works: Believed to block D2 dopamine receptors.

Contraindications (reasons you shouldn't take it): Hypersensitivity to drug or class, bone marrow depression, and Parkinson's disease (disorder of the brain that affects movement and coordination); should not be used by patients taking sedatives.

Possible side effects and warnings: Can cause seizures, low platelet count, bone marrow suppression, and neuroleptic malignant syndrome (life-threatening muscle rigidity, fever, vital sign instability, and cognitive changes such as delirium). Should be used with caution in women with liver failure, low blood pressure, or glaucoma.

How it can affect pregnant women: There are no adequate reports or well-controlled studies in pregnant women. Based on a long clinical experience, chlorpromazine seems safe and is effective when used during pregnancy for the indications listed above. However there are other, better-studied medications for the same indications.

How it can affect a developing embryo or fetus: There are no adequate reports or well-controlled studies in human fetuses. Chlorpromazine rapidly crosses the placenta, and a temporary extrapyramidal syndrome (spasticity of fine-motor movements) has been reported in newborns of women given chlorpromazine during labor. There is no evidence that chlorpromazine causes birth defects. Rodent studies have not found any serious birth effects, although learning and behavioral abnormalities were reported in some studies. However, animal studies are not necessarily good indicators of how a drug will behave in humans.

Breast-feeding: There are no adequate reports or well-controlled studies in nursing women. Although chlorpromazine is excreted into human breast milk, occasional doses are probably compatible with breast-feeding.

Potential drug interactions: Interaction between the following medications and chlorpromazine has the potential to impact the effect of one or more of the drugs. In some instances the interaction can be dangerous or life-threatening and must be avoided: abarelix, amiodarone, apomorphine, azithromycin, cinacalcet, ciprofloxacin, cisapride, clarithromycin, dofetilide, dolasetron, duloxetine, erythromycin, fluconazole, ibutilide, imatinib, lithium, lopinavir, methadone, palonosetron, pimozide, pindolol, posaconazole, propanalol, ritonavir, sotalol, tacrolimus, tamoxifen, thiazide diuretics, class 1A antiarrythmics.

What the FDA says about use in pregnancy: Category C (see Appendix).

What the available evidence suggests about breast-feeding safety: Probably safe.

The bottom line for you:

- Chlorpromazine may be used during pregnancy and while breast-feeding when better-studied medications are ineffective or unavailable.

CHLORPROPAMIDE

Brand names: Arodoc, Chlordiabet, Chlorprosil, Diabenil, Diabinese, Diamide, Diatanpin, Dibetes, Gliconorm, Glycermin, Glymese, Insilange, Meldian, Mellitos, Milligon, Norgluc, Normoglic, Orodiabin, Promide, Tanpinin

Drug classes: Antidiabetic agent; Sulfonylurea

Indications (what it is used for): Type II diabetes, diabetes insipidus (lack of antidiuretic hormone).

How it works: Stimulates insulin release from the pancreas.

Contraindications (reasons you shouldn't take it): Hypersensitivity to drug or class, diabetic ketoacidosis (lack of insulin prevents body using sugar as a fuel), sulfonamides allergy.

Possible side effects and warnings: Can cause low blood glucose, bone marrow suppression, anemia, low platelet count, cholestatic jaundice, liver dysfunction, blurred vision, nausea, vomiting, weight gain, itching, and photosensitivity. Should be used with caution in women with liver or kidney dysfunction.

How it can affect pregnant women: There are no adequate reports or well-controlled studies of chlorpropamide in pregnant women. Although some oral hypoglycemic drugs are safe and provide excellent control of blood glucose from the first trimester on, chlorpropamide crosses the placenta and should be avoided during pregnancy.

How it can affect a developing embryo or fetus: Although some oral hypoglycemic agents do not efficiently cross the placenta and are safe to use during pregnancy, chlorpropamide crosses the placenta and can cause low blood glucose levels in the fetus or newborn. It has also been shown to reduce birth weight and increase mortality in babies born to diabetic women. There are alternative medications that cross the placenta less readily and are better choices for maternal therapy.

Breast-feeding: Although there are no adequate studies in nursing mothers, chlorpropamide enters the breast milk, and low blood glucose has been reported in breast-feeding babies.

Potential drug interactions: Interaction between the following medications and chlorpropamide has the potential to impact the effect of one or more of the drugs. In some instances the interaction can be dangerous or life-threatening and must be avoided: beta-adrenergic blockers, barbiturates, calcium channel blockers, chloramphenicol, corticosteroids, coumarins, diuretics, estrogens, isoniazid, miconazole, monoamine oxidase inhibitors (MAOIs), nicotinic acid, nonsteroidal anti-inflammatory drugs (NSAIDs), oral contraceptives, phenytoin, probenecid, salicylates, sulfonamides, phenothiazines, thyroid products.

What the FDA says about use in pregnancy: Category C (see Appendix).

What the available evidence suggests about breast-feeding safety: Not safe.

The bottom line for you:

- There are alternative medications that cross the placenta less readily and are better choices for treating type II diabetes during pregnancy and while breast-feeding.

CHLORZOXAZONE

Brand names: Biomioran, Eze D.S., Myoforte, Paraflex, Parafon Forte DSC, Relaxazone, Relax-DS, Remular, Strifon Forte DSC

Drug class: Muscle relaxant

Indications (what it is used for): Muscle spasms.

How it works: Depresses activity of the central nervous system.

Contraindications (reasons you shouldn't take it): Hypersensitivity to drug or class, alcohol consumption.

Possible side effects and warnings: Can cause nausea, vomiting, diarrhea, loss of appetite, headache, severe weakness, unusual increase in sweating, fainting, breathing difficulties, irritability, convulsions, feeling of paralysis, and loss of consciousness. Should be used with caution in women with liver or kidney failure.

How it can affect pregnant women: There is no published data with chlorzoxazone during pregnancy. However, chlorzoxazone is an old drug that has been used during pregnancy without apparent harm.

How it can affect a developing embryo or fetus: There are no adequate reports or well-controlled studies in human fetuses. It is unknown whether chlorzoxazone crosses the human placenta. No

studies looking for birth defects have been performed on rodents.

Breast-feeding: There is no published data in nursing women. It is unknown whether chlorzoxazone enters human breast milk.

Potential drug interactions: No clinically significant interactions currently identified.

What the FDA says about use in pregnancy: Category C (see Appendix).

What the available evidence suggests about breast-feeding safety: Unknown.

The bottom line for you:

- Chlorzoxazone has been used during pregnancy for decades and has not been associated with adverse outcomes.
- However, there are other agents that have been better studied during pregnancy, which may provide effective symptom relief.
- There is not enough information to reach a conclusion on the safety of chlorzoxazone while breast-feeding. Its side effects in adults are potentially worrisome, and breast-fed newborns should be observed closely.

CHOLERA VACCINE

Brand names: None

Drug class: Vaccine

Indications (what it is used for): Prevention of cholera when traveling to cholera-endemic areas.

How it works: Stimulates immune system to produce disease-fighting antibodies.

Contraindications (reasons you shouldn't take it): Hypersensitivity to drug or class; any acute illness, such as a cold or fever.

Possible side effects and warnings: Can cause skin redness; hardness, pain, or tenderness at the site of injection; malaise, headache, and mild to moderate temperature elevations that may persist for 1 or 2 days. Intravenous injection of the vaccine should be avoided.

How it can affect pregnant women: Cholera vaccine is a sterile suspension of killed *V. cholerae* (the bacterium that causes cholera). Only oral vaccines are available. There are no adequate reports or well-controlled studies of cholera vaccine in pregnant women.

How it can affect a developing embryo or fetus: There are no adequate reports or well-controlled studies in human fetuses. It is likely that the antibodies produced by pregnant women in response to the vaccine cross the human placenta and provide some protection to the newborn. There is no evidence of fetal harm. Rodent studies have not been performed.

Breast-feeding: There are no adequate reports or well-controlled studies in nursing women. Cholera vaccine–induced antibodies enter human breast milk.

Potential drug interactions: Cholera and yellow fever vaccines given within 3 weeks of each other decreases the antibody responses to both.

What the FDA says about use in pregnancy: Category C (see Appendix).

What the available evidence suggests about breast-feeding safety: Safe.

The bottom line for you:

- Although the inactivated vaccine is not expected to have any adverse effects, its safety in pregnancy has not been directly studied. Therefore, the benefits of vaccine must be carefully weighed against any potential adverse effects before it is given to a pregnant woman.
- It is reasonable to assume that this vaccine can be used safely in nursing mothers.

CHOLESTYRAMINE

Brand names: Choles, Cholybar, Cuemid, Questran, Questran Light

Drug class: Antihyperlipidemic; Bile acid sequestrant

Indications (what it is used for): Hypercholesterolemia (high cholesterol and lipids).

How it works: Binds intestinal bile acids in a nonabsorbable complex.

Contraindications (reasons you shouldn't take it): Hypersensitivity to drug or class, bile duct obstruction.

Possible side effects and warnings: Can cause severe constipation, flatulence, gastric pain, loss of appetite, heartburn, headache, rash, fatigue, and weight loss. Should be used with caution in women experiencing constipation.

How it can affect pregnant women: Cholestyramine binds bile acids and other substances such as fat-soluble vitamins. It is sometimes used for the treatment of cholestasis of pregnancy (a severe, itchy rash due to the backup of bile in the liver, most commonly occurring in the third trimester), but its effectiveness has long been questioned. In the only randomized trial conducted, it was not as effective as ursodeoxycholic acid.

How it can affect a developing embryo or fetus: There are no adequate reports or well-controlled studies in human fetuses. Cholestyramine is not absorbed from the mother's bowels but may interfere with the woman's uptake of fat-soluble vitamins and result in a deficiency in the fetus. Rodent studies found no evidence that cholestyramine increases the risk of infertility, miscarriage, birth defects, or low birth weight. However, animal studies are not necessarily good indicators of how a drug will behave in humans.

Breast-feeding: There is no published data with cholestyramine in nursing women. However, it is unlikely to impact breast-feeding as it is not absorbed from the gut.

Potential drug interactions: Interaction between the following medications and cholestyramine has the potential to impact the effect of one or more of the drugs. In some instances the interaction can be dangerous or life-threatening and must be avoided: phenylbutazone, warfarin, thiazide diuretics, propranolol, tetracycline, penicillin G, phenobarbital, thyroid and thyroxin preparations, estrogens and progestins, digitalis. Cholestyramine may interfere with normal fat digestion and absorption and thus prevent absorption of fat-soluble vitamins such as A, D, E, and K.

What the FDA says about use in pregnancy: Category C (see Appendix).

What the available evidence suggests about breast-feeding safety: Safe.

The bottom line for you:

- There are superior medications for the treatment of cholestasis during pregnancy.

CIMETIDINE

Brand names: Beamat, Cimebec, Cimetegal, Cimetidine in Sodium Chloride, Cimewet, Ciwidine, Edalene, Gerucim, Paoweian, Procimeti, Proctospre, Tagagel, Tagamed, Tagamet, Tagamin, Tratol, Ulcinfan, Ulpax, Valmagen, Wergen

Drug classes: Antihistamine, H2; Anti-ulcer agent

Indications (what it is used for): Peptic ulcer disease, gastroesophageal reflux disease (GERD), Zollinger-Ellison syndrome (tumors in the pancreas).

How it works: Blocks histamine H2 receptors, whose activation produces the symptoms.

Contraindications (reasons you shouldn't take it): Hypersensitivity to drug or class.

Possible side effects and warnings: Can cause low white blood cell and/or low platelet count, bone marrow suppression, headache, diarrhea, vomiting, rash, and liver failure.

How it can affect pregnant women: Evidence documenting the safety of acid-suppressing drugs during pregnancy is very limited. GERD and/or heartburn occurs in 45–85% of pregnant women in part because of high progesterone and estrogen levels. The treatment for GERD consists of reducing gastric acidity starting with lifestyle and dietary changes. If these fail, antacids or sucralfate are first-line medical therapies, followed by histamine receptor blockers.

How it can affect a developing embryo or fetus: There are no adequate reports or well-controlled studies of cimetidine in human fetuses. Studies of drugs prescribed for large groups of women generally conclude that there is no increased risk of birth defects or preterm birth (before 37 weeks). Rodent studies found a link between cimetidine and problems such as undescended testicles and incomplete genital development in males. However, animal studies are not necessarily good indicators of how a drug will behave in humans.

Breast-feeding: There are no adequate reports or well-controlled studies in nursing women. Cimetidine enters human breast milk, but the levels should be safe for a breast-feeding baby. However, the amount of medication excreted into breast milk is lower for similar agents such as famotidine and nizatidine.

Potential drug interactions: Interaction between the following medications and cimetidine has the potential to impact the effect of one or more of the drugs. In some instances the interaction can be dangerous or life-threatening and must be avoided: warfarin, ketoconazole, phenytoin, propranolol, nifedipine, chlordiazepoxide, diazepam, certain tricyclic antidepressants, lidocaine, theophylline, metronidazole.

What the FDA says about use in pregnancy: Category B (see Appendix).

What the available evidence suggests about breast-feeding safety: Safe.

The bottom line for you:

- After lifestyle modifications, antacids and antacid/alginic acid combinations or sucralfate are the first choice for treating heartburn and GERD during pregnancy.
- If symptoms are not adequately relieved or complications develop, treatment with cimetidine or ranitidine may be considered.
- Cimetidine is safe for use while breast-feeding.

CIPROFLOXACIN

Brand names: Ciloxan, Cipro, Cyprobay

Drug classes: Antibiotic; Fluoroquinolone

Indications (what it is used for): Anthrax, cystitis (bladder inflammation), enteric fever (bacterial infection spread through contaminated food, drink, or water; also called typhoid fever), drug-resistant tuberculosis, Q fever (infection with the bacterium *Coxiella burnetii,* transmitted by farm animals).

How it works: Kills bacteria by interfering with DNA replication.

Contraindications (reasons you shouldn't take it): Hypersensitivity to drug or class.

Possible side effects and warnings: Can cause seizures, infection of the colon, psychosis, hypersensitivity (excess reaction), nausea, vomiting, dizziness, rash, sensitivity to light, itching, agitation, confusion, tendonitis, joint pain, and liver damage. Should be used with caution in women with kidney or liver failure, dehydration, diabetes, or seizure disorder, or sun exposure.

How it can affect pregnant women: There are no adequate reports or well-controlled studies in pregnant women. Fluoroquinolone antibiotics are a very potent group. Fluoroquinolone therapy is widely used as a treatment for gonorrhea in pregnant (and nonpregnant) women because it is relatively inexpensive and requires only one dose administered orally. However, gonorrhea is becoming increasingly resistant to ciprofloxacin, and it is no longer recommended for this indication. Ciprofloxacin has the best safety profile of second-line drugs for drug-resistant tuberculosis. It is the drug of choice for prevention among pregnant women who have been exposed to *Bacillus anthracis* (anthrax) but show no symptoms. Ciprofloxacin has also been used to treat Q fever during pregnancy.

How it can affect a developing embryo or fetus: There are no adequate reports or well-controlled studies in human fetuses. Small amounts of ciprofloxacin cross the human placenta, and short courses of ciprofloxacin appear to have caused no fetal problems in clinical experience. As a class, the new quinolones do not appear to be associated with an increased risk of malformation or musculoskeletal problems in humans. When long-term treatment is called for, follow-up and newborn MRI of the joints may be warranted to assure there has been no cartilage or bone damage.

Breast-feeding: There are no adequate reports or well-controlled studies in breast-feeding mothers. Ciprofloxacin enters human breast milk and is concentrated in the milk at levels higher than those found in the mother's blood. Although the American Academy of Pediatrics considers it safe for breast-feeding, there is a report of a breast-fed newborn of a mother taking ciprofloxacin who developed *C. difficile* pseudomembranous colitis (diarrhea caused by a bacterial infection related to the use of antibiotics). It is probably best to avoid ciprofloxacin during breast-feeding if there are reasonable alternatives.

Potential drug interactions: Interaction between the following medications and ciprofloxacin has the potential to impact the effect of one or more of the drugs. In some instances the interaction can be dangerous or life-threatening and must be avoided: glyburide, theophylline, magnesium- and/or aluminum-containing antacids, sucralfate, didanosine chewable/buffered tablets or pediatric powder, methotrexate, metoclopramide, nonsteroidal anti-inflammatory drugs (NSAIDs), phenytoin, probenicid, warfarin, and products containing calcium, iron, or zinc.

What the FDA says about use in pregnancy: Category C (see Appendix).

What the available evidence suggests about breast-feeding safety: Possibly unsafe.

The bottom line for you:

- Ciprofloxacin appears safe and effective for the treatment of certain bacterial infections during pregnancy. However, there are usually alternative agents with which there is more experience during pregnancy and breast-feeding.
- Fluroquinolones are no longer recommended for the treatment of gonorrhea.
- Although the risk is small, ciprofloxacin probably should be avoided while breast-feeding.

CISAPRIDE

Brand names: Propulsid, Viprasen
Drug class: Gastrointestinal, stimulant
Indications (what it is used for): GERD (gastroesophageal reflux disease).
How it works: Stimulates stomach motility (movement).
Contraindications (reasons you shouldn't take it): Hypersensitivity to drug or class; irregular, fast, or slow heart rate, including sinus node dysfunction and bradycardia; AV block (impaired conduction between atria and ventricles of the heart); congestive heart failure, ventricular arrhythmia.
Possible side effects and warnings: Can cause severe irregular heart rate, bone marrow failure, low platelet count, anemia, liver failure, headache, nausea, vomiting, fatigue, and depression. Should be used with caution in women with electrolyte imbalances or an abnormal ECG.
How it can affect pregnant women: Gastroesophageal reflux disease and/or heartburn occurs in 45–85% of pregnant women in part because of high progesterone and estrogen levels. The treatment for GERD consists of reducing gastric acidity starting with lifestyle and dietary changes. If these fail, antacids or sucralfate are first-line medical therapies, followed by histamine receptor blockers. There are no adequate reports or well-controlled studies of cisapride in pregnant women. It is reserved for patients with severe symptoms.
How it can affect a developing embryo or fetus: There are no adequate reports or well-controlled studies in human fetuses. In population studies (studies of a large group of people taken from the larger population), there are no differences in maternal history, birth weight, gestational age at delivery, and rates of live births, miscarriage, fetal distress, or major or minor malformations among the group of pregnant women exposed to cisapride compared with women who did not take the drug. It is unknown whether cisapride crosses the human placenta, but it has been shown to cross other animal placentas. Rodent studies suggest that fetal exposure to cisapride may be associated with decreased fertility in adulthood. However, animal studies are not necessarily good indicators of how a drug will behave in humans.
Breast-feeding: Although cisapride enters human breast milk, the amount is small and unlikely to have any clinical effect.
Potential drug interactions: Interaction between the following medications or substances and cisapride has the potential to impact the effect of one or more of the drugs. In some instances the interaction can be dangerous or life-threatening and must be avoided: any medications that inhibit the enzyme CYP3A4; anticholinergic compounds, such as belladonna and dicyclomine; clarithromycin and erythromycin; furosemide; grapefruit and grapefruit juice; troleandomycin; nefazodone; indinavir and ritonavir; fluconazole, itraconazole, and oral ketoconazole; thiazides; certain antiarrhythmics; maptrotiline; certain antipsychotic medications, such as sertindole; bepridil, sparfloxacin.
What the FDA says about use in pregnancy: Category C (see Appendix).
What the available evidence suggests about breast-feeding safety: Likely safe.
The bottom line for you:
- Because of the relatively small clinical experience, cisapride should be reserved for pregnant or breast-feeding women with severe symptoms unresponsive to other therapies.

CISATRACURIUM

Brand name: Tracrium
Drug classes: Anesthesia, adjunct; Musculoskeletal agent; Neuromuscular blocker, nondepolarizing
Indications (what it is used for): Surgical paralysis.
How it works: Blocks nerve conduction to the muscle.
Contraindications (reasons you shouldn't take it): Hypersensitivity to drug or class.

Possible side effects and warnings: Can cause cardiovascular collapse, slow heart rate, low blood pressure, rash, flushing, and hives, all due to histamine release and high blood pressure. Should be used with caution in women with liver or kidney dysfunction, low blood pressure, cardiovascular disease, or electrolyte abnormalities.

How it can affect pregnant women: There are no adequate reports or well-controlled studies of cisatracurium in pregnant women.

How it can affect a developing embryo or fetus: There are no adequate reports or well-controlled studies of cisatracurium in human fetuses. Atracurium (a related medication) is used when necessary to facilitate surgical procedures on fetuses. Although small amounts cross the human placenta, its use during cesarean section is not associated with negative effects on the newborn. In theory, cisatracurium could be toxic to a fetus if it was needed to facilitate long-term paralysis of a critically ill pregnant woman such as a trauma victim.

Breast-feeding: There are no adequate reports or well-controlled studies in nursing women. It is unknown whether cisatracurium enters human breast milk. Considering that it is typically used only during surgery, it is unlikely to affect a breast-feeding newborn.

Potential drug interactions: Isoflurane or enflurane administered with nitrous oxide/oxygen may prolong the duration of action of cisatracurium, as well as aminoglycosides, tetracyclines, bacitracin, polymyxins, lincomycin, clindamycin, and colistin, magnesium salts, lithium, local anesthetics, procainamide, quinidine.

What the FDA says about use in pregnancy: Category B (see Appendix).

What the available evidence suggests about breast-feeding safety: Likely safe.

The bottom line for you:

- Cisatracurium is considered safe for limited use during pregnancy and while breast-feeding.

CISPLATIN

Brand names: Asiplatin, Platinol

Drug class: Antineoplastic

Indications (what it is used for): Chemotherapy for cancers, including ovary, bladder, lung, esophageal, cervical, breast, gastric, lymphoma, myeloma, and sarcoma.

How it works: Prevents the processing of DNA for cell growth and duplication.

Contraindications (reasons you shouldn't take it): Hypersensitivity to drug or class, bone marrow suppression, pregnancy and breast-feeding.

Possible side effects and warnings: Can cause kidney, liver, ear, or eye toxicities; nerve damage; seizures; anemia; low potassium or glucose; blurred vision; tingling; muscle weakness and severe loss of muscle control; rash; hives; and loss of taste. Should be used with caution in women with kidney or liver failure, neuropathy (nerve damage), hearing impairment, or bone marrow suppression.

How it can affect pregnant women: There are no adequate reports or well-controlled studies in pregnant women. Women being treated with cisplatin are advised to avoid pregnancy during treatment due to concerns about fetal harm (see "How it can affect a developing embryo or fetus," below). Cisplatin has been used during pregnancy for women diagnosed with life-threatening ovarian or other malignancies. The published literature consists mostly of case reports and small collections of patients, but good outcomes are common among them. The patients must be monitored closely because pregnant women and their offspring can have altered protein binding and, as a result, are at increased risk of toxicity from the medication.

How it can affect a developing embryo or fetus: There are no adequate reports or well-controlled studies in human fetuses. Cisplatin crosses the human placenta. Malformations in children of women treated with cisplatin are rare but have been reported after first-trimester exposure. Cisplatin caused birth defects and damage to mouse embryos.

However, animal studies are not necessarily good indicators of how a drug will behave in humans.

Breast-feeding: Cisplatin enters human breast milk but at concentrations at or below a detectable level; it is generally considered compatible with breast-feeding.

Potential drug interactions: Cisplatin can increase blood levels of anticonvulsant medications.

What the FDA says about use in pregnancy: Category D (see Appendix).

What the available evidence suggests about breast-feeding safety: Safe.

The bottom line for you:

- Women being treated with cisplatin should avoid pregnancy.
- However, given cisplatin's evidence of relative safety during pregnancy, treatment should not be delayed when cure is possible if a woman becomes pregnant during treatment or is diagnosed with a life-threatening malignancy during pregnancy.
- Cisplatin is generally considered safe for use while breast-feeding.

CITALOPRAM

Brand name: Celexa

Drug classes: Antidepressant; SSRI

Indications (what it is used for): Depression.

How it works: Serotonin reuptake inhibition.

Contraindications (reasons you shouldn't take it): Hypersensitivity to drug or class, use of monamine oxidase inhibitors (MAOIs).

Possible side effects and warnings: Can cause kidney, eye, or ear toxicities; neuropathy; seizures; anemia; low potassium or glucose levels. Citalopram should be used with caution in women who have been seriously contemplating or discussing suicide, or those with seizure disorder, mania, or liver or kidney dysfunction. The drug should not be stopped abruptly. Women should talk to their healthcare provider about how to taper off.

How it can affect pregnant women: Depression is common during and after pregnancy but often goes unrecognized and untreated. Depression can be made worse by pregnancy or delivery, and suicide is a not uncommon cause of maternal death. Pregnancy is not a reason to discontinue antidepressant drugs if the medication is effective and needed. A woman being treated for depression who becomes pregnant should not discontinue medication abruptly on her own but rather discuss her treatment and condition with her medical provider. A woman being treated for depression who discovers she has become pregnant should not discontinue medication on her own, but rather discuss her treatment and condition with her medical provider.

How it can affect a developing embryo or fetus: There are no adequate reports or well-controlled studies in human fetuses. Citalopram crosses the human placenta, achieving a higher blood level in the fetus than sertraline or paroxetine (similar antidepressants). Some studies have shown a small increase in the risk of heart defects in embryos exposed to SSRIs in the first trimester but current study suggests it is not dose dependent (the risk does not increase or decrease as the dose does, suggesting other factors may play a role in creating the defect). The safest approach for all SSRIs is probably to avoid them in the first trimester. Women with moderate to severe depression responsive to their medication, however, should continue treatment during pregnancy as the benefit outweighs the possible risks to mother and child.

SSRI use late in pregnancy may double the risk of persistent pulmonary hypertension (high blood pressure affecting the lungs) during the newborn period (which, at 2 in 1000 births, is low to begin with). SSRI exposure during the third trimester and until delivery may also lead to a withdrawal syndrome during the first few days of life, requiring extra care. Symptoms in the newborn may include problems breathing, jitteriness, increased muscle tone, irritability, altered sleep patterns, tremors, and poor eating. In most cases, these symptoms are mild and disappear within two weeks with no treatment. Symptoms can occur in up to 30% of exposed newborns, and although they occur at all doses, may occur more often with higher doses. The risk does not outweigh the benefit of needed therapy.

Breast-feeding: Citalopram enters human breast milk, but the concentration in the breast-fed newborn is very low and likely poses no threat. A few cases of side effects such as drowsiness or fussiness have been reported, but no adverse effects on development have been found in infants followed for up to a year. There is no need to discontinue breast-feeding if citalopram is required. Drugs with lower excretion into breast milk may be preferred, especially while nursing a preterm infant. Related to citalopram, escitalopram offers lower infant exposure and adverse reactions are less likely.

Potential drug interactions: Interaction between the following medications and citalopram has the potential to impact the effect of one or more of the drugs. In some instances the interaction can be dangerous or life-threatening and must be avoided: aspirin, metoprolol, nonsteroidal anti-inflammatory drugs (NSAIDs), sumatriptan.

What the FDA says about use in pregnancy: Category C (see Appendix).

What the available evidence suggests about breast-feeding safety: Likely safe.

The bottom line for you:

- Although there are alternative agents with which there is more experience during pregnancy and while breast-feeding, citalopram may be used when necessary to treat clinically significant depression.
- Citalopram is probably safe for use while breast-feeding. In some instances, escitalopram may be preferred.

CLARITHROMYCIN

Brand names: Biaxin, Biaxin XL, Klacid XL
Drug classes: Antibiotic; Macrolide
Indications (what it is used for): Bacterial infections.
How it works: Kills bacteria by blocking their ability to synthesize proteins.
Contraindications (reasons you shouldn't take it): Hypersensitivity to drug or class.
Possible side effects and warnings: Can cause life-threatening allergic reaction, Stevens-Johnson syndrome (a rare but serious skin reaction to medication), irregular heart rate, nausea, abdominal pain, diarrhea, infection of the colon, heartburn, headache, and rash. Should be used with caution in women with liver dysfunction or kidney failure.
How it can affect pregnant women: There are no adequate reports or well-controlled studies of clarithromycin in pregnant women. It is used to treat lower respiratory tract infections, genitourinary tract infections, skin infections, neutropenia (abnormally low level of one type of white blood cell), AIDS-related infections, acute maxillary sinusitis (inflammation of the sinuses), and active duodenal ulcer. Clarithromycin has been used successfully during pregnancy for the treatment of Q fever (infection with the bacterium *Coxiella burnetii,* transmitted by farm animals), Mediterranean spotted fever (bacterial infection caused by *Rickettsia*), and *Mycobacterium avium* (serious bacterial infection affecting the lymph nodes, central nervous system, and bone marrow).
How it can affect a developing embryo or fetus: There are no adequate reports or well-controlled studies in human fetuses. Clarithromycin crosses the human placenta to a greater degree than similar antibiotics, making it a good choice for the treatment of genital *Mycoplasma* and *Ureaplasma* infections as these bacteria are thought by some to play a role in preterm birth (before 37 weeks) by infecting the membranes and fetus. Postmarketing studies (studies done by a drug's manufacturer after the drug is

on the market) reveal no increased risk of birth defects or restricted fetal growth. Animal studies are similarly reassuring when using clinical dosing. However, animal studies are not necessarily good indicators of how drugs will behave in humans.

Breast-feeding: There are no adequate reports or well-controlled studies in nursing women. Clarithromycin enters human breast milk, reaching levels in the breast-fed newborn as high as 75% of the mother's concentration.

Potential drug interactions: Interaction between the following medications and clarithromycin has the potential to impact the effect of one or more of the drugs. In some instances the interaction can be dangerous or life-threatening and must be avoided: theophylline, carbamazepine, dihydroergotamine, ergotamine, lovastatin, oral anticoagulants, ritonavir, simvastatin, triazolam, zidovudine, astemizole, cisapride, pimozide, terfenadine.

What the FDA says about use in pregnancy: Category C (see Appendix).

What the available evidence suggests about breast-feeding safety: Generally considered safe; observe for diarrhea.

The bottom line for you:

- Clarithromycin may be used during pregnancy with relative safety.
- High placental transfer during the first trimester makes clarithromycin an attractive treatment for *Mycoplasma* and *Ureaplasma* infections.
- Clarithromycin is generally considered safe for use while breast-feeding.

CLAVULANATE POTASSIUM

Brand names: Augmentin, Augmentin ES-600, Augmentin XR

Drug class: Anti-infective

Indications (what it is used for): Combined with penicillins, amoxicillin, and ticarcillin to broaden their antibacterial spectrum to cover certain gram-negative bacteria.

How it works: Inactivates the enzyme beta-lactamase, which enables the bacteria to become resistant to the plain antibiotic.

Contraindications (reasons you shouldn't take it): Hypersensitivity to drug or class.

Possible side effects and warnings: Can cause nausea, vomiting, diarrhea, abdominal pain, colitis, loss of appetite, and infection of the colon. At high doses, it can cause seizures, platelet dysfunction, hemolytic anemia, encephalitis (inflammation of the brain), and nephritis (inflammation in the kidneys). For warnings, see penicillins, amoxicillin, and ticarcillin.

How it can affect pregnant women: See penicillins, amoxicillin, and ticarcillin.

How it can affect a developing embryo or fetus: There are no well-controlled studies in human fetuses. Clavulanate crosses the human placenta. Rodent studies have found no evidence that clavulanate potassium causes birth defects or restricted fetal growth when it is given in conjunction with penicillin or amoxicillin. (See penicillins, amoxicillin, and ticarcillin.)

Breast-feeding: Although there are no reports specifically addressing the passage of clavulanate into the breast milk, it is generally considered compatible with breast-feeding.

Potential drug interactions: May reduce the efficacy of oral contraceptives.

What the FDA says about use in pregnancy: Category B (see Appendix).

What the available evidence suggests about breast-feeding safety: Safe.

The bottom line for you:

- Clavulanate is combined with penicillin, amoxicillin, and ticarcillin to broaden their antibacterial spectrum to include certain resistant gram-negative bacteria.
- It is considered safe for use during pregnancy and while breast-feeding.

CLEMASTINE

Brand names: Allerhist-1, Contac 12-Hour Allergy, Tavist, Tavist-1

Drug class: Antihistamine, H1

Indications (what it is used for): Stuffy nose, hives.

How it works: Antagonizes central and peripheral H1 receptors responsible for the symptoms of the cold or allergy.

Contraindications (reasons you shouldn't take it): Hypersensitivity to drug or class, asthma, alcohol intolerance.

Possible side effects and warnings: Can cause seizures, life-threatening allergic reaction, sedation, drowsiness, dizziness, bone marrow suppression, dry mouth, extreme sleepiness, confusion, weakness, ringing in the ears, blurred vision, enlarged pupils, flushing, fever, shaking, inability to sleep, hallucinations, and possibly seizures. Should be used with caution in women with glaucoma.

How it can affect pregnant women: There are no adequate reports or well-controlled studies of clemastine during pregnancy.

How it can affect a developing embryo or fetus: There are no adequate reports or well-controlled studies in human fetuses. It is unknown whether clemastine crosses the human placenta. Overdoses of some antihistamines can produce symptoms of toxicity in newborns, including excitement, hyperreflexia (overresponsive reflexes), tremors, ataxia (lack of muscle coordination), fever, seizures, fixed dilated pupils, dry mouth, and facial flushing.

Breast-feeding: Clemastine enters breast milk. There is one case of a 10-week-old breast-feeding baby whose mother was taking clemastine who then developed drowsiness, irritability, refusal to feed, and neck stiffness.

Potential drug interactions: Interaction between the following medications and clemastine has the potential to impact the effect of one or more of the drugs. In some instances the interaction can be dangerous or life-threatening and must be avoided: monoamine oxidase inhibitors (MAOIs); central nervous system depressants such as barbiturates, tranquilizers, alcohol.

What the FDA says about use in pregnancy: Category B (see Appendix).

What the available evidence suggests about breast-feeding safety: Possibly unsafe.

The bottom line for you:

- There are alternative antihistamines with which there is more experience during pregnancy and while breast-feeding.

CLINDAMYCIN

Brand names: Cleocin, Cleocin Phosphate, Cleocin T, Clinda-Derm, Euroclin, Turimycin

Drug classes: Antibiotic; Dermatologic Lincosamide

Indications (what it is used for): Bacterial infections.

How it works: Kills bacteria by inhibiting their ability to make proteins.

Contraindications (reasons you shouldn't take it): Hypersensitivity to drug or class, colitis.

Possible side effects and warnings: Can cause diarrhea, low platelet count, life-threatening allergic reaction, esophagitis, infection of the colon, nausea, vomiting, rash, and jaundice. Should be used with caution in women with liver or kidney failure.

How it can affect pregnant women: Clindamycin is used for the treatment of serious infections caused by anaerobes (bacteria that can survive without oxygen), respiratory tract infections, postpartum endometritis (inflammation of the uterine lining after delivery), pneumonitis (inflammation in the lungs), and soft-tissue infections caused by streptococci and staphylococci. Oral clindamycin cures bacterial vaginosis 90% during pregnancy and two-thirds of treated women maintain normal flora throughout the remainder of the pregnancy. Clearance (how fast the drug passes through the body) is increased during pregnancy, and as a result, higher doses may be necessary. When combined with gentamicin to treat premature preterm rupture of membranes (PPROM, water breaking before 37 weeks), clindamycin significantly lowers the risk of an intrauterine infection. It is the antibiotic of choice to prevent a newborn from contracting group B streptococcus from a mother who is positive for group B strep but allergic to penicillin.

How it can affect a developing embryo or fetus: There are no adequate reports or well-controlled studies in human fetuses. Clindamycin crosses the human placenta and achieves high enough levels in the fetus to treat susceptible bacteria. There are no reports linking clindamycin with birth defects in humans or rodents.

Breast-feeding: Clindamycin enters human breast milk. Although there are case reports of nursing newborns experiencing bloody stools when their mothers were treated with clindamycin, it is usually considered compatible with breast-feeding.

Potential drug interactions: Clindamycin has neuromuscular-blocking properties that may enhance the action of other neuromuscular-blocking agents. Clindamycin may interfere with the action of erythromycin.

What the FDA says about use in pregnancy: Category B (see Appendix).

What the available evidence suggests about breast-feeding safety: Likely safe.

The bottom line for you:

- Clindamycin is safe and effective (either alone or combined with gentamicin) for a variety of pregnancy-related infections.
- Clindamycin is generally considered compatible with breast-feeding.

CLOFIBRATE

Brand names: None; discontinued in the U.S.
Drug class: Antihyperlipidemic
Indications (what it is used for): Hypercholesterolemia (high cholesterol and triglycerides).
How it works: Blocks lipid metabolism.

Contraindications (reasons you shouldn't take it): Severe kidney or liver toxicity, gallbladder disease, primary biliary cirrhosis.

Possible side effects and warnings: Can cause mild abdominal and bowel irritation, muscle pain, increased liver enzymes, gallstones, water retention, and breast enlargement. Should be used with caution in women with significant kidney or liver dysfunction, rhabdomyolysis (breakdown of muscle fibers), or high potassium levels (with preexisting kidney insufficiency).

How it can affect pregnant women: There are no adequate reports or well-controlled studies of clofibrate in pregnant women, and there is little information on its effect on cholesterol metabolism during human pregnancy. Because so little is known, women of childbearing age taking clofibrate should use effective contraception. Hypercholesterolemia is not an immediate threat in most women being treated for it, so it is usually acceptable to stop therapy during pregnancy. In women planning a pregnancy, clofibrate should be withdrawn several months before conception if deemed medically safe.

How it can affect a developing embryo or fetus: There are no adequate reports or well-controlled studies in human fetuses. It is unknown whether clofibrate crosses the human placenta. It does cross the rodent placenta and alters fetal cholesterol metabolism. Although no animal studies found evidence that clofibrate causes birth defects, rabbit studies found that the fetal blood level is higher than that in the mother. However, animal studies are not necessarily good indicators of how a drug will behave in humans.

Breast-feeding: There is no published data in nursing women. It is unknown whether clofibrate enters human breast milk. Animal studies note an increase in mortality among nursing offspring.

Potential drug interactions: Interaction between the following medications and clofibrate has the potential to impact the effect of one or more of the drugs. In some instances the interaction can be dangerous or life-threatening and must be avoided: oral anticoagulants, phenytoin, other fibrates, tolbutamide, lovastatin.

What the FDA says about use in pregnancy: Category C (see Appendix).

What the available evidence suggests about breast-feeding safety: Unsafe.

The bottom line for you:

- It is unlikely that a pregnant or breast-feeding woman would require treatment with clofibrate.
- Until there is additional information, it should be used during pregnancy and while breast-feeding only if there are no other reasonable options.

CLOMIPHENE

Brand names: Clomid, Clomifene, Milophene, Serophene

Drug classes: Hormone; Stimulant, ovarian

Indications (what it is used for): To induce ovulation.

How it works: Binds to estrogen receptors with both stimulatory and inhibitory effects, resulting in ovulation.

Contraindications (reasons you shouldn't take it): Hypersensitivity to drug or class, pregnancy, abnormal uterine bleeding, adrenal gland dysfunction, thyroid disease, pituitary tumor, endometrial cancer.

Possible side effects and warnings: Can cause thromboembolism (blood clot in a blood vessel), ovarian hyperstimulation syndrome (swollen and painful ovaries), multiple pregnancy, ovarian enlargement, nausea, vomiting, hot flashes, abdominal distention, breast tenderness, blurred vision, headache, and abnormal uterine bleeding. Should be used with caution in women with polycystic ovary syndrome (PCOS—an endocrine abnormality leading to cystic ovaries and infertility) or liver disease.

How it can affect pregnant women: There are no reasons to prescribe clomiphene during pregnancy since its purpose is to stimulate ovulation to achieve pregnancy. For women who are trying to become pregnant using clomiphene, there is a risk of ovarian hyperstimulation and an increased incidence of multiple or ectopic pregnancies (pregnancies established in the fallopian tubes where the embryo and fetus cannot develop properly).

How it can affect a developing embryo or fetus: There are no adequate reports or well-controlled studies in human fetuses. It is unknown whether clomiphene crosses the human placenta. Clomid is a first-line treatment for women who have difficulties with ovulation. Although a range of fetal abnormalities have been reported in pregnancies that resulted from clomiphene-induced ovulation, no discernible pattern has emerged that directly implicates Clomid, and limited clinical experience suggests that there is no difference in the overall rates of birth defects among newborns of women who conceived after clomiphene treatment. It is generally considered a safe therapy.

Breast-feeding: There is no published data in nursing women. It is unknown whether clomiphene is excreted in human milk, but it is possible that it may inhibit breast-feeding. Until more information becomes available, women using clomiphene should not breast-feed.

Potential drug interactions: No clinically significant interactions identified.

What the FDA says about use in pregnancy: Category X (see Appendix).

What the available evidence suggests about breast-feeding safety: Unsafe.

The bottom line for you

- Clomiphene should not be used during pregnancy or when planning to breast-feed.
- Women who are considering using clomiphene to stimulate ovulation should have a pregnancy test first.

CLOMIPRAMINE

Brand name: Anafranil
Drug class: Antidepressant; Tricyclic

Indications (what it is used for): Obsessive-compulsive disorder, depression.

How it works: Inhibits reuptake of the neurotransmitters norepinephrine and serotonin, which are related to mood.

Contraindications (reasons you shouldn't take it): Hypersensitivity to drug or class, history of heart attack, glaucoma, pheochromocytoma (adrenal gland tumor), recent use of monoamine oxidase inhibitors (MAOIs), and serious thoughts of suicide.

Possible side effects and warnings: Can cause dry mouth, sedation, headache, constipation, and seizures. Should be used with caution in women with liver or kidney dysfunction or seizure disorder.

How it can affect pregnant women: Depression is common during and after pregnancy but often goes unrecognized and untreated. Depression can be made worse by pregnancy or delivery, and suicide is a not uncommon cause of maternal death. Pregnancy is not a reason to discontinue antidepressant drugs if the medication is effective and needed. A woman being treated for depression who becomes pregnant should not discontinue medication abruptly on her own but rather discuss her treatment and condition with her medical provider. Pregnancy may increase the dose needed to be effective, and women with a history of depression have a higher rate of recurrence after delivery. There are no adequate reports or well-controlled studies of clomipramine in pregnant women. A variety of withdrawal symptoms may occur with abrupt discontinuation. Recent population-based studies have revealed the use of tricyclic antidepressants may significantly increase the risk of preeclampsia (high blood pressure and protein in the urine during pregnancy and complications associated with it) by 2–3 times. Although there are alternative medications, women of reproductive age are frequently prescribed tricyclic antidepressants (TCAs).

How it can affect a developing embryo or fetus: There are no adequate reports or well-controlled studies in human fetuses. Clomipramine and its major metabolite (a product that it is broken down into) cross the human placenta. Withdrawal symptoms, including jitteriness, tremor, and seizures, are reported in newborns whose mothers took clomipramine up through delivery. Rodent studies found no evidence of birth defects or low birth weight despite the use of doses higher than those used clinically. However, animal studies are not necessarily good indicators of how a drug will behave in humans.

Breast-feeding: Since only trace amounts of clomipramine are found in human breast milk, it is likely compatible with breast-feeding.

Potential drug interactions: Interaction between the following medications and clomipramine has the potential to impact the effect of one or more of the drugs. In some instances the interaction can be dangerous or life-threatening and must be avoided: anticholinergic or sympathomimetic drugs; guanethidine, clonidine, or similar agents; haloperidol; any medication that inhibits the activity of the enzyme CYP2D6, such as quinidine, cimetidine, phenothiazines, propafenone, flecainide, fluoxetine, sertraline, fluvoxamine, and paroxetine; warfarin, digoxin.

What the FDA says about use in pregnancy: Category C (see Appendix).

What the available evidence suggests about breast-feeding safety: Likely safe.

The bottom line for you:

- Depression is a serious and often unrecognized problem during pregnancy and after delivery.
- Pregnancy is not a reason to discontinue needed and effective therapy.
- Clomipramine may be used during pregnancy and while breast-feeding to treat clinically significant depression.

CLONAZEPAM

Brand name: Klonopin
Drug classes: Anxiolytic; Benzodiazepine

Indications (what it is used for): Petit mal seizures (absence epilepsy), anxiety, periodic involuntary leg movement, neuralgia (nerve pain).

How it works: Binds to benzodiazepine receptors.

Contraindications (reasons you shouldn't take it): Hypersensitivity to drug or class.

Possible side effects and warnings: Can cause respiratory depression, low white blood cell count, liver failure, loss of muscle coordination, confusion, visual changes, drowsiness, and behavioral changes. Should be used with caution in women with liver disease.

How it can affect pregnant women: There are no adequate reports or well-controlled studies in pregnant women. In case reports, clonazepam was unrelated to complications of pregnancy, labor, or delivery.

How it can affect a developing embryo or fetus: There are no adequate reports or well-controlled studies in human fetuses. Clonazepam crosses the human placenta. In a case control study, birth defects were reported in 13% of infants whose mothers took clonazepam during pregnancy in combination with other antiepileptic drugs; however, there was no pattern of defects. Most studies conclude that there is no increased risk of birth defects, but they have limitations. Exposure in the late third trimester and during labor may pose greater risks because of newborn withdrawal syndrome, which, while rare, can persist from hours to months after birth. Affected babies may show mild sedation, low muscle tone, reluctance to suck, apnea spells (intermittently stopping breathing), cyanosis (a blue tinge to the skin resulting from low oxygen levels), and impaired responses to cold when uncovered.

Breast-feeding: There are no adequate reports or well-controlled studies in nursing mothers. Clonazepam enters human breast milk. A single case report suggests that a breast-feeding baby could ingest a clinically relevant amount, but no newborn levels are reported. Breast-feeding need not be discontinued if clonazepam is required by the mother. Infants should be monitored for drowsiness, adequate weight gain, and developmental milestones, especially in younger, exclusively breast-fed infants whose mothers are a using combination of drugs. Monitoring of the infant's blood level may be indicated if excessive sedation occurs.

Potential drug interactions: Interaction between the following medications and clonazepam has the potential to impact the effect of one or more of the drugs. In some instances the interaction can be dangerous or life-threatening and must be avoided: phenytoin; carbamazepine; phenobarbital; narcotics; barbiturates; nonbarbiturate hypnotics; anti-anxiety agents; the phenothiazine, thioxanthene, and butyrophenone classes of antipsychotic agents; monoamine oxidase inhibitors (MAOIs); tricyclic antidepressants; other anticonvulsant drugs; alcohol.

What the FDA says about use in pregnancy: Category D (see Appendix).

What the available evidence suggests about breast-feeding safety: Possibly unsafe.

The bottom line for you:

- At this point, there is no substantive evidence that clonazepam use by itself can result in birth defects.
- Exposure in the late third trimester and during labor and should be avoided when possible to prevent newborn withdrawal syndrome.
- Breast-feeding is reasonable as long as the infant is monitored for adverse effects.

CLONIDINE

Brand names: Catapres, Catapres-TTS, Duraclon

Drug classes: Adrenergic agonist, central alpha-2; Antihypertensive

Indications (what it is used for): High blood pressure.

How it works: Blocks an alpha receptor in the brain associated with hypertension.

Contraindications (reasons you shouldn't take it): Hypersensitivity to drug or class.

Possible side effects and warnings: Can cause drowsiness, dry mouth and eyes, constipation, headache, rash, nausea, and swelling. Should be used with caution in women with cardiovascular disease or liver or kidney failure.

How it can affect pregnant women: There are no adequate reports or well-controlled studies in pregnant women. Drug clearance is increased by pregnancy, often requiring an increased dose or a shorter time between doses. A decrease in maternal heart rate increases the risk of a low-birth-weight baby. Women withdrawing from a variety of illicit narcotics may benefit from clonidine initially and then methadone if symptoms persist. The combination of epidural clonidine with bupivacaine and fentanyl for pain control during labor improves analgesia and reduces the need for added medication and the frequency of shivering. A similar beneficial effect is reported when clonidine is combined with spinal morphine to provide pain relief after cesarean section.

How it can affect a developing embryo or fetus: There are no adequate reports or well-controlled studies in human fetuses. Clonidine readily crosses the placenta, achieving levels in the fetus that are similar to those of the mother. Newborns of women receiving clonidine during labor are not sedated, but they may experience temporary low blood pressure. Clonidine does not negatively affect fetal heart rate. Rodent studies are reassuring, showing no increase in birth defects or low birth weight. However, animal studies are not necessarily good indicators of how a drug will behave in humans.

Breast-feeding: Clonidine is concentrated in human breast milk. Caution is advised.

Potential drug interactions: Interaction between the following medications and clonidine has the potential to impact the effect of one or more of the drugs. In some instances the interaction can be dangerous or life-threatening and must be avoided: alcohol, barbiturates, or other sedating drugs; narcotic analgesics; tricyclic antidepressants; beta-blockers; digitalis; calcium channel blockers.

What the FDA says about use in pregnancy: Category C (see Appendix).

What the available evidence suggests about breast-feeding safety: Possibly unsafe.

The bottom line for you:

- Clonidine may be used with relative safely during pregnancy for management of substance abuse or as a component of labor analgesia.
- Women who must take clonidine for control of their blood pressure may breast-feed, but only with regular monitoring of the newborn by the pediatrician.

CLORAZEPATE

Brand names: Gen-Xene, Mendon, Nevracten, Tranxene

Drug classes: Anxiolytic; Benzodiazepine; Sedative

Indications (what it is used for): Anxiety, alcohol withdrawal.

How it works: Enhances the effects of the neurotransmitter GABA by binding to benzodiazepine receptors.

Contraindications (reasons you shouldn't take it): Hypersensitivity to drug or class, substance abuse, glaucoma, acute angina (chest pain), serious thoughts of suicide.

Possible side effects and warnings: Can cause liver damage, drowsiness, headache, low blood pressure, and dry mouth.

How it can affect pregnant women: There are no adequate reports or well-controlled studies in pregnant women. There are other options available with which there is more experience during pregnancy and while breast-feeding.

How it can affect a developing embryo or fetus: There are no adequate reports or well-controlled studies in pregnant women. Clorazepate appears to cross the placenta more slowly than other benzodiazepines (20% compared to 85% for diazepam). There is no credible evidence that clorazepate causes birth defects in humans. The lowest effective dose of clorazepate should be used during delivery, because high doses are associated with floppy infant syndrome (limpness when a baby is lying down that may not ever resolve).

Breast-feeding: Clorazepate is excreted into human breast milk at low concentrations. As with other benzodiazepines, caution is advised while breast-feeding.

Potential drug interactions: Interaction between the following medications and clorazepate has the potential to impact the effect of one or more of the drugs. In some instances the interaction can be dangerous or life-threatening and must be avoided: hypnotic medications, barbiturates, narcotics, phenothiazines, monoamine oxidase inhibitors (MAOIs), other antidepressants.

What the FDA says about use in pregnancy: Category D (see Appendix).

What the available evidence suggests about breast-feeding safety: Unknown.

The bottom line for you:

- Clorazepate should be used during pregnancy and breast-feeding only if the benefit to the woman justifies the potential risk of floppy infant syndrome.
- There are other drug options available with which there is more experience during pregnancy and while breast-feeding.

CLOTRIMAZOLE

Brand names: Canastene, Clomaz, Clomine, Fungicide, Gyne-Lotrimin, Lotrimin, Mycelex, Mycelex-G

Drug classes: Antifungal, topical; Dermatologic

Indications (what it is used for): Tinea pedis (athlete's foot), tinea cruris (jock itch), tinea versicolor (fungal rash on the trunk), tinea corporis (fungal infection on the arms or legs), cutaneous and vulvovaginal candidiasis (yeast infection).

How it works: Alters membrane permeability of the fungus.

Contraindications (reasons you shouldn't take it): Hypersensitivity to drug or class.

Possible side effects and warnings: Can cause skin inflammation, burning, swelling, itching, and vaginal irritation.

How it can affect pregnant women: There are no adequate reports or well-controlled studies in pregnant women. Vaginal yeast infection is common during pregnancy. A 7-day course of treatment may be necessary during pregnancy rather than the shorter courses effective for nonpregnant women. Topical clotrimazole appears more effective than nystatin for treating symptomatic vaginal candidiasis in pregnancy.

How it can affect a developing embryo or fetus: There are no adequate reports or well-controlled studies in human fetuses. It is unknown whether clotrimazole crosses the human placenta. However, since the medication is applied topically, there is limited systemic absorption in the mother, so the maternal blood level is unlikely to be clinically significant. Rodent studies are reassuring, revealing no increased risk of birth defects or underweight babies. However, animal studies are not necessarily good indicators of how a drug will behave in humans.

Breast-feeding: There are no adequate reports or well-controlled studies in nursing mothers. It is unknown whether clotrimazole enters human breast milk. However, considering the low level of the medication in maternal blood after topical or vaginal application, it is unlikely that a breast-feeding baby would ingest a clinically significant amount.

Potential drug interactions: No clinically significant interactions identified.

What the FDA says about use in pregnancy: Category B (see Appendix).

What the available evidence suggests about breast-feeding safety: Likely safe.

The bottom line for you:

- There is no evidence that either vaginal yeast infection or clotrimazole in pregnancy is harmful to the baby.
- A longer course of treatment (7 days) may be necessary for vaginitis during pregnancy.

- Clotrimazole is likely safe for use while breast-feeding.

CLOZAPINE

Brand names: Clozaril, Entumin, Etumine
Drug class: Antipsychotic
Indications (what it is used for): Atypical psychosis, schizophrenia.
How it works: May interfere with the D2 dopamine receptors.
Contraindications (reasons you shouldn't take it): Hypersensitivity to drug or class, myocarditis (inflammation of the heart muscle), myeloproliferative disorder (abnormal growth of blood cells in the bone marrow), glaucoma, central nervous system depression.
Possible side effects and warnings: Can cause bone marrow suppression, low white blood cell count, neuroleptic malignant syndrome (life-threatening muscle rigidity, fever, vital sign instability, and cognitive changes such as delirium), blood clots, constipation, irregular heart rate, and cardiac arrest. Should be used with caution in women with kidney or liver damage, seizure or cardiac disease, or bone marrow suppression.
How it can affect pregnant women: Psychosis places a mother and her fetus at risk. Clinical experience suggests that most current psychotropic drugs are relatively safe for use in pregnancy. Clozapine is a relatively new medication for treatment-resistant schizophrenia. The published data during pregnancy is limited to case reports. It may be effective in patients experiencing positive (hallucinations, delusions, bizarre behavior, hostility) and negative (withdrawal, blunted emotions, lack of motivation, inability to experience pleasure or enjoyment) symptoms.
How it can affect a developing embryo or fetus: There are no adequate reports or well-controlled studies in the human fetus. It is unknown whether clozapine crosses the human placenta. Rodent studies have found no evidence of birth defects or restricted fetal growth despite the use of doses higher than those used clinically. However, animal studies are not necessarily good indicators of how a drug will behave in humans.
Breast-feeding: There are no adequate reports or well-controlled studies in nursing women. Clozapine enters human breast milk, although it is estimated that a nursing infant would ingest a clinically small amount of drug. However, there is a report of 4 infants who experienced side effects that reversed when the breast-feeding was stopped. As a precaution, the drug should be given at the lowest effective dose, breast-feeding avoided during peak drug levels, and the infant monitored for any adverse effects.
Potential drug interactions: Interaction between the following medications and clozapine has the potential to impact the effect of one or more of the drugs. In some instances the interaction can be dangerous or life-threatening and must be avoided: cimetidine, caffeine, erythromycin, fluvoxamine, central nervous system depressants, medications for blood pressure, atropines, phenytoin, nicotine, rifampin, drugs that suppress bone marrow production, epinephrine.
What the FDA says about use in pregnancy: Category B (see Appendix).
What the available evidence suggests about breast-feeding safety: Unknown.
The bottom line for you:

- Psychosis places a mother and her fetus at risk.
- If clozapine is required, it should be used at the lowest possible dose and given in divided doses to minimize peaks of medication and any potential adverse effect for the fetus or newborn.
- Women who must remain on clozapine probably should not breast-feed. If they choose to do so, the infant should be observed closely for side effects and blood levels checked if appropriate.

CODEINE

Brand name: None
Drug classes: Analgesic, narcotic; Antitussive

Indications (what it is used for): Antitussive, expectorant.
How it works: Opiate receptor stimulant.
Contraindications (reasons you shouldn't take it): Hypersensitivity to drug or class.
Possible side effects and warnings: Can cause dizziness, euphoria, nausea, vomiting, constipation, dry mouth, urinary retention, and itching. Should be used with caution in women with liver or kidney dysfunction, increased intracranial pressure, hypothyroidism, acute alcoholism, or chronic lung disease.
How it can affect pregnant women: There are no adequate reports or well-controlled studies in pregnant women. Codeine is converted in the body into morphine. Combining codeine with a nonsteroidal anti-inflammatory drug significantly enhances pain relief. It is commonly used alone and in combination with other agents to relieve episiotomy pain after delivery.
How it can affect a developing embryo or fetus: There are no adequate reports or well-controlled studies in human fetuses. Morphine readily crosses the placenta. Opioids in general have recently been associated with a small to moderate increase in the risk of a variety of birth defects, but the research lumped together a number of drugs; isolated studies of codeine have not revealed any evidence of increased malformations. Newborn withdrawal syndrome has been reported. Rodent studies are reassuring, revealing no increase in birth defects. However, animal studies are not necessarily good indicators of how a drug will behave in humans.
Breast-feeding: There are no adequate reports or well-controlled studies in nursing mothers. Codeine and its metabolite morphine are excreted in human breast milk. Breast-feeding newborns have low plasma levels of the drug during the first few days of life, in part because there is a low concentration in milk and in part due to the small amount of milk produced after delivery. Thus, moderate codeine use (up to 60 mg daily) is probably compatible with breast-feeding shortly after delivery. Thereafter, codeine abuse could lead to high levels in the newborn.
Potential drug interactions: Interaction between the following medications and codeine has the potential to impact the effect of one or more of the drugs. In some instances the interaction can be dangerous or life-threatening and must be avoided: other narcotic analgesics, general anesthetics, phenothiazines, tranquilizers, sedative-hypnotics, other central nervous system depressants (including alcohol).
What the FDA says about use in pregnancy: Category C (see Appendix).
What the available evidence suggests about breast-feeding safety: Safe.
The bottom line for you:
- Codeine is effective and safe when used during pregnancy and while breast-feeding for a brief duration.
- Prolonged use should be avoided if breast-feeding.

COLESEVELAM
Brand name: Welchol
Drug classes: Antihyperlipidemic; Bile acid sequestrant
Indications (what it is used for): Hypercholesterolemia (high levels of cholesterol and triglycerides).
How it works: Binds bile acids in the intestine.
Contraindications (reasons you shouldn't take it): Hypersensitivity to drug or class.
Possible side effects and warnings: Can cause nausea, bloating, belching, flatulence, and weight loss. Should be used with caution in women with constipation, very high triglycerides (above 300 mg/dL), dysphagia (difficulty swallowing), or a history of major gastrointestinal surgery.
How it can affect pregnant women: There is no published data with colesevelam during pregnancy. Though colesevelam is not absorbed out of the maternal bowel, it could potentially lead to poor

absorption of fat-soluble vitamins important for a successful pregnancy. However, pregnant rabbits and rats were unaffected by its use.

How it can affect a developing embryo or fetus: There are no adequate reports or well-controlled studies in human fetuses. There should be no direct effect of the drug on the fetus since little of the drug is absorbed out of the bowel. Rodent studies are reassuring, revealing no evidence of fetal toxicity. However, animal studies are not necessarily good indicators of how a drug will behave in humans.

Breast-feeding: There are no adequate reports or well-controlled studies in pregnant women. Colesevelam is not absorbed into the systemic circulation, which suggests that a direct effect on breast-feeding is not possible. However, prolonged use could induce vitamin malabsorption in the mother and decrease the milk concentration of vitamins A, D, and K.

Potential drug interactions: Colesevelam decreases the clearance of verapamil.

What the FDA says about use in pregnancy: Category B (see Appendix).

What the available evidence suggests about breast-feeding safety: Likely safe.

The bottom line for you:
- Colesevelam is likely safe for use during pregnancy.
- There are other medications with which there is more experience while breast-feeding.

COLESTIPOL

Brand name: Colestid

Drug classes: Antihyperlipidemic; Bile acid sequestrant

Indications (what it is used for): Hypercholesterolemia (high cholesterol and triglycerides), digitoxin overdose.

How it works: Binds bile acids in the intestine.

Contraindications (reasons you shouldn't take it): Hypersensitivity to drug or class.

Possible side effects and warnings: Can cause nausea, bloating, belching, flatulence, and weight loss. Should be used with caution in women with constipation or impaired vitamin absorption.

How it can affect pregnant women: There are no adequate reports or well-controlled studies in pregnant women. Colestipol is used to reduce cholesterol in patients with primary hypercholesterolemia who do not respond adequately to diet adjustments. Little if any drug is absorbed from the mother's bowel. Chronic use of colestipol may lead to increased bleeding secondary to the hypoprothrombinemia (a blood-clotting problem) of vitamin K deficiency.

How it can affect a developing embryo or fetus: There are no adequate reports or well-controlled studies in human fetuses. However, little is absorbed systemically by the mother, so it should not cause direct fetal harm at the recommended dosages. Rodent studies show no evidence of toxicity. However, animal studies are not necessarily good indicators of how a drug will behave in humans.

Breast-feeding: There are no adequate reports or well-controlled studies in breast-feeding women. Colestipol is not absorbed into the systemic circulation, which suggests that a direct effect on breast-feeding is not possible. However, prolonged use could induce vitamin malabsorption by the mother and decrease the milk concentration of vitamins A, D, and K.

Potential drug interactions: Interaction between the following medications and colestipol has the potential to impact the effect of one or more of the drugs. In some instances the interaction can be dangerous or life-threatening and must be avoided: chlorothiazide, tetracycline, furosemide, penicillin G, hydrochlorothiazide, gemfibrozil.

What the FDA says about use in pregnancy: Category B (see Appendix).

What the available evidence suggests about breast-feeding safety: Likely safe.

The bottom line for you:
- Colestipol is probably safe during pregnancy and while breast-feeding if required for the

health of the mother; vitamin status should be monitored closely.

CORTISONE
Brand names: Cortisyl, Cortone
Drug class: Corticosteroid
Indications (what it is used for): Adrenal insufficiency, inflammation.
How it works: Unknown.
Contraindications (reasons you shouldn't take it): Hypersensitivity to drug or class, congestive heart failure, active untreated infections.
Possible side effects and warnings: Can cause adrenal insufficiency, psychosis, immunosuppression, peptic ulcer, congestive heart failure, osteoporosis, pseudotumor cerebri (increased pressure in the brain unrelated to a tumor), pancreatitis, low potassium, high blood pressure, bruising, acne, and impaired wound healing. Should be used with caution in women with a seizure disorder, diabetes, high blood pressure, osteoporosis, or liver dysfunction.
How it can affect pregnant women: There are no adequate reports or well-controlled studies in pregnant women. In early pregnancy, estrogen increases the synthesis of a protein that binds steroids, which means that women who need cortisone to treat conditions such as Cushing's syndrome require higher doses. It has been suggested (but not convincingly shown) that chronic steroid administration increases the incidence of maternal infection. Women who receive a short-term burst of even more potent steroids to enhance fetal lung development, such as those used with preterm premature rupture of membranes (PPROM, water breaking before 37 weeks) have no increased risk of chorioamnionitis (an infection of the fetal membranes). Cortisone has been used to treat first-trimester hyperemesis (severe morning sickness), but there are other agents available that are believed to be safer for the fetus for this indication.
How it can affect a developing embryo or fetus: There are no adequate reports or well-controlled studies in human fetuses. There is almost complete conversion of cortisol to cortisone by the placenta, and it is readily transferred to the fetus. The evidence overall is that corticosteroids may be a weak teratogen (a substance that can cause birth defects) when taken in the first trimester. The most recent meta-analysis concluded that there is a small but real increase in the risk of cleft lip or palate after first-trimester exposure to prednisone, a cortisone-like drug. There is no increased risk of anomalies when steroids are begun after organ formation (after 11 weeks). Women exposed to topical cortisone during pregnancy experience no increase in birth defects. A few small studies suggested a possible relationship between long-term steroid use during pregnancy and poor fetal growth; however, it is hard to tell if that was the result of the medication or the disease it was being used to treat.
Breast-feeding: There are no adequate reports or well-controlled studies in breast-feeding women. Cortisone is a normal component of breast milk, but it is unclear whether maternal treatment increases the concentration.
Potential drug interactions: Interaction between the following medications and cortisone has the potential to impact the effect of one or more of the drugs. In some instances the interaction can be dangerous or life-threatening and must be avoided: anticoagulants, phenobarbital, phenytoin, rifampin, troleandomycin, ketoconazole, high-dose aspirin.
What the FDA says about use in pregnancy: Category C (see Appendix).
What the available evidence suggests about breast-feeding safety: Unknown.
The bottom line for you:
- A short course of oral or intravenous cortisone is probably safe during pregnancy and breast-feeding.
- The fetuses of women taking oral cortisone long term should undergo a detailed sonographic exam at 20 weeks and be followed for adequate placental performance.

CROMOLYN

Brand names: Cromoglicic Acid, Cromogloz, Gastrocrom, Inostral, Intal, NasalCrom, Opticrom

Drug classes: Antiasthmatic; Mast cell stabilizer; Ophthalmic

Indications (what it is used for): Mastocytosis (a rare but serious skin disorder), food allergies, inflammatory bowel disease, chronic and exercise-induced asthma, allergic rhinitis, and conjunctivitis.

How it works: Inhibits mast cell degranulation (release), although unclear if this is how it treats asthma.

Contraindications (reasons you shouldn't take it): Hypersensitivity to drug or class.

Possible side effects and warnings: Can cause bronchospasm, life-threatening allergic reaction, dry throat or throat irritation, bitter taste, cough, wheezing, and dizziness. Should be used with caution in women with an irregular heart rate.

How it can affect pregnant women: Asthma is a common disease in life and in pregnancy. Approximately one-third of pregnant women with asthma get worse during pregnancy, one-third get better, and one-third remain clinically unchanged. Well-controlled asthma does not affect pregnancy outcome, but poorly controlled asthma may increase the risk of preterm birth (before 37 weeks) or low birth weight. There are no adequate reports or well-controlled studies of cromolyn in pregnant women. Intranasal corticosteroids are considered first-line therapy in pregnancy, followed by first-generation antihistamines. Typically, cromolyn is prescribed if those measures prove inadequate.

Certain medications used during labor and delivery have the potential to worsen asthma, including nonselective beta-blockers, some prostaglandins (used to induce labor), and ergonovine (used to control blood loss after delivery).

How it can affect a developing embryo or fetus: There are no adequate reports or well-controlled studies in human fetuses. It is unknown whether cromolyn crosses the human placenta. Rodent studies are reassuring, revealing no increase in birth defects or low birth weight. However, animal stud-

ies are not necessarily good indicators of how a drug will behave in humans.

Breast-feeding: There are no adequate reports or well-controlled studies in breast-feeding women. It is unknown whether cromolyn enters human breast milk.

Potential drug interactions: No clinically significant interactions identified.

What the FDA says about use in pregnancy: Category B (see Appendix).

What the available evidence suggests about breast-feeding safety: Likely safe.

The bottom line for you:
- Cromolyn is probably safe for use during pregnancy and while breast-feeding.

CYANOCOBALAMIN

Brand names: Antipernicin, B-12-1000, Berubigen, Betalin 12, Betlovex, Blu-12, Cobal, Cobalparen, Cobavite, Cobex, Cobolin-M, Compensal, Corubeen, Corubin, Cpc-Carpenters, Crystamine, Crysti-12, Cyanocob, Cyanoject, Cyano-Plex, Cyomin, Cytacon, Cytaman, Depinar, Depo-Cobolin, Docemine, Dodecamin, La-12, Lifaton, Nascobal, Neurin-12, Neurodex, Neuroforte-R, Norivite, Ottovit, Pan B-12, Primabalt, Rubesol-1000, Rubisol, Rubivite, Rubramin Pc, Ruvite, Shovite, Sytobex, Vibal, Vibisone, Vitabee 12, Vita Liver, Vitamin B_{12}, Vita-Plus B-12, Yobramin

Drug classes: Hematinic; Vitamin/mineral

Indications (what it is used for): Vitamin B_{12} deficiency, pernicious anemia.

How it works: Cyanocobalamin is an enzyme involved in major biochemical reactions.

Contraindications (reasons you shouldn't take it): Hypersensitivity to drug or class.

Possible side effects and warnings: Can cause life-threatening allergic reaction, blood clots, itching, diarrhea, and hives. Should be used with caution in women experiencing itching, diarrhea, or hives.

How it can affect pregnant women: Cyanocobalamin is required for proper red blood cell formation, neurological function, and DNA synthesis. There are no adequate reports or well-controlled studies in pregnant women. Deficiency has been linked to early miscarriage in several small studies but not confirmed in others. It is likely that normal to slightly low levels in isolation are not associated with adverse pregnancy outcomes. The recommended daily intake is 2.6 mcg per day during pregnancy, an amount typically exceeded in standard prenatal vitamins. Cyanocobalamin deficiency and a related rise in homocysteine are long-term significant risk factors for cardiovascular disease and may, in genetically predisposed women, increase the risk of adverse pregnancy outcome.

How it can affect a developing embryo or fetus: There are no adequate reports or well-controlled studies in human fetuses. There is efficient transfer of cyanocobalamin to the fetus by 16 weeks of pregnancy. Increased folate intake prior to and during pregnancy reduces the risk of neural tube defects and possibly other fetal malformations, and it appears that one of the beneficial effects of folate may come from an enzyme that depends on cyanocobalamin to function properly.

Breast-feeding: Although there are no adequate reports or well-controlled studies, cyanocobalamin is generally considered safe for breast-feeding women. The recommended daily intake is 2.8 mcg per day.

Potential drug interactions: Chloramphenical may decrease the efficacy of cyanocobalamin. Omeprazole may decrease cyanocobalamin's absorption.

What the FDA says about use in pregnancy: Category C (see Appendix).

What the available evidence suggests about breast-feeding safety: Safe.

The bottom line for you:

- Cyanocobalamin is contained in most prenatal vitamin tablets, although the evidence that it improves pregnancy outcome overall is weak. It may have beneficial effects as part of a comprehensive balance in micronutrients.

CYCLAMATE
Not available in the U.S.

Brand name: None

Drug class: Artificial sweetener

Indications (what it is used for): Food sweetener.

How it works: Stimulation of the sweet receptors.

Contraindications (reasons you shouldn't take it): Hypersensitivity.

Possible side effects and warnings: None.

How it can affect pregnant women: Cyclamate was removed from food products in the U.S. and Canada in the 1970s after several animal studies suggested that it posed an increased risk of bladder cancer in rats fed the maximum dietary level. However, there are no adequate or well-controlled studies in human subjects, and epidemiologic study does not suggest that it resulted in increased cancer rates in humans. Although still banned in the U.S., it is currently available in Canada and Europe. The scientific community is reviewing current data, which may support cyclamate approval again.

How it can affect a developing embryo or fetus: No adequate or well-controlled studies have been performed in human fetuses. Cyclamate crosses the human placenta. Rodent studies are reassuring, revealing no increase in either birth defects or underweight fetuses. However, animal studies are not necessarily good indicators of how a drug will behave in humans.

Breast-feeding: There is no published data in nursing women. It is unknown whether cyclamate enters human breast milk.

Potential drug interactions: No clinically relevant drug interactions have been found.

What the FDA says about use in pregnancy: No assigned category (see Appendix).

What the available evidence suggests about breast-feeding safety: Unknown.

The bottom line for you:

- There is inadequate data to state whether cyclamate is safe during pregnancy and while breast-feeding.

CYCLOBENZAPRINE

Brand names: Flexeril

Drug class: Muscle relaxant

Indications (what it is used for): Muscle spasm.

How it works: Believed to increase the release of the neurotransmitter norepinephrine in the brain, which inhibits muscle contractions.

Contraindications (reasons you shouldn't take it): Hypersensitivity to drug or class, use of mono-amine oxidase inhibitors (MAOIs) within 14 days, hyperthyroidism, recent heart attack, irregular heart rate.

Possible side effects and warnings: Can cause irregular heart rate, seizures, heart attack, hepatitis, nausea, vomiting, dry mouth, dizziness, weakness, heartburn, blurred vision, drowsiness, fatigue, constipation, and nervousness. Should be used with caution in women with glaucoma.

How it can affect pregnant women: Although there is no published data during pregnancy, a long clinical experience suggests that any risks are small.

How it can affect a developing embryo or fetus: There are no adequate reports or well-controlled studies in human fetuses. It is unknown whether cyclobenzaprine crosses the human placenta. Although there is no published experience during pregnancy, a long clinical experience suggests that any risks are small. Rodent studies are reassuring, revealing no increase in either birth defects or low birth weight. However, animal studies are not necessarily good indicators of how a drug will behave in humans.

Breast-feeding: There is no published data in nursing women. It is unknown whether cyclobenzaprine enters human breast milk.

Potential drug interactions: Interaction between the following medications or substances and cyclobenzaprine has the potential to impact the effect of one or more of the drugs. In some instances the interaction can be dangerous or life-threatening and must be avoided: monoamine oxidase inhibitors (MAOIs), alcohol, barbiturates, and other central nervous system depressants.

What the FDA says about use in pregnancy: Category B (see Appendix).

What the available evidence suggests about breast-feeding safety: Unknown.

The bottom line for you:

- Although there is no published data during pregnancy, the long clinical experience during pregnancy suggests there is no significant risk to mother or child.

- It is unknown whether cyclobenzaprine enters human breast milk. As the drug is related to tricyclic antidepressants and some of those drugs reach high milk levels, it is perhaps best not to nurse while taking the drug.

CYCLOPHOSPHAMIDE

Brand names: Cytokan, Cytoxan, Endoxon, Neosar, Neosar for Injection

Drug classes: Antineoplastic, alkylating agent; Antirheumatic

Indications (what it is used for): Chemotherapy for cancer: ovary, bladder, lung, esophagus, cervix, breast, gastric, lymphoma, myeloma, sarcoma, gestational trophoblastic disease, mycosis fungoides (T cell lymphoma); immune disorders such as rheumatoid arthritis.

How it works: Prevents DNA from being read, causing cell death.

Contraindications (reasons you shouldn't take it): Hypersensitivity to drug or class, bone marrow depression.

Possible side effects and warnings: Can cause nausea, vomiting, infertility, congestive heart failure, malignancy, low white blood cell and/or platelet counts, cardiomyopathy (disease of the heart muscle), hair loss, rash, headache, dizziness, and stomatitis (inflammation of the mucous membranes of the mouth). Should be used with caution in women with kidney or liver failure, low white blood cell or platelet counts, or who have had recent radiation or recent chemotherapy.

How it can affect pregnant women: Cyclophosphamide is used to treat cancer and other malignancies of the ovary, breast, and blood and lymph systems. It can cause temporary or permanent sterility. There is also a risk the treatment will lead to the development of an additional tumor. Although there are no adequate reports or well-controlled studies in pregnant women, multiple case reports demonstrate that cyclophosphamide can be used for the treatment of a life-threatening malignancy during pregnancy with a good outcome for mother and child.

How it can affect a developing embryo or fetus: There are no adequate reports or well-controlled studies in human fetuses. Cyclophosphamide crosses the human placenta, although large studies have not convincingly demonstrated an association with birth defects in humans; treatment in the first trimester may increase the chance of miscarriage. There are reports of newborns whose mothers were treated during pregnancy experiencing bone marrow suppression and even secondary cancers.

Breast-feeding: Cyclophosphamide enters human breast milk in high concentration and is generally considered incompatible with breast-feeding. Low white blood cell counts have been reported in breast-fed children.

Potential drug interactions: The anesthesiologist should be notified if a woman has been treated with cyclophosphamide within 10 days of general anesthesia. The activities of cyclophosphamide are increased by high doses of phenobarbital.

What the FDA says about use in pregnancy: Category D (see Appendix).

What the available evidence suggests about breast-feeding safety: Not safe.

The bottom line for you:

- The treatment of life-threatening cancer generally should not be delayed because of pregnancy. A sizable clinical experience with cyclophosphamide supports its relatively safe use during pregnancy. Serious complications in the newborn are rare, and the possibility of maternal death obviously is far worse.

- Women undergoing treatment should not breast-feed.

CYCLOSERINE

Brand names: Cyclorin, Seromycin
Drug class: Antimycobacterial
Indications (what it is used for): Tuberculosis (active pulmonary and extrapulmonary).
How it works: Interferes with the synthesis of the bacterial cellular wall.
Contraindications (reasons you shouldn't take it): Epilepsy, depression, severe anxiety, psychosis, severe kidney insufficiency, alcoholism.
Possible side effects and warnings: None reported. Should be used with caution in women with drowsiness, headache, mental confusion, tremors, dizziness, loss of memory, or psychoses.
How it can affect pregnant women: There are no adequate reports or well-controlled studies of cycloserine in pregnant women. The published data is limited to case reports, which have found no obvious pregnancy-related adverse effects.
How it can affect a developing embryo or fetus: There are no adequate reports or well-controlled studies in human fetuses. It is unknown whether cycloserine crosses the human placenta. No cycloserine-related birth defects have been found in the fetuses of treated women.
Breast-feeding: Although cycloserine is excreted into human breast milk in small quantities, no adverse effects have been reported and it is generally considered safe while breast-feeding.
Potential drug interactions: Interaction between the following medications and cycloserine has the potential to impact the effect of one or more of the drugs. In some instances the interaction can be dangerous or life-threatening and must be avoided: ethionamide, alcohol, isoniazid.
What the FDA says about use in pregnancy: Category C (see Appendix).
What the available evidence suggests about breast-feeding safety: Safe.

The bottom line for you:

- Cycloserine may be used with relative safety during pregnancy and while breast-feeding for the treatment of active tuberculosis.

CYCLOSPORINE

Brand names: Ciclosporin, Neoral, Sandimmune, SangCy

Drug class: Immunosuppressant

Indications (what it is used for): Prevention of transplant organ rejection, ulcerative colitis.

How it works: Believed to inhibit T lymphocyte immune cells.

Contraindications (reasons you shouldn't take it): Hypersensitivity to drug or class, high blood pressure.

Possible side effects and warnings: Can cause seizures; low platelet and/or low white blood cell counts; infection; high glucose, potassium, or uric acid levels. Should be used with caution in women with liver or kidney failure.

How it can affect pregnant women: There are no adequate reports or well-controlled studies in pregnant women. Treatment with cyclosporine for steroid refractory ulcerative colitis (inflammation of the colon that does not respond to corticosteroid medications) during pregnancy can be considered effective and safe. Successful pregnancy after solid organ transplantation is common. Women planning pregnancy after transplant should consider the following criteria for optimal outcomes: (1) good transplant graft function; (2) no evidence of rejection; (3) waiting a minimum of 1–2 years after transplantation; and (4) either no or well-controlled high blood pressure. Preeclampsia (high blood pressure and protein in the urine during pregnancy and complications associated with it) complicates about 30% of pregnancies after kidney transplant. Your physician should monitor your blood pressure, kidney function, protein in the urine, and weight at least every 2 weeks until the third trimester, and then every week.

How it can affect a developing embryo or fetus: There are no adequate reports or well-controlled studies in human fetuses. Less than 5% of the maternal dose crosses to the fetus, suggesting that fetal exposure is low. However, some drugs are known to increase the fetal cyclosporine level by promoting the transfer. Most children of women treated with an immunosuppressive during pregnancy have normal growth and development. Children born to women who have received transplants and are taking cyclosporine have normal kidney function despite prolonged exposure in utero. Some studies suggest a higher risk of stillbirth, preterm delivery (before 37 weeks), and low birth weight in transplant patients treated with cyclosporine. Whether this is due to the disease or the cyclosporine is unknown. Preliminary evidence suggests that prenatal exposure to immunosuppressive drugs does not have a profound effect on the developing immune system.

Breast-feeding: There are no adequate reports or well-controlled studies in nursing mothers. Too little cyclosporine is excreted into human breast milk to produce a measurable level in the breast-fed newborn.

Potential drug interactions: Interaction between the following medications or substances and cyclosporine has the potential to impact the effect of one or more of the drugs. In some instances the interaction can be dangerous or life-threatening and must be avoided: gentamicin, tobramycin, vancomycin, trimethoprim with sulfamethoxazole, melphalan, amphotericin B, azapropazon, diclofenac, naproxen, sulindac, cimetidine, ranitidine, tacrolimus, CYP3A inhibitors (e.g., diltiazem, nicardipine, verapamil, fluconazole, itraconazole, ketoconazole, clarithromycin, erythromycin, quinupristin/daldopristin, methylprednisolone, allopurinol, bromocriptine, danazol, metoclopramide, colchicine, amiodarone, indinavir, nelfinavir, ritonavir, saquinavir), grapefruit and grapefruit juice, nafcillin, rifampin, carbamazepine, phenobarbital, phenytoin, octreotide, ticlopidine, orlistat, St. John's wort, digoxin, colchicine, prednisolone, HMG-CoA reductase inhibitors (statins), potassium-sparing diuretics. For detailed information on cyclosporine drug interactions, please contact Novartis Medical Affairs Department at 888-669-6682.

What the FDA says about use in pregnancy: Category C (see Appendix).

What the available evidence suggests about breast-feeding safety: Likely safe.

The bottom line for you:

- Cyclosporine may be used with relative safety during pregnancy and while breast-feeding in transplant patients and women with steroid-resistant ulcerative colitis.
- Women with kidney transplants are at particular risk for preeclampsia (high blood pressure and protein in the urine during pregnancy and complications associated with it), which threatens their health and that of the fetus. They should be monitored closely throughout pregnancy.

CYPROHEPTADINE

Brand names: Actinal, Cyheptin, Huavine, Ioukmin, Nekomin, Oractine, Periactin, Setomin

Drug classes: Antihistamine, H1; Antihistamine, sedating

Indications (what it is used for): Allergic rhinitis.

How it works: Central and peripheral H1 receptor antagonist, serotonin receptor antagonist.

Contraindications (reasons you shouldn't take it): Hypersensitivity to drug or class, gastric ulcer, glaucoma, use of monoamine oxidase inhibitors (MAOIs) within 14 days, bladder neck obstruction.

Possible side effects and warnings: Can cause bone marrow suppression, dry mouth, nausea, vomiting, urinary retention, dizziness, headache, rash, diarrhea, weight gain, and glucose intolerance (prediabetes).

How it can affect pregnant women: There are no adequate reports or well-controlled studies in pregnant women. Cyproheptadine is mostly used to prevent or relieve stuffy nose, skin itching, hives, and tissue swelling. It is also used to for a myriad of problems unrelated to pregnancy, including stimulating appetite in women with anorexia nervosa and preventing migraines.

How it can affect a developing embryo or fetus: There are no adequate reports or well-controlled studies in human fetuses. It is unknown whether cyproheptadine crosses the human placenta. Rodent studies are reassuring, revealing no evidence of birth defects or low-birth-weight newborns. However, animal studies are not necessarily good indicators of how a drug will behave in humans. Although cyproheptadine is an old drug, there are other, better-studied options for use during pregnancy.

Breast-feeding: There is no published data in nursing women. It is unknown whether cyproheptadine enters human breast milk.

Potential drug interactions: Interaction between the following medications and cyproheptadine has the potential to impact the effect of one or more of the drugs. In some instances the interaction can be dangerous or life-threatening and must be avoided: monoamine oxidase inhibitors (MAOIs) or other central nervous system depressants such as hypnotics, sedatives, tranquilizers, antianxiety agents, or alcohol.

What the FDA says about use in pregnancy: Category B (see Appendix).

What the available evidence suggests about breast-feeding safety: Unknown.

The bottom line for you:

- There are better-studied alternatives for use during pregnancy and while breast-feeding.

CYTARABINE

Brand names: Cytosar-U, Tarabine PFS

Drug class: Antineoplastic, antimetabolite

Indications (what it is used for): Leukemia.

How it works: Interferes with the RNA and DNA production in cancer cells, inhibiting their growth.

Contraindications (reasons you shouldn't take it): Hypersensitivity to drug or class, pregnancy, infertility.

Possible side effects and warnings: Can cause anemia, bruising, nausea, vomiting, hair loss, low white blood cell count, bone marrow suppression, and pancreatitis. Should be used with caution in women with kidney or liver failure.

How it can affect pregnant women: The coexistence of leukemia and pregnancy is extremely rare. There are no adequate reports or well-controlled studies in pregnant women. Cytarabine is used during pregnancy to achieve remission of acute episodes of leukemia. Once remission is achieved, the dose should be readjusted.

How it can affect a developing embryo or fetus: There are no adequate reports or well-controlled studies in human fetuses. Cytarabine appears to cross the human placenta and has been associated with defects in the fetus, including flattening of the skull and underdevelopment of the skull and face, premature fusion of the sutures leading to a deformation of the skull, low birth weight, a low white blood cell count, and abnormal liver tests in the newborn. Children born without any of these defects appear to mature normally. In addition, the manufacturer of the medication has compiled 32 cases where cytarabine was administered during pregnancy. Most were normal, although 5 were preterm. Two cases of congenital abnormalities involving the limbs were noted. Seven (mostly the preterm babies) had various problems including evidence of bone marrow suppression and electrolyte abnormalities.

Breast-feeding: There are no adequate reports or well-controlled studies in nursing women. It is unknown whether cytarabine enters human breast milk.

Potential drug interactions: Cytarabine may decrease the effectiveness of gentamicin for certain *Klebsiella pneumoniae* strains. May reduce fluorocytosine efficacy.

What the FDA says about use in pregnancy: Category D (see Appendix).

What the available evidence suggests about breast-feeding safety: Unknown.

The bottom line for you:

- Cytarabine is at least a modest human teratogen (substance that can cause birth defects), which suggests that therapy should be delayed if possible during fetal organ formation. However, cytarabine should not be delayed when it is needed to treat severe maternal disease after the first 11–12 weeks of pregnancy.

- It is not known whether cytarabine is safe for use while breast-feeding.

DACARBAZINE

Brand name: DTIC-Dome

Drug class: Antineoplastic, alkylating agent

Indications (what it is used for): Melanoma, Hodgkin's disease.

How it works: Primary action appears to be alkylation of nucleic acids (damage to the cancer cells' DNA).

Contraindications (reasons you shouldn't take it): Hypersensitivity to drug or class.

Possible side effects and warnings: Can cause low white blood cell or platelet counts, hair loss, loss of appetite, nausea and vomiting, liver toxicity, diarrhea, fever, muscle aches, liver or kidney dysfunction, and sensitivity to light. Should be used with caution in women with liver or kidney dysfunction.

How it can affect pregnant women: There are no adequate reports or well-controlled studies in pregnant women. Treatment during pregnancy is typically reserved for life-threatening disease. There are many reports of dacarbazine use during pregnancy with a good outcome.

How it can affect a developing embryo or fetus: There are no adequate reports or well-controlled studies in human fetuses. It is unknown whether dacarbazine crosses the human placenta. No increase in birth defects has been reported in human fetuses, although the experience is relatively small.

Long-term follow-up studies of children exposed in utero in the first trimester are reassuring.

Breast-feeding: There are no adequate reports or well-controlled studies in nursing women. It is unknown whether dacarbazine enters human breast milk.

Potential drug interactions: No clinically significant drug interactions have been identified.

What the FDA says about use in pregnancy: Category C (see Appendix).

What the available evidence suggests about breast-feeding safety: Unknown.

The bottom line for you:

- Dacarbazine may be used during pregnancy and considered while breast-feeding when treatment is needed for life-threatening melanoma or Hodgkin's disease.

DACLIZUMAB

Brand name: Zenapax

Drug classes: Immunosuppressant; Monoclonal antibody

Indications (what it is used for): To prevent rejection of transplanted kidney.

How it works: Blocks the IL-2 receptor, which is involved in rejection.

Contraindications (reasons you shouldn't take it): Hypersensitivity to drug or class.

Possible side effects and warnings: Can cause pulmonary edema (fluid in the lungs), renal tubular necrosis, nausea, vomiting, diarrhea, constipation, abdominal or chest pain, heartburn, tremor, headache, edema, dizziness, burning during urination, shortness of breath, fever, acne, and cough.

How it can affect pregnant women: There is no published data in pregnant women. Perhaps because of the lack of study, the FDA recommends that women who could become pregnant use contraception during therapy and for at least 4 months after completion of therapy.

How it can affect a developing embryo or fetus: There are no adequate reports or well-controlled studies in human fetuses. It is unknown whether daclizumab crosses the human placenta, though IgG (immunoglobulin G) class molecules do cross. No birth defects have been reported in human fetuses exposed to daclizumab, but its use is uncommon and there have been no animal studies investigating its effects on the fetus.

Breast-feeding: There are no published reports in nursing mothers. It is unknown whether daclizumab enters human breast milk. Considering that the drug is destroyed by stomach acid, it seems unlikely to pose a major risk to the breast-fed newborn.

Potential drug interactions: Interaction between the following medications and daclizumab has the potential to impact the effect of one or more of the drugs. In some instances the interaction can be dangerous or life-threatening and must be avoided: cyclosporine, mycophenolate mofetil, corticosteroids, antilymphocyte antibody therapy.

What the FDA says about use in pregnancy: Category C (see Appendix).

What the available evidence suggests about breast-feeding safety: Unknown.

The bottom line for you:

- Daclizumab should be used during pregnancy and breast-feeding only when needed to preserve the mother's transplanted organ.
- The FDA recommends that women who could become pregnant use contraception during therapy and for at least 4 months afterward.
- Although there is inadequate study to state with certainty, the available information suggests that the risk of daclizumab to a breast-fed baby is small.

DACTINOMYCIN

Brand name: Cosmegen

Drug class: Antineoplastic, antibiotic

Indications (what it is used for): Gestational trophoblastic disease (GTN; tumors that develop from placental tissue), Wilms' tumor (a type of cancer of the kidney), uterine carcinoma, Ewing's sarcoma (malignant bone tumor).

How it works: Inhibits RNA and protein synthesis so cells cannot grow.

Contraindications (reasons you shouldn't take it): Hypersensitivity to drug or class, herpes zoster, varicella (chickenpox) infection.

Possible side effects and warnings: Can cause aplastic anemia, low platelet and/or white blood cell counts, flushing, hair loss, acute folliculitis (rash caused by inflammation of hair follicles), nausea, vomiting, fever, lethargy, abdominal pain, muscle aches, loss of appetite, liver damage, gastrointestinal ulceration, pharyngitis, and stomatitis (inflammation of the mucous linings of the mouth). Should be used with caution in women with liver or kidney dysfunction.

How it can affect pregnant women: There are no adequate reports or well-controlled studies of dactinomycin in pregnant women. Dactinomycin is typically given to nonpregnant women who have a malignancy. There appears to be little if any impact on future fertility based on the experience of women treated for germ cell ovarian cancer. It is used during pregnancy only for newly diagnosed malignant disease, and the earliest reported use is at 15 weeks. There were no associated adverse outcomes.

How it can affect a developing embryo or fetus: There are no adequate reports or well-controlled studies in human fetuses. It is unknown whether dactinomycin crosses the human placenta. No birth defects have been reported in humans, although no first-trimester exposures are reported. Rodent studies do provide evidence it can cause birth defects and harm embryos. However, animal studies are not necessarily good indicators of how a drug will behave in humans.

Breast-feeding: There is no published data in nursing women. It is unknown whether dactinomycin enters human breast milk. It is generally considered incompatible with breast-feeding until studies are able to demonstrate its safety.

Potential drug interactions: Dactinomycin may interfere with procedures used to determine antibacterial drug levels.

What the FDA says about use in pregnancy: Category D (see Appendix).

What the available evidence suggests about breast-feeding safety: Unknown.

The bottom line for you:

- Dactinomycin should be used during pregnancy only to treat life-threatening maternal disease.
- Until here is new information, breast-feeding should be avoided during treatment with dactinomycin.

DALTEPARIN

Brand name: Fragmin

Drug class: Anticoagulant; Low-molecular-weight heparin

Indications (what it is used for): Prevention and treatment of deep vein thrombosis (blood clot in a vein), unstable angina (chest pain caused by poor blood flow).

How it works: Inhibits clot formation.

Contraindications (reasons you shouldn't take it): Hypersensitivity to drug or class, active bleeding, low platelet count, use of epidural catheters, antibodies to drug, prosthetic heart valve, spinal puncture.

Possible side effects and warnings: Can cause bleeding, low platelet count, fever, itching, osteoporosis, easy bruising, nosebleeds, injection site reaction, and liver damage. Should be used with caution in women with diabetic retinopathy, liver or kidney dysfunction, recent surgery, pregnancy, gastrointestinal bleeding, or history of stroke.

How it can affect pregnant women: Dalteparin is a heparin (class of drugs that inhibit drug clotting) derivative that is injected once or twice daily to prevent or treat deep vein thrombosis. These agents are increasingly popular for the treatment of various disorders during pregnancy, although evidence for their superiority or effectiveness over the cheaper unfractionated heparin remains limited. The therapeutic dose of dalteparin is based on maternal weight and women vary widely in their requirements, as the drug passes through the body more rapidly during pregnancy. Because of the long effect on clotting, many obstetricians substitute the shorter-acting unfractionated heparin for dalteparin after 36 weeks of pregnancy. Otherwise, many anesthesiologists wait 12 hours before either placing an epidural catheter or reinitiating dalteparin to prevent hematoma formation.

How it can affect a developing embryo or fetus: Neither dalteparin nor unfractionated heparin crosses the placenta and therefore neither poses a threat to an embryo or fetus.

Breast-feeding: Only trace amounts of dalteparin enter human breast milk. It is highly unlikely that treatment would have any clinically relevant effect on a nursing infant.

Potential drug interactions: Dalteparin should be used with care in women receiving oral anticoagulants, platelet inhibitors, and thrombolytic agents because of increased risk of bleeding.

What the FDA says about use in pregnancy: Category B (see Appendix).

What the available evidence suggests about breast-feeding safety: Safe.

The bottom line for you:

- Dalteparin is safe for use during pregnancy and while breast-feeding.

DANAZOL

Brand names: Danocrine, Danatrol, Danogen, Danokrin, Ectopal, Zoldan-A

Drug class: Hormone, other gynecologic

Indications (what it is used for): Endometriosis (uterine tissue growing outside the uterus), fibrocystic breast disease, hereditary angioedema (swelling underneath the skin).

How it works: Alters communication between the pituitary and ovary.

Contraindications (reasons you shouldn't take it): Hypersensitivity to drug or class, undiagnosed genital bleeding, porphyria (a rare group of blood disorders), pregnancy, breast-feeding.

Possible side effects and warnings: Can cause altered lipid levels, contraceptive failure, pseudotumor cerebri (increased pressure in the brain unrelated to a tumor), weight gain, acne, edema, hair growth or loss, hoarseness, menstrual irregularities, flushing, sweating, vaginal dryness, decreased breast size, high blood pressure, anxiety, and thromboembolism (blood clot in a blood vessel). Should be used with caution in women with liver, kidney, or heart dysfunction, or with epilepsy or migraine.

How it can affect pregnant women: Danazol should not be used during pregnancy. It should be discontinued if you become pregnant. Danazol is not an effective contraceptive.

How it can affect a developing embryo or fetus: There are no adequate reports or well-controlled studies in human fetuses. It is unknown whether danazol crosses the human placenta. Although the FDA classifies danazol as category X, there is no reason to terminate a pregnancy when the fetus has been exposed to danazol without evidence of fetal damage. Rather, exposed fetuses should undergo a detailed ultrasound examination. Exposure to danazol after 8 weeks can promote the development of male sex characteristics in female fetuses, causing such abnormalities as a deformed vagina, an enlarged clitoris, labial fusion, and ambiguous genitalia. The latter three can be identified before 20 weeks with ultrasound.

Breast-feeding: There is no published data in nursing women. It is unknown whether danazol enters human breast milk. It should not be taken while breast-feeding.

Potential drug interactions: Prolongation of bleeding time occurs in women already on warfarin. Danazol may increase the effects of carbamazepine.

What the FDA says about use in pregnancy: Category X (see Appendix).

What the available evidence suggests about breast-feeding safety: Possibly unsafe.

The bottom line for you:
- There are no indications for danazol during pregnancy. A pregnancy test is recommended immediately prior to initiating therapy and effective contraception recommended during treatment.
- If a woman being treated with danazol becomes pregnant, she should undergo detailed ultrasound examination between 18 and 20 weeks to look for possible fetal abnormalities.
- Until there is new information, breast-feeding should be avoided during treatment with danazol.

DAPSONE

Brand names: Avlosulfon, Dapsoderm-X, Dapson
Drug class: Antimycobacterial
Indications (what it is used for): *Pneumocystis carinii* pneumonia (PCP), dermatitis, herpetiformis (chronic blistering of the skin), malaria suppression, leprosy (Hansen's disease).
How it works: Unknown; kills or slows the growth of bacteria.
Contraindications (reasons you shouldn't take it): Hypersensitivity to drug or class.
Possible side effects and warnings: Can cause hemolysis (breakdown of red blood cells), aplastic anemia, peripheral neuropathy (nerve damage causing numbness, tingling, or pain in the hands and feet), nausea, vomiting, abdominal pain, pancreatitis, dizziness, blurred vision, ringing in the ears, sleeplessness, fever, headache, fatigue, weakness, psychosis, kidney problems; exfoliative dermatitis, erythema multiforme and toxic epidermal necrolysis (skin disorders), light sensitivity, drug-induced lupuslike syndrome, and infectious mononucleosis–like syndrome. Should be used with caution in women with heart, liver, or kidney dysfunction, or G6PD deficiency.
How it can affect pregnant women: There are no adequate reports or well-controlled studies of dapsone in pregnant women. Either alone or in combination with pyrimethamine, trimethoprim-sulfamethoxazole, or pentamidine, dapsone is the regimen most commonly used to prevent potentially lethal PCP in immunocompromised women. When used to treat leprosy, it should be administered in combination with one or more antileprosy drugs to avoid resistance. Malaria is a significant risk during pregnancy. Dapsone should be considered for women with resistance to chloroquine and pyrimethaminesulfadoxine. Most reported adverse effects are associated with long-term use. A total of 924 pregnancies were identified during which the woman was treated with dapsone. Mild degrees of hemolysis consistently occurred in women who underwent continued therapy, although adverse effects were less likely with intermittent treatment.
How it can affect a developing embryo or fetus: There are no adequate reports or well-controlled studies in human fetuses. Transfer across the human placenta likely occurs, as there are reports of newborns having high levels of methemoglobinemia (an oxidized hemoglobin that does not release oxygen to the tissues) following dapsone exposure in the womb. Although very high methemoglobin levels could pose a risk to the fetus, harm has not been demonstrated; rather, dapsone use during pregnancy is associated with higher birth weights. Dapsone does not appear to cause birth defects in humans.
Breast-feeding: Enough dapsone is excreted into breast milk to cause hemolysis in newborns. In geographic locales where breast-feeding is essential, the infant should be monitored for hemolysis and breast-feeding should be stopped if hemolysis occurs.
Potential drug interactions: Interaction between the following medications and dapsone has the potential to impact the effect of one or more of the drugs. In some instances the interaction can be dangerous or life-threatening and must be avoided: rifampin, folic acid antagonists such as pyrimethamine.

What the FDA says about use in pregnancy: Category C (see Appendix).

What the available evidence suggests about breast-feeding safety: Possibly safe if under close monitoring by the child's physician.

The bottom line for you:

- Dapsone may be safe for use during pregnancy and while breast-feeding.
- Hemolysis in newborns is the most common adverse effect and they should be closely monitored for it.

DAUNORUBICIN

Brand names: Cerubidine, DaunoXome

Drug class: Antineoplastic, antibiotic

Indications (what it is used for): HIV-associated Kaposi's sarcoma (cancer that causes patches of abnormal tissue to grow under the skin), acute myeloid leukemia, acute lymphoblastic leukemia.

How it works: Inhibits the enzyme topoisomerase and binds DNA so that the cell cannot divide or produce the substances it needs to survive.

Contraindications (reasons you shouldn't take it): Hypersensitivity to drug or class.

Possible side effects and warnings: Can cause bone marrow suppression, liver and heart toxicity, hair loss, nausea, vomiting, diarrhea, back pain, flushing, chest tightness, and fever. Should be used with caution in women with liver, kidney, or heart dysfunction, or with myelosuppression.

How it can affect pregnant women: Daunorubicin is an antibiotic used to target solid tumors like Kaposi's sarcoma. It is also used in combination with other drugs for the treatment of breast cancer. There are no adequate reports or well-controlled studies of daunorubicin in pregnant women. There are, however, multiple case reports of its use during pregnancy with successful outcomes.

How it can affect a developing embryo or fetus: There are no adequate reports or well-controlled studies in human fetuses. Modest amounts of daunorubicin cross the human placenta. There are mul-

tiple reports of its use during pregnancy, including in the first trimester, with either no evidence of an adverse fetal effect or, on occasion, evidence only of bone marrow suppression (anemia, low platelet and white blood cell count). Although children are more sensitive than adults to daunorubicin-mediated heart damage, there are no such reports in exposed fetuses. Short-term follow-up of newborns exposed in the womb suggest normal development.

Breast-feeding: Clinically negligible amounts of daunorubicin are excreted into human breast milk.

Potential drug interactions: No clinically significant drug interactions have been identified.

What the FDA says about use in pregnancy: Category D (see Appendix).

What the available evidence suggests about breast-feeding safety: Likely safe.

The bottom line for you:

- Daunorubicin may be used during pregnancy and while breast-feeding for the treatment of life-threatening maternal disease with low risk to the fetus or newborn.

DELAVIRDINE

Brand name: Rescriptor

Drug classes: Nonnucleoside reverse transcriptase inhibitor (NNRTI); Retroviral

Indications (what it is used for): HIV.

How it works: NNRTI prevents the viral nucleic acid from directing the actions of the human nucleic acid.

Contraindications (reasons you shouldn't take it): Hypersensitivity to drug or class.

Possible side effects and warnings: Can cause skin rash (in up to 20% of patients), swelling under the skin, Stevens-Johnson syndrome (a rare but serious skin reaction to medication), anemia, gastrointestinal bleeding, pancreatitis, low platelet or white blood cell counts, fatigue, nausea, vomiting, diarrhea, abdominal pain, blood in the urine, dry skin, liver damage, flulike symptoms, slow heart rate, headache, anxiety, and edema (swelling).

How it can affect pregnant women: There are no adequate reports or well-controlled studies in pregnant women. Delavirdine may be beneficial as a part of salvage therapy (treatment when other therapies have failed) with protease inhibitors since it increases the blood levels of many of them.

How it can affect a developing embryo or fetus: There are no adequate reports or well-controlled studies in human fetuses. It is unknown whether delavirdine crosses the human placenta. In rodents, studies using doses higher than the recommended human dose found that delavirdine damages the embryo and causes holes in the heart wall, which, if large, can be life-threatening. However, animal studies are not necessarily good indicators of how a drug will behave in humans.

Breast-feeding: There is no published data in nursing women. It is unknown whether delavirdine enters human breast milk. If infant formula is available, breast-feeding is not recommended when a mother is HIV positive because HIV can be transmitted to the newborn in the breast milk.

Potential drug interactions: Delavirdine has numerous drug interactions; tell your health-care provider and pharmacist about all medications you are taking before starting delaviridine. Or, if you are on delaviridine, make sure all your providers and pharmacists know that before adding another medication. Delavirdine inhibits the breakdown of many drugs (e.g., antiarrhythmics, calcium channel blockers, sedative-hypnotics), and serious and/or life-threatening interactions may result. Further, some drugs reduce delavirdine levels, increasing the possibility of drug resistance.

What the FDA says about use in pregnancy: Category C (see Appendix).

What the available evidence suggests about breast-feeding safety: Unknown.

The bottom line for you:

- Delavirdine may be used during pregnancy if needed to treat HIV-positive women who have a positive viral load.
- If infant formula is available, breast-feeding is not recommended when a mother is HIV positive because HIV can be transmitted to the newborn in the breast milk.
- If you are being treated with delavirdine, talk to your physician about being registered with the Antiretroviral Pregnancy Registry (1-800-258-4263). Your participation helps increase the information available on delavirdine and pregnancy.

DEMECLOCYCLINE

Brand names: Bioterciclin, Clortetrin, Declomycin, Ledermycin

Drug classes: Antibiotic; Tetracyclic

Indications (what it is used for): Bacterial infection.

How it works: Slows growth of bacteria by inhibiting protein synthesis.

Contraindications (reasons you shouldn't take it): Hypersensitivity to drug or class, diabetes insipidus (lack of antidiuretic hormone).

Possible side effects and warnings: Can cause sensitivity to light, diabetes insipidus, pseudotumor cerebri (increased pressure in the brain unrelated to a tumor), low platelet count, hemolytic anemia, liver or kidney dysfunction, enterocolitis (inflammation of the colon), and vaginal yeast infection. Should be used with caution in women with liver or kidney dysfunction.

How it can affect pregnant women: There are no adequate reports or well-controlled studies of demeclocycline during pregnancy.

How it can affect a developing embryo or fetus: There are no adequate reports or well-controlled studies in human fetuses. It is unknown whether demeclocycline crosses the human placenta. Other related tetracycline drugs can cause a permanent discoloration of the child's teeth (yellow-gray/brown) when given during the latter half of pregnancy, or during childhood prior to 8 years of age.

Breast-feeding: There is no published data in nursing women. Although it is unknown whether demeclocycline enters human breast milk, other tetracyclines do cross. Based on the potential of its being excreted into breast milk and discoloring teeth, demeclocycline is generally considered incompatible with breast-feeding.

Potential drug interactions: Tetracyclines may depress prothrombin activity, necessitating a decrease in the dose of anticoagulants. They may interfere with the bactericidal action of penicillins and may render oral contraceptives less effective. Breakthrough bleeding has been reported.

What the FDA says about use in pregnancy: Category D (see Appendix).

What the available evidence suggests about breast-feeding safety: Avoid until more information becomes available.

The bottom line for you:

- There are alternative agents with greater experience during pregnancy and while breast-feeding that do not pose such risks to the fetus or newborn.

DESIPRAMINE

Brand names: Deprexan, Norpramin, Pertofrane
Drug classes: Antidepressant; Tricyclic (TCA)
Indications (what it is used for): Depression.
How it works: Unknown.
Contraindications (reasons you shouldn't take it): Hypersensitivity to drug or class, use of monoamine oxidase inhibitors (MAOIs) within 14 days, coronary artery disease.
Possible side effects and warnings: Can cause stroke, heart attack, irregular heartbeat, low platelet count, seizures, urinary retention, and glaucoma. Should be used with caution in women with heart disease, glaucoma, thyroid disease, or seizure disorder.
How it can affect pregnant women: Depression is common during and after pregnancy but often goes unrecognized and untreated. Depression can be made worse by pregnancy or delivery, and suicide is a not uncommon cause of maternal death. Pregnancy is not a reason to discontinue antidepressant drugs if the medication is effective and needed. A woman being treated for depression who becomes pregnant should not discontinue medication abruptly on her own but rather discuss her treatment and condition with her medical provider. Pregnancy may increase the dose needed to be effective, and women with a history of depression have a higher rate of recurrence after delivery.

Tricyclic antidepressants, which include desipramine, continue to be widely used during pregnancy, but they remain inadequately studied. There are no adequate reports or well-controlled studies of desipramine in pregnant women. Recent population based studies have revealed the use of tricyclic antidepressants may significantly increase the risk of preeclampsia by 2–3 times. Women vary greatly in how they metabolize TCAs during pregnancy, which means their physician needs to monitor them and adjust dosage when necessary.

How it can affect a developing embryo or fetus: There are no adequate reports or well-controlled studies in human fetuses. It is unknown whether desipramine crosses the human placenta. No evidence of birth defects was found in rhesus monkey fetuses exposed to imipramine (a related medication); however, there was a high incidence of maternal toxicity and miscarriage. There have been many studies of brain function in offspring exposed during pregnancy, but they have not yielded consistent results. However, animal studies are not necessarily good indicators of how a drug will behave in humans.

Breast-feeding: Limited experience suggests that desipramine is excreted in small quantities into human breast milk, but it does not reach detectable levels in breast-feeding newborns. No adverse effects have been reported. It is suggested that breast-fed newborns be watched closely for evidence of side effects.

Potential drug interactions: Desipramine has numerous drug interactions and it is imperative that your physician knows all the medications you are taking (including over-the-counter) before deciding to prescribe desipramine. Interaction between the following medications and desipramine has the potential to impact the effect of one or more of the drugs. In some instances the interaction can be dangerous or life-threatening and must be avoided: CYP2D6 inhibitors, including quinidine, cimetidine, other antidepressants, phenothiazines, the class IC antiarrhythmics propafenone and flecainide, all SSRIs (e.g., fluoxetine, sertraline, paroxetine), and anticholinergic or sympathomimetic drugs. The response to alcohol may be exaggerated while taking desipramine. Alcohol consumption is not recommended during pregnancy.

What the FDA says about use in pregnancy: No assigned category (see Appendix).

What the available evidence suggests about breast-feeding safety: Safe.

The bottom line for you:

- Tricyclic antidepressants such as desipramine are effective second-line therapies (i.e., when SSRIs are ineffective) for postpartum depression.
- Pregnancy is not a reason to discontinue psychotropic drugs when they are truly needed and providing a clear benefit.
- Desipramine is probably safe to use while breast-feeding, but it is suggested that newborns be watched closely for evidence of side effects.

DESMOPRESSIN

Brand names: DDAVP Desmopressin, Octim
Drug classes: Antidiuretic; Hormone
Indications (what it is used for): Diabetes insipidus (lack of antidiuretic hormone), von Willebrand disease and factor VIII deficiency (both hereditary bleeding disorders), bed-wetting.

How it works: A synthetic version of the naturally occurring hormone vasopressin, which controls the reabsorption of molecules in the tubules of the kidneys.

Contraindications (reasons you shouldn't take it): Hypersensitivity to drug or class, coronary artery disease, type IIB von Willebrand disease.

Possible side effects and warnings: Can cause low blood sodium levels, swelling of the brain, stuffy nose, flushing, abdominal pain, and blood clots. Should be used with caution in women who have an electrolyte imbalance.

How it can affect pregnant women: Desmopressin replaces the missing hormone in women with diabetes insipidus. It is effective treatment for women who develop temporary diabetes insipidus during late pregnancy and/or right after delivery. Desmopressin also triggers the release of a missing clotting protein complex, factor VIII, in women with some types of von Willebrand disease. It is given prior to surgery to maintain hemostasis (the ability for blood to clot and stop bleeding) during the procedure and immediately afterward. Desmopressin does not cause uterine contractions. The rate of postpartum hemorrhage is especially high in women with some types of von Willebrand disease up to 5 weeks after delivery, and desmopressin can help reduce that risk.

How it can affect a developing embryo or fetus: There are no adequate reports or well-controlled studies in human fetuses. There is no detectable transfer of desmopressin across the placenta at doses used clinically. No adverse fetal effects have been reported when desmopressin is used in pregnancy, and rodent studies are equally reassuring.

Breast-feeding: There are no adequate reports or well-controlled studies in nursing women. A single study found minimal levels of desmopressin in human breast milk after one nasal spray dose. Considering the dose and dosing frequency, it is unlikely that a significant quantity reaches a breast-feeding newborn. It has been used to treat diabetes insipidus during labor and delivery.

Potential drug interactions: Large doses of desmopressin may increase the response to other pressor agents.

What the FDA says about use in pregnancy: Category B (see Appendix).

What the available evidence suggests about breast-feeding safety: Safe.

The bottom line for you:

- Desmopressin is effective therapy during pregnancy or while breast-feeding for women with diabetes insipidus and some types of von Willebrand disease.

DEXAMETHASONE

Brand names: Aeroseb-Dex, Corotason, Curson, Decaderm, Decadron, Decarex, Decaspray, Decofluor, Desigdron, Dexone, Dms, Hexadrol, Isopto, Lebedex, Lozusu, Maxidex, Millicorten, Mymethasone, Predni, Taidon

Drug class: Corticosteroid

Indications (what it is used for): Accelerating fetal lung maturity, adrenal insufficiency, inflammatory states, congenital adrenal hyperplasia (the fetus makes excess male hormones), allergic reactions, testing for Cushing's syndrome (high levels of cortisol and related compounds), cerebral edema (swelling of the brain), shock.

How it works: Unknown.

Contraindications (reasons you shouldn't take it): Hypersensitivity to drug or class, fungal infections, untreated infections (however, may be used in patients under treatment for tuberculous meningitis [infection of the meninges with tuberculosis]), and breast-feeding.

Possible side effects and warnings: Can cause immunosuppression (leaving you more susceptible to infections), pancreatitis, fluid retention, heart failure, pseudotumor cerebri (increased pressure in the brain unrelated to a tumor), myositis (inflammation of skeletal muscles), Cushing's syndrome, decreased carbohydrate tolerance, osteoporosis, liver dysfunction, blood clots, sleeplessness, and anxiety. Should be used with caution in women with seizure disorder, diabetes, high blood pressure, osteoporosis, or liver dysfunction.

How it can affect pregnant women: Dexamethasone is widely used during pregnancy to accelerate

fetal lung maturity when the pregnancy is at high risk for preterm delivery (before 37 weeks). Most large studies conclude that the risk of infection in women after premature preterm rupture of membranes (PPROM, water breaking before 37 weeks) is not increased by dexamethasone. It may cause a temporary abnormal glucose tolerance test and will worsen diabetes mellitus. Large doses, such as those given to help fetal lungs mature, are associated with an increased risk for pulmonary edema (fluid in the lungs) in the mother, especially when combined with a tocolytic agent (a drug to delay or stop preterm labor) and the mother has an underlying infection. It is also given to women with severe preeclampsia (high blood pressure and protein in the urine during pregnancy and complications associated with it) who require preterm delivery. Women treated longer than a few days should be monitored closely for high blood pressure or glucose intolerance, and must be given higher, "stress," doses of the medication during labor and after delivery. Dexamethasone is an effective treatment for nausea after general anesthesia for pregnancy termination. It may also reduce itching in women with cholestasis of pregnancy (a severe, itchy rash due to the backup of bile in the liver, most commonly occurs in the third trimester).

How it can affect a developing embryo or fetus: Corticosteroids such as dexamethasone are used to improve the health and survival of a baby born preterm and shorten hospitalization by helping to speed the maturation of the lungs and bowel. Dexamethasone readily crosses the human placenta unmetabolized, exposing the fetus to the potent parent compound. One study concluded that children subjected to multiple doses of dexamethasone to enhance lung maturity were more likely to develop brain and neurodevelopmental abnormalities by age 2. However, this result was not confirmed by subsequent study. Low amniotic fluid volume may follow extensive use and women treated for more than a week during pregnancy should be monitored for low amniotic fluid levels. Dexamethasone has also been used to treat fetal heart rhythm abnormalities associated with maternal autoimmune diseases such as lupus erythematosus (a chronic inflammatory disease in which the immune system attacks the body's own tissues and organs). Infants of women treated for more than a week immediately prior to delivery should be carefully observed for signs of hypoadrenalism (inadequate steroid production). Dexamethasone can prevent or reduce masculinization of a female fetus affected by congenital adrenal hyperplasia if begun by 6–7 weeks. The drug is continued until a definitive fetal diagnosis of gender is made by DNA analysis of chorionic villi or amniocytes at 11–15 weeks.

The evidence overall is that corticosteroids may be a weak teratogen (a substance that can cause birth defects) when taken in the first trimester. The most recent meta-analysis concluded that there was a small but real increase in the risk of cleft lip or palate after first-trimester exposure to prednisone. There is no increased risk of anomalies when steroids are begun after organ formation (after 11 weeks). Women exposed to topical cortisone during pregnancy experience no increase in birth defects. A few small studies suggested a possible relationship between long-term steroid use during pregnancy and poor fetal growth; however, it is hard to tell if that was the result of the medication or the disease it was being used to treat.

Breast-feeding: There are no adequate reports or well-controlled studies in breast-feeding women. Dexamethasone is excreted into human breast milk, but the impact on the newborn is unknown. Other corticosteroids are generally considered safe for breast-feeding. Dexamethasone given to enhance fetal lung maturity is unlikely to have a clinically relevant effect on a breast-feeding newborn.

Potential drug interactions: Interaction between the following medications and dexamethasone has the potential to impact the effect of one or more of the drugs. In some instances the interaction can be dangerous or life-threatening and must be avoided: macrolide antibiotics, anticholinesterase agents, warfarin, isoniazid, cholestyramine, cyclosporine, CYP3A4 inducers (e.g., barbiturates, phenytoin, carbamazepine, rifampin), CYP3A4 inhibitors (e.g., ketoconazole, erythromycin), other drugs metabolized by CYP3A4 (e.g., indinavir, erythromycin), aspirin and other nonsteroidal anti-inflammatory drugs (NSAIDs).

What the FDA says about use in pregnancy: Category C (see Appendix).

What the available evidence suggests about breast-feeding safety: Unknown.

The bottom line for you:

- Dexamethasone is effective for the reduction of severe complications of preterm birth.
- There is some evidence that first-trimester exposure or chronic therapy in a pregnant woman can present certain risks to the fetus. A detailed ultrasound and a consultation with a perinatologist is advised.
- Other corticosteroids are generally considered safe to use while breast-feeding. There is no specific information on dexamethasone.

DEXCHLORPHENIRAMINE

Brand names: Dexchlor, Dex-Cpm, Mylaramine, Polaramine

Drug classes: Antihistamine, H1; Decongestant

Indications (what it is used for): Allergic rhinitis (stuffy, runny nose due to allergies), anaphylaxis (life-threatening allergic reaction).

How it works: Blocks central and peripheral H1 receptors, whose activation causes the symptoms.

Contraindications (reasons you shouldn't take it): Hypersensitivity to drug or class.

Possible side effects and warnings: Can cause low blood pressure, dry mouth, nausea, vomiting, and constipation. Should be used with caution in women with a bowel obstruction or who are taking sedative medications.

How it can affect pregnant women: Dexchlorpheniramine is the active metabolite of chlorpheniramine. There are no adequate reports or well-controlled studies in pregnant women, and its safety during pregnancy is not established. However, chlorpheniramine is widely available in over-the-counter preparations and has not been implicated in adverse effects during pregnancy.

How it can affect a developing embryo or fetus: There are no adequate reports or well-controlled studies in human fetuses, and it is unknown whether dexchlorpheniramine crosses the human placenta. However, large follow-up studies of women who have taken dexchlorpheniramine suggest that it does not cause birth defects. Rodent studies are generally reassuring despite the use of doses higher than those used clinically. However, animal studies are not necessarily good indicators of how a drug will behave in humans.

Breast-feeding: There are no adequate reports or well-controlled studies in nursing women. It is unknown whether dexchlorpheniramine enters human breast milk. There are no reports of adverse effects on breast-feeding newborns despite widespread use of the medication.

Potential drug interactions: May cause severe low blood pressure when given in conjunction with a monoamine oxidase inhibitor (MAOI). Sedative effects are increased by alcohol and other sedative drugs. The action of oral anticoagulants may be inhibited by antihistamines.

What the FDA says about use in pregnancy: Category B (see Appendix).

What the available evidence suggests about breast-feeding safety: Unknown, but likely safe.

The bottom line for you:

- Dexchlorpheniramine may be used with relative safety during pregnancy.
- Small, occasional doses of dexchlorpheniramine are not likely to cause any adverse effects in breast-fed infants. Larger doses or more prolonged use might cause effects in the infant or decrease the milk supply, particularly in combination with pseudoephedrine or before breast-feeding is well established. A single bedtime dose after the last feeding may be adequate for many and minimize any effects of the drug.

DEXMETHYLPHENIDATE

Brand name: Focalin

Drug class: Central nervous system stimulant

Indications (what it is used for): Attention deficit disorder.

How it works: Unknown; stimulates the brain.

Contraindications (reasons you shouldn't take it): Hypersensitivity to drug or class, history of severe anxiety, glaucoma, motor tics, monoamine oxidase inhibitor (MAOI) use within 14 days.

Possible side effects and warnings: Can cause seizures, dependency, irregular heart rate, angina, palpitations, low platelet or white blood cell counts, nervousness, sleeplessness, abdominal pain, headache, dizziness, blurred vision, loss of appetite, weight loss, and rash. Should be used with caution in women with cardiovascular disease, high blood pressure, seizure disorder, psychosis, substance abuse, or hyperthyroidism.

How it can affect pregnant women: There are no published reports of dexmethylphenidate use during pregnancy.

How it can affect a developing embryo or fetus: There are no adequate reports or well-controlled studies in human fetuses. It is unknown whether dexmethylphenidate crosses the human placenta. There is concern that exposure in the womb could lead to behavioral abnormalities based on rodent and human study of related drugs (amphetamine and methamphetamine).

Breast-feeding: There is no published data in nursing women. It is unknown whether dexmethylphenidate enters human breast milk.

Potential drug interactions: Interaction between the following medications and dexmethylphenidate has the potential to impact the effect of one or more of the drugs. In some instances the interaction can be dangerous or life-threatening and must be avoided: drugs used to treat high blood pressure, oral anticoagulants, anticonvulsants (e.g., pheno-barbital, phenytoin, primidone), antidepressants, clonidine. Should not be used within 2 weeks of taking a monoamine oxidase inhibitor (MAOI).

What the FDA says about use in pregnancy: Category C (see Appendix).

What the available evidence suggests about breast-feeding safety: Unknown; likely safe if used cautiously.

The bottom line for you:

- Most patients with attention deficit disorder can avoid treatment during at least the first trimester. For those who are truly debilitated, dexmethylphenidate is a therapeutic option during pregnancy and while breast-feeding.

DEXTROAMPHETAMINE

Brand names: Amphaetex, Das, Dexampex, Dexedrina, Dexedrine, Dextrostat, Ferndex, Oxydess, Spancap No. 1

Drug classes: Adrenergic agonist; Amphetamine; Central nervous system stimulant

Indications (what it is used for): Attention-deficit/hyperactivity disorder, narcolepsy, obesity.

How it works: Unknown; stimulates the brain.

Contraindications (reasons you shouldn't take it): Hypersensitivity to drug or class, high blood pressure, glaucoma, hyperthyroidism, Tourette's syndrome (involuntary movements and vocalizations).

Possible side effects and warnings: Can cause irregular heart rate, palpitation, sleeplessness, irritability, dry mouth, diarrhea, tremor, loss of appetite, and personality changes. Should be avoided in women with uncontrolled hypertension and used with caution in women with mild high blood pressure.

How it can affect pregnant women: There are no adequate reports or well-controlled studies of dextroamphetamine in pregnant women. There are case reports of its use for the treatment of narcolepsy (sudden attacks of sleep) during pregnancy. Since amphetamines are used to decrease appetite, its use during pregnancy should be discouraged.

How it can affect a developing embryo or fetus: There are no adequate reports or well-controlled studies in human fetuses. Amphetamines cross the human placenta. One report describes a tracheo-esophageal fistula (part of the trachea and esophagus are joined), and anal atresia (a missing anus) in the newborn of a mother who took dextroamphetamine throughout the first trimester. Epidemiologic study reveals that birth weight is unaffected if the drug is stopped prior to 28 weeks of pregnancy but is significantly lower if the drug is continued.

Breast-feeding: Amphetamines are excreted in human breast milk and are generally considered best to avoid while breast-feeding.

Potential drug interactions: Interaction between the following medications or substances and dextroamphetamine has the potential to impact the effect of one or more of the drugs. In some instances the interaction can be dangerous or life-threatening and must be avoided: medications that alter acidity in the stomach or of the urine (including guanethidine, reserpine, ascorbic acid, fruit juices, ammonium chloride, sodium acid phosphate, sodium bicarbonate, acetazolamide, and some thiazides), desipramine, protriptyline, other tricyclic antidepressants (TCAs), monoamine oxidase inhibitors (MAOIs), metabolite of furazolidone, meperidine, propoxyphene.

What the FDA says about use in pregnancy: Category C (see Appendix).

What the available evidence suggests about breast-feeding safety: Use with caution.

The bottom line for you:

- Except for perhaps narcolepsy, there are no indications for dextroamphetamine during pregnancy and while breast-feeding that would prevent a pregnant woman from temporarily stopping use of the medication to eliminate any possible harm to the fetus or breast-feeding baby.

DEXTROMETHORPHAN

Brand names: Aquabid-Dm, Biophen-Dm, Bio-Tuss Dm, Broncot, Dectuss DM, Equi-Tuss Dm,

Fenex Dm, Gani-Tuss-Dm Nr, Genophen-Dm Elixir, Guaibid Dm, Guiadrine Dm, Guaifenesin Dm, Guaifenesin W/Dextromethorphan, Humibid DM, Iodur-Dm, Iofen-Dm Nf, Iogan-Dm, Iophen D-C, Iophen-DM, Io Tuss-Dm, Iotuss-Dm, Mucobid Dm, Muco-Fen-Dm, Myodine Dm, Numobid Dx, Oridol Dm, Pancof-HC, Phenergan w/Dextromethorphan, Phen-Tuss DM, Pherazine DM, Promethazine w/DM, Prothazine, Q-Mibid-Dm, RobafenDm, Roganidin-Dm, Sil-O-Tuss Dm, Sudal-DM, Tosmar Dm, Tri-Onex Dm, Tusnel, Tusside, Tussidin Dm, Tussidin Dm Nr, Tussin Dm, Tussi-Organidin DM, Tussi-Organidin DM NR, Tussi-Organidin DM-S NR, Tussi-R-Gen Dm, Tusso-DM

Drug classes: Antitussive; Expectorant

Indications (what it is used for): Cough.

How it works: Suppression of the cough center.

Contraindications (reasons you shouldn't take it): Hypersensitivity to drug or class, use of monoamine oxidase inhibitors (MAOIs) within 14 days.

Possible side effects and warnings: Can lead to abuse or cause serotonin syndrome (drug reaction causing excessive levels of serotonin in the blood), sedation, dizziness, and abdominal pain. Should be used with caution in women taking serotonergic drugs.

How it can affect pregnant women: There are no adequate reports or well-controlled studies of dextromethorphan in pregnant women. It is found in many over-the-counter preparations, often with a decongestant, and no adverse pregnancy outcomes have been reported with its appropriate use.

How it can affect a developing embryo or fetus: There are no adequate reports or well-controlled studies in human fetuses. It is unknown whether dextromethorphan crosses the human placenta. The wide and long-term clinical experience suggests that any fetal risk of dextromethorphan-containing cough preparations is small when used as recommended. Rodent studies are reassuring.

Breast-feeding: There are no adequate reports or well-controlled studies in nursing women. It is un-known whether dextromethorphan enters human breast milk. However, the wide and long-term clinical experience suggests that any risk to a breast-feeding newborn is small.

Potential drug interactions: No clinically relevant drug interactions are currently identified.

What the FDA says about use in pregnancy: Category C (see Appendix).

What the available evidence suggests about breast-feeding safety: Safe.

The bottom line for you:

- Dextromethorphan may be used with minimal risk during pregnancy and while breast-feeding.

DIATRIZOATE

Brand names: Amidotrizoate, Angiovist 282, Berlex, Bolus Infusion Set, Burron Infusion Set, Cystografin, Cystografin Dilute, Cystografin Dilute w/Set, Hypaque, Hypaque-Cysto, Hypaque-Cysto 100Ml/300Ml, Hypaque-Cysto 250Ml/500Ml, Hypaque Meglumine, Reno-M-30, Reno-M-60, Reno-M-Dip, Urovist Cysto, Urovist Cysto 100Ml in 300Ml, Urovist Cysto 300Ml in 500Ml, Urovist Cysto Pediatric, Urovist Meglumine, Urovist Meglumine DIU/CT

Drug class: Diagnostic, nonradioactive

Indications (what it is used for): Retrograde cysto-urethrography (diatrizoate is injected into the bladder or fallopian tubes so they can be seen during X-rays or CT scans).

How it works: Radiographic contrast agent, shows up as a bright color on an imaging test to illuminate certain parts of the anatomy and show any abnormalities.

Contraindications (reasons you shouldn't take it): Hypersensitivity to drug or class.

Possible side effects and warnings: Can cause hematuria (red blood cells in the urine), retrograde infection, kidney failure, hypersensitivity, and life-threatening allergic reaction. Should be used with caution in women who have a sensitivity to iodine or a urinary tract infection.

How it can affect pregnant women: There are no adequate reports or well-controlled studies of diatrizoate in pregnant women. Diatrizoate is a contrast agent frequently used to study bladder structure or function and to check for obstructions in the fallopian tubes. In the past, it was used for a variety of fetal-imaging studies.

How it can affect a developing embryo or fetus: There are no adequate reports or well-controlled studies in human fetuses. It is unknown whether diatrizoate crosses the human placenta. After preterm delivery, diatrizoate is used to diagnose any intestinal problems in the newborn.

Breast-feeding: A single report suggests that a small amount of diatrizoate may be excreted into human breast milk. However, considering the indication and dosing, one-time diatrizoate use is unlikely to pose a clinically significant risk to a breast-feeding newborn.

Possible Potential drug interactions: No clinically significant interactions are currently identified.

What the FDA says about use in pregnancy: Category C (see Appendix).

What the available evidence suggests about breast-feeding safety: Likely safe.

The bottom line for you:

● Diatrizoate should be used during pregnancy and breast-feeding only if the benefit to the woman justifies the potential risk to the embryo, fetus, or newborn.

DIAZEPAM

Brand names: Alupram, Anlin, Baogin, Britazepam, Centrazepam, Chuansuan, Desloneg, Diastat, Diatran, Dizac, Euphorin, Evacalm, Jinpanfan, Mandro, Meval, Nellium, Nerozen, Nixtensyn, Notense, Parzam, Pomin, Rival, Tensium, Tranquil, Valitran, Valium, Valrelease, Winii, Zepaxid

Drug classes: Anxiolytic; Benzodiazepine; Muscle relaxant

Indications (what it is used for): Anxiety, alcohol withdrawal, seizure disorder, status epilepticus (constant or near-constant seizures), muscle spasm.

How it works: Binds benzodiazepine and possibly GABA receptors centrally.

Contraindications (reasons you shouldn't take it): Hypersensitivity to drug or class, glaucoma, central nervous system depression, shock, coma, and barbiturate or alcohol use.

Possible side effects and warnings: Can cause severe burning and vascular irritation, withdrawal syndrome if stopped abruptly, liver toxicity, low blood counts, low blood pressure, nausea, vomiting, vertigo, blurred vision, and rash. Should be used with caution in women with kidney, liver, or lung dysfunction, or with psychosis.

How it can affect pregnant women: There are no adequate reports or well-controlled studies of diazepam in pregnant women. It is a beneficial addition to IV fluids and vitamins for the treatment of first-trimester hyperemesis gravidarum (severe morning sickness leading to dehydration and malnourishment). Diazepam is less effective than magnesium sulfate for the prevention and treatment of eclamptic convulsions (convulsions related to severe pre-eclampsia). Sometimes pregnancy brings out chorea (tics) in women who are predisposed to them, and benzodiazepines may aid chorea control. Diazepam is also used to lower anxiety in women undergoing surgical procedures.

How it can affect a developing embryo or fetus: There are no adequate reports or well-controlled studies in human fetuses. Diazepam rapidly crosses the human placenta, achieving a level equal to that of the mother within 15 minutes and exceeding it within several hours of administration. Several studies have suggested an increased risk of fetal malformation with use in the first trimester, but they were not confirmed by more comprehensive studies. Postnatal follow-up of exposed children up to 4 years is likewise reassuring, revealing no adverse effects on brain development. Decreased fetal movement frequently accompanies intravenous administration, and prolonged central nervous system depression may occur in newborns who were exposed to it in the womb, apparently due to their inability to metabolize diazepam. They may also display floppy infant syndrome (a laxness to muscles when lying down) or marked withdrawal symptoms such as mild sedation, low muscle tone, reluctance to suck, apnea (pauses in breathing), cyanosis (blue-tinged skin due to low oxygen levels), and impaired responses to cold stress. These symptoms are treatable but may persist for hours to months after birth and should be monitored. In general, the shortest course and lowest dose are recommended during pregnancy.

Breast-feeding: Diazepam is excreted into human breast milk to a limited degree. The maximum newborn exposure is estimated to be 3% of the maternal dose. Problems may arise in preterm infants or if the maternal dose is particularly high.

Potential drug interactions: Interaction between the following medications and diazepam has the potential to impact the effect of one or more of the drugs. In some instances the interaction can be dangerous or life-threatening and must be avoided: phenothiazines, narcotics, barbiturates, MAOIs, and other antidepressants; valproate; potential inhibitors of CYP2CI9 (e.g., cimetidine, quinidine, tranylcypromine) and CYP3A4 (e.g., ketoconazole, troleandomycin, clotrimazole); inducers of CYP2CI9 (e.g., rifampin) and CYP3A4 (e.g., carbamazepine, phenytoin, dexamethasone, phenobarbital); CYP2CI9 substrates (e.g., omeprazole, propranolol, imipramine); CYP3A4 substrates (e.g., cyclosporine, paclitaxel, terfenadine, theophylline, warfarin).

What the FDA says about use in pregnancy: Category D (see Appendix).

What the available evidence suggests about breast-feeding safety: Likely safe.

The bottom line for you:

- Many of the indications for diazepam during pregnancy and while breast-feeding have alternative agents that are considered to have a higher safety margin.

- However, there appears little risk for its use during limited procedures to enhance maternal comfort. Such use will have no impact on breast-feeding.

DIAZOXIDE

Brand names: Hyperstat, Proglycem

Drug classes: Antihypertensive; Antihypoglycemic

Indications (what it is used for): High blood pressure.

How it works: Directly relaxes peripheral arteriole smooth muscle.

Contraindications (reasons you shouldn't take it): Hypersensitivity to drug or class, sulfonamides or thiazide diuretics.

Possible side effects and warnings: Can cause irregular heartbeat, seizures, heart attack, high blood sugar, weakness, low blood pressure, nausea, vomiting, and congestive heart failure. Should be used with caution in women with coronary artery disease.

How it can affect pregnant women: Treating high blood pressure during pregnancy requires a careful balance between maintaining maternal health and avoiding potential harmful side effects to the fetus from treatment. Diazoxide has been used for the treatment of severe high blood pressure during pregnancy but is also associated with a high risk of low blood pressure and the fetal distress that results from poor placental blood flow. Smaller, more frequent dosing reduces that risk, but there are many alternatives, including labetalol, nifedipine, ketanserin, hydralazine, and nitroprusside, which appear to be equally effective with lower complication rates.

How it can affect a developing embryo or fetus: There are no adequate reports or well-controlled studies in human fetuses. Diazoxide crosses the human placenta but is not known to adversely affect the fetus if placental blood flow is not affected. Rodent studies are generally reassuring, with no increase in birth defects or low birth weight. However, animal studies are not necessarily good indicators of how a drug will behave in humans.

Breast-feeding: There is no published data in nursing women. It is unknown whether diazoxide enters human breast milk.

Potential drug interactions: Interaction between the following medications and diazoxide has the potential to impact the effect of one or more of the drugs. In some instances the interaction can be dangerous or life-threatening and must be avoided: bilirubin; warfarin; thiazides and other diuretics; other blood-pressure-lowering medications such as hydralazine, reserpine, methyldopa, beta-blockers, prazosin, minoxidil, nitrites, and other papaverinelike compounds.

What the FDA says about use in pregnancy: Category C (see Appendix).

What the available evidence suggests about breast-feeding safety: Unknown.

The bottom line for you:

- There are many alternatives (e.g., labetalol, nifedipine, ketanserin) for the treatment of chronic and acute high blood pressure during pregnancy that are equally effective but less likely to cause dangerously low blood pressure in the mother (which can threaten fetal health).
- There is not enough information to conclude that diazoxide is either safe or unsafe to use during breast-feeding. Considering its clinical uses during pregnancy, exposure during delivery should not pose a risk to the breast-feeding newborn.

DICLOFENAC

Brand names: Berifen Gel, Blesin, Cataflam, Clofen, Diclofenac Sodium, Oritaren, Silino, Voltaren

Drug class: Analgesic, nonnarcotic; Nonsteroidal anti-inflammatory drug (NSAID); Ophthalmic

Indications (what it is used for): Dysmenorrhea (severe menstrual pain), mild to moderate pain, rheumatoid arthritis or osteoarthritis, ankylosing spondylitis (inflammation of joints in the spine).

How it works: Inhibits the synthesis of prostaglandins, substances related to inflammation.

Contraindications (reasons you shouldn't take it): Hypersensitivity to drug or class, NSAID-induced asthma, nasal polyps, gastrointestinal bleeding.

Possible side effects and warnings: Can cause life-threatening allergic reaction, bleeding, bronchospasm, low platelet count, Stevens-Johnson syndrome (a rare but serious skin reaction to medication), impaired liver or kidney function, abdominal pain, itching, drowsiness, and ringing in the ears. Should be used with caution in women with high blood pressure, nasal polyps, or congestive heart failure, or with a history of gastrointestinal bleeding.

How it can affect pregnant women: There are no adequate reports or well-controlled studies in pregnant women. Diclofenac is a short-acting NSAID that can lower fever, reduce inflammation, and lessen pain. Its pain-relieving properties are similar to other NSAIDs. It is useful during pregnancy for arthritic pain and after delivery for pain related to episiotomy or C-section. Like other NSAIDs, diclofenac alters kidney function and can increase the toxicity of certain drugs, such as digoxin. Diclofenac does not interfere with cervical ripening induced by misoprostol. It is sometimes used for pain relief during egg collection in women undergoing in vitro fertilization (IVF), and does affect implantation or pregnancy rates. It should not be used to prevent preterm birth.

How it can affect a developing embryo or fetus: There are no adequate reports or well-controlled studies in human fetuses. Diclofenac rapidly crosses the human placenta even in the first trimester, reaching the same concentration in the fetus as it does in the mother. Other NSAIDs have been associated with gastroschisis (a condition treated by surgery in which the fetus's intestines protrude through a hole in the abdominal wall) when used in the first trimester. When used in the third trimester, diclofenac, like most NSAIDs, is associated with narrowing or (rarely) closure of the ductus arteriosus, a critical fetal blood vessel directing blood away from the lung. Its closure leads to tricuspid valve incompetence (leaky valve between the right atrium and right ventricle), heart failure, and high blood pressure in the lungs, all of which could cause long-term damage. Stopping the drug appears to reverse this process. It is best to avoid repeated dosing of NSAIDs after 32 weeks. Rodent studies are generally reassuring, having found no evidence of birth defects or low birth weight. However, animal studies are not necessarily good indicators of how a drug will behave in humans.

Breast-feeding: There are no adequate reports or well-controlled studies of diclofenac in nursing women. Most NSAIDs enter human breast milk to some extent. The chemical structure and preliminary study suggest that any passage will be low and that occasional use is without clinically significant risk. However, ibuprofen is generally preferred for breast-feeding women.

Potential drug interactions: Interaction between the following medications and diclofenac has the potential to impact the effect of one or more of the drugs. In some instances the interaction can be dangerous or life-threatening and must be avoided: aspirin, cyclosporine, ACE inhibitors, lithium, coumarins.

What the FDA says about use in pregnancy: Category C (see Appendix).

What the available evidence suggests about breast-feeding safety: Likely safe.

The bottom line for you:
- There are alternative agents with which there is more experience during pregnancy and while breast-feeding.
- However, diclofenac is reasonably safe for use during pregnancy in the second and third trimesters and while breast-feeding as a short-term analgesic.
- It is wise to avoid diclofenac in the first trimester and sustained use should be avoided after 32 weeks.

DICLOXACILLIN

Brand names: Dacocillin, Dycill, Dynapen, Maclicine, Orbenin, Pathocil, Staphcillin

Drug classes: Antibiotic; Penicillin

Indications (what it is used for): Bacterial infections, osteomyelitis (infection of the bone), mastitis (infection in the tissue of the breast, common during breast-feeding).

How it works: Kills bacteria by inhibiting the synthesis of cell walls.

Contraindications (reasons you shouldn't take it): Hypersensitivity to drug or class.

Possible side effects and warnings: Can cause seizures, infection of the colon, anemia, low platelet or white blood cell counts, abdominal pain, nausea, vomiting, diarrhea, dizziness, fatigue, fever, and liver damage. Should be used with caution in women who are allergic to cephalosporin or who have kidney or liver dysfunction, Epstein-Barr virus (a virus of the herpes family), or cytomegalovirus infection.

How it can affect pregnant women: There are no adequate reports or well-controlled studies of dicloxacillin in pregnant women. Dicloxacillin is an excellent drug for the treatment of postpartum mastitis (infection in the tissue of breast, usually related to breast-feeding). Penicillin-derived drugs have proved safe for use during pregnancy.

How it can affect a developing embryo or fetus: There are no adequate reports or well-controlled studies in human fetuses. Dicloxacillin crosses the human placenta, but the fetal concentrations are relatively low. Rodent studies are reassuring, revealing no increase in birth defects or low birth weight. However, animal studies are not necessarily good indicators of how a drug will behave in humans.

Breast-feeding: The transfer of dicloxacillin/cloxacillin to breast milk is minimal. In most cases, women with mastitis can continue to breast-feed (even from the affected breast) during treatment.

Possible Potential drug interactions: Tetracycline-class medications should be avoided.

What the FDA says about use in pregnancy: Category B (see Appendix).

What the available evidence suggests about breast-feeding safety: Safe.

The bottom line for you:

- Dicloxacillin is safe for use during pregnancy and is a drug of choice for the treatment of postpartum mastitis.

DICYCLOMINE

Brand names: Antispas, A-Spas, Bentyl, Bo-Cyclomine, Coochil, Dedoxia, Diciclomina, Dicyclocot, Magesan, Medispag

Drug classes: Anticholinergic; Gastrointestinal

Indications (what it is used for): Irritable bowel syndrome.

How it works: Decreases bowel motility by inhibiting smooth-muscle contractility.

Contraindications (reasons you shouldn't take it): Hypersensitivity to drug or class, ulcerative colitis, bowel paralysis, myasthenia gravis (an autoimmune disease causing muscle weakness), acid reflux, glaucoma.

Possible side effects and warnings: Can cause drowsiness, blurred vision, respiratory distress, fast heart rate, hives, confusion, constipation, dilated pupils, nausea, vomiting, fever, psychosis, and excessive sensitivity to light. Should be used with caution in women with cardiovascular disease or hyperthyroidism.

How it can affect pregnant women: There are no adequate reports or well-controlled studies of dicyclomine in pregnant women.

How it can affect a developing embryo or fetus: There are no adequate reports or well-controlled studies in human fetuses. It is unknown whether dicyclomine crosses the human placenta. Dicyclomine was a component of Bendectin, a popular drug no longer marketed in the U.S. used to treat nausea and vomiting during pregnancy. It initially consisted of doxylamine, dicyclomine, and pyridoxine; dicyclomine was dropped in 1976. Bendectin was ultimately discontinued in 1983 after an onslaught of lawsuits suggesting that it caused birth defects. Subsequent studies found no difference in the rate of birth defects between mothers who had taken Bendectin during the first trimester and those who had not. An FDA panel concluded that there was no connection between Bendectin use and birth defects.

Breast-feeding: There is no published data in nursing women. Dicyclomine is excreted in human milk in relatively low amounts. Although newborn levels have not been measured, there are case reports of severe respiratory symptoms in newborns directly treated with dicyclomine for colic, so it is generally considered incompatible with breast-feeding.

Potential drug interactions: Interaction between the following medications and dicyclomine has the potential to impact the effect of one or more of the drugs. In some instances the interaction can be dangerous or life-threatening and must be avoided: amantadine, antiarrhythmic agents such as quinidine, antihistamines, antipsychotic agents, benzodiazepines, digoxin, metoclopramide, monoamine oxidase inhibitors (MAOIs), narcotic analgesics such as meperidine, nitrates and nitrites, sympathomimetic agents, tricyclic antidepressants. Antacids may interfere with the absorption of dicyclomine and should be avoided.

What the FDA says about use in pregnancy: Category B (see Appendix).

What the available evidence suggests about breast-feeding safety: Possibly unsafe.

The bottom line for you:

- Dicyclomine has been well studied and is considered safe for use during pregnancy, although there are alternative agents for nausea and vomiting that are more effective.
- Dicyclomine probably should be avoided while breast-feeding until there is more information on its safety.

DIDANOSINE

Brand names: DDI, Videx, Videx EC

Drug classes: Antiviral; Nucleoside reverse transcriptase inhibitor

Indications (what it is used for): HIV.

How it works: Inhibits nucleoside reverse transcriptase, preventing the virus from reproducing.

Contraindications (reasons you shouldn't take it): Hypersensitivity to drug or class, history of pancreatitis, neuropathy (nerve damage).

Possible side effects and warnings: Can cause pancreatitis, nerve damage, liver damage, inflammation of the optic nerve, low platelet count, diabetes, nausea, vomiting, diarrhea, rhabdomyolysis (breakdown of muscle fibers), rash, abdominal pain, joint pain, and loss of appetite. Should be used with caution in women who have gout, neuropathy, or kidney or liver dysfunction, or are using neurotoxic medications.

How it can affect pregnant women: There are no adequate reports or well-controlled studies of didanosine in pregnant women. HIV-positive women with more than 400 viral particles per milliliter of blood respond faster and stay responsive for 4 years when given a multidrug regimen treatment including didanosine, stavudine, and nelfinavir compared to zidovudine, lamivudine, and nelfinavir. However, fatal side effects have been reported on rare occasions in pregnant women who were given a combination of didanosine and stavudine. Avoid. Didanosine is a cause of diabetes. Women taking didanosine should have their blood sugar levels monitored frequently, especially when it is combined with other drugs such as pentamidine and dapsone, which themselves cause high blood sugars. Didanosine does not cure HIV, nor does it reduce the risk of HIV transmission by sexual contact or blood contamination.

How it can affect a developing embryo or fetus: There are no adequate reports or well-controlled studies in human fetuses. In the laboratory, didanosine rapidly crosses the human placenta. It is estimated that human fetal levels would be high enough to treat viral infection. Rodent studies have shown no evidence of birth defects or low birth weight despite the use of doses higher than those used clinically. However, animal studies are not necessarily good indicators of how a drug will behave in humans.

Breast-feeding: There is no published data in nursing women. It is unknown whether didanosine enters human breast milk. If infant formula is available, breast-feeding is not recommended because HIV can be transmitted to the newborn in the breast milk.

Potential drug interactions: Didanosine has numerous recognized drug interactions, and all prescribers should know what medications you are taking before adding didanosine. Likewise, you should tell all health-care practitioners and pharmacists if you are taking didanosine.

What the FDA says about use in pregnancy: Category B (see Appendix).

What the available evidence suggests about breast-feeding safety: Unknown.

The bottom line for you:

- Didanosine is used during pregnancy as part of an effective cocktail of drugs to achieve an undetectable level of HIV. Avoid using with stavudine.
- If infant formula is available, breast-feeding is not recommended when a mother is HIV positive because HIV can be transmitted to the newborn in the breast milk.
- Women who need to take didanosine during pregnancy are encouraged to register with the Antiretroviral Pregnancy Registry (1-800-258-4263). Your participation helps increase the information available on didanosine and pregnancy.

DIENESTROL

Brand names: DV, Estraguard, Ortho Dienoestrol

Drug classes: Estrogen; Hormone

Indications (what it is used for): Atrophic vaginitis (thinning of vaginal membranes due to low estrogen).

How it works: Activates the estrogen receptors to produce a feminizing response.

Contraindications (reasons you shouldn't take it): Hypersensitivity to drug or class, history of blood clots, cancer (ovarian, uterine, breast), unexplained vaginal bleeding, pregnancy.

Possible side effects and warnings: Can cause depression, blood clots, stroke, heart attack, endometrial cancer, gallbladder disease, pancreatitis, high blood pressure, nausea, vomiting, abnormal uterine bleeding, migraine, libido change, an increase in size of uterine fibromyomas (noncancerous tumors, aka fibroids), vaginal yeast infection, and breast tenderness. Should be used with caution in women over the age of 35 who smoke or women with liver or kidney dysfunction or a history of depression.

How it can affect pregnant women: Dienestrol is a synthetic nonsteroidal estrogen suitable for intravaginal use. Estrogen should not be used during pregnancy because it increases the pregnancy-related risk of the side effects noted above. Estrogens are not effective for the prevention or treatment of threatened or habitual miscarriage. The 1985 DES Task Force concluded that use of DES (diethylstilbestrol, a similar synthetic estrogen) during pregnancy was associated with a subsequent increased risk of breast cancer in the mothers, although a cause-and-effect relationship remains unconfirmed. There is no evidence that natural estrogens are less hazardous than synthetic estrogens at equivalent doses.

How it can affect a developing embryo or fetus: There are no adequate reports or well-controlled studies in human fetuses. It is unknown whether dienestrol crosses the human placenta. Estrogens should not be used during pregnancy since they are associated with an increased risk of congenital defects in the reproductive organs of the fetus and possibly other birth defects. Studies of female offspring of women who received DES during pregnancy have found an increased risk of vaginal adenosis (an abnormality of the vagina), squamous cell dysplasia of the uterine cervix, and clear cell vaginal cancer later in life; males have an increased risk of urogenital abnormalities and possibly testicular cancer later in life.

Breast-feeding: There is no published data in nursing women. It is unknown whether dienestrol enters human breast milk. Estrogens are usually considered incompatible with breast-feeding and may suppress milk production.

Potential drug interactions: No clinically significant drug interactions have been identified. However, estrogen affects many body responses.

What the FDA says about use in pregnancy: Category X (see Appendix).

What the available evidence suggests about breast-feeding safety: Possibly unsafe.

The bottom line for you:

- Dienestrol should not be used during pregnancy or while breast-feeding.

DIETHYLPROPION

Brand names: Depletite, Diethylpropion HCl, Dietil, Dipro, Durad, M-Orexic, Radtue, Tenuate, Tenuate Dospan, Tepanil

Drug classes: Anorexiant; Central nervous system stimulant

Indications (what it is used for): Obesity.

How it works: Suppresses appetite by an unknown mechanism.

Contraindications (reasons you shouldn't take it): Hypersensitivity to drug or class, use of monoamine oxidase inhibitors (MAOIs) within 14 days, cardiovascular disease, glaucoma, hyperthyroidism.

Possible side effects: Can cause pulmonary high blood pressure, irregular heart rate, psychosis, dry mouth, constipation, and restlessness.

How it can affect pregnant women: There are no adequate reports or well-controlled studies of diethylpropion in pregnant women. The published data consists of isolated case reports that appear to have been normal. Weight loss is not recommended during pregnancy.

How it can affect a developing embryo or fetus: There are no adequate reports or well-controlled

studies in human fetuses. It is unknown whether diethylpropion crosses the human placenta. There have been reports of newborns whose mothers used diethylpropion during pregnancy experiencing withdrawal after birth. There is a single case report of a newborn with skeletal malformations after maternal use of diethylpropion in the first month of pregnancy. None of these reports are strong enough to attribute the problem to the diethypropion.

Breast-feeding: There are no adequate reports or well-controlled studies in nursing women. Diethylpropion is excreted into human breast milk, although how much remains unclear.

Potential drug interactions: Interaction between the following medications and diethylpropion has the potential to impact the effect of one or more of the drugs. In some instances the interaction can be dangerous or life-threatening and must be avoided: glucose-lowering drugs (e.g., insulin), drugs to lower high blood pressure, phenothiazines. Use while undergoing general anesthesia may result in arrhythmias (irregular heartbeats).

What the FDA says about use in pregnancy: Category B (see Appendix).

What the available evidence suggests about breast-feeding safety: Unknown.

The bottom line for you:

- There is no clinical indication for diethylpropion during pregnancy. Despite the FDA category, the available information is too limited to allow conclusions on safety.
- Considering its indication and until there is additional study, it is best to avoid diethylpropion while breast-feeding.

DIETHYLSTILBESTROL

Brand name: Stilphostrol
Drug class: Antineoplastic; Estrogen; Hormone
Indications (what it is used for): Metastatic breast cancer.
How it works: Activates the estrogen receptors.

Contraindications (reasons you shouldn't take it): Hypersensitivity to drug or class, history of blood clots, cancer (ovarian, uterine, breast), unexplained vaginal bleeding, pregnancy.

Possible side effects and warnings: Can cause depression, nervousness, dizziness, chest pain, shortness of breath, nausea, vomiting, leg edema (swelling), erythema nodosum (painful skin inflammation), decreased sex drive, fatigue, and increased clotting factor production. Should be used with caution in women over the age of 35 who smoke or women with cardiovascular disease, coronary artery disease, seizure disorder, liver tumor, high calcium levels, or glucose intolerance.

How it can affect pregnant women: Diethylstilbestrol (DES) was given to some 3 million pregnant women in the U.S. and in the Netherlands between 1947 and 1975 under the mistaken belief that it prevented miscarriage. The 1985 DES Task Force concluded that use of DES during pregnancy was associated with a subsequent increased risk of breast cancer in the mothers, although a cause-and-effect relationship remains unconfirmed. There is no evidence that natural estrogens are less hazardous than synthetic estrogens at equivalent doses.

How it can affect a developing embryo or fetus: There are no adequate reports or well-controlled studies in human fetuses. It is unknown whether dienestrol crosses the human placenta. Estrogens should not be used during pregnancy since they are associated with an increased risk of congenital defects in the reproductive organs and possibly other birth defects. Studies of female offspring of women who received DES during pregnancy have found an increased risk of vaginal adenosis (an abnormality of the vagina), squamous cell dysplasia of the uterine cervix, and clear cell vaginal cancer later in life; males have an increased risk of urogenital abnormalities and possibly testicular cancer later in life.

Breast-feeding: Estrogens generally should not be used while breast-feeding and may suppress milk production.

Potential drug interactions: No clinically significant drug interactions have been currently identified. However, estrogen affects many body responses.

What the FDA says about use in pregnancy: Category X (see Appendix).

What the available evidence suggests about breast-feeding safety: Probably not safe.

The bottom line for you:

- Diethylstilbestrol should not be used during pregnancy and while breast-feeding.

DIFLUNISAL

Brand names: Dolobid, Dopanone, Fluodonil, Noaldol

Drug classes: Analgesic, nonnarcotic; NSAID; Salicylate

Indications (what it is used for): Mild to moderate pain, osteoarthritis, rheumatoid arthritis.

How it works: Reduces the synthesis of prostaglandins (natural substances that play a role in inflammation).

Contraindications (reasons you shouldn't take it): Hypersensitivity to drug or class, asthma, hives, aspirin-precipitated rhinitis

Possible side effects and warnings: Can cause peptic ulcer, gastrointestinal bleeding, low platelet count, Stevens-Johnson syndrome (a rare but serious skin reaction to medication), nephritis (inflammation in the kidneys), and liver or kidney failure. Should be used with caution in women with nasal polyps, gastrointestinal bleeding, high blood pressure, heart failure, or liver or kidney disease.

How it can affect pregnant women: Diflunisal is a nonsteroidal anti-inflammatory drug (NSAID) that can reduce inflammation, lower fevers, and lessen pain. Like many NSAIDs, it interferes with blood clotting by inhibiting the action of platelets. There are no adequate reports of diflunisal in pregnant women. Diflunisal is more effective than aspirin for relieving the pain after episiotomy.

How it can affect a developing embryo or fetus: There are no adequate reports or well-controlled studies in human fetuses. It is unknown whether diflunisal crosses the human placenta. Rodent studies found that diflunisal can harm embryos and cause skeletal malformations when given at 1 to 8 times the maximum recommended human dose. In humans, other NSAIDs are associated with a narrowing or (rarely) closure of the ductus arteriosus, a critical fetal blood vessel directing blood away from the lungs. Its closure leads to tricuspid valve incompetence (leaky valve between the right atrium and right ventricle), heart failure, and high blood pressure in the lungs, all of which could cause long-term damage. Stopping the drug appears to reverse the process. It is best to avoid repeated dosing of NSAIDs after 32 weeks.

Breast-feeding: There is no published data in nursing women. Small quantities of diflunisal are excreted into human milk, but it is unlikely occasional use poses a clinically significant risk to a breast-feeding newborn.

Potential drug interactions: Interaction between the following medications and diflunisal has the potential to impact the effect of one or more of the drugs. In some instances the interaction can be dangerous or life-threatening and must be avoided: acetaminophen, oral anticoagulants, cyclosporine, methotrexate.

What the FDA says about use in pregnancy: Category C (see Appendix).

What the available evidence suggests about breast-feeding safety: Likely safe.

The bottom line for you:

- Diflunisal and other NSAIDs are probably safe if used occasionally during pregnancy and while breast-feeding.
- Similar to other NSAIDs, it is wise to avoid diflunisal in the first trimester and sustained use should be avoided in the third trimester.

DIGITOXIN

Brand names: Coramedan, Crystodigin

Drug classes: Antiarrhythmic; Cardiac glycoside; Inotrope

Indications (what it is used for): Heart failure, fast or irregular heart rate.

How it works: Slows the preparation of the heart cell for contraction.

Contraindications (reasons you shouldn't take it): Hypersensitivity to drug or class, ventricular tachycardia (rapid heartbeat that begins in the ventricles), heart disease, and hypersensitive carotid sinus syndrome.

Possible side effects and warnings: Can cause digitalis intoxication (nausea, vomiting, visual disturbance, electrolyte abnormalities, and slow heart rate). Should be used with caution in women with low potassium levels or liver or kidney failure.

How it can affect pregnant women: There are no adequate reports or well-controlled studies of digitoxin in pregnant women. Digitoxin works similarly to digitalis, but is cleared from the body more rapidly during pregnancy. This means that women taking digitoxin during pregnancy may need a higher dose than usual and should have blood levels checked periodically.

How it can affect a developing embryo or fetus: There are no adequate reports or well-controlled studies in human fetuses. Digoxin and digitoxin cross the human placenta and achieve levels in the fetus that are slightly lower than those in the mother. However, the human placenta is rich in digoxin receptors, which means that most of the digoxin/digitoxin given to the mother never reaches the fetus. Fetal heart failure, one suggested indication for its use in pregnancy, further increases placental digitoxin binding, which means that the mother's level must be at near toxic levels (for her) before the fetal concentration begins to rise. Toxic fetal levels can lead to a slow fetal heart rate.

Breast-feeding: There is no published data in nursing women. It is unknown whether digitoxin enters human breast milk.

Potential drug interactions: Interaction between the following medications and digitoxin has the potential to impact the effect of one or more of the drugs. In some instances the interaction can be dangerous or life-threatening and must be avoided: potassium-depleting diuretics, quinidine, verapamil, amiodarone, erythromycin, propafenone, indomethacin, itraconazole, alprazolam, spironolactone, antacids, kaolin, sulfasalazine, neomycin, cholestyramine, certain anticancer drugs, metoclopramide, rifampin, succinylcholine.

What the FDA says about use in pregnancy: Category C (see Appendix).

What the available evidence suggests about breast-feeding safety: Unknown.

The bottom line for you:

- Digitoxin can be used safely during pregnancy if needed for the benefit of mother or fetus.
- There are, however, alternative digoxin-type agents with shorter elimination times, which may be preferable depending on the indication.
- Its safety while breast-feeding is unknown.

DIGOXIN

Brand names: Digacin, Digitek, Lanicor, Lanoxicaps, Lanoxin

Drug classes: Antiarrhythmic; Cardiac glycoside; Inotrope

Indications (what it is used for): Congestive heart failure, atrial fibrillation/flutter, paroxysmal atrial tachycardia, fetal arrhythmia.

How it works: Slows the preparation of the heart cell for contraction.

Contraindications (reasons you shouldn't take it): Hypersensitivity to drug or class, ventricular fibrillation, ventricular tachycardia, atrioventricular accessory pathway, sick sinus syndrome.

Possible side effects and warnings: Can cause hallucinations, blurred vision, low platelet count, irregular or slow heart rate, delirium, and abnormal potassium levels. Should be used with caution in women with slow heart rate, atrioventricular block, prior heart attack, cardiomyopathy (disease of the heart muscle), constrictive pericarditis (inflammation of the membrane covering the heart), or kidney or liver damage.

How it can affect pregnant women: There is a long clinical experience with digoxin for the treatment of benign arrhythmias and cardiomyopathy during pregnancy and postpartum. A full cardiovascular evaluation is recommended whenever starting digoxin. Potential stimulants, such as smoking (which is never recommended during pregnancy), caffeine, and alcohol (which is never recommended during pregnancy), should be eliminated during treatment because they can cause abnormal heart rhythms. Although no antiarrhythmic drug is completely safe during pregnancy, most are well tolerated and add little risk. Women with peripartal cardiomyopathy (weakened heart muscle associated with pregnancy) who have persistently abnormal ventricular function must be continuously treated with digoxin, diuretics, and anticoagulants and, like patients with dilated cardiomyopathy (heart too weak to pump blood efficiently), may ultimately require heart transplantation.

How it can affect a developing embryo or fetus: There are no adequate reports or well-controlled studies in human fetuses. Digoxin and digitoxin cross the human placenta and achieve levels in the fetus that are slightly lower than those in the mother. However, the human placenta is rich in digoxin receptors, which means that much of the digitoxin/digoxin is bound up in the placenta and never reaches the fetus.

Fetal heart failure is one indication for digoxin's use in pregnancy, and it increases placental digitoxin binding, requiring the mother's level to be higher than usual. Digoxin is generally considered first-line therapy for the treatment of fetal supraventricular tachycardia (a dangerously fast heart rate that can cause heart failure) absent heart failure. Direct fetal digoxin administration can be successful if more traditional intensive trials of transplacental therapy with digoxin, flecainide, verapamil, and procainamide, either separately or in combination, fail. Transplacental digoxin therapy has also been used to improve the strength of heart contraction in fetuses whose normal pacemaker is blocked due to scars. Despite adequate therapy and improvement in the fetal health, many fetuses require pacemaker implantation or heart transplantation after birth.

Breast-feeding: There are no adequate reports or well-controlled studies in nursing women. Though low levels of digoxin enter human breast milk, an unsupplemented breast-fed newborn would have levels below those used to treat a condition.

Potential drug interactions: Interaction between the following medications and digoxin has the potential to impact the effect of one or more of the drugs. In some instances the interaction can be dangerous or life-threatening and must be avoided: potassium-depleting diuretics, quinidine, verapamil, amiodarone, erythromycin, propafenone, indomethacin, itraconazole, alprazolam, spironolactone, antacids, kaolin, sulfasalazine, neomycin, cholestyramine, certain anticancer drugs, metoclopramide, rifampin, succinylcholine.

What the FDA says about use in pregnancy: Category C (see Appendix).

What the available evidence suggests about breast-feeding safety: Safe.

The bottom line for you:

- Digoxin has a long clinical track record of treating both maternal and fetal heart failure and heart rhythm abnormalities; it is one of the safest antiarrhythmics to use during pregnancy.
- Digoxin is considered safe for use while breast-feeding.

DIHYDROERGOTAMINE
Brand names: D.H.E. 45, Migranal
Drug classes: Ergot alkaloid; Migraine agent
Indications (what it is used for): Migraine and cluster headache.
How it works: Constricts dilated blood vessels in the brain that cause headache.

Contraindications (reasons you shouldn't take it): Hypersensitivity to drug or class, coronary artery disease, uncontrolled high blood pressure, basilar migraine, peripheral vascular disease (reduced blood flow to areas other than the heart or brain), cerebrovascular disease (narrowing of blood vessels that supply the brain), having taken a 5-HT1 agonist drug within the past 24 hours, severe liver or kidney dysfunction, simultaneous use of vessel constrictor medications, sepsis.

Possible side effects and warnings: Can cause high blood pressure, peripheral or intestinal artery spasm, coronary artery spasm, heart attack, chest pain, rapid or slow heart rate, nausea, vomiting, numbness in fingers and toes, leg weakness, and itching. Should be used with caution in women who have cardiac risk factors.

How it can affect pregnant women: Fifty to 90% of women who suffer migraines experience improvement during pregnancy, mainly during the second and third trimesters. A higher percentage of women who have menstrual migraine experience this improvement compared to women with other types of migraines. Dihydroergotamine is effective for the treatment of menstrual migraine. Unfortunately, dihydroergotamine can cause uterine contractions and is considered contraindicated (should not be used) during pregnancy.

How it can affect a developing embryo or fetus: There are no adequate reports or well-controlled studies in human fetuses. It is unknown whether dihydroergotamine crosses the human placenta. In one animal and one human study, the evidence suggested that it crosses the placenta and interferes with placental blood flow.

Breast-feeding: There is no published data in nursing women. It is unknown whether dihydroergotamine enters human breast milk. A related drug, ergotamine, is excreted into breast milk and can have adverse effects on a breast-fed newborn. It is thus reasonable to stop breast-feeding until the treated headache has resolved.

Potential drug interactions: Notify your pharmacist and physician of your current medications. Interaction between the following medications and dihydroergotamine has the potential to impact the effect of one or more of the drugs. In some instances the interaction can be dangerous or life-threatening and must be avoided: peripheral vasoconstrictors, propranolol, nicotine.

What the FDA says about use in pregnancy: Category X (see Appendix).

What the available evidence suggests about breast-feeding safety: Probably unsafe.

The bottom line for you:

- Dihydroergotamine should not be used during pregnancy, because it causes uterine contractions.
- If required while breast-feeding, it is safest to discontinue feeding and to pump and discard the milk until the headache resolves and the treatment is completed.
- There are alternative agents with which there is more experience during both pregnancy and breast-feeding.

DIHYDROTACHYSTEROL

Brand names: DHT, Hytakerol, Tachyrol
Drug class: Vitamin/mineral
Indications (what it is used for): Osteoporosis, low calcium level, kidney osteodystrophy (kidneys fail to reabsorb sufficient sufficient calcium from the urine, leading to bones becoming weak and brittle).
How it works: Stimulates bone mineralization as well as intestinal calcium and phosphorus absorption.
Contraindications (reasons you shouldn't take it): Hypersensitivity to drug or class, high calcium or vitamin D levels.
Possible side effects and warnings: Can cause high calcium levels, kidney damage, convulsions, excessive thirst, nausea, vomiting, loss of appetite, anemia, weakness, and metastatic calcifications (deposit of calcium salts in nonbone tissue). Should be used with caution in women with kidney stones, high phosphorus, or high vitamin D levels.

How it can affect pregnant women: There are no adequate reports or well-controlled studies of dihydrotachysterol (vitamin D) in pregnant women, although it is part of most prenatal vitamin preparations. Dihydrotachysterol and calcitriol are both effective for the management of hypoparathyroidism (abnormally low levels of parathyroid hormone) during pregnancy, although the dose required typically needs to be increased during the second half of pregnancy.

How it can affect a developing embryo or fetus: There are no adequate reports or well-controlled studies in human fetuses. It is not known whether dihydrotachysterol crosses the human placenta, nor is it known whether dihydrotachysterol increases fetal calcium. Rodent studies suggest that it may cross and increase the transfer of calcium to the fetus.

Breast-feeding: There are no adequate reports or well-controlled studies in nursing women. Even though dihydrotachysterol increases the calcium in breast milk, excessively high calcium levels are not seen in breast-fed newborns. However, hypercalcemia (high calcium levels) has been reported in breast-feeding women being treated for hypoparathyroid.

Potential drug interactions: Interaction between the following medications and dihydrotachysterol has the potential to impact the effect of one or more of the drugs. In some instances the interaction can be dangerous or life-threatening and must be avoided: thiazide diuretics.

What the FDA says about use in pregnancy: Category C (see Appendix).

What the available evidence suggests about breast-feeding safety: Likely safe.

The bottom line for you:
- Dihydrotachysterol may be used during pregnancy and while breast-feeding.
- Vitamin D is included in most prenatal vitamins.
- In hypoparathyroid women, both mother and infant should be monitored for high calcium levels during breast-feeding.

DILTIAZEM

Brand names: Cardizem, Clarute, Dilacor XR, Lacerol, Tiazac

Drug classes: Antiarrhythmic, class IV; Calcium channel blocker

Indications (what it is used for): Angina (chest pain), atrial arrhythmias.

How it works: Blocks calcium channels to slow pacemaker activity.

Contraindications (reasons you shouldn't take it): Hypersensitivity to drug or class, atrioventricular block, low blood pressure, slow heart rate, sick sinus syndrome (a group of heart rhythm disorders), current or prior heart attack.

Possible side effects and warnings: Can cause edema (swelling); headache; nausea; vomiting; dizziness; weakness; rash; flushing; heart block; pulmonary congestion; sensitivity to light; hives; dry mouth; shortness of breath; hyperuricemia (high uric acid in the blood); joint pain; ringing in the ears; erythema multiforme, Stevens-Johnson syndrome, and toxic epidermal necrolysis (rare but serious skin disorders). Should be used with caution in women with liver or kidney damage.

How it can affect pregnant women: There are no adequate reports or well-controlled studies of diltiazem in pregnant women. Diltiazem is used in pregnant and nonpregnant women for the treatment of cardiac rhythm emergencies. Diltiazem can reduce uterine contractions and dilate arteries. Diltiazem has no advantage over nifedipine to slow or stop labor. Recently, a relationship between oral erythromycin and sudden cardiac death was reported in patients also receiving strong (CYP3A inhibitors (e.g. diltiazem). Pregnant women are often prescribed erythromycin following preterm premature rupture of the membranes (PPROM, water breaking before 37 weeks), so it is important to know if a woman is taking diltiazem during pregnancy.

How it can affect a developing embryo or fetus: There are no adequate reports or well-controlled studies in human fetuses. It is unknown whether diltiazem crosses the human placenta; it rapidly crosses the rabbit placenta. Rodent studies have observed an increased rate of malformations of the skeleton and aortic arch at doses much higher than the maximum recommended human dose. However, animal studies are not necessarily good indicators of how a drug will behave in humans.

Breast-feeding: There are no adequate reports or well-controlled studies in nursing women. Diltiazem enters human breast milk and may reach levels similar to those in the mother. Although considered safe for breast-feeding women, it may be wise to use another calcium channel blocker that is not excreted to such a degree.

Potential drug interactions: Interaction between the following medications and diltiazem has the potential to impact the effect of one or more of the drugs. In some instances the interaction can be dangerous or life-threatening and must be avoided: CYP3A4 substrates (such as erythromycin), medications known to affect heart function, midazolam, triazolam, buspirone, carbamazepine, rifampin.

What the FDA says about use in pregnancy: Category C (see Appendix).

What the available evidence suggests about breast-feeding safety: Likely safe.

The bottom line for you:

- Diltiazem should be used during pregnancy and breast-feeding only if the benefit to the woman justifies the potential risk to the fetus or newborn.
- Because erythromycin involves CYP3A4, it should be avoided in women receiving diltiazem.
- In the event of preterm premature rupture of membranes (water breaking before 37 weeks), ampicillin plus sulbactam is the preferred treatment.

DIMENHYDRINATE

Brand names: Amosyt, Biodramina, Di-Men, Dimeno, Dimetabs, Dinate, Dommanate, Dramamine, Dramanate, Dramavance, Dramocen, Dramoject, Dymenate, Hydrate, Marmine, Or-Dram, Shodram, T-Circ, Travelgum, Wehamine

Drug classes: Anticholinergic; Antiemetic; Antivertigo

Indications (what it is used for): Motion sickness, migraine headache.

How it works: Unknown.

Contraindications (reasons you shouldn't take it): Hypersensitivity to drug or class.

Possible side effects and warnings: Can cause drowsiness, headache, fatigue, increased appetite, abdominal pain, nausea, vomiting, diarrhea, increased bronchial secretion, loss of appetite, and nervousness. Should be used with caution in women with seizure disorder or glaucoma, or who are using medications that are toxic to the ear.

How it can affect pregnant women: There are no adequate reports or well-controlled studies of dimenhydrinate in pregnant women. Even though it is a popular medication in many countries for the relief of nausea and vomiting during pregnancy, the practice is essentially unstudied. In one study, both ginger and dimenhydrinate were equally effective/ineffective. Although both dimenhydrinate and diphenhydramine are considered treatment options for severe migraine headache in pregnancy, some research has found an increase in uterine contractions.

How it can affect a developing embryo or fetus: There are no adequate reports or well-controlled studies in human fetuses. It is unknown whether dimenhydrinate crosses the human placenta. Population studies (studies of a large group of people taken from the larger population) reveal no evidence that dimenhydrinate increases the risk of fetal abnormalities when given at any stage of pregnancy. Rodent studies are similarly reassuring. However, animal studies are not necessarily good indicators of how a drug will behave in humans.

Breast-feeding: There is no adequate published data in nursing women. Dimenhydrinate is excreted into human breast milk in small quantities. However, there is a long clinical experience with breast-feeding women taking dimenhydrinate without adverse effects.

Potential drug interactions: Interaction between

the following medications and dimenhydrinate has the potential to impact the effect of one or more of the drugs. In some instances the interaction can be dangerous or life-threatening and must be avoided: azelastine, dexmedetomidine, pramlintide.

What the FDA says about use in pregnancy: Category B (see Appendix).

What the available evidence suggests about breast-feeding safety: Likely safe.

The bottom line for you:

- Dimenhydrinate may be safe to use during pregnancy and while breast-feeding for the treatment of motion sickness and migraine.

DINOPROSTONE (VAGINAL SUPPOSITORY)

Brand names: Cervidil, Prepidil, Prostin E2, Prostin E2 Vaginal Suppository

Drug classes: Oxytocic; Prostaglandin

Indications (what it is used for): Cervical ripening.

How it works: Unknown.

Contraindications (reasons you shouldn't take it): Hypersensitivity to drug or other oxytocics, vaginal delivery contraindicated, undiagnosed vaginal bleeding, high uterine muscle tone, frequent uterine contractions, fetal distress, imminent delivery, fetus too large for the pelvis, prior cesarean section or other major uterine surgery, grand multiparity (5 or more previous pregnancies).

Possible side effects and warnings: Can cause bronchospasm, irregular or slow heart rate, high blood pressure, uterine rupture, high acid levels in the fetal blood, premature rupture of the membranes (water breaking before labor begins), nausea, vomiting, diarrhea, headache, uterine contractions, dizziness, flushing, fever, cough, chills, and shortness of breath. Should be used with caution in women whose water has already broken or who have asthma, increased intraocular pressure, or liver or kidney dysfunction.

How it can affect pregnant women: Dinoprostone is the naturally occurring form of prostaglandin E2. It is used orally, vaginally, or intracervically to ripen (open) the cervix for delivery or pregnancy termination. Complications include frequent uterine contractions and uterine rupture. It is not recommended for outpatient use since the medication may bring on frequent uterine contractions. Misoprostol and dinoprostone are equally safe for the induction of labor. However, misoprostol is more efficient, may be associated with a lower cesarean rate, and is significantly cheaper. Dinoprostone has also been used to treat postpartum hemorrhage occurring when the uterus fails to contract. The safety profile of dinoprostone is good; it has been used successfully in women with a wide range of medical complications.

How it can affect a developing embryo or fetus: There are no adequate reports or well-controlled studies in human fetuses. It is unknown whether dinoprostone crosses the human placenta. The effects that have been reported in the fetus appear to be complications of uterine activity rather than direct effects of the medication.

Breast-feeding: There is no published data in nursing women. It is unknown whether dinoprostone enters human breast milk. However, considering that it is used for a short period of time and at low doses, dinoprostone is unlikely to pose a clinically significant risk to a breast-feeding newborn.

Potential drug interactions: Dinoprostone may increase the effect of other labor-inducing medications and should not be used simultaneously.

What the FDA says about use in pregnancy: Category C (see Appendix).

What the available evidence suggests about breast-feeding safety: Safe.

The bottom line for you:

- Dinoprostone is used during pregnancy for cervical ripening in preparation for labor induction.
- Other prostaglandin compounds, such as misoprostol, have similar efficacy, the same degree of safety, but lower cost.

DIPHENHYDRAMINE

Brand names: Allerdryl 50, Allergia-C, Allergina, Amidryl, Banophen, Beldin, Belix, Bena-D10, Benadryl, Benadryl Steri-Dose, Benahist, Benapon, Ben-A-Vance, Bendramine, Benoject, Ben-Rex, Bydramine, Dibenil, Dimidril, Diphen, Diphenacen-50, Diphenhist, Dytuss, Fynex, Genahist, Hydramine, Hydril, Hyrexin, Noradryl, Norafed, Nordryl, Pharm-A-Dry, Restamin, Shodryl, Tega Dryl, Truxadryl, Tusstat, Uad Dryl, Wehdryl

Drug class: Antihistamine

Indications (what it is used for): Antihistamine, life-threatening allergic reaction, dystonic reactions (severe muscle contractions), sedation, sleeplessness, motion sickness.

How it works: Blocks histamine receptors, whose activation causes the symptoms.

Contraindications (reasons you shouldn't take it): Hypersensitivity to drug or class, simultaneous use of alcohol.

Possible side effects and warnings: Can cause drowsiness, dry mouth, nausea, vomiting, headache, abdominal pain, fever, and diarrhea. Should be used with caution in women with increased intraocular pressure, asthma, overactive thyroid, cardiovascular disease, or peptic ulcer.

How it can affect pregnant women: There are no adequate reports or well-controlled studies of diphenhydramine in pregnant women despite a long history of use in obstetrics. Diphenhydramine is a popular sleep aid during pregnancy and is also used treat allergic reactions and migraine.

How it can affect a developing embryo or fetus: There are no adequate reports or well-controlled studies in human fetuses. Although diphenhydramine crosses the human placenta, there is no evidence of increased fetal risk if administered during any stage of pregnancy. It may cause depressed breathing in newborns if administered during labor shortly before birth. Rodent studies are reassuring, revealing no increase in malformations or low birth weight. However, animal studies are not necessarily good indicators of how a drug will behave in humans.

Breast-feeding: There is no published data in nursing women. It is unknown whether diphenhydramine enters human breast milk. Irritability is the most common adverse reaction reported in the newborns of women using antihistamines while breast-feeding.

Potential drug interactions: Other central nervous system depressants such as hypnotics, sedatives, tranquilizers, and alcohol increase the sedating effects of diphenhydramine. Monoamine oxidase inhibitors (MAOIs) may prolong and intensify the anticholinergic (drying) effects of diphenhydramine.

What the FDA says about use in pregnancy: Category B (see Appendix).

What the available evidence suggests about breast-feeding safety: Safe.

The bottom line for you:

- Diphenhydramine appears safe and effective for selected uses during pregnancy and while breast-feeding.

DIPYRIDAMOLE

Brand name: Persantine

Drug class: Platelet inhibitor

Indications (what it is used for): Prevention of blood clots, angina (chest pain), and heart valve disease.

How it works: Blocks platelets from adhering to the vessel wall and stimulates dilation of arteries.

Contraindications (reasons you shouldn't take it): Hypersensitivity to drug or class.

Possible side effects and warnings: Can cause low blood pressure, heart attack, irregular or rapid heart rate, bronchospasm, rash, shortness of breath, nausea, vomiting, flushing, and diarrhea. Should be used with caution in women with low blood pressure.

How it can affect pregnant women: Pregnancy greatly increases the risk of blood clots. Dipyridamole has been used extensively during pregnancy with apparent safety over the years. Dipyridamole is also used to treat essential thrombocythemia (overproduction of platelets by the bone marrow) during pregnancy.

How it can affect a developing embryo or fetus: There are no adequate reports or well-controlled studies in human fetuses. It is unknown whether dipyridamole crosses the human placenta. It had been thought that dipyridamole could reduce the risk of the fetus not growing properly in the womb, but studies reveal that it does not improve upon the beneficial effect of aspirin. Rodent studies are reassuring, revealing no increase in malformations or low birth weight. However, animal studies are not necessarily good indicators of how a drug will behave in humans.

Breast-feeding: There is no adequate published data in nursing women. Although dipyridamole enters human breast milk, there is no evidence of any harmful effects to newborns that would necessitate stopping breast-feeding during treatment.

Potential drug interactions: May interact badly with adenosine and cholinesterase inhibitors.

What the FDA says about use in pregnancy: Category B (see Appendix).

What the available evidence suggests about breast-feeding safety: Likely safe.

The bottom line for you:

• Dipyridamole appears safe during pregnancy and while breast-feeding.

DISOPYRAMIDE

Brand name: Norpace

Drug class: Antiarrhythmic, class IA

Indications (what it is used for): Irregular heart rate originating in the ventricles, hypertrophic cardiomyopathy (thickening of the heart muscles).

How it works: Slows the preparation of the heart muscle for contraction.

Contraindications (reasons you shouldn't take it): Hypersensitivity to drug or class, unresponsive heart failure, internally blocked heartbeat, congestive heart failure, cardiomyopathy (disease of the heart muscle).

Possible side effects and warnings: Can cause congestive heart failure, irregular heart rate, low platelet count, low blood pressure, dizziness, blurred vision, nausea, vomiting, diarrhea, abdominal pain, dry mucous membranes, anxiety, urinary retention, itching, rash, and constipation. Should be used with caution in women with low blood glucose or abnormal rapid heart rates.

How it can affect pregnant women: There are no adequate reports or well-controlled studies of disopyramide in pregnant women. Pregnancy increases the percentage of free drug in the body, which increases the risks of side effects. Use during pregnancy has been associated with hemorrhage, low blood pressure, and uterine contractions that can lead to fetal distress. Preterm labor (before 37 weeks) has been reported. Women taking disopyramide during pregnancy need to be carefully monitored for these adverse effects.

How it can affect a developing embryo or fetus: There are no adequate reports or well-controlled studies of disopyramide in human fetuses. It crosses the human placenta, achieving about one-third of the mother's level. No associated birth defects have been reported. Rodent studies were generally reassuring, although the highest doses were associated with damage to the embryo and poor fetal growth. However, animal studies are not necessarily good indicators of how a drug will behave in humans.

Breast-feeding: There are no adequate reports or well-controlled studies of disopyramide during breast-feeding. The amount of disopyramide in breast milk is too small to produce a clinically relevant level in a breast-fed newborn.

Potential drug interactions: Interaction between the following medications and disopyramide has the potential to impact the effect of one or more of the drugs. In some instances the interaction can be dangerous or life-threatening and must be avoided: phenytoin, other antiarrhythmic drugs (e.g., quinidine, procainamide, lidocaine, propranolol), verapamil, clarithromycin, erythromycin, CYP3A4 inhibitors.

What the FDA says about use in pregnancy: Category C (see Appendix).

What the available evidence suggests about breast-feeding safety: Likely safe.

The bottom line for you:

- Because of the risk of contractions, disopyramide should be avoided during pregnancy unless there are no other options.
- Disopyramide is probably safe for use while breast-feeding.

DISULFIRAM

Brand names: Antabuse, Antadict, Aversan, Disulfiram, Tetmosol

Drug class: Antialcoholic

Indications (what it is used for): Alcohol dependence.

How it works: Inhibits an enzyme necessary to break down alcohol.

Contraindications (reasons you shouldn't take it): Hypersensitivity to drug or class, alcohol use within the last 12 hours, metronidazole use, coronary artery disease, psychosis.

Possible side effects and warnings: Can cause cardiovascular collapse, irregular heart rate, seizure, coma, psychosis, optic neuritis (inflammation of the optic nerve), hepatitis, rash, drowsiness, fatigue, headache, and a metallic/garliclike taste. Should be used with caution in women with diabetes, a history of seizures, or liver or kidney damage.

How it can affect pregnant women: Alcohol is the most commonly used human teratogen (substance that causes birth defects), and alcohol abuse is increasingly more common among reproductive-age women. There are no adequate reports or well-controlled studies of disulfiram in pregnant women. Disulfiram deters alcohol consumption by causing severe nausea and vomiting. The safety of disulfiram during pregnancy is not established. The published literature consists mostly of case reports and small series of pregnancies that generally conclude that the drug is effective.

How it can affect a developing embryo or fetus: There are no adequate reports or well-controlled studies in human fetuses. It is unknown whether disulfiram crosses the human placenta. There are several case reports of limb abnormalities in children born to alcoholic women treated with disulfiram during pregnancy. It is unknown whether the defects were related to alcohol, disulfiram, or neither. In the laboratory, disulfiram damages embryos by interfering with DNA synthesis and anatomical development.

Breast-feeding: There is no published data in nursing women. It is unknown whether disulfiram enters human breast milk.

Potential drug interactions: Interaction between the following medications and disulfiram has the potential to impact the effect of one or more of the drugs. In some instances the interaction can be dangerous or life-threatening and must be avoided: phenytoin-like drugs, oral anticoagulants, isoniazid.

What the FDA says about use in pregnancy: Category C (see Appendix).

What the available evidence suggests about breast-feeding safety: Unknown.

The bottom line for you:

- Alcohol is the most commonly used substance that causes birth defects. If disulfiram can help, it constitutes a smaller risk than alcohol.
- There is not enough information to determine the safety of disulfiram during breast-feeding.

DIVALPROEX

Brand name: Depakote

Drug classes: Anticonvulsant; Migraine

Indications (what it is used for): Seizures, mania, bipolar disease, major depression, migraine prevention.

How it works: Multiple actions; exact mechanism unknown.

Contraindications (reasons you shouldn't take it): Hypersensitivity to drug or class, liver damage or disease.

Possible side effects and warnings: Can cause fetal neural tube (brain and spinal cord) defects, nausea, vomiting, diarrhea, abdominal pain, liver damage, pancreatitis, syndrome of inappropriate antidiuretic hormone secretion (excess release of a hypothalamus produced hormone stored in the pituitary gland that decreases urination), low sodium level, low platelet and white and red blood cell counts, bleeding, psychosis, Stevens-Johnson syndrome (a rare but serious skin reaction to medication), heartburn, hair loss, tremors, appetite changes, sleeplessness, swelling, blurred vision, and ringing in the ears. Should be used with caution in women with kidney damage, bone marrow suppression, bleeding tendencies, and congenital metabolic disorders.

How it can affect pregnant women: Women on medication for a seizure disorder should (when possible) plan their pregnancies, discuss the optimal medication with their neurologist, and begin appropriate supplemental folate therapy before conception (4 mg per day) to minimize the risk of birth defects. The concern over the risks of birth defects associated with antiseizure medications must be weighed against the risks of continued seizures to both the mother and fetus. Women who become pregnant while being treated should not stop treatment on their own but rather meet quickly with their doctor before making a decision.

Divalproex is a form of valproic acid that becomes valproate when digested. There are no adequate reports or well-controlled studies of divalproex in pregnant women. Valproate is a recognized human teratogen (a substance that can cause birth defects). Women who are planning pregnancy should switch to a different drug if possible (although vaproate is sometimes the only drug that can control seizures, and seizures in pregnancy may have worse consequences than the medications that treat them). Divalproex causes birth defects and learning disabilities, especially at high doses. Women who become pregnant while taking valproate should talk with their doctor immediately and be offered appropriate screening (1st and 2nd trimester ultrasound and second trimester biochemistry), although screening and scans do not find all birth defects. If it is necessary during

pregnancy, divalproate should be taken in divided doses to avoid peaks (see valproic acid) that pose the greatest risk to the fetus. Research shows that people taking valproate for bipolar disorder have a higher risk of suicide than those taking lithium. Pregnant women being treated with divalproate should have their blood levels monitored during pregnancy in case dose adjustments are necessary.

How it can affect a developing embryo or fetus: There are no adequate reports or well-controlled studies in human fetuses. Valproate and its metabolites (the products the drug is broken into after it enters the body) cross the placenta and are concentrated in fetal plasma. Valproate is known to cause birth defects, and combination with other anticonvulsants increases the risks of malformation. It is associated with a variety of major and minor malformations, including a 20 times increase in neural tube defects, cleft lip and palate, cardiovascular abnormalities, defects of the genitals and urinary system, developmental delay, endocrinologic disorders, limb defects, and autism. Research suggests that there are more adverse outcomes during pregnancy with valproate compared to other antiepileptic drugs. In one small but population-based study, all children exposed to valproate had minor, and some of them major, cognitive or neurologic problems. For women who fail other antiepileptic drug therapy and require valproate, the dose should be limited if possible. Doctors should prescribe the lowest effective dose and divide doses to minimize peak drug levels and the risks associated with them. (See valproic acid.)

Breast-feeding: There are no adequate reports or well-controlled studies in nursing women. Although small amounts of valproate are excreted into human breast milk, the blood level achieved in the breast-fed newborn is not clinically significant. (See valproic acid.)

Potential drug interactions: New interactions are continuously reported; the following is only a partial list. Interaction between the following medications and valproate has the potential to impact the

A-to-Z Drug Directory | 157

effect of one or more of the drugs. In some instances the interaction can be dangerous or life-threatening and must be avoided: drugs that affect the expression of liver enzymes (e.g., phenytoin, carbamazepine, phenobarbital, primidone), aspirin, felbamate, rifampin, clonazepam, diazepam, ethosuximide, lamotrigine, zidovudine.

What the FDA says about use in pregnancy: Category D (see Appendix).

What the available evidence suggests about breast-feeding safety: Safe.

The bottom line for you:

- There are more adverse pregnancy outcomes from valproate exposure in pregnancy than from any other antiepileptic drug. Alternative agents should be used whenever possible.

- Women who become pregnant while taking divalproex should not discontinue the medication on their own but should speak to their healthcare provider immediately about the possibility of switching medications, taking supplemental folic acid, and planning a detailed ultrasound to look for any possible abnormalities.

- If treatment with divalproate is absolutely necessary, it should be used alone and in divided doses to minimize peak blood levels and thus the risk to an embryo or fetus.

- Alternative drugs should be used for the treatment of migraine headaches.

DOBUTAMINE

Brand name: Dobutrex

Drug classes: Adrenergic agonist; Inotrope

Indications (what it is used for): Heart failure.

How it works: Activates the beta-adrenergic receptors in the heart to improve the force of contraction.

Contraindications (reasons you shouldn't take it): Hypersensitivity to drug or class, narrowing of the outlet to the aorta, high blood pressure.

Possible side effects and warnings: Can cause abnormal heart rate, phlebitis (inflammation of the veins), low or high blood pressure, nausea, vomit-

ing, headache, chest pain, palpitations, and shortness of breath. Should be used with caution in women with a history of recent heart attack, abnormal heart rate, or sulfite allergy.

How it can affect pregnant women: There are no adequate reports or well-controlled studies of dobutamine in pregnant women. Dobutamine is recommended for pregnant women with idiopathic (unexplained) dilated heart failure. It can also be used to test heart function in women who have previously suffered peripartal cardiomyopathy (occurs in the final month of pregnancy or within 5 months after delivery) and want to know the risks of recurrence in another pregnancy.

How it can affect a developing embryo or fetus: There are no adequate reports or well-controlled studies in human fetuses. Dobutamine crosses the human placenta. There are reports of its use for a particular pregnancy complication of identical twins that share blood supplies. Rodent studies are reassuring, revealing no increase in birth defects or low birth weight. However, animal studies are not necessarily good indicators of how a drug will behave in humans.

Breast-feeding: There is no published data in nursing women. It is unknown whether dobutamine enters human breast milk.

Potential drug interactions: Studies suggest that the use of dobutamine with nitroprusside may require the dose of each drug be lower than if used alone.

What the FDA says about use in pregnancy: No assigned category (see Appendix).

What the available evidence suggests about breast-feeding safety: Unknown.

The bottom line for you:

- Dobutamine may be used safely during pregnancy and while breast-feeding for the treatment of potentially life-threatening problems.

DOCETAXEL

Brand name: Taxotere

Drug class: Anti-neoplastic, antimitotic

Indications (what it is used for): Breast cancer, lung cancer, gestational choriocarcinoma (cancer that develops from placental tissue).

How it works: Blocks cell division.

Contraindications (reasons you shouldn't take it): Hypersensitivity to drug or class, bone marrow depression.

Possible side effects and warnings: Can cause low platelet or blood cell counts, marrow suppression, rash, edema (swelling), stomatitis (inflammation of the mucous linings of the mouth). Should be used with caution in women with kidney or liver damage.

How it can affect pregnant women: There are no adequate reports or well-controlled studies of docetaxel in pregnant women. Several case reports document successful pregnancies.

How it can affect a developing embryo or fetus: There are no adequate reports or well-controlled studies in human fetuses. It is unknown whether docetaxel crosses the human placenta. Although there is no evidence that it causes birth defects in humans, rodent studies have found damage to the embryo and fetus at doses far lower than those used in humans. However, animal studies are not necessarily good indicators of how a drug will behave in humans.

Breast-feeding: There is no published data in nursing women. It is unknown whether docetaxel enters human breast milk. It is generally considered incompatible with breast-feeding since it affects cell growth. Women who wish to breast-feed should wait at least 11 hours after their last dose to do so.

Potential drug interactions: Interaction between the following medications and docetaxel has the potential to impact the effect of one or more of the drugs. In some instances the interaction can be dangerous or life-threatening and must be avoided: cyclosporine, erythromycin, ketoconazole, terfenadine, and troleandomycin.

What the FDA says about use in pregnancy: Category D (see Appendix).

What the available evidence suggests about breast-feeding safety: Possibly unsafe.

The bottom line for you:

- Docetaxel may be used cautiously during pregnancy and while breast-feeding to treat a life-threatening maternal disease.

DOCUSATE CALCIUM

Brand names: Colace, Ediclone, Kasof, Laxagel, Prenate-90, Rapilax, Regulax, Surfak, Wasserlax

Drug class: Laxative

Indications (what it is used for): Constipation.

How it works: Retains moisture and fat within the large bowel.

Contraindications (reasons you shouldn't take it): Hypersensitivity to drug or class, impacted stool, mineral oil use, colitis, bowel obstruction.

Possible side effects and warnings: Can cause bitter taste, nausea, rash, diarrhea, throat irritation, and intestinal obstruction. Should be used with caution in women with nausea or vomiting.

How it can affect pregnant women: Although there are no adequate or well-controlled studies of docusate in pregnancy, there is a long clinical experience with virtually no reported complications. Docusate is often used after delivery to avoid constipation after an episiotomy repair.

How it can affect a developing embryo or fetus: Docusate is not absorbed systemically from the bowel and thus cannot cross the placenta and reach the fetus.

Breast-feeding: Docusate is not absorbed systemically from the bowel and thus will not enter human breast milk.

Potential drug interactions: No clinically relevant drug interactions are currently identified.

What the FDA says about use in pregnancy: Category C (see Appendix).

What the available evidence suggests about breast-feeding safety: Safe.

Bottom line for you:

- Docusate is safe during pregnancy and while breast-feeding.

DOLASETRON MESYLATE

Brand name: Anzemet

Drug classes: Antiemetic; Serotonin receptor antagonist

Indications (what it is used for): Severe nausea or vomiting due to chemotherapy or anesthesia.

How it works: Blocks serotonin receptors, which activate the symptoms.

Contraindications (reasons you shouldn't take it): Hypersensitivity to drug or class.

Possible side effects and warnings: Can cause irregular heart rate, headache, diarrhea, abdominal pain, fever, fatigue, dizziness, liver damage, low white blood cell count, high blood pressure, pain, drowsiness, and urinary retention. Should be used with caution in women with hypomagnesemia (low blood magnesium levels) or preexisting heart rate abnormalities.

How it can affect pregnant women: There is no published data with dolasetron during pregnancy.

How it can affect a developing embryo or fetus: There are no adequate reports or well-controlled studies in human fetuses. It is unknown whether dolasetron crosses the placenta. Rodent studies are reassuring, revealing no increase in malformations or low birth weight. However, animal studies are not necessarily good indicators of how a drug will behave in humans.

Breast-feeding: There is no published data in nursing women. It is unknown whether dolasetron enters human breast milk.

Potential drug interactions: The risk of a clinically significant drug interaction seems low for drugs commonly used in chemotherapy or surgery since dolasetron is eliminated by multiple routes.

What the FDA says about use in pregnancy: Category B (see Appendix).

What the available evidence suggests about breast-feeding safety: Unknown.

The bottom line for you:

- Dolasetron is likely safe for use during pregnancy and, based on its drug class, while breast-feeding. However, there are many alternative agents with which there is more experience.

DOPAMINE

Brand name: Intropin

Drug classes: Adrenergic agonist; Inotrope

Indications (what it is used for): Shock, unresponsive congestive heart failure.

How it works: Stimulates vascular and heart adrenergic and dopaminergic receptors that contract blood vessels to raise blood pressure and make the heart pump more effectively.

Contraindications (reasons you shouldn't take it): Hypersensitivity to drug or class, sulfites, ventricular fibrillation, pheochromocytoma (adrenal gland tumor).

Possible side effects and warnings: Can cause life-threatening allergic reaction, asthma, gangrene, low or high blood pressure, abnormal heart rate, chest pain, blood vessel contraction, shortness of breath, kidney damage, headache, and anxiety. Should be used with caution in women with diabetes, occlusive vascular diseases, or Raynaud's disease (disorder in which blood vessels are prone to spasm, which causes discoloration of the fingers, toes, and occasionally other areas often triggered by cold), or who are taking monoamine oxidase inhibitors (MAOIs).

How it can affect pregnant women: Dopamine is a natural catecholamine (a stress hormone) that increases the strength of heart contraction and the rate of contraction. There are no adequate reports or well-controlled studies of dopamine use in pregnant women. It is used only when the mother is critically ill.

How it can affect a developing embryo or fetus: There are no adequate reports or well-controlled studies in human fetuses. However, a mother dying or in shock is not healthy for a fetus. Rodent studies are reassuring, revealing no increase in malformations or low birth weight. However, animal studies are not necessarily good indicators of how a drug will behave in humans.

Breast-feeding: There is no published data in nursing women. It is unknown whether dopamine enters human breast milk.

Potential drug interactions: Interaction between the following medications and dopamine has the potential to impact the effect of one or more of the drugs. In some instances the interaction can be dangerous or life-threatening and must be avoided: cyclopropane or halogenated anesthetics, monoamine oxidase inhibitors (MAOIs), butyrophenones (such as haloperidol), phenothiazines, vasoconstricting agents (such as ergonovine), oxytocic drugs.

What the FDA says about use in pregnancy: Category C (see Appendix).

What the available evidence suggests about breast-feeding safety: Unknown.

The bottom line for you:

- Dopamine may be used during pregnancy and while breast-feeding for serious illness in the mother.

DOXEPIN

Brand names: Silenor, Sinequan, Zonalon
Drug classes: Antidepressant; Tricyclic
Indications (what it is used for): Depression, anxiety, itching (topical).
How it works: Exact mechanism unknown; inhibits catecholamine reuptake.
Contraindications (reasons you shouldn't take it): Hypersensitivity to drug or class, glaucoma, urinary retention.
Possible side effects and warnings: Can cause dry mouth, blurred vision, constipation, urinary retention, drowsiness, confusion, disorientation, hallucinations, numbness and tingling, irregular gait, seizures, abnormal white blood cell or platelet counts, bruising, lowered libido, rash, and loss of appetite. Should be used with caution in women under the age of 24 and over the age of 65.

How it can affect pregnant women: Depression is common during and after pregnancy but often goes unrecognized and untreated. Depression can be made worse by pregnancy or delivery, and suicide is a not uncommon cause of maternal death. Pregnancy is not a reason to discontinue antidepressant drugs if the medication is effective and needed. A woman being treated for depression who becomes pregnant should not discontinue medication abruptly on her own but rather discuss her treatment and condition with her medical provider. Pregnancy may increase the dose needed to be effective, and women with a history of depression have a higher rate of recurrence after delivery. There are no adequate reports or well-controlled studies of doxepin in pregnant women. Recent population based studies have revealed the use of tricyclic antidepressants may significantly increase the risk of preeclampsia by 2–3 times.

How it can affect a developing embryo or fetus: There are no adequate reports or well-controlled studies in human fetuses. It is unknown whether doxepin crosses the human placenta.

Breast-feeding: There are no adequate reports or well-controlled studies in nursing women. Although only small amounts of doxepin and its active metabolite (the product it is broken down to in the body) enter breast milk, one report described apnea (interruption in breathing) and drowsiness in a newborn even though the newborn blood doxepin level was just into the detectable range. Caution is advised.

Potential drug interactions: Interaction between the following medications and doxepin has the potential to impact the effect of one or more of the drugs. In some instances the interaction can be dangerous or life-threatening and must be avoided: CYP2D6 inhibitors (e.g., quinidine, cimetidine) and CYP2D6 substrates (many other antidepressants, phenothiazines, and the class 1C antiarrhythmics propafenone and flecainide), SSRIs (e.g., fluoxetine, sertraline, paroxetine), monoamine oxidase inhibitors (MAOIs). Doxepin is metabolized by CYP2D6. CYP2D6 is reduced in 7–10% of Caucasians ("poor metabolizers"), causing higher than expected blood levels of tricyclic antidepressants. Drugs that inhibit CYP2D6 render normal metabolizers poor metabolizers.

What the FDA says about use in pregnancy: Category C (see Appendix).

What the available evidence suggests about breast-feeding safety: Possibly unsafe.

The bottom line for you:

- Doxepin should be used during pregnancy and while breast-feeding only if the severity of the mother's depression mandates its use. Topical use for itching is unlikely to pose a significant clinical risk.

- There are other medications with which there is greater experience during pregnancy and while breast-feeding.

DOXORUBICIN

Brand name: Adriamycin

Drug class: Antineoplastic, antibiotic

Indications (what it is used for): Cancer (bladder, breast, bronchogenic, gastric, ovary, thyroid, bone, leukemia, lymphoma, Hodgkin's disease [a type of cancer of the lymphatic system], Wilms' tumor [a type of cancer of the kidney], neuroblastoma [a type of cancer in nerve tissue]).

How it works: Interferes with DNA synthesis, leading to cell death.

Contraindications (reasons you shouldn't take it): Hypersensitivity to drug or class; high bilirubin; cardiomyopathy (disease of the heart muscle); congestive heart failure; marrow failure; prior completed course of doxorubicin, idarubicin, or daunorubicin.

Possible side effects and warnings: Can cause cyclophosphamide toxicity, irregular heart rate, hair loss, hyperpigmentation (skin darkening), nausea, vomiting, stomatitis (inflammation of the mucous linings of the mouth), leukemia, fever, chills, hives, and neurotoxicity. Should be used with caution in women with liver damage or who are undergoing radiation therapy.

How it can affect pregnant women: There are no adequate reports or well-controlled studies of doxorubicin in pregnant women. Women diagnosed with breast cancer during pregnancy are frequently treated in the first trimester with a drug regimen including fluorouracil, doxorubicin, and cyclophosphamide. These drugs may cause irreversible heart toxicity during or even months after therapy. So far, doxorubicin does not appear to impair future fertility based on women attempting pregnancy after surviving Hodgkin's disease without recurrence.

How it can affect a developing embryo or fetus: Although there are no adequate reports or well-controlled studies in human fetuses, there are numerous reports whose interpretations are complicated by the fact that doxorubicin is often given with other medications. Birth defects reported after first-trimester exposure include no opening in the anus, rectovaginal fistula (a hole between the rectum and the vagina), abnormally shaped face, premature closure of the skull sutures, underdeveloped fingers or toes, and sloughing skin. Rarely fetal death has been reported 36 hours after treatment with doxorubicin when given with a variety of other neoplastic agents. The lack of a pattern suggests that the death may not have been caused by the doxorubicin. Women treated during the second and third trimesters of pregnancy experience little increase in the rates of complications during labor and delivery, and their newborns do well. There has been no long-term follow-up of exposed fetuses, so we do not have good information on any possible long-term effects of fetal exposure.

Breast-feeding: There are no adequate reports or well-controlled studies in nursing women. Doxorubicin is concentrated in human breast milk, but the amount ingested and absorbed by a breast-feeding newborn is clinically insignificant. Although this amount appears negligible, some experts still consider the use of doxorubicin during breast-feeding contraindicated because if the concentration of doxorubicin got high enough, it could slow the growth rate of cells in the newborn that would normally be rapidly growing.

Potential drug interactions: Interaction between the following medications and doxorubicin has the potential to impact the effect of one or more of the drugs. In some instances the interaction can be dangerous or life-threatening and must be avoided: other cytotoxic drugs, paclitaxel, progesterone, cardioprotectant, fluorouracil, cyclophosphamide, cytarabine.

What the FDA says about use in pregnancy: Category D (see Appendix).

What the available evidence suggests about breast-feeding safety: Likely safe.

The bottom line for you:

- Doxorubicin is used during pregnancy for the treatment of life-threatening diseases. Most exposed pregnancies are successful, especially when treatment begins after the first trimester.
- Doxorubicin is likely safe while breast-feeding, but you should consult your pediatrician first.

DOXYCYCLINE

Brand names: Doxy, Doxy-100, Doxychel, Doxycycline Hyclate, Monodox, Vibramycin, Vibra-Tabs
Drug classes: Antibiotic; Tetracycline
Indications (what it is used for): Gonorrhea, chlamydia, pelvic inflammatory disease, malaria, Lyme disease, anthrax.
How it works: Slows bacterial growth by inhibiting protein synthesis.
Contraindications (reasons you shouldn't take it): Hypersensitivity to drug or class, pregnancy.
Possible side effects and warnings: Can cause low white blood cell or platelet counts; liver or kidney damage; appetite loss; acid reflux; nausea; vomiting; infection of the colon; diarrhea; stomatitis (inflammation of the mucous linings of the mouth); swollen, discolored tongue; black hairy tongue; hoarseness or trouble swallowing; dizziness; headache; and tooth discoloration in children. Should be

used with caution in women with liver or kidney damage. (See tetracycline.)

How it can affect pregnant women: Doxycycline is a broad-spectrum antibiotic. When penicillin is contraindicated (cannot be used), tetracycline-class antibiotics are alternatives for the treatment of gonorrhea, syphilis, Vincent's infection (trench mouth), and *Actinomyces* species. Doxycycline may be less damaging to the liver than tetracycline. There are no adequate reports or well-controlled studies of doxycycline in pregnant women. It is generally avoided during pregnancy because of fetal considerations.

How it can affect a developing embryo or fetus: There are no adequate reports or well-controlled studies in human fetuses. Doxycycline crosses the human placenta and may cause a yellow-gray-brown tooth discoloration in adults after they were exposed during pregnancy or as children. It is unlikely that topically applied doxycycline during pregnancy achieves a blood level high enough to cause this effect. Rodent studies are generally reassuring, revealing no evidence of birth defects, but there is some increase in miscarriage at high doses. However, animal studies are not necessarily good indicators of how a drug will behave in humans.

Breast-feeding: There are no adequate reports or well-controlled studies in nursing women. Doxycycline enters human breast milk, and clinical experience suggests that it is incompatible with breast-feeding.

Potential drug interactions: Interaction between the following medications and doxycyline has the potential to impact the effect of one or more of the drugs. In some instances the interaction can be dangerous or life-threatening and must be avoided: antacids, anticoagulant therapy, penicillin, barbiturates, carbamazepine, phenytoin, methoxyflurane. Doxycycline may render oral contraceptives less effective.

What the FDA says about use in pregnancy: Category D (see Appendix).

What the available evidence suggests about breast-feeding safety: Unsafe.

The bottom line for you:

- Intravenous, intramuscular, and oral doxycycline should be avoided during pregnancy whenever possible because of their effect on the fetal tooth coloration.
- Doxycycline is not safe for use while breast-feeding.

DRONABINOL

Brand name: Marinol

Drug class: Antiemetic

Indications (what it is used for): Nausea or vomiting associated with chemotherapy, AIDS-related loss of appetite.

How it works: Activates cannabinoid receptors to stimulate appetite.

Contraindications (reasons you shouldn't take it): Hypersensitivity to drug or class.

Possible side effects and warnings: Can cause anxiety, fast heart rate, euphoria, dizziness, dry mouth, mood disturbances, loss of muscle coordination, paranoia, orthostatic low blood pressure (blood pressure that drops upon standing up, often causes dizziness, light-headedness), hallucinations, facial flush, and conjunctivitis. Should be used with caution in women with schizophrenia.

How it can affect pregnant women: There are no adequate reports or well-controlled studies of dronabinol in pregnant women. Animal studies revealed evidence of decreased maternal weight gain.

How it can affect a developing embryo or fetus: There are no adequate reports or well-controlled studies in human fetuses. It is unknown whether dronabinol crosses the human placenta. Animal studies suggested a decreased number of offspring, increased fetal mortality, and early resorptions (loss of an embryo). However, animal studies are not necessarily good indicators of how a drug will behave in humans.

Breast-feeding: There is no published data in nursing women. It is unknown whether dronabinol enters human breast milk. If infant formula is available, breast-feeding is not recommended when a mother is HIV positive because HIV can be transmitted to the newborn in the breast milk.

Potential drug interactions: Interaction between the following medications and dronabinol has the potential to impact the effect of one or more of the drugs. In some instances the interaction can be dangerous or life-threatening and must be avoided: amphetamines, cocaine, and other sympathomimetic medications that can produce high blood pressure or a fast heart rate; amitriptyline; tricyclic antidepressants such as amoxapine, atropine, or desipramine; scopolamine, antihistamines, and other anticholinergic drugs; central nervous system depressants such as barbiturates, benzodiazepine, ethanol, lithium, opioids, buspirone, and muscle relaxants.

What the FDA says about use in pregnancy: Category C (see Appendix).

What the available evidence suggests about breast-feeding safety: Unknown.

The bottom line for you:

- There are alternative medications with which there is more experience during pregnancy and while breast-feeding.
- If infant formula is available, breast-feeding is not recommended when a mother is HIV positive because HIV can be transmitted to the newborn in the breast milk

DROPERIDOL

Brand name: Inapsine

Drug classes: Anesthetic, adjunct; Antivertigo; Anxiolytic; Sedative

Indications (what it is used for): Nausea or vomiting during surgery.

How it works: Unknown; blocks adrenergic and dopaminergic receptors, whose activation may cause the nausea and vomiting.

Contraindications (reasons you shouldn't take it): Hypersensitivity to drug or class, abnormal heart rhythms.

Possible side effects and warnings: Can cause tardive dyskinesia (involuntary body movements), abnormal heart rhythm, low blood pressure, bronchospasm, laryngospasm, delirium, drowsiness, chills, anxiety, nightmares, fever, and high blood pressure. Should be used with caution in women with a previous reaction to drugs causing tardive dyskinesia, low blood pressure, central nervous system depression, congestive heart failure, slow heart rate, low magnesium or potassium levels, liver or kidney damage, or alcohol abuse, or who are taking diuretics.

How it can affect pregnant women: There are no adequate reports or well-controlled studies of droperidol in pregnant women. It has been used in emergency rooms for the acute management of migraine headache with success similar to that of meperidine. Droperidol reduces the incidence of itching, nausea, and vomiting after epidural morphine. The addition of metoclopramide appears to increase its efficacy.

How it can affect a developing embryo or fetus: There are no adequate reports or well-controlled studies in human fetuses. It is unknown whether droperidol crosses the human placenta. Rodent studies are reassuring, revealing no increase in malformations or low birth weight. However, animal studies are not necessarily good indicators of how a drug will behave in humans.

Breast-feeding: There is no published data in nursing women. It is unknown whether droperidol enters human breast milk. However, considering that it is used only during surgery, its short-term use is unlikely to pose a significant risk to a breast-feeding baby.

Potential drug interactions: Interaction between the following medications and droperidol has the potential to impact the effect of one or more of the drugs. In some instances the interaction can be dangerous or life-threatening and must be avoided: any drug with the potential to prolong the QT interval (the time it takes for the left and right ventricles of the heart to conduct an impulse and prepare for the next impulse), class I or III antiarrhythmics, antihistamines, antimalarials, calcium channel blockers, neuroleptics, antidepressants, drugs known to induce low magnesium or potassium (these include diuretics, laxatives, and steroid hormones), other CNS-depressant drugs (e.g., barbiturates, tranquilizers, opioids, and general anesthetics).

What the FDA says about use in pregnancy: Category C (see Appendix).

What the available evidence suggests about breast-feeding safety: Likely safe.

The bottom line for you:

- Droperidol has long been an inexpensive and effective medication for prevention of nausea and vomiting associated with cesarean section.

ECONAZOLE NITRATE

Brand name: Spectazole

Drug classes: Antifungal; Dermatologic

Indications (what it is used for): Athlete's foot and yeast infections of the skin.

How it works: Damages the fungus cell wall, leading to cell death.

Contraindications (reasons you shouldn't take it): Hypersensitivity to drug or class.

Possible side effects and warnings: Can cause burning, itching, redness, and rash.

How it can affect pregnant women: Econazole has been used successfully for the treatment of *Candida* vaginitis (vaginal yeast infections), but it is less effective than clotrimazole. There are no adequate reports or well-controlled studies of econazole in pregnant women, but when administered vaginally, there is very little systemic absorption of the drug.

How it can affect a developing embryo or fetus: There are no adequate reports or well-controlled studies in human fetuses. It is unknown whether econazole crosses the human placenta. The results of the only study of pregnant women using the vaginally administered drug found no evidence of birth defects or any other adverse pregnancy outcome. Considering the dose and how it is given, it is unlikely the maternal blood level could cause harm to a developing embryo or fetus. Rodent studies are reassuring, having found no increase in either birth defects or low birth weight despite the use of doses higher than those used clinically. However, animal studies are not necessarily good indicators of how a drug will behave in humans.

Breast-feeding: There is no published data in nursing women. It is unknown whether econazole enters human breast milk. It is present in rodent breast milk after high oral doses. Considering that econazole is usually used for a limited period of time at a low dose that is administered vaginally, it seems unlikely to pose a clinically significant risk to a breast-feeding baby.

Potential drug interactions: No clinically significant interactions are currently identified.

What the FDA says about use in pregnancy: Category C (see Appendix).

What the available evidence suggests about breast-feeding safety: Likely safe.

The bottom line for you:

- Econazole is likely safe for the treatment of vaginal yeast infection during pregnancy and while breast-feeding, although there are other antifungal agents that are more effective and with which there is more experience.

EFAVIRENZ

Brand name: Sustiva
Drug classes: Antiviral; Nonnucleoside reverse transcriptase inhibitor
Indications (what it is used for): HIV infection.
How it works: Prevents the virus from reproducing.
Contraindications (reasons you shouldn't take it): Hypersensitivity to drug or class.
Possible side effects and warnings: Can cause Stevens-Johnson syndrome and erythema multiforme (skin disorders), rash, drowsiness, inability to sleep, abnormal dreams, high cholesterol and triglyceride levels, diarrhea, nausea, vomiting, fever, and liver damage. Should be used with caution in women who have liver damage or who are taking cisapride, triazolam, midazolam, or astemizole.

How it can affect pregnant women: There are no adequate reports or well-controlled studies of efavirenz in pregnant women. There are several case series of HIV-infected women who conceived while taking efavirenz, but preconception planning is advised for women taking efavirenz. It is common practice to switch women who are pregnant or are trying to get pregnant from efavirenz to another nonnucleoside reverse transcriptase inhibitor with which there is more experience during pregnancy and that has not been associated with an increased risk of birth defects. Efavirenz can decrease the effectiveness of oral contraceptives. Women taking efavirenz are encouraged to use a backup barrier method of contraception.

How it can affect a developing embryo or fetus: There are no adequate reports or well-controlled studies in human fetuses. Efavirenz crosses the placenta, achieving levels in the fetus that are similar to those of the mother. There are reports associating first-trimester use with several birth defects, including spina bifida and cleft lip and palate.

Breast-feeding: Efavirenz enters human breast milk. If infant formula is available, breast-feeding is not recommended when a mother is HIV positive because HIV can be transmitted to the newborn in the breast milk. However, none of the children breast-fed by efavirenz-treated women who have been studied became infected while breast-feeding.

Potential drug interactions: Interaction between the following medications and efavirenz has the potential to impact the effect of one or more of the drugs. In some instances the interaction can be dangerous or life-threatening and must be avoided: CYP34A substrates; drugs metabolized by the isozomes CYP2C9, 2C19, and 3A4; drugs that alter

CYP3A4 (such as phenobarbital, rifampin, rifabutin); astemizole; midazolam; triazolam; cisapride; ergot derivatives; voriconazole; atazanavir; clarithromycin; indinavir; lopinavir; methadone; saquinavir; sertraline; ritonavir.

What the FDA says about use in pregnancy: Category D (see Appendix).

What the available evidence suggests about breast-feeding safety: Possibly safe.

The bottom line for you:
- The early experience with efavirenz during pregnancy is concerning; it is likely a human teratogen (a substance that causes birth defects).
- There are alternative agents with which there is more experience during pregnancy and while breast-feeding.
- If infant formula is available, breast-feeding is not recommended when a mother is HIV positive because HIV can be transmitted to the newborn in the breast milk.
- Women who have taken efavirenz during pregnancy are encouraged to register with the Antiretroviral Pregnancy Registry (1-800-258-4263) to help gain a better understanding of the effects of efavirenz during pregnancy.

ELETRIPTAN

Brand names: Relpax
Drug class: Serotonin receptor agonist
Indications (what it is used for): Migraine headache.
How it works: Binds to serotonin receptors, causing brain blood vessels to contract.
Contraindications (reasons you shouldn't take it): Hypersensitivity to drug or class, uncontrolled high blood pressure, cerebrovascular disease (narrowing of blood vessels that supply the brain), ischemic heart disease, coronary spasm, basilar or hemiplegic migraines, peripheral vascular disease (reduced blood flow to areas other than the heart or brain), ischemic bowel (reduced blood flow to the bowel), or use of other ergotamine compounds.

Possible side effects and warnings: Can cause sudden, life-threatening high blood pressure, heart attack, coronary spasm, dangerous heart rhythms, stroke, peripheral vascular ischemia (restricted blood supply to areas other than the brain or heart), bowel ischemia, nausea, vomiting, cramping, heartburn, trouble swallowing, sleepiness, headache, tingling, chest or jaw or neck pain or pressure. Should be used with caution in women with cardiac risk factors.

How it can affect pregnant women: Fifty to 90% of women who suffer migraines experience improvement during pregnancy, mainly during the second and third trimesters. A higher percentage of women who have menstrual migraine experience this improvement compared to women with other types of migraines. There is no published data with eletriptan during pregnancy. Triptans, as a group, may be associated with preterm birth and are best avoided at the extremes of prematurity (before 28 weeks) until more data is available.

How it can affect a developing embryo or fetus: There are no adequate reports or well-controlled studies in human fetuses. It is unknown whether eletriptan crosses the human placenta. An increased risk of birth defects has not been reported for any drug in this class. In some rodents, doses of eletriptan more than 6 times the maximum recommended human dose administered during the period of organ formation were associated with low birth weight and skeletal abnormalities. However, animal studies are not necessarily good indicators of how a drug will behave in humans.

Breast-feeding: Eletriptan is excreted in human breast milk, but the amount reaching the milk is small. It is unlikely that a breast-fed child will ingest a clinically significant amount.

Potential drug interactions: Interaction between the following medications and eletriptan has the potential to impact the effect of one or more of the drugs. In some instances the interaction can be dangerous or life-threatening and must be avoided: ergot-type medications (e.g., dihydroergotamine, methysergide), other 5-HT1 agonists.

What the FDA says about use in pregnancy: Category C (see Appendix).

What the available evidence suggests about breast-feeding safety: Likely safe.

The bottom line for you:

- Eletriptan should be avoided during pregnancy if possible, especially before 28 weeks. There are alternative agents with a more reassuring safety profile.

- Eleptriptan is likely safe for use while breast-feeding.

ENALAPRIL

Brand names: Renitec, Vasotec

Drug class: ACEI/A2R-antagonist (ACE inhibitor)

Indications (what it is used for): High blood pressure, congestive heart failure, heart attack, kidney disease.

How it works: Inhibits the action of a protein that causes blood vessels to contract.

Contraindications (reasons you shouldn't take it): Hypersensitivity to drug or class, renal artery narrowing.

Possible side effects and warnings: Can cause swelling under the skin, low blood pressure, kidney failure, high potassium level, liver damage, low white blood cell count, pancreatitis, dizziness, nausea, vomiting, fatigue, heartburn, rash, hives, and muscle aches. Use with caution in women with kidney disease, low blood volume, severe congestive heart failure, or collagen vascular disease.

How it can affect pregnant women: When pregnancy is discovered, enalapril should be immediately replaced with another suitable blood-pressure-lowering medication not associated with fetal damage (see "How it can affect a developing embryo or fetus").

How it can affect a developing embryo or fetus: There are no adequate reports or well-controlled studies in human fetuses. Enalapril crosses the human placenta. Exposure to agents like enalapril that interfere with the actions of renin and angiotensin (integral to the regulation of blood pressure) is associated with poor skull formation, reversible or irreversible kidney failure, and fetal death, as well as low amniotic fluid volume, prematurity, and low birth weight. These findings are reported even after first-trimester exposure (which was previously thought to be low risk).

Breast-feeding: Trace amounts of enalapril are detected in breast milk. Until further study, enalapril should be given at the lowest possible dose if required while breast-feeding, and exposed infants monitored for possible adverse effects.

Potential drug interactions: Interaction between the following medications and enalapril has the potential to impact the effect of one or more of the drugs. In some instances the interaction can be dangerous or life-threatening and must be avoided: diuretics, agents that release renin, nonsteroidal anti-inflammatory drugs (NSAIDs), lithium.

What the FDA says about use in pregnancy: Category D (see Appendix).

What the available evidence suggests about breast-feeding safety: Unknown.

The bottom line for you:

- Enalapril is a known teratogen (a substance that can cause birth defects). It and other medications that inhibit the action of renin and/or angiotensin should be avoided during pregnancy.

- If treatment with enalapril is absolutely necessary during pregnancy and while breast-feeding, the lowest possible dose should be used and the fetus/newborn monitored closely for adverse effects.

ENOXAPARIN

Brand name: Lovenox

Drug classes: Anticoagulant; Low-molecular-weight heparin

Indications (what it is used for): Prevents and treats blood clots in the mother or placenta.

How it works: Accelerates natural anticoagulants in the body.

Contraindications (reasons you shouldn't take it): Hypersensitivity to drug or class, active bleeding, low platelet count.

Possible side effects and warnings: Can cause epidural/spinal hematoma, low platelet count, paralysis, congestive heart failure, pneumonia, anemia, hemorrhage, fever, bleeding or bruising at the injection site, blood in the urine, and liver damage. Should be used with caution in women with diabetic retinopathy or kidney disease.

How it can affect pregnant women: The incidence of blood clots (both pulmonary embolus and clots in the leg veins) is higher during pregnancy and for the first 6 weeks after delivery (as high as 1% of all pregnancies and 3% after cesarean section). Pregnancy increases the clearance (how fast a drug is eliminated from your body) of both heparin and drugs like enoxaparin, which means that the dose will need to be increased as a pregnancy advances. Heparin-like drugs cause bone thinning at a rate similar to heparin, although they may be less likely to cause low platelet counts. Enoxaparin has also been used to prevent blood clots during pregnancy in women with congenital clotting abnormalities or a mechanical heart valve or antiphospholipid syndrome (the immune system mistakenly produces antibodies against normal blood proteins). The manufacturer specifically discourages the use of enoxaparin with mechanical heart valves since there have been multiple deaths. Women who are treated for the prevention of blood clots or pulmonary embolus are at risk after an epidural or spinal block of developing a collection of blood that compresses the spinal cord and causes paralysis. Because the effects of enoxaparin cannot be easily reversed, women are often switched to unfractionated heparin at 36 weeks of pregnancy. Otherwise, the next injection should be withheld until contractions begin, or injections discontinued 12 hours prior to a planned delivery. Enoxaparin should be also discontinued 12 hours before placement of an epidural or spinal block, and not be restarted until about 12 hours after removal of an indwelling epidural catheter.

How it can affect a developing embryo or fetus: Enoxaparin does not cross the human placenta and therefore poses no direct risk to the human fetus.

Breast-feeding: There are no adequate reports or well-controlled studies in nursing women. Enoxaparin is unlikely to enter the breast milk because of its large molecular size. Even if it did, the child's stomach acids would break it down.

Potential drug interactions: Any medications that can increase the risk of bleeding should be discontinued prior to beginning enoxaparin. These include anticoagulants; platelet inhibitors including aspirin; salicylates; nonsteroidal anti-inflammatory drugs (NSAIDs), including ketorolac; dipyridamole; sulfinpyrazone.

What the FDA says about use in pregnancy: Category B (see Appendix).

What the available evidence suggests about breast-feeding safety: Likely safe.

The bottom line for you:

- Enoxaparin is safe to use during pregnancy and while breast-feeding.
- The dose must be monitored periodically to be sure the amount given is optimal.
- Enoxaparin is more expensive than unfractionated heparin with likely equal efficacy and a similar risk of bone thinning during long-term therapy.

EPHEDRINE

Brand names: None listed but often an ingredient in over-the-counter medications

Drug classes: Adrenergic agonist; Bronchodilator; Decongestant, nasal

Indications (what it is used for): Nasal decongestant, support blood pressure after epidural analgesia.

How it works: Causes release of epinephrine and norepinephrine from nerve endings, which stimulates adrenergic receptors and causes blood vessels to constrict.

Contraindications (reasons you shouldn't take it): Hypersensitivity to drug or class, overactive thyroid, porphyria (a rare group of blood disorders), coronary artery disease, hypertension, use of a monoamine oxidase inhibitor (MAOI) within 14 days.

Possible side effects and warnings: Can cause irregular or fast heart rate, sleeplessness, nervousness, and dizziness. Should be used with caution in women with glaucoma, irregular heart rate, or overactive thyroid.

How it can affect pregnant women: There are no adequate reports or well-controlled studies of ephedrine in pregnant women. It is considered the drug of choice to treat low blood pressure associated with an epidural or a spinal block, where it helps preserve blood flow to the fetus. When overused as part of a decongestant, ephedrine may worsen the high blood pressure associated with preeclampsia (high blood pressure and protein in the urine during pregnancy and complications associated with it).

How it can affect a developing embryo or fetus: There are no adequate reports or well-controlled studies in human fetuses. Ephedrine apparently crosses the placenta, but the long clinical experience with the drug, both in over-the-counter preparations and during labor, is reassuring, finding no birth defects or fetal harm.

Breast-feeding: There are no adequate reports or well-controlled studies in nursing women. Less than 1% of the dose taken by the mother is excreted into the breast milk, and it is generally considered safe during breast-feeding. However, ephedrine use can decrease milk production.

Potential drug interactions: Interaction between the following medications and ephedrine has the potential to impact the effect of one or more of the drugs. In some instances the interaction can be dangerous or life-threatening and must be avoided: bromocriptine, atomoxetine, insulin.

What the FDA says about use in pregnancy: Category C (see Appendix).

What the available evidence suggests about breast-feeding safety: Likely safe but can decrease milk volume.

The bottom line for you:
- Ephedrine is considered safe during pregnancy to treat an occasional stuffy nose or to treat the low blood pressure associated with an epidural or a spinal block.
- Although safe for the breast-fed newborn, it may decrease the mother's milk supply.

EPINEPHRINE
Brand names: Adrenalin Chloride, Ana-Guard, Epifrin, EpiPen, Glaucon, Philip, Racepinephrine, Sus-Phrine

Drug classes: Adrenergic agonist; Bronchodilator; Inotrope; Ophthalmic; Pressor

Indications (what it is used for): Severe asthma, life-threatening allergic reaction, cardiac stoppage.

How it works: Potent activator of a- and b-adrenoceptors, which cause the symptoms.

Contraindications (reasons you shouldn't take it): Hypersensitivity to drug or class, narrow-angle glaucoma, coronary artery disease, cerebrovascular disease (narrowing of blood vessels that supply the brain), sulfite allergy.

Possible side effects and warnings: Can cause stroke, brain hemorrhage, irregular or rapid heart rate, high blood pressure, tremors, nausea, vomiting, and headache. Should be used with caution in women with asthma or an overactive thyroid.

How it can affect pregnant women: Epinephrine is commonly used for the relief of severe bronchospasm due to allergy. There are no adequate reports or well-controlled studies in pregnant women. Epinephrine is often mixed with local anesthetic agents used during pregnancy or delivery to prolong the anesthetic action.

How it can affect a developing embryo or fetus: There are no adequate reports or well-controlled studies in human fetuses. Epinephrine is a natural substance and rapidly crosses the human placenta. It has been shown to cause birth defects in rodents at high doses, likely by interfering with maternal and/or fetal blood flow. However, animal studies are not necessarily good indicators of how a drug will behave in humans.

Breast-feeding: There is no published data in nursing women. It is unknown whether epinephrine enters human breast milk. However, considering that it is usually used in limited doses and is rapidly destroyed by stomach acid when orally ingested, epinephrine use is unlikely to pose a clinically significant risk to a breast-feeding baby.

Potential drug interactions: Interaction between the following medications and epinephrine has the potential to impact the effect of one or more of the drugs. In some instances the interaction can be dangerous or life-threatening and must be avoided: digitalis, mercurial diuretics, or other drugs that sensitize the heart to arrhythmias; tricyclic antidepressants; certain antihistamines (e.g., chlorpheniramine, diphenhydramine, tripelennamine); levothyroxine.

What the FDA says about use in pregnancy: Category C (see Appendix).

What the available evidence suggests about breast-feeding safety: Safe.

The bottom line for you:

- Epinephrine is safe during pregnancy and while breast-feeding at the recommended doses.

EPOETIN ALFA

Brand names: EPO, Epogen, Eprex, Erythropoietin, Procrit

Drug classes: Hematopoietic agent; Hormone

Indications (what it is used for): To reduce the need for transfusion because of AZT therapy, chronic kidney failure, or chemotherapy.

How it works: Stimulates the production of red blood cells.

Contraindications (reasons you shouldn't take it): Hypersensitivity to drug or class.

Possible side effects and warnings: Can cause severe high blood pressure, rapid heart rate, congestive heart failure, heart attack, stroke, blood clots, seizures, headache, joint pain, fever, diarrhea, nausea, vomiting, dizziness, rash, tingling, and shortness of breath. Should be used with caution in women with high blood pressure; iron, folate, or vitamin B_{12} deficiency; congestive heart failure; coronary artery disease; seizure disorder; or sickle-cell anemia.

How it can affect pregnant women: There are no adequate reports or well-controlled studies of epoetin in pregnant women. Epoetin is used to boost the effectiveness of iron treatment for pregnant women with anemia due to iron deficiency. It has been used safely and effectively to treat a pregnant woman with sickle-cell disease whose religion forbade blood transfusions.

How it can affect a developing embryo or fetus: There are no adequate reports or well-controlled studies in human fetuses. It does not appear to cross the human placenta.

Breast-feeding: There is no published data in nursing women. It is unknown whether epoetin enters human breast milk, although the natural form, erythropoietin, is a normal component of breast milk.

Potential drug interactions: None currently identified.

What the FDA says about use in pregnancy: Category C (see Appendix).

What the available evidence suggests about breast-feeding safety: Likely safe.

The bottom line for you:

- Epoetin should be safe for use during pregnancy and while breast-feeding if alternative, less expensive maternal therapy fails to resolve the anemia.

EPOPROSTENOL

Brand name: Flolan

Drug classes: Antihypertensive; Platelet inhibitor; Prostaglandin; Vasodilator

Indications (what it is used for): Pulmonary hypertension.

How it works: Directly dilates blood vessels.

Contraindications (reasons you shouldn't take it): Hypersensitivity to the drug or class, congestive heart failure, pulmonary edema.

Possible side effects and warnings: Can cause pulmonary edema, sudden pulmonary hypertension, low platelet count, headache, nausea, vomiting, anxiety, rapid heart rate, low blood pressure, chest pain, diarrhea, tingling, and shortness of breath.

How it can affect pregnant women: Idiopathic (unexplained) pulmonary hypertension (high blood pressure in the lungs) is a rare, progressive condition that can be fatal in as many as 50% of cases, and it may be worsened by pregnancy. Epoprostenol is a synthetic prostacyclin that dilates the pulmonary blood vessels. It has been used with success to treat women during pregnancy and after delivery. It is also used to treat persistent pulmonary hypertension in newborns.

How it can affect a developing embryo or fetus: There are no adequate reports or well-controlled studies in human fetuses. It is unknown whether epoprostenol crosses the human placenta. However, the placenta and fetus already make large quantities of the natural version of prostacyclin, and there is no reason to suspect that it will be harmful to an embryo or fetus unless the mother's blood pressure is too low. Rodent studies reveal no evidence of birth defects or low birth weight despite the use of doses higher than those used clinically. However, animal studies are not necessarily good indicators of how a drug will behave in humans.

Breast-feeding: There is no published data in nursing women. It is unknown whether epoprostenol is excreted into human breast milk, although prostacyclin is a normal component of it.

Potential drug interactions: Interaction between the following medications and epoprostenol has the potential to impact the effect of one or more of the drugs. In some instances the interaction can be dangerous or life-threatening and must be avoided: diuretics, blood-pressure-lowering medications, or other vasodilators; furosemide; digoxin.

What the FDA says about use in pregnancy: Category B (see Appendix).

What the available evidence suggests about breast-feeding safety: Likely safe.

The bottom line for you:

- Epoprostenol may be used in pregnant and breast-feeding women who have life-threatening pulmonary hypertension.

EPROSARTAN MESYLATE

Brand name: Teveten

Drug classes: Antihypertensive; AT-1 antagonist

Indications (what it is used for): High blood pressure.

How it works: Blocks the angiotensin receptor, whose activation causes blood vessel constriction and hypertension.

Contraindications (reasons you shouldn't take it): Hypersensitivity to drug or class, pregnancy.

Possible side effects and warnings: Can cause severe high blood pressure, rapid heart rate, congestive heart failure, heart attack, stroke, blood clots, seizures, headache, joint pain, fever, diarrhea, nausea, vomiting, shortness of breath, dizziness, rash, and tingling. Should be used with caution in women with a narrow renal artery, intravascular volume depletion, or congestive heart failure.

How it can affect pregnant women: There is no published data with eprosartan during pregnancy. However, extensive experience with other drugs that block or interfere with the renin-angiotensin system (integral to the regulation of blood pressure) indicates that it is a teratogen (a substance that can cause birth defects) and should be avoided during pregnancy unless there are no other options.

How it can affect a developing embryo or fetus: There are no adequate reports or well-controlled

studies in human fetuses. It is unknown whether eprosartan crosses the human placenta. Similar drugs are proven teratogens. Adverse fetal effects reported with similar medications include underdeveloped skull, reversible or irreversible kidney failure, low amniotic fluid, prematurity, low birth weight, and death. These findings are reported even after late first-trimester exposure.

Breast-feeding: There is no published data in nursing women. It is unknown whether eprosartan enters human breast milk; it is excreted into rodent breast milk. Until further study, it should be given at the lowest possible dose if required while breast-feeding, and infants should be monitored for possible adverse effects.

Potential drug interactions: No clinically significant drug interactions currently identified.

What the FDA says about use in pregnancy: Category D (see Appendix).

What the available evidence suggests about breast-feeding safety: Unknown.

The bottom line for you:

- Eprosartan and drugs that inhibit the action of angiotensin are all likely causes of major birth defects and should be avoided during pregnancy.
- There are alternative agents with which there is more experience during pregnancy and while breast-feeding.

ERGOCALCIFEROL

Brand names: Biocatines D2 masiva, Deltalin, Drisdol, Radiostol, Vitamin D

Drug class: Vitamin/mineral

Indications (what it is used for): Rickets, hypoparathyroidism, hereditary low phosphate levels.

How it works: Ergocalciferol is converted first in the liver and then in the kidneys to the active form of vitamin D. Vitamin D2 stimulates the absorption of calcium and phosphorus from the bowels and thus bone thickening.

Contraindications (reasons you shouldn't take it): Hypersensitivity, certain kidney diseases, high calcium or vitamin A levels.

Possible side effects and warnings: Can cause high calcium levels, nausea, vomiting, loss of appetite, anemia, weakness, and kidney dysfunction. Should be used with caution in women with kidney dysfunction and/or stones, or with cerebrovascular disease (narrowing of blood vessels that supply the brain).

How it can affect pregnant women: Ergocalciferol is a regulator of calcium. There are few well-controlled studies of ergocalciferol in pregnant women. Many studies reveal a high rate of vitamin D deficiency in pregnant women, and supplementation is recommended, although the amount is debated. Veiled or dark-skinned pregnant women have an increased risk of deficiency, since exposure to sunlight helps our bodies manufacture vitamin D. The RDA (recommended daily allowance) during pregnancy is 400–600 IU; the safety of larger doses is unknown. Oral supplementation in vitamin D–deficient women raises the levels of vitamin D in the blood. There is a long clinical experience of ergocalciferol supplementation during pregnancy and breast-feeding without complications. There are no adequate reports or well-controlled studies in pregnant women. In one study, women who took 4,000 IU daily in their second and third trimesters experienced a lower rate of pregnancy-related complications compared to women who took 400 IU every day.

How it can affect a developing embryo or fetus: There are no adequate reports or well-controlled studies in human fetuses. It is unknown whether ergocalciferol crosses the human placenta. However, maternal vitamin D supplementation does not significantly increase the level in the newborn. Toxic levels of vitamin D (consistently taking a much higher dose than the RDA during pregnancy) have been associated in fetuses with a particular type of heart disease that narrows the aortic valve, causes an elflike appearance, and results in mental retardation. Newborns with low vitamin D often have markers predictive of future allergies.

Breast-feeding: There are no adequate reports or well-controlled studies in nursing women. It is likely that supplementation is safe during breast-feeding. Vitamin D is normally found in breast milk, and ergocalciferol use has little effect on the level of vitamin D metabolites. There is a single report of a woman given large doses of vitamin D in whom 25-hydroxycholecalciferol (the circulating form of vitamin D, which promotes the absorption of calcium) was identified in her milk, and her child developed high calcium levels.

Potential drug interactions: Mineral oil interferes with the absorption of fat-soluble vitamins, such as vitamin D. Thiazide diuretic use in hypoparathyroid patients being treated with ergocalciferol may cause high calcium levels.

What the FDA says about use in pregnancy: Category C (see Appendix).

What the available evidence suggests about breast-feeding safety: Likely safe.

The bottom line for you

- Vitamin D supplementation is recommended during pregnancy and may reduce the risk of adverse outcomes. Most multivitamin supplements (prenatal or otherwise) and calcium supplements contain vitamin D in one form or another. The RDA during pregnancy is 400–600 IU. Check the label and speak with your health-care provider before deciding to take an additional amount.
- There are many forms of vitamin D sold. Base your supplementation on the number of units of vitamin per pill.

ERGOTAMINE

Brand names: Ergomar, Ergostat, Medihaler-Ergotamine, Wigrettes
Drug class: Ergot alkaloid
Indications (what it is used for): To stop or prevent a migraine headache.

How it works: Likely constricts blood vessels (dilation of the blood vessels is associated with the headache).

Contraindications (reasons you shouldn't take it): Hypersensitivity to drug or class, peripheral vascular disease (reduced blood flow to areas other than the heart or brain), coronary artery disease, high blood pressure, liver or kidney dysfunction, severe itching, bacterial infection in the blood, pregnancy.

Possible side effects and warnings: Can cause nausea, vomiting, leg weakness, muscle aches, numbness and tingling of the fingers and toes, pain over the heart, transient changes in heart rate, swelling, and itching. Should be used with caution in breast-feeding women.

How it can affect pregnant women: Fifty to 90% of women who suffer migraines experience improvement during pregnancy, mainly during the second and third trimesters. A higher percentage of women who have menstrual migraine experience this improvement compared to women with other types of migraines. There are no adequate reports or well-controlled studies in pregnant women. Ergotamine causes strong uterine contractions and can cause miscarriage. Some studies note increased rates of preterm birth and low birth weight in women taking ergotamine. Ergotamine constricts both arteries and veins in many organs. By reducing the diameter of the blood vessel, which in turn reduces blood flow, it ends the migraine. However, the same event in the uterus can lead to miscarriage or preterm birth depending on the gestational age.

How it can affect a developing embryo or fetus: There are no adequate reports or well-controlled studies in human fetuses. It is unknown whether ergotamine crosses the human placenta, but it is a potent contractor of the uterus and uterine blood vessels, resulting in miscarriage or preterm birth. Although ergotamine is not likely a direct cause of birth defects, the severe contractions or vasoconstriction associated with excess drug could lead to a lack of oxygen and fetal death. It has also been associated with a set of birth defects called Möbius syndrome, an extremely rare congenital neurological disorder characterized by facial paralysis and the inability to move the eyes from side to side.

Breast-feeding: There are no adequate reports or well-controlled studies in nursing women. Ergotamine is excreted into human breast milk. Theoretically, excessive dosing or prolonged use of ergotamine could inhibit breast-feeding by decreasing blood flow. Although generally considered incompatible with breast-feeding, the only published study found no effect on milk production or infant weight gain.

Potential drug interactions: When combined with other vasoconstrictor drugs, ergotamine can cause dangerous high blood pressure.

What the FDA says about use in pregnancy: Category X (see Appendix).

What the available evidence suggests about breast-feeding safety: Possibly not safe.

The bottom line for you

- Ergotamine should be avoided during pregnancy.
- Although the risks while breast-feeding are probably small, there are alternative agents for which there is a higher safety profile and more experience.

ERYTHROMYCIN

Brand names: Akne-Mycin, A/T/S, C-Solve-2, Del-Mycin, Dumotrycin, E-Base, Emgel, Endo-eritrin, Erisone, Eritomicina, Erycette, Erygel, Erythra-Derm, ETS, Ilotycin, Mercina, PCE, Proterytrin, Retcin, Romycin, Sansac, Staticin, T-Stat

Drug classes: Antibiotic; Dermatologic; Macrolide; Ophthalmic

Indications (what it is used for): Prolonging pregnancy after preterm premature rupture of the membranes (PPROM, water breaking before 37 weeks); treatment of some sexually transmitted diseases; prevention of rheumatic heart disease, bacterial endocarditis, and neonatal group B streptococcal infection.

How it works: Inhibits protein synthesis by the bacteria so they cannot grow and divide.

Contraindications (reasons you shouldn't take it): Hypersensitivity to drug or class, use of cisapride or astemizole.

Possible side effects and warnings: Can cause a life-threatening allergic reaction, liver damage, jaundice, blood clots, abnormal or irregular heart rate, low blood pressure, nausea, vomiting, diarrhea, itching, loss of appetite, and abdominal pain. Should be used with caution in women with myasthenia gravis (an autoimmune disease causing muscle weakness) or liver dysfunction.

How it can affect pregnant women: Erythromycin decreases the risk of infection in women with PPROM, but it does not help women who have preterm labor but whose water has not broken. In that case, it may even increase the risk of neurodevelopmental complications in the newborn. Erythromycin reduces the frequency of preterm birth in women early in pregnancy who have bacteria in their urine or symptomatic vaginitis. Erythromycin is an effective alternative therapy for the treatment of chlamydia. Erythromycin is not recommended for the treatment of syphilis during pregnancy because the amount crossing the placenta is low and it is unlikely to treat or prevent fetal infection. A relationship between oral erythromycin and sudden cardiac death was reported in patients also taking strong inhibitors of CYP3A, such as nitroimidazole antifungal agents, diltiazem, nifedipine, verapamil, and troleandomycin. Because of this, care is needed in using erythromycin for PPROM, as there is a growing practice of using nifedipine to delay preterm birth.

How it can affect a developing embryo or fetus: There are no adequate reports or well-controlled studies in human fetuses. Erythromycin crosses the human placenta, reaching a level of about one-third the mother's concentration. This level is too low to treat such fetal infections as syphilis. Rodent studies reveal no evidence of birth defects or low birth weight despite the use of doses higher than those used clinically. However, animal studies are not necessarily good indicators of how a drug will behave in humans.

Breast-feeding: There are no adequate reports or well-controlled studies in nursing women. Erythromycin is excreted into human breast milk, achieving a milk level similar to that of the mother's blood.

Potential drug interactions: Interaction between the following medications and erythromycin has the potential to impact the effect of one or more of the drugs. In some instances the interaction can be dangerous or life-threatening and must be avoided: theophylline, oral anticoagulants, ergotamine, dihydroergotamine, triazolam, midazolam, alfentanil, astemizole, bromocriptine, carbamazepine, cisapride, cyclosporine, disopyramide, hexobarbital, lovastatin, phenytoin, tacrolimus, terfenadine, valproate.

What the FDA says about use in pregnancy: Category B (see Appendix).

What the available evidence suggests about breast-feeding safety: Safe.

The bottom line for you:

- Erythromycin is generally considered safe for use during pregnancy and while breast-feeding.
- Erythromycin is the treatment of choice for PPROM to prolong the time before infection sets in and triggers labor.
- It should probably be avoided in women taking a calcium channel blocker (e.g., to slow preterm labor) and in women in preterm labor with intact membranes (the water has not broken).
- Erythromycin may reduce the chance of preterm birth in women with asymptomatic bacteriuria (bacteria in the urine without the usual symptoms of urinary tract infection) or symptomatic lower genital tract infections.

ESCITALOPRAM

Brand name: Lexapro
Drug classes: Antidepressant; SSRI (selective serotonin reuptake inhibitor)

Indications (what it is used for): Depression, anxiety (generalized).

How it works: Inhibits the reuptake of serotonin, a chemical in nerves involved in regulating mood.

Contraindications (reasons you shouldn't take it): Hypersensitivity to drug or class, citalopram hypersensitivity or use, or use of a monoamine oxidase inhibitor (MAOI) within 14 days.

Possible side effects and warnings: Can cause serotonin syndrome (drug reaction causing excessive levels of serotonin in the blood), withdrawal syndrome, mania, low sodium, sleeplessness, sleepiness, sweating, fatigue, dizziness, dry mouth, loss of sex drive, inability to achieve orgasm, decreased appetite, constipation, diarrhea, heartburn, cholestasis (slow or blocked flow of bile from the liver), and abdominal pain. Should be used with caution in women with liver or kidney damage, history of mania, or seizure disorder, or who are at risk for suicide.

How it can affect pregnant women: Depression is common during and after pregnancy but often goes unrecognized and untreated. Depression can be made worse by pregnancy or delivery, and suicide is a not uncommon cause of maternal death. Pregnancy is not a reason to discontinue antidepressant drugs if the medication is effective and needed. A woman being treated for depression who becomes pregnant should not discontinue medication abruptly on her own but rather discuss her treatment and condition with her medical provider. Pregnancy may increase the dose needed to be effective, and women with a history of depression have a higher rate of recurrence after delivery.

The published data with escitalopram during pregnancy consists mostly of inadequately documented case reports. Limited study suggests increased metabolism during the second half of pregnancy. If true, continued effectiveness may require an increase in the dose. As for most psychotropic drugs, using only one medication and the lowest effective quantity taken in divided doses to minimize the peaks may reduce any potential risk associated with the medication.

How it can affect a developing embryo or fetus: There are no adequate reports or well-controlled studies in human fetuses. It is unknown whether escitalopram crosses the human placenta. Citalopram, a closely related chemical, does cross the human placenta, achieving a fetal level that is about a tenth of the mother's. This degree of transfer is significantly lower than with fluoxetine (another SSRI), which suggests that lower fetal exposure will occur with escitalopram. Some studies have shown a small increase in the risk of heart defects in embryos exposed to SSRIs in the first trimester but current study suggests it is not dose dependent (the risk does not increase or decrease as the dose does, suggesting other factors may play a role in creating the defect). The safest approach for all SSRIs is probably to avoid them in the first trimester, if medically prudent. Women with moderate to severe depression responsive to their medication, however, should continue treatment during pregnancy as the benefit outweighs the possible risks to mother and child.

SSRI use late in pregnancy may double the risk of persistent pulmonary hypertension (high blood pressure affecting the lungs) during the newborn period (which, at 2 in 1000 births, is low to begin with). SSRI exposure during the third trimester and until delivery may also lead to a withdrawal syndrome during the first few days of life, requiring extra care. Symptoms in the newborn may include problems breathing, jitteriness, increased muscle tone, irritability, altered sleep patterns, tremors, and poor eating. In most cases, these symptoms are mild and disappear within 2 two weeks with no treatment. These symptoms occur in up to 30% of exposed newborns, and, although they can occur at all doses, may occur more often with higher doses. The risk does not outweigh the benefit of needed therapy.

Rodent studies found no evidence of birth defects despite the use of doses higher than those used clinically. However, animal studies are not necessarily a good indicator of how a drug will behave in humans.

Breast-feeding: There is no published data in nursing women with escitalopram. However, in one study, citalopram was found in breast milk but undetectable in a breast-fed newborn. In two other reports of infants exposed to citalopram, sleepiness, decreased feeding, and weight loss were described. Caution is advised.

Potential drug interactions: Interaction between the following medications and escitalopram has the potential to impact the effect of one or more of the drugs. In some instances the interaction can be dangerous or life-threatening and must be avoided: ketoconazole, desipramine, cimetidine, sumatriptan, nonsteroidal anti-inflammatory drugs (NSAIDs), aspirin.

What the FDA says about use in pregnancy: Category C (see Appendix).

What the available evidence suggests about breast-feeding safety: Probably safe.

The bottom line for you:

- Depression may be life-threatening during pregnancy and after delivery; pregnancy and breast-feeding are not reasons to discontinue needed therapy.
- Although there are alternative agents with which there is more experience during pregnancy and breast-feeding, escitalopram may be used when necessary to treat clinically significant depression in pregnancy.
- Until more information is available, it is best to observe the newborn closely while breast-feeding.

ESOMEPRAZOLE

Brand name: Nexium

Drug classes: Antiulcer; Gastrointestinal; Proton pump inhibitor

Indications (what it is used for): GERD (gastroesophageal reflux disease), erosive esophagitis, *H. pylori* infection.

How it works: Reduces release of acid from the stomach lining.

Contraindications (reasons you shouldn't take it): Hypersensitivity to drug or class.

Possible side effects and warnings: Can cause liver dysfunction, diarrhea, and headache. Should be used with caution in women with liver dysfunction or if it is needed long-term.

How it can affect pregnant women: Esomeprazole is similar to omeprazole. There are no adequate reports or well-controlled studies in pregnant women. GERD and/or heartburn occurs in 45–85% of pregnant women in part because of high progesterone and estrogen levels. The treatment for GERD consists of reducing gastric acidity starting with lifestyle and dietary changes. If these fail, antacids or sucralfate are first-line medical therapies, followed by histamine receptor blockers. Proton pump inhibitors such as esomeprazole are being used with increasing frequency during pregnancy, though additional study is needed.

How it can affect a developing embryo or fetus: It is unknown whether esomeprazole crosses the human placenta. In several studies of pregnant women (totaling almost 1,000 pregnancies), there was no increase in the rate of birth defects or adverse pregnancy outcomes. Rodent studies are likewise reassuring, with no increase in birth defects or low birth weight despite the use of doses higher than those used clinically. However, animal studies are not necessarily good indicators of how a drug will behave in humans.

Breast-feeding: There is no published data in nursing women. It is unknown whether esomeprazole is excreted into human breast milk. It likely behaves like omeprazole, where only clinically insignificant amounts of the drug are found in breast milk.

Potential drug interactions: Interaction between the following medications and esomeprazole has the potential to impact the effect of one or more of the drugs. In some instances the interaction can be dangerous or life-threatening and must be avoided: warfarin, atazanavir, ketoconazole, iron salts, digoxin, clarithromycin, amoxicillin.

What the FDA says about use in pregnancy: Category B (see Appendix).

What the available evidence suggests about breast-feeding safety: Likely safe.

The bottom line for you:

- Based on existing information on esomeprazole and experience with the related medication omeprazole, esomeprazole may be used safely during pregnancy and while breast-feeding for the treatment of acid reflux that is unresponsive to diet and antacid therapy.

ESTRADIOL

Brand names: Alora, Climara, Estrace, Estraderm, Estring, Fempatch, Vivelle

Drug classes: Estrogen; Hormone

Indications (what it is used for): Contraception (in combination with a progesterone-type agent), vasomotor symptoms of menopause, osteoporosis prevention, atrophic vaginitis, primary ovarian failure, breast cancer palliation.

How it works: A natural estrogen that binds to estrogen receptors, triggering the development and maintenance of female sex characteristics; also triggers responses to estrogen that are not dependent on binding an estrogen receptor.

Contraindications (reasons you shouldn't take it): Vaginal bleeding of an unknown cause, blood clots, estrogen-dependent breast cancer, pregnancy.

Possible side effects and warnings: Can cause blood clots, stroke, heart attack, endometrial and breast cancer, gallbladder disease, pancreatitis, high blood pressure, breast tenderness, liver tumor, bloating, nausea, vomiting, headache, dizziness, depression, weight gain, libido changes, intolerance to contact lenses, migraine, and rash. Should be used with caution in women over the age of 35 who smoke and/or women who are breast-feeding, or who suffer from liver dysfunction.

How it can affect pregnant women: There is no indication for estradiol during pregnancy.

How it can affect a developing embryo or fetus: There are no adequate reports or well-controlled studies in human fetuses. Although other synthetic/environmental estrogens (e.g., diethylstilbestrol) are recognized causes of birth defects, few studies support this effect for estradiol. There is no evidence of significant fetal harm after inadvertent exposure during the first trimester.

Breast-feeding: Although estradiol is excreted into breast milk and has been reported to reduce the amount of milk produced, it is not effective as an inhibitor of milk production. Estrogen-containing contraceptives can be started after the sixth week of breast-feeding when the lipid and clotting profiles of the mother have returned to normal.

Potential drug interactions: Interaction between the following medications or substances and estradiol has the potential to impact the effect of one or more of the drugs. In some instances the interaction can be dangerous or life-threatening and must be avoided: St. John's wort, phenobarbital, carbamazepine, rifampin, erythromycin, clarithromycin, ketoconazole, itraconazole, ritonavir, grapefruit and grapefruit juice.

What the FDA says about use in pregnancy: Category X (see Appendix).

What the available evidence suggests about breast-feeding safety: Safe.

The bottom line for you:
- There is no indication for estradiol during pregnancy.
- There is also no clear evidence that inadvertent exposure to estradiol in the first trimester causes birth defects.
- Estrogens, as a category, when taken in the first few weeks after delivery, may decrease milk production and increase the risk of blood clots.

ESTROGENS, CONJUGATED

Brand names: Azumon, Conjugen, Emopremarin, Mannest, Menopak-E, Ovest, Premarin, Trepova
Drug classes: Estrogen; Hormone

Indications (what it is used for): Primary ovarian failure, vasomotor symptoms of menopause, osteoporosis.

How it works: Binds to estrogen receptors, triggering the development and maintenance of female sex characteristics; also triggers responses to estrogen that are not dependent on binding an estrogen receptor.

Contraindications (reasons you shouldn't take it): Vaginal bleeding of an unknown cause, blood clots, estrogen-dependent breast cancer, pregnancy.

Possible side effects and warnings: Can cause blood clots, stroke, heart attack, endometrial and breast cancer, gallbladder disease, pancreatitis, high blood pressure, breast tenderness, liver tumor, bloating, nausea, vomiting, headache, dizziness, depression, weight gain, libido changes, intolerance to contact lenses, migraine, and rash. Should be used with caution in women over the age of 35 who smoke and/or women who are breast-feeding, or who suffer from liver dysfunction.

How it can affect pregnant women: There are no indications for conjugated estrogens during pregnancy.

How it can affect a developing embryo or fetus: There are no adequate reports or well-controlled studies in human fetuses. Although other synthetic/environmental estrogens (e.g., diethylstilbestrol) are recognized causes of birth defects, few studies support this effect for conjugated estrogens. There is no evidence of significant fetal harm after inadvertent exposure during the first trimester.

Breast-feeding: Although conjugated estrogens are excreted into breast milk and have been reported to reduce the amount of milk produced, they are not effective as inhibitors of milk production. Estrogen-containing contraceptives can be started after the sixth week of breast-feeding when the lipid and clotting profiles of the mother have returned to normal.

Potential drug interactions: Interaction between the following medications and conjugated estrogens has the potential to impact the effect of one or more of the drugs. In some instances the interaction can be dangerous or life-threatening and must be avoided: St. John's wort, phenobarbital, carbamazepine, rifampin, erythromycin, clarithromycin, ketoconazole, itraconazole, ritonavir, grapefruit and grapefruit juice.

What the FDA says about use in pregnancy: Category X (see Appendix).

What the available evidence suggests about breast-feeding safety: Safe.

The bottom line for you:

- There is no indication for conjugated estrogens during pregnancy.
- There is also no clear evidence that inadvertent exposure in the first trimester causes birth defects.
- Estrogens as a category, when taken in the first few weeks after delivery, may decrease milk production and increase the risk of blood clots.

ESTROGENS, ESTERIFIED

Brand names: Amnestrogen, Estratab, Evex, Femogen, Menest

Drug classes: Estrogen; Hormone

Indications (what it is used for): Hormone replacement, vasomotor symptoms of menopause, osteoporosis prevention, atrophic vaginitis, primary ovarian failure, breast cancer palliation.

How it works: Binds to estrogen receptors, triggering the development and maintenance of female sex characteristics; also triggers responses to estrogen that are not dependent on binding an estrogen receptor.

Contraindications (reasons you shouldn't take it): Vaginal bleeding of an unknown cause, blood clots, estrogen-dependent breast cancer, pregnancy.

Possible side effects and warnings: Can cause blood clots, stroke, heart attack, endometrial and breast cancer, gallbladder disease, pancreatitis, high blood pressure, breast tenderness, liver tumor, bloating, nausea, vomiting, headache, dizziness, depression, weight gain, libido changes, intolerance to contact lenses, migraine, and rash. Should be used

with caution in women over the age of 35 who smoke and/or women who are breast-feeding, or who suffer from liver dysfunction.

How it can affect pregnant women: Esterified estrogens are prepared from plants. There are no indications for esterified estrogens during pregnancy. There are no clear physiologic advantages to using plant estrogens over other types.

How it can affect a developing embryo or fetus: There are no adequate reports or well-controlled studies in human fetuses. Although other synthetic/environmental estrogens (e.g., diethylstilbestrol) are recognized causes of birth defects, few studies support this effect for esterified estrogens. There is no evidence of significant fetal harm after inadvertent exposure during the first trimester.

Breast-feeding: Although esterified estrogens are excreted into breast milk and have been reported to reduce the amount of milk produced, they are not effective as inhibitors of milk production. Estrogen-containing contraceptives can be started after the sixth week of breast-feeding when the lipid and clotting profiles of the mother have returned to normal.

Potential drug interactions: Interaction between the following medications or substances and esterified estrogens has the potential to impact the effect of one or more of the drugs. In some instances the interaction can be dangerous or life-threatening and must be avoided: St. John's wort, phenobarbital, carbamazepine, rifampin, erythromycin, clarithromycin, ketoconazole, itraconazole, ritonavir, grapefruit and grapefruit juice.

What the FDA says about use in pregnancy: Category X (see Appendix).

What the available evidence suggests about breast-feeding safety: Safe.

The bottom line for you:

- There is no indication for esterified estrogens during pregnancy.
- There is also no clear evidence that inadvertent exposure in the first trimester causes birth defects.
- Estrogens as a category, when taken in the first few weeks after delivery, may decrease

milk production and increase the risk of blood clots.

ESTROPIPATE

Brand names: Harmonet, Ogen, Ortho-Est

Drug classes: Estrogen; Hormone

Indications (what it is used for): Vasomotor symptoms of menopause, osteoporosis prevention, hormone replacement for hypogonadism (diminished production of sex hormones by the ovaries).

How it works: Binds to estrogen receptors, triggering the development and maintenance of female sex characteristics; also triggers responses to estrogen that are not dependent on binding an estrogen receptor.

Contraindications (reasons you shouldn't take it): Vaginal bleeding of an unknown cause, blood clots, estrogen-dependent breast cancer, pregnancy.

Possible side effects and warnings: Can cause blood clots, stroke, heart attack, endometrial and breast cancer, gallbladder disease, pancreatitis, high blood pressure, breast tenderness, liver tumor, bloating, nausea, vomiting, headache, dizziness, depression, weight gain, libido changes, intolerance to contact lenses, migraine, and rash. Should be used with caution in women over the age of 35 who smoke and/or women who are breast-feeding, or who suffer from liver dysfunction.

How it can affect pregnant women: There are no indications for estropipate during pregnancy.

How it can affect a developing embryo or fetus: There are no adequate reports or well-controlled studies in human fetuses. Other synthetic/environmental estrogens (e.g., diethylstilbestrol) are recognized causes of birth defects, but there is no clear evidence of significant fetal harm after inadvertent exposure to estropipate during the first trimester.

Breast-feeding: Although other estrogens (e.g. estradiol) are excreted into breast milk and have been reported to reduce the amount of milk produced, they are not effective as an inhibitor of milk production. Estrogen-containing contraceptives can be started after the sixth week of breast-feeding when the lipid and clotting profiles of the mother have returned to normal.

Potential drug interactions: Interaction between the following medications and substances and estropipate has the potential to impact the effect of one or more of the drugs. In some instances the interaction can be dangerous or life-threatening and must be avoided: St. John's wort, phenobarbital, carbamazepine, rifampin, erythromycin, clarithromycin, ketoconazole, itraconazole, ritonavir, grapefruit and grapefruit juice.

What the FDA says about use in pregnancy: Category X (see Appendix).

What the available evidence suggests about breast-feeding safety: Safe.

The bottom line for you:

- There is no indication for estropipate during pregnancy.
- There is also no clear evidence that inadvertent exposure in the first trimester causes birth defects.
- Estrogens as a category, when taken in the first few weeks after delivery, may decrease milk production and increase the risk of blood clots.

ETHAMBUTOL

Brand names: Afimocil, Carnotol, Cidanbutol, Coxytol, Danbutol, Myambutol

Drug class: Antimycobacterial

Indications (what it is used for): Mycobacterial infection, such as tuberculosis.

How it works: Inhibits growing mycobacteria.

Contraindications (reasons you shouldn't take it): Hypersensitivity to drug or class, optic neuritis (inflammation of the optic nerve).

Possible side effects and warnings: Can cause low platelet count, optic and/or peripheral neuropathy, loss of appetite, nausea, vomiting, joint pain, abdominal pain, fever, headache, hallucinations, itching, and liver dysfunction. Should be used with caution in women who have liver dysfunction or ophthalmologic disorders.

How it can affect pregnant women: Untreated tuberculosis poses a significant threat to mother, fetus, and family. Pregnant women may be reluctant to start treatment because of a general fear of medication and, early in pregnancy, because of morning sickness. What information exists suggests that all 4 first-line drugs for the treatment of tuberculosis (isoniazid, rifampin, ethambutol, and pyrazinamide) have excellent safety records in pregnancy.

How it can affect a developing embryo or fetus: There are no adequate reports or well-controlled studies in human fetuses. Ethambutol reportedly crosses the human placenta, reaching levels in the fetus similar to those in the mother. There are no reports of adverse fetal effects. Rodent studies are reassuring, revealing no evidence of birth defects or low birth weight despite the use of doses higher than those used clinically. However, animal studies are not necessarily good indicators of how a drug will behave in humans.

Breast-feeding: There are no adequate reports or well-controlled studies in nursing women. Only small quantities of ethambutol are excreted into breast milk, and it is generally considered compatible with breast-feeding.

Potential drug interactions: Antacids may reduce the absorption of ethambutol if given within 4 hours of taking the medication.

What the FDA says about use in pregnancy: Category C (see Appendix).

What the available evidence suggests about breast-feeding safety: Safe.

The bottom line for you:
- Pregnancy does not affect the need to treat mycobacterial infection. Ethambutol is considered safe and effective during pregnancy and while breast-feeding.

ETHINYL ESTRADIOL
Brand names: Estinyl, Feminone
Drug classes: Estrogen; Hormone

Indications (what it is used for): Contraception (when combined with a progesterone-type agent), hot flashes, osteoporosis prevention, atrophic vaginitis, primary ovarian failure, breast cancer palliation.

How it works: Binds to estrogen receptors, triggering the development and maintenance of female sex characteristics; also triggers responses to estrogen that are not dependent on binding an estrogen receptor.

Contraindications (reasons you shouldn't take it): Vaginal bleeding of an unknown cause, blood clots, estrogen-dependent breast cancer, pregnancy.

Possible side effects and warnings: Can cause blood clots, stroke, heart attack, endometrial and breast cancer, gallbladder disease, pancreatitis, high blood pressure, breast tenderness, liver tumor, bloating, nausea, vomiting, headache, dizziness, depression, weight gain, libido changes, intolerance to contact lenses, migraine, and rash. Should be used with caution in women over the age of 35 who smoke and/or women who are breast-feeding or who suffer from liver dysfunction.

How it can affect pregnant women: There are no indications for ethinyl estradiol during pregnancy.

How it can affect a developing embryo or fetus: There are no adequate reports or well-controlled studies in human fetuses. Other synthetic/environmental estrogens (e.g., diethylstilbestrol) are recognized causes of birth defects, but there is no clear evidence of significant fetal harm after inadvertent exposure during the first trimester.

Breast-feeding: Although other estrogens (e.g. estradiol) are excreted into breast milk and have been reported to reduce the amount of milk produced, they are not effective as an inhibitor of milk production. Estrogen-containing contraceptives can be started after the sixth week of breast-feeding when the lipid and clotting profiles of the mother have returned to normal.

Potential drug interactions: Interaction between the following medications and ethinyl estradiol has the potential to impact the effect of one or more of the drugs. In some instances the interaction can be dangerous or life-threatening and must be avoided: St. John's wort, phenobarbital, carbamazepine, rifampin, erythromycin, clarithromycin, ketoconazole, itraconazole, ritonavir, grapefruit and grapefruit juice.

What the FDA says about use in pregnancy: Category X (see Appendix).

What the available evidence suggests about breast-feeding safety: Safe.

The bottom line for you:

- There is no indication for ethinyl estradiol during pregnancy.
- There is also no clear evidence that inadvertent exposure in the first trimester causes birth defects.
- Estrogens as a category, when taken in the first few weeks after delivery, may decrease milk production and increase the risk of blood clots.

ETHOSUXIMIDE

Brand names: Thosutin, Zarontin

Drug classes: Anticonvulsant; Succinimide

Indications (what it is used for): Treatment of absence epilepsy (petit mal).

How it works: Increases the threshold for seizure development.

Contraindications (reasons you shouldn't take it): Hypersensitivity to drug or class.

Possible side effects and warnings: Can cause bone marrow suppression, hemolytic anemia, systemic lupus erythematosus (a chronic inflammatory disease in which the immune system attacks the body's own tissues and organs), Stevens-Johnson syndrome (a rare but serious skin reaction to medication), loss of appetite, heartburn, nausea, vomiting, diarrhea, irritability, headache, dizziness, rash, facial hair growth, and excess gum growth. Should be used with caution in women with bone marrow depression, liver or kidney damage, mixed seizures, or porphyria (a group of rare blood disorders). Do not stop taking the drug abruptly.

How it can affect pregnant women: Women on medication for a seizure disorder should (when possible) plan their pregnancies, discuss the optimal medication with their neurologist, and begin appropriate supplemental folate therapy before conception (4 mg per day) to minimize the risk of birth defects. The risks of birth defects associated with antiseizure medications must be weighed against the risks of continued seizures to both the mother and fetus. Women who become pregnant during treatment should not stop the drug on their own but rather meet quickly with their doctor before making a decision.

Ethosuximide is used in the treatment of petit mal epilepsy. Epilepsy affects the menstrual cycle, aspects of contraception, fertility, pregnancy, and bone health in women. It is common for seizure frequency to vary throughout the menstrual cycle, influenced by the hormones estrogen and progesterone. Around the time of ovulation, the estrogen level peaks; a few days before menstruation, the progesterone level peaks. There are no adequate reports or well-controlled studies of ethosuximide in pregnant women.

How it can affect a developing embryo or fetus: There are no adequate reports or well-controlled studies in human fetuses. Ethosuximide crosses the human placenta, achieving a level in the fetus that is similar to that of the mother. Based predominantly on population studies (studies of a large group of people taken from the larger population), the likelihood that ethosuximide taken alone is a potent teratogen (substance that causes birth defects) is low. However, its combination with other antiepileptic agents may increase the risk.

Breast-feeding: There are no adequate reports or well-controlled studies in nursing women. Ethosuximide is freely excreted into human breast milk, but the levels are low in breast-fed newborns. It is generally considered safe for breast-feeding.

Potential drug interactions: May interact with other antiepileptic drugs, altering their effectiveness.

What the FDA says about use in pregnancy: No assigned category (see Appendix).

What the available evidence suggests about breast-feeding safety: Likely safe.

The bottom line for you:

- Ethosuximide may be used during pregnancy and while breast-feeding when the mother's safety requires treatment of her seizure disorder.

ETIDOCAINE HYDROCHLORIDE

Brand name: Duranest

Drug class: Anesthetic, local

Indications (what it is used for): Anesthesia for minor surgery.

How it works: Prevents nerve transmission so that pain is not felt.

Contraindications (reasons you shouldn't take it): Hypersensitivity to drug or class.

Possible side effects and warnings: Can cause low maternal blood pressure and rapid heart rate, convulsions, nervousness, light-headedness, and slow fetal heart rate if used for a paracervical block (an anesthetic procedure). Should be used with caution in women who are experiencing shock, or who have heart block, peripheral vascular disease (reduced blood flow to areas other than the heart or brain), or high blood pressure.

How it can affect pregnant women: Etidocaine is a rapid-onset, long-acting local anesthetic agent that produces a strong motor block when used for epidural or spinal anesthesia. Because a motor block is undesired during labor, it is not typically used for labor epidural analgesia but is sometimes used to repair lacerations after vaginal delivery. There are no adequate reports or well-controlled studies of etidocaine in pregnant women.

How it can affect a developing embryo or fetus: There are no adequate reports or well-controlled studies in human fetuses. Local anesthetics may cross the placenta when used for epidural, pudendal, caudal nerve, or paracervical blocks. Etidocaine does cross the human placenta, and a slow fetal heart rate leading to emergency cesarean delivery has been reported after paracervical block with etidocaine as well as with similar drugs. Rodent studies are reassuring, revealing no evidence of birth defects or low birth weight despite the use of doses higher than those used clinically. However, animal studies are not necessarily good indicators of how a drug will behave in humans.

Breast-feeding: There is no published data in nursing women. It is unknown whether etidocaine enters human breast milk. Considering that it is typically used for a specific period of time around surgical events, it is unlikely to pose a clinically significant risk to a breast-feeding baby.

Potential drug interactions: None currently identified.

What the FDA says about use in pregnancy: Category B (see Appendix).

What the available evidence suggests about breast-feeding safety: Likely safe.

The bottom line for you:

- Etidocaine is safe to use as a local anesthetic during pregnancy and while breast-feeding for some purposes.

ETODOLAC

Brand name: Lodine

Drug classes: Analgesic, nonnarcotic; NSAID

Indications (what it is used for): Mild to moderate pain, osteoarthritis, rheumatoid arthritis.

How it works: Inhibits enzymes that produce inflammation in the joints.

Contraindications (reasons you shouldn't take it): Hypersensitivity to drug or other nonsteroidal anti-inflammatory drugs (NSAIDs).

Possible side effects and warnings: Can cause a life-threatening allergic reaction, gastrointestinal bleeding, kidney failure or inflammation, low white blood cell and/or platelet count, liver damage, Stevens-Johnson syndrome (a rare but serious skin reaction to medication), heartburn, nausea, constipation, ringing in the ears, and fluid retention. Should be used with caution in women with gastrointestinal bleeding, high blood pressure, or congestive heart failure.

How it can affect pregnant women: Etodolac is a nonsteroidal anti-inflammatory drug that provides pain relief and lowers fever. There is no published data during human pregnancy. Some NSAIDS may increase the risk of a first-trimester pregnancy loss, and it is best to avoid all in the first trimester. (See indomethacin.)

How it can affect a developing embryo or fetus: There are no adequate reports or well-controlled studies in human fetuses. It is unknown whether etodolac crosses the human placenta. The structure of the drug suggests that it is likely to pose risks similar to those of indomethacin, which readily crosses the placenta and, if taken too long, constricts the fetal ductus arteriosus (a critical fetal blood vessel directing blood away from the lungs), potentially increasing strain on the fetal heart, decreasing blood flow to the kidneys, urination and ultimately amniotic fluid levels. Stopping the drug appears to reverse this process. Rodent studies performed with indomethacin at doses approximating the maximum recommended human dose were associated with an increased prevalence of limb birth defects. Higher than recommended doses in rodents delayed labor and increased the rate of miscarriage (see indomethacin). However, animal studies are not necessarily good indicators of how a drug will behave in humans.

Breast-feeding: There is no published data in nursing women. It is not known whether etodolac is excreted into human breast milk (see indomethacin).

Potential drug interactions: Interaction between the following medications and etodolac has the potential to impact the effect of one or more of the drugs. In some instances the interaction can be dangerous or life-threatening and must be avoided: ACE inhibitors, lithium, cyclosporine, digoxin, methotrexate, aspirin, furosemide, thiazides, phenylbutazone, warfarin.

What the FDA says about use in pregnancy: Category C (see Appendix).

What the available evidence suggests about breast-feeding safety: Unknown.

The bottom line for you:

- There are alternative agents with which there is more experience during pregnancy and while breast-feeding.

ETOMIDATE

Brand name: Amidate

Drug class: Anesthetic, general

Indications (what it is used for): Induction of general anesthesia.

How it works: Unknown.

Contraindications (reasons you shouldn't take it): Hypersensitivity to drug or class.

Possible side effects and warnings: Can cause shock, jerking movements, nausea, vomiting, apnea, and injection site reactions.

How it can affect pregnant women: Etomidate is a short-acting hypnotic drug used to initiate general anesthesia for cesarean delivery in women with co-existing heart disease.

How it can affect a developing embryo or fetus: There are no adequate reports or well-controlled studies of etomidate in human fetuses. Transfer across the rodent placenta occurs, reaching concentrations roughly equal to those in the mother's blood. Because the drug is typically used after the first trimester, there is no risk of birth defects.

Breast-feeding: There is no published data in breast-feeding. It is unknown whether etomidate enters human breast milk. However, considering that it is used for a specific period of time around a surgical event and its short duration, it is unlikely that a breast-fed baby would ingest clinically relevant amounts.

Potential drug interactions: May increase central nervous system (CNS) depression when used with other CNS depressants.

What the FDA says about use in pregnancy: Category C (see Appendix).

What the available evidence suggests about breast-feeding safety: Likely safe.

The bottom line for you:

- Etomidate appears safe for use during pregnancy and while breast-feeding for women who have heart problems.

ETRETINATE

Brand name: Tegison

Drug classes: Dermatologic; Retinoid

Indications (what it is used for): Severe psoriasis.

How it works: Unknown.

Contraindications (reasons you shouldn't take it): Hypersensitivity to drug or class.

Possible side effects and warnings: Can cause increased intracranial pressure not related to a tumor, liver damage, corneal opacities, and high lipid levels. Should be used with caution in women with liver dysfunction.

How it can affect pregnant women: Psoriasis is not a life-threatening condition, and the use of etretinate is absolutely contraindicated (should not be taken) during pregnancy. Women should be tested for pregnancy within 2 weeks of initiating therapy and use effective contraception while they are being treated with etretinate. Drug levels may persist for years after treatment, though the relevance of these levels to subsequent pregnancy outcome is unknown. There are no published studies of etretinate in pregnant women. Several reports note normal outcomes years after treatment has ended.

How it can affect a developing embryo or fetus: Etretinate causes birth defects in humans. Multiple organ systems are susceptible to damage, including the spine (spina bifida), the face (dysmorphia), skeleton (limbs and digits), and the brain (microcephaly; a smaller than normal head, which can cause developmental issues). If a woman becomes pregnant while taking etretinate, she should discontinue treatment immediately and speak to her physician about getting a detailed fetal evaluation by a skilled fetal sonographer to search for adverse effects.

Breast-feeding: There is no published data in nursing women. It is unknown whether etretinate enters human breast milk. It is excreted into rodent milk.

Potential drug interactions: No clinically relevant interactions are currently identified.

What the FDA says about use in pregnancy: Category X (see Appendix).

What the available evidence suggests about breast-feeding safety: Unknown.

The bottom line for you:

- Etretinate should not be taken during pregnancy.
- If you become pregnant while taking etretinate, you should discontinue treatment immediately and speak to your physician about getting a detailed fetal sonogram to search for adverse effects.
- Safety while breast-feeding is unknown. It is best to avoid.

FACTOR IX

Brand names: Alphanine, Bebulin VH, Immuno, Konyne 80, Mononine, Profilnine SD, Proplex T

Drug classes: Blood-clotting factor; Blood component, substitute

Indications (what it is used for): Factor IX deficiency (prevention and control of bleeding), treatment of anticoagulant overdose.

How it works: Replaces factor IX, a protein critical to blood clotting.

Contraindications (reasons you shouldn't take it): Hypersensitivity to mouse proteins, liver dysfunction, abnormal clotting.

Possible side effects and warnings: Can cause blood clots, viral disease, flushing, tingling, fever, chills, nausea, vomiting, hives, headache, blood pressure changes, and injection site reaction. Should be used with caution in women who have a tendency toward excessive clotting.

How it can affect pregnant women: Factor IX is first synthesized or extracted from human plasma and then purified to reduce the risk of virus transmission. There are no adequate reports or well-controlled studies in pregnant women. The published literature consists of case series and single reports. Factor IX deficiency is inherited usually on the X chromosome, so deficiency is rare in women. The life of factor IX is short. Postpartum hemorrhage (hemorrhage after delivery) is the most common complication, and it occurs more often in women who received fewer than 4 days of factor IX replacement.

How it can affect a developing embryo or fetus: There are no adequate reports or well-controlled studies of factor IX in human fetuses. The large size of the factor IX molecules makes it unlikely to cross the placenta.

Breast-feeding: There are no adequate reports or well-controlled studies in nursing women. It is unknown whether factor IX enters human breast milk. However, any factor IX swallowed by the newborn would be degraded by the digestive process and have no effect.

Potential drug interactions: None currently identified.

What the FDA says about use in pregnancy: Category C (see Appendix).

What the available evidence suggests about breast-feeding safety: Safe.

The bottom line for you:
- Factor IX replacement is safe for use during pregnancy or while breast-feeding.

FAMCICLOVIR

Brand name: Famvir
Drug class: Antiviral
Indications (what it is used for): Treatment of genital herpes and herpes zoster.
How it works: Inhibits the ability of the virus to make more DNA.
Contraindications (reasons you shouldn't take it): Hypersensitivity to drug or class.

Possible side effects and warnings: Can cause headache, nausea, vomiting, diarrhea, fatigue, itching, tingling, and flatulence. Should be used with caution in women with kidney dysfunction.

How it can affect pregnant women: There are no adequate reports or well-controlled studies in pregnant women. Drugs in this class decrease both asymptomatic shedding and the likelihood of clinical recurrence of herpes virus in both nonpregnant and pregnant women. Drug clearance (how fast it passes through the body) increases as pregnancy advances, meaning that the dose may need to be increased to maintain effectiveness.

How it can affect a developing embryo or fetus: There are no adequate reports or well-controlled studies in human fetuses. It is unknown whether famciclovir crosses the human placenta. Rodent studies are reassuring, revealing no evidence of birth defects or low birth weight despite the use of doses higher than those used clinically. However, animal studies are not necessarily good indicators of how a drug will behave in humans.

Breast-feeding: There is no published data in nursing women. It is unknown whether famciclovir is excreted in human breast milk. It is concentrated in rat milk.

Potential drug interactions: Interaction between the following medications and famciclovir has the potential to impact the effect of one or more of the drugs. In some instances the interaction can be dangerous or life-threatening and must be avoided: probenecid or other drugs eliminated by active kidney tubular secretion, and drugs metabolized by aldehyde oxidase.

What the FDA says about use in pregnancy: Category B (see Appendix).

What the available evidence suggests about breast-feeding safety: Unknown.

The bottom line for you:
- There is more experience with acyclovir during pregnancy and while breast-feeding.
- Women taking famciclovir during pregnancy are encouraged to register with the Famciclovir

Registry (1-888-669-6682) maintained by the manufacturer to help gain a better understanding of the efficacy and safety of famciclovir during pregnancy.

FAMOTIDINE

Brand name: Pepcid

Drug classes: Antihistamine, H2; Gastrointestinal

Indications (what it is used for): Treatment of GERD (gastroesophageal reflux disease), heartburn, gastric ulcer disease, and Zollinger-Ellison syndrome (tumors in the pancreas).

How it works: Blocks the histamine 2 receptor, the stimulation of which leads to the symptoms.

Contraindications (reasons you shouldn't take it): Hypersensitivity to drug or class, phenylketonuria (an inherited amino acid disorder).

Possible side effects and warnings: Can cause bone marrow suppression, jaundice, bronchospasm, headache, taste changes, constipation, diarrhea, acne, dizziness, dry skin, swelling around the eyes, muscle aches, liver and kidney damage, and ringing in the ears. Should be used with caution in women with kidney dysfunction.

How it can affect pregnant women: GERD (or heartburn) is common during pregnancy, and antacids are typically the first-choice drugs for treatment. However, when unsuccessful, H2 antagonists such as famotidine may be helpful. There are no adequate reports or well-controlled studies of famotidine in pregnant women. One epidemiologic study concluded that the use of H2 antagonists during pregnancy was associated with a higher prevalence of preterm birth (before 37 weeks), but this remains unproved. Its use in rodents around the time of ovulation reduces the rate of embryo implantation. However, animal studies are not necessarily good indicators of how a drug will behave in humans.

How it can affect a developing embryo or fetus: There are no adequate reports or well-controlled studies in human fetuses. Famotidine crosses the placenta, achieving a level in the fetus that is about half that of the mother. Rodent studies are reassuring, revealing no evidence of birth defects or low birth weight despite the use of doses higher than those used clinically. However, animal studies are not necessarily good indicators of how a drug will behave in humans.

Breast-feeding: There are no adequate reports or well-controlled studies in nursing women. Famotidine is excreted into human breast milk to a lesser extent than cimetidine and ranitidine, and is thus the preferred agent during breast-feeding. The daily infant dose is low enough that any clinical effect will be minimal.

Potential drug interactions: None identified currently.

What the FDA says about use in pregnancy: Category B (see Appendix).

What the available evidence suggests about breast-feeding safety: Safe.

The bottom line for you:

- Until more information is available, famotidine should probably be avoided midcycle in women attempting to become pregnant.
- H2 blockers are second-choice therapies (after antacids have failed) for the treatment of GERD (heartburn) during pregnancy.
- Although famotidine is considered safe and effective for the treatment of GERD and peptic ulcer disease during pregnancy and while breast-feeding, there are alternative agents with which there is more experience during pregnancy and breast-feeding.

FELBAMATE

Brand names: Felbatol, Taloxa

Drug class: Anticonvulsant

Indications (what it is used for): Second-line therapy for seizure disorders.

How it works: Unknown.

Contraindications (reasons you shouldn't take it): Hypersensitivity to drug or class.

Possible side effects and warnings: Can cause aplastic anemia, liver failure, loss of appetite, nausea, vomiting, headache, sleeplessness, dizziness, sleepiness, constipation, nervousness, tremors, double vision, depression, abdominal pain, and lack of gross-muscle control. Should be used with caution in women with liver or kidney dysfunction, or with a history of blood disorders.

How it can affect pregnant women: Women on medication for a seizure disorder should (when possible) plan their pregnancies, discuss the optimal medication with their neurologist, and begin appropriate supplemental folate therapy before conception (4 mg per day) to minimize the risk of birth defects. The risks of birth defects associated with antiseizure medications must be weighed against the risks of continued seizures to both the mother and fetus. Women who become pregnant during treatment should not stop treatment on their own but rather meet quickly with their doctor before making a decision.

There are no adequate reports or well-controlled studies of felbamate in pregnant women. Enzyme-inducing antiepileptic drugs such as felbamate can reduce the effectiveness of hormonal contraceptives, increasing the risk of an unplanned pregnancy. Patients should use either a higher-hormone-content oral contraceptive or a second method such as a condom. Drug dose adjustments are often necessary during pregnancy.

How it can affect a developing embryo or fetus: Uncontrolled seizures are a risk to the woman and her fetus. There are no adequate reports or well-controlled studies in human fetuses. It is unknown whether felbamate crosses the human placenta. It does cross the rodent placenta, but rodent studies are reassuring, revealing no evidence of birth defects despite the use of doses higher than those used clinically. An increased incidence of low birth weight was seen. However, animal studies are not necessarily good indicators of how a drug will behave in humans.

Breast-feeding: There are no adequate reports or well-controlled studies in nursing women. Felbamate is excreted into human breast milk, although the amount and impact on newborns remain to be clarified. Felbamate is excreted into rodent breast milk, and there is a higher death rate in breast-fed pups whose mothers received felbamate. If a mother chooses to breast-feed, her infant should be monitored for possible adverse effects, the drug should be given at the lowest effective dose, and breast-feeding should be avoided at times of peak drug levels.

Potential drug interactions: Interaction between the following medications and felbamate has the potential to impact the effect of one or more of the drugs. In some instances the interaction can be dangerous or life-threatening and must be avoided: phenytoin, valproate, carbamazepine, carbamazepine-epoxide, and other antiepileptics.

What the FDA says about use in pregnancy: Category C (see Appendix).

What the available evidence suggests about breast-feeding safety: Unknown.

The bottom line for you:

- Felbamate is a second-line (second-choice) treatment for several seizure disorders. Although experience with it during pregnancy is limited, it appears so far to be relatively safe.
- During pregnancy and while breast-feeding, it should be used alone (when possible) and at the lowest effective dose.

FELODIPINE

Brand name: Plendil

Drug classes: Antihypertensive; Calcium channel blocker

Indications (what it is used for): Chronic hypertension (high blood pressure).

How it works: Blocks the movement of calcium into the muscle cell, preventing muscle contraction.

Contraindications (reasons you shouldn't take it): Hypersensitivity to drug or class.

Possible side effects and warnings: Can cause swelling, headache, flushing, dizziness, nausea, abdominal pain, diarrhea, runny nose, chest pain, palpitations, muscle cramps, and weakness. Should be used with caution in women with liver dysfunction or congestive heart failure.

How it can affect pregnant women: There are no adequate reports or well-controlled studies of felodipine in pregnant women. The published data consists of isolated case reports where felodipine was used successfully and without adverse effect for the treatment of severe high blood pressure during pregnancy. In general, calcium channel blockers delay delivery by 48 to 96 hours and prolong pregnancy in rabbits.

How it can affect a developing embryo or fetus: There are no adequate reports or well-controlled studies in human fetuses. It is unknown whether felodipine crosses the human placenta. Felodipine is associated in rodents with an increased prevalence of birth defects involving the fingers and toes, possibly related to the mother's low blood pressure with a resulting decrease in placental blood flow. However, animal studies are not necessarily good indicators of how a drug will behave in humans.

Breast-feeding: There is no published data in nursing women. It is unknown whether felodipine enters human breast milk. It is excreted into rodent milk.

Potential drug interactions: Interaction between the following medications or substances and felodipine has the potential to impact the effect of one or more of the drugs. In some instances the interaction can be dangerous or life-threatening and must be avoided: CYP3A4 inhibitors (e.g., ketoconazole, itraconazole, erythromycin, grapefruit and grapefruit juice, cimetidine), long-term anticonvulsant therapy (e.g., phenytoin, carbamazepine, phenobarbital).

What the FDA says about use in pregnancy: Category C (see Appendix.)

What the available evidence suggests about breast-feeding safety: Unknown.

The bottom line for you:
- There are other agents with a superior safety profile and with which there is more experience during pregnancy and while breast-feeding.

FENOFIBRATE

Brand name: Tricor

Drug class: Antihyperlipidemic

Indications (what it is used for): Hyperlipidemia (high levels of blood lipids such as cholesterol and triglycerides).

How it works: Interferes with triglyceride synthesis.

Contraindications (reasons you shouldn't take it): Hypersensitivity to drug or class, liver or kidney dysfunction, gallbladder disease.

Possible side effects and warnings: Can cause hepatitis or liver damage, pancreatitis, gallstones, muscle inflammation or pain, abdominal pain, headache, constipation, runny nose, and nausea. Should be used with caution in women taking oral anticoagulants.

How it can affect pregnant women: There are no adequate reports or well-controlled studies of fenofibrate in pregnant women. One rodent study concluded that pregnant and nonpregnant rats respond differently to fenofibrate, and that high maternal doses were associated with delayed delivery. Since high lipid levels are not usually life-threatening in the short term, it is probably best to stop fenofibrate during pregnancy.

How it can affect a developing embryo or fetus: There are no adequate reports or well-controlled studies in human fetuses. It is unknown whether fenofibrate crosses the human placenta. In rodents, fenofibrate caused low birth weight when given at doses equivalent to the maximum recommended human dose and was associated with fetal death and birth defects at higher doses. However, animal studies are not necessarily good indicators of how a drug will behave in humans.

Breast-feeding: There is no published data in nursing women. It is unknown whether fenofibrate enters human breast milk.

Potential drug interactions: Interaction between the following medications and fenofibrate has the potential to impact the effect of one or more of the drugs. In some instances the interaction can be dangerous or life-threatening and must be avoided: anticoagulants such as warfarin, HMG-CoA reductase inhibitors, cyclosporine. Women should take fenofibrate at least 1 hour before or 4–6 hours after a bile acid–binding resin (cholestryamine, colesevelam, colestipol).

What the FDA says about use in pregnancy: Category C (see Appendix).

What the available evidence suggests about breast-feeding safety: Unknown.

The bottom line for you:

- There is too little experience with fenofibrate to determine its safety during pregnancy or while breast-feeding.
- Hyperlipidemia is not usually life-threatening in the near term, so stopping medication during pregnancy is suggested.
- If treatment is necessary, there are alternative agents with which there is more experience during pregnancy and while breast-feeding.

FENOPROFEN

Brand name: Nalfon

Drug classes: Analgesic, nonnarcotic; NSAID (nonsteroidal anti-inflammatory drug)

Indications (what it is used for): Arthritis, mild to moderate pain.

How it works: Inhibits the enzymes cyclooxygenase and lipoxygenase to reduce the synthesis of prostaglandins involved in inflammation.

Contraindications (reasons you shouldn't take it): Hypersensitivity to drug or class, NSAID-induced asthma.

Possible side effects and warnings: Can cause life-threatening allergic reactions, bowel bleeding, kidney failure, bronchospasm, low platelet or white blood cell counts, liver toxicity, heartburn, nausea, headache, constipation, abdominal pain, dizziness, rash, fluid retention, and ringing in the ears. Should be used with caution in women with bowel bleeding, high blood pressure, congestive heart failure, or nasal polyps.

How it can affect pregnant women: Fenoprofen is a nonsteroidal anti-inflammatory and fever-reducing medication. There are no adequate reports or well-controlled studies of fenoprofen in pregnant women. Similar to other NSAIDs, it is effective for the relief of episiotomy pain. In rodents, fenoprofen prolonged labor; related compounds such as indomethacin are used to slow or stop preterm labor.

How it can affect a developing embryo or fetus: There are no adequate reports or well-controlled studies in human fetuses. It is unknown whether fenoprofen crosses the human placenta. NSAIDS as a group have the potential to decrease blood flow to the fetal kidneys (and thus decrease fetal urination) and constrict the ductus arteriosus (an important fetal blood vessel that carries blood away from the unused lungs) when used consistently after 32 weeks. Its closure leads to tricuspid valve incompetence, heart failure, and high blood pressure in the lungs, all of which can cause long-term damage. Stopping the medication appears to reverse this process. Fenoprofen prolongs pregnancy in rodents, as do other NSAIDs.

Breast-feeding: There is no published data in nursing women. It is unknown whether fenoprofen enters human breast milk.

Potential drug interactions: Interaction between the following medications and fenoprofen has the potential to impact the effect of one or more of the drugs. In some instances the interaction can be dangerous or life-threatening and must be avoided: ACE inhibitors, furosemide, thiazides, lithium, methotrexate, warfarin, phenobarbital, drugs that are albumin-bound, hydantoins, sulfonamides, sulfonylureas.

What the FDA says about use in pregnancy: Category C, before 30 weeks gestation; D, 30 weeks and after (see Appendix).

What the available evidence suggests about breast-feeding safety: Unknown.

The bottom line for you:

- Fenoprofen offers no clear advantage over other NSAIDs with which there is more experience during pregnancy and while breast-feeding.

FENTANYL

Brand names: Fentanyl Oralet, Oralet, Sublimaze

Drug classes: Analgesic, narcotic; Anesthetic, general

Indications (what it is used for): Anesthesia, preoperative analgesia, regional anesthesia, postoperative pain relief.

How it works: Binds to various opiate receptors.

Contraindications (reasons you shouldn't take it): Hypersensitivity to drug or class.

Possible side effects and warnings: Can cause respiratory depression or arrest, addiction, laryngospasm, bronchospasm, irregular or slow heart rate, cardiac arrest, bowel paralysis, nausea, vomiting, weakness, dry mouth, confusion, sweating, euphoria, itching, and low blood pressure. Should be used with caution in women with liver, kidney, or lung dysfunction; bowel obstruction; low blood pressure; gallbladder disease; seizure disorder; or inflammatory bowel disease, or who are taking a central nervous system depressant.

How it can affect pregnant women: Fentanyl is a short-acting narcotic with considerable risk for abuse. It is often combined with a local anesthetic during labor to minimize the muscle weakness from epidural anesthesia. In fetuses that are presenting bottom first in late pregnancy, fentanyl used in a spinal block increases the chance of turning the breech baby so its head is down. Fentanyl is often used in conjunction with a cervical block for anesthesia during pregnancy termination.

How it can affect a developing embryo or fetus: There are no adequate reports or well-controlled studies in human fetuses. Fentanyl rapidly crosses the human placenta, achieving the same level as it does in the mother. It has been used for analgesia during fetal surgery. Rodent studies are generally reassuring, revealing no evidence of birth defects or low birth weight despite the use of doses higher than those used clinically. However, animal studies are not necessarily good indicators of how a drug will behave in humans.

Breast-feeding: There are no adequate reports or well-controlled studies in nursing women. Fentanyl enters human breast milk, but any fentanyl ingested will likely be digested and not pose a clinical risk to a breast-feeding newborn.

Potential drug interactions: Interaction between the following medications and fentanyl has the potential to impact the effect of one or more of the drugs. In some instances the interaction can be dangerous or life-threatening and must be avoided: potent CYP3A4 inhibitors such as macrolide antibiotics (e.g., erythromycin, clarithromycin), azole antifungal agents (e.g., ketoconazole, itraconazole), protease inhibitors (e.g., ritanovir, nelfinavir), diltiazem, and nefazadone; CYP3A4 inducers (e.g., rifampin, carbamazepine, phenytoin, St. John's wort); other central nervous system depressants, including but not limited to other opioids, sedatives, hypnotics, tranquilizers (e.g., benzodiazepines), general anesthetics, phenothiazines, skeletal muscle relaxants, and alcohol; monoamine oxidase inhibitors (MAOIs).

What the FDA says about use in pregnancy: Category C (see Appendix).

What the available evidence suggests about breast-feeding safety: Safe.

The bottom line for you:

- Fentanyl is a short-acting narcotic widely used during pregnancy for short-term pain control mostly for surgical procedures (typically for cesarean delivery). It has no effect on the newborn by the time breast-feeding begins.

FERROUS GLUCONATE

Brand name: Fergon

Drug classes: Hematinic; Vitamin/mineral

Indications (what it is used for): Iron deficiency and supplementation.

How it works: Iron is an essential part of many proteins, including hemoglobin.

Contraindications (reasons you shouldn't take it): Hypersensitivity to drug or class, iron overload, liver damage due to excess iron, hemolytic anemia, thalassemia (inherited blood disorder), peptic ulcer disease, ulcerative colitis.

Possible side effects and warnings: Can cause heartburn, nausea, vomiting, diarrhea, constipation, and dark stools. Long-term use of higher levels may lead to iron overload.

How it can affect pregnant women: Though iron supplementation is widely practiced during pregnancy throughout the industrialized world, there is no convincing evidence that it improves long- or short-term outcomes. And although severe anemia is an important cause of maternal death, there is no convincing evidence of the risks of mild to moderate anemia. One U.S. study of women with inadequate iron stores before pregnancy concluded that birth weight was higher and the chance of preterm birth lower with supplementation. Women with disorders of iron use (e.g., thalassemia) should not be supplemented because of the risk of iron overload.

How it can affect a developing embryo or fetus: There is no evidence that maternal iron supplementation influences the fetal iron status.

Breast-feeding: Maternal iron supplementation does not alter the iron concentration in breast milk.

Potential drug interactions: Interaction between the following medications and ferrous glucanate has the potential to impact the effect of one or more of the drugs. In some instances the interaction can be dangerous or life-threatening and must be avoided: cefdinir, didanosine, levodopa, mycophenolate, penicillamine, quinolones, tetracycline, thyroid hormones.

What the FDA says about use in pregnancy: No assigned category (see Appendix).

What the available evidence suggests about breast-feeding safety: Safe.

The bottom line for you:
- Although the risk of routine iron supplementation during pregnancy and while breast-feeding is probably minimal, there is no clear improvement in outcome from supplementation.
- Women with thallasemia should not take iron supplements.

FEXOFENADINE
Brand name: Allegra

Drug class: Antihistamine, H1

Indications (what it is used for): Allergic rhinitis, hives.

How it works: Selectively blocks the H1 receptor, the action of which causes the allergic symptoms.

Contraindications (reasons you shouldn't take it): Hypersensitivity to drug or class.

Possible side effects and warnings: Can cause painful menstruation, drowsiness, nausea, flulike symptoms, heartburn, and fatigue. Should be used with caution in women with kidney dysfunction.

How it can affect pregnant women: Fexofenadine is a second-generation antihistamine effective for the symptomatic relief of allergic rhinitis. Although often preferred in general for its nonsedating properties, there are no published controlled trials or population studies of fexofenadine during pregnancy.

How it can affect a developing embryo or fetus: There are no adequate reports or well-controlled studies in human fetuses. Although the small size of its molecule suggests that fexofenadine can cross the human placenta, it is unknown whether it does. And although there is no evidence of birth defects in rodents, there is an increase in low birth weight and lower survival of offspring of rodents fed high doses during pregnancy. However, animal studies are not necessarily good indicators of how a drug will behave in humans.

Breast-feeding: There is no published data in nursing women. It is unknown whether fexofenadine enters human breast milk. Clinically insignificant levels of terfenadine, a drug converted in the body to fexofenadine, are found in breast milk. It is likely to be the same with fexofenadine. Thus, the risk to a breast-feeding newborn is likely negligible.

Potential drug interactions: Use with ketoconazole or erythromycin increases the blood plasma level of fexofenadine. Fexofenadine should not be taken 2 hours before or after aluminum- or magnesium-containing antacids. Grapefruit, orange, and apple juice (or those fruits in large amounts) may reduce the effectiveness of fexofenadine.

What the FDA says about use in pregnancy: Category C (see Appendix).

What the available evidence suggests about breast-feeding safety: Likely safe.

The bottom line for you:

- Although this class of drugs appears safe for use during pregnancy and while breast-feeding, there are alternative agents, including inhaled steroids and first-generation antihistamines such as chlorpheniramine, with which there is much more experience.

FILGRASTIM

Brand name: Neupogen
Drug classes: Biologic response modifier; Hematopoietic agent
Indications (what it is used for): Severe and chronic low white blood cell counts or AIDS; low counts due to chemotherapy or bone marrow transplantation.
How it works: Stimulates the colonies of white blood cells to produce more.
Contraindications (reasons you shouldn't take it): Hypersensitivity to drug or class, hypersensitivity to *E. coli* proteins.
Possible side effects and warnings: Can cause life-threatening allergic reaction; low platelet counts; nausea and vomiting; musculoskeletal, abdominal, and bone pain; rash; low blood pressure; and localized swelling. Should be used with caution in women with liver or kidney dysfunction.

How it can affect pregnant women: There are no adequate reports or well-controlled studies of filgrastim in pregnant women. Filgrastim is used to treat life-threatening conditions, and it has been used successfully in a limited number of pregnant women without obvious adverse effects.

How it can affect a developing embryo or fetus: There are no adequate reports or well-controlled studies in human fetuses. It is unknown whether filgrastim crosses the human placenta. There is no evidence to suggest it causes birth defects in humans, although rodent studies using high doses revealed evidence of damage to embryos and low birth weight. However, animal studies are not necessarily good indicators of how a drug will behave in humans.

Breast-feeding: There are no adequate reports or well-controlled studies in nursing women. It is unknown whether filgrastim enters human breast milk.

Potential drug interactions: Drug interactions have not been fully evaluated. Drugs that may potentiate the release of neutrophils (white blood cells), such as lithium, should be used with caution.

What the FDA says about use in pregnancy: Category C (see Appendix).

What the available evidence suggests about breast-feeding safety: Unknown.

The bottom line for you:

- Filgrastim should be used only for the life-threatening conditions it treats.

FLAVOXATE

Brand name: Urispas
Drug classes: Anticholinergic; Antispasmodic
Indications (what it is used for): Bladder spasm.
How it works: Blocks specific nerve receptors (the muscarinic receptors) whose stimulation causes bladder spasm.
Contraindications (reasons you shouldn't take it): Hypersensitivity to drug or class, bowel obstruction, bowel bleeding, difficulty swallowing.
Possible side effects and warnings: Can cause low white blood cell count, nausea, vomiting, dry mouth,

constipation, dizziness, blurred vision, rapid heart rate, palpitations, headache, drowsiness, burning with urination, hives, and fever.

How it can affect pregnant women: There is no published data with flavoxate during pregnancy. In nonpregnant women, flavoxate increases and then subsequently decreases uterine contractions.

How it can affect a developing embryo or fetus: There are no adequate reports or well-controlled studies in human fetuses. It is unknown whether flavoxate crosses the placenta. Rodent studies are reassuring, revealing no evidence of birth defects or low birth weight despite the use of doses higher than those used clinically. However, animal studies are not necessarily good indicators of how a drug will behave in humans.

Breast-feeding: There is no published data in nursing women. It is unknown whether flavoxate enters human breast milk.

Potential drug interactions: Flavoxate may alter the absorption of numerous drugs by slowing motility in the gastrointestinal tract.

What the FDA says about use in pregnancy: Category B (see Appendix).

What the available evidence suggests about breast-feeding safety: Unknown.

The bottom line for you:

- Although the risk of flavoxate is likely low, there are few, if any, indications for its use during pregnancy and while breast-feeding.

FLECAINIDE

Brand name: Tambocor

Drug class: Antiarrhythmic, class IC

Indications (what it is used for): To suppress a dangerous heart rate irregularity.

How it works: Depresses the responsiveness of the heart cell to electrical stimulation.

Contraindications (reasons you shouldn't take it): Hypersensitivity to drug or class, cardiogenic shock, heart block.

Possible side effects and warnings: Can cause abnormal heart rates, congestive heart failure, cardiac arrest, dizziness, blurred vision, heartburn, headache, nausea, vomiting, fatigue, weakness, constipation, and chest pain. Should be used with caution in women with congestive heart failure, irregular heart rhythms, or liver or kidney dysfunction.

How it can affect pregnant women: There are no adequate reports or well-controlled studies of flecainide in pregnant women. Flecainide has been used successfully for the treatment of maternal arrhythmias (irregular heart rates) during pregnancy. Limited experience suggests that it is eliminated from the bloodstream faster during pregnancy, thus requiring a higher dose to be effective.

How it can affect a developing embryo or fetus: There are no adequate reports or well-controlled studies in human fetuses. Flecainide rapidly crosses the placenta; it is also concentrated in amniotic fluid and thus may recirculate if swallowed by the fetus. It is an accepted drug for the treatment of abnormal fetal heart rates above 200 beats per minute.

Breast-feeding: Although flecainide is concentrated in human breast milk, the quantity of milk consumed would be unlikely to produce a clinically significant level in a breast-feeding baby.

Potential drug interactions: Interaction between the following medications and flecainide has the potential to impact the effect of one or more of the drugs. In some instances the interaction can be dangerous or life-threatening and must be avoided: digoxin; propranolol; amiodarone; CYP11D6 inhibitors, such as quinidine.

What the FDA says about use in pregnancy: Category C (see Appendix).

What the available evidence suggests about breast-feeding safety: Safe.

The bottom line for you:

- Flecainide is one of the drugs of choice for the treatment of fetuses with a sustained heart rate above 200 beats per minute.
- Flecainide may be used with relative safety during pregnancy and while breast-feeding for treatment of dangerous maternal heart rhythms.

FLU VACCINE, see INFLUENZA VACCINE

FLUCONAZOLE

Brand name: Diflucan
Drug class: Antifungal
Indications (what it is used for): Candidiasis (yeast infection), cryptococcal meningitis.
How it works: Inhibits cell activities, leading to the fungus's death.
Contraindications (reasons you shouldn't take it): Hypersensitivity to drug or class; use of astemizole, cisapride, or terfenidine.
Possible side effects and warnings: Can cause liver toxicity, seizures, angioedema (swelling under the skin), Stevens-Johnson syndrome (a rare but serious skin reaction to medication), bone marrow suppression, nausea, vomiting, headache, rash, dizziness, diarrhea, heartburn, and taste changes. Should be used with caution in women with liver or kidney dysfunction.
How it can affect pregnant women: There are no adequate reports or well-controlled studies of fluconazole in pregnant women. It has been used for the treatment of life-threatening coccidioidomycosis (a fungal disease) during pregnancy and *Candida* sepsis (a yeast infection in the blood) after delivery.
How it can affect a developing embryo or fetus: There are no adequate reports or well-controlled studies in human fetuses. It is unknown whether fluconazole crosses the human placenta. When taken orally for short periods of time, fluconazole is unlikely to pose a significant risk of birth defects. However, there are 4 reports of children whose mothers were treated intravenously who developed a rare pattern of birth defects including abnormal face and skull development, cleft palate, bowing of the thigh bones, thin ribs and long bones, joint contractures, and congenital heart disease. Fluconazole does not appear to increase the risks of low birth weight or preterm birth, and it is used for the treatment of newborn yeast infection acquired during vaginal delivery. Rodent studies using doses higher than the maximum recommended human dose found that fluconazole caused a number of birth defects. However, animal studies are not necessarily good indicators of how a drug will behave in humans.
Breast-feeding: There are no adequate reports or well-controlled studies in nursing women. Fluconazole reaches similar concentrations in human breast milk as it does in the mother's blood. It is generally recommended that breast-feeding be avoided.
Potential drug interactions: Interaction between the following medications and fluconazole has the potential to impact the effect of one or more of the drugs. In some instances the interaction can be dangerous or life-threatening and must be avoided: oral hypoglycemic agents, tolbutamide, glyburide and glipizide, sulfonylurea oral hypoglycemic agents, coumarin-type anticoagulants, phenytoin, cyclosporine, rifampin, theophylline, cimetidine, hydrochlorothiazide, zidovudine.
What the FDA says about use in pregnancy: Category C (see Appendix) for a one-time 150mg dose; category D (see Appendix) otherwise.
What the available evidence suggests about breast-feeding safety: Possibly unsafe.
The bottom line for you:
- Fluconazole may be a weak teratogen (substance that can cause birth defects) and its use either orally or intravenously should be avoided during pregnancy.
- There are alternative agents with which there is more experience during pregnancy and while breast-feeding.

FLUDROCORTISONE

Brand name: Florinef
Drug class: Corticosteroid
Indications (what it is used for): Inadequate production of corticosteroids by the adrenal glands; low blood pressure caused by changing positions, such as from sitting to standing.
How it works: Blocks inflammation.

Contraindications (reasons you shouldn't take it): Hypersensitivity to drug or class, systemic fungal infection.

Possible side effects and warnings: Can cause inadequate production of corticosteroids by the adrenal glands, steroid psychosis (psychotic reactions to steroid use, aka 'roid rage), immunosuppression, peptic ulcer disease, nausea, vomiting, diarrhea, headache, dizziness, sleeplessness, mood swings, anxiety, low potassium levels, high glucose levels, acne, Cushingoid features, skin atrophy, and poor wound healing. Should be used with caution in women with congestive heart failure, liver or kidney dysfunction, diabetes, high blood pressure, tuberculosis, or osteoporosis.

How it can affect pregnant women: There are no adequate reports or well-controlled studies of fludrocortisone in pregnant women. It has been used without complication for the treatment of inadequate production of corticosteroids by the adrenal glands during pregnancy. Women being treated for congenital abnormality of adrenal function causing them to lose salt conceive and complete pregnancies successfully while taking fludrocortisone.

How it can affect a developing embryo or fetus: There are no adequate reports or well-controlled studies in human fetuses. The best evidence is that corticosteroids are weak teratogens (substances that can cause birth defects) when taken in the first trimester. Although there is no increase in major birth defects, the rates of both cleft lip and cleft palate are increased. There is no increase in risk of anomalies when steroids are begun after organ formation (after 11 weeks) or if given only topically. A few small studies suggested a possible relationship between long-term steroid use during pregnancy and poor fetal growth; however, it is hard to tell if that was the result of the medication or the disease it was being used to treat.

Breast-feeding: There is no published data in nursing women. It is unknown whether fludrocortisone enters human breast milk, though other corticosteroids are excreted at low concentrations into milk.

Potential drug interactions: Interaction between the following medications and fludrocortisone has the potential to impact the effect of one or more of the drugs. In some instances the interaction can be dangerous or life-threatening and must be avoided: potassium-sensitive drugs (e.g., digitalis), oral anticoagulants, antidiabetic agents, aspirin, barbiturates, phenytoin, rifampin, vaccines, estrogen.

What the FDA says about use in pregnancy: Category C (see Appendix).

What the available evidence suggests about breast-feeding safety: Unknown.

The bottom line for you:

- Fludrocortisone may be used during pregnancy and while breast-feeding for replacement treatment of women with adrenal insufficiency.
- Large doses should probably be avoided in the first trimester.

FLUMAZENIL

Brand names: Marzicon, Romazicon

Drug class: Antidote

Indications (what it is used for): Benzodiazepine overdose.

How it works: Blocks the benzodiazepine receptors, reversing their effect.

Contraindications (reasons you shouldn't take it): Hypersensitivity to drug or class, overdose of more than one medication, tricyclic antidepressant overdose.

Possible side effects and warnings: Can cause withdrawal syndrome; seizures; irregular, slow, or fast heart rate; dizziness; nausea; vomiting; sweating; blurred vision; headache; anxiety; fatigue; shivering; confusion. Should be used with caution in women with a history of seizures, alcoholism, or psychiatric illness.

How it can affect pregnant women: There are no adequate reports or well-controlled studies of flumazenil in pregnant women. The published literature is limited to case reports where it was used successfully for the treatment of benzodiazepine overdose during pregnancy.

How it can affect a developing embryo or fetus: There are no adequate reports or well-controlled studies in human fetuses. Flumazenil can reverse an overdose of maternally administered diazepam in both the fetus and newborn. Rodent studies revealed no evidence of birth defects. Behavioral changes were noted in rat pups after late-pregnancy exposure. However, animal studies are not necessarily good indicators of how a drug will behave in humans.

Breast-feeding: There is no published data in nursing women. It is unknown whether flumazenil enters human breast milk. Considering the indication, limited or one-time flumazenil use is unlikely to pose a clinically significant risk to a breast-feeding newborn.

Potential drug interactions: Interaction between the following medications and flumazenil has the potential to impact the effect of one or more of the drugs. In some instances the interaction can be dangerous or life-threatening and must be avoided: mixed drug overdose; tricyclic antidepressants; chronic benzodiazepine treatment; nonbenzodiazepine agonists such as zopiclone, triazolopyridazines, and others.

What the FDA says about use in pregnancy: Category C (see Appendix).

What the available evidence suggests about breast-feeding safety: Unknown, but likely safe.

The bottom line for you:

- Flumazenil is likely safe for use during pregnancy and while breast-feeding to treat life-threatening benzodiazepine overdose.

FLUNISOLIDE

Brand names: AeroBid, Nasalide, Nasarel
Drug class: Corticosteroid, inhalation
Indications (what it is used for): Asthma prevention, allergic runny nose.

How it works: Unknown.

Contraindications (reasons you shouldn't take it): Hypersensitivity to drug or class, status asthmaticus (severe and potentially life-threatening asthma attack), respiratory infection.

Possible side effects and warnings: Can cause inadequate production of corticosteroids by the adrenal glands, nausea, vomiting, diarrhea, headache, sore throat, nasal congestion, heartburn, flulike symptoms, palpitations, abdominal pain, loss of appetite, peripheral edema (swelling in the limbs), dizziness, cough, eczema, and high blood pressure.

How it can affect pregnant women: Asthma is a common disease in life and in pregnancy. Approximately one-third of pregnant women with asthma get worse during pregnancy, one-third get better, and one-third remain clinically unchanged. Well-controlled asthma does not affect pregnancy outcome, but poorly controlled asthma may increase the risk of preterm birth (before 37 weeks) or low birth weight. There is no published data with flunisolide during pregnancy, although inhaled corticosteroids are a cornerstone of asthma prevention and used widely during pregnancy without apparent adverse effects. Inhaled corticosteroids are the preventative medication of choice for pregnant women with persistent asthma unless their condition is well controlled by cromolyn or nedocromil.

Certain medications used during labor and delivery have the potential to worsen asthma, including nonselective beta-blockers, some prostaglandins (used to induce labor), and ergonovine (used to control blood loss after delivery).

How it can affect a developing embryo or fetus: There are no adequate reports or well-controlled studies in human fetuses. It is unknown whether flunisolide crosses the human placenta. In rodents, flunisolide doses at 100 times the maximum recommended human dose can damage the fetus. Although oral or intravenous administered corticosteroids (as opposed to inhaled steroids) can cause birth defects in some rodents and may be a weak teratogen (substance that causes birth defects) in humans, the low concentration of inhaled flunisolide absorbed systemically suggests that the risk of harmful effects on a fetus is low.

Breast-feeding: There is no published data in nursing women. It is unknown whether flunisolide enters human breast milk. Considering the amount absorbed systemically by the mother, it is unlikely that the blood level achieved in a breast-feeding newborn will be clinically relevant.

Potential drug interactions: None currently identified.

What the FDA says about use in pregnancy: Category C (see Appendix).

What the available evidence suggests about breast-feeding safety: Unknown, but likely safe.

The bottom line for you:

- Inhaled corticosteroids are a safe and effective first-line treatment of moderate to severe asthma during pregnancy and while breast-feeding.

FLUOCINOLONE TOPICAL

Brand name: Synalar
Drug classes: Corticosteroid; Dermatologic
Indications (what it is used for): Steroid-responsive dermatitis (rash).
How it works: Unknown.
Contraindications (reasons you shouldn't take it): Hypersensitivity to drug or class.
Possible side effects and warnings: Can cause inadequate production of corticosteroids by the adrenal glands; irritated, burning, itching, dry, and fragile skin; inflammation of hair follicles; excess hair growth; acne; loss of skin color; stretch marks.
How it can affect pregnant women: There is no published data with fluocinolone during pregnancy.
How it can affect a developing embryo or fetus: There are no adequate reports or well-controlled studies in human fetuses. It is unknown whether fluocinolone crosses the human placenta. Although oral or intravenous administered corticosteroids (as opposed to inhaled steroids) can cause birth defects

in some rodents and may be a weak teratogen (substance that causes birth defects) in humans, the low concentration of topically applied fluocinolone, which is absorbed systemically, suggests that the risk of harmful effects on a fetus is low.

Breast-feeding: There are no reports in nursing women. It is unknown whether fluocinolone enters human breast milk. However, considering the low amount that is absorbed systemically with topical use, it is unlikely that the blood level achieved in a breast-feeding baby would be clinically significant.

Potential drug interactions: Topical steroids may increase psoriasis symptoms when combined with anthralin.

What the FDA says about use in pregnancy: Category C (see Appendix).

What the available evidence suggests about breast-feeding safety: Unknown, but likely safe.

The bottom line for you:

- Fluocinolone is probably safe for topical use during pregnancy and while breast-feeding.

FLUOROURACIL

Brand name: Adrucil
Drug classes: Antimetabolite; Antineoplastic
Indications (what it is used for): Malignant tumors including breast, colon, basal cell, and placenta.
How it works: Inhibits both DNA and RNA synthesis, which are necessary for cell growth and replication.
Contraindications (reasons you shouldn't take it): Hypersensitivity to drug or class, myelosuppression (decreased bone marrow activity), serious infection, recent surgery.
Possible side effects and warnings: Can cause low platelet or white blood cell counts, bone marrow suppression, bowel bleeding, nausea, vomiting, diarrhea, loss of appetite, inflammation of the small intestine, hair loss, rash, light sensitivity, redness of the skin, sores in the mouth, lethargy, malaise, headache, and confusion. Should be used with caution in

women with liver or kidney dysfunction, who have used alkylating agents in the past, or who have coronary artery disease.

How it can affect pregnant women: There are no adequate reports or well-controlled studies of fluorouracil in pregnant women. Fluorouracil is most commonly used during pregnancy in the second and third trimesters for the treatment of metastatic breast cancer, where it is often combined with doxorubicin and cyclophosphamide. Treatment during pregnancy can be associated with successful outcomes.

How it can affect a developing embryo or fetus: There are no adequate reports or well-controlled studies in human fetuses. Fluorouracil apparently crosses the human placenta, since maternal administration can lead to fetal immune suppression. The few published epidemiologic studies support the multiple case reports of normal pregnancy outcome after early exposure. Little is known about the long-term effects of intrauterine exposure to fluorouracil. Although it should be used only when the mother's survival is at risk, breast cancer can sometimes be treated during the second and third trimesters with a modest risk of short-term fetal complications.

Breast-feeding: There is no published data in nursing women. It is unknown whether fluorouracil enters human breast milk.

Potential drug interactions: Leucovorin may increase the toxicity of fluorouracil.

What the FDA says about use in pregnancy: Category D (see Appendix).

What the available evidence suggests about breast-feeding safety: Unknown.

The bottom line for you:

- Fluorouracil can be used with relative safety in the second and third trimesters when the mother's survival is at risk.

FLUOXETINE

Brand names: Prozac, Sarafem
Drug classes: Antidepressant; Selective serotonin reuptake inhibitor (SSRI)

Indications (what it is used for): Depression, premenstrual dysphoric syndrome, obsessive-compulsive disorder, bulimia, postpartum depression.

How it works: Selectively inhibits reuptake of serotonin, a neurotransmitter related to mood.

Contraindications (reasons you shouldn't take it): Hypersensitivity to drug or class, use of a monoamine oxidase inhibitor (MAOI) during the prior 2 weeks.

Possible side effects and warnings: Can cause sleeplessness, nausea, diarrhea, tremor, headache, loss of appetite, anxiety, dry mouth, decreased libido, delayed or absent orgasm, abnormal dreams, sedation, sweating, and itching. Should be used with caution in women with liver or kidney dysfunction, a history of seizures, or suicide threats.

How it can affect pregnant women: Depression is common during and after pregnancy but often goes unrecognized and untreated. Depression can be made worse by pregnancy or delivery, and suicide is a not uncommon cause of maternal death. Pregnancy is not a reason to discontinue antidepressant drugs if the medication is effective and needed. A woman being treated for depression who becomes pregnant should not discontinue medication abruptly on her own, but rather discuss her treatment and condition with her medical provider. Fluoxetine breakdown appears increased by pregnancy and many pregnant women require an increase in their dose to maintain effectiveness. Fluoxetine is as effective as a course of counseling in the short term for the treatment for postpartum depression.

How it can affect a developing embryo or fetus: There are no adequate reports or well-controlled studies in human fetuses. Fluoxetine crosses the human placenta, reaching levels similar to those in the mother. The level is similar to that reached with citalopram but higher than that reached with sertraline or paroxetine. Some studies have shown a small increase in the risk of heart defects in embryos exposed to SSRIs in the first trimester but current study suggests it is not dose dependent (the risk does not increase or decrease as the dose does, suggesting other factors may play a role in creating the defect). The safest approach for all SSRIs is probably to avoid them in the first trimester. Women with moderate to severe depression responsive to their medication, however, should continue treatment during pregnancy as the benefit outweighs the possible risks to mother and child.

SSRI use late in pregnancy may double the risk of persistent pulmonary hypertension (high blood pressure affecting the lungs) during the newborn period (which, at 2 in 1000 births, is low to begin with). SSRI exposure during the third trimester and until delivery may also lead to a withdrawal syndrome during the first few days of life, requiring extra care. Symptoms in the newborn may include problems breathing, jitteriness, increased muscle tone, irritability, altered sleep patterns, tremors, and poor eating. In most cases, these symptoms are mild and disappear within 2 two weeks with no treatment. These symptoms can occur in up to 30% of exposed newborns, and, although they can occur at all doses, occur more often with higher doses. The risk does not outweigh the benefit of needed therapy. Exposure throughout pregnancy does not adversely affect learning, language development, or temperament of preschool and early-school-age children.

Rodent studies are reassuring from the standpoint of birth defects, although the rates of low birth weight and stillbirth are higher in rats treated with doses higher than those used clinically. Mild behavioral changes are seen in some rodents, which may or may not be long term. However, animal studies are not necessarily good indicators of how a drug will behave in humans.

Breast-feeding: Newborn blood levels are typically low in women taking 20 mg or less per day. Thus, breast-feeding is not contraindicated with maternal doses in this range.

Potential drug interactions: Interaction between the following medications and fluoxetine has the potential to impact the effect of one or more of the drugs. In some instances the interaction can be dangerous or life-threatening and must be avoided: medications metabolized by the CYP2D6 system (including but not limited to flecainide, vinblastine, and tricyclic antidepressants), thioridazine, phenytoin, carbamazepine, antipsychotics, diazepam, alprazolam, lithium, imipramine, desipramine, sumatriptan, nonsteroidal anti-inflammatory drugs (NSAIDs), aspirin, warfarin.

What the FDA says about use in pregnancy: Category C (see Appendix).

What the available evidence suggests about breast-feeding safety: Likely safe at daily doses less than 20 mg.

The bottom line for you:

- Women with moderate to severe depression responsive to their medication should continue their antidepressant medication during pregnancy as the benefit outweighs the possible risks to mother and child.
- Fluoxetine may be used while breast-feeding.

FLUPHENAZINE

Brand names: Permitil, Prolixin
Drug classes: Antipsychotic; Phenothiazine
Indications (what it is used for): Psychosis (e.g., chronic schizophrenia).
How it works: Unclear.
Contraindications (reasons you shouldn't take it): Hypersensitivity to drug or class, central nervous system depression, bone marrow depression, profound low blood pressure, pheochromocytoma (adrenal gland tumor).
Possible side effects and warnings: Can cause seizures, neuroleptic malignant syndrome (life-threatening muscle rigidity, fever, vital sign instability, and cognitive changes such as delirium), bone marrow suppression, cholestatic jaundice, nausea, loss of appetite, headache, depression, high prolactin levels, involuntary body movements, sedation, pseudoparkinsonism, drowsiness, blurred vision, dry mouth, constipation, light sensitivity, and in-

ability to urinate. Should be used with caution in women with liver dysfunction, seizure disorder, myasthenia gravis (an autoimmune disease causing muscle weakness), Parkinson's disease (disorder of the brain that affects movement and coordination), or severe cardiovascular disease.

How it can affect pregnant women: Fluphenazine is a long-acting antipsychotic typically used in institutional settings. There are no adequate reports or well-controlled studies in pregnant women.

How it can affect a developing embryo or fetus: There are no adequate reports or well-controlled studies in human fetuses. It is unknown whether fluphenazine crosses the human placenta. Series of self-reported pregnancy exposures have not revealed an increased risk of adverse outcomes. Rodent studies revealed bone and central nervous system malformations. These risks are greater when fluphenazine is combined with diphenylhydantoin. However, animal studies are not necessarily good indicators of how a drug will behave in humans.

Breast-feeding: There is no published data in nursing women. It is unknown whether fluphenazine enters human breast milk.

Potential drug interactions: Interaction between the following medications and fluphenazine has the potential to impact the effect of one or more of the drugs. In some instances the interaction can be dangerous or life-threatening and must be avoided: antacids, beta-blockers, barbiturates, orphenadrine, bromocriptine, antimalarial drugs, tricyclic antidepressants (TCAs), levodopa, meperidine. Fluphenazine may increase the effects of other drugs that cause drowsiness, including antidepressants, alcohol, antihistamines, sedatives, pain relievers, anxiety medicines, and muscle relaxants.

What the FDA says about use in pregnancy: Category C (see Appendix).

What the available evidence suggests about breast-feeding safety: Unknown.

The bottom line for you:
- Fluphenazine may be used during pregnancy if necessary.

- There is presently no data to determine its safety while breast-feeding. Discuss other options with your pediatrician.

FLURAZEPAM

Brand names: Dalmane, Fluleep, Midorm, Niotal, Paxane

Drug classes: Benzodiazepine; Hypnotic; Sedative

Indications (what it is used for): Short-term relief of insomnia.

How it works: Activates benzodiazepine receptors, triggering sleep.

Contraindications (reasons you shouldn't take it): Hypersensitivity to drug or class, pregnancy.

Possible side effects and warnings: Can cause coma, dependence, sedation, dizziness, lack of gross-muscle control, confusion, headache, nausea, and liver injury. Should be used with caution in women with liver or lung dysfunction or with sleep apnea.

How it can affect pregnant women: There are no adequate reports or well-controlled studies of flurazepam in pregnant women. Flurazepam lingers in the bloodstream for up to 4 days, and sedation the day after taking it is common. There are other hypnotics with better pharmacologic and safety profiles, such as zolpidem. Prolonged use of most hypnotics is not advised. Flurazepam has generally been replaced by improved agents such as eszopiclone and zolpidem.

How it can affect a developing embryo or fetus: There are no adequate reports or well-controlled studies in human fetuses. Flurazepam crosses the human placenta. There is weak data that benzodiazepines such as diazepam and chlordiazepoxide may be associated with an increased risk of malformations from first-trimester exposure. Mood depression was reported in the newborn of a woman taking flurazepam for 10 days prior to delivery. The long-term neurologic effects of in utero exposure are unknown.

Breast-feeding: There are no adequate reports or well-controlled studies in nursing women. Older abstracts suggest that flurazepam enters human breast milk.

Potential drug interactions: Interaction between the following medications and flurazepam has the potential to impact the effect of one or more of the drugs. In some instances the interaction can be dangerous or life-threatening and must be avoided: phenothiazines, narcotics, barbiturates, monoamine oxidase inhibitors (MAOIs), antidepressants, cimetidine, valproate, inhibitors of CYP2CI9 (e.g., cimetidine, quinidine, tranylcypromine) and CYP3A4 (e.g., clotrimazole, ketoconazole, troleandomycin), inducers of CYP2CI9 (e.g., rifampin) and CYP3A4 (e.g., carbamazepine, dexamethasone, phenobarbital, phenytoin), substrates of CYP2CI9 (e.g., imipramine, omeprazole, propranolol) and CYP3A4 (e.g., cyclosporine, paclitaxel, terfenadine, theophylline, warfarin).

What the FDA says about use in pregnancy: Category X (see Appendix).

What the available evidence suggests about breast-feeding safety: Possibly safe; observe newborn closely for sedation.

The bottom line for you:

- Although there is no firm evidence that flurazepam causes birth defects, there is no indication for its use during pregnancy. There are other hypnotics, such as zolpidem and escopiclone, with better pharmacologic and safety profiles.
- There are sleep aids for which there is more experience during breastfeeding. Flurazepam is considered relatively safe for use while breast-feeding, though newborns should be observed closely for any signs of sedation.

FLUTICASONE

Brand names: Cutivate, Flonase, Flonase Aq, Flovent, Flunase, Zoflut

Drug classes: Corticosteroid, inhalation; Corticosteroid, topical; Dermatologic

Indications (what it is used for): Asthma prevention.

How it works: Blocks inflammation.

Contraindications (reasons you shouldn't take it): Hypersensitivity to drug or class, acute asthma, status asthmaticus (severe and potentially life-threatening asthma attack).

Possible side effects and warnings: Can cause inadequate production of corticosteroids by the adrenal glands, bronchospasm, glaucoma, cataracts, Cushingoid features, headache, nasal congestion, sinusitis, and sore throat.

How it can affect pregnant women: Asthma is a common disease in life and in pregnancy. Approximately one-third of pregnant women with asthma get worse during pregnancy, one-third get better, and one-third remain clinically unchanged. Well-controlled asthma does not affect pregnancy outcome, but poorly controlled asthma may increase the risk of preterm birth (before 37 weeks) or low birth weight. Inhaled corticosteroids are considered the preventative medication of choice for pregnant women with persistent asthma unless their condition is well controlled by cromolyn or nedocromil. Budesonide and beclomethasone are considered the first-line treatments.

There are no adequate reports or well-controlled studies of fluticasone in pregnant women. However, neither inhaled nor nasal corticosteroids increase the rates of adverse pregnancy outcomes. Fluticasone is commonly used during pregnancy for asthma; case series are reassuring. Once-daily budesonide nasal spray, fluticasone nasal spray, mometasone furoate nasal spray, and triamcinolone aqueous nasal spray have similar effectiveness and safety profiles for allergic rhinitis and are used during pregnancy.

Certain medications used during labor and delivery have the potential to worsen asthma, including nonselective beta-blockers, some prostaglandins (used to induce labor), and ergonovine (used to control blood loss after delivery).

How it can affect a developing embryo or fetus: There are no adequate reports or well-controlled studies in human fetuses. It is unknown whether fluticasone crosses the human placenta. However, neither inhaled nor nasal corticosteroids alone adversely affect fetal growth or placental function. Although oral or intravenous administered corticosteroids (as opposed to inhaled steroids) can cause birth defects in some rodents and may be a weak teratogen (substance that causes birth defects) in humans, the low concentration of inhaled fluocinolone absorbed systemically suggests that the risk of a harmful effect on a fetus is low.

Breast-feeding: There are no adequate reports or well-controlled studies in nursing women. It is unknown whether fluticasone enters human breast milk. Measurable but small amounts enter rat breast milk. Considering the small amount that is absorbed systemically, it is unlikely that the milk level achieved is clinically relevant to a breast-feeding baby.

Potential drug interactions: Interaction between the following medications and fluticasone has the potential to impact the effect of one or more of the drugs. In some instances the interaction can be dangerous or life-threatening and must be avoided: ritonavir and ketoconazole.

What the FDA says about use in pregnancy: Category C (see Appendix).

What the available evidence suggests about breast-feeding safety: Safe.

The bottom line for you:

● Fluticasone is safe and effective for use during pregnancy and while breast-feeding for the prevention of asthma.

FLUVASTATIN

Brand names: Lescol, Lescol XL

Drug classes: Antihyperlipidemic; HMG-CoA reductase inhibitor

Indications (what it is used for): Hypercholesterolemia (high cholesterol and triglycerides), mixed dyslipidemia, secondary prevention of cardiac events.

How it works: Blocks HMG-CoA reductase, a key enzyme in cholesterol synthesis.

Contraindications (reasons you shouldn't take it): Hypersensitivity to drug or class, active liver disease, pregnancy.

Possible side effects and warnings: Can cause pancreatitis, liver toxicity, constipation, heartburn, flatulence, nausea, diarrhea, abdominal pain, muscle ache, muscle weakness, and muscle breakdown. Should be used with caution in women with liver or kidney disease or a history of alcohol abuse.

How it can affect pregnant women: There are no adequate reports or well-controlled studies of fluvastatin in pregnant women. Hyperlipidemia is a chronic illness, and discontinuing treatment during pregnancy is unlikely to compromise long-term health. The published data is confined to a case report with a normal pregnancy outcome.

How it can affect a developing embryo or fetus: Cholesterol and related substances are building blocks for the placenta and fetus, which is why there might be concern about using drugs to block their production during pregnancy. There are no adequate reports or well-controlled studies in human fetuses. It is not known whether fluvastatin crosses the placenta. In rodents, fluvastatin was associated with delayed and abnormal skeletal development. Similar-class drugs are associated with rare reports of malformations; however, there is no pattern of abnormalities in humans to suggest that the drug is the cause of those defects.

Breast-feeding: There are no adequate reports or well-controlled studies in nursing women. Fluvastatin is apparently concentrated in human breast milk. The effect on a breast-feeding baby is unknown.

Potential drug interactions: Interaction between the following medications and fluvastatin has the potential to impact the effect of one or more of the drugs. In some instances the interaction can be dangerous or life-threatening and must be avoided: CYP3A4 inhibitors/substrates, such as cyclosporine, erythromycin, and itraconazole; phenytoin; cholestyramine; diclofenac; glibenclamide; glyburide; cimetidine; ranitidine; omeprazole; rifampicin.

What the FDA says about use in pregnancy: Category X (see Appendix).
What the available evidence suggests about breast-feeding safety: Unknown.
The bottom line for you:
- Fluvastatin is at present considered contraindicated during pregnancy, although there is scant evidence of risk.
- Breast-feeding is best avoided until there is new information.

FOLIC ACID

Brand names: Acido, Folasic, Folicet, Folico, Folvite, Nifolin, Renal Multivit Form Forte/Zinc
Drug classes: Hematinic; Vitamin/mineral
Indications (what it is used for): Pregnancy supplementation, primary prevention of various birth defects including spina bifida (an opening in the spine), treatment of megaloblastic anemia (anemia with larger than normal red blood cells).
How it works: Required for hemoglobin and DNA synthesis.
Contraindications (reasons you shouldn't take it): Anemia of unknown cause.
Possible side effects and warnings: Can cause nausea, vomiting, loss of appetite, flatulence, irritability, altered sleep pattern, skin redness, rash, and itching.
How it can affect pregnant women: The widespread folate supplementation in food products in the U.S. has been associated with reduced the rates of preterm birth and low birth weight. Low folate and vitamin B_6 reserves, especially when combined, may increase the risk of miscarriage. HIV-positive women also show improved pregnancy outcomes when supplemented with folate.
How it can affect a developing embryo or fetus: A wide range of birth defects are linked to folate deficiency, and their risk is decreased by folate supplementation. Spina bifida and other neural tube defects plus several other pregnancy complications are linked to impaired folate metabolism. It is suggested that high levels of folate supplementation might also blunt the negative impact of antiepileptic drugs on the fetus. Evidence has emerged that vitamin B_{12} deficiency may also increase the risk of fetal neural tube defects.
Breast-feeding: Maternal folate stores are depleted during breast-feeding. Supplementation minimizes maternal loss and increases the level of folate in milk.
Potential drug interactions: None currently identified.
What the FDA says about use in pregnancy: Category A (see Appendix).
What the available evidence suggests about breast-feeding safety: Safe.
The bottom line for you:
- Pre-conception folate supplementation reduces the incidence of neural tube defects and possibly other birth defects.
- Although folate is an ingredient in all prenatal vitamins, women who have previously had a fetus with a neural tube defect require higher folate doses (4 mg daily) before conception than typically prescribed during pregnancy to decrease recurrence.
- Pre-conception folate supplementation may reduce the rate of miscarriage when both parents are carriers of a gene mutation that predisposes them to inefficient folate metabolism.

FONDAPARINUX

Brand name: Arixtra
Drug class: Anticoagulant
Indications (what it is used for): Prevention of blood clots after surgery.
How it works: Selectively activates antithrombin, a protein that inhibits blood clotting,
Contraindications (reasons you shouldn't take it): Hypersensitivity to drug or class, active bleeding, body weight under 100 pounds, poor kidney

function, low platelet count, receiving intramuscular medicines, bacterial endocarditis (infection of the heart valve), epidural or spinal analgesia.

Possible side effects and warnings: Can cause hemorrhage, low platelet count, epidural or spinal hematoma, paralysis, injection site pain, and liver damage. Should be used with caution in women with kidney dysfunction, history of bowel bleeding, hemorrhagic stroke, heparin-induced low platelets, active or recent peptic ulcer disease, and diabetic retinopathy.

How it can affect pregnant women: Fondaparinux is the first of a new class of antithrombotic agents developed to prevent and treat blood clots. Fondaparinux is rapidly absorbed and can be dosed once a day in nonpregnant patients. The current data in pregnancy, though encouraging, is confined to case reports. It is unknown whether pregnancy affects the clearance (how fast it travels through your body) of fondaparinux.

How it can affect a developing embryo or fetus: There are no adequate reports or well-controlled studies in human fetuses. Laboratory studies suggest that fondaparinux does not cross the human placenta, meaning that the fetus is not directly at risk.

Breast-feeding: There are no adequate reports or well-controlled studies in nursing women. It is unknown whether fondaparinux enters human breast milk. Oral absorption from the gut will be low.

Potential drug interactions: None currently identified.

What the FDA says about use in pregnancy: Category B (see Appendix).

What the available evidence suggests about breast feeding safety: Likely safe.

The bottom line for you:

- There is no published data during pregnancy and while breast-feeding, there are alternative agents with which there is more experience.

FORMOTEROL, INHALED

Brand names: Foradil Aerolizer

Drug classes: Adrenergic agonist; Bronchodilator

Indications (what it is used for): Prevention of an asthma episode, treatment of exercise-induced asthma, maintenance of chronic obstructive pulmonary disease (COPD).

How it works: Activates the beta-2 receptors to relax the bronchioles.

Contraindications (reasons you shouldn't take it): Hypersensitivity to drug or class, acute asthma.

Possible side effects and warnings: Can cause irregular heart rate, paradoxical bronchospasm (constriction of the airways after treatment with a bronchodilator), low potassium level, nervousness, tremors, headache, dry mouth, nausea, dizziness, sleeplessness, chest pain, muscle cramps, heartburn, and hoarseness. Should be used with caution in women with an irregular heart rate, cardiovascular disease, high blood pressure, diabetes, low potassium level, or a seizure disorder.

How it can affect pregnant women: Asthma is a common disease in life and in pregnancy. Approximately one-third of pregnant women with asthma get worse during pregnancy, one-third get better, and one-third remain clinically unchanged. Well-controlled asthma does not affect pregnancy outcome, but poorly controlled asthma may increase the risk of preterm birth (before 37 weeks) or low birth weight. Inhaled corticosteroids are the preventative medication of choice for pregnant women with persistent asthma unless their condition is well controlled by cromolyn or nedocromil.

Formoterol is a long-acting agent used for asthma prevention; not for acute treatment. There are no adequate reports or well-controlled studies of formoterol in pregnant women. In one small study of 33 pregnant women, no adverse effects or decrease in effectiveness was noted.

Certain medications used during labor and delivery have the potential to worsen asthma, including nonselective beta-blockers, some prostaglandins (used to induce labor), and ergonovine (used to control blood loss after delivery).

How it can affect a developing embryo or fetus: There are no adequate reports or well-controlled studies of formoterol in human fetuses. Rodent studies are reassuring, revealing problems only with a dose more than 2,000 times the maximum recommended clinical dose. However, animal studies are not necessarily good indicators of how a drug will behave in humans.

Breast-feeding: There is no published data in nursing women. It is unknown whether formoterol enters human breast milk. The transfer of similar agents, such as terbutaline, is very low.

Potential drug interactions: Interaction between the following medications and formoterol has the potential to impact the effect of one or more of the drugs. In some instances the interaction can be dangerous or life-threatening and must be avoided: other adrenergic drugs, xanthine derivatives, steroids, monoamine oxidase inhibitors (MAOIs), tricyclic antidepressants (TCAs), drugs known to prolong the QTc interval, beta-blockers.

What the FDA says about use in pregnancy: Category C (see Appendix).

What the available evidence suggests about breast-feeding safety: Unknown, but likely safe.

The bottom line for you:

- The limited information available suggests that formoterol may be safe to use during pregnancy and while breast-feeding, although there are other agents with which there is more experience.

FOSCARNET

Brand name: Foscavir

Drug class: Antiviral

Indications (what it is used for): Acyclovir-resistant herpes simplex virus, cytomegalovirus retinitis, AIDS.

How it works: Selectively blocks viral replication.

Contraindications (reasons you shouldn't take it): Hypersensitivity to drug or class.

Possible side effects and warnings: Can cause kidney failure; pancreatitis; bone marrow suppression; bronchospasm; seizures; nausea; vomiting; diarrhea; fever, headache; weakness; and low levels of calcium, phosphate, and magnesium. Should be used with caution in women with kidney dysfunction, malnutrition, or central nervous system disorders.

How it can affect pregnant women: There are no adequate reports or well-controlled studies of foscarnet in pregnant women, and the indications for using the medication are limited. Foscarnet was used successfully during pregnancy in one AIDS patient for the treatment of drug-resistant herpes genital simplex virus and in another HIV-infected woman with severe nerve pain.

How it can affect a developing embryo or fetus: There are no adequate reports or well-controlled studies in human fetuses. It is unknown whether foscarnet crosses the human placenta. Rodent studies reveal only a modest increase in minor skeletal abnormalities. However, animal studies are not necessarily good indicators of how a drug will behave in humans.

Breast-feeding: There is no published data in nursing women. It is unknown whether foscarnet enters human breast milk.

Potential drug interactions: Combined use of foscarnet and pentamidine may cause dangerously low calcium levels. Treatment with other drugs known to influence serum calcium concentrations should be done with extreme caution.

What the FDA says about use in pregnancy: Category C (see Appendix).

What the available evidence suggests about breast-feeding safety: Unknown.

The bottom line for you:

- Foscarnet may be used during pregnancy for these serious disorders.
- There is presently no data to determine its safety while breast-feeding. Discuss other options with your pediatrician.

FOSINOPRIL

Brand name: Monopril
Drug class: ACEI/A2R-antagonist
Indications (what it is used for): High blood pressure, congestive heart failure, acute heart attack, kidney disease.
How it works: Inhibits an enzyme that produces one of many proteins that increase blood pressure.
Contraindications (reasons you shouldn't take it): Hypersensitivity to drug or class, hereditary or ACE-related angioedema, pregnancy.
Possible side effects and warnings: Can cause angioedema (swelling under the skin), low blood pressure, kidney failure, liver toxicity, low white blood cell count, pancreatitis, cough, dizziness, fatigue, high potassium level, nausea, vomiting, musculoskeletal pain, and cold symptoms. Should be used with caution in women with renal artery stenosis, kidney dysfunction, severe heart failure, connective tissue disease, dehydration, or low sodium.
How it can affect pregnant women: Fosinopril is a long-acting drug that is part of a class of drugs that are known teratogens (substances that can cause birth defects). Although there is no published data with fosinopril during pregnancy, there are almost always other options. Women taking fosinopril before conception should switch medications if planning pregnancy.
How it can affect a developing embryo or fetus: There are no adequate reports or well-controlled studies in human fetuses. It is unknown whether fosinopril crosses the human placenta. However, this class of drugs is known to have adverse effects on the kidneys of human fetuses, leading to disability or death. They should not be used during pregnancy.
Breast-feeding: There is no published data in nursing women. The manufacturer reports low levels of fosinopril in human breast milk.
Potential drug interactions: Interaction between the following medications and fosinopril has the potential to impact the effect of one or more of the drugs. In some instances the interaction can be dangerous or life-threatening and must be avoided: diuretics, potassium-sparing diuretics (e.g., amiloride, spironolactone, triamterene), potassium supplements, lithium, antacids.
What the FDA says about use in pregnancy: Category D (see Appendix).
What the available evidence suggests about breast-feeding safety: Unknown.
The bottom line for you:

- All drugs that inhibit aspects of the renin-angiotensin system (integral to the regulation of blood pressure), such as fosinopril, should be avoided during pregnancy unless there is no other safe option for the mother.
- There are almost always alternative agents with which there is more experience during pregnancy and while breast-feeding.

FROVATRIPTAN

Brand name: Froval
Drug class: Migraine
Indications (what it is used for): Migraine headache.
How it works: Activates a serotonin receptor on blood vessels, causing them to contract.
Contraindications (reasons you shouldn't take it): Hypersensitivity to drug or class, coronary artery disease, cerebrovascular disease (narrowing of blood vessels that supply the brain), peripheral vascular disease (reduced blood flow to areas other than the heart or brain), ischemic bowel disease (reduced blood flow to the bowel), uncontrolled high blood pressure, hemiplegic or basilar migraine, use of an ergot or 5-HT1 agonist (other medications for migraine) within 24 hours.
Possible side effects and warnings: Can cause acute heart attack, coronary vasospasm, irregular heart rate, subarachnoid hemorrhage (bleeding between the skull and the surface of the brain), severe life-threatening high blood pressure, stroke, bowel damage, dizziness, fatigue, flushing, tingling, dry mouth, bone pain, heartburn, neck or jaw tightness, and chest pressure. Should be used with caution in women who have heart problems.

How it can affect pregnant women: Fifty to 90% of women who suffer migraines experience improvement during pregnancy, mainly during the second and third trimesters. A higher percentage of women who have menstrual migraine experience this improvement compared to women with other types of migraines. There is no published data with frovatriptan during pregnancy.

How it can affect a developing embryo or fetus: There are no adequate reports or well-controlled studies of frovatriptan in human fetuses.

Breast-feeding: There is no published data in nursing women. It is unknown whether frovatriptan enters human breast milk. Considering the limited dosing regimen and the safety of similar-class medications, frovatriptan is likely compatible with breast-feeding. A treated woman may pump and discard her milk for 24 hours after treatment and then resume breast-feeding.

Potential drug interactions: Interaction between the following medications and frovatriptan has the potential to impact the effect of one or more of the drugs. In some instances the interaction can be dangerous or life-threatening and must be avoided: ergot-containing drugs, other 5-HT1B/1D agonists, selective serotonin reuptake inhibitors (SSRIs; e.g., fluoxetine, fluvoxamine, paroxetine, sertraline).

What the FDA says about use in pregnancy: Category C (see Appendix).

What the available evidence suggests about breast-feeding safety: Unknown, but likely safe.

The bottom line for you:

- There are alternative agents with which there is more experience during pregnancy.
- While breast-feeding, it would be reasonable to pump and discard milk for 24 hours after treatment.

FUROSEMIDE

Brand name: Lasix
Drug class: Diuretic, loop

Indications (what it is used for): Fluid accumulation in the lungs or peripheral edema (swelling in the limbs), high blood pressure, high calcium level.

How it works: Blocks the reabsorption of sodium and chloride from urine in the kidneys.

Contraindications (reasons you shouldn't take it): Hypersensitivity to drug or class, hypersensitivity to sulfonamides, no urine output, hepatic coma (loss of consciousness due to liver failure), electrolyte imbalance.

Possible side effects and warnings: Can cause low potassium, metabolic alkalosis (too much bicarbonate in the blood), low blood pressure when sitting or standing, hearing impairment, low white blood cell or platelet counts, pancreatitis, jaundice, worsening of lupus, inflammation of the blood vessels, erythema multiforme (a skin disorder), hemolytic anemia, dizziness, nausea, vomiting, weakness, cramps, high uric acid or glucose levels, ringing in the ears, tingling, and light sensitivity. Should be used with caution in women with severe kidney disease, a history of a recent acute heart attack, diabetes, lupus erythematosus (a chronic inflammatory disease in which the immune system attacks the body's own tissues and organs), a history of pancreatitis, or who are taking medications that may affect hearing.

How it can affect pregnant women: There are no adequate reports or well-controlled studies of furosemide in pregnant women. It is a drug of choice for the treatment of congestive heart failure and/or fluid accumulation in the lung during pregnancy. The long clinical experience is reassuring.

How it can affect a developing embryo or fetus: There are no adequate reports or well-controlled studies in human fetuses. Furosemide crosses the human placenta, achieving levels in the fetus similar to those in the mother. It is unclear, however, whether or when during pregnancy the fetal kidneys are responsive to it.

Breast-feeding: There are no adequate reports or well-controlled studies in nursing women. Furosemide does enter human breast milk in small amounts that would be poorly absorbed by a breast-feeding newborn. It is unlikely that one-time or limited use would cause harm during breast-feeding.

Potential drug interactions: Interaction between the following medications and furosemide has the potential to impact the effect of one or more of the drugs. In some instances the interaction can be dangerous or life-threatening and must be avoided: aminoglycoside antibiotics, ethacrynic acid, salicylates, tubocurarine, succinylcholine, lithium, blood-pressure-lowering medications, ganglionic or peripheral adrenergic-blocking drugs, sucralfate, indomethacin.

What the FDA says about use in pregnancy: Category C (see Appendix).

What the available evidence suggests about breast-feeding safety: Likely safe.

The bottom line for you:

- Furosemide may be used during pregnancy and breast-feeding with relative safety.

GABAPENTIN

Brand name: Neurontin
Drug class: Anticonvulsant
Indications (what it is used for): Seizures (partial), nerve pain, shingles (painful skin rash due to the virus that causes chickenpox).
How it works: Unknown.
Contraindications (reasons you shouldn't take it): Hypersensitivity to drug or class.
Possible side effects and warnings: Can cause low white blood cell count, dizziness, sleepiness, fatigue, poor coordination of muscle movements, tremors, blurred vision, nausea, vomiting, nervousness, slurred speech, weight gain, and heartburn. Should be used with caution in women with kidney dysfunction. Avoid abrupt withdrawal.
How it can affect pregnant women: Women on medication for a seizure disorder should (when possible) plan their pregnancies, discuss the optimal medication with their neurologist, and begin appropriate supplemental folate therapy before concep-

tion (4 mg per day) to minimize the risk of birth defects. The risks of birth defects associated with antiseizure medications must be weighed against the risks of continued seizures to both the mother and fetus. Women who become pregnant during treatment should not stop treatment on their own but rather meet quickly with their doctor before making a decision.

Gabapentin is a second-generation anticonvulsant used mainly as an addition to other first-line drugs. There is little published data during pregnancy. The limited study available suggests that gabapentin may have a higher safety margin than the first-generation agents phenytoin and carbamazepine, and may require a dose adjustment during pregnancy. Gabapentin has also been used successfully for chronic headache during early pregnancy. Gabapentin has been given for restless leg syndrome, a disorder reportedly increased during pregnancy.

How it can affect a developing embryo or fetus: Seizures pose a risk to mother and fetus. There are no adequate reports or well-controlled studies of gabapentin in human fetuses. Gabapentin crosses the human placenta and is concentrated in the fetus at a level around 1½ times the maternal level. There was no evidence of an increased risk of birth defects in a small postmarketing study (study done by a drug's manufacturer after the drug is on the market). Rodent studies showed an increase in minor malformations when given at doses that are multiples of the maximum recommended clinical dose. However, animal studies are not necessarily good indicators of how a drug will behave in humans.

Breast-feeding: There are no adequate reports or well-controlled studies in nursing women. Gabapentin is excreted into human breast milk, achieving levels similar to the mother's. Although the blood level of breast-fed infants is 10–15% of the mother's level, no adverse effects have been observed. When required, the drug should be given at the lowest effective dose, breast-feeding avoided at times of peak drug levels, and the infant monitored for possible adverse effects.

Potential drug interactions: Interaction between the following medications and gabapentin has the potential to impact the effect of one or more of the drugs. In some instances the interaction can be dangerous or life-threatening and must be avoided: naproxen, morphine, cimetidine. It is recommended that gabapentin be taken at least 2 hours after antacid use.

What the FDA says about use in pregnancy: Category C (see Appendix).

What the available evidence suggests about breast-feeding safety: Unknown, but likely safe.

The bottom line for you:

- Limited study suggests that gabapentin is not a major cause of birth defects and is safer than first-generation anticonvulsants.
- Based on this limited evidence, the benefits of gabapentin therapy appear to outweigh the potential risks to the fetus.
- If needed while breast-feeding, the drug should be given at the lowest effective dose, breast-feeding avoided at times of peak drug levels, and the infant monitored for possible adverse effects.

GADOVERSETAMIDE

Brand name: Optimark

Drug class: Diagnostics, nonradioactive

Indications (what it is used for): MRI.

How it works: A component of the drug shifts the magnetic field created by a MRI, allowing an anatomical structure to be seen more clearly.

Contraindications (reasons you shouldn't take it): Hypersensitivity to drug or class.

Possible side effects and warnings: Can cause body discomfort, headache, abdominal pain, weakness, back pain, flushing, nausea, vomiting, diarrhea, heartburn, dizziness, tingling, runny nose, and taste alteration. Should be used with caution in women with hemolytic anemia or kidney disease.

How it can affect pregnant women: There is no published data with gadoversetamide during pregnancy.

How it can affect a developing embryo or fetus: There are no adequate reports or well-controlled studies in human fetuses. It is unknown whether gadoversetamide crosses the human placenta; it does cross the rodent placenta. Limited rodent studies are reassuring, revealing no increase in birth defects or low birth weight. However, animal studies are not necessarily good indicators of how a drug will behave in humans.

Breast-feeding: There is no published data in nursing women. It is unknown whether gadoversetamide enters human breast milk. It is excreted in rat breast milk. After injection with gadoversetamide, breast-feeding women may consider pumping and discarding their milk for the first 72 hours after the MRI.

Potential drug interactions: Drug interactions with other contrast agents and other drugs have not been studied.

What the FDA says about use in pregnancy: Category C (see Appendix).

What the available evidence suggests about breast-feeding safety: Unknown.

The bottom line for you:

- Gadoversetamide may be used during pregnancy and while breast-feeding when the severity of the maternal problem warrants.
- After injection with gadoversetamide, breast-feeding women may consider pumping and discarding their milk for the first 72 hours after the MRI.

GANCICLOVIR

Brand name: Cytovene

Drug class: Antiviral

Indications (what it is used for): Inflammation of the retina caused by cytomegalovirus.

How it works: Inhibits viral replication.

Contraindications (reasons you shouldn't take it): Hypersensitivity to drug or class, bone marrow depression.

Possible side effects and warnings: Can cause seizures, coma, low white or red blood cell or platelet counts, kidney or liver damage, fever, diarrhea, nausea, vomiting, sweating, chills, itching, tingling, and peripheral nerve damage. Should be used with caution in women with kidney dysfunction.

How it can affect pregnant women: There are no adequate reports or well-controlled studies during pregnancy. Case reports include successful use in the first trimester of two women with transplant-associated cytomegalovirus, as well as use in the third trimester for cytomegalovirus hepatitis.

How it can affect a developing embryo or fetus: There are no adequate reports or well-controlled studies in human fetuses. Ganciclovir crosses the human placenta and has been administered directly to cytomegalovirus-infected fetuses, although it did not cure the infection. Ganciclovir is the drug of choice for treatment after birth of newborn with cytomegalovirus; it does not cure the infection, but it reduces the risk of viral damage. In some rodents, it is associated with birth defects involving the palate, eyes, kidneys, and brain. However, animal studies are not necessarily good indicators of how a drug will behave in humans.

Breast-feeding: There are no adequate reports or well-controlled studies in nursing women. It is unknown whether ganciclovir enters human breast milk; it does enter rat breast milk. Considering that ganciclovir is used to treat newborns, it is usually considered safe when breast-feeding.

Potential drug interactions: Interaction between the following medications and ganciclovir has the potential to impact the effect of one or more of the drugs. In some instances the interaction can be dangerous or life-threatening and must be avoided: didanosine, zidovudine, probenecid, imipenem-cilastatin, drugs that inhibit replication of rapidly dividing cell populations (e.g., amphotericin B, dapsone, doxorubicin, flucytosine, pentamidine, trimethoprim-sulfamethoxazole combinations, vinblastine, vincristine, other nucleoside analogs).

What the FDA says about use in pregnancy: Category C (see Appendix).

What the available evidence suggests about breast-feeding safety: Likely safe.

The bottom line for you:
- Ganciclovir may be used during pregnancy when there is symptomatic maternal or fetal disease.
- Considering its use in newborns, ganciclovir is likely safe for use while breast-feeding.

GATIFLOXACIN

Brand name: Tequin

Drug classes: Antibiotic; Quinolone

Indications (what it is used for): Bacterial infection, uncomplicated gonorrhea.

How it works: Kills bacteria.

Contraindications (reasons you shouldn't take it): Hypersensitivity to drug or class, abnormal heart rhythm.

Possible side effects and warnings: Can cause infection of the colon, superinfection, vaginitis, seizures, tendonitis, psychosis, nausea, vomiting, diarrhea, abdominal pain, headache, heartburn, dizziness, light-headedness, inability to sleep, rash, anxiety, confusion, liver damage, agitation, and light sensitivity. Should be used with caution in women with cardiovascular disease or proarrhythmic condition, or who are taking class IA or III antiarrhythmic agents.

How it can affect pregnant women: There is no published data with gatifloxacin during pregnancy.

How it can affect a developing embryo or fetus: There are no adequate reports or well-controlled studies in human fetuses. It is unknown whether gatifloxacin crosses the human placenta. Rodent studies using multiples of the maximum recommended human dose revealed an increased risk of skeletal abnormalities and death in newborns. However, animal studies are not necessarily good indicators of how a drug will behave in humans.

Breast-feeding: There is no published data in nursing women. It is unknown whether gatifloxacin enters human breast milk. Gatifloxacin does enter rat milk, and caution is suggested until further study has been done.

Potential drug interactions: Interaction between the following medications and gatifloxacin has the potential to impact the effect of one or more of the drugs. In some instances the interaction can be dangerous or life-threatening and must be avoided: glyburide, digoxin, probenecid, nonsteroidal anti-inflammatory drugs (NSAIDs).

What the FDA says about use in pregnancy: Category C (see Appendix).

What the available evidence suggests about breast-feeding safety: Unknown.

The bottom line for you:

- Gatifloxacin may be used during pregnancy and while breast-feeding when the seriousness of infection requires it. However, there are other agents with more experience and higher safety profiles.

GEMFIBROZIL

Brand names: Lopid, Tripid

Drug class: Antihyperlipidemic

Indications (what it is used for): Reduces high triglycerides, high cholesterol.

How it works: Decreases the production of triglycerides and cholesterol.

Contraindications (reasons you shouldn't take it): Hypersensitivity to drug or class, gallbladder disease, liver dysfunction.

Possible side effects and warnings: Can cause muscle inflammation and/or breakdown, gallstones, cholestatic jaundice, low platelet or red blood cell counts, acute appendicitis, irregular heart rate, liver damage, nausea, vomiting, heartburn, abdominal pain, diarrhea, and fatigue. Should be used with caution in women with kidney dysfunction or who are already taking a statin class of drug.

How it can affect pregnant women: There are no adequate reports or well-controlled studies of gemfibrozil in pregnant women. Hyperlipidemia (high triglycerides and cholesterol) is a chronic illness and stopping therapy during pregnancy is unlikely in most instances to alter the long-term course of the disease. There are case reports documenting uncomplicated use of gemfibrozil during pregnancy.

How it can affect a developing embryo or fetus: Cholesterol and related substances are building blocks for the placenta and fetus, which is why there might be concern about using drugs to block their production during pregnancy. There are no adequate reports or well-controlled studies of gemfibrozil in human fetuses. It crosses the human placenta and achieves therapeutic levels in the fetus. In a single report, the levels of essential fatty acids in the fetal blood were normal. Rodent studies revealed an increase in skeletal abnormalities at a dose greater than twice the maximum recommended clinical dose. However, animal studies are not necessarily good indicators of how a drug will behave in humans.

Breast-feeding: There are no adequate reports or well-controlled studies in nursing women. It is unknown whether gemfibrozil enters human breast milk. Some rodents showed decreased weight during the newborn period and while weaning.

Potential drug interactions: Interaction between the following medications and gemfibrozil has the potential to impact the effect of one or more of the drugs. In some instances the interaction can be dangerous or life-threatening and must be avoided: HMG-CoA reductase inhibitors, anticoagulants, regaplinide, itraconazole.

What the FDA says about use in pregnancy: Category C (see Appendix).

What the available evidence suggests about breast-feeding safety: Unknown.

The bottom line for you:

- In most instances, statin therapy can be withheld during pregnancy without significant risk to the mother.

- It is unknown whether gemfibrozil is safe to use while breast-feeding.

GENTAMICIN

Brand names: Garamycin, Genoptic, Gentacidin, Gentak, G-Myticin, Ocu-Mycin

Drug classes: Aminoglycoside; Antibiotic; Dermatologic; Ophthalmic; Otic

Indications (what it is used for): Bacterial infection, prevention of endocarditis (inflammation of the lining of the heart).

How it works: Kills bacteria by blocking protein synthesis.

Contraindications (reasons you shouldn't take it): Hypersensitivity to drug or class.

Possible side effects and warnings: Can cause kidney, ear, or nerve toxicity; low platelet counts; bone marrow suppression; inflammation of the colon; increased pressure in the brain; nausea; vomiting; rash; itching; weakness; tremors; muscle cramps; loss of appetite; edema (swelling); headache; diarrhea; heartburn; and ringing in the ears. Should be used with caution in women with kidney dysfunction, a cochlear implant, or myasthenia gravis (an autoimmune disease causing muscle weakness), or who are taking drugs that may damage kidney function.

How it can affect pregnant women: Gentamicin is commonly used in pregnant women for the treatment of infections such as those in the kidney. Combined with clindamycin, it is the standard treatment for infection of the uterus during labor or after delivery.

How it can affect a developing embryo or fetus: There are no adequate reports or well-controlled studies in human fetuses. Gentamicin crosses the human placenta, reaching a level in the fetus similar to that of the mother. In rats, gentamicin interfered with kidney growth and function in fetuses when given at multiples of the maximum recommended clinical dose. However, animal studies are not necessarily good indicators of how a drug will behave in humans, and there is little evidence that gentamicin causes damage in human fetuses.

Breast-feeding: Gentamicin enters human breast milk; however, only trace amounts are absorbed by the breast-feeding child.

Potential drug interactions: Drugs that decrease kidney function increase the risk of gentamicin toxicity.

What the FDA says about use in pregnancy: Category C (see Appendix).

What the available evidence suggests about breast-feeding safety: Safe.

The bottom line for you:

- Gentamicin is widely used during pregnancy and while breast-feeding without evidence of excess toxicity to mother, fetus, or newborn.

GLATIRAMER ACETATE

Brand name: Copaxone

Drug class: Immunomodulator

Indications (what it is used for): Relapsing MS (multiple sclerosis).

How it works: Unknown.

Contraindications (reasons you shouldn't take it): Hypersensitivity to drug or class, hypersensitivity to mannitol.

Possible side effects and warnings: Can cause injection site reactions, temporary chest pain, back pain, flulike symptoms, skin redness, infection, weakness, itching, anxiety, nausea, vomiting, inability to sleep, muscle tension, shortness of breath, rash, sweating, and palpitations. Should be used with caution in women who are immunosuppressed.

How it can affect pregnant women: A number of postmarketing studies (studies done by a drug's manufacturer after the drug is on the market) published over the past few years indicate that glatiramer acetate is safe and effective during pregnancy.

How it can affect a developing embryo or fetus: There are no adequate reports or well-controlled studies in human fetuses. It is unknown whether glatiramer crosses the human placenta. Rodent studies are reassuring, revealing no evidence of birth defects or reduced birth weight despite use of doses higher than those used clinically. However, animal studies are not necessarily good indicators of how a drug will behave in humans.

Breast-feeding: There is no published data in nursing women. It is unknown whether glatiramer enters human breast milk.

Potential drug interactions: None currently identified.

What the FDA says about use in pregnancy: Category B (see Appendix).

What the available evidence suggests about breast-feeding safety: Unknown.

The bottom line for you:

- Limited study indicates that glatiramer is relatively safe and effective during pregnancy.
- There is presently no data to determine its safety while breast-feeding. Discuss other options with your pediatrician.

GLIMEPIRIDE

Brand name: Amaryl

Drug classes: Hypoglycemic; Sulfonylurea

Indications (what it is used for): Type II diabetes.

How it works: Stimulates the release of insulin by the pancreas.

Contraindications (reasons you shouldn't take it): Hypersensitivity to drug or class, diabetic ketoacidosis (lack of insulin prevents body using sugar as a fuel).

Possible side effects and warnings: Can cause low blood sugar, bone marrow suppression, dizziness, weakness, nausea, and headache. Should be used with caution in women with hypersensitivity to sulfonamides.

How it can affect pregnant women: There are no adequate reports or well-controlled studies of glimepiride in pregnant women. The published data is limited to case reports.

How it can affect a developing embryo or fetus: There are no adequate reports or well-controlled studies in human fetuses. It is unknown whether glimepiride crosses the human placenta. Evidence

suggests that other second-generation sulfonylureas cross poorly. There is one case report describing a newborn with persistent low blood sugars after long-term in utero exposure. Rodent studies are reassuring, revealing no evidence of birth defects or reduced birth weights despite the use of doses higher than those used clinically. However, animal studies are not necessarily good indicators of how a drug will behave in humans.

Breast-feeding: There are no adequate reports or well-controlled studies in nursing women. It is unknown whether glimepiride enters human breast milk. Its chemical structure suggests that the risk to the newborn will be low.

Potential drug interactions: Interaction between the following medications and glimepiride has the potential to impact the effect of one or more of the drugs. In some instances the interaction can be dangerous or life-threatening and must be avoided: non-steroidal anti-inflammatory drugs (NSAIDs), drugs that are highly protein bound (e.g., salicylates, sulfonamides, chloramphenicol, coumarins, probenecid, monoamine oxidase inhibitors [MAOIs], and beta-blockers), thiazides and other diuretics, corticosteroids, phenothiazines, thyroid products, estrogens, oral contraceptives, phenytoin, nicotinic acid, sympathomimetics, isoniazid, miconazole, oral hypoglycemic agents.

What the FDA says about use in pregnancy: Category C (see Appendix).

What the available evidence suggests about breast-feeding safety: Unknown.

The bottom line for you:

- Glimepiride should be tested further before being used during pregnancy or while breast-feeding. Glyburide is the second-generation sulfonylurea of choice for gestational and type II diabetes.

GLIPIZIDE

Brand names: Glucotrol, Glucotrol XL, Minidab

Drug classes: Hypoglycemic; Sulfonylurea

Indications (what it is used for): Type II diabetes.

How it works: Stimulates insulin release from the pancreas.

Contraindications (reasons you shouldn't take it): Hypersensitivity to drug or class, diabetic keto-acidosis (lack of insulin prevents body using sugar as a fuel), type I diabetes.

Possible side effects and warnings: Can cause low blood sugar, bone marrow suppression, dizziness, weakness, nausea, and headache. Should be used with caution in women with a hypersensitivity to sulfonamides.

How it can affect pregnant women: There is no published data with glipizide during pregnancy.

How it can affect a developing embryo or fetus: There are no adequate reports or well-controlled studies in human fetuses. About 6% of the maternal dose of glipizide crosses the human placenta, significantly more than with glyburide. No birth defects were found in rodents. However, animal studies are not necessarily good indicators of how a drug will behave in humans.

Breast-feeding: Glipizide is not excreted into human breast milk.

Potential drug interactions: Interaction between the following medications and glipizide has the potential to impact the effect of one or more of the drugs. In some instances the interaction can be dangerous or life-threatening and must be avoided: nonsteroidal anti-inflammatory drugs (NSAIDs), drugs that are highly protein bound (e.g., salicylates, sulfonamides, chloramphenicol, coumarins, probenecid, monoamine oxidase inhibitors [MAOIs], and beta-blockers), thiazides and other diuretics, corticosteroids, phenothiazines, thyroid products, estrogens, oral contraceptives, phenytoin, nicotinic acid, sympathomimetics, isoniazid, miconazole, fluconazole, oral hypoglycemic agents.

What the FDA says about use in pregnancy: Category C (see Appendix).

What the available evidence suggests about breast-feeding safety: Safe.

The bottom line for you:

- Glipizide should not be used during pregnancy because of its greater degree of placental transport. Glyburide is the second-generation sulfonylurea of choice for gestational and type II diabetes.

- Based on the limited data available, the exposure of infants to glipizide through breast milk is expected to be minimal.

- Women with type II diabetes treated with sulfonylureas should not be discouraged from breast-feeding. The benefits of breast-feeding greatly outweigh the risks, if any, of these medications. The baby should, however, be monitored for signs of hypoglycemia (low blood sugar).

GLUCAGON

Brand name: GlucaGen

Drug classes: Antihypoglycemic; Hormone

Indications (what it is used for): Severe low blood sugar.

How it works: Converts liver glycogen to glucose.

Contraindications (reasons you shouldn't take it): Hypersensitivity to drug or class.

Possible side effects and warnings: Can cause high blood sugar, low blood pressure, nausea, vomiting, hives, and respiratory difficulty. Should be used with caution in women taking insulin or who have epinephrine-producing tumors.

How it can affect pregnant women: There are no adequate reports or well-controlled studies in pregnant women. There is, however, a long, reassuring clinical experience of glucagon use during pregnancy, typically in diabetic women with insulin-induced severe low blood sugar.

How it can affect a developing embryo or fetus: There are no adequate reports or well-controlled studies in human fetuses. Glucagon does not appear to cross the human placenta. Rodent studies are reassuring, revealing no evidence of birth defects or low birth weight despite the use of doses higher than those used clinically. However, animal studies are not necessarily good indicators of how a drug will behave in humans.

Breast-feeding: There is no published data with glucagon in nursing women. It is unknown whether it is excreted in human breast milk. However, glucagon is destroyed in the gut and therefore cannot reach a breast-feeding baby's bloodstream.

Potential drug interactions: None currently identified.

What the FDA says about use in pregnancy: Category B (see Appendix).

What the available evidence suggests about breast-feeding safety: Safe.

The bottom line for you:

- Glucagon is safe for use during pregnancy and while breast-feeding to treat severe low blood sugar.

GLYBURIDE

Brand names: DiaBeta, Micronase

Drug classes: Hypoglycemic; Sulfonylurea

Indications (what it is used for): Type II diabetes.

How it works: Stimulates insulin release from the pancreas.

Contraindications (reasons you shouldn't take it): Hypersensitivity to drug or class, diabetic ketoacidosis (lack of insulin prevents body using sugar as a fuel), type I diabetes, kidney insufficiency.

Possible side effects and warnings: Can cause low blood sugar, bone marrow suppression or red blood cell breakdown, hepatitis, nausea, pain in the upper abdomen, dizziness, blurred vision, heartburn, rash, light sensitivity, low sodium level, and headache. Should be used with caution in women with liver or kidney dysfunction, hypersensitivity to sulfonamides, thyroid disease, or adrenal insufficiency.

How it can affect pregnant women: Glyburide is a safe and effective alternative to insulin during pregnancy in women with either gestational or type II diabetes. The degree of control achieved can be as good as or better than insulin, with less impact on lifestyle.

How it can affect a developing embryo or fetus: Less than 2% of the maternal glyburide dose crosses over to the fetus. Low blood sugars in a newborn after birth are less common than after insulin treatment. There is no evidence that glyburide is a cause of birth defects. Rodent studies are reassuring, revealing no evidence of birth defects or low birth weight. However, animal studies are not necessarily good indicators of how a drug will behave in humans.

Breast-feeding: Glyburide is not excreted into human breast milk.

Potential drug interactions: Interaction between the following medications and glyburide has the potential to impact the effect of one or more of the drugs. In some instances the interaction can be dangerous or life-threatening and must be avoided: nonsteroidal anti-inflammatory drugs (NSAIDs), other drugs that are highly protein bound (e.g., salicylates, sulfonamides, chloramphenicol, probenecid, coumarins, monoamine oxidase inhibitors [MAOIs], and beta-adrenergic blocking agents), thiazides and other diuretics, corticosteroids, phenothiazines, thyroid products, estrogens, oral contraceptives, phenytoin, nicotinic acid, sympathomimetics, calcium channel blockers, isoniazid, oral miconazole, oral hypoglycemic agents.

What the FDA says about use in pregnancy: Category C (see Appendix).

What the available evidence suggests about breast-feeding safety: Safe.

The bottom line for you:

- Glyburide is a safe and effective alternative to insulin during pregnancy for women with gestational or Type II diabetes.
- The exposure of infants to second-generation sulfonylureas like glyburide through breast milk is minimal.
- Women with type II diabetes treated with sulfonylureas should not be discouraged from breast-

feeding. The benefits of breast-feeding greatly outweigh the risks, if any, of these medications. The baby should, however, be monitored for signs of hypoglycemia (low blood sugar).

GLYCERIN
Brand name: None
Drug class: Laxative
Indications (what it is used for): Constipation.
How it works: Irritates the bowel, increasing both motility and water content.
Contraindications (reasons you shouldn't take it): Hypersensitivity to drug or class, no urine production, low blood volume, pulmonary edema (fluid in the lungs).
Possible side effects and warnings: Can cause diarrhea, headache, nausea, and rectal irritation. Should be used with caution in women with abdominal pain or liver or kidney dysfunction.
How it can affect pregnant women: There are no adequate reports or well-controlled studies of glycerin in pregnant women. Maternal risks are related to chronic abuse of the product, which leads to worse bowel motility when withdrawn.
How it can affect a developing embryo or fetus: There are no adequate reports or well-controlled studies in human fetuses. However, the fetus is unlikely to be exposed significantly since maternal absorption of glycerin out of the gut is low.
Breast-feeding: There is no published data in nursing women. However, maternal systemic absorption of glycerin is low, suggesting that the risk to a breast-feeding newborn is minimal.
Potential drug interactions: None currently identified.
What the FDA says about use in pregnancy: Category C (see Appendix).
What the available evidence suggests about breast-feeding safety: Safe.
The bottom line for you:
- Glycerin is a traditional and safe remedy for

constipation during pregnancy and while breast-feeding when taken occasionally.

GLYCOPYRROLATE
Brand name: Robinul
Drug classes: Anesthetic, adjunct; Anticholinergic; Gastrointestinal
Indications (what it is used for): Peptic ulcer disease, assisting general anesthesia, reversal of paralysis.
How it works: Blocks the acetylcholine receptors on nerves.
Contraindications (reasons you shouldn't take it): Hypersensitivity to drug or class, glaucoma, bowel obstruction, paralyzed bowel, myasthenia gravis (a neuromuscular disorder involving muscle weakness), ulcerative colitis, unstable cardiovascular system.
Possible side effects and warnings: Can cause low blood pressure when standing, constipation, dry mouth, pupil dilation, blurred vision, inability to urinate, nausea, sleeplessness, weakness, palpitations, dizziness, headache, confusion, and abdominal pain. Should be used with caution in women with liver dysfunction.
How it can affect pregnant women: Glycopyrrolate reduces nausea in pregnant women after spinal anesthesia. It also reduces the risk of low blood pressure after epidural anesthesia.
How it can affect a developing embryo or fetus: There are no adequate reports or well-controlled studies in human fetuses. It is unknown whether glycopyrrolate crosses the human placenta. Rodent studies are reassuring, revealing no evidence of birth defects or low birth weight despite the use of doses higher than those used clinically. However, animal studies are not necessarily good indicators of how a drug will behave in humans.
Breast-feeding: There is no published data in nursing women. It is unknown whether glycopyrrolate enters human breast milk. Considering that its use

is mostly limited to the time of general anesthesia, it is unlikely to pose a risk to a breast-feeding newborn.

Potential drug interactions: Interaction between the following medications and glycopyrrolate has the potential to impact the effect of one or more of the drugs. In some instances the interaction can be dangerous or life-threatening and must be avoided: injection with other anticholinergics or medications with anticholinergic activity, such as phenothiazines, antiparkinson drugs, or tricyclic antidepressants. There are no known drug interactions with the tablet form.

What the FDA says about use in pregnancy: Category B (see Appendix).

What the available evidence suggests about breast-feeding safety: Unknown, but probably safe.

The bottom line for you:

- Glycopyrrolate is commonly used during pregnancy and while breast-feeding as an adjunct to anesthesia without apparent adverse effect.

GRANISETRON HYDRO-CHLORIDE

Brand name: Kytril

Drug classes: Antiemetic; antivertigo agent; serotonin receptor antagonist

Indications (what it is used for): Severe nausea and vomiting associated with chemotherapy, radiation, or spinal anesthesia.

How it works: Selectively blocks the 5-HT3 receptors, which are centrally involved in causing nausea.

Contraindications (reasons you shouldn't take it): Hypersensitivity to drug or class.

Possible side effects and warnings: Can cause bone marrow suppression, headache, weakness, sleepiness, diarrhea, constipation, fever, rash, high blood pressure, taste changes, hair loss, and liver damage.

How it can affect pregnant women: Nausea and vomiting are common after spinal anesthesia.

Granisetron is at least as good as droperidol and metoclopramide for prevention. The addition of dexamethasone further enhances its efficacy. There are also several reports of its successful use in pregnant women receiving chemotherapy for a malignancy.

How it can affect a developing embryo or fetus: There are no adequate reports or well-controlled studies in human fetuses. It is unknown whether granisetron crosses the placenta. Rodent studies are reassuring, revealing no evidence of birth defects or low birth weight despite the use of doses higher than those used clinically. However, animal studies are not necessarily good indicators of how a drug will behave in humans.

Breast-feeding: There is no published data in nursing women. It is unknown whether granisetron enters human breast milk.

Potential drug interactions: Interaction between the following medications and granisetron has the potential to impact the effect of one or more of the drugs. In some instances the interaction can be dangerous or life-threatening and must be avoided: inducers or inhibitors of hepatic CYP enzymes.

What the FDA says about use in pregnancy: Category B (see Appendix).

What the available evidence suggests about breast-feeding safety: Likely safe.

The bottom line for you:

- Granisetron is safe and effective during pregnancy and likely safe while breast-feeding.

- However, there are cheaper and often as effective agents available for the treatment of severe nausea and vomiting, especially for pregnant women undergoing cancer therapy or receiving a spinal anesthetic.

GRISEOFULVIN

Brand names: Brofulin, Fulvicin U/F, Fulvina, Grifulin, Grifulvin V, Grisactin, Grisactin Ultra, Griseofulvin Ultramicrosize, Gris-Peg, Microfulvin, Microgris, Sporostatin, Taidin/Fulvicin P/G, Ultragris, Ultramicrosize Griseofulvin

Drug class: Antifungal

Indications (what it is used for): Fungal infections including tinea corporis (arms or legs), tinea capitis (scalp), tinea cruris (jock itch), tinea pedis (athlete's foot), tinea unguium (finger- and toenails).

How it works: Increases the skin resistance to fungal invasion.

Contraindications (reasons you shouldn't take it): Hypersensitivity to drug or class, porphyria (a rare group of blood disorders).

Possible side effects and warnings: Can cause liver toxicity, low white blood cell count, nausea, headache, rash, hives, light sensitivity, lupuslike syndrome, thrush (yeast infection of the mouth), tingling, dizziness, fatigue, inability to sleep, protein in the urine, flatulence, and diarrhea. Should be used with caution in women with penicillin allergy or liver dysfunction.

How it can affect pregnant women: There are no adequate reports or well-controlled studies in pregnant women. Plasma levels of estrogens and progestins used in oral contraceptives are decreased by griseofulvin, which means it can decrease contraceptive effectiveness. Griseofulvin interferes with chromosome distribution during cell replication, to the maturation of egg and sperm. As a result, men are cautioned to delay fathering children for 6 months after completing therapy, and women should wait at least 1 month before trying to conceive.

How it can affect a developing embryo or fetus: There are no adequate reports or well-controlled studies in human fetuses. It is unknown whether griseofulvin crosses the human placenta. Epidemiologic studies are limited but reveal no evidence of increased birth defects.

Breast-feeding: There are no adequate reports or well-controlled studies of griseofulvin in nursing women. It is unknown whether it is excreted in human breast milk.

Potential drug interactions: Interaction between the following medications and griseofulvin has the potential to impact the effect of one or more of the drugs. In some instances the interaction can be dangerous or life-threatening and must be avoided: warfarin-type anticoagulant therapy, barbiturates, alcohol. Griseofulvin may reduce the effectiveness of oral contraceptives and increase the incidence of breakthrough bleeding.

What the FDA says about use in pregnancy: Category C (see Appendix).

What the available evidence suggests about breast-feeding safety: Unknown.

The bottom line for you:

- Because there is little information about the safety of griseofulvin and since most indications for the medication can wait until after delivery for treatment, griseofulvin should be avoided during pregnancy and while breast-feeding.

GUAIFENESIN

Brand names: Fenesin, Fenex La, Humibid L.A., Mucinex, Mucobid-L.A., Muco-Fen LA, Organidin Nr, Pneumomist, Prolex, Touro Ex, Tussin

Drug classes: Antitussive; Expectorant

Indications (what it is used for): Cough suppression, expectorant.

How it works: Increases the quantity and decreases the viscosity of respiratory tract secretions.

Contraindications (reasons you shouldn't take it): Hypersensitivity to drug or class.

Possible side effects and warnings: Can cause drowsiness, nausea, vomiting, rash, and headache.

How it can affect pregnant women: Guaifenesin is a common component in many over-the-counter cough remedies. There are no adequate reports or well-controlled studies in pregnant women. The long clinical experience during pregnancy suggests relative safety.

How it can affect a developing embryo or fetus: There are no adequate reports or well-controlled studies in human fetuses. It is unknown whether guaifenesin crosses the human placenta. Limited epidemiologic study provides no evidence that guaifenesin causes birth defects. The long clinical experience during pregnancy suggests relative safety. Rodent pregnancy studies have not been performed.

Breast-feeding: There is no published data with guaifenesin in nursing women. It is unknown whether this drug is excreted in human breast milk. The long clinical experience during breast-feeding suggests relative safety.

Potential drug interactions: None currently identified.

What the FDA says about use in pregnancy: Category C (see Appendix).

What the available evidence suggests about breast-feeding safety: Unknown, probably safe.

The bottom line for you:
- The long clinical experience with guaifenesin suggests that it is safe for occasional use during pregnancy and while breast-feeding.

GUANETHIDINE

Brand names: Antipres, Declindin, Ingadine, Ismelin, Normalin, Sanotensin

Drug classes: Adrenergic antagonist, peripheral; Antihypertensive

Indications (what it is used for): Moderate to severe high blood pressure, including that due to kidney disease.

How it works: Interferes with catecholamine release by nerves.

Contraindications (reasons you shouldn't take it): Hypersensitivity to drug or class, pheochromocytoma (adrenal gland tumor), congestive heart failure not due to hypertension, concurrent use of monoamine oxidase inhibitors (MAOIs).

Possible side effects and warnings: Can cause low blood pressure, chest pain, shortness of breath, diarrhea, nausea, vomiting, dry mouth, depression, tremor, blurred vision, weakness, muscle aches, dermatitis, and weight gain. Should be used with caution in women undergoing surgery, who have fever, need it for chronic treatment, or have kidney

dysfunction, peptic ulcer disease, a recent heart attack, or coronary artery disease.

How it can affect pregnant women: Low blood pressure (which can occur if there is overtreatment with guanethidine) is a major concern during pregnancy since it reduces uterine blood flow. There are other medications with fewer side effects; this medication is used during pregnancy only when the mother's life is at risk.

How it can affect a developing embryo or fetus: There are no adequate reports or well-controlled studies in human fetuses. It is unknown whether guanethidine crosses the human placenta.

Breast-feeding: There are no adequate reports or well-controlled studies in nursing women. Guanethidine does enter human breast milk at very low concentrations, which probably pose no risk to a breast-feeding child.

Potential drug interactions: Interaction between the following medications and guanethidine has the potential to impact the effect of one or more of the drugs. In some instances the interaction can be dangerous or life-threatening and must be avoided: rauwolfia derivatives (e.g., reserpine), thiazides, amphetamines, tricyclic antidepressants (TCAs), phenothiazines, oral contraceptives. Monoamine oxidase inhibitors (MAOIs) should be discontinued at least 1 week before starting on guanethidine.

What the FDA says about use in pregnancy: Category C (see Appendix).

What the available evidence suggests about breast-feeding safety: Likely safe.

The bottom line for you:
- There are alternative agents for which there is a higher safety margin and with which there is more experience during pregnancy and while breast-feeding.

GUANFACINE HYDROCHLORIDE

Brand names: Entulic, Tenex

Drug classes: Adrenergic antagonist, central; Antihypertensive

Indications (what it is used for): Hypertension, migraine headache, heroin withdrawal.

How it works: Blocks alpha-2 adrenergic receptors in the brain.

Contraindications (reasons you shouldn't take it): Hypersensitivity to drug or class.

Possible side effects and warnings: Can cause fatigue, weakness, sleepiness, dizziness, constipation, and headache. Should be used with caution in women with liver dysfunction or coronary artery disease, or who have had a recent heart attack.

How it can affect pregnant women: There are no well-controlled trials of guanfacine during pregnancy. It is not generally recommended for the treatment of preeclamptic hypertension (severe high blood pressure and complications associated with it during pregnancy), in part because it takes a long time to begin working. There are other agents that are typically more effective.

How it can affect a developing embryo or fetus: There are no adequate reports or well-controlled studies of guanfacine in human fetuses. It is not known if guanfacine crosses the human placenta. There are no reports of fetal abnormalities.

Breast-feeding: There is no published data in nursing women. It is unknown whether guanfacine enters human breast milk.

Potential drug interactions: Interaction between the following medications and guanfacine has the potential to impact the effect of one or more of the drugs. In some instances the interaction can be dangerous or life-threatening and must be avoided: microsomal enzyme inducers such as phenobarbital or phenytoin .

What the FDA says about use in pregnancy: Category B (see Appendix).

What the available evidence suggests about breast-feeding safety: Unknown.

The bottom line for you:

- There are alternative agents with which there is more experience during pregnancy and while breast-feeding.

HAEMOPHILUS INFLUENZAE VACCINE

Brand names: ActHIB, HibTITER, OmniHIB, PedvaxHIB, ProHIBIT

Drug class: Vaccine

Indications (what it is used for): Maternal susceptibility to *Haemophilus influenzae* virus.

How it works: Promotes antibody production against part of the virus.

Contraindications (reasons you shouldn't take it): Hypersensitivity to drug or class, hypersensitivity to diphtheria vaccine or thimerosal, acute febrile illness (sudden onset of fever).

Possible side effects and warnings: Can cause redness, allergic reaction, and fever. Use with caution in immunosuppressed women.

How it can affect pregnant women: There are no adequate reports or well-controlled studies in pregnant women.

How it can affect a developing embryo or fetus: There are no adequate reports or well-controlled studies of *H. influenzae* conjugate vaccine in human fetuses. Although animal studies have not been conducted, there is no evidence that the vaccine components either cross the placenta or pose a risk to the human fetus. However, the maternal antibodies produced in response to the vaccine do cross the placenta and provide some immunity to the fetus and newborn. Maternal immunization does not interfere with subsequent newborn immunization, and the child should still have the recommended number of vaccinations.

Breast-feeding: There is no published data with *H. influenzae* conjugate vaccine in nursing women. It is likely that *H. influenzae* antibodies enter human breast milk. It is unknown whether they convey any protection to the nursing newborn.

Potential drug interactions: None currently identified.

What the FDA says about use in pregnancy: Category C (see Appendix).

What the available evidence suggests about breast-feeding safety: Unknown, but likely safe.

The bottom line for you:
- The vaccine is safe and effective when given in the third trimester and reduces *H. influenzae* infections in newborns.
- It is likely safe when given to breast-feeding women.

HALCINONIDE TOPICAL

Brand names: Dermalog, Halog, Halog-E

Drug classes: Corticosteroid, topical; Dermatologic

Indications (what it is used for): Steroid-responsive dermatitis (skin inflammation).

How it works: Unknown.

Contraindications (reasons you shouldn't take it): Hypersensitivity to drug or class.

Possible side effects and warnings: Can cause adrenal suppression, burning, itching, contact dermatitis, inflammation of hair follicles, dry skin, acne, infection, and skin atrophy.

How it can affect pregnant women: There is no published data with halcinonide during pregnancy. Halcinonide reduces scar formation and may be used by women after cesarean section.

How it can affect a developing embryo or fetus: Although there are no adequate reports or well-controlled studies in human fetuses, the quantity of halcinonide absorbed systemically is unlikely to pose a risk to the fetus even if it does cross the placenta.

Breast-feeding: There is no published data in nursing women. It is unknown whether halcinonide enters human breast milk. The amount absorbed by the mother suggests that the level in breast milk will not be significant for a breast-feeding baby.

Potential drug interactions: No clinically relevant interactions currently identified.

What the FDA says about use in pregnancy: Category C (see Appendix).

What the available evidence suggests about breast-feeding safety: Likely safe.

The bottom line for you:
- Halcinonide may be used with relative safety for the treatment of dermatitis during pregnancy and while breast-feeding.

HALOPERIDOL

Brand names: Einalon, Haldol, Haloperidol Lactate, Pacedol, Pericate, Seranase

Drug class: Antipsychotic

Indications (what it is used for): Psychosis, Tourette's syndrome (involuntary movements and vocalizations).

How it works: Unknown.

Contraindications (reasons you shouldn't take it): Hypersensitivity to drug or class, central nervous system depression, coma, Parkinson's disease (disorder of the brain that affects movement and coordination).

Possible side effects and warnings: Can cause irregular heart rate, seizures, neuroleptic malignant syndrome (life-threatening muscle rigidity, fever, vital sign instability, and cognitive changes such as delirium), involuntary repetitive body movements, involuntary contraction and spasm of muscles, pneumonia, fever, jaundice, insomnia, drowsiness, anxiety, menstrual irregularities, and a milky discharge from the nipples not related to childbirth or pregnancy. Should be used with caution in women with liver dysfunction, seizure disorder, severe hyperthyroidism, or cardiovascular disease.

How it can affect pregnant women: There are no adequate reports or well-controlled studies of haloperidol in pregnant women. There is, however, a long clinical experience during pregnancy suggesting a wide margin of safety. It has been used with success in the first trimester to treat severe nausea and vomiting. Haloperidol has also been used to treat chorea gravidarum (involuntary abnormal movements that occur during pregnancy). It is as effective for the treatment of schizophrenia as olanzapine but costs significantly less.

How it can affect a developing embryo or fetus: There are no adequate reports or well-controlled studies in human fetuses. More than half the maternal dose of haloperidol crosses the human placenta, but there is no evidence that it increases the risks of birth defects. There may be an increased rate of pre-term birth (before 37 weeks).

Breast-feeding: There are no adequate reports or well-controlled studies in nursing women. Haloperidol enters human breast milk, and in breast-feeding infants it can achieve therapeutic levels. As the impact of haloperidol on a newborn is unclear and limited study suggests an impact on neurodevelopment, breast-feeding is best avoided.

Potential drug interactions: Patients receiving both lithium and haloperidol should be closely monitored for a potential life-threatening reaction.

What the FDA says about use in pregnancy: Category C (see Appendix).

What the available evidence suggests about breast-feeding safety: Possibly unsafe.

The bottom line for you:
- Haloperidol is a drug of choice for the treatment of acute or chronic psychosis during pregnancy based on clinical experience and in comparison to its alternatives.
- It is probably best to avoid haloperidol if breast-feeding or avoid breast-feeding if haloperidol is the only therapeutic choice.

HALOTHANE

Brand names: Anestane, Fluothane
Drug class: Anesthetic, general
Indications (what it is used for): General anesthesia.
How it works: Unknown; disrupts the neuronal lipid membrane.
Contraindications (reasons you shouldn't take it): Hypersensitivity to drug or class, history of malignant hyperthermia (a rare life-threatening rise in body temperature, usually triggered by exposure to some general anesthetics), halothane-induced jaundice, or hepatitis.

Possible side effects and warnings: Can cause malignant hyperthermia, irregular or rapid heart rate, cardiac arrest, blue or purple coloration of the skin or mucous membranes due to low oxygen, hypoxia (inadequate oxygen supply), muscle rigidity, low blood pressure, liver or kidney toxicity, seizures, muscle breakdown, and carbon monoxide toxicity. Should be used with caution in women who have a head injury, liver dysfunction, irregular heart rate, increased intracranial pressure, pheochromocytoma (adrenal gland tumor), or myasthenia gravis (an autoimmune disease causing muscle weakness).

How it can affect pregnant women: Halothane is an inhaled anesthetic agent for which there is a long clinical experience during pregnancy. The main advantage of halothane and related compounds is that they relax the uterus, which is helpful in some emergencies. They should not be used for routine vaginal or cesarean delivery.

How it can affect a developing embryo or fetus: Halothane rapidly crosses the human placenta, reaching a level in the fetus similar to that of the mother within minutes.

Breast-feeding: There is no published data in nursing women. It is unknown whether halothane enters human breast milk. Considering the indication, one-time halothane use is unlikely to pose a clinically significant risk to a breast-feeding baby.

Potential drug interactions: May react with numerous other drugs given with it. Be sure your anesthesiologist has a list of all your medications.

What the FDA says about use in pregnancy: Category C (see Appendix).

What the available evidence suggests about breast-feeding safety: Safe.

The bottom line for you:
- Halothane has a long history of use during pregnancy but has been generally replaced by newer agents that have less toxicity.
- Halothane exposure at delivery is not a contraindication for breast-feeding.

HEPARIN

Brand names: Heparin Flush, Heparin Lok-Pak, Heparin Porcine, Hepflush, Liquaemin Sodium, Sodium Heparin

Drug class: Anticoagulant

Indications (what it is used for): Treatment and prevention of blood clots, treatment of thrombophilias (blood disorders that promote blood clotting), antiphospholipid syndrome (the immune system mistakenly produces antibodies against normal blood proteins).

How it works: Blocks clot formation.

Contraindications (reasons you shouldn't take it): Hypersensitivity to drug or class, active bleeding, blood vessel damage, spinal or epidural anesthesia.

Possible side effects and warnings: Can cause bleeding, bruising, low platelet count, thin bones, irritation at injection site, ulceration, fever, chills, itching, hives, and runny nose. It should be used with caution in women who have recently received spinal or epidural anesthesia or have severe high blood pressure, peptic ulcer disease, history of bowel bleeding, or kidney dysfunction.

How it can affect pregnant women: Heparin is a natural product that consists of many different variations of a protein. It is an anticoagulant of choice during pregnancy. Despite the long history of clinical use during pregnancy, there are no adequate reports or well-controlled studies in pregnant women.

How it can affect a developing embryo or fetus: There are no adequate reports or well-controlled studies in human fetuses. Heparin does not cross the placenta and is not associated with an adverse fetal outcome.

Breast-feeding: Heparin is not excreted into breast milk because of the large size of the heparin molecule.

Potential drug interactions: The effect of heparin can be increased or decreased by other drugs occasionally used with it. These include warfarin and dicumarol, aspirin, dextran, dipyridamole, hydroxychloroquine, ibuprofen, indomethacin, and phenylbutazone. Be sure your pharmacist and physician know all other drugs you are using.

What the FDA says about use in pregnancy: Category C (see Appendix).

What the available evidence suggests about breast-feeding safety: Safe.

The bottom line for you:

- Heparin is an anticoagulant of choice during pregnancy. There are pragmatic reasons a doctor will choose one type of heparin versus another, often related to availability or the reason the medication is needed.
- Heparin is safe for use while breast-feeding.

HEPATITIS A VACCINE

Brand names: Havrix, Vaqta

Drug class: Vaccine

Indications (what it is used for): Maternal susceptibility to hepatitis A.

How it works: Forms antibodies to inactivated virus.

Contraindications (reasons you shouldn't take it): Hypersensitivity to drug or class, febrile illness (illness with a fever).

Possible side effects and warnings: Can cause life-threatening allergic reaction, local reaction, fever, rash, sore throat, abdominal pain, joint pain, muscle pain, enlarged lymph nodes, light sensitivity, and dizziness. Should be used with caution in women who are immunosuppressed.

How it can affect pregnant women: The vaccine consists of inactivated virus. There are no reported adverse effects on mother or fetus. Women should be vaccinated during pregnancy if they are traveling to areas where the hepatitis A virus (HAV; so-called infectious hepatitis) is endemic, such as parts of Africa, Central and South America, and Asia; are older than 30 and with chronic liver disease; waiting for or have received liver transplants, or are working with nonhuman primates who may carry the infection. HAV vaccination of chronic HCV (hepatitis C) carrier women substantially reduces their risks of disease and death. Immunoglobulin provides a safe alternative for short-term protection during pregnancy if there is too little time for the vaccine to work.

How it can affect a developing embryo or fetus: There are no adequate reports or well-controlled studies of HAV vaccine in human fetuses. HAV is rarely transmitted to the fetus and is not a known cause of birth defects. The antibodies produced in response to vaccination cross the placenta and may provide some protection to the newborn.

Breast-feeding: There are no adequate reports or well-controlled studies in nursing women. It is unknown whether the vaccine's inactivated virus enters human breast milk. The vaccine is generally considered safe with breast-feeding. It is likely that vaccine-stimulated antibodies do enter breast milk, which may provide the newborn some protection.

Potential drug interactions: Hepatitis A vaccine should be administered with a different syringe and at a different injection site when given with other vaccines or IgG (immunoglobulin G). It should be used with caution in women on anticoagulant therapy.

What the FDA says about use in pregnancy: Category C (see Appendix).

What the available evidence suggests about breast-feeding safety: Likely safe.

The bottom line for you:

- Hepatitis A vaccine may be used during pregnancy and while breast-feeding.

HEPATITIS B IMMUNE GLOBULIN

Brand names: BatHEP B, H-big, Hyperhep, Nabi-HB

Drug class: Antisera

Indications (what it is used for): Used in susceptible women to prevent infection with hepatitis B after exposure to the virus.

How it works: Passive immunization.

Contraindications (reasons you shouldn't take it): Hypersensitivity to drug or class.

Possible side effects and warnings: Can cause swelling and redness at the injection site, headache, a feeling of general uneasiness or being "out of sorts," nausea, diarrhea, muscle aches, and life-threatening allergic reaction. Should be used with caution in women with a history of allergy to other vaccines, or with low platelet count or another bleeding disorder.

How it can affect pregnant women: Women (pregnant or not) benefit if exposed to infected household contacts, an infected sexual partner, or blood from infected individuals. Immune globulin should be given with hepatitis B vaccine to trigger permanent immunity.

How it can affect a developing embryo or fetus: There are no adequate reports or well-controlled studies of hepatitis B immune globulin in human fetuses. There is no reason to expect the immunoglobulin to be harmful. Further, its administration to susceptible women appears to reduce the incidence of HBV in newborns, although there is controversy on whether giving the immunoglobulin to infected women in the third trimester reduces transmission to their newborns. Nevertheless, babies of women who have hepatitis B should be vaccinated before leaving the hospital, and again at 1–4 months and 12–18 months.

Breast-feeding: Vaccinated women have higher immunoglobulin levels in their breast milk, which may provide their newborns some protection.

Potential drug interactions: It is unknown whether administration of hepatitis B immune globulin can interfere with the immune response to live virus vaccines. Therefore, vaccination with live virus vaccines should be deferred until approximately 3 months after administration of hepatitis B immune globulin (human). It may be necessary to revaccinate women who received immunoglobulin shortly after live virus vaccination.

What the FDA says about use in pregnancy: Category C (see Appendix).

What the available evidence suggests about breast-feeding safety: Safe.

The bottom line for you:
- Hepatitis B immune globulin is effective and of minimal risk to a fetus or newborn. It should be used during pregnancy and while breast-feeding whenever indicated.

HEPATITIS B VACCINE, RECOMBINANT

Brand names: Engerix-B, Recombivax HB
Drug class: Vaccine
Indications (what it is used for): To provide immunity to hepatitis B.
How it works: Creates an active immune response.
Contraindications (reasons you shouldn't take it): Hypersensitivity to drug or class.
Possible side effects and warnings: Can cause a general feeling of uneasiness or being "out of sorts," headache, fever, nausea, vomiting, abdominal pain, runny nose, joint pain, muscle pain, Guillain-Barré syndrome (the body's immune system attacks the nerves), Bell's palsy (facial paralysis), insomnia, arthritis, Stevens-Johnson syndrome (a rare but serious skin reaction to medication), and injection site reactions such as redness, itching, swelling, and nodule formation. It should be used with caution in women with multiple sclerosis.
How it can affect pregnant women: Hepatitis B vaccine appears safe and effective during pregnancy, and immunization may help protect the fetus. Postpartum vaccination is also effective. The number of at-risk patients is large, and many practitioners recommend routine vaccination. However, vaccination can usually be delayed until after delivery for most indications unless the risk of infection is especially great (e.g., travel to areas where the virus is endemic).
How it can affect a developing embryo or fetus: There are no adequate reports or well-controlled studies of hepatitis B vaccine in human fetuses. The antibodies transferred across the placenta provide temporary immunity in more than half of the newborns of women vaccinated during pregnancy. Neonatal vaccination is 95% effective. There does not appear to be any substantive difference among recombinant vaccines.
Breast-feeding: There are no adequate reports or well-controlled studies in nursing women. It is unknown whether hepatitis B vaccine enters human breast milk, but breast-fed newborns of vaccinated women have higher hepatitis B antibody levels.
Potential drug interactions: No clinically relevant interactions currently identified.
What the FDA says about use in pregnancy: Category C (see Appendix).
What the available evidence suggests about breast-feeding safety: Safe.
The bottom line for you:
- Hepatitis B vaccine is noninfectious, and is safe and effective during pregnancy and while breast-feeding.

HEXACHLOROPHENE

Brand name: pHisoHex
Drug classes: Antiseptic; Dermatologic
Indications (what it is used for): Skin or wound cleansing.
How it works: Chemical inactivation of bacteria.
Contraindications (reasons you shouldn't take it): Hypersensitivity to drug or class.
Possible side effects and warnings: None listed.
How it can affect pregnant women: Hexachlorophene is contained in some vaginal lubricants including those sold over the counter and was in the past used to cleanse skin before surgery. It is not recommended during pregnancy because it is effective against only a narrow range of bacteria. In addition, it is absorbed across the skin and high levels can be neurotoxic.
How it can affect a developing embryo or fetus: There are no adequate reports or well-controlled studies in human fetuses. Hexachlorophene crosses the human placenta and in rodents accumulated in the spinal cord and brain. Hexachlorophene contained in vaginal lubricants is variably absorbed across the mucosa, achieving detectable levels in

blood of both the mother and fetus. Because of the risk of hexachlorophene toxicity in the newborn, hexachlorophene-free lubricants should be used during labor for pelvic examinations.

Breast-feeding: There is no published data in nursing women. It is unknown whether hexachlorophene enters human breast milk. The long clinical experience suggests that it is likely safe.

Potential drug interactions: No clinically relevant interactions currently identified.

What the FDA says about use in pregnancy: Category C (see Appendix).

What the available evidence suggests about breast-feeding safety: Unknown; likely safe.

The bottom line for you:

- Hexachlorophene should be avoided during pregnancy. There are better alternatives (e.g., chlorhexidine, ovidoneiodine).
- Occasional hexachlorophene exposure is likely safe while breast-feeding.

HYDRALAZINE

Brand names: Apresoline, Apresrex, Dralzine, Hyperex, Ipolina, Naselin, Nepresol, Solezorin, Sulesorin, Supres, Zinepress

Drug classes: Antihypertensive; Vasodilator

Indications (what it is used for): Moderate to severe high blood pressure, congestive heart failure.

How it works: Unknown.

Contraindications (reasons you shouldn't take it): Hypersensitivity to drug or class, coronary artery disease, mitral valve disease (heart valve between left atrium and ventricle does not work properly).

Possible side effects and warnings: Can cause low white blood cell counts, lupuslike syndrome, palpitations, rapid heart rate, headache, angina, flushing, nausea, vomiting, diarrhea, and peripheral edema (swelling in the limbs). Should be used with caution in women with kidney dysfunction or cardiovascular disease.

How it can affect pregnant women: Hydralazine is one of the most widely used drugs for the treatment of sudden and severe high blood pressure during pregnancy such as that seen in women with severe preeclampsia (high blood pressure and protein in the urine during pregnancy and complications associated with it). Comparative study suggests that other commonly used agents, such as nifedipine and labetolol, are equally effective for blood pressure control and have less risk of lowering blood pressure too much.

How it can affect a developing embryo or fetus: Hydralazine crosses the human placenta and reaches levels in the fetus similar to or higher than those of the mother. The impact of the drug on the human fetus is unknown. Limited use during the first trimester reveals no evidence of birth defects.

Breast-feeding: There are no adequate reports or well-controlled studies in nursing women. Hydralazine enters human breast milk, but the amount ingested by the breast-feeding newborn is clinically insignificant.

Potential drug interactions: Interaction between the following medications and hydralazine has the potential to impact the effect of one or more of the drugs. In some instances the interaction can be dangerous or life-threatening and must be avoided: monoamine oxidase inhibitors (MAOIs). Dangerously low blood pressure levels may occur when diazoxide and hydralazine are injected at the same time.

What the FDA says about use in pregnancy: Category C (see Appendix).

What the available evidence suggests about breast-feeding safety: Safe.

The bottom line for you:

- Hydralazine remains a drug of choice for the treatment of acute high blood pressure during pregnancy, although alternative agents may have less risk of causing dangerously low blood pressure. As a result, hydralazine is often used after the first drug selected has failed to produce the desired response. The selection of an antihypertensive should be based on the doctor's experience and familiarity with a particular drug and on what is known about adverse effects. Other medications are preferable for the treatment of chronic high blood pressure during pregnancy.

- Hydralazine is generally considered safe for use while breast-feeding.

HYDROCHLOROTHIAZIDE

Brand names: Aquazide H, Esidrix, Hydrodiuril, Hydro Par, Microzide, Oretic

Drug classes: Antihypertensive; Diuretic; Thiazide

Indications (what it is used for): Hypertension, peripheral edema (swelling in the limbs).

How it works: Prevents the reabsorption of salt by the kidneys from the urine.

Contraindications (reasons you shouldn't take it): Hypersensitivity to drug or class, hypersensitivity to sulfonamides, poor kidney function.

Possible side effects and warnings: Can cause bone marrow failure; low platelet and/or white blood cell counts; kidney failure; high levels of sugar, uric acid, calcium, and/or lipids; headache; dizziness; low blood pressure when standing; nausea; vomiting; abdominal pain; tingling; and pancreatitis. Should be used with caution in women with liver or kidney dysfunction.

How it can affect pregnant women: There are no adequate reports or well-controlled studies in pregnant women. Thiazides and related diuretics are rarely administered today during the first trimester. In the past, these drugs were mistakenly given routinely in the second or third trimester to prevent or treat preeclampsia (high blood pressure and protein in the urine during pregnancy and complications associated with it). They are ineffective, but fortunately adverse fetal effects were rare. Low-dose diuretics are the most effective first-line treatment for chronic high blood pressure and the prevention of cardiovascular disease morbidity and mortality in nonpregnant women, but they are avoided during pregnancy because they interfere with some important pregnancy changes. Thus, thiazides should not

be started during pregnancy but they may be continued if already in use.

How it can affect a developing embryo or fetus: Hydrochlorothiazide crosses the human placenta, achieving levels in the fetus that can equal those of the mother. Although there is no evidence that they cause birth defects based on a long clinical experience, hydrochlorothiazide can cause temporary newborn electrolyte abnormalities, low platelet counts, and high blood sugars when given around the time of delivery. Rodent studies are reassuring, revealing no evidence of birth defects or low birth weight despite the use of doses higher than those used clinically. However, animal studies are not necessarily good indicators of how a drug will behave in humans.

Breast-feeding: There are no adequate reports or well-controlled studies in nursing women. Small quantities of hydrochlorothiazide can be detected in human breast milk but it is generally considered safe.

Potential drug interactions: Interaction between the following medications and hydrochlorothiazide has the potential to impact the effect of one or more of the drugs. In some instances the interaction can be dangerous or life-threatening and must be avoided: other antihypertensive agents; alcohol, barbiturates, and narcotics; antidiabetic drugs (oral agents and insulin); corticosteroids; lithium; nonsteroidal anti-inflammatory drugs (NSAIDs).

What the FDA says about use in pregnancy: Category B (see Appendix).

What the available evidence suggests about breast-feeding safety: Safe.

The bottom line for you:

- Although diuretics are no longer first-line therapy for the treatment of high blood pressure during pregnancy, hydrochlorothiazide remains a drug of choice for the treatment of heart failure unrelated to hypertension, and if initiated prior to pregnancy, may be continued.
- Hydrochlorothiazide is generally considered safe for use while breast-feeding.

HYDROCODONE

Brand names: Histussin-HC, Hycodan, Hycomar, Hydrocodone Compound, Hydrocone/Mycodone, Hydromet, Hydropane, Hydrotropine, Mycodone, Tussigon, Vicodin

Drug classes: Analgesic, narcotic; Antitussive; Narcotic; Sedative

Indications (what it is used for): Cough, acute pain.

How it works: Binds opioid receptors in the central nervous system.

Contraindications (reasons you shouldn't take it): Hypersensitivity to drug or class, glaucoma.

Possible side effects and warnings: Can cause dizziness, respiratory depression, euphoria, sedation, confusion, nausea, vomiting, constipation, dry mouth, urinary retention, itching, slow or fast heart rates, and increased pressure within the eye. It should be used with caution in women with increased intracranial pressure, liver or kidney dysfunction, history of addiction to or dependence on a drug, head injury, or abdominal pain.

How it can affect pregnant women: Hydrocodone is a modified codeine that also includes homatropine in the tablet to discourage abuse. There are no adequate reports or well-controlled studies in pregnant women. The pain relief produced by combination with ibuprofen is superior to that achieved with ibuprofen alone. Similar to codeine, hydrocodone is more effective for the relief of uterine cramping than for episiotomy pain.

How it can affect a developing embryo or fetus: There are no adequate reports or well-controlled studies in human fetuses. Hydrocodone presumably crosses the human placenta. At doses above those typically prescribed, it can cause newborn respiratory depression (slowed or inadequate breathing) at birth. Although not observed in humans, rodent studies revealed low birth weight at doses higher than typical but below those required to cause maternal toxicity. However, animal studies are not necessarily good indicators of how a drug will behave in humans.

Breast-feeding: There are no adequate reports or well-controlled studies in nursing women. It is unknown whether hydrocodone enters human breast milk. However, codeine and its metabolite morphine are excreted in human breast milk. Breast-feeding newborns whose mothers are using hydrocodone have low plasma levels during the first few days of life, in part because it has a low concentration in milk, and in part due to the small amount of milk initially produced by the breast-feeding woman. Thus, moderate hydrocodone use after delivery is probably compatible with breast-feeding.

Potential drug interactions: Interaction between the following medications and hydrocodone has the potential to impact the effect of one or more of the drugs. In some instances the interaction can be dangerous or life-threatening and must be avoided: other narcotic analgesics, general anesthetics, phenothiazines, tranquilizers, sedative-hypnotics, and other central nervous depressants (including alcohol).

What the FDA says about use in pregnancy: Category C (see Appendix).

What the available evidence suggests about breast-feeding safety: Safe.

The bottom line for you:

- Hydrocodone is an effective analgesic suitable during pregnancy and while breast-feeding.
- Like all narcotics, hydrocodone has the potential for abuse and should be used only for the relief of pain or a short-term cough.

HYDROCORTISONE

Brand names: Acticort, Aeroseb-Hc, Ala-Cort, Ala-Scalp, Albacort, Allercort, Alphaderm, Anusol-Hc, Balneol-Hc, Beta-Hc, Cetacort, Coracin, Coreton, Cort-Dome, Cortef, Cortenema, Cortes, Cortril, Cotacort, Dermol Hc, Eldecort, Epicort, Flexicort, Glycort, H-Cort, Hi-Cor, Hidroaltesona, Hidromar, Hidrotisona, Hycort, Hycortole, Hydrocortemel, Hydrocortone, Hydro-Tex, Hymac, Hytone, IVocort, Lacticare, Lemoderm, Lidex, Nogenic Hc, Nutracort, Otozonbase, Penecort, Proctocort,

Procto-Hc, Rederm, S-T Cort, Stie-Cort, Synacort, Tega-Cort, Texacort, Topisone

Drug classes: Corticosteroid, topical; Dermatologic

Indications (what it is used for): Inflammatory disorders, steroid-responsive dermatitis, and itching.

How it works: Unknown.

Contraindications (reasons you shouldn't take it): Hypersensitivity to drug or class, systemic fungal infection.

Possible side effects and warnings: Excess can cause adrenal insufficiency, steroid psychosis (psychotic reactions to steroid use; aka 'roid rage'), immunosuppression, menstrual irregularities, congestive heart failure, peptic ulcer disease, bloating, appetite change, swelling, nausea, vomiting, indigestion, headache, mood swings, insomnia, anxiety, acne, skin atrophy, high blood pressure, low potassium and high glucose levels, and impaired wound healing. It should be used with caution in women with diabetes, high blood pressure, seizure disorder, osteoporosis, liver dysfunction, or tuberculosis.

How it can affect pregnant women: Hydrocortisone is a naturally occurring steroid hormone made in the adrenal gland. When used topically, it is unlikely to lose much risk.

How it can affect a developing embryo or fetus: There are no adequate reports or well-controlled studies in human fetuses. Topical steroids (mild to moderate potency) do not pose a risk to the fetus. Pregnancy outcomes after maternal exposure to intranasal corticosteroids are limited, but pharmacological studies show much less of the medication is absorbed systemically after intranasal administration, suggesting it's safety during pregnancy is at least comparable with that of inhaled corticosteroid.

The best evidence is that systemic corticosteroids (those taken by mouth or by injection) are weak teratogens (substances that cause birth defects) when taken in the first trimester. Although there is no increase in major birth defects, the rates of both cleft lip and cleft palate are increased. There is no increase in risk of anomalies when steroids are begun after organ formation (after 11 weeks). A few small studies suggested a possible relationship between long-term steroid use during pregnancy and poor fetal growth; however, it is hard to tell if that was the result of the medication or the disease it was being used to treat.

Breast-feeding: There is no published data in nursing women. It is unknown whether hydrocortisone enters human breast milk. Glucocorticoids are a normal component of breast milk, although it is not known whether maternal ingestion increases the natural concentration. The long clinical experience is reassuring.

Potential drug interactions: Corticosteroids have a wide range of effects and it is important that your physician and pharmacist know all drugs you are taking. Interaction between the following medications and hydrocortisone has the potential to impact the effect of one or more of the drugs. In some instances the interaction can be dangerous or life-threatening and must be avoided: drugs that induce liver enzymes (e.g., phenobarbital, phenytoin, rifampin), drugs that can inhibit the metabolism of corticosteroids (e.g., troleandomycin, ketoconazole), aspirin, and oral anticoagulants.

What the FDA says about use in pregnancy: Category C (see Appendix).

What the available evidence suggests about breast-feeding safety: Likely safe.

The bottom line for you:

- Hydrocortisone may be used during pregnancy and while breast-feeding for the treatment of significant disease in the mother.
- Topical or over-the-counter hydrocortisone likely poses no risk to a fetus or newborn.

HYDROMORPHONE

Brand names: Dilaudid, Dilaudid-HP, Hydromorphone Hcl, Hydrostat

Drug classes: Analgesic; Narcotic

Indications (what it is used for): Moderate to severe pain, cough.

How it works: Binds to and stimulates multiple opiate receptors.

Contraindications (reasons you shouldn't take it): Hypersensitivity to drug or class, increased intracranial pressure, respiratory depression.

Possible side effects and warnings: Can cause respiratory depression, cessation of breathing, central nervous system depression, sedation, drowsiness, dizziness, loss of appetite, nausea, vomiting, constipation, low blood pressure when standing, psychological and physical dependence, and urethral spasm. It should be used with caution in women with liver or kidney dysfunction.

How it can affect pregnant women: Hydromorphone plus a local anesthetic (e.g., bupivacaine) is a popular epidural anesthetic during labor. Similar to morphine, it enhances the sensory blockade, allowing for a lower concentration of local anesthetic to be effective. The result is a decrease in motor block (aka walking epidural). There are no well-controlled studies of women receiving hydromorphone chronically during pregnancy.

How it can affect a developing embryo or fetus: There are no adequate reports or well-controlled studies in human fetuses. When given intravenously, hydromorphone rapidly crosses the placenta, achieving the same level in the fetus as it does in the mother.

Breast-feeding: There are no adequate reports or well-controlled studies in nursing women. Small quantities of hydromorphone enter human breast milk. Considering the dose and pattern of clinical use, hydromorphone is compatible with breast-feeding.

Potential drug interactions: Interaction between the following medications and hydromorphone has the potential to impact the effect of one or more of the drugs. In some instances the interaction can be dangerous or life-threatening and must be avoided: other central nervous system (CNS) depressants (e.g., sedatives or hypnotics, general anesthetics, phenothiazines, tranquilizers, alcohol), opioid agonist-antagonist agents (e.g., buprenorphine, butorphanol, nalbuphine, pentazocine).

What the FDA says about use in pregnancy: Category C (see Appendix).

What the available evidence suggests about breast-feeding safety: Likely safe.

The bottom line for you:
- Hydromorphone is a popular agent for labor epidural analgesia in combination with a local anesthetic. It is given intravenously or intramuscularly for relief of severe pain.
- It is likely safe while breast-feeding.

HYDROQUINONE TOPICAL

Brand names: Aida, Banquin, Eldopaque Forte, Eldoquin Forte, Epocler, Hydroxyquinone, Melanex, Melanol, Melpaque HP, Melquin, Nuquin HP, Solaquin Forte

Drug classes: Depigmenting; Dermatologic

Indications (what it is used for): Melasma (hyperpigmentation: dark skin discoloration) associated with pregnancy, use of oral contraceptives, and hormone replacement therapy. It is used after pregnancy, not during.

How it works: Suppresses the skin cells' ability to make dark pigment.

Contraindications (reasons you shouldn't take it): Hypersensitivity to drug or class, hypersensitivity to sulfites.

Possible side effects and warnings: Can cause contact dermatitis, dry and/or cracking skin, irritation, and burning.

How it can affect pregnant women: There are no adequate reports or well-controlled studies of hydroquinone in pregnant women. Although the actual amount absorbed across the skin into the bloodstream is small, there are no indications that require its use during pregnancy. Postpartum, hydroquinone is often used for the treatment of melasma.

How it can affect a developing embryo or fetus: There are no adequate reports or well-controlled studies in human fetuses. Hydroquinone crosses the human placenta, but the amount of hydroxyquinone absorbed into the mother's blood is small and its use during pregnancy has not been associated with an increase in adverse pregnancy outcomes. It did cause birth defects in chicks and some rodents, and can cause chromosome abnormalities in human cells grown in the laboratory. However, animal studies are not necessarily good indicators of how a drug will behave in humans.

Breast-feeding: There is no published data in nursing women. It is unknown whether hydroquinone enters human breast milk. The low absorption of drug across the mother's skin indicates that it poses no risk, although treatment can be delayed until weaning.

Potential drug interactions: No clinically relevant interactions currently identified.

What the FDA says about use in pregnancy: Category C (see Appendix).

What the available evidence suggests about breast-feeding safety: Likely safe.

The bottom line for you:

- There are no indications that require hydroquinone use during pregnancy or while breast-feeding. However, unintended and brief exposure and use while breast-feeding should be safe.

HYDROXYCHLOROQUINE

Brand name: Plaquenil

Drug classes: Antimalarial; Antiprotozoal; Antirheumatic; Immunomodulator

Indications (what it is used for): Systemic lupus erythematosus (SLE; a chronic inflammatory disease in which the immune system attacks the body's own tissues and organs), treatment and prevention of malaria, rheumatoid arthritis.

How it works: Unknown

Contraindications (reasons you shouldn't take it): Hypersensitivity to drug or class, porphyria (a rare group of blood disorders), visual field changes.

Possible side effects and warnings: Can cause bone marrow depression, low platelet or white blood cell counts, seizures, visual changes, deafness, exfoliative dermatitis, dizziness, nausea, vomiting, diarrhea, headache, loss of muscle coordination, itching, and weight loss.

How it can affect pregnant women: There are no adequate reports or well-controlled studies in pregnant women. Some experts recommend discontinuing hydroxychloroquine in pregnant women with connective tissue diseases, even though it has been long used for malaria prevention during pregnancy. It is reasonable to continue using the drug, considering that it takes up to 2 months for the body to clear it, and lupus flares, which are detrimental to pregnancy outcome, occur after discontinuation.

How it can affect a developing embryo or fetus: There are no adequate reports or well-controlled studies in human fetuses. However, several large clinical series in women with either malaria or SLE are reassuring, having found no increase in birth defects or low birth weight. Although there is no substantive evidence of birth defects in rodents, hydroxychloroquine crosses the placenta and is deposited in the pigmented fetal tissues. However, animal studies are not necessarily good indicators of how a drug will behave in humans.

Breast-feeding: There are no adequate reports or well-controlled studies in nursing women. The concentration of hydroxychloroquine in human breast milk is very low and should not pose a threat to a breast-fed newborn.

Potential drug interactions: No relevant drug interactions currently identified.

What the FDA says about use in pregnancy: Category C (see Appendix).

What the available evidence suggests about breast-feeding safety: Likely safe.

The bottom line for you:
- The additional risk imposed by hydroxychloroquine on pregnancy appears modest, and the drug should not be withheld when necessary.
- Hydroxychloroquine is considered safe for use while breast-feeding.

HYDROXYUREA
Brand names: Droxea, Hydrea
Drug class: Antineoplastic, miscellaneous
Indications (what it is used for): Sickle-cell disease (disorder of hemoglobin, which delivers oxygen throughout the body), essential thrombocythemia (overproduction of platelets by the bone marrow), polycythemia vera (bone marrow makes too many red blood cells), HIV infection, resistant chronic myelogenous leukemia, head and neck tumors, solid tumors.
How it works: Unclear; inhibits DNA synthesis.
Contraindications (reasons you shouldn't take it): Hypersensitivity to drug or class, bone marrow depression.
Possible side effects and warnings: Can cause bone marrow depression, leukemia, pulmonary fibrosis (inflammation and/or scarring of the lungs), dermatomyositis (inflammatory muscle disease), mouth ulcers, anorexia, nausea, vomiting, diarrhea, constipation, skin redness, painful urination, headache, dizziness, hallucinations, seizures, hair loss, and skin inflammation. It should be used with caution in women with kidney dysfunction or who are taking myelosuppressive agents.
How it can affect pregnant women: There are no adequate reports or well-controlled studies of hydroxyurea in pregnant women. Published data is limited to case reports and small series of patients with sickle-cell disease, thrombocythemia, and leukemia, which typically document successful outcomes.
How it can affect a developing embryo or fetus: There are no adequate reports or well-controlled studies in human fetuses. It is unknown whether hydroxyurea crosses the human placenta. Hydroxyurea caused birth defects in a wide variety of animal models. It also caused low birth weight and impaired learning in rats. However, animal studies are not necessarily good indicators of how a drug will behave in humans. The human experience, which consists of case reports and small case series, suggests that the risks to the human fetus are overestimated.
Breast-feeding: There are no adequate reports or well-controlled studies in nursing women. Hydroxyurea does enter human breast milk, although there is only one limited report. Because of its ability to damage DNA, hydroxyurea is best avoided while breast-feeding until there is additional information available.
Potential drug interactions: Use with other myelosuppressive agents or radiation may increase the likelihood of bone marrow depression or other adverse events.
What the FDA says about use in pregnancy: Category D (see Appendix).
What the available evidence suggests about breast-feeding safety: Possibly unsafe.
The bottom line for you:
- Although the risk of hydroxyurea during pregnancy appears overestimated, it should be used only for the treatment of life-threatening maternal illness.
- Until there is more information, it is probably best to avoid breast-feeding while taking hydroxyurea.

HYDROXYZINE
Brand names: Atarax, Atazina, Hyzine, Neucalm 50, Vistacot, Vistaril, Vistazine
Drug classes: Antiemetic; Antihistamine, H1; Antivertigo agent; Anxiolytic; Hypnotic; Sedative
Indications (what it is used for): Anxiety, itching, nausea, vomiting, sedation, insomnia.
How it works: Blocks histamine 1 receptors, whose activation causes the symptoms.

Contraindications (reasons you shouldn't take it): Hypersensitivity to drug or class.

Possible side effects and warnings: Can cause seizures, wheezing, shortness of breath, drowsiness, dry mouth, loss of muscle coordination, headache, agitation, slurred speech, and bitter taste. It should be used with caution in women with asthma.

How it can affect pregnant women: Although there are no adequate reports or well-controlled studies in pregnant women, hydroxyzine remains a first-line treatment of itching and nausea during pregnancy. It is often administered with narcotic agents to reduce the narcotic-associated nausea. Hydroxyzine reduces the itching associated with epidural or spinal morphine and morphine analogs. It is superior to droperidol for relief of nausea associated with general anesthesia.

How it can affect a developing embryo or fetus: There are no adequate reports or well-controlled studies in human fetuses. It is unknown whether hydroxyzine crosses the human placenta, although its use is associated with a sedating effect on the fetal heart rate. Epidemiologic studies of women taking hydroxyzine for allergy symptoms are reassuring, having found no evidence of an increase in birth defects or low birth weight.

Breast-feeding: There is no published data in nursing women. It is unknown whether hydroxyzine enters human breast milk.

Potential drug interactions: Interaction between the following medications and hydroxyzine has the potential to impact the effect of one or more of the drugs. In some instances the interaction can be dangerous or life-threatening and must be avoided: monoamine oxidase inhibitors (MAOIs), pramlintide, dexmedetomidine.

What the FDA says about use in pregnancy: Category C (see Appendix).

What the available evidence suggests about breast-feeding safety: Unknown.

The bottom line for you:
- The long clinical experience suggests that hydroxyzine is safe during pregnancy.
- There has been no objective study of hydroxyzine use while breast-feeding. It is unlikely that its occasional use during labor would pose a risk to a newborn. Otherwise, it is probably best to avoid.

HYOSCYAMINE

Brand names: A-Spas SL, Anaspaz, Cystospaz-M, Donnamar, Ed-Spaz, Gastrosed, Hyco, Hyosol SL, Hyospaz, Levbid, Levsin, Levsinex, Liqui-Sooth, Medispaz, Pasmex, Setamine, Spasdel

Drug classes: Anticholinergic; Antispasmodic; Gastrointestinal

Indications (what it is used for): Bowel or bladder spasm.

How it works: Anticholinergic agent.

Contraindications (reasons you shouldn't take it): Hypersensitivity to drug or class, glaucoma, ulcerative colitis, toxic megacolon (enlarged colon due to infection), unstable cardiovascular disease, autonomic neuropathy (nerve disorder that affects involuntary body functions), myasthenia gravis (an autoimmune disease causing muscle weakness).

Possible side effects and warnings: Can cause paralytic ileus (intestinal obstruction), increased intraocular pressure, heatstroke, confusion, blurred vision, urinary retention, dry mouth, constipation, rapid heart rate, headache, loss of taste, and lack of sweating. Should be used with caution during hot weather and in women with liver or kidney dysfunction, hyperthyroidism, irregular heart rate, coronary artery disease, congestive heart failure, stomach reflux, or pulmonary disease.

How it can affect pregnant women: There is no published data with hyoscyamine during pregnancy.

How it can affect a developing embryo or fetus: There are no adequate reports or well-controlled

studies in human fetuses. Hyoscyamine reportedly crosses the human placenta. Rodent studies into the potential for birth defects have not been conducted.
Breast-feeding: There is no published data in nursing women. The trace amounts of hyoscyamine excreted into human breast milk are too low to be clinically relevant.
Potential drug interactions: Interaction between the following medications and hyoscyamine has the potential to impact the effect of one or more of the drugs. In some instances the interaction can be dangerous or life-threatening and must be avoided: other antimuscarinics, amantadine, haloperidol, phenothiazines, monoamine oxidase inhibitors (MAOIs), tricyclic antidepressants, antihistamines. Antacids may interfere with absorption; take hyoscyamine before meals and antacids after meals.
What the FDA says about use in pregnancy: Category C (see Appendix).
What the available evidence suggests about breast-feeding safety: Likely safe.
The bottom line for you:

- There is too little information on hyoscyamine during pregnancy to conclude either safety or danger to the fetus. An alternative should be sought.
- Hyoscyamine is likely safe for use while breast-feeding.

IBUPROFEN

Brand names: Advil, Alaxan, Artril, Bloom, Brofen, Dolofen, Emflam, Fenspan, Ibren, Ibugen, Ibuprohm, Ibu-Tab, Ifen, Motrin, Nobafon, Paduden, Paxofen, Profen, Prontalgin, Tarein
Drug classes: Analgesic, nonnarcotic; Antipyretic; Nonsteroidal anti-inflammatory (NSAID)
Indications (what it is used for): Mild to moderate pain, fever, painful menstrual period, osteoarthritis, rheumatoid arthritis.
How it works: Reduces the production of prostaglandins, substances that cause pain or cramping.

Contraindications (reasons you shouldn't take it): Hypersensitivity to drug or class, aspirin- or NSAID-induced asthma, third-trimester pregnancy.
Possible side effects and warnings: Can cause kidney failure, fluid retention, heartburn, bowel bleeding, bronchospasm, low platelet or white blood cell counts, interstitial nephritis (inflammation in the kidneys), liver toxicity, Stevens-Johnson syndrome (a rare but serious skin reaction to medication), nausea, constipation, abdominal pain, headache, dizziness, rash, ringing in the ears, and drowsiness. It should be used with caution in women with high blood pressure, congestive heart failure, history of bowel bleeding, or nasal polyps.
How it can affect pregnant women: About 5% of women use ibuprofen around conception or during pregnancy. Two studies have found an increased risk of miscarriage with the use of NSAIDs early in pregnancy, although several other studies did not. The association is stronger if the initial use occurs around conception or if it lasts more than a week. Thus, there are concerns that ibuprofen may interfere with implantation of the fetus. Although a clear risk has not been established, women who are trying to conceive may wish to avoid ibuprofen. Ibuprofen is better than acetaminophen for the relief of pain associated with pregnancy termination, miscarriage, delivery, and episiotomy. The addition of hydrocodone significantly enhances the pain-relieving properties of ibuprofen. There is epidemiologic evidence linking chronic ibuprofen use to postpartum hemorrhage. It is best to avoid ibuprofen in the first trimester and sustained exposure in the third trimester out of concern for its fetal effects.
How it can affect a developing embryo or fetus: There are no adequate reports or well-controlled studies in human fetuses. Ibuprofen crosses the human placenta and fetal levels reflect the mother's level. Chronic use is associated with narrowing or (rarely) closure of the ductus arteriosus, a critical

fetal blood vessel directing blood away from the lungs. Its closure leads to tricuspid valve incompetence, heart failure, and high blood pressure in the lungs, all of which could cause long-term damage. Stopping the drug appears to reverse this process. It is best to avoid repeated dosing of NSAIDs after 32 weeks. A few studies have suggested a possible association with the use of ibuprofen in early pregnancy and a risk for certain birth defects. Two studies, but not all, suggest a small increased risk for gastroschisis (an infant's intestines protrude from a hole in the abdominal wall, which can be repaired surgically) with the use of ibuprofen in the first trimester. These studies suggest that ibuprofen use in the first trimester raises the risk of having a baby with gastroschisis 2 to 4 times. A small increased risk for heart defects has been reported in 3 studies looking at prescriptions in early pregnancy.

Breast-feeding: There are no adequate reports or well-controlled studies in nursing women. Only small amounts of ibuprofen are excreted into human breast milk and it is likely safe for the breast-feeding newborn.

Potential drug interactions: Interaction between the following medications and ibuprofen has the potential to impact the effect of one or more of the drugs. In some instances the interaction can be dangerous or life-threatening and must be avoided: couramin, lithium.

What the FDA says about use in pregnancy: Category C, before 30 weeks gestation, category D, 30 weeks and after (see Appendix).

What the available evidence suggests about breast-feeding safety: Safe.

The bottom line for you:

- Taking ibuprofen near or following conception may increase the risk of spontaneous miscarriage, and first-trimester exposure may increase by a small amount the risk of bowel defects in the fetus. It should be avoided in the first trimester.
- Single-ingredient acetaminophen use during the first trimester does not appear to increase the risk of major birth defects. It may decrease the risk of selected defects when used for an illness involving a fever. As such, acetaminophen is the fever-reducing agent and pain reliever of choice in the first trimester if one must be used.
- Ibuprofen probably poses minimal risk when taken occasionally after the first trimester.
- After 32 weeks, there is a small risk that prolonged use of ibuprofen or related drugs could cause a fetal cardiovascular problem. Acetaminophen is preferred after this time for pain relief.
- Ibuprofen is an excellent pain reliever after delivery, although its efficacy is similar to that of other NSAIDs.
- Ibuprofen is safe for use while breast-feeding.

IDARUBICIN

Brand name: Idamycin

Drug class: Antineoplastic, antibiotic

Indications (what it is used for): Acute myelogenous leukemia.

How it works: Interferes with DNA synthesis.

Contraindications (reasons you shouldn't take it): Hypersensitivity to drug or class, prior mediastinal radiation (radiation to the chest), prior use of daunorubicin or doxorubicin.

Possible side effects and warnings: Can cause congestive heart failure, heart attack, irregular heart rate, seizures, tissue damage near the site of injection, bone marrow suppression, bleeding, inflammation of the colon, abdominal pain, infection, nausea, vomiting, diarrhea, hair loss, inflammation of the digestive tract lining, rash, itching, shortness of breath, confusion, sleepiness, cough, fever, and headache.

How it can affect pregnant women: There are no adequate reports or well-controlled studies in pregnant women. The published data is limited to case reports and short series of patients. Its efficacy is apparently unaffected by pregnancy.

How it can affect a developing embryo or fetus: There are no adequate reports or well-controlled studies in human fetuses. Idarubicin crosses the human placenta, and there are a number of case reports of fetal heart damage when idarubicin is taken with multiple other drugs. Idarubicin caused damage to rodent embryos and birth defects in studies using doses lower than the maximum recommended human dose. However, animal studies are not necessarily good indicators of how a drug will behave in humans.

Breast-feeding: There are no adequate reports or well-controlled studies in nursing women. It is unknown whether idarubicin enters human breast milk. However, considering its ability to cause heart damage, it is best to avoid breast-feeding while idarubicin is administered.

Potential drug interactions: No drug interactions currently identified.

What the FDA says about use in pregnancy: Category D (see Appendix).

What the available evidence suggests about breast-feeding safety: Unknown.

The bottom line for you:
- Idarubicin poses a significant risk to the fetal heart and should be avoided unless maternal survival depends on its use.
- Until there is additional information on its safety, it is best to avoid breast-feeding.

IDOXURIDINE

Brand names: Dendrid, Imavate, Presamine
Drug classes: Antiviral; Ophthalmic
Indications (what it is used for): HSV keratitis (herpes simplex virus inflammation of the cornea).
How it works: Inhibits DNA synthesis.
Contraindications (reasons you shouldn't take it): Hypersensitivity to drug or class.
Possible side effects and warnings: Can cause cloudy cornea, tear duct occlusions, blurred vision, and light sensitivity.
How it can affect pregnant women: There is no published data with idoxuridine during pregnancy. The quantity of drug absorbed into the mother's bloodstream is unknown.
How it can affect a developing embryo or fetus:

There are no adequate reports or well-controlled studies in human fetuses. It is unknown whether idoxuridine crosses the human placenta. Rodent studies revealed evidence of increased malformations and embryo death after both injection into the mother or placement onto the eye. However, animal studies are not necessarily good indicators of how a drug will behave in humans.

Breast-feeding: There is no published data in nursing women. It is unknown whether idoxuridine enters human breast milk. Considering topical use, the maternal blood level is likely low. Until there is additional information, it is best not to breast-feed during treatment.

Potential drug interactions: Interaction between the following medications and idoxuridine has the potential to impact the effect of one or more of the drugs. In some instances the interaction can be dangerous or life-threatening and must be avoided: boric acid.

What the FDA says about use in pregnancy: Category C (see Appendix).

What the available evidence suggests about breast-feeding safety: Unknown.

The bottom line for you:
- Idoxuridine causes birth defects in animals and should be used only to preserve the mother's vision.
- Until there is additional information on its safety, it is best to avoid breast-feeding.

IMIPENEM-CILASTIN

Brand name: Primaxin
Drug classes: Antibiotic; Carbapenem
Indications (what it is used for): Serious bacterial infection.
How it works: Kills sensitive bacteria by weakening the cell wall.
Contraindications (reasons you shouldn't take it): Hypersensitivity to drug or class.
Possible side effects and warnings: Can cause infection of the colon, seizures, low platelet or white

blood cell counts, rash, diarrhea, low urine output, inflammation in the veins, rapid heart rate, yeast infection, urine discoloration, gastroenteritis, liver or kidney damage, nausea, and vomiting. It should be used with caution in women who have cephalosporin allergy, kidney dysfunction, or a seizure disorder.

How it can affect pregnant women: Imipenem-cilastin is a combination that kills a broad range of bacteria. However, imipenem-cilastin is not considered first-line therapy because of its high cost. There are no adequate reports or well-controlled studies in pregnancy. The clearance (how fast the drug moves through your system) of imipenem-cilastin increases during pregnancy, suggesting that the dose should be increased. Although imipenem-cilastin effectively prevents infection in women undergoing non-elective cesarean delivery, it is no better than any other antibiotic used for this purpose.

How it can affect a developing embryo or fetus: There are no adequate reports or well-controlled studies in human fetuses. Imipenem-cilastin crosses the human placenta, achieving a level in the fetus about one-third that of the mother. Rodent studies are reassuring, revealing no evidence of birth defects or low birth weight despite the use of doses higher than those used clinically. However, animal studies are not necessarily good indicators of how a drug will behave in humans.

Breast-feeding: There are no adequate reports or well-controlled studies in nursing women. Small amounts of imipenem-cilastin are excreted into human breast milk, and it is generally considered compatible with breast-feeding.

Potential drug interactions: Generalized seizures have been reported in patients who received ganciclovir and imipenem-cilastin.

What the FDA says about use in pregnancy: Category C (see Appendix).

What the available evidence suggests about breast-feeding safety: Safe.

The bottom line for you:

- Imipenem-cilastin is safe and effective during pregnancy and while breast-feeding, although

there are less expensive medications with which there is more experience.

IMIPRAMINE

Brand names: Imipramine HCl, Imiprin, Janimine, Surplix, Tofnil, Tofranil, Tofranil-Pm

Drug classes: Antidepressant; Tricyclic

Indications (what it is used for): Depression, chronic pain, panic disorder.

How it works: Inhibits neuroepinephrine and serotonin reuptake, both chemicals related to mood.

Contraindications (reasons you shouldn't take it): Hypersensitivity to drug or class, monoamine oxidase inhibitor (MAOI) use within 14 days, recovery from a heart attack.

Possible side effects and warnings: Can cause heart attack, stroke, seizures, blood disorders, low platelet or white blood cell counts, dry mouth, drowsiness, confusion, disorientation, blurred vision, and increased appetite. It should be used with caution in women with a history of seizure, glaucoma, coronary artery disease, thyroid disease, or liver dysfunction, or who are at risk of suicide.

How it can affect pregnant women: Depression is common during and after pregnancy but often goes unrecognized. Depression can be made worse by pregnancy or delivery, and suicide is not an uncommon cause of maternal death. Pregnancy is not a reason to discontinue psychotropic drugs that are needed and effective. A woman being treated for depression who becomes pregnant should not discontinue medication abruptly on her own but rather discuss her treatment and condition with her medical provider. Recent population based studies have revealed the use of tricyclic antidepressants may significantly increase the risk of preeclampsia by 2–3 times. Imipramine has been used extensively for the treatment of depression during pregnancy but is poorly studied. Most health-care providers recommend that pregnant women use newer antidepressants, which have been more thoroughly studied in pregnancy.

How it can affect a developing embryo or fetus: There are no adequate reports or well-controlled studies in human fetuses. Imipramine presumably crosses the human placenta, as it rapidly crosses the rodent placenta and is distributed throughout the fetus. Although rodent studies are generally reassuring, showing no increase in birth defects, behavioral studies suggest that prenatal exposure to imipramine may alter a variety of newborn responses to stress after delivery. However, animal studies are not necessarily good indicators of how a drug will behave in humans.

Breast-feeding: There are no adequate reports or well-controlled studies in nursing women. The amount of imipramine excreted into human breast milk is likely clinically insignificant.

Potential drug interactions: Interaction between the following medications and imipramine has the potential to impact the effect of one or more of the drugs. In some instances the interaction can be dangerous or life-threatening and must be avoided: CYP2D6 inhibitors, including cimetidine and quinidine; other antidepressants; phenothiazines; class 1C antiarrhythmics propafenone and flecainide; all SSRIs (e.g., fluoxetine, paroxetine, sertraline). Seven to 10% of Caucasians are what are called poor metabolizers; they have higher than expected plasma concentrations of TCAs when given usual doses.

What the FDA says about use in pregnancy: Category D (see Appendix).

What the available evidence suggests about breast-feeding safety: Likely safe.

The bottom line for you:

- Imipramine may be used during pregnancy and while breast-feeding for the treatment of significant depression, though some newer drugs may have better safety profiles.
- As for most psychotropic drugs, it is best if the medication is used alone, at the lowest effective dose, and given in divided doses to minimize the exposure risks to the fetus.

IMIQUIMOD

Brand name: Aldara

Drug classes: Antiviral; Dermatologic; Immunomodulator

Indications (what it is used for): Genital warts, premalignant skin lesions.

How it works: Unknown.

Contraindications (reasons you shouldn't take it): Hypersensitivity to drug or class.

Possible side effects and warnings: Can cause burning, hypopigmentation, itching, and pain in treated areas; fatigue; flulike symptoms; headache; and diarrhea.

How it can affect pregnant women: The published data with imiquimod during pregnancy is limited to case reports and small series of patients. It has been used with apparent safety and efficacy for the treatment of genital warts during pregnancy. There are no reports currently of its use for other premalignant skin lesions during pregnancy.

How it can affect a developing embryo or fetus: There are no adequate reports or well-controlled studies in human fetuses. It is unknown whether imiquimod crosses the human placenta if absorbed into the mother's bloodstream; nor are there studies on systemic absorption. The limited human studies and the rodent studies are reassuring, revealing no evidence of an increase in birth defects or low birth weight. However, animal studies are not necessarily a good indicator of how a drug will behave in humans.

Breast-feeding: There is no data in nursing women. However, it is unlikely, considering the dose and that it is administered topically, that any significant concentration of imiquimod enters human breast milk.

Potential drug interactions: No clinically significant interactions currently identified.

What the FDA says about use in pregnancy: Category C (see Appendix).

What the available evidence suggests about breast-feeding safety: Likely safe.

The bottom line for you:

- Imiquimod is likely of minimal risk for the topical treatment of genital warts or other skin disorders during pregnancy.
- There are alternative treatments for some of the skin problems, which do not include drugs.
- Despite the absence of direct study, a breast-feeding newborn's exposure to any imiquimod would be too low to produce any clinical effects.

IMMUNE GLOBULIN

Brand names: Biogam, Carimune, Gamimune N 5%, Gamimune N 10%, Gammagard S/D, Gammar-P I.V., Immune Globulin, Iveegam En, Panglobulin, Polygam S/D, Sandoglobulin, Venoglobulin-S 5%, Venoglobulin-S 10%

Drug class: Immune globulin

Indications (what it is used for): Immune thrombocytopenia (ITP; immune-mediated low platelet count), alloimmune thrombocytopenia (ATP; maternal-fetal platelet incompatibility), primary immune deficiency diseases, B-cell chronic lymphocytic leukemia.

How it works: Unknown.

Contraindications (reasons you shouldn't take it): Hypersensitivity to drug or class, acute or chronic kidney failure.

Possible side effects and warnings: Can cause life-threatening allergic reaction, hives, low blood pressure, headache, fatigue, chills, backache, leg cramps, light-headedness, fever, flushing, nausea, vomiting, blood clots, aseptic meningitis (inflammation of the membranes surrounding the brain, without bacterial infection), kidney dysfunction or failure, and death. Should be used with caution in women who are over 65 or who have selective IgA (immunoglobulin A) deficiency, diabetes, volume depletion (loss of water and salts from cells), sepsis, use of known kidney-damaging drugs, or cerebrovascular disease (narrowing of blood vessels that supply the brain), or who have had a prior blood clot.

How it can affect pregnant women: IV immune globulin (human) is a sterile, highly purified IgG immune globulin extracted from human plasma. The manufacturing process dramatically reduces the risk of transmitting any virus. There are few well-controlled studies in pregnant women. In addition to the indications listed below, immune globulin has been successfully used during pregnancy for dermatomyositis (inflammatory muscle disease), Churg-Strauss vasculitis (inflammation of blood vessels), Guillain-Barré syndrome (the body's immune system attacks the nerves), and acquired hemophilia A. It is also used for ITP, a common hematologic disease in young women. Although ITP is a risk to both mother and newborn, there is no convincing evidence that it poses a risk to the fetus. Maternal immune globulin therapy is the primary treatment for fetal ATP (see "How it can affect a developing embryo or fetus") and has been used on occasion for severe RBC alloimmunization (Rh disease; caused by an immune response of the Rh- mother to her Rh+ fetus). Immune globulin appears ineffective for the treatment of recurrent miscarriage when there is no direct evidence of a significant immune abnormality.

How it can affect a developing embryo or fetus: There are no adequate and well-controlled studies in human fetuses. Animal studies have not been done. IV immune globulin crosses the human placenta, and the treatment of fetuses at risk for ATP is cost-effective and reduces the severity of fetal low platelet counts and the risk of a fetal brain hemorrhage. Children with ATP treated as fetuses have better long-term developmental outcomes than untreated children. With Rh disease, therapy does not necessarily eliminate the need for fetal transfusion, but it does appear to delay the gestational age at which it must be started.

Breast-feeding: There are no adequate reports or well-controlled studies in nursing women. It is unknown whether immune globulin enters human breast milk, although endogenous (produced normally by the mother) immunoglobulins are a normal component of breast milk.

Potential drug interactions: Should be administered separately from other drugs and IV solutions. Antibodies in immune globulin may interfere with patient's responses to live vaccines such as those for measles, mumps, and rubella.

What the FDA says about use in pregnancy: Category C (see Appendix).

What the available evidence suggests about breast-feeding safety: Safe.

The bottom line for you:

- Immune globulin is safe and effective during pregnancy and while breast-feeding.

INDINAVIR

Brand names: Crixivan, MK-639

Drug classes: Antiviral; Protease inhibitor

Indications (what it is used for): HIV infection.

How it works: Inhibits the destruction of proteins that interfere with viral replication.

Contraindications (reasons you shouldn't take it): Hypersensitivity to drug or class; history of kidney stones; concurrent use of astemizole, cisapride, midazolam, or triazolam.

Possible side effects and warnings: Can cause kidney stones; diabetes; nausea; vomiting; diarrhea; abdominal pain; sleeplessness; headache; high bilirubin, lipids, or glucose; loss of appetite; dry mouth; weakness; taste changes; and fatty tissue damage. Should be used with caution in women with liver dysfunction or diabetes.

How it can affect pregnant women: Indinavir reduces the level of circulating HIV to an undetectable level, especially when combined with other treatments such as a nucleoside analog or a reverse transcriptase inhibitor. Its clearance (how quickly it moves through the body) is increased during pregnancy and a dose adjustment may be necessary.

How it can affect a developing embryo or fetus: Indinavir crosses the human placenta, although fetal exposure is likely low. In one series of patients, the majority of pregnancies treated had an adverse outcome, but it was unclear whether those outcomes were a result of the treatment or the disease. Although most premarketing rodent birth defect studies were reassuring, in one animal study, indinavir was associated with delayed growth and skeletal and eye abnormalities. However, animal studies are not necessarily good indicators of how a drug will behave in humans.

Breast-feeding: There is no adequate data in nursing women. Indinavir does enter human breast milk, and breast-feeding is usually not recommended when a mother is HIV positive (if infant formula is available) because HIV can be transmitted to the newborn in the breast milk.

Potential drug interactions: Interaction between the following medications and indinavir has the potential to impact the effect of one or more of the drugs. In some instances the interaction can be dangerous or life-threatening and must be avoided: delavirdine, efavirenz, itraconazole, ketoconazole, rifampin, calcium channel blockers.

What the FDA says about use in pregnancy: Category C (see Appendix).

What the available evidence suggests about breast-feeding safety: Unsafe.

The bottom line for you:

- The primary goal during pregnancy is to reduce the circulating maternal HIV virus to undetectable levels. Although there are more commonly used combination antiviral therapies, indinavir may be used during pregnancy if needed (for example, because of drug resistance with another combination).

- Pregnant women taking antiretroviral therapy are encouraged to register with the Antiretroviral Pregnancy Registry (1-800-258-4263) to help increase the amount of information available about indinavir and other antiretrovirals during pregnancy.

- If infant formula is available, breast-feeding is usually not recommended when a mother is HIV positive because HIV can be transmitted to the newborn in the breast milk.

INDOMETHACIN

Brand name: Indocin

Drug classes: Analgesic, nonnarcotic; Antiarthritic; Nonsteroidal anti-inflammatory (NSAID)

Indications (what it is used for): Menstrual pain, mild to moderate pain, osteoarthritis or rheumatoid arthritis, inhibition of labor contractions.

How it works: Reduces the production of prostaglandins, which cause the pain or cramping.

Contraindications (reasons you shouldn't take it): Hypersensitivity to drug or class, aspirin- or NSAID-induced asthma, third-trimester pregnancy.

Possible side effects and warnings: Can cause kidney failure, fluid retention, heartburn, bowel bleeding, bronchospasm, low platelet and/or white blood cell count, interstitial nephritis (inflammation in the kidneys), liver toxicity, Stevens-Johnson syndrome (a rare but serious skin reaction to medication), nausea, constipation, abdominal pain, headache, dizziness, rash, ringing in the ears, and drowsiness. It should be used with caution in women with high blood pressure, congestive heart failure, a history of bowel bleeding, or nasal polyps.

How it can affect pregnant women: Indomethacin is used off-label (used to treat a condition not approved by the FDA) for the treatment of preterm labor (before 37 weeks). It prolongs pregnancy by 48–96 hours compared to sugar pills, allowing time to administer corticosteroids to help the lungs of the fetus mature and, in some circumstances, to administer magnesium sulfate to decrease the risk of cerebral palsy. However, indomethacin is no better for that purpose than calcium channel blockers such as nifedipine, which have stronger safety profiles. Indomethacin reduces the kidneys' excretion of water and can cause sudden weight gain and swelling during pregnancy. Indomethacin should also probably be avoided in women at risk for delivery within 24 hours, as it can prolong the mother's bleeding time.

How it can affect a developing embryo or fetus: Indomethacin crosses the placenta, and the level in the fetus reflects that of the mother. A third of the fetuses exposed to indomethacin for a week or more develop low amniotic fluid levels and/or show evidence of constriction of a blood vessel that diverts blood from the unused fetal lung. Since indomethacin has not been proved to be an effective long-term treatment for preterm labor or incompetent cervix, these adverse effects are completely avoidable. Because indomethacin reduces fetal urination, it may on occasion be used to treat excess amniotic fluid levels of unknown cause. It should not, however, be used in identical twin pregnancies where one twin has too much fluid and the other too little; indomethacin can lead to fetal kidney shutdown. The longer the fetal kidneys are exposed to indomethacin, the longer the effect of indomethacin lasts after finally being discontinued.

Breast-feeding: There are no adequate reports or well-controlled studies in nursing women. The quantity of indomethacin excreted into human breast milk is too low to have a clinically significant effect on a nursing newborn.

Potential drug interactions: Interaction between the following medications and indomethacin has the potential to impact the effect of one or more of the drugs. In some instances the interaction can be dangerous or life-threatening and must be avoided: diflunisal, other NSAIDs, oral anticoagulants, probenecid, lithium, digoxin, beta-adrenoceptors.

What the FDA says about use in pregnancy: Category B (see Appendix).

What the available evidence suggests about breast-feeding safety: Safe.

The bottom line for you:

- Indomethacin can slow spontaneous preterm labor and thus allow time for the administration of corticosteroids.
- It is wise to avoid indomethacin in the first trimester.
- Indomethacin has significant effects on the fetal and, at times, the maternal kidney and cardiovascular systems. Prolonged use should be avoided at all times and especially after 32 weeks.
- Indomethacin is safe for use while breast-feeding.

INFLIXIMAB

Brand name: Remicade

Drug classes: Anti-inflammatory; Antirheumatic; Inflammatory bowel disease agent; Monoclonal antibody; Tumor necrosis factor (TNF) modulator

Indications (what it is used for): Crohn's disease (inflammatory bowel disease), rheumatoid arthritis.

How it works: An antibody that binds and inhibits tumor necrosis factor, whose action leads to the symptoms.

Contraindications (reasons you shouldn't take it): Hypersensitivity to drug or class, hypersensitivity to mouse proteins, active infection.

Possible side effects and warnings: Can cause infection in the bloodstream, opportunistic infections, worsening of congestive heart failure, chest pain, serum sickness–like reaction, lupuslike syndrome, fever, chills, muscle aches, backache, joint pain, dizziness, nausea, vomiting, heartburn, itching, rash, upper respiratory infection, urinary tract infection, high or low blood pressure, facial or hand edema (swelling), and liver damage. It should be used with caution in women who are pregnant or who have multiple sclerosis, chronic or recurrent infections, latent tuberculosis, or demyelinating disease (damage to the myelin sheath that surrounds nerve fibers in the brain and spinal cord).

How it can affect pregnant women: There are no adequate reports or well-controlled studies of infliximab use during pregnancy. The current experience is limited to case reports and small series of patients, which reported good outcomes.

How it can affect a developing embryo or fetus: There are no adequate reports or well-controlled studies in human fetuses. It appears that infliximab crosses the human placenta. Limited case reports are reassuring. Infliximab levels persist in the fetus even if discontinued 10 or more weeks prior to delivery. However, no adverse effects have been reported.

Breast-feeding: There are no adequate reports or well-controlled studies in nursing women. No drug was detected in the breast milk of 2 women studied over multiple time points.

Potential drug interactions: Use with etanercept (another TNF-a–blocking agent) and anakinra (an interleukin-1 antagonist) increases the risks of serious infection and low white blood cell counts.

What the FDA says about use in pregnancy: Category B (see Appendix).

What the available evidence suggests about breast-feeding safety: Likely safe.

The bottom line for you:

- Infliximab should be used during pregnancy and while breast-feeding only if the benefit to the mother justifies the potential risk to the fetus or newborn. Early experience in women with medically significant diseases has been reassuring.

INFLUENZA VACCINE

Brand names: Fluimmune, Fluogen, Flu Shield, Flushield, Fluvirin, Fluzone

Drug class: Vaccine

Indications (what it is used for): No immunity to the strains of flu virus.

How it works: Produces immunity against the virus.

Contraindications (reasons you shouldn't take it): Hypersensitivity to drug or class, hypersensitivity to eggs, past history of Guillain-Barré syndrome (the body's immune system attacks the nerves), fever.

Possible side effects and warnings: Can cause infection in the bloodstream, opportunistic infections, worsening of heart failure, chest pain, serum sickness–like reaction, lupuslike syndrome, fever, chills, muscle aches, backache, joint pain, dizziness, nausea, vomiting, heartburn, itching, rash, upper respiratory infection, urinary tract infection, high or low blood pressure, facial or hand swelling, and liver damage.

How it can affect pregnant women: The vaccine consists of an inactivated virus. Pregnant women are more susceptible to viral respiratory diseases, and the most common one is influenza. Pregnant women are more likely than nonpregnant women to die from influenza. It is estimated that 1–2 hospitalizations can be prevented for every 1,000 pregnant women vaccinated. Thus, all women who intend to become pregnant or who are pregnant should receive the influenza vaccine. It may be given in any trimester.

How it can affect a developing embryo or fetus: There are no adequate reports or well-controlled studies in human fetuses. It is unknown whether influenza vaccine crosses the human placenta, but vaccine-stimulated IgG (immunoglobulin G) does, perhaps providing a level of immunity for the newborn. Maternal influenza vaccination reduces respiratory illness rates in their infants by more than 2 times for up to 6 months of age. One study of influenza vaccination of more than 2,000 pregnant women demonstrated no adverse fetal effects. There is no evidence that it causes birth defects.

Breast-feeding: There is no published data in nursing women. It is unknown whether influenza vaccine enters human breast milk. Influenza vaccine is considered safe for breast-feeding and it is likely that the maternal IgG is excreted into the breast milk, which might be beneficial to the newborn.

Potential drug interactions: The influenza vaccine can increase the effect of warfarin and increase the risk of bleeding.

What the FDA says about use in pregnancy: Category C (see Appendix).

What the available evidence suggests about breast-feeding safety: Safe.

The bottom line for you:
- Unless there is a contraindication (reason a woman should not receive the vaccination), all pregnant women should receive the influenza vaccine prior to flu season.

INSULIN, RECOMBINANT HUMAN
Brand names: Humulin R, L, N, and U
Drug classes: Antidiabetic agent; Hypoglycemic

Indications (what it is used for): Diabetes.
How it works: Lowers glucose by stimulating its uptake, blocking its production in the liver, inhibiting fat and protein breakdown, and increasing protein synthesis.
Contraindications (reasons you shouldn't take it): Hypersensitivity to drug or class, low blood glucose.
Possible side effects and warnings: Can cause low blood glucose and potassium levels, fat breakdown, itching, rash, and a reaction at the injection site. It should be used with caution in women with low potassium, kidney or liver dysfunction, or thyroid disorder. Only the R form of insulin should be given via IV.
How it can affect pregnant women: Recombinant insulin is produced by bacteria containing the human insulin gene. It is then modified chemically to produce three types of insulin with differing absorption patterns. There is a large body of clinical data using human recombinant insulin during pregnancy. Careful monitoring of glucose levels coupled with active regulation of the insulin dose is crucial for the best pregnancy outcome. Achieving normal blood glucose levels (fasting >55 and <85mg/dL, premeal <90mg/dL and 2h after the meal <110mg/dL) leads to improved pregnancy outcomes. An insulin infusion may be desirable at times during hospitalization.
How it can affect a developing embryo or fetus: Insulin does not cross the placenta. Women with insulin-requiring diabetes who do not have good control of their condition before pregnancy are at increased risk of having a child with a structural malformation, especially one involving the spine/brain, heart, or kidneys. The higher the average blood glucose level, the higher the risk. Normalization of glucose prior to conception reduces the risk to lower than that of an average woman without diabetes. High average glucose levels increase the risk for a range of adverse pregnancy outcomes and may lead to abnormally large newborns who have metabolic abnormalities and poor heart function. In

adulthood, these offspring are at increased risk for diabetes, obesity, high blood pressure, and heart disease. Clearly, it is critical that blood glucose be controlled prior to conception and during pregnancy.

Breast-feeding: There are no adequate reports or well-controlled studies in nursing women. It is unknown whether human recombinant insulin enters human breast milk. Human insulin is a normal component of breast milk. A wide body of clinical data with similar insulin preparations suggests that it is compatible with breast-feeding. Breast-feeding women may require dose or meal adjustments or both.

Potential drug interactions: Many drugs affect glucose metabolism and may necessitate an insulin dose adjustment. Interaction between the following medications and human recombinant insulin has the potential to impact the effect of one or more of the drugs. In some instances the interaction can be dangerous or life-threatening and must be avoided: drugs that can increase the risk of low glucoses, including fluoxetine, monoamine oxidase inhibitors (MAOIs), oral hypoglycemic agents, salicylates, somatostatin analogs (e.g., octreotide), and sulfonamide antibiotics; drugs that increase the risk of high glucoses, including corticosteroids, diuretics, isoniazid, niacin, phenothiazine derivatives, somatropin, sympathomimetic agents (e.g., epinephrine, salbutamol, terbutaline), and thyroid hormones; sympatholytic drugs, such as beta-blockers, clonidine, guanethidine, and reserpine.

What the FDA says about use in pregnancy: Category B (see Appendix).

What the available evidence suggests about breast-feeding safety: Safe.

The bottom line for you:

- The goal for a diabetic woman is normal glucose levels throughout pregnancy. Failure to accomplish this places the mother at risk for multiple pregnancy complications and the baby at high risk for birth defects and multiple diseases in adulthood.

- Human recombinant insulin is a mainstay for the treatment of hyperglycemia in pregnant and breast-feeding women.

INSULIN, SEMISYNTHETIC HUMAN

Brand name: Velosulin BR

Drug classes: Antidiabetic agent; Hypoglycemic

Indications (what it is used for): Diabetes.

How it works: Lowers glucose by stimulating its uptake, blocking its production in the liver, inhibiting fat and protein breakdown, and increasing protein synthesis.

Contraindications (reasons you shouldn't take it): Hypersensitivity to drug or class, low blood glucose. It should not be administered via IV.

Possible side effects and warnings: Can cause low blood glucose and potassium levels, fat breakdown, itching, rash, and a reaction at the injection site. It should be used with caution in women with low potassium, kidney or liver dysfunction, or thyroid disorder.

How it can affect pregnant women: Human semisynthetic insulin is produced from pork insulin that is chemically converted into the human structure. It is functionally the same as regular recombinant human insulin. There are no published reports of its use during pregnancy. Insulin selection is often a matter of physician preference and cost. Careful monitoring of glucose levels coupled with active regulation of the insulin dose is crucial for the best outcome.

How it can affect a developing embryo or fetus: Insulin does not cross the placenta. Women with insulin-requiring diabetes who do not have good control of their condition before pregnancy are at increased risk of bearing a child with a structural malformation, especially involving the spine/brain, heart, or kidneys. The higher the average blood glucose level, the greater the risk. Normalization of glucose prior to conception reduces the risk to a level below the risk of an average woman without diabetes. High average glucose levels increase the risk for a range of adverse pregnancy outcomes and may lead to abnormally large newborns who have metabolic abnormalities and poor heart function. In adulthood, these offspring are at increased risk for diabetes, obesity, high blood pressure, and cardiac disease. Clearly, it is critical that blood glucose be controlled prior to conception and during pregnancy.

Breast-feeding: There is no published data in nursing women. It is unknown whether human semisynthetic insulin enters human breast milk, although natural insulin is a normal component of breast milk. A long clinical experience with similar insulin preparations suggests that it is compatible with breast-feeding. Breast-feeding women may require dose or meal adjustments or both.

Potential drug interactions: Many drugs affect glucose metabolism and may necessitate an insulin dose adjustment. Interaction between the following medications and human semisynthetic insulin has the potential to impact the effect of one or more of the drugs. In some instances the interaction can be dangerous or life-threatening and must be avoided: drugs that can increase the risk of low glucoses, including fluoxetine, monoamine oxidase inhibitors (MAOIs), oral hypoglycemic agents, salicylates, somatostatin analogs (e.g., octreotide), and sulfonamide antibiotics; drugs that increase the risk of high glucoses, including corticosteroids, diuretics, isoniazid, niacin, phenothiazine derivatives, somatropin, sympathomimetic agents (e.g., epinephrine, salbutamol, terbutaline), and thyroid hormones; sympatholytic drugs such as beta-blockers, clonidine, guanethidine, and reserpine.

What the FDA says about use in pregnancy: Category B (see Appendix).

What the available evidence suggests about breast-feeding safety: Safe.

Bottom line for you:
- The goal for a diabetic woman is normal glucose levels throughout pregnancy. Failure to accomplish this places mother at risk for multiple pregnancy complications and the baby at high risk for birth defects and for multiple diseases in adulthood.
- Insulin selection is often a matter of time to peak effect, physician preference, and cost.

INSULIN ASPART
Brand name: NovoLog
Drug classes: Antidiabetic agent; Hypoglycemic
Indications (what it is used for): Diabetes.
How it works: Lowers the glucose by stimulating its uptake, blocking its production in the liver, inhibiting fat and protein breakdown, and increasing protein synthesis.
Contraindications (reasons you shouldn't take it): Hypersensitivity to drug or class, low blood glucose.
Possible side effects and warnings: Can cause low blood glucose and potassium levels, fat breakdown, itching, rash, and a reaction at the injection site. It should be used with caution in women with low potassium, kidney or liver dysfunction, or thyroid disorder.
How it can affect pregnant women: Insulin aspart is a rapidly acting human-type insulin with an effect that lasts up to 5 hours. It is similar to insulin lispro, which is similar to regular human insulin in controlling the after-meal glucose level without increasing the risk of a premeal low blood glucose. Its added advantage over regular human insulin is that it can be taken immediately before the meal. Insulin aspart is at least as safe and effective as regular human insulin when used with neutral protamine Hagedorn (NPH) insulin in pregnant women with type I diabetes and potentially offers benefits in terms of after-meal control and the prevention of severe low blood glucose. Careful monitoring of glucose levels coupled with frequent adjustments of the insulin dose are crucial for the best outcome.
How it can affect a developing embryo or fetus: Insulin does not cross the placenta. Women with insulin-requiring diabetes who do not have good

control of their condition before pregnancy are at increased risk of bearing a child with a structural malformation, especially one involving the spine/brain, heart, or kidneys. The higher the average blood glucose level, the greater the risk. Normalization of glucose prior to conception reduces the risk to a level below the risk of an average woman without diabetes. High average glucose levels increase the risk for a range of adverse pregnancy outcomes and may lead to abnormally large newborns who have metabolic abnormalities and poor heart function. In adulthood, these offspring are at increased risk for diabetes, obesity, high blood pressure, and cardiac disease. Clearly, it is critical that blood glucose be controlled prior to conception and during pregnancy.

Breast-feeding: There is no published data in nursing women. It is unknown whether insulin aspart enters human breast milk, although insulin is a normal component of breast milk. A long clinical experience with similar insulin preparations suggests that it is compatible with breast-feeding. Breast-feeding women may require dose or meal adjustments or both.

Potential drug interactions: Many drugs affect glucose metabolism and may necessitate an insulin dose adjustment. Interaction between the following medications and insulin aspart has the potential to impact the effect of one or more of the drugs. In some instances the interaction can be dangerous or life-threatening and must be avoided: drugs that can increase the risk of low glucoses, including fluoxetine, monoamine oxidase inhibitors (MAOIs), oral hypoglycemic agents, salicylates, somatostatin analogs (e.g., octreotide), and sulfonamide antibiotics; drugs that increase the risk of high glucoses, including corticosteroids, diuretics, isoniazid, niacin, phenothiazine derivatives, somatropin, sympathomimetic agents (e.g., epinephrine, terbutaline), and thyroid hormones; sympatholytic drugs such as beta-blockers, clonidine, guanethidine, and reserpine.

What the FDA says about use in pregnancy: Category B (see Appendix).

What the available evidence suggests about breast-feeding safety: Safe.

The bottom line for you:

- The goal for a diabetic woman is normal glucose levels throughout pregnancy. Failure to accomplish this places the mother at risk for multiple pregnancy complications and the baby at high risk for birth defects and for multiple diseases in adulthood.
- Insulin selection is often a matter of time to peak effect, physician preference, and cost.

INSULIN GLARGINE

Brand name: Lantus

Drug classes: Antidiabetic agent; Hypoglycemic

Indications (what it is used for): Diabetes.

How it works: Lowers the glucose by stimulating its uptake, blocking its production in the liver, inhibiting fat and protein breakdown, and increasing protein synthesis.

Contraindications (reasons you shouldn't take it): Hypersensitivity to drug or class, low blood glucose. It should not be administered via IV.

Possible side effects and warnings: Can cause low blood glucose and potassium levels, fat breakdown, itching, rash, and a reaction at the injection site. It should be used with caution in women with low potassium, kidney or liver dysfunction, or thyroid disorder.

How it can affect pregnant women: Insulin glargine is a long-acting recombinant insulin producing a fairly steady level for up to 24 hours. There are no adequate reports or well-controlled studies in pregnant women. Because insulin requirements during pregnancy change rapidly, its long-acting profile makes it a poor choice. Although the published data is confined to case reports and small series of patients, they include apparent successes when used for a constant low-level release to maintain glucose levels between meals. Careful monitoring of glucose levels coupled with active regulation of the insulin dose is crucial for the best outcome.

How it can affect a developing embryo or fetus: Insulin does not cross the placenta. Women with insulin-requiring diabetes who do not have good control of their condition before pregnancy are at increased risk of bearing a child with a structural malformation, especially involving the spine/brain, heart, or kidneys. The higher the average blood glucose level, the greater the risk. Normalization of glucose prior to conception lowers the risk to a level below the risk of an average woman without diabetes. High average glucose levels increase the risk for a range of adverse pregnancy outcomes and may lead to abnormally large newborns who have metabolic abnormalities and poor heart function. In adulthood, these offspring are at increased risk for diabetes, obesity, high blood pressure, and cardiac disease. Clearly, it is critical that blood glucose be controlled prior to conception and during pregnancy.

Breast-feeding: There is no published data in nursing women. It is unknown whether human semisynthetic insulin enters human breast milk, although insulin is a normal component of breast milk. A long clinical experience with similar insulin preparations suggests that it is compatible with breast-feeding. Breast-feeding women may require dose or meal adjustments or both.

Potential drug interactions: Many drugs affect glucose metabolism and may necessitate an insulin dose adjustment. Interaction between the following medications and insulin glargine has the potential to impact the effect of one or more of the drugs. In some instances the interaction can be dangerous or life-threatening and must be avoided: drugs that can increase the risk of low glucoses, including fluoxetine, monoamine oxidase inhibitors (MAOIs), oral hypoglycemic agents, salicylates, somatostatin analogs (e.g., octreotide), and sulfonamide antibiotics; drugs that increase the risk of high glucoses, including corticosteroids, diuretics, isoniazid, niacin, phenothiazine derivatives, somatropin, sympathomimetic agents (e.g., epinephrine, salbutamol, terbutaline), and thyroid hormones; sympatholytic drugs such as beta-blockers, clonidine, guanethidine, and reserpine.

What the FDA says about use in pregnancy: Category C (see Appendix).

What the available evidence suggests about breast-feeding safety: Safe.

The bottom line for you:

- The goal for a diabetic woman is normal glucose levels throughout pregnancy. Failure to accomplish this places the mother at risk for multiple pregnancy complications and the baby at high risk for birth defects and for multiple diseases in adulthood.

- Insulin selection is often a matter of time to peak effect, physician preference, and cost.

INSULIN LISPRO

Brand name: Humalog

Drug classes: Antidiabetic agent; Hypoglycemic

Indications (what it is used for): Diabetes.

How it works: Lowers the glucose by stimulating its uptake, blocking its production in the liver, inhibiting fat and protein breakdown, and increasing protein synthesis.

Contraindications (reasons you shouldn't take it): Hypersensitivity to drug or class, low blood glucose.

Possible side effects and warnings: Can cause low blood glucose and potassium levels, fat breakdown, itching, rash, and a reaction at the injection site. It should be used with caution in women with low potassium, kidney or liver dysfunction, or thyroid disorder.

How it can affect pregnant women: Insulin lispro is a rapidly acting human insulin analog with the same potency as regular human insulin. In nonpregnant patients, insulin lispro is superior to regular human insulin for the control of after-meal glucose levels without increasing the risk of a low premeal blood glucose. Insulin lispro's added advantage over regular human insulin is that it can be taken immediately before the meal, rather than the 30–60 minute wait necessary for regular insulin. The published data suggests that similar pregnancy outcomes are obtained with fewer hypoglycemic episodes compared to regular human insulin. Although there are no adequate reports or well-controlled studies in pregnant women, many state that either this agent or insulin aspart should replace regular human insulin in combination with an intermediate-duration-acting insulin because of its preferable release profile. Careful monitoring of glucose levels coupled with active regulation of the insulin dose is crucial for the best outcome.

How it can affect a developing embryo or fetus: Insulin does not cross the placenta. Women with insulin-requiring diabetes who do not have good control of their condition before pregnancy are at increased risk of bearing a child with a structural malformation, especially involving the spine/brain, heart, or kidneys. The higher the average blood glucose level, the greater the risk. Normalization of glucose prior to conception lowers the risk to a level below the risk of an average woman without diabetes. High average glucose levels increase the risk for a range of adverse pregnancy outcomes and may lead to abnormally large newborns who have metabolic abnormalities and poor heart function. In adulthood, these offspring are at increased risk to develop diabetes, obesity, high blood pressure, and cardiac disease. Clearly, it is critical that blood glucose be controlled prior to conception and during pregnancy.

Breast-feeding: There is no published data with insulin lispro in nursing women. It is unknown whether insulin lispro enters human breast milk, although insulin is a normal component of breast milk. A long clinical experience with similar insulin preparations suggests that it is compatible with breast-feeding. Breast-feeding women may require dose or meal adjustments or both.

Potential drug interactions: Many drugs affect glucose metabolism and may necessitate an insulin dose adjustment. Interaction between the following medications and insulin lispro has the potential to impact the effect of one or more of the drugs. In some instances the interaction can be dangerous or life-threatening and must be avoided: drugs that can increase the risk of low glucoses, including fluoxetine, monoamine oxidase inhibitors (MAOIs), oral hypoglycemic agents, salicylates, somatostatin analogs (e.g., octreotide), and sulfonamide antibiotics; drugs that increase the risk of high glucoses, include corticosteroids, diuretics, isoniazid, niacin, phenothiazine derivatives, somatropin, sympathomimetic agents (e.g., epinephrine, salbutamol, terbutaline), and thyroid hormones; sympatholytic drugs, such as beta-blockers, clonidine, guanethidine, and reserpine.

What the FDA says about use in pregnancy: Category B (see Appendix).

What the available evidence suggests about breast-feeding safety: Safe.

The bottom line for you:

- The goal for a diabetic woman is normal glucose levels throughout pregnancy. Failure to accomplish this places the mother at risk for multiple pregnancy complications and the the baby at high risk for birth defects and for multiple diseases in adulthood.
- Insulin selection is often a matter of time to peak effect, physician preference, and cost.

INTERFERON ALFA-2B, RECOMBINANT

Brand name: Intron A

Drug classes: Antineoplastic, interferon; Antiviral, interferon; Immunomodulator

Indications (what it is used for): Condyloma acuminatum (genital warts), chronic hepatitis B or C infection, AIDS-associated Kaposi's sarcoma (cancer that causes patches of abnormal tissue to grow under the skin), hairy cell leukemia.

How it works: Unknown.

Contraindications (reasons you shouldn't take it): Hypersensitivity to drug or class, autoimmune hepatitis.

Possible side effects and warnings: Can cause low white blood cell, red blood cell, and/or platelet counts; seizures; lung or liver toxicity; delirium; suicidal thoughts; irregular heart rate; cardiomyopathy (disease of the heart muscle); heart attack; bleeding in the gastrointestinal tract; high blood pressure; peripheral neuropathy; flulike symptoms; rash, loss of appetite; abdominal pain; diarrhea; joint pain; dry mouth; cough; dizziness; headache; tingling or numbness of the skin; mood swings; anxiety; and injection site reaction. It should be used with caution in women who are taking bone marrow–suppressing agents or who have bone marrow suppression, seizure disorder, heart disease, severe liver or kidney dysfunction, depression, disorder of the central nervous system, diabetes, thyroid disorders, kidney or liver toxic agents, or an autoimmune disorder.

How it can affect pregnant women: There are no adequate reports or well-controlled studies in pregnant women. Case reports document the use of interferon alfa-2b during pregnancy for the treatment of chronic hepatitis C infection and essential thrombocythemia (overproduction of platelets by the bone marrow).

How it can affect a developing embryo or fetus: There are no adequate reports or well-controlled studies in human fetuses. It is unknown whether interferon alfa-2b crosses the placenta, although most other interferons do not. Rodent studies are reassuring, revealing no evidence of birth defects or low birth weight despite the use of doses higher than those used clinically. However, it increased the risk of miscarriage in rhesus monkeys when given at multiples of the maximum recommended human dose. Animal studies are not necessarily good indicators of how a drug will behave in humans.

Breast-feeding: There are no adequate reports or well-controlled studies in nursing women. Only a scant quantity of interferon alfa-2b enters human breast milk and is likely clinically insignificant. If infant formula is available, breast-feeding is usually not recommended for an HIV-positive mother because HIV can be transmitted to the newborn in the breast milk.

Potential drug interactions: Interaction between the following medications and interferon alfa-2b has the potential to impact the effect of one or more of the drugs. In some instances the interaction can be dangerous or life-threatening and must be avoided: theophylline. Interferons may increase the potential nerve, blood, or heart toxic side effects of other medications.

What the FDA says about use in pregnancy: Category C (see Appendix).

What the available evidence suggests about breast-feeding safety: Unknown; likely safe unless the mother is HIV positive.

The bottom line for you:

- Interferon alfa-2b should be used during pregnancy and while breast-feeding only if the benefit to the woman justifies the potential risk to the fetus or newborn.
- If a woman becomes pregnant or plans to become pregnant while taking interferon alfa-2b, it may be wise to consider discontinuing therapy at least during the first trimester.
- If infant formula is available, breast-feeding is usually not recommended when a mother is HIV positive because HIV can be transmitted to the newborn in the breast milk.

INTERFERON ALFACON-1

Brand name: Infergen

Drug classes: Antiviral, interferon; Immunomodulator

Indications (what it is used for): Chronic hepatitis C virus infection with compensated liver disease (the liver is damaged but still able to function).

How it works: Unknown.

Contraindications (reasons you shouldn't take it): Hypersensitivity to drug or class, hypersensitivity to *E. coli*–derived products, decompensated liver disease (the liver is no longer able to function), autoimmune hepatitis.

Possible side effects and warnings: Can cause depression, suicide or suicidal thoughts, high blood pressure, irregular heart rate, chest pain, heart attack, low white blood cell and/or platelet counts, eye disorders, and hypothyroidism. It should be used with caution in women with preexisting cardiac disease, low white blood cell levels, or autoimmune disorders.

How it can affect pregnant women: Interferon alfacon-1 is a non–naturally occurring recombinant type I interferon. There is no published data during pregnancy.

How it can affect a developing embryo or fetus: There are no reports or well-controlled studies in human fetuses. It is unknown whether interferon alfacon-1 crosses the human placenta; most other interferons do not. Although rodent studies are reassuring, revealing no evidence of birth defects or low birth weight despite the use of doses higher than those used clinically, there was an increase in early miscarriage in both rodents and some monkeys. However, animal studies are not necessarily good indicators of how a drug will behave in humans.

Breast-feeding: There is no published data in nursing women. It is unknown whether interferon alfacon-1 enters human breast milk.

Potential drug interactions: No formal drug interaction studies have been conducted. Interferon alfacon-1 should be used cautiously in patients receiving drugs that cause myelosuppression or are metabolized by certain liver enzymes. Interferons may increase the potential nerve, blood, or heart toxic side effects of other medications.

What the FDA says about use in pregnancy: Category C (see Appendix).

What the available evidence suggests about breast-feeding safety: Unknown.

The bottom line for you:

- If a woman becomes pregnant or plans to become pregnant while taking interferon alfacon-1, it may be wise to consider discontinuing therapy at least during the first trimester.
- Interferon alfacon-1 should be used during pregnancy and breast-feeding only if the benefit to the woman justifies the potential risk to the fetus or newborn.

INTERFERON ALFA-N3

Brand name: Alferon N

Drug classes: Antiviral, interferon; Immunomodulator

Indications (what it is used for): Condyloma acuminatum (genital warts).

How it works: Unknown.

Contraindications (reasons you shouldn't take it): Hypersensitivity to drug or class, hypersensitivity to egg proteins or neomycin.

Possible side effects and warnings: Can cause flulike symptoms; fever; sweating; itching; dizziness; sleeplessness; joint, muscle, and/or back pain; and headache. It should be used with caution in women with unstable angina, congestive heart failure, chronic obstructive pulmonary disease (COPD), diabetes, blood clots or a clotting disorder, low white blood cell counts, or seizure disorder.

How it can affect pregnant women: Interferon alfa-N3 is derived from human white blood cells. There is no published data with interferon alfa-N3 during pregnancy.

How it can affect a developing embryo or fetus: There are no adequate reports or well-controlled studies in human fetuses. It is unknown whether interferon alfa-N3 crosses the placenta, although most other interferons do not. Rodent studies of birth defects have not been performed. Topical application is unlikely to produce a blood level in the mother that would pose a risk to a fetus.

Breast-feeding: There is no published data in nursing women. It is unknown whether interferon alfa-N3 enters human breast milk.

Potential drug interactions: Interferons may increase the potential nerve, blood, or heart toxic side effects of other medications.

What the FDA says about use in pregnancy: Category C (see Appendix).

What the available evidence suggests about breast-feeding safety: Unknown.

The bottom line for you:

- There is too little information on interferon alfa-N3 to guide its use during pregnancy.
- Interferon alfa-N3 should be used during pregnancy and breast-feeding only if the benefit to the woman justifies the potential risk to the fetus or newborn.

INTERFERON BETA-1A

Brand names: Avonex, Rebif

Drug classes: Immunomodulator; Neurologic

Indications (what it is used for): Relapsing multiple sclerosis (MS).

How it works: Unknown.

Contraindications (reasons you shouldn't take it): Hypersensitivity to drug or class

Possible side effects and warnings: Can cause seizures, cardiac arrest, hemorrhage, anemia, weakness, diarrhea, fever, chills, flulike symptoms, liver damage, depression, suicidal thoughts, and injection site reaction. It should be used with caution in women with a seizure disorder or depression.

How it can affect pregnant women: There are no adequate reports or well-controlled studies of interferon beta-1a in pregnant women. The relapse frequency for MS decreases during pregnancy and increases after delivery. Menstrual irregularities occurred in monkeys treated with 100 times the maximum recommended human dose. Ovulation stopped, and there were decreased levels of the hormone progesterone noted in some animals given the medication. These effects were reversed by discontinuing the drug. Treatment with twice the recommended weekly dose had no effect on cycle duration or ovulation.

How it can affect a developing embryo or fetus: There are no adequate reports or well-controlled studies in human fetuses. It is unknown whether interferon beta-1a crosses the placenta; most other interferons do not. Limited animal study suggests increased rates of early miscarriage and low birth weight. There was no evidence of increased birth defects in either rodent or monkey studies. However, animal studies are not necessarily good indicators of how a drug will behave in humans.

Breast-feeding: There is no published data in nursing women. It is unknown whether interferon beta-1a enters human breast milk.

Potential drug interactions: Due to its potential to cause a low white blood cell count, proper monitoring of patients is required if interferon beta-1a is given in combination with myelosuppressive agents. Interferons may increase the potential nerve, blood, or heart toxic side effects of other medications.

What the FDA says about use in pregnancy: Category C (see Appendix).

What the available evidence suggests about breast-feeding safety: Unknown.

The bottom line for you:

- If a woman becomes pregnant or plans to become pregnant while taking interferon beta-1a, it may be wise to consider discontinuing therapy at least during the first trimester.
- Interferon beta-1a should be used during pregnancy and breast-feeding only if the benefit to the woman justifies the potential risk to the fetus or newborn.

INTERFERON BETA-1B, RECOMBINANT

Brand names: Betaferon, Betaseron

Drug classes: Immunomodulator; Neurologic

Indications (what it is used for): Relapsing multiple sclerosis (MS).

How it works: Unknown.

Contraindications (reasons you shouldn't take it): Hypersensitivity to drug or class.

Possible side effects and warnings: Can cause shock, seizures, cardiac arrest, irregular heart rate, anemia, muscle aches, weakness, fever, chills, flulike symptoms, nausea, diarrhea, heartburn, and injection site reaction. It should be used with caution in women with a seizure disorder or depression.

How it can affect pregnant women: There are no adequate reports or well controlled studies of interferon beta-1b during pregnancy. The relapse frequency for MS decreases during pregnancy and increases after delivery. Menstrual irregularities occurred in monkeys treated with 100 times the maximum recommended human dose. Ovulation stopped, and progesterone levels were lowered in some animal studies. These effects reversed after stopping the drug. Treatment with twice the recommended dose had no effect on cycle duration or ovulation.

How it can affect a developing embryo or fetus: There are no adequate reports or well-controlled studies in human fetuses. It is unknown whether interferon beta-1b crosses the human placenta; most other interferons do not. There was no evidence of increased birth defects in either rodent or monkey studies. Limited animal study suggests increased rates of early miscarriage and low birth weight when other interferons are given. However, animal studies are not necessarily good indicators of how a drug will behave in humans.

Breast-feeding: There is no published data in nursing women. It is unknown whether interferon beta-1b enters human breast milk.

Potential drug interactions: Due to its potential to cause a low white blood cell count, proper monitoring of patients is required if interferon beta-1a is given in combination with myelosuppressive agents. Interferons may increase the potential nerve, blood, or heart toxic side effects of other medications.

What the FDA says about use in pregnancy: Category C (see Appendix).

What the available evidence suggests about breast-feeding safety: Unknown.

The bottom line for you:

- If a woman becomes pregnant or plans to become pregnant while taking interferon beta-1b, it may be wise to consider discontinuing therapy at least during the first trimester.
- Interferon beta-1b should be used during pregnancy and breast-feeding only if the benefit to the woman justifies the potential risk to the fetus or newborn.

INTERFERON GAMMA-1B, RECOMBINANT

Brand name: Actimmune
Drug class: Immunomodulator
Indications (what it is used for): Chronic granulomatous disease (hereditary disease of the immune system); severe, malignant osteopetrosis (bones become abnormally dense and prone to breakage).
How it works: Unknown.
Contraindications (reasons you shouldn't take it): Hypersensitivity to drug or class, hypersensitivity to *E. coli* products.
Possible side effects and warnings: Can cause fever, headache, rash, chills, fatigue, diarrhea, nausea and vomiting, muscle aches, joint pain, and local injection site reactions. It should be used with caution in women with preexisting heart disease, low white blood cell counts, or a seizure disorder.
How it can affect pregnant women: There is no published data with interferon gamma-1b during pregnancy.
How it can affect a developing embryo or fetus: There are no adequate reports or well-controlled studies in human fetuses. It is unknown whether interferon gamma-1b crosses the human placenta; most other interferons do not. Studies in pregnant primates treated with intravenous doses 2–100 times the maximum recommended human dose revealed no birth defects. Interferon gamma-1b increased the rate of miscarriage in primates given 100 times the maximum recommended human dose. However, animal studies are not necessarily good indicators of how a drug will behave in humans.
Breast-feeding: There is no published data in nursing women. It is unknown whether interferon gamma-1b enters human breast milk.
Potential drug interactions: Due to its potential to cause a low white blood cell count, proper monitoring

of patients is required if interferon beta-1a is given in combination with myelosuppressive agents. Interferons may increase the potential nerve, blood, or heart toxic side effects of other medications.

What the FDA says about use in pregnancy: Category C (see Appendix).

What the available evidence suggests about breast-feeding safety: Unknown.

The bottom line for you:

- If a woman becomes pregnant or plans to become pregnant while taking interferon gamma-1b, it may be wise to consider discontinuing therapy at least during the first trimester.
- Interferon gamma-1b should be used during pregnancy and breast-feeding only if the benefit to the woman justifies the potential risk to the fetus or newborn.

IOHEXOL

Brand name: Omnipaque

Drug class: Diagnostic, radiopharmaceutical

Indications (what it is used for): Radiography, CT scanning.

How it works: Iodine-containing contrast medium used to illuminate parts of the body during a diagnostic-imaging test.

Contraindications (reasons you shouldn't take it): Hypersensitivity to drug or class.

Possible side effects and warnings: Can cause temporary weakness and vomiting.

How it can affect pregnant women: Iohexol is a contrast medium used extensively in clinical radiology. There are no adequate reports or well-controlled studies of iohexol in pregnant women. Side effects are rare, even in patients with a history of iodine sensitivity or adverse reactions to other contrast agents.

How it can affect a developing embryo or fetus: There are no adequate reports or well-controlled studies in human fetuses. Iohexol crosses the human placenta and has been used to identify fetal birth defects. No adverse effects are reported.

Breast-feeding: There are no adequate reports or well-controlled studies in nursing women. Small quantities of iohexol enter human breast milk, but these kinds of medications are poorly absorbed orally. As a result, iohexol seems to pose little risk to a breast-feeding newborn.

Potential drug interactions: Interaction between the following medications and iohexol has the potential to impact the effect of one or more of the drugs. In some instances the interaction can be dangerous or life-threatening and must be avoided: drugs that lower the seizure threshold, especially phenothiazine derivatives including those used for antihistaminic or antinauseant properties; monoamine oxidase inhibitors (MAOIs); tricyclic antidepressants (TCAs); central nervous system stimulants; psychoactive drugs described as analeptics, major tranquilizers, or antipsychotic drugs.

What the FDA says about use in pregnancy: Category B (see Appendix).

What the available evidence suggests about breast-feeding safety: Safe.

The bottom line for you:

- Iohexol is probably safe for use during pregnancy and while breast-feeding.

IPECAC SYRUP

Brand name: None

Drug classes: Antidote; Emetic; Toxicology agent

Indications (what it is used for): To trigger vomiting.

How it works: Induces vomiting by both local and central nervous system stimulation.

Contraindications (reasons you shouldn't take it): Hypersensitivity to drug or class, unconsciousness.

Possible side effects and warnings: Can cause heart damage with chronic use, diarrhea, choking, drowsiness, cough, heartburn, central nervous system depression, lethargy, and muscle weakness. It should be used with caution in women who have ingested gasoline, kerosene, or volatile oil alkali or acid.

How it can affect pregnant women: There is no published data with ipecac during pregnancy. Although there is a long clinical experience with its use to treat pregnant and nonpregnant patients who have ingested toxic substances, ipecac syrup is no longer recommended for routine management of outpatient ingestions of medications or other chemicals. There is no evidence from clinical studies that ipecac improves the outcome of poisoned patients, and its routine administration in emergency rooms should be abandoned. Ipecac may delay the use, or reduce the effectiveness of, activated charcoal, oral antidotes, and whole bowel irrigation—other methods for treating the ingestion of toxic chemicals.

How it can affect a developing embryo or fetus: There are no adequate reports or well-controlled studies in human fetuses. It is unknown if ipecac crosses the human placenta. Rodent studies for birth defects have not been performed.

Breast-feeding: There are no adequate reports or well-controlled studies in nursing women. It is unknown whether ipecac enters human breast milk.

Potential drug interactions: Ipecac may decrease adsorption by activated charcoal.

What the FDA says about use in pregnancy: Category C (see Appendix).

What the available evidence suggests about breast-feeding safety: Safe.

The bottom line for you:

- There are superior alternatives for the treatment of oral poisoning.

IPRATROPIUM BROMIDE

Brand names: Atrovent, Disne-Asmol

Drug classes: Anticholinergic; Bronchodilator

Indications (what it is used for): Bronchospasm, rhinitis (stuffy nose), rhinorrhea (runny nose).

How it works: Blocks activation of the cholinergic receptors that cause the symptoms.

Contraindications (reasons you shouldn't take it): Hypersensitivity to drug or class, hypersensitivity to soybeans or peanuts.

Possible side effects and warnings: Can cause cough, bronchospasm when used with the inhaler, headache, palpitations, nervousness, dizziness, nausea, dry mouth, pharyngitis, rash, blurred vision, and upper respiratory tract infection. It should be used with caution in women with narrow-angle glaucoma.

How it can affect pregnant women: The published data with ipratropium bromide during pregnancy is limited to case reports. Mild asthma during pregnancy is managed with inhaled beta-2 agonists; therapy for moderate asthma includes inhaled cromolyn, inhaled beclomethasone, and oral theophylline. Severe asthma should be treated with oral corticosteroids at the lowest effective dose. The management of acute asthma includes nebulized beta-2 agonists, ipratropium, and IV methylprednisolone alone or in combination as required.

How it can affect a developing embryo or fetus: There are no adequate reports or well-controlled studies in human fetuses. It is unknown whether ipratropium crosses the human placenta. Rodent studies are reassuring, revealing no evidence of birth defects or low birth weight despite the use of doses higher than those used clinically. The highest doses (1,000 times the maximum recommended human dose) were associated with damage to the rodent embryo. However, animal studies are not necessarily good indicators of how a drug will behave in humans.

Breast-feeding: There is no published data in nursing women. It is unknown whether ipratropium enters human breast milk. However, ipratropium is poorly absorbed systemically after inhalation and is unlikely to achieve a clinically relevant amount in breast milk.

Potential drug interactions: Other anticholinergic medications may increase the effects of ipratropium bromide.

What the FDA says about use in pregnancy: Category B (see Appendix).

What the available evidence suggests about breast-feeding safety: Safe.

The bottom line for you:

- Ipratropium is an effective agent for the management of acute asthma and likely safe for use during pregnancy and while breast-feeding.
- However, there are alternative agents with which there is more experience during pregnancy and breast-feeding.

IRON DEXTRAN

Brand names: Dexferrum, Feostat, Heparan, Imexon, Infed, Iodex, Norefmi, Orferon, Pri-Dextra, Proferdex

Drug classes: Hematinic; Mineral

Indications (what it is used for): Iron deficiency and supplementation.

How it works: Essential component in many proteins, including hemoglobin.

Contraindications (reasons you shouldn't take it): Hypersensitivity to drug or class, anemia not associated with iron deficiency.

Possible side effects and warnings: Can cause chest pain, abdominal pain, convulsions, nausea and vomiting, seizures, headache, blood in the urine, low blood pressure, hives, respiratory arrest, shortness of breath, joint pain, and arthritis. It should be used with caution in women with heart or liver disease, kidney infection, or rheumatoid arthritis.

How it can affect pregnant women: There is no evidence that iron supplementation improves pregnancy outcome in the industrialized world. Iron dextran is more effective than oral treatment in correcting anemia and reducing the need for transfusion in both pregnant and nonpregnant women. It is especially useful in women who have had bypass surgery for weight reduction. The intramuscular administration at monthly intervals for 3 doses appears effective and well tolerated and may be used in women who cannot tolerate oral iron. Folic acid supplementation is recommended.

How it can affect a developing embryo or fetus: There are no adequate reports or well-controlled studies of iron dextran in human fetuses. Iron crosses the placenta, and there is some evidence that maternal iron dextran IV supplementation increases fetal iron stores.

Breast-feeding: Maternal iron supplementation does not alter the concentration of iron in breast milk.

Potential drug interactions: Interaction between the following medications and iron dextran has the potential to impact the effect of one or more of the drugs. In some instances the interaction can be dangerous or life-threatening and must be avoided: A-tocopherol (vitamin E).

What the FDA says about use in pregnancy: Category C (see Appendix).

What the available evidence suggests about breast-feeding safety: Safe.

The bottom line for you:

- When required in women who cannot tolerate oral iron or who cannot absorb it, iron dextran is safe and effective for use during pregnancy and while breast-feeding if appropriate precautions are taken.

ISOCARBOXAZID

Brand name: Marplan

Drug classes: Antidepressant; Monoamine oxidase inhibitor (MAOI)

Indications (what it is used for): Depression.

How it works: Inhibits MAO, an enzyme involved in depression.

Contraindications (reasons you shouldn't take it): Hypersensitivity to drug or class; cerebrovascular or cardiovascular disease; pheochromocytoma (adrenal gland tumor); liver or kidney disease; current or recent use of other MAOIs, tricyclic antidepressants (TCAs), selective serotonin reuptake inhibitors (SSRIs), and buspirone; sympathomimetics; meperidine; dextromethorphan; foods rich in tyramine; anesthetics; antihypertensives; caffeine; and central nervous system depressants.

Possible side effects and warnings: Can cause low blood pressure, hepatotoxicity, lower seizure threshold, dry mouth, nausea, diarrhea, dizziness, and fainting. It should be used with caution in women who drink alcohol, have kidney dysfunction, or experience frequent headaches.

How it can affect pregnant women: Depression is common during and after pregnancy but often goes unrecognized. Depression can be made worse by pregnancy or delivery, and suicide is a not uncommon cause of maternal death. Pregnancy is not a reason to discontinue antidepressant drugs if the medication is effective and needed. A woman being treated for depression who becomes pregnant should not discontinue medication abruptly on her own but rather discuss her treatment and condition with her medical provider. There are no adequate reports or well-controlled studies of isocarboxazid in pregnant women, and there are other medications for depression with which there is more experience during pregnancy.

How it can affect a developing embryo or fetus: There are no adequate reports or well-controlled studies in human fetuses. It is unknown whether isocarboxazid crosses the human placenta; it does cross the rat placenta. Rodent studies of birth defects have not been performed. Prolonged treatment during rodent pregnancy is associated with behavioral changes in the offspring. However, animal studies are not necessarily good indicators of how a drug will behave in humans.

Breast-feeding: There is no published data in nursing women. It is unknown whether isocarboxazid enters human breast milk.

Potential drug interactions: Interaction between the following medications and isocarboxazid has the potential to impact the effect of one or more of the drugs. In some instances the interaction can be dangerous or life-threatening and must be avoided: disulfiram or other psychotropic medications.

What the FDA says about use in pregnancy: Category C (see Appendix).

What the available evidence suggests about breast-feeding safety: Unknown.

The bottom line for you:

- Isocarboxazid should be used during pregnancy and breast-feeding only if the benefit to the woman justifies the potential risk to the fetus or newborn.
- There are alternative agents with which there is more experience during pregnancy and while breast-feeding.

ISOFLURANE

Brand name: Forane
Drug class: Anesthetic, general
Indications (what it is used for): Induction and maintenance of anesthesia.
How it works: Unknown.
Contraindications (reasons you shouldn't take it): Hypersensitivity to drug or class, history of malignant hyperthermia (a rare life-threatening rise in body temperature, usually triggered by exposure to some general anesthetics).
Possible side effects and warnings: Can cause malignant hyperthermia, muscle rigidity, rapid or irregular heart rate, blue or purple skin due to inadequate oxygen, increased pressure in the brain, liver toxicity, shivering, nausea and vomiting, delirium, and uterine relaxation. It should be used with caution in women with a head injury, increased pressure in the brain, myasthenia gravis (an autoimmune disease causing muscle weakness), or cardiac risk factors.
How it can affect pregnant women: There are no adequate reports or well-controlled studies in pregnant women. Isoflurane has been used clinically without complication in pregnancy for many years. Like other halogenated anesthetic agents, isoflurane relaxes the uterus, increasing the obstetrician's ability to perform intrauterine manipulation but also the risk of postpartum hemorrhage.
How it can affect a developing embryo or fetus: There are no adequate reports or well-controlled studies in human fetuses. Isoflurane rapidly crosses the human placenta, achieving similar concentrations

in mother and fetus. It has been used for fetal surgery and to facilitate intrauterine maneuvers. Rodent studies suggest that isoflurane can have a range of adverse effects on the fetus. For this reason, and despite the absence of human data, isoflurane is typically reserved for specific indications.

Breast-feeding: There is no published data in nursing women. It is unknown whether isoflurane enters human breast milk. However, considering the indications and dosing, one-time isoflurane use is unlikely to pose a clinically significant risk to a breast-feeding newborn.

Potential drug interactions: Isoflurane increases the relaxant effect of all muscle relaxants.

What the FDA says about use in pregnancy: Category C (see Appendix).

What the available evidence suggests about breast-feeding safety: Unknown, but likely safe.

The bottom line for you:

- There is large clinical experience with isoflurane for general anesthesia during pregnancy. Any negative effects on the human fetus have escaped detection, at least to date. Because rodent studies have raised concerns for the fetus, isoflurane is typically reserved for specific indications such as when uterine relaxation is necessary.

ISONIAZID

Brand names: Abdizide, Dipicin, Eutizon, Fetefu, INH, Isonicid, Laniazid, Niazid, Nydrazid, Nydrazyd, Rimifon

Drug class: Antimycobacterial

Indications (what it is used for): Prevention and treatment of tuberculosis (TB).

How it works: Blocks the growth and reproduction of the bacteria that cause TB.

Contraindications (reasons you shouldn't take it): Hypersensitivity to drug or class, acute liver disease.

Possible side effects and warnings: Can cause bone marrow suppression, inflammation of the optic nerve, peripheral neuropathy (nerve damage

causing numbness, tingling or pain in the hands and feet), liver toxicity, seizures, nausea and vomiting, pain in the upper abdomen, diarrhea, dizziness, rash, acne, euphoria, agitation, and ringing in the ears. It should be used with caution in women with liver or kidney dysfunction or who drink alcohol.

How it can affect pregnant women: Untreated TB in pregnancy is a significant threat to mother, fetus, and family. Women with untreated HIV along with TB are at particular risk. There are no adequate reports or well-controlled studies of isoniazid in pregnant women. There is a wide variation in how quickly people break down isoniazid by a method called acetylation. About half of blacks and whites are so-called slow acetylators; the rest are rapid acetylators. Most Eskimos and Asians are rapid acetylators. Slow acetylation may lead to higher blood levels and increase the risk of toxicity from the drug. The risk of isoniazid-induced liver inflammation is age-related and increased by alcohol use. All 4 first-line drugs for the treatment of TB (isoniazid, rifampin, ethambutol, and pyrazinamide) have an excellent safety record in pregnancy. Supplemental pyridoxine reduces the chance of nerve damage.

How it can affect a developing embryo or fetus: There are no adequate reports or well-controlled studies in human fetuses. Isoniazid crosses the human placenta but is not associated with an increased risk of malformations. Rodent studies are reassuring, revealing no evidence of birth defects or low birth weight despite the use of doses higher than those used clinically. However, animal studies are not necessarily good indicators of how a drug will behave in humans.

Breast-feeding: There are no adequate reports or well-controlled studies in nursing women. Only scant amounts of isoniazid are excreted into human breast milk. It is generally considered compatible with breast-feeding.

Potential drug interactions: Interaction between the following medications and isoniazid has the potential to impact the effect of one or more of the drugs. In some instances the interaction can be dangerous or life-threatening and must be avoided: insulin or other hypoglycemic agents, carbidopa, levodopa, fentanyl anesthesia.

What the FDA says about use in pregnancy: Category C (see Appendix).

What the available evidence suggests about breast-feeding safety: Safe.

The bottom line for you:

- Isoniazid is considered safe for use during pregnancy and while breast-feeding.

ISOTRETINOIN

Brand name: Accutane

Drug classes: Acne agent; Dermatologic; Retinoid

Indications (what it is used for): Severe cystic acne, keratinization disorders (skin cells lose their moisture and form a hard layer).

How it works: Unknown.

Contraindications (reasons you shouldn't take it): Hypersensitivity to drug or class, hypersensitivity to parabens, pregnancy.

Possible side effects and warnings: Can cause major birth defects, depression, psychosis, suicidal thoughts, liver damage, pseudotumor cerebri (increased pressure in the brain), keratinization disorders (skin cells lose their moisture and form a hard layer), inflammation in the blood vessels, cataracts, hearing impairment, bone marrow suppression, high triglyceride levels, inflammatory bowel disease, pancreatitis, blood clots, seizures, dry skin, skin fragility, itching, severe nosebleeds, pink eye, photosensitivity, joint pain, peeling of the palms, decreased night vision, ringing in the ears, and nail bed changes. It should be used with caution in women with a psychiatric disorder, who are breast-feeding or exposed to bright sunlight, or have a seizure disorder, elevated lipids, history of pancreatitis, or diabetes.

How it can affect pregnant women: Isotretinoin should not be used during pregnancy. In order to avoid the administration of isotretinoin during pregnancy, only manufacturer-approved physicians may prescribe it. Although many fail to do so, patients must be capable of complying with mandatory contraceptive measures. Women should not take St. John's wort, which can reduce the effectiveness of oral contraceptives, increasing the risk of an unplanned pregnancy. It is critical that women of childbearing age select and commit to using two forms of effective contraception simultaneously unless absolute abstinence is the chosen method, or the patient has undergone a tubal ligation or hysterectomy, or her male partner has had a vasectomy. In a study of 8,609 women between 13 and 45 years of age given their first prescription for isotretinoin, 90 became pregnant. Of these, 76 terminated their pregnancies, 3 miscarried, and 2 experienced trauma during delivery resulting in the death of their newborns. There were only 9 live births; one had an abnormality of the face and neck.

How it can affect a developing embryo or fetus: There are no adequate reports or well-controlled studies in human fetuses. Both isotretinoin and its active metabolites (substances the medication breaks down inside the body) cross the human placenta and are recognized human teratogens (substances that can cause birth defects). Multiple organ systems are affected, including the central nervous system, cardiovascular system, and endocrine glands. Mental retardation without external malformation has also been reported.

Breast-feeding: There is no published data in nursing women. It is unknown whether isotretinoin enters human breast milk. Considering its effect on the fetus, breast-feeding is contraindicated.

Potential drug interactions: Interaction between the following medications and isotretinoin has the potential to impact the effect of one or more of the drugs. In some instances the interaction can be dangerous or life-threatening and must be avoided: tetracyclines, vitamin A supplements.

What the FDA says about use in pregnancy: Category X (see Appendix).

What the available evidence suggests about breast-feeding safety: Not safe.

The bottom line for you:
- Isotretinoin is a well-documented cause of birth defects in humans and should not be used during pregnancy or while breast-feeding.
- If a woman becomes pregnant while taking isotretinoin, she should meet promptly with her obstetrician to discuss her options.

ISRADIPINE

Brand name: DynaCirc

Drug classes: Antihypertensive; Calcium channel blocker; Dihydropyridine

Indications (what it is used for): High blood pressure.

How it works: Inhibits the entry of calcium into smooth-muscle cells, which is required for their contraction.

Contraindications (reasons you shouldn't take it): Hypersensitivity to drug or class.

Possible side effects and warnings: Can cause palpitations, rapid heart rate, headache, low blood pressure, dizziness, fatigue, swelling, flushing, rash, urinary frequency, nausea and vomiting. Should be used with caution in women with congestive heart failure.

How it can affect pregnant women: There are no adequate reports or well-controlled studies in pregnant women. Isradipine has been used with success to treat preeclampsia (high blood pressure and protein in the urine during pregnancy and complications associated with it) prior to delivery with efficacy similar to methyldopa.

How it can affect a developing embryo or fetus: There are no adequate reports or well-controlled studies in human fetuses. Although isradipine crosses the human placenta and achieves a level that approximates 25% of the mother's level, the fetal circulation appears unaffected. Rodent studies are reassuring, revealing no evidence of birth defects despite the use of doses higher than those used clinically. However, animal studies are not necessarily good indicators of how a drug will behave in humans.

Breast-feeding: There is no published data in nursing women. It is unknown whether isradipine enters human breast milk.

Potential drug interactions: Interaction between the following medications and israpidine has the potential to impact the effect of one or more of the drugs. In some instances the interaction can be dangerous or life-threatening and must be avoided: cimetidine, fentanyl anesthesia.

What the FDA says about use in pregnancy: Category C (see Appendix).

What the available evidence suggests about breast-feeding safety: Unknown.

The bottom line for you:
- Calcium channel antagonists are effective for the control of high blood pressure during pregnancy. However, there are alternative agents with which there is more experience in pregnancy and breast-feeding.

IVERMECTIN

Brand names: Mectizan, Stromectol

Drug class: Antiparasitic

Indications (what it is used for): Strongyloidiasis (roundworm infection), onchocerciasis (river blindness, a parasitic disease), scabies.

How it works: Increases cell membrane permeability in nerves and muscles, leading to the parasites' death.

Contraindications (reasons you shouldn't take it): Hypersensitivity to drug or class.

Possible side effects and warnings: Can cause itching, fever, swelling, rash, swollen lymph nodes, dizziness, chest pain, abdominal distention, rapid heart rate, abnormal eye sensation, low blood pressure, and liver dysfunction.

How it can affect pregnant women: There are no adequate reports or well-controlled studies of ivermectin in pregnant women. The few published cases report no adverse effects. Further, there have been several mass exposures of pregnant women during community-based treatment of onchocerciasis. No increase in adverse pregnancy outcomes was noted.

How it can affect a developing embryo or fetus: There are no adequate reports or well-controlled studies in human fetuses. It is not known whether ivermectin crosses the human placenta. In several mass exposures of pregnant women during community-based treatment of onchocerciasis there was no increase in miscarriage or birth defects.

Breast-feeding: There are no adequate reports or well-controlled studies in nursing women. A limited amount of ivermectin reaches human breast milk and is unlikely to pose a clinically significant risk to the breast-feeding infant.

Potential drug interactions: No clinically significant drug interactions currently identified.

What the FDA says about use in pregnancy: Category C (see Appendix).

What the available evidence suggests about breast-feeding safety: Likely safe.

The bottom line for you:
- Ivermectin may be used safely during pregnancy and while breast-feeding.

KANAMYCIN

Brand names: Kantrex, Klebcil
Drug classes: Aminoglycoside; Antibiotic
Indications (what it is used for): Bacterial infection.
How it works: Blocks protein synthesis, leading to cell destruction.
Contraindications (reasons you shouldn't take it): Hypersensitivity to drug or class.
Possible side effects and warnings: Can cause kidney damage, hearing loss, ringing in the ears, inflammation of the colon, pressure inside the skull, itching, nausea and vomiting, diarrhea, weakness, tremors, muscle cramps, loss of appetite, swelling, dizziness, and low white blood cell and/or platelet counts. Should be used with caution in women with myasthenia gravis (an autoimmune disease causing muscle weakness), renal dysfunction, or vestib-

ular or cochlear implant, or who are taking other kidney-damaging drugs.

How it can affect pregnant women: There are no adequate reports or well-controlled studies in pregnant women. Kanamycin is a second-line choice for the treatment of tuberculosis but is otherwise not used widely during pregnancy.

How it can affect a developing embryo or fetus: There are no well-controlled studies in human fetuses. Case reports suggest that transfer across the human placenta is incomplete. Although there is no evidence that kanamycin causes birth defects, nerve damage in the eye was reported in one instance when an in utero–exposed newborn was treated again after birth.

Breast-feeding: There are no adequate reports or well-controlled studies in nursing women. Kanamycin enters human breast milk but is generally considered compatible with breast-feeding.

Potential drug interactions: Interaction between the following medications and kanamycin has the potential to impact the effect of one or more of the drugs. In some instances the interaction can be dangerous or life-threatening and must be avoided: beta-lactam-type antibiotics (penicillins, cephalosporins), diuretics, other antibiotics that are neurotoxic or toxic to the kidneys.

What the FDA says about use in pregnancy: Category D (see Appendix).

What the available evidence suggests about breast-feeding safety: Likely safe.

The bottom line for you:
- Kanamycin is a second choice for the treatment of tuberculosis during pregnancy.
- For most other indications, there are alternative agents with which there is more experience during pregnancy and while breast-feeding.

KETAMINE

Brand name: Ketalar
Drug class: Anesthesia, general
Indications (what it is used for): Induction of anesthesia.

How it works: Unknown.

Contraindications (reasons you shouldn't take it): Hypersensitivity to drug or class, high blood pressure, elevated intracranial pressure, glaucoma, thyrotoxicosis (overactivity of the thyroid gland), congestive heart failure, psychosis.

Possible side effects and warnings: Can cause increased intracranial pressure, laryngospasm, increased intraocular pressure, low or high blood pressure, slow heart rate, poor heart function, delirium, excess saliva, nausea and vomiting, tremors, double vision, involuntary eye movements, twitching, depressed reflexes, and hallucinations. Should be used with caution in women with liver dysfunction or gastroesophageal reflux disease (GERD).

How it can affect pregnant women: Ketamine is a rapid-acting general anesthetic. There are no adequate reports or well-controlled studies in pregnant women. It is popular for cesarean delivery for women who are bleeding heavily or have asthma (the increased release of catecholamines improves bronchospasm), or if the fetus is thought to have an increased acid level. Women given ketamine for cesarean delivery have a lower need for pain medication postoperatively compared to those who received thiopental. There is reportedly an increased incidence of dreaming during anesthesia. Ketamine has also been used in women undergoing C-section with spinal analgesia. In some studies, low-dose ketamine given intravenously with a spinal provided longer analgesia after the cesarean section and lower postoperative need for pain relief.

How it can affect a developing embryo or fetus: There are no adequate reports or well-controlled studies in human fetuses. A number of rodent studies suggest that ketamine may alter behavior after delivery and affect the sense of taste. In sheep, ketamine reduced the adverse effects of poor brain blood flow. For this reason, ketamine may be of use with low oxygen levels in a fetus.

Breast-feeding: There are no adequate reports or well-controlled studies in nursing women. It is unknown whether ketamine enters human breast milk. However, considering how it is used, it is unlikely that a clinically significant amount of drug remains in breast milk 48 hours after surgery.

Potential drug interactions: Prolonged recovery time may occur if barbiturates and/or narcotics are used at the same time as ketamine.

What the FDA says about use in pregnancy: Category D (see Appendix).

What the available evidence suggests about breast-feeding safety: Likely safe.

The bottom line for you:
- Ketamine appears safe and effective when used during pregnancy and while breast-feeding.

KETOCONAZOLE

Brand names: Fugen, Funazole, Fungazol, Funginox, Nizoral, Zoralin

Drug class: Antifungal

Indications (what it is used for): Fungal infections such as tinea versicolor (skin), tinea capitis (scalp), tinea corporis (ringworm, usually on the arms, legs, or trunk), tinea cruris (jock itch), tinea pedis (athlete's foot), and candidiasis (yeast infection).

How it works: Inhibits cell membrane synthesis, killing the fungus.

Contraindications (reasons you shouldn't take it): Hypersensitivity to drug or class; low stomach acid production; fungal meningitis; use of astemizole, cisapride, or terfenadine.

Possible side effects and warnings: Can cause liver failure or toxicity, adrenal insufficiency, nausea and vomiting, diarrhea, dizziness, headache, lethargy, nervousness, sleepiness, hemolytic anemia, low white blood cell and/or platelet counts, and rash. Should be used with caution in women who have liver dysfunction or are taking drugs that can be toxic to the liver.

How it can affect pregnant women: There are no adequate reports or well-controlled studies in pregnant women. Ketoconazole inhibits the activities of aromatase, an enzyme essential for the production of sex hormones. Although the drug is absorbed when applied topically, the blood level achieved is relatively low.

How it can affect a developing embryo or fetus: There are no adequate reports or well-controlled studies in human fetuses. Several studies suggest that ketoconazole interferes with ovarian synthesis of progesterone by inhibiting the enzyme aromatase, which means that it could theoretically interfere with implantation and maintenance of the embryo in early pregnancy. Limited epidemiological studies are reassuring, showing no evidence that it causes birth defects or low birth weight. In rodent studies, ketoconazole caused maternal toxicity along with hand and foot malformations of offspring when given at 10 times the maximum recommended clinical dose. However, animal studies are not necessarily good indicators of how a drug will behave in humans.

Breast-feeding: Only a trace amount of maternally administered ketoconazole enters human breast milk, and it is generally considered safe during breast-feeding.

Potential drug interactions: Interaction between the following medications and ketoconazole has the potential to impact the effect of one or more of the drugs. In some instances the interaction can be dangerous or life-threatening and must be avoided: terfenadine, astemizole, cisapride, cyclosporine, tacrolimus, methylprednisolone, midazolam, triazolam, oral hypoglycemic agents, rifampin, isoniazid, alcohol.

What the FDA says about use in pregnancy: Category C (see Appendix).

What the available evidence suggests about breast-feeding safety: Safe.

The bottom line for you:
- Topical ketoconazole may be used during pregnancy and while breast-feeding.
- Intravenous ketoconazole should be reserved for life-threatening fungal infections.

KETOPROFEN

Brand names: Alrhumat, Kefenid, Orudis, Oruvail

Drug classes: Analgesic, nonnarcotic; Nonsteroidal anti-inflammatory drug (NSAID)

Indications (what it is used for): Mild to moderate pain, fever, dysmenorrhea (pain during menstruation), osteoarthritis, and rheumatoid arthritis.

How it works: Reduces the synthesis of prostaglandins, which cause the cramping and pain.

Contraindications (reasons you shouldn't take it): Hypersensitivity to drug or class, aspirin- or NSAID-induced asthma.

Possible side effects and warnings: Can cause kidney failure, fluid retention, heartburn, gastrointestinal bleeding, bronchospasm, inflammation in the kidneys, liver toxicity, Stevens-Johnson syndrome (a rare but serious skin reaction to medication), headache, nausea, constipation, abdominal pain, dizziness, rash, low white blood cell and/or platelet counts, ringing in the ears, and drowsiness. Should be used with caution in women with high blood pressure, congestive heart failure, nasal polyps, or liver or kidney dysfunction, or a history of gastrointestinal bleeding.

How it can affect pregnant women: There are no adequate reports or well-controlled studies in pregnant women. Ketoprofen provides effective pain relief after both vaginal and cesarean delivery; its efficacy is similar to that of other NSAIDs.

How it can affect a developing embryo or fetus: There are no adequate reports or well-controlled studies in human fetuses. Ketoprofen rapidly crosses the placenta, reaching a level equal to that of the mother. Most other NSAIDs decrease fetal urine production and are associated with premature closure or narrowing of a blood vessel that shunts blood away from the lungs. Its closure leads to tricuspid valve incompetence, heart failure, and high blood pressure in the lungs, all of which could cause long-term damage. Stopping the drug appears to reverse this process. A case report suggests that ketoprofen has the same actions. It is best to avoid repeated dosing of NSAIDs after 32 weeks' gestation. Acute kidney failure is reported in preterm infants whose mothers received ketoprofen prior to delivery. Rodent studies revealed no evidence of birth defects or low birth weight. However, animal studies are not necessarily good indicators of how a drug will behave in humans.

Breast-feeding: Low concentrations of ketoprofen are found in human breast milk, but the amount consumed by a breast-fed infant is clinically irrelevant.

Potential drug interactions: Interaction between the following medications and ketoprofen has the potential to impact the effect of one or more of the drugs. In some instances the interaction can be dangerous or life-threatening and must be avoided: ACE inhibitors, furosemide, thiazides, diuretics, lithium, probenecid, warfarin.

What the FDA says about use in pregnancy: Category C (see Appendix).

What the available evidence suggests about use breast-feeding safety: Safe.

The bottom line for you:

- Ketoprofen is an excellent agent for pain relief during delivery. However, there are other NSAIDs with which there is more experience during pregnancy that are unassociated with strong effects on the kidney.
- Ketoprofen is safe for use while breast-feeding.
- As with all NSAIDs, sustained use should be avoided after 32 weeks.

KETOROLAC TROMETHAMINE

Brand names: Acular, Acular PF, Toradol

Drug classes: Analgesic, nonnarcotic; Nonsteroidal anti-inflammatory drug (NSAID)

Indications (what it is used for): Moderate to severe pain.

How it works: Reduces the synthesis of prostaglandins, which cause the cramping and pain.

Contraindications (reasons you shouldn't take it): Hypersensitivity to drug or class, aspirin- or NSAID-induced asthma, cerebrovascular hemorrhage. Should not be used 7 days before and after surgery, to avoid excess bleeding.

Possible side effects and warnings: Can cause kidney failure, fluid retention, heartburn, gastrointestinal bleeding, bronchospasm, inflammation in the kidneys, liver toxicity, Stevens-Johnson syndrome (a rare but serious skin reaction to medication), headache, nausea, constipation, abdominal pain, dizziness, rash, low white blood cell and/or platelet counts, ringing in the ears, and drowsiness. Should be used with caution in women with high blood pressure, congestive heart failure, a history of gastrointestinal bleeding, nasal polyps, or liver or kidney dysfunction.

How it can affect pregnant women: Ketorolac is indicated for the management of pain that otherwise would require an opioid for relief. There are no adequate reports or well-controlled studies in pregnant women. It should not be used to inhibit labor.

How it can affect a developing embryo or fetus: There are no adequate reports or well-controlled studies in human fetuses. It is unknown whether ketorolac crosses the placenta. Most other NSAIDs decrease fetal urine production and are associated with premature closure or narrowing of a blood vessel that shunts blood away from the lungs. Its closure leads to tricuspid valve incompetence, heart failure, and high blood pressure in the lungs, all of which could cause long-term damage. Stopping the drug appears to reverse this process. It is not known whether ketorolac has the same actions. It is best to avoid repeated dosing of NSAIDs after 32 weeks' gestation. Rodent studies are reassuring, revealing no evidence of birth defects or low birth weight. However, animal studies are not necessarily good indicators of how a drug will behave in humans.

Breast-feeding: Small quantities of ketorolac enter human breast milk.

Potential drug interactions: Interaction between the following medications and ketorolac has the potential to impact the effect of one or more of the drugs. In some instances the interaction can be dangerous or life-threatening and must be avoided: furosemide, probenecid, lithium, methotrexate, psychoactive drugs (e.g., alprazolam, fluoxetine, thiothixene).

What the FDA says about use in pregnancy: Category C (see Appendix).

What the available evidence suggests about breast-feeding safety: Safe.

The bottom line for you:

- Ketorolac is an excellent analgesic, but there are other NSAIDs with which there is more experience during pregnancy and while breast-feeding.

LABETALOL

Brand names: Coreton, Normadate, Normodyne, Trandate

Drug classes: Adrenergic antagonist; Alpha- and beta-blocker; Antihypertensive

Indications (what it is used for): High blood pressure.

How it works: Blocks both alpha- and beta-adrenergic receptors, whose activation causes the high blood pressure.

Contraindications (reasons you shouldn't take it): Hypersensitivity to drug or class, asthma, congestive heart failure, cardiogenic shock, slow or irregular heart rate, liver toxicity, low blood glucose level.

Possible side effects and warnings: Can cause liver damage, systemic lupus erythematosus (SLE; a chronic inflammatory disease in which the immune system attacks the body's own tissues and organs), bronchospasm, dizziness, nausea and vomiting, fatigue, heartburn, runny nose, shortness of breath, swelling, low blood pressure when sitting or standing, itching, and kidney damage. Should be used with caution in women with chest pain, diabetes, or liver or kidney dysfunction, or who have had recent major surgery, have a history of heart attack, or use cocaine. The medication should not be withdrawn abruptly.

How it can affect pregnant women: High blood pressure complicates 5–10% of pregnancies and is a leading cause of death and disability for both mother and child. Severe high blood pressure should be treated rapidly to reduce the chance of stroke, death, and possibly eclampsia (seizures brought on by severe high blood pressure in pregnancy) in preeclamptic women. Labetalol is better tolerated than methyldopa and provides more efficient control of blood pressure. Although there is no consensus as to whether mild to moderate chronically high blood pressure should be treated during pregnancy, the risks of temporary severe high blood pressure (hospitalization of mother and child after birth, protein in the mother's urine at delivery, respiratory distress in the newborn) may all be decreased by treatment. Labetalol is the drug of choice for women with high blood pressure who have a rapid heart rate, and it has a lower risk than intravenous hydralazine of causing dangerously low blood pressure. It is also used during pregnancy to control the side effects of hyperthyroidism (an overactive thyroid).

How it can affect a developing embryo or fetus: Labetalol crosses the human placenta, reaching a level in the fetus that is about half that of the mother. At typical doses, labetalol does not alter blood flow through the placenta and through the fetus. A slow heart rate, low blood pressure, low blood glucose level, and a thickening of the heart muscles are all reported in either the fetuses or newborns of women who took large doses of labetalol chronically by mouth or intravenously. Fetal death has also been reported when a mother's blood pressure dropped profoundly and rapidly in response to intravenous labetalol. This overresponse can be minimized by adequate hydration. Overall, newborn outcome is similar to that achieved with hydralazine, another medication often used in the past to treat severe high blood pressure before birth. Rodent studies are reassuring, revealing no evidence of birth defects or excess low birth weight despite the use of doses higher than those used clinically. However, animal studies are not necessarily good indicators of how a drug will behave in humans.

Breast-feeding: There is no consistent relationship

between the maternal blood level of labetalol and the concentrations found in breast milk. There is a risk that treatment with labetalol during breast-feeding could cause a low blood glucose level in the newborn; this can be minimized by supplementing with glucose-fortified formula.

Potential drug interactions: Labetalol has the potential to interact dangerously (in some cases, fatally) with a number of medications, including anesthetic agents, tricyclic antidepressants (TCAs), beta-agonists (used for the treatment of asthma), cimetidine, nitroglycerine, and calcium agonists such as verapamil.

What the FDA says about use in pregnancy: Category C (see Appendix).

What the available evidence suggests about breast-feeding safety: Safe.

The bottom line for you:

- Labetalol is an effective agent for the treatment of sudden high blood pressure and severe hyperthyroidism during labor.
- It is a first-line oral treatment for chronically high blood pressure during pregnancy.
- Low blood glucose level is the most common adverse effect for the newborn, which can be minimized by supplementing with glucose-fortified formula.

LACTULOSE

Brand names: Acilac, C-Cephulose, Cephulac, Cholac, Constilac, Constulose, Duphalac, Enulose, Evalose, Generlac, Heptalac, Laxilose

Drug classes: Gastrointestinal; Laxative

Indications (what it is used for): Constipation, liver encephalopathy (liver is no longer able to remove toxic substances from the blood).

How it works: Increases stool water content and traps ammonium ions in the bowels.

Contraindications (reasons you shouldn't take it): Hypersensitivity to drug or class, galactosemia (inability to use the sugar galactose).

Possible side effects and warnings: Can cause a

buildup of acid in the blood, abdominal distention and pain, belching, diarrhea, loss of appetite, nausea and vomiting, electrolyte disorders, and flatulence. It should be used with caution in women with diabetes or low potassium levels.

How it can affect pregnant women: Constipation is common during pregnancy. Lactulose helps restore normal bowel habits. Women with lactose intolerance actually tolerate lactulose better in the third trimester because pregnancy slows bowel motility. It is used by some doctors to maintain a soft stool after deliveries that are complicated by tearing into the rectum.

How it can affect a developing embryo or fetus: There are no adequate reports or well-controlled studies of lactulose in human fetuses. Because little lactulose is absorbed by the mother, it is unlikely that the mother's blood concentration will reach a clinically relevant level that could present a risk to a fetus.

Breast-feeding: There is no published data in nursing women. It is unknown whether lactulose enters human breast milk. Because so little is absorbed by the mother, it is unlikely that the milk concentration could reach a clinically relevant level for a breast-feeding baby.

Potential drug interactions: Avoid neomycin and other laxatives.

What the FDA says about use in pregnancy: Category B (see Appendix).

What the available evidence suggests about breast-feeding safety: Safe.

The bottom line for you:

- Most laxatives are relatively safe during pregnancy and while breast-feeding.

LAMIVUDINE

Brand names: Epivir, Epivir HBV, 3TC

Drug classes: Antiviral; Nucleoside reverse transcriptase inhibitor

Indications (what it is used for): HIV infection, hepatitis B infection (HBV).

How it works: Inhibits the protein reverse transcriptase, necessary for the virus to replicate.

Contraindications (reasons you shouldn't take it): Hypersensitivity to drug or class.

Possible side effects and warnings: Can cause an accumulation of acid in the blood, fatty liver or toxicity, pancreatitis, neuropathy (nerve pain), low white blood cell or platelet counts, muscle breakdown, and worsening of hepatitis B. It should be used with caution in women with liver or kidney dysfunction, pancreatitis, or who are on long-term lamivudine therapy or are obese.

How it can affect pregnant women: There are no adequate reports or well-controlled studies of lamivudine in pregnant women. Triple therapy (zidovudine, lamivudine, nevirapine) is a highly effective treatment for HIV, and therapy that reduces the viral load lowers the risk of a mother transmitting the virus to her child. The goal of treatment is an undetectable viral load. Liver toxicity, which occurs usually within 5 months of beginning therapy, is a major concern during pregnancy. It is most severe if a mother also has hepatitis B and C. Lamivudine is one of two drugs used for the treatment of hepatitis B during pregnancy; interferon alfa-2b is the other. The initial response to lamivudine is better than the response to treatment with interferon alfa-2b.

How it can affect a developing embryo or fetus: An estimated 1 million children are born each year to HIV-infected mothers. Without maternal treatment, about 25% become infected. Maternal zidovudine reduces the rate of transmission to the newborn to less than 10%, with an even greater reduction if combined with lamivudine. Newborns are typically treated with both zidovudine and lamivudine within 12 hours of birth to prevent transmission of the virus.

Mitochondrial disorders (disorders caused by dysfunctional mitochondria, the "powerhouses" of the cell) have been reported in children exposed in utero to some reverse transcriptase enzyme inhibitors (e.g., zidovudine). Rodent studies are reassuring, revealing no evidence of birth defects or very low birth weight despite the use of doses higher than those used clinically. Given the great benefit of preventing HIV transmission from mother to child, these highly successful drugs will continue to be used during pregnancy; however, some evidence for gene toxicity suggests that exposed children should be closely observed into adulthood for the early detection of cancers due to the gene damage.

Breast-feeding: There are no adequate reports or well-controlled studies in nursing women. Lamivudine is excreted into human breast milk. If infant formula is available, breast-feeding is usually not recommended when a mother is HIV positive because HIV can be transmitted to the newborn in the breast milk. Antiretroviral agents administered during the third trimester and after delivery reach levels in breast milk that are similar to or higher than plasma concentrations and can significantly reduce HIV levels. This supports the idea of treating the mother to reduce the risk of breast-feeding-associated transmission in areas where there is no formula.

Potential drug interactions: The combined use of lamivudine and zalcitabine is not recommended.

What the FDA says about use in pregnancy: Category C (see Appendix).

What the available evidence suggests about breast-feeding safety: Not safe.

The bottom line for you:

- A cocktail of lamivudine, zidovudine, and nevirapine significantly reduces the risk of mother-to-child transmission both during pregnancy and after delivery, and it remains a standard treatment for adult HIV infection.
- Pregnant women should be monitored closely for liver toxicity after initiating therapy.
- Pregnant women treated for HIV are encouraged to register with the Antiretroviral Pregnancy Registry (1-800-258-4263) to help gather important information about the safety and efficacy of the treatment during pregnancy. The registry can also be a good source of information on taking the medication during pregnancy.
- If infant formula is available, breast-feeding is usually not recommended when a mother is HIV

positive because HIV can be transmitted to the newborn in the breast milk. In areas where formula is not available, treatment during breast-feeding may help reduce the risk of transmission.

LAMOTRIGINE

Brand name: Lamictal
Drug class: Anticonvulsant
Indications (what it is used for): Seizures (partial).
How it works: Unknown.
Contraindications (reasons you shouldn't take it): Hypersensitivity to drug or class.
Possible side effects and warnings: Can cause rash (in some cases, life-threatening), menstrual cramps, dizziness, lack of muscle coordination, sleepiness, blurred or double vision, headache, nausea and vomiting, heartburn, runny nose, anxiety, pain, weight loss, chest pain, infection, bone marrow failure, hemolytic anemia, liver failure, difficulty using language to communicate, confusion, and involuntary eye movement. Should be used with caution in women with liver or kidney dysfunction or who have an allergy to valproate. Avoid abrupt withdrawal of the medication.
How it can affect pregnant women: Women on medication for a seizure disorder should (when possible) plan their pregnancies. They should discuss the optimal medication with their neurologist and begin appropriate supplemental folate therapy before conception (4 mg per day) to minimize the risk of birth defects. The risks of birth defects associated with antiseizure medications must be weighed against the risks of continued seizures to both the mother and fetus. Women who become pregnant during treatment should not stop treatment on their own but should meet quickly with their doctor before making a decision.

There are no adequate reports or well-controlled studies of lamotrigine during pregnancy. However, lamotrigine is by far the most extensively studied of the newer antiepileptic drugs. Its clearance from the body (how fast the body processes and eliminates the drug) is increased during pregnancy, and many women require a higher dose to maintain seizure control. Lamotrigine is an inhibitor of folate production (which is necessary for the growth of a healthy baby), so folate supplementation before conception is wise. The most frequent adverse maternal effect is skin rash, typically in the first month of treatment.
How it can affect a developing embryo or fetus: There are no adequate reports or well-controlled studies in human fetuses. Lamotrigine crosses the human placenta, achieving levels similar to those in the mother. Women taking anticonvulsant medication of any type have twice the risk of having a child with a birth defect compared to the normal risk of 2–4%. Rodent studies are reassuring, revealing no evidence of birth defects or increased low birth weight at doses similar to those used clinically. However, the highest doses caused maternal and fetal toxicity characterized by low birth weight and heart dilation. Animal studies are not necessarily good indicators of how a drug will behave in humans.

A recently completed post-marketing study revealed that the combination of valproate and lamotrigine posed a particularly high risk for birth defects (12%). There was no evidence lamotrigine alone or in combination with other anticonvulsants increased the overall rate of birth defects. Using only one medication at the lowest effective amount, given in divided doses to avoid the peak levels, helps minimize those risks.
Breast-feeding: Nursed infants have blood levels approximating 30% of the mother's plasma level. Although no adverse effects have been reported, breast-fed infants should be monitored closely. The concentration of lamotrigine in milk is highest 1 to 4 hours after the dose. The drug should be given at the lowest effective dose and breast-feeding avoided at times of peak drug levels.

Potential drug interactions: Avoid combining with other anticonvulsants such as carbamazepine, oxcarbazepine, valproate, phenobarbital, phenytoin, primidone, or rifampin. Dosage adjustments may be necessary for women taking oral contraceptives. There is the potential for decreased contraceptive efficacy and women should promptly report changes in their menstrual pattern (e.g., breakthrough bleeding).

What the FDA says about use in pregnancy: Category C (see Appendix).

What the available evidence suggests about breast-feeding safety: Likely safe.

The bottom line for you:

- When necessary for seizure control, lamotrigine is a reasonable option for use during pregnancy.
- Folate supplementation prior to conception may reduce the risk of associated birth defects.
- Lamotrigine is well tolerated and drug interactions are modest.
- Lamotrigine is likely safe for use while breast-feeding when coupled with close observation.

LANSOPRAZOLE

Brand names: Lopral, Ogastro, Prevacid, Zoton

Drug classes: Gastrointestinal; Proton pump inhibitor

Indications (what it is used for): Gastroesophageal reflux disease (GERD), esophagitis, gastric or duodenal ulcer, *H. pylori* infection (bacterial infection of the stomach), hypersecretory conditions, stress ulcer, ulcer prevention.

How it works: Blocks the release of stomach acid.

Contraindications (reasons you shouldn't take it): Hypersensitivity to drug or class.

Possible side effects and warnings: Can cause liver failure, a variety of blood disorders; Stevens-Johnson syndrome, toxic epidermal necrolysis, and erythema multiforme (all skin disorders); pancreatitis; headache; diarrhea; weakness; yeast infection; chest pain; cerebrovascular disease (narrowing of blood vessels that supply the brain); high or low blood pressure; heart attack; and palpitations. Should be used with caution in women who have been using it for a long time or who have liver dysfunction.

How it can affect pregnant women: Gastroesophageal reflux disease and/or heartburn occurs in 45–85% of pregnant women in part because of high progesterone and estrogen levels. The treatment for GERD consists of reducing gastric acidity starting with lifestyle and dietary changes. If these fail, antacids or sucralfate are first-line medical therapies, followed by histamine receptor blockers. Ranitidine is generally preferred because of its documented efficacy and safety profile in pregnancy, even in the first trimester. Proton pump inhibitors such as lansoprazole are reserved for when these approaches do not work. In those cases, proton pump inhibitors are considered effective and safe treatment for GERD without reported adverse effects.

How it can affect a developing embryo or fetus: There are no well-controlled studies in human fetuses. It is unknown whether lansoprazole crosses the human placenta. Epidemiologic and postmarketing studies (studies done by a drug's manufacturer after the drug is on the market) are reassuring, and rodent studies revealed no evidence of birth defects or low birth weight despite the use of doses higher than those used clinically. However, animal studies are not necessarily good indicators of how a drug will behave in humans.

Breast-feeding: There is no published data in nursing women. It is unknown whether lansoprazole enters human breast milk. It is excreted into rodent milk.

Potential drug interactions: Interaction between the following medications and lansoprazole has the potential to impact the effect of one or more of the drugs. In some instances the interaction can be dangerous or life-threatening and must be avoided: ampicillin, digoxin, iron, ketoconazole, theophylline, warfarin.

What the FDA says about use in pregnancy: Category B (see Appendix).

What the available evidence suggests about breast-feeding safety: Unknown.

The bottom line for you:

- Lansoprazole is generally considered safe and effective for use during pregnancy and while breast-feeding if other treatments fail.

LETROZOLE

Brand name: Femara

Drug class: Antineoplastic, aromatase inhibitor

Indications (what it is used for): Breast cancer.

How it works: Inhibits aromatase, a protein that makes estrogens.

Contraindications (reasons you shouldn't take it): Hypersensitivity to drug or class.

Possible side effects and warnings: Can cause blood clots, muscle pain, nausea and vomiting, fatigue, joint pain, abdominal pain, cough, chest pain, hot flashes, diarrhea, viral infection, swelling, high blood pressure, and loss of appetite. Should be used with caution in women with kidney dysfunction.

How it can affect pregnant women: Breast cancer is not infrequently detected and treated in pregnant women. Letrozole is a nonsteroidal aromatase inhibitor that significantly lowers estrogen levels in women with estrogen-sensitive breast cancer. Letrozole has also been used to treat infertility associated with poor response to FSH (follicle-stimulating hormone) administration. Letrozole is more than 95% effective for medical termination of a pregnancy under 9 weeks gestation when combined with misoprostil.

How it can affect a developing embryo or fetus: There are no well-controlled studies in human fetuses. It is unknown whether letrozole crosses the human placenta. The limited clinical experience suggests that there is no difference in the overall rates of major and minor congenital malformations (birth defects) among newborns of women who conceived after letrozole or clomiphene treatments. Since estrogen affects placental blood vessel growth in humans, letrozole could impact embryo implantation. Letrozole use during rodent pregnancy was toxic to embryos and fetuses and caused birth defects even at low doses. However, animal studies are not necessarily good indicators of how a drug will behave in humans.

Breast-feeding: There is no published data in nursing women. It is unknown whether letrozole enters human breast milk.

Potential drug interactions: Interaction between the following medications and letrozole has the potential to impact the effect of one or more of the drugs. In some instances the interaction can be dangerous or life-threatening and must be avoided: tamoxifen.

What the FDA says about use in pregnancy: Category X (see Appendix).

What the available evidence suggests about breast-feeding safety: Unknown.

The bottom line for you:

- Letrozole is a secondary agent for the treatment of breast cancer and is used during pregnancy only for life-threatening disease, since estrogen is important for the woman's adaptation to pregnancy.
- The risk of birth defects is likely small, though the risk of miscarriage is high with first trimester exposure.
- As women taking letrozole have breast cancer, it is likely that breast-feeding is not an option.

LEUCOVORIN

Brand names: Calcium folinate, citrovorum factor, Lerderfoline, Ledervorin-Calcium, Wellcovorin

Drug classes: Antidote; Toxicology; Vitamin/mineral

Indications (what it is used for): Rescue from profound folate inhibition.

How it works: Bypasses folate blockers.

Contraindications (reasons you shouldn't take it): Hypersensitivity to drug or class, vitamin B_{12} deficiency, pernicious anemia (intestines cannot absorb vitamin B_{12}), megaloblastic anemia (anemia with larger than normal red blood cells).

Possible side effects and warnings: Can cause life-threatening allergic reaction, seizures, fainting, nausea and vomiting, and hives. Should be used with caution in women with a seizure disorder.

How it can affect pregnant women: Leucovorin is used if a woman develops unregulated growth of the placenta, which can be either benign or cancerous. Most women are treated with surgery, but some require chemotherapy with methotrexate. Methotrexate blocks the generation of folic acid, which the tumor needs for growth, but the medication can persist in the woman's tissue for long periods after treatment. Leucovorin overcomes that block of folic acid synthesis caused by methotrexate, minimizing the toxicity associated with the medication. This enables high doses of methotrexate to be used.

How it can affect a developing embryo or fetus: There are no adequate reports or well-controlled studies in human fetuses. Folate is quickly transferred across the placenta, and most prenatal vitamins contain 0.8 mg. A wide range of birth defects are linked to folate deficiency, including spina bifida (an opening in the spine) and other fetal neural tube defects, and 4 mg of folate daily prior to conception can help prevent their recurrence in women with a history of them. In fact, mass folate supplementation in the nation's food sources has been associated with a reduction in the rate of numerous birth defects. It is suggested that high levels of folate supplementation might also blunt the negative impact of antiepileptic drugs on the fetus. Evidence has emerged that vitamin B12 deficiency may also increase the risk of fetal neural tube defects. Studies of birth defects in rodents have not been conducted.

Breast-feeding: There is no published data in nursing women. It is unknown whether leucovorin enters human breast milk. Folate does.

Potential drug interactions: Interaction between the following medications and leucovorin has the potential to impact the effect of one or more of the drugs. In some instances the interaction can be dangerous or life-threatening and must be avoided: phenobarbital, phenytoin, primidone, 5-fluorouracil, methotrexate.

What the FDA says about use in pregnancy: Category C (see Appendix).

What the available evidence suggests about breast-feeding safety: Unknown.

The bottom line for you:

- Leucovorin is used during pregnancy and while breast-feeding only in women being treated with methotrexate for life-threatening disease.

LEUPROLIDE

Brand names: Lupron, Procren

Drug class: Antineoplastic, hormone modifier

Indications (what it is used for): Endometriosis, uterine fibroids.

How it works: Inhibits the release of the gonadotropins from the pituitary by suppressing ovarian hormone production.

Contraindications (reasons you shouldn't take it): Hypersensitivity to drug or class, undiagnosed vaginal bleeding.

Possible side effects and warnings: Can cause angina (chest pain), irregular heart rate, heart attack, blood clots in the lungs, spinal cord compression, paralysis, bone density loss, erythema multiforme (a skin disorder), decreased sex drive, thyroid enlargement, anxiety, blurred vision, lethargy, memory disorder, mood swings, itching, nervousness, numbness, tingling, cough, pleural rub (squeaking or grating sounds when breathing), pneumonia, dry skin, bruising, hair loss, local skin reactions, pigmentation, skin lesions, scarring in the lungs, burning with urination, incontinence, low white blood cell count, coughing up blood, pelvic fibrosis, hair growth, and low blood protein levels. Should be used with caution in women with bone metastases, osteoporosis, psychiatric disorder, or depression.

How it can affect pregnant women: Gonadotropin-releasing agonists are important treatments for infertility and are often used with IVF (in vitro fertilization). There are no adequate reports or well-controlled studies of leuprolide during pregnancy, nor are there indications for its use after conception has been achieved.

How it can affect a developing embryo or fetus: There are no adequate reports or well-controlled studies in human fetuses. It is unknown whether leuprolide crosses the human placenta. No birth defects are reported in women inadvertently exposed to leuprolide during pregnancy. Theoretically, early exposure of a male fetus could lead to a very small penis, since leuprolide interferes with the action of testosterone; however, there are no reports of this happening. Rodent studies revealed an increase in the rate of major birth defects and low birth weight as the dose increased. However, animal studies are not necessarily good indicators of how a drug will behave in humans.

Breast-feeding: There is no published data in nursing women. It is unknown whether leuprolide enters human breast milk. There is no indication for its use while breast-feeding.

Potential drug interactions: No clinically relevant drug interactions currently identified.

What the FDA says about use in pregnancy: Category X (see Appendix).

What the available evidence suggests about breast-feeding safety: Unknown.

The bottom line for you:

- Leuprolide should not be used during pregnancy. Barrier contraception (e.g., condom, diaphragm) is recommended if therapy is initiated for indications other than infertility.
- There is no indication for leuprolide while breast-feeding.
- No malformations (birth defects) have been reported in women inadvertently exposed to leuprolide.

LEVETIRACETAM
Brand name: Keppra
Drug class: Anticonvulsant

Indications (what it is used for): Partial-onset seizure disorder.

How it works: Unknown.

Contraindications (reasons you shouldn't take it): Hypersensitivity to drug or class.

Possible side effects and warnings: Can cause nausea and vomiting, suicide attempts, psychosis, low white blood cell count, bone marrow suppression, sleepiness, weakness, dizziness, lack of muscle coordination, agitation, anxiety, behavior changes, anemia, cough, runny nose, and double vision. Should be used with caution in women with kidney dysfunction or depression. Avoid stopping the drug abruptly.

How it can affect pregnant women: Women on medication for a seizure disorder should (when possible) plan their pregnancies, discuss the optimal medication with their neurologist, and begin appropriate supplemental folate therapy before conception (4 mg per day) to minimize the risk of birth defects. The risks of birth defects associated with antiseizure medications must be weighed against the risks of continued seizures to both the mother and fetus. Women who become pregnant during treatment should not stop treatment on their own but should meet quickly with their doctor before making a decision.

Studies of small groups of women indicate that levetiracetam is well tolerated during pregnancy. The maternal clearance of the drug from the body (how fast the body processes and eliminates it) increases, which often necessitates a higher dose as a pregnancy advances.

How it can affect a developing embryo or fetus: There are no adequate reports or well-controlled studies in human fetuses. In a series of 11 exposed pregnancies, there were 3 newborns with low birth weight. Levetiracetam crosses the human placenta. In the laboratory, combining the antiseizure medications carbamazepine or topiramate with phenytoin can increase cell death. This illustrates the increased risk of using more than one anticonvulsant during pregnancy. In contrast, cotreatment with levetiracetam and carbamazepine does not enhance cell death in the developing brain. Thus, it may be possible to avoid the risk of fetal brain damage by choosing the right combination of drugs. Levetiracetam, alone or in combination, is a promising candidate for the treatment of seizures during pregnancy and for newborn seizure disorders. Rodent studies conducted using doses in excess of the maximum recommended human dose have been harmful to embryos and increased the prevalence of skeletal malformations. However, animal studies are not necessarily good indicators of how a drug will behave in humans.

Breast-feeding: Levetiracetam enters human breast milk. The plasma levels in breast-fed newborns are between 10–15% of the mother's level and likely do not pose a risk to a breast-feeding infant. There are, however, alternative agents with which there is more experience during pregnancy and while breast-feeding.

Potential drug interactions: Laboratory data indicate that levetiracetam is unlikely to produce, or be subject to, drug interactions.

What the FDA says about use in pregnancy: Category C (see Appendix).

What the available evidence suggests about breast-feeding safety: Unknown.

The bottom line for you:

- Levetiracetam should be used during pregnancy and while breast-feeding only if the benefit to the woman justifies the potential risk to the embryo, fetus, or newborn. There are alternative agents with which there is more experience.
- A breast-fed newborn whose mother is taking levetiracetam should be watched closely for sleepiness and poor feeding.
- Women being treated with levetiracetam during pregnancy are encouraged to register with the UCB Antiepileptic Drugs (AED) Pregnancy Registry (1-888-537-7734) to help gather better information on pregnancy outcomes. The registry can also be a source of information for women undergoing treatment.

LEVOFLOXACIN

Brand names: Cravit, Lesacin, Levaquin, Quixin
Drug classes: Antibiotic; Quinolone
Indications (what it is used for): Bacterial infections susceptible to the antibiotic.
How it works: Inhibits bacterial topoisomerase IV and DNA gyrase, required for DNA replication, transcription, repair, and recombination.
Contraindications (reasons you shouldn't take it): Hypersensitivity to drug or class, prolongation of the QT interval, use of other antiarrhythmic drugs.
Possible side effects and warnings: Can cause tendon inflammation and rupture, nausea and vomiting, vaginal yeast infection, phototoxicity (skin and/or eye reaction to sunlight and other forms of light), infection of the colon, anemia, seizures, psychosis, joint pain, restlessness, light-headedness, anxiety, agitation, confusion, liver dysfunction, heartburn, and taste changes. Should be used with caution in women with liver or kidney dysfunction, seizure disorders, dehydration, low levels of potassium in the blood, diabetes, a slow heart rate, or deterioration of the heart muscle. Avoid sun exposure while using levofloxacin.
How it can affect pregnant women: There are no adequate reports or well-controlled studies of levofloxacin in pregnant women. Levofloxacin has fewer adverse gastrointestinal or nervous system side effects than other quinolones. Levofloxacin should not be used for the treatment of gonorrhea because resistant strains have developed. Vaginal yeast infection is a side effect more frequently associated with quinolones such as levofloxacin than with other antibiotics.
How it can affect a developing embryo or fetus: There are no adequate reports or well-controlled studies in human fetuses. Only a small amount (less than 4%) of maternal levofloxacin (and ofloxacin) crosses the human placenta, making it a poor drug to treat infection in the amniotic fluid. Some, but not all, quinolones produced bone joint inflammation, interfering with cartilage growth in the exposed

offspring of mice, dogs, and rabbits, and it is this toxicity that led to their restricted use in pregnant women. Use of quinolones during the first trimester of human pregnancy has not been associated with an increased risk of birth defects or musculoskeletal conditions. Rodent studies of levofloxacin are reassuring, revealing no evidence of increased birth defects despite the use of doses higher than those used clinically. An increased rate of low birth weight is reported. However, animal studies are not necessarily good indicators of how a drug will behave in humans.

Breast-feeding: Levofloxacin enters breast milk, but breast-fed newborns have levels below those being prescribed for children.

Potential drug interactions: Because the following medications can reduce the effectiveness of levofloxacin, they should be taken 2 hours before or after taking levofloxacin: antacids containing magnesium or aluminum, sucralfate, iron, multivitamin preparations with zinc. Interaction between the following medications and levofloxacin has the potential to impact the effect of one or more of the drugs. In some instances the interaction can be dangerous or life-threatening and must be avoided: nonsteroidal anti-inflammatory drugs (NSAIDs), warfarin, antidiabetic agents. Some quinolones, including levofloxacin, may produce false positive urine screening results for opiates.

What the FDA says about use in pregnancy: Category C (see Appendix).

What the available evidence suggests about breast-feeding safety: Likely safe.

The bottom line for you:

- Although quinolones in general appear safe during the first trimester, their widespread use during the second and third trimesters should await further study because of the potential for causing tendon damage in children.
- If a quinolone is necessary for maternal indications, levofloxacin is a reasonable choice since it is poorly transported to the fetus, minimizing any risk.

- There are alternative agents with which there is more experience during pregnancy.
- Levofloxacin is likely safe for use while breast-feeding.

LEVORPHANOL

Brand name: Levo-Dromoran
Drug class: Analgesic, narcotic
Indications (what it is used for): Pain.
How it works: Binds to opiate receptors to generate its effects.
Contraindications (reasons you shouldn't take it): Hypersensitivity to drug or class, depressed breathing, heart attack, low blood pressure.
Possible side effects and warnings: Can cause nausea, vomiting, respiratory distress, bronchospasm, double vision, mood disturbance, itching, flushing, rash, constipation, biliary (bile duct) spasm, and dry mouth. Should be used with caution in women with liver or kidney dysfunction, drug dependency, or a seizure disorder.
How it can affect pregnant women: Levorphanol is similar to morphine but 4–6 times stronger. There is no published data during pregnancy.
How it can affect a developing embryo or fetus: There are no adequate reports or well-controlled studies in human fetuses. Levorphanol's chemical structure suggests that it rapidly crosses the placenta. Rodents exposed in the uterus to levorphanol showed tolerance to the drug after birth.
Breast-feeding: There is no published data in nursing women. It is unknown whether levorphanol enters human breast milk, but its chemical structure suggests that it does.
Potential drug interactions: Interaction between the following medications and levorphanol has the potential to impact the effect of one or more of the drugs. In some instances the interaction can be dangerous or life-threatening and must be avoided: other central nervous system (CNS) depressants (including sedatives, hypnotics, general anesthetics, droperidol, phenothiazines or other tranquilizers, and

ethanol/alcohol), monoamine oxidase inhibitors (MAOIs), neuromuscular blocking agents, cimetidine.

What the FDA says about use in pregnancy: Category C (see Appendix).

What the available evidence suggests about breast-feeding safety: Unknown.

The bottom line for you:

- There are alternative agents with which there is more experience during pregnancy and while breast-feeding.
- The risks of levorphanol during pregnancy and breast-feeding are likely similar to those of morphine.

LEVOTHYROXINE

Brand names: Levo-T, Levothroid, Levoxyl, L-Thyroxine, Novothyrox, Synthroid, Synthrox, Throxinique, Thyradin, Thyroxine

Drug class: Hormone, thyroid

Indications (what it is used for): Hypothyroidism; coma, a life-threatening complication of hypothyroidism.

How it works: Increases overall metabolism.

Contraindications (reasons you shouldn't take it): Hypersensitivity to drug or class, extremely high thyroid hormone levels, adrenal insufficiency.

Possible side effects and warnings: Can cause weight loss, increased appetite, rapid or irregular heart rate, nervousness, diarrhea, congestive heart failure, high blood pressure, angina, abdominal cramps, sweating, tremors, sleeplessness, heat intolerance, fever, menstrual irregularities, and hair loss. It should be used with caution in women with high blood pressure or cardiovascular disease.

How it can affect pregnant women: Hypothyroidism (an underactive thyroid) affects 4–10% of women. However, many signs and symptoms of hypothyroidism are mimicked by pregnancy, so its diagnosis should always be confirmed by laboratory tests. Levothyroxine is a standard replacement during pregnancy, and the dose required to maintain normal levels often increases as a pregnancy advances. Hypothyroidism without any symptoms is more common in women who are pregnant with multiple gestations.

How it can affect a developing embryo or fetus: Thyroid hormones are essential for normal brain development. Both maternal and fetal thyroid hormones play a role in that normal development. Both high and low fetal thyroid hormone levels can affect brain development. Although the transport of maternal thyroid hormone across the placenta is low, its importance is illustrated by the fact that most newborns born without a thyroid have no sign of hypothyroidism at birth (meaning that they received some benefit form their mother's thyroid hormones), and maternal hypothyroidism during early and mid-pregnancy is associated with nerve-related damage in newborns.

In some studies, the children of women with subclinical hypothyroidism (low thyroid function but no symptoms) in the first half of pregnancy had lower mean Mental Developmental Index scores during the first year of life, although it is unknown whether thyroxine supplementation diminishes that risk.

Graves' disease, where the mother makes an antibody that can cross the placenta and stimulate the fetal thyroid, is fairly common. Most fetuses whose mothers are being treated with propylthiouracil for Graves' disease do not have normal thyroid function since the propylthiouracil also crosses the placenta, potentially lowering thyroid levels in the fetus. Levothyroxine can be used to treat a fetus that is hypothyroid as a result of a mother being treated for Graves' disease. Women with Graves' Disease should be seen by a perinatologist.

Breast-feeding: There are no adequate reports or well-controlled studies in nursing women. Levothyroxine is excreted at low concentrations into human breast milk. The effect on a breast-feeding newborn is debated. It is unknown whether maternal supplementation increases thyroid hormone in the milk. Some reports suggest that the levels in breast milk are sufficient to treat hypothyroidism in newborns.

Potential drug interactions: Levothyroxine has the potential to interact badly with a long list of medications (too many to list here). Be sure that your doctor and pharmacist know all medications you are taking (prescription and over the counter) and are aware of levothyroxine interactions.

What the FDA says about use in pregnancy: Category A (see Appendix).

What the available evidence suggests about breast-feeding safety: Safe.

The bottom line for you:

- Thyroid abnormalities during pregnancy pose a risk to fetal and newborn neurologic development and require treatment.
- Levothyroxine is a drug of choice for the treatment of hypothyroidism during pregnancy and while breast-feeding.

LIDOCAINE

Brand names: Alphacaine, Leostesin, Rucaina, Xylocaina, Xylocaine

Drug classes: Anesthetic, local; Anesthetic, topical; Antiarrhythmic, class IB

Indications (what it is used for): Irregular heart rate (ventricular), local anesthesia, postherpetic nerve pain (a complication of shingles, caused by the chickenpox virus).

How it works: Prevents the nerve impulse from traveling by stabilizing nerve membranes.

Contraindications (reasons you shouldn't take it): Hypersensitivity to drug or class, Wolff-Parkinson-White syndrome (abnormally rapid heart rhythm), sinoatrial or atrial-ventricular block, Stokes-Adams syndrome (insufficient blood flow to the brain due to an abnormal heart rate causing fainting). Allergic reactions are rare.

Possible side effects and warnings: Can cause ringing in the ears, blurred vision, light-headedness, impaired swallowing, seizures, respiratory arrest, heart rate irregularities, cardiovascular collapse, asthma, coma, tremors, confusion, low blood pressure, hallucinations, agitation, and nausea and vomiting. Should be used with caution in women with liver or kidney dysfunction, slow heart rate, congestive heart failure, or high blood pressure.

How it can affect pregnant women: Injected lidocaine has been used for decades to provide analgesia at delivery. Sprayed lidocaine is not effective for killing pain the in the perineum, although the topical application of 2% lidocaine gel decreases perineal pain in women with genital herpes. Maternal spinal or epidural block with lidocaine (and most local anesthetics) may cause low blood pressure. Both the quality and the duration of anesthesia are improved by the addition of fentanyl. Lidocaine is a second option for the treatment of irregular ventricular heart rates after failed electrical cardioversion.

How it can affect a developing embryo or fetus: Lidocaine rapidly crosses the human placenta. The results of newborn neurobehavioral examinations after the mother received continuous epidural analgesia are conflicting. Some suggest a decrease in newborn muscle strength and tone, while others find no effect. There are no reports of associated malformations (birth defects) with exposure during pregnancy. Rodent studies are reassuring, revealing no evidence of birth defects despite the use of doses higher than those used clinically. However, animal studies are not necessarily good indicators of how a drug will behave in humans.

Breast-feeding: Lidocaine is excreted into breast milk, but the maternal systemic levels are low. Considering the dose and how it is administered, it is unlikely that a breast-feeding newborn would ingest clinically relevant amounts.

Potential drug interactions: Interaction between the following medications and lidocaine has the potential to impact the effect of one or more of the drugs. In some instances the interaction can be dangerous or life-threatening and must be avoided: class I antiarrhythmic drugs (e.g., mexiletine, tocainide).

What the FDA says about use in pregnancy: Category B (see Appendix).

What the available evidence suggests about breast-feeding safety: Safe.

The bottom line for you:
- Lidocaine is considered safe and effective during pregnancy and while breast-feeding.

LINDANE

Brand names: Aphtiria, Hexicid, Kwell, Lorexane, Scabex

Drug classes: Anti-infective; Dermatologic; Scabicide/pediculicide

Indications (what it is used for): Scabies (mites), pediculosis (lice, aka crabs).

How it works: Kills the adults and eggs.

Contraindications (reasons you shouldn't take it): Hypersensitivity to drug or class, inflamed skin, seizure disorder, pregnancy, breast-feeding.

Possible side effects and warnings: Can cause seizures, neurotoxicity, dizziness, eczema, inflamed and itchy skin, anxiety, sleeplessness, and low white blood cell counts. Use only the lotion for scabies; use only the shampoo for lice. Do not repeat.

How it can affect pregnant women: Lindane (g-hexachlorocyclohexane) is a popular over-the-counter treatment for scabies and pediculosis, though it should be used only after other treatments such as permethrin have failed. The number of suspected adverse reactions is small considering that over 10 million ounces of 1% lindane are sold annually. Almost all suspected adverse drug reactions involve misuse of the medication. There are no adequate reports or well-controlled studies of lindane in pregnant women. However, lindane is stored in fat, which can serve as a depot for sustained release of the medication, and rodent studies showed a loss of coordinated uterine contractions. For this reason, the manufacturer says the medication should not be used during pregnancy.

How it can affect a developing embryo or fetus: There are no adequate reports or well-controlled studies in human fetuses. Lindane likely is stored in, and crosses to some degree, the human placenta. It is a known neurotoxin (substance that can damage nerves). There is a case report in which a woman attempted suicide at 16 weeks of pregnancy by orally ingesting lindane (it's normally applied topically); the result was fetal death and vaginal bleeding. Fortunately, the maternal blood level after topical application (cream or shampoo) is low. Rodent studies are reassuring, revealing no evidence of birth defects or low birth weight despite the use of doses higher than those used clinically. Transfer across the rabbit placenta was poor. However, animal studies are not necessarily good indicators of how a drug will behave in humans.

Breast-feeding: There are no adequate reports or well-controlled studies in nursing women. Lindane is found in human breast milk both from environmental sources and after topical use. There are no reported adverse effects on newborns. Lindane is excreted into human milk at low concentrations. It is unlikely that a breast-feeding newborn would ingest a clinically relevant amount. And since the treatment is short-lived, a newborn can also be supplemented for 2 days if the level of concern is high.

Potential drug interactions: Oils may increase the absorption of lindane; therefore, simultaneous use of creams, ointments, or oils should be avoided. If an oil-based hairdressing is used, it is recommended that the hair be shampooed, rinsed, and dried before application of lindane shampoo.

What the FDA says about use in pregnancy: Category C (see Appendix).

What the available evidence suggests about breast-feeding safety: Likely safe.

The bottom line for you:
- Should be reserved for use after permethrin has failed to treat head lice or scabies during pregnancy or while breast-feeding. It is important to follow the directions closely.

LIOTHYRONINE

Brand names: Cytomel, Triostat

Drug class: Hormone, thyroid

Indications (what it is used for): Coma due to a lack of thyroid hormone.

How it works: Unknown; increases metabolism.

Contraindications (reasons you shouldn't take it): Hypersensitivity to drug or class, heart attack, very high levels of thyroid hormone, adrenal insufficiency.

Possible side effects and warnings: Can cause headache, irritability, nervousness, sweating, rapid or irregular heart rate, increased bowel motility, menstrual irregularities, shock, sleeplessness, tremors, weight loss, heat intolerance, and sweating. It should be used with caution in women with angina, high blood pressure, diabetes, or kidney failure.

How it can affect pregnant women: Liothyronine is a synthetic form of the T3 thyroid hormone. It may be used for the treatment of myxedema coma, a potentially lethal form of severe hypothyroidism (low levels of thyroid hormone), although most experts recommend treatment with intravenous levothyroxine instead. There are no adequate reports or well-controlled studies of liothyronine in pregnant women. There are no reports of myxedema coma during pregnancy.

How it can affect a developing embryo or fetus: There are no adequate reports or well-controlled studies of liothyronine in human fetuses. Transfer of natural T3 across the human placenta is low but likely clinically important to the fetus.

Breast-feeding: It is unknown whether liothyronine enters human breast milk. However, several studies conclude the amount of natural thyroid hormone present in human milk is too low to clinically affect a breast-feeding newborn. It is unknown whether supplementation with liothyronine increases that level.

Potential drug interactions: Interaction between the following medications and liothyronine has the potential to impact the effect of one or more of the drugs. In some instances the interaction can be dangerous or life-threatening and must be avoided: vitamin K–dependent clotting factors, insulin, oral hypoglycemics, estrogens or estrogen-containing oral contraceptives, imipramine and other tricyclic antidepressants (TCAs), digitalis, ketamine, catecholamines such as epinephrine and norepinephrine, vasopressors, and cholestyramine.

What the FDA says about use in pregnancy: Category A (see Appendix).

What the available evidence suggests about breast-feeding safety: Safe.

The bottom line for you:

- Liothyronine may be used during pregnancy and while breast-feeding if the benefit to the woman justifies the potential risk to the embryo, fetus, or newborn.

LIOTRIX

Brand names: Euthroid, Thyrolar

Drug class: Hormone, thyroid

Indications (what it is used for): Hypothyroidism.

How it works: Unknown; increases metabolism.

Contraindications (reasons you shouldn't take it): Hypersensitivity to drug or class, heart attack, very high thyroid hormone levels, adrenal insufficiency.

Possible side effects and warnings: Can cause headache, irritability, nervousness, sweating, rapid or irregular heart rate, increased bowel motility, menstrual irregularities, shock, sleeplessness, tremors, weight loss, heat intolerance, and sweating. Should be used with caution in women with chest pain, high blood pressure, diabetes, or kidney failure.

How it can affect pregnant women: Hypothyroidism (an underactive thyroid) affects 4–10% of women. However, many signs and symptoms of hypothyroidism are mimicked by pregnancy, so its diagnosis should always be confirmed by laboratory tests. Liotrix is a combination of two synthetic thyroid hormones: levothyroxine (T4) and liothyronine (T3). There are no adequate reports or well-controlled studies of liotrix in pregnant women. Liotrix is one of the standard replacements during pregnancy, and the dose required to maintain normal levels often increases as a pregnancy advances. Hypothyroidism without any symptoms is more common in women who are pregnant with multiples.

How it can affect a developing embryo or fetus: There are no adequate reports or well-controlled studies of liotrix in human fetuses. Transfer of natural T3 across the human placenta is low but likely clinically important to the fetus. Thyroid hormones are essential for normal brain development. Both maternal and fetal thyroid hormones play a role in that normal development. Both high and low fetal thyroid hormone levels can affect brain development. Although the transport of maternal thyroid hormone across the placenta is low, its importance is illustrated by the fact that most newborns born without a thyroid have no sign of hypothyroidism at birth (meaning that they received some benefit from their mother's thyroid hormones), and maternal hypothyroidism during early and midpregnancy is associated with nerve-related damage in newborns.

In some studies, the children of women with subclinical hypothyroidism (low thyroid function but no symptoms) in the first half of pregnancy had lower mean Mental Developmental Index scores during the first year of life, although it is unknown whether thyroxine supplementation diminishes that risk.

Breast-feeding: There are no adequate reports or well-controlled studies in nursing women. It is unknown whether liotrix enters human breast milk. However, several studies conclude the amount of natural thyroid hormone present in human milk is too low to clinically affect a breast-feeding newborn. It is unknown whether supplementation with liotrix increases that level.

Potential drug interactions: See levothyroxine and liothronine individually.

What the FDA says about use in pregnancy: Category A (see Appendix).

What the available evidence suggests about breast-feeding safety: Safe.

The bottom line for you:

- Liotrix may be used safely during pregnancy and while breast-feeding.

LISINOPRIL

Brand names: Prinivil, Zestril

Drug classes: ACEI/A2R antagonist; Antihypertensive

Indications (what it is used for): High blood pressure, congestive heart failure, heart attack.

How it works: Interferes with the generation of angiotensin, a protein that constricts arteries, thus causing hypertension.

Contraindications (reasons you shouldn't take it): Hypersensitivity to drug or class, history of angioedema (swelling beneath the skin), pregnancy.

Possible side effects and warnings: Can cause fetal and newborn illness and death, decreased blood volume, weakness, fever, numbness or tingling, dizziness, heartburn, gastroenteritis, palpitations, rapid heart rate, liver toxicity, low white blood cell count, high potassium level, swelling, diarrhea, chest pain, cough, liver damage, itching, and rash. Should be used with caution in women with narrowing of the renal artery, liver or kidney dysfunction, low sodium level, congestive heart failure, or collagen vascular disease (disease of the connective tissue).

How it can affect pregnant women: There are no adequate reports or well-controlled studies of lisinopril in pregnant women. In general, any drug that blocks a protein in the pathway activating angiotensin is contraindicated throughout pregnancy because of fetal damage (see "How it can affect a developing embryo or fetus"). The lowest effective dose should be used if lisinopril or another ACE inhibitor is necessary for blood pressure control during pregnancy.

How it can affect a developing embryo or fetus: There are no adequate reports or well-controlled studies in human fetuses. Lisinopril crosses the human placenta. Although no adverse effects have been reported after first-trimester exposure to lisinopril, most other ACE inhibitors have been well documented to cause fetal harm after first-trimester exposure. Later exposure is associated with underdevelopment of the skull, reversible or irreversible kidney failure, no urine output, low amniotic fluid volume, low birth weight, and persistent opening of the ductus arteriosus (a critical fetal blood vessel that draws blood away from the lungs), and fetal death. Lisinopril should be discontinued if low amniotic fluid volume is detected unless it is necessary to save the life of the mother. The fetus and newborn should be carefully monitored for any adverse effects of low amniotic fluid, such as kidney damage. If the newborn is showing low urine production despite adequate blood pressure, the child may benefit from washing out the drug either by complete blood replacement or peritoneal dialysis.

Breast-feeding: There is no published data in nursing women. It is unknown whether lisinopril enters human breast milk. Two similar drugs, enalapril and captopril, are considered safe for use while breast-feeding.

Potential drug interactions: Interaction between the following medications and lisinopril has the potential to impact the effect of one or more of the drugs. In some instances the interaction can be dangerous or life-threatening and must be avoided: diuretics, nonsteroidal anti-inflammatory drugs (NSAIDs) indomethacin, potassium-sparing diuretics (e.g., amiloride, spironolactone, triamterene), potassium supplements, potassium-containing salt substitutes, and lithium.

What the FDA says about use in pregnancy: Category D (see Appendix).

What the available evidence suggests about breast-feeding safety: Likely safe.

The bottom line for you:

- ACE inhibitors are well-established teratogens (substances that can cause birth defects) and should not be used at any time in pregnancy unless there are no other options to protect the life of the mother.
- When a mother's disease requires treatment with lisinopril, the lowest effective dose should be used, followed by close monitoring of the fetus.
- Lisinopril is probably safe to use while breast-

feeding. Enalapril and captopril are suitable alternatives.

LITHIUM CARBONATE

Brand names: Calith, Eskalith, Eskalith CR, Hypnorex, Hyponrex, Lilipin, Lilitin, Lithane, Litheum, Lithobid, Lithocarb, Lithonate, Lithotabs, Manialit, Phasal

Drug class: Antipsychotic

Indications (what it is used for): Bipolar disorder, acute mania, schizoaffective disorder (hallucinations or delusions, mania or depression), low white blood cell count associated with chemotherapy.

How it works: Unknown.

Contraindications (reasons you shouldn't take it): Hypersensitivity to drug or class, inability to attend the doctor appointments necessary to monitor lithium level, pregnancy.

Possible side effects and warnings: Can cause tremors, twitching, involuntary muscular contractions and relaxations, excess muscle tone, lack of coordination of muscle movements, hyperactive reflexes, blackouts, seizures, sustained muscle contractions causing twisting and repetitive movements or abnormal postures, jerky resistance to passive movement, slurred speech, dizziness, involuntary eye movement, incontinence of urine or feces, sleepiness, restlessness, confusion, stupor, coma, tongue movements, tics, ringing in the ears, hallucinations, poor memory, slowed intellectual functioning, excess urination, diarrhea, vomiting, gastritis, salivary gland swelling, abdominal pain, excessive salivation, flatulence, drowsiness, irregular or slow heart rate, low blood pressure, circulatory collapse, kidney dysfunction, hair loss, anesthesia of skin, acne, psoriasis, enlarged thyroid, severe hypothyroidism, and hyperparathyroidism. Should be used with caution in women with liver or kidney dysfunction, abnormal blood volume, thyroid disorder, or coronary artery disease.

How it can affect pregnant women: Lithium is used for the treatment of psychiatric disorders, especially for the long-term prevention of recurrent mania and bipolar depression, and to reduce the risk of suicidal behavior. Among patients with a bipolar disorder, the risk of a suicide attempt is lower during treatment with lithium than with divalproex. Pregnancy and the period after delivery are times of great risk for recurrence of bipolar disease.

Recommendations during pregnancy include discontinuing therapy for at least the first trimester, switching to a medication with a safer profile (e.g., tricyclic antidepressants), using smaller doses of lithium, and avoiding sodium restriction or diuretics while under treatment. However, the discontinuation of a mood stabilizer during pregnancy, particularly abruptly, carries a high risk of a dramatic and rapid worsening of the bipolar disease. Doctors must balance the relative risks of exposing a fetus to medication with the high risk of maternal recurrence if therapy is stopped. The dose needs to be monitored throughout pregnancy (weekly, starting at 35 weeks), and therapy either discontinued or decreased by one-quarter in the 2 to 3 days before delivery.

How it can affect a developing embryo or fetus: Lithium crosses the placenta, achieving levels in the fetus similar to those in the mother. The main adverse fetal effects attributable to lithium are heart defects and increased birth weight; folate supplementation may help lessen those effects. A targeted ultrasound performed between 18 and 23 weeks by a fetal medicine expert is recommended to watch for any abnormalities.

Infants delivered with higher lithium concentrations have significantly lower Apgar scores (a test done to assess the newborn's transition to life outside the uterus), longer hospital stays, and higher rates of central nervous system and neuromuscular complications. The complications often attributed to lithium include poor respiratory effort and blue lips and skin, heart rate rhythm disturbances, nephrogenic diabetes insipidus (inability of the kidneys to remove water from urine because of a lack of anti diuretic hormone), thyroid dysfunction and goiter,

low blood glucose level, decreased muscle tone and lethargy, excess amniotic fluid, jaundice, and high birth weight. As a result, the delivery of a mother taking lithium should be considered high risk. Withholding lithium therapy for 24–48 hours before delivery decreases the maternal lithium to a safe level for the newborn. The results of long-term follow-up studies are otherwise reassuring, as are the most recent epidemiologic studies. Animal studies using doses producing blood levels similar to therapeutic human levels have not reported any abnormalities, although higher doses have produced brain and skeletal abnormalities. However, animal studies are not necessarily good indicators of how a drug will behave in humans.

Breast-feeding: Lithium is excreted into human milk and can be measured in the nursing newborn. Typically, the levels are low and no serious adverse events are reported. As a precaution, the infant should be closely followed by a pediatrician, and his or her lithium level should be checked during the first month.

Potential drug interactions: Interaction between the following medications and lithium has the potential to impact the effect of one or more of the drugs. In some instances the interaction can be dangerous or life-threatening and must be avoided: haloperidol, diuretics, nonsteroidal anti-inflammatory drugs (NSAIDs), indomethacin, piroxicam, metronidazole, ACE inhibitors (e.g., captopril, enalapril), angiotensin II receptor antagonists (e.g., losartan), calcium channel blockers, selective serotonin reuptake inhibitors (SSRIs), acetazolamide, urea, xanthine preparations, alkalinizing agents, and iodide preparations.

What the FDA says about use in pregnancy: Category D (see Appendix).

What the available evidence suggests about breast-feeding safety: Safe.

The bottom line for you:

- Women on lithium therapy who could become pregnant should use adequate contraception and talk with their doctors before attempting to become pregnant.

- Good-quality studies suggest that lithium is at worst a weak human teratogen (substance that causes birth defects).
- Lithium is a preferred medication for patients with typical bipolar disorder and those who are at high risk for severe depression or depression combined with persistent suicidal thoughts during pregnancy. Lithium blood levels should be monitored during pregnancy.
- Women who take lithium during pregnancy should undergo a detailed ultrasound by a skilled perinatologist between 18 and 23 weeks to look for any abnormalities.
- Typically, the lithium levels in breast-fed newborns are low. As a precaution, the infant should be closely followed by a pediatrician and the lithium levels checked during the first month.

LOPERAMIDE

Brand names: Arret, Beamodium, Chisen, Hocular, Imode, Imodium, Lorico, Motilen

Drug classes: Antidiarrheal; Gastrointestinal

Indications (what it is used for): Diarrhea.

How it works: Inhibits bowel motility.

Contraindications (reasons you shouldn't take it): Hypersensitivity to drug or class, bloody diarrhea, pseudomembranous colitis (a bacterial infection of the colon typically associated with antibiotic usage).

Possible side effects and warnings: Can cause pseudomembranous colitis (antibiotic associated diarrhea), abdominal pain and distention, loss of bowel motility, constipation, nausea and vomiting, drowsiness, dizziness, dry mouth, fatigue, and skin rash. Should be used with caution in women who have had diarrhea for more than 48 hours or who have liver, kidney, or inflammatory bowel disease.

How it can affect pregnant women: Loperamide is a popular and effective agent for the treatment of diarrhea and associated symptoms. It has been used in pregnancy without complication. Loperamide reduces the incidence of diarrhea and nausea in women undergoing second-trimester pregnancy termination. One study noted that its use during pregnancy increased the risk of placenta previa (the placenta covers the cervix), overweight newborns, and cesarean delivery. These observations have yet to be confirmed but do not appear plausible from a physiologic perspective.

How it can affect a developing embryo or fetus: Quality human studies suggest that loperamide use during pregnancy is not associated with an increased risk of major birth defects, although a recent study of self-reported cases noted an increase in hypospadias (the urethra develops on the underside of the penis) when used during early pregnancy.

Breast-feeding: Although there are no adequate reports or well-controlled studies in nursing women, loperamide is generally considered safe for breast-feeding women.

Potential drug interactions: No clinically relevant interactions currently identified.

What the FDA says about use in pregnancy: Category C (see Appendix).

What the available evidence suggests about breast-feeding safety: Safe.

The bottom line for you:

- Loperamide is generally considered safe for use during pregnancy and while breast-feeding.

LORACARBEF

Brand name: Lorabid

Drug classes: Antibiotic; Cephalosporin, second-generation

Indications (what it is used for): Bacterial infections due to sensitive bacteria.

How it works: Inhibits cell wall synthesis, causing the death of the bacteria.

Contraindications (reasons you shouldn't take it): Hypersensitivity to drug or class, pseudomembranous colitis (bacterial infection of the colon).

Possible side effects and warnings: Can cause penicillin allergy, kidney dysfunction, antibiotic-associated colitis, and seizures.

How it can affect pregnant women: Loracarbef is used to treat lower respiratory tract infections, genitourinary tract infections, skin infections, and septicemia (bacteria in the blood), and to prevent infection after surgery. Although cephalosporins are usually considered safe during pregnancy, there is no published data with loracarbef during pregnancy.

How it can affect a developing embryo or fetus: There are no adequate reports or well-controlled studies of loracarbef in human fetuses. Other cephalosporins cross the human placenta. Rodent studies are reassuring, revealing no evidence of birth defects or low birth weight despite the use of doses higher than those used clinically. However, animal studies are not necessarily good indicators of how a drug will behave in humans.

Breast-feeding: There is no published data in nursing women. It is unknown whether loracarbef enters human breast milk. Most cephalosporins are excreted into breast milk, but they are considered safe for use while breast-feeding.

Potential drug interactions: Interaction between the following medications and loracarbef has the potential to impact the effect of one or more of the drugs. In some instances the interaction can be dangerous or life-threatening and must be avoided: probenecid.

What the FDA says about use in pregnancy: Category B (see Appendix).

What the available evidence suggests about breast-feeding safety: Likely safe.

The bottom line for you:

- Loracarbef is probably safe for use during pregnancy and breast-feeding, although there are alternative antibiotics with which there is more experience.

LORATADINE

Brand names: Alavert, Claritin, Claritin Redi-Tabs

Drug class: Antihistamine, H1

Indications (what it is used for): Allergic runny nose, hives.

How it works: Blocks peripheral H1 receptors, whose activation causes the symptoms.

Contraindications (reasons you shouldn't take it): Hypersensitivity to drug or class.

Possible side effects and warnings: Can cause bronchospasm, hepatitis, fatigue, headache, sleepiness, dry mouth, nervousness, and abdominal pain. Should be used with caution in women with liver or kidney dysfunction.

How it can affect pregnant women: Loratadine is a second-generation antihistamine with minimal sedating effect. It is a first-line agent for the treatment of runny nose due to allergy. There are no adequate reports or well-controlled studies of loratadine in pregnant women. Based on its chemical structure, it is likely safe for use during pregnancy.

How it can affect a developing embryo or fetus: There are no adequate reports or well-controlled studies in human fetuses. It is unknown whether loratadine crosses the human placenta. However, quality human studies reveal no adverse outcomes. In 2002, a Swedish study observed that the prevalence of hypospadias (the urethra develops on the underside of the penis) was twice that of the general population among male infants exposed to loratadine while in the uterus. However, the CDC analyzed data from the National Birth Defects Prevention Study and concluded that there was no increased risk for hypospadias. This conclusion was confirmed by a recent Danish study.

Breast-feeding: Loratadine and its active metabolite (the product the body breaks it down into) pass easily into human breast milk, reaching levels almost equivalent to those in the mother's bloodstream. However, the total dose absorbed by a breast-feeding newborn is clinically insignificant.

Potential drug interactions: No clinically relevant interactions currently identified.

What the FDA says about use in pregnancy: Category B (see Appendix).

What the available evidence suggests about breast-feeding safety: Safe.

The bottom line for you:
- Loratadine is considered safe for use in pregnancy and while breast-feeding.

LORAZEPAM

Brand names: Almazine, Aplacassee, Ativan, Bonton, Lorat, Lozepam, Nervistopl, Sedizepan, Wintin

Drug classes: Anticonvulsant; Anxiolytic; Benzodiazepine

Indications (what it is used for): Anxiety, sleeplessness, status epilepticus (constant or near-constant seizures).

How it works: Stimulates benzodiazepine receptors to relieve anxiety and sleeplessness.

Contraindications (reasons you shouldn't take it): Hypersensitivity to drug or class, glaucoma, alcohol intoxication, depressive disorder, psychosis.

Possible side effects and warnings: Can cause cardiovascular collapse, respiratory depression, withdrawal syndrome, blood abnormalities, gangrene, drug dependency, sedation, dizziness, weakness, lack of muscle coordination, depression, nausea and/or vomiting, loss of memories created after taking the drug, headache, sleep disturbances, double vision, involuntary eye movement, agitation, urinary incontinence, changes in appetite, delirium, and pain at the injection site. Should be used with caution in women with liver, lung, or kidney dysfunction, or who are abusing drugs.

How it can affect pregnant women: There is growing appreciation that the suggested risks of lorazepam during pregnancy are smaller than previously thought. Women in need of the therapy should not be denied it solely because they are pregnant. Although nonpharmacologic approaches (treatments and strategies that do not require drugs) to the treatment of sleeplessness are the preferred first choice, intermediate-acting benzodiazepines such as lorazepam may be useful if first-line medications fail.

How it can affect a developing embryo or fetus: There are no adequate reports or well-controlled studies in human fetuses. Lorazepam crosses the human placenta. High peak concentrations can be avoided by dividing the total daily dose into 2 or 3 smaller doses. Although there are many studies of benzodiazepine use in human pregnancy, data on the potential to cause birth defects and the effects on the newborn development and behavior are limited and conflicting. There is no clear evidence of an increase in birth defects. Benzodiazepine use in the third trimester or during labor may cause floppy baby syndrome or newborn withdrawal after birth. These symptoms can include mild sedation, low muscle tone, episodes where the newborn stops breathing, blue tinge to skin from low oxygen, impaired metabolic responses to cold stress, and reluctance to suck, all of which may persist for hours to months after birth but generally resolve without long-lasting effects. Rodent studies are for the most part reassuring, revealing no evidence of birth defects or low birth weight despite the use of doses higher than those used clinically. Prenatal exposure of fetal rodents to some benzodiazepines was associated with behavioral and neurochemical alterations in the period after delivery that may persist into adulthood. Studies in humans have shown a similar effect at least up until 18 months of age.

Breast-feeding: Small amounts of lorazepam are excreted into human breast milk, although the dose ingested by a breast-feeding baby should be clinically insignificant. Using the lowest effective quantity in divided doses to minimize drug peaks would further reduce any theoretic risk.

Potential drug interactions: Interaction between the following medications and lorazepam has the potential to impact the effect of one or more of the drugs. In some instances the interaction can be dangerous or life-threatening and must be avoided: alcohol, phenothiazines, barbiturates, monoamine oxidase inhibitors (MAOIs), scopolamine, and other antidepressants.

What the FDA says about use in pregnancy: Category D (see Appendix).

What the available evidence suggests about breast-feeding safety: Safe.

The bottom line for you:

- Benzodiazepines have historically been prescribed too much. They should be avoided where possible during pregnancy.
- Although there are alternative agents for which there is both more experience and a clearer safety profile during pregnancy and while breast-feeding, lorazepam may be an appropriate choice for women when there is a clear need for the medication.

LOVASTATIN

Brand names: Altocor, Lofacol, Mevacor

Drug classes: Antihyperlipidemic; HMG-CoA reductase inhibitor; Statin

Indications (what it is used for): High cholesterol and triglycerides, prevention of cardiovascular events.

How it works: Inhibits the action of the enzyme HMG-CoA reductase, thus lowering the levels of cholesterol products in the blood.

Contraindications (reasons you shouldn't take it): Hypersensitivity to drug or class, active liver disease, liver dysfunction, pregnancy, breast-feeding.

Possible side effects and warnings: Can cause muscle breakdown, liver toxicity, heartburn, constipation, flatulence, abdominal pain, rash, weakness, and muscle pain. Should be used with caution in women with liver or kidney dysfunction or alcoholism.

How it can affect pregnant women: There are no adequate reports or well-controlled studies of lovastatin in pregnant women. The limited information available on the effect of HMG-CoA reductase inhibitors on pregnancy suggests that outcomes are similar to those of women who did not take it. However, high cholesterol and triglycerides is a chronic problem, and discontinuation of lovastatin during pregnancy is unlikely to worsen the long-term outcome of the woman being treated.

How it can affect a developing embryo or fetus: Cholesterol and other products of the cholesterol biosynthesis are essential to fetal development, so a drug that greatly reduces their building blocks could pose a risk to the fetus. There are no adequate reports or well-controlled studies of lovastatin in human fetuses. It is unknown whether it crosses the human placenta, and there is only limited study.

Lower-quality studies tend to raise the most concern. One review of 70 first-trimester exposures noted 31 adverse outcomes, including 22 newborns with structural birth defects, 4 with low birth weight, and 5 fetal deaths. Cerivastatin and lovastatin were associated with 4 reports of severe defects of the central nervous system. Simvastatin, lovastatin, and atorvastatin were all associated with reports of limb deficiencies. None were reported after exposure to pravastatin, however, which is poorly transported across the placenta. A more recent survey of 225 lovastatin-exposed pregnancies followed from the first trimester onward concluded that the rate of birth defects was similar to the rate of women who did not take lovastatin.

Breast-feeding: There is no published data in nursing women. Small quantities of lovastatin apparently enter human breast milk. Statin drugs inhibited prolactin release in the rat brain, and theoretically could interfere with the initiation of breast-feeding.

Potential drug interactions: Interaction between the following medications or substances and lovastatin has the potential to impact the effect of one or more of the drugs. In some instances the interaction can be dangerous or life-threatening and must be avoided: inhibitors of CYP3A4 (an enzyme that breaks down lovastatin), such as clarithromycin, erythromycin, or grapefruit or grapefruit juice; HIV protease inhibitors; itraconazole; ketoconazole; nefazodone; telithromycin; gemfibrozil; other fibrates; niacin; cyclosporine; amiodarone; verapamil; warfarin and coumarin anticoagulants.

What the FDA says about use in pregnancy: Category X (see Appendix).

What the available evidence suggests about breast-feeding safety: Unknown.

The bottom line for you:

- Lovastatin is not recommended during pregnancy or while breast-feeding until further studies better determine its safety.
- If an accidental exposure to lovastatin occurs during pregnancy, there is no justification for termination of pregnancy out of fear of fetal deformities, and women who require lovastatin treatment during pregnancy should feel reassured the fetal risk is likely small.
- There is inadequate information available to make a recommendation on the safety of breast-feeding.

MAGNESIUM CITRATE

Brand name: None
Drug class: Laxative
Indications (what it is used for): Constipation.
How it works: Unknown.
Contraindications (reasons you shouldn't take it): Hypersensitivity to drug or class, appendicitis, sudden severe pain in the abdomen that may require surgery, bowel obstruction.
Possible side effects and warnings: Can cause abdominal cramps, flatulence, diarrhea, low blood pressure, high blood magnesium level, and respiratory disturbances. Should be used with caution in women with kidney dysfunction or electrolyte disturbances.
How it can affect pregnant women: There are no adequate reports or well-controlled studies of magnesium citrate in pregnant women. Magnesium citrate reduces the frequency of leg cramps at night in nonpregnant women.
How it can affect a developing embryo or fetus: There are no adequate reports or well-controlled studies of magnesium citrate in human fetuses. Magnesium ions freely cross the placenta.
Breast-feeding: Magnesium is normally present in human breast milk. It is unknown whether magnesium citrate increases the natural magnesium content of the milk. Considering what it is used for and the typical dosage, limited use is unlikely to pose a

clinically significant risk to a breast-feeding baby.
Potential drug interactions: Calcium channel blockers should be avoided. Doxercalciferol may increase the risk of hypermagnesemia (too much magnesium in the blood).
What the FDA says about use in pregnancy: Category B (see Appendix).
What the available evidence suggests about breast-feeding safety: Likely safe.
The bottom line for you:

- Magnesium citrate is considered safe if used occasionally during pregnancy and while breast-feeding.

MAGNESIUM SULFATE

Brand name: None
Drug classes: Anticonvulsant; Electrolyte replacement
Indications (what it is used for): Ventricular arrhythmia, eclampsia (seizures associated with high blood pressure developed during pregnancy and protein in the urine), low serum (blood) magnesium level.
How it works: Inhibits calcium release and blocks calcium influx.
Contraindications (reasons you shouldn't take it): Hypersensitivity to drug or class, kidney failure, impaired heart function.
Possible side effects and warnings: Can cause respiratory failure, cardiovascular collapse, depressed heart function, fluid in the lungs, low body temperature, depressed reflexes, low blood pressure, drowsiness, nausea, vomiting, low blood calcium levels, high blood potassium levels, flushing, blurred vision, sweating, muscle weakness, sedation, and confusion. Should be used with caution in women with kidney dysfunction or electrolyte disturbances.
How it can affect pregnant women: Magnesium sulfate is rapidly eliminated from the body through the kidneys. The toxicity of magnesium is linked to its blood level, and poor kidney function is a common cause of toxicity. Too much magnesium is a

cause of maternal death. It is used to treat the following conditions.

Preeclampsia: Magnesium sulfate halves the risk of eclampsia in women with moderate to severe preeclampsia and is more effective than phenytoin and diazepam. It is also the drug of choice for the control of seizures. It remains unclear whether magnesium sulfate is beneficial for the treatment of mild preeclampsia. Magnesium sulfate does not prevent the worsening of preeclampsia during labor, and about 10–15% of preeclamptic women become eclamptic, despite treatment.

Preterm labor: No drug used to treat labor before 37 weeks actually stops real preterm labor. The benefit of such drugs is buying time to administer corticosteroids to help the fetus's lungs mature. Magnesium sulfate is the most commonly used tocolytic (medication to slow or stop preterm labor) in the U.S. Unfortunately, several in-depth analyses concluded it is both ineffective and potentially dangerous as an agent to prevent preterm birth or even delay delivery. For example, one review found that the risk of perinatal death was higher for women being treated with magnesium sulfate.

How it can affect a developing embryo or fetus: Magnesium crosses the placenta and increases the fetal blood level. It remains unclear whether magnesium sulfate alters the fetal heart rate during labor. Magnesium sulfate has a protective effect on the fetal brain, reducing the risk of cerebral palsy in preterm infants when being used at the time of birth. There is no clear evidence of adverse effects from short-term magnesium sulfate therapy. Respiratory depression may occur if newborn levels are very high at birth.

Breast-feeding: Magnesium is normally present in human breast milk. It is unknown whether magnesium sulfate increases the natural magnesium content of the milk. Considering what it is used for and the typical dose, limited use is unlikely to pose a clinically significant risk to a breast-feeding baby.

Potential drug interactions: Magnesium increases the effects of barbiturates, narcotics, hypnotics (or systemic anesthetics), or other central nervous system (CNS) depressants.

What the FDA says about use in pregnancy: Category A (see Appendix).

What the available evidence suggests about breast-feeding safety: Safe.

The bottom line for you:

- Magnesium sulfate is superior to phenytoin and diazepam for preventing eclamptic convulsions. It also reduces the risk of subsequent cerebral palsy in at-risk pregnancies.

- Magnesium sulfate is not an effective inhibitor of preterm labor and has worse safety and cost profiles compared to alternatives such as nifedipine and indomethacin. It should not be used for this purpose.

- Magnesium sulfate has no impact on breast-feeding.

MANNITOL

Brand names: Osmitrol, Resectisol

Drug class: Diuretic, osmotic

Indications (what it is used for): Prevention and treatment of low urine production due to sudden kidney failure, cerebral edema (swelling of the brain).

How it works: Increases the rate at which the kidneys filter blood.

Contraindications (reasons you shouldn't take it): Hypersensitivity to drug or class, lack of urine output, progressive kidney failure after mannitol initiation, no response to the initial bolus of mannitol, pulmonary edema (fluid in the lungs), severe dehydration, intracranial hemorrhage, and progressive heart failure.

Possible side effects and warnings: Can cause seizures, heart failure, cardiovascular collapse, fluid in the lungs, sudden kidney failure, central nervous system depression, coma, fluid imbalance, rapid heart rate, dehydration, electrolyte disorders, accumulation of acid in the blood, blurred vision, blood clots, hives, fever, dry mouth, thirst, runny nose, death of skin tissue, chest pain, and water intoxication. Should be used with caution in women with kidney dysfunction.

How it can affect pregnant women: There are no adequate reports or well-controlled studies of mannitol in pregnant women. Most published data is limited to case reports of women undergoing surgery for causes unrelated to pregnancy (intracranial hemorrhage or brain tumors) or for hypermagnesemia (too much magnesium in the blood). Mannitol has also been used for the treatment of posterior reversible encephalopathy.

How it can affect a developing embryo or fetus: There are no adequate reports or well-controlled studies in human fetuses. Mannitol crosses the human placenta. Rodent birth defect studies have not been performed. Studies of pregnant sheep revealed that the administration of mannitol to the mother can alter the amount of amniotic fluid. However, animal studies are not necessarily good indicators of how a drug will behave in humans.

Breast-feeding: There is no published literature in nursing women. It is unknown whether mannitol enters human breast milk.

Potential drug interactions: No clinically relevant drug interactions identified.

What the FDA says about use in pregnancy: Category C (see Appendix).

What the available evidence suggests about breast-feeding safety: Unknown.

The bottom line for you:

- Mannitol is typically indicated in life-threatening situations and its benefits to the woman outweigh any potential risk to the embryo, fetus, or newborn.

MAZINDOL

Brand names: Mazanor, Sanorex
Drug classes: Anorexiant; Central nervous system stimulant
Indications (what it is used for): Weight loss.

How it works: Appetite suppression.

Contraindications (reasons you shouldn't take it): Hypersensitivity to drug or class, arteriosclerosis (hardening of the arteries), cardiovascular disease, high blood pressure, high thyroid hormone levels, glaucoma, and anxiety.

Possible side effects and warnings: Can cause palpitations, rapid heart rate, high blood pressure, psychosis, sleeplessness, euphoria, loss of control of movements, depressed mood, tremors, headaches, Tourette's syndrome (involuntary movements and vocalizations), dry mouth, diarrhea, constipation, anorexia, and decreased sex drive. Should be used with caution in women who are substance abusers.

How it can affect pregnant women: Mazindol behaves like an amphetamine. Its effectiveness in obese nonpregnant women is at best modest, and tolerance develops. There is no published data during pregnancy, and there are no indications for its use during pregnancy.

How it can affect a developing embryo or fetus: There are no adequate reports or well-controlled studies in human fetuses. It is unknown whether mazindol crosses the human placenta. Rodent studies suggest that it causes rib abnormalities when taken at multiples of the maximum recommended clinical daily dose. However, animal studies are not necessarily good indicators of how a drug will behave in humans.

Breast-feeding: There is no published data in nursing women. It is unknown whether mazindol enters human breast milk.

Potential drug interactions: Interaction between the following medications and manzindol has the potential to impact the effect of one or more of the drugs. In some instances the interaction can be dangerous or life-threatening and must be avoided: guanethidine, exogenous catecholamines.

What the FDA says about use in pregnancy: Category C (see Appendix).

What the available evidence suggests about breast-feeding safety: Unknown.

The bottom line for you:
- There are no indications for mazindol during pregnancy or while breast-feeding.

MEBENDAZOLE
Brand names: Bendosan, Damaben, Drivermide, Fugacar, Ovex, Vermox
Drug class: Anthelmintic
Indications (what it is used for): Infection with pinworm, whipworm, hookworm, roundworm, capillariasis.
How it works: Causes glucose depletion, leading to the parasites' death.
Contraindications (reasons you shouldn't take it): Hypersensitivity to drug or class, use in children under the age of 2.
Possible side effects and warnings: Can cause swelling under the skin, seizures, reduced white blood cell count, abdominal pain, nausea, vomiting, diarrhea, fever, dizziness, headache, rash, itching, hair loss, and convulsions.
How it can affect pregnant women: Treatment of reproductive-age women is strongly recommended in areas of widespread hookworm infection (Africa and Southeast Asia) and its related anemia. In some endemic areas, treatment of all pregnant women after the first trimester effectively reduces the incidence of low birth weight and newborn death related to infection.
How it can affect a developing embryo or fetus: There are no adequate reports or well-controlled studies in human fetuses. It is unknown whether mebendazole crosses the human placenta. It is rare for a child to be born with a parasitic infection. The largest prospective study (a study that follows a group of individuals for a period of time) of 140 first-trimester exposures found no increase in birth defects or other adverse outcomes There are no reported harmful effects after second- or third-trimester exposures. Rodent studies suggest that mebendazole can damage embryos and cause birth defects at fairly low doses. However, animal studies are not necessarily good indicators of how a drug will behave in humans.
Breast-feeding: There is no published data in nursing women. It is unknown whether mebendazole enters human breast milk.
Potential drug interactions: No clinically relevant interactions identified.
What the FDA says about use in pregnancy: Category C (see Appendix).
What the available evidence suggests about breast-feeding safety: Unknown.
The bottom line for you:
- Mebendazole is considered safe and effective during pregnancy. Treatment is beneficial for women in Africa and Southeast Asia where intestinal parasites are widespread.
- The risk, if any, of mebendazole to the breast-fed newborn is unknown.

MECHLORETHAMINE
Brand name: Mustargen
Drug class: Antineoplastic, alkylating agent
Indications (what it is used for): Hodgkin's disease stages III–IV (advanced stages of a type of cancer of the lymphatic system), chronic myelocytic and chronic lymphocytic leukemia, mycosis fungoides (T cell lymphoma), polycythemia vera (bone marrow makes too many red blood cells), lymphosarcoma.
How it works: Alkylating agent that prevents cell division.
Contraindications (reasons you shouldn't take it): Hypersensitivity to drug or class, suppurative (producing pus) inflammation.
Possible side effects and warnings: Can cause blood clots; life-threatening allergic reaction; nausea; vomiting; depression; hemolytic anemia; skin eruption; delayed, absent, or abnormal menstruation.
How it can affect pregnant women: There are no adequate reports or well-controlled studies of mechlorethamine in pregnant women. Based on limited published data, mechlorethamine may be used

during pregnancy with a good outcome. Hodgkin's disease does not affect the normal progress of pregnancy, and termination of pregnancy is usually unnecessary. Women or adolescents treated before they are ready to conceive may experience decreased gonadal function and may want to consider some type of fertility preservation before beginning therapy.

How it can affect a developing embryo or fetus: There are no adequate reports or well-controlled studies in human fetuses. It is unknown whether mechlorethamine crosses the human placenta. Chemotherapy treatment at full doses in even the first trimester can end with a good outcome. Children of women treated for hematologic malignancies during pregnancy with a variety of cytotoxic agents, including mechlorethamine, have normal birth weights as well as normal learning and educational performances. There is no increase in the prevalence of either acute leukemia or congenital, neurologic, and psychological abnormalities in the children born to treated women.

Breast-feeding: There is no published data in nursing women. It is unknown whether mechlorethamine enters human breast milk.

Potential drug interactions: No clinically relevant drug interactions identified.

What the FDA says about use in pregnancy: Category D (see Appendix).

What the available evidence suggests about breast-feeding safety: Unknown.

The bottom line for you:

- Mechlorethamine can be administered even during the first trimester with good outcome. Long-term follow-up of children exposed in utero to chemotherapy is reassuring.
- The safety of mechlorethamine while breast-feeding is unknown.

MECLIZINE

Brand names: Ancolan, Antivert, Duramesan, EnVert, Meclicot, Meclizine, Meclozine, Medivert, Yonyun

Drug classes: Antiemetic; Antihistamine, H1; Antivertigo agent

Indications (what it is used for): Motion sickness.

How it works: Blocks acetylcholine and histamine 1 receptors, the activation of which causes the symptoms.

Contraindications (reasons you shouldn't take it): Hypersensitivity to drug or class.

Possible side effects and warnings: Can cause rapid heart rate, hallucinations, jaundice, hearing damage, agitation, confusion, anxiety, low blood pressure, blurred vision, dry mouth, loss of appetite, nausea, vomiting, diarrhea, rash, and constipation. Should be used with caution in women with bowel or bladder obstruction or who are taking other central nervous system depressants.

How it can affect pregnant women: There are no adequate reports or well-controlled studies of meclizine in pregnant women. Meclizine effectively reduces nausea and vomiting associated with emergency hormonal contraception (so-called morning-after pill). It is commonly used in several European countries for the treatment of first trimester morning sickness.

How it can affect a developing embryo or fetus: There are no adequate reports or well-controlled studies in human fetuses. It is unknown whether meclizine crosses the human placenta. Long-term and extensive clinical experience reveals little evidence that meclizine is a human teratogen (substance that can cause birth defects). One population-based study in Sweden of more than 16,000 first-trimester exposures reported improved pregnancy outcomes compared to people who did not take the medication. Rodent studies conducted with doses 25–50 times the maximum recommended clinical dose revealed an increase in cleft lip and palate. However, animal studies are not necessarily good indicators of how a drug will behave in humans.

Breast-feeding: There are no adequate reports or well-controlled studies in nursing women. It is unknown whether meclizine enters human breast milk, although it is generally considered safe while breast-feeding.

Potential drug interactions: No clinically relevant drug interactions identified.

What the FDA says about use in pregnancy: Category B (see Appendix).

What the available evidence suggests about breast-feeding safety: Safe.

The bottom line for you:

- Meclizine is considered safe and effective during pregnancy for the treatment of morning sickness unresponsive to vitamin B6.
- The safety of meclizine while breast-feeding is unknown but considered safe based on a long clinical experience.

MECLOFENAMATE

Brand name: Meclomen

Drug classes: Analgesic, nonnarcotic; Nonsteroidal anti-inflammatory drug (NSAID)

Indications (what it is used for): Pain, painful menstruation, osteoarthritis, rheumatoid arthritis, ankylosing spondylitis (inflammation of joints in the spine), gout

How it works: Blocks cyclooxygenase and lipoxygenase, the enzymes that are responsible for the creation of prostaglandins, substances involved in inflammation and pain.

Contraindications (reasons you shouldn't take it): Hypersensitivity to drug or class, NSAID-induced asthma.

Possible side effects and warnings: Can cause a life-threatening allergic reaction, gastrointestinal bleeding, bronchospasm, kidney or liver damage or failure, Stevens-Johnson syndrome (a rare but serious skin reaction to medication), an extremely low white blood cell count, abdominal pain, constipation, headache, dizziness, rash, hives, drowsiness, swelling, ringing in the ears, lupus- and serum sickness–like symptoms. Should be used with caution in women with nasal polyps, bowel bleeding, high blood pressure, heart failure, or asthma.

How it can affect pregnant women: Meclofenamate is a nonsteroidal agent that can lessen inflammation, relieve pain, and lower fevers. There are no adequate reports or well-controlled studies of meclofenamate in pregnant women. It should not be used for the treatment of preterm labor. It is a popular analgesic for the pain after vaginal delivery.

How it can affect a developing embryo or fetus: There are no adequate reports or well-controlled studies in human fetuses. It is unknown whether meclofenamate crosses the human placenta. Similar-class agents do cross and have, on rare occasions, been associated with a narrowing or closure of the ductus arteriosus, a critical blood vessel directing blood away from the fetal lungs. Its closure leads to tricuspid valve incompetence, heart failure, and high blood pressure in the lungs, all of which can cause long-term damage. Stopping the drug appears to reverse this process. Because of the potential for premature closure of the fetal ductus arteriosus after maternal use of NSAIDs, chronic meclofenamate treatment during pregnancy is not recommended without fetal monitoring. Rodent studies revealed that meclofenamate, like aspirin and other NSAIDs, can cause minor skeletal malformations (e.g., extra ribs, delayed calcification of bones) but no major birth defects. However, animal studies are not necessarily good indicators of how a drug will behave in humans.

Breast-feeding: There is no published data in nursing women. Meclofenamate enters human breast milk.

Potential drug interactions: Aspirin or warfarin use with meclofenamate increases the risk of gastrointestinal bleeding.

What the FDA says about use in pregnancy: Category C, first and second trimesters; Category D, third trimester (see Appendix).

What the available evidence suggests about breast-feeding safety: Unknown; likely safe.

The bottom line for you:

- Similar to other NSAIDs, meclofenamate poses minimal risk when used occasionally during pregnancy and while breast-feeding.

- Similar to other NSAIDs, it is wise to avoid meclofenamate in the first trimester and sustained use should be avoided in the third trimester.

MEDROXYPROGESTERONE

Brand names: Amen, Aragest, Asconale, Clinovir, Curretab, Cycrin, Depo-Provera, Med-Pro, Provera
Drug classes: Antineoplastic, hormone; Contraceptive; Hormone
Indications (what it is used for): Abnormal menses, hormone replacement, contraception.
How it works: Blocks the release of gonadotropins, which are critical for ovulation, while making the endometrium hostile to implantation.
Contraindications (reasons you shouldn't take it): Hypersensitivity to drug or class, pregnancy, blood clots, breast cancer, undiagnosed vaginal bleeding, liver failure, and retained abortion.
Possible side effects and warnings: Can cause blood clots, stroke, heart attack, liver tumors, gallbladder disease, cholestatic jaundice, high blood pressure, stroke, absent menstruation, nausea, vomiting, breast tenderness, weight gain, headache, swelling, depression, rash, itching, changes in sex drive, appetite changes, acne, excessive hair growth, hair loss, and inflammation of the optic nerve. Should be used with caution in women with cerebrovascular disorders, liver dysfunction, or heart failure, or who are breast-feeding.
How it can affect pregnant women: Medroxyprogesterone is a popular and effective contraceptive; irregular bleeding and absence of menstruation are the most common side effects. It can be combined with an injectable estrogen to minimize irregular bleeding. Medroxyprogesterone does not appear to alter long-term fertility after it is discontinued. Because it is used for contraception, it is inevitable that women whose pregnancies were unrecognized until after the first trimester are exposed to medroxyprogesterone. Medications such as medroxyprogesterone were long used during early pregnancy in the mistaken belief that they prevented miscarriage. Medroxyprogesterone is also commonly used as a secondary treatment of endometrial cancer or adenomatous hyperplasia, especially in young women who wish to preserve fertility.

How it can affect a developing embryo or fetus: There are no adequate reports or well-controlled studies of medroxyprogesterone in human fetuses. In utero exposure of male fetuses to some progestational agents like medroxyprogesterone may double the risk of hypospadias (the urethra develops on the underside of the penis). Although there is insufficient data to quantify the risk for the female fetus, some progestational agents may cause slight masculinization of the external genitalia (e.g., labia adhesion). Other defects have not been noted in either humans or rodents. After first-trimester exposure, women should undergo a detailed ultrasound between 18 and 22 weeks to screen for ambiguous genitalia in the fetus.
Breast-feeding: Trace amounts of medroxyprogesterone are excreted into human breast milk. Its administration for contraception is usually delayed until 3 days after delivery since progesterone withdrawal is thought to help stimulate the initiation of milk production. When given this way, medroxyprogesterone does not appear to suppress lactation or affect a nursing newborn.
Potential drug interactions: None clinically significant.
What the FDA says about use in pregnancy: Category X (see Appendix).
What the available evidence suggests about breast-feeding safety: Safe.
The bottom line for you:
- Medroxyprogesterone should not be given during pregnancy.
- If it is done so mistakenly, the pregnancy will likely be unaffected. But women exposed in the first trimester should undergo a detailed ana-

tomic ultrasound between 18 and 22 weeks to check for ambiguous fetal genitalia.
- Medroxyprogesterone is safe for use while breast-feeding.

MEFENAMIC ACID

Brand names: Coslan, Ponsfen, Ponstel
Drug classes: Analgesic, nonnarcotic; Nonsteroidal anti-inflammatory drug (NSAID)
Indications (what it is used for): Pain, painful menstruation, osteoarthritis, rheumatoid arthritis, ankylosing spondylitis (inflammation of joints in the spine), gout (joint inflammation as a result of uric acid buildup in the blood).
How it works: Blocks cyclooxygenase and lipoxygenase, enzymes that are responsible for the creation of prostaglandins, substances involved in the inflammation and pain.
Contraindications (reasons you shouldn't take it): Hypersensitivity to drug or class, NSAID-induced asthma.
Possible side effects and warnings: Can cause a life-threatening allergic reaction, gastrointestinal bleeding, bronchospasm, kidney or liver damage or failure, Stevens-Johnson syndrome (a rare but serious skin reaction to medication), an extremely low white blood cell count, abdominal pain, constipation, headache, dizziness, rash, hives, drowsiness, swelling, ringing in the ears, lupus- and serum sickness–like symptoms. Should be used with caution in women with nasal polyps, bowel bleeding, high blood pressure, heart failure, or asthma.
How it can affect pregnant women: Mefenamic acid is a nonsteroidal agent that can reduce inflammation, pain, and fevers. There are no adequate reports or well-controlled studies of mefenamic acid in pregnant women. Mefenamic acid rapidly decreases uterine cramps in women with painful menstruation. In one small, randomized trial, the prevalence of preterm labor (before 37 weeks) was significantly reduced by mefenamic acid compared

with a placebo. This observation has not subsequently been tested adequately. It should not be used for this indication.
How it can affect a developing embryo or fetus: There are no adequate reports or well-controlled studies in human fetuses. Mefenamic acid crosses the human placenta, achieving a fetal level about one-third of the maternal level. Similar-class medications have been associated, on rare occasions, with a narrowing or closure of the ductus arteriosus, a critical blood vessel directing blood away from the fetal lungs. Its closure leads to tricuspid valve incompetence, heart failure, and high blood pressure in the lungs, all of which can cause long-term damage. Stopping the medication appears to reverse this process. Because of the potential for premature closure of the ductus arteriosus after maternal use of NSAIDs, chronic mefenamic acid treatment during pregnancy is not recommended without fetal monitoring. Rodent studies have found no evidence of birth defects or low birth weight despite the use of doses higher than those used clinically. However, animal studies are not necessarily good indicators of how a drug will behave in humans.
Breast-feeding: The trace amounts of mefenamic acid excreted into breast milk pose no clinical risk to a breast-feeding baby.
Potential drug interactions: Interaction between the following medications and mefenamic acid has the potential to impact the effect of one or more of the drugs. In some instances the interaction can be dangerous or life-threatening and must be avoided: CYP2C9 inhibitors, furosemide, lithium, thiazides, methotrexate, warfarin, antacids containing magnesium hydroxide, and oral anticoagulants.
What the FDA says about use in pregnancy: Category C (see Appendix).
What the available evidence suggests about breast-feeding safety: Safe.
The bottom line for you:
- When used occasionally, mefenamic acid appears safe for use during pregnancy and while

breast-feeding, although continuous use likely has the same adverse effects as other NSAIDs.

- Similar to other NSAIDs, it is wise to avoid mefenemic acid in the first trimester and sustained use should be avoided in the third trimester.

MEFLOQUINE

Brand name: Lariam
Drug class: Antiprotozoal
Indications (what it is used for): Malaria prevention and treatment.
How it works: Unknown.
Contraindications (reasons you shouldn't take it): Hypersensitivity to drug or class, depression, psychosis, serious life-threatening infections.
Possible side effects and warnings: Can cause seizures, hallucinations, erythema multiforme and Stevens-Johnson syndrome (both skin disorders), irregular heart rate, encephalopathy (brain disease or malfunction causing an altered mental state), dizziness, fainting, muscle pain, nausea, vomiting, fever, headache, chills, diarrhea, itching, weakness, transient emotional disturbances, and hair loss. Should be used with caution in women with seizures, psychiatric disorder, liver dysfunction, or a cardiac conduction disease.
How it can affect pregnant women: Malaria remains an important cause of maternal and newborn illness and death in areas where it is endemic (parts of Africa, Southeast Asia, and South America). The parasite is increasingly resistant to more traditional treatments such as chloroquine, and mefloquine is the most effective medication for the prevention of chloroquine-resistant malaria. In endemic areas, the World Health Organization favors mefloquine administration in pregnant women from 16 weeks onward. Mefloquine and quinine are the only antimalarials generally available for the treatment of drug-resistant malaria during pregnancy. Prospective studies (studies that follow a group of individuals for a period of time) show that mefloquine in combination with artesunate is more effective than quinine for the treatment of multidrug-resistant malaria during pregnancy. Many of the adverse effects of mefloquine result from primary liver damage or thyroid disturbances in the mother.

How it can affect a developing embryo or fetus: Mefloquine given during early pregnancy for the prevention of malaria is not associated with an increased risk of birth defects and is not an indication for pregnancy termination. Similarly, second-trimester exposure is not associated with adverse reactions. Rodent studies revealed that mefloquine at doses higher than those used in humans is a teratogen (substance that can cause birth defects). However, animal studies are not necessarily good indicators of how a drug will behave in humans.
Breast-feeding: There are no adequate reports or well-controlled studies in nursing women. The small amount of the drug detected in breast milk is not clinically relevant.
Potential drug interactions: Interaction between the following medications and mefloquine has the potential to impact the effect of one or more of the drugs. In some instances the interaction can be dangerous or life-threatening and must be avoided: chloroquine, quinidine, quinine, halofantrine, anticonvulsants (e.g., carbamazepine, phenobarbital, phenytoin, valproic acid), and oral live typhoid vaccine.
What the FDA says about use in pregnancy: Category C (see Appendix).
What the available evidence suggests about breast-feeding safety: Safe.
The bottom line for you:

- Mefloquine is an effective medication for the prevention of chloroquine-resistant falciparum malaria. WHO favors mefloquine prevention in pregnant women who live in endemic areas from 16 weeks of pregnancy onward.
- Use of mefloquine in pregnant women has not been associated with birth defects.
- Mefloquine is safe for use while breast-feeding.

MEGESTROL

Brand names: Magace, Megace, Niagestine

Drug classes: Antineoplastic; Hormone/hormone modifier; Hormone, other gynecologic; Progestin

Indications (what it is used for): Breast cancer, endometrial cancer (palliative), AIDS wasting syndrome.

How it works: Blocks the release of gonadotropins, which are critical for ovulation, while making the endometrium (lining of the uterus) hostile to implantation.

Contraindications (reasons you shouldn't take it): Hypersensitivity to drug or class, first-trimester pregnancy.

Possible side effects and warnings: Can cause weight gain, blood clots, stroke, adrenal suppression, abdominal pain, absence of menstruation, nausea, vomiting, breast tenderness, weight gain, headache, swelling, depression, rash, itching, libido changes, appetite changes, acne, excessive hair growth, hair loss, constipation, and cardiomyopathy (disease of the heart muscle). Should be used with caution in women with recurrent or metastatic cancer or thromboembolic disease (blood clot in the brain).

How it can affect pregnant women: Megestrol is a synthetic hormone related to progesterone used for both cancer treatment and as an implantable contraceptive. There are no adequate reports or well-controlled studies of megestrol in pregnant women, nor are there any indications for its use during pregnancy. Many case reports document successful pregnancy in women with endometrial cancer whose uterus was preserved for a subsequent pregnancy by megestrol. As a treatment for weight loss in cancer patients, megestrol should be started only after other treatable causes are sought and addressed.

How it can affect a developing embryo or fetus: There are no adequate reports or well-controlled studies in human fetuses. It is unknown whether megestrol crosses the human placenta. There are case reports of abnormalities in exposed offspring, including hypospadias in male children (the urethra develops on the underside of the penis).

Breast-feeding: There are no adequate reports or well-controlled studies in nursing women. The small quantities of megestrol excreted into human breast milk are not clinically relevant.

Potential drug interactions: Interaction between the following medications and megestrol has the potential to impact the effect of one or more of the drugs. In some instances the interaction can be dangerous or life-threatening and must be avoided: indinavir.

What the FDA says about use in pregnancy: Category D (tablet); X (suspension) (see Appendix).

What the available evidence suggests about breast-feeding safety: Safe.

The bottom line for you:

- There are no indications for megestrol use during pregnancy. However, accidental exposure to megestrol is not a reason for pregnancy termination, but the fetus should undergo a detailed second-trimester ultrasound by a skilled specialist to search for abnormalities of the genitalia.

- Megestrol is safe for use while breast-feeding.

MELATONIN

Brand name: None

Drug class: Hormone, antioxidant

Indications (what it is used for): Sleep promotion (jet lag), sleeplessness, seasonal affective disorder.

How it works: Directly influences the sleep-wake cycle.

Contraindications (reasons you shouldn't take it): Hypersensitivity to drug or class.

Possible side effects and warnings: Can cause fatigue, depression, coronary artery constriction, and itching. It may decrease fertility. Should be used with caution in women with cardiovascular disease.

How it can affect pregnant women: There are no adequate reports or well-controlled studies of melatonin in pregnant women. Melatonin is a natural hormone with antioxidant properties produced by the pineal gland. Its secretion is stimulated by the dark and inhibited by light. Secretion disturbances have been associated with depression. Rodent studies suggest that melatonin is involved in the initiation of labor without having a direct effect on progesterone secretion.

How it can affect a developing embryo or fetus: There are no adequate reports or well-controlled studies in human fetuses. Melatonin rapidly crosses the human placenta, where it inhibits arterial narrowing caused by oxidized lipids. In rodents, melatonin provided limited protection of the fetal brain after low blood flow. However, animal studies are not necessarily good indicators of how a drug will behave in humans.

Breast-feeding: There are no adequate reports or well-controlled studies of melatonin in nursing women. Naturally occurring melatonin is undetectable in both human and rodent breast milk during exposure to light, but it increases rapidly after darkness. Naturally occurring melatonin is believed responsible for shifting the newborn to the circadian rhythm of the mother.

Potential drug interactions: No clinically relevant interactions identified.

What the FDA says about use in pregnancy: No assigned category (see Appendix).

What the available evidence suggests about breast-feeding safety: Safe.

The bottom line for you:

- Melatonin is generally considered safe for occasional use during pregnancy and while breast-feeding.

MELPHALAN

Brand name: Alkeran

Drug class: Antineoplastic, alkylating agent

Indications (what it is used for): Multiple myeloma (bone marrow cancer), ovarian cancer.

How it works: Binds DNA so that new proteins cannot be made and rapidly growing cells die.

Contraindications (reasons you shouldn't take it): Hypersensitivity to drug or class, hyper-

sensitivity to chlorambucil, resistance to melphalan.

Possible side effects and warnings: Can cause bone marrow suppression, nausea, vomiting, diarrhea, pulmonary fibrosis (scarring of the lungs), interstitial pneumonitis (a lung disease), skin hypersensitivity, inflammation of the blood vessels, hair loss, hemolytic anemia, severe life-threatening allergic reaction, oral sores, and sterility. Should be used with caution in women with kidney failure, low white and/or red blood cell and/or platelet counts.

How it can affect pregnant women: There are no adequate reports or well-controlled studies of melphalan in pregnant women. Case reports of its use during pregnancy are associated with good outcomes. Melphalan is also used for malignant trophoblastic disease (tumors that develop from the placenta) that is resistant to methotrexate. It is sometimes paired with actinomycin D and methotrexate, and the combination of the three makes patients more susceptible to life-threatening complications than if methotrexate is used alone. Women cured of trophoblastic disease or ovarian cancer (usually stages 1A–C) using a drug regimen that includes melphalan can go on to have successful pregnancies.

How it can affect a developing embryo or fetus: There are no adequate reports or well-controlled studies in human fetuses. It is unknown whether melphalan crosses the human placenta. Rodent studies revealed damage to the embryo as well as birth defects involving the central nervous system and skeleton. However, animal studies are not necessarily good indicators of how a drug will behave in humans.

Breast-feeding: There is no published data in nursing women. It is unknown whether melphalan enters human breast milk.

Potential drug interactions: Interaction between the following medications and melphalan has the potential to impact the effect of one or more of the drugs. In some instances the interaction can be dangerous or life-threatening and must be avoided: cisplatin, cyclosporine.

What the FDA says about use in pregnancy: Category D (see Appendix).

What the available evidence suggests about breast-feeding safety: Unknown.

The bottom line for you:

- Melphalan is an effective part of multidrug regimens for the treatment of life-threatening malignant diseases. Case reports of its use during pregnancy reveal that good outcomes are possible, but prudence suggests delaying administration until the second trimester when possible.

- The safety of melphalan while breast-feeding is unknown.

MEPERIDINE

Brand names: Demerol, Doloneurin

Drug classes: Analgesic, narcotic; Anesthetic, adjunct

Indications (what it is used for): Pain, preoperative sedation, obstetric analgesia.

How it works: Binds opioid receptors in the central nervous system (CNS) to block or lessen the response to pain.

Contraindications (reasons you shouldn't take it): Hypersensitivity to drug or class, use of a monoamine oxidase inhibitor (MAOI) within 14 days.

Possible side effects and warnings: Can cause respiratory depression and arrest, cardiac arrest, palpitations, irregular heart rate, dependency, abuse, vomiting, sweating, shock, agitation, disorientation, euphoria, dysphoria, weakness, dry mouth, flushing, visual disturbances, constipation, biliary tract spasm, low blood pressure, fainting, itching, skin rashes, and pain at the site of injection. Should be used with caution in women who have respiratory, liver, or kidney dysfunction; seizure disorder; head injury; hypothyroidism; atrial flutter; or convulsions.

How it can affect pregnant women: Meperidine is a synthetic narcotic similar in activity to morphine. Historically, meperidine was perhaps the most commonly used parenteral (not administered by mouth) opioid during labor for pain relief. However, well-designed studies demonstrate that the incidence of cesarean delivery in nulliparous women (women having their first child) with epidural analgesia is similar to IV meperidine but that epidural analgesia provides superior pain relief, less sedation, and no risk of newborn respiratory depression. When used for early labor analgesia, meperidine increases the acid level (lowers the pH) in the umbilical cord blood of newborns, perhaps because of decreased maternal breathing. Postoperatively, meperidine offers high-quality pain relief with few side effects.

How it can affect a developing embryo or fetus: Meperidine crosses the human placenta and significantly decreases variation in the fetal heart rate, which is also associated with an increase in the level of acid in the fetal blood, presumably because it decreases maternal breathing. Meperidine reaches its highest concentration in the fetal tissues 2–3 hours after being given to the mother, correlating with the clinical observation that the maximum risk of newborn breathing depression occurs 2–3 hours after maternal injection. There is a risk that the newborn may require resuscitation. The greater the time interval from drug injection to delivery (up to 4 hours), the lower the newborn's performance on the Brazelton Neonatal Behavioral Assessment Scale, suggesting that he or she is sedated.

Breast-feeding: Meperidine is excreted into human breast milk, with peak levels occurring about 2 hours after administration. Although a single dose of meperidine has little impact on a nursing infant, repeated administration leads to sedation. Nursing infants exposed to morphine are more alert and oriented than those exposed repeatedly to meperidine. This makes morphine the preferred narcotic for breast-feeding mothers.

Potential drug interactions: Interaction between the following medications and meperidine has the potential to impact the effect of one or more of the drugs. In some instances the interaction can be dangerous or life-threatening and must be avoided:

other central nervous system (CNS) depressants, including sedatives or hypnotics, general anesthetics, phenothiazines, other tranquilizers, and ethanol; agonist-antagonist analgesics (e.g., buprenorphine, butorphanol, nalbuphine, pentazocine); acyclovir; cimetidine; phenytoin; ritonavir.

What the FDA says about use in pregnancy: Category C (see Appendix).

What the available evidence suggests about breast-feeding safety: Safe, but there are better alternatives.

The bottom line for you:

- The long clinical experience with meperidine during pregnancy and while breast-feeding is overall reassuring. If repetitive doses are necessary while breast-feeding, morphine is a better choice.
- Repeated use during labor leads to the accumulation of meperidine and normeperidine in fetal tissues, reaching a maximum about 3 hours after administration. Newborn breathing depression may occur 2–3 hours after maternal administration.

MERCAPTOPURINE

Brand name: Purinethol

Drug classes: Antineoplastic, antimetabolite; Immunomodulator

Indications (what it is used for): Crohn's disease (inflammatory bowel disease), ulcerative colitis, acute lymphocytic and acute myelogenous leukemia.

How it works: Multiple biochemical effects leading to cell death.

Contraindications (reasons you shouldn't take it): Hypersensitivity to drug or class, kidney dysfunction.

Possible side effects and warnings: Can cause bone marrow suppression, liver toxicity, kidney stones, diarrhea, fever, nausea, vomiting, loss of appetite, jaundice, abdominal pain, swelling, and bleeding. Should be used with caution in women with bone marrow suppression.

How it can affect pregnant women: There are no adequate reports or well-controlled studies of mercaptopurine in pregnant women. Mercaptopurine and azathioprine are the immunomodulatory agents most commonly encountered during pregnancy in women with inflammatory bowel disease. Both drugs require caution. Mercaptopurine is also used as an adjunct to prevent organ rejection after transplantation.

Inflammatory bowel disease can be challenging during pregnancy. Women with symptom-free disease are likely to have an uncomplicated pregnancy, whereas those with symptoms are more likely to experience a worsening of their disease and are at risk for miscarriage, stillbirth, and a low-birth-weight baby. In women considering pregnancy, a flare should be treated aggressively and remission accomplished before conception. A woman who unexpectedly conceives while her disease is active should be treated aggressively, as remission provides the greatest hope for a favorable outcome.

The treatment of acute myelogeous leukemia typically involves a complex drug regimen that includes mercaptopurine. Multiple case reports suggest that the use of mercaptopurine can produce a complete and sustained remission culminating in the delivery of a normally developed infant.

How it can affect a developing embryo or fetus: There are no adequate reports or well-controlled studies of mercaptopurine in human fetuses. It likely crosses the human placenta since temporary severe newborn bone marrow suppression is reported. The impact of first-trimester mercaptopurine use on fetal development is controversial. Lower-quality studies have concluded that there is no increased risk of birth defects. However, a more recent, higher-quality study that included all cases in a specific population concluded that risk of malformation is increased more than 6 times. In a second recent report, the incidence of fetal loss was higher in women with inflammatory bowel disease previously treated with mercaptopurine compared to those who had not been treated with the medication. Whether this was related to their older age at conception, longer duration of disease, more severe disease at the outset of pregnancy, or use of mercaptopurine cannot be determined. Although it is suggested that mercaptopurine increases the risk of miscarriage, it proved a poor agent to induce miscarriage in one study.

Exposure during the second and third trimesters does affect the fetal immune system, and birth weight may be reduced. Toxic effects on the newborn pancreas, liver, and lymphocytes are reported. Rodent studies found an increased incidence of cleft palate, small chin and tongue, short limbs, and gut herniation. Zinc supplementation reduced the risk in rodents of an adverse effect. However, animal studies are not necessarily good indicators of how a drug will behave in humans.

Breast-feeding: There is no published data in nursing women. It is unknown whether mercaptopurine enters human breast milk.

Potential drug interactions: Interaction between the following medications and mercaptopurine has the potential to impact the effect of one or more of the drugs. In some instances the interaction can be dangerous or life-threatening and must be avoided: allopurinol, trimethoprim-sulfamethoxazole, and warfarin.

What the FDA says about use in pregnancy: Category D (see Appendix).

What the available evidence suggests about breast-feeding safety: Unknown; best to avoid.

The bottom line for you:
- Mercaptopurine is a commonly used drug for the treatment of inflammatory bowel disease.
- Women with ulcerative colitis should conceive when their disease is quiet, if possible.
- It is reasonable to assume that mercaptopurine is a weak to modest teratogen (substance that can cause birth defects) and should be avoided in the first trimester when medically feasible. Zinc supplementation may reduce the risk of an adverse effect.

- Until the impact is known, it is best to avoid immunosuppressive medications while breast-feeding.

MEROPENEM

Brand name: Merrem IV
Drug classes: Antibiotic; Carbapenem
Indications (what it is used for): Treatment of infection from susceptible bacteria.
How it works: Inhibits cell wall synthesis, leading to bacterial death.
Contraindications (reasons you shouldn't take it): Hypersensitivity to drug or class, penicillin allergy.
Possible side effects and warnings: Can cause seizures, *C. difficile* colitis (diarrhea caused by a bacterial infection related to the use of antibiotics), back pain, abdominal pain, chest pain, bacterial infection in the blood, shock, fever, liver failure, congestive heart failure, rapid or slow heart rate, high or low blood pressure, heart attack, blood clots, fainting, anemia, peripheral swelling, low oxygen levels in the blood, sleeplessness, agitation, delirium, confusion, dizziness, seizure, kidney failure, painful urination, shortness of breath, injection site reaction, rash, itching, and constipation. Should be used with caution in women with a seizure disorder or kidney dysfunction.
How it can affect pregnant women: There are few adequate reports or well-controlled studies of meropenem in pregnant women. One multicenter study concluded that meropenem is an effective and safe alternative to clindamycin-gentamicin for the treatment of women with acute obstetric infections.
How it can affect a developing embryo or fetus: There are no adequate reports or well-controlled studies in human fetuses. Meropenem crosses the human placenta, but the levels achieved are inadequate to treat a fetus for an infection. Rodent and monkey studies are reassuring, revealing no evidence of birth defects or low birth weight despite the use of doses higher than those used clinically.

However, animal studies are not necessarily good indicators of how a drug will behave in humans.

Breast-feeding: There is no published data in nursing women. It is unknown whether meropenem enters human breast milk. Most penicillins are considered safe for use while breast-feeding.

Potential drug interactions: Interaction between the following medications and meropenem has the potential to impact the effect of one or more of the drugs. In some instances the interaction can be dangerous or life-threatening and must be avoided: probenicid, valproic acid.

What the FDA says about use in pregnancy: Category B (see Appendix).

What the available evidence suggests about breast-feeding safety: Unknown, but most penicillins are considered safe.

The bottom line for you:

- Meropenem is safe and effective for the treatment of bacterial infection during pregnancy. However, there are alternative agents with which there is more experience.
- Most penicillins are considered safe for use while breast-feeding.

MESALAMINE

Brand names: Asacol, Pentasa, Rowasa
Drug classes: Gastrointestinal; Salicylate
Indications (what it is used for): Ulcerative colitis, Crohn's disease (inflammatory bowel disease).
How it works: Unknown.
Contraindications (reasons you shouldn't take it): Hypersensitivity to drug or class, hypersensitivity to salicylates.
Possible side effects and warnings: Can cause bloody diarrhea, fever, headache, rash, a life-threatening allergic reaction, bone marrow suppression, kidney damage, inflammation in the kidneys and/or the heart, peptic ulcer, hepatitis, peripheral nerve pain, Stevens-Johnson syndrome (a rare but serious skin reaction to medication), headache, abdominal pain, heartburn, nausea, vomiting, flatu-lence, constipation, diarrhea, weakness, back pain, joint pain, runny nose, dry mouth, painful menstruation, hair loss, and flulike symptoms. Should be used with caution in women with kidney or liver dysfunction, pyloric stenosis (narrowing of the opening between stomach and small intestine), or who are taking bowel movement suppressants.

How it can affect pregnant women: Inflammatory bowel disease can be challenging during pregnancy. Women with symptom-free disease are likely to have an uncomplicated pregnancy, whereas those with symptoms are more likely to suffer a worsening of their disease and are at risk for miscarriage, stillbirth, and a low-birth-weight baby. This is truer for patients with Crohn's disease than those with ulcerative colitis. In women considering pregnancy, a flare should be treated aggressively and remission accomplished before conception. A woman who unexpectedly conceives while her disease is active should be treated aggressively, as remission provides the greatest hope for a favorable outcome. Most women with adverse effects from sulfasalazine tolerate mesalamine. Mesalamine is at least equivalent or superior to sulfasalazine, and superior to placebo in inducing remission of acute inflammatory bowel disease. It is also comparable to sulfasalazine and superior to placebo for long-term maintenance of remission.

How it can affect a developing embryo or fetus: There are no adequate reports or well-controlled studies in human fetuses. Although it is unknown whether mesalamine crosses the human placenta, only trace amounts of the active metabolite (substance the body breaks the medication down into) are found in the fetus. The greatest threat to a normal pregnancy is active disease; therefore, treatment is preferable. Inflammatory bowel disease is associated with increased rates of prematurity and low birth weight. Disease severe enough to require treatment with mesalamine or steroids is associated with lower birth weights than milder disease.

Breast-feeding: There are no adequate reports or well-controlled studies in nursing women. Although it is unknown whether mesalamine enters human breast milk, only trace amounts of its active metabolite are excreted into the milk.

Potential drug interactions: No clinically relevant interactions identified.

What the FDA says about use in pregnancy: Category B (see Appendix).

What the available evidence suggests about breast-feeding safety: Safe.

The bottom line for you:

- Mesalamine is a first-line medication for the treatment of inflammatory bowel disease during pregnancy and while breast-feeding.

- Mesalamine does not appear to pose a major risk for birth defects.

MESTRANOL

Brand names: Genora, Micronor, Nelova, Norethin, Norinyl, Ortho-Novum

Drug classes: Contraceptive; Estrogen; Hormone

Indications (what it is used for): Contraception, painful menstruation, dysfunctional uterine bleeding, endometriosis (the endometrium, which lines the uterus, grows outside the uterus), polycystic ovary syndrome (PCOS, multiple cysts inside the ovary leading to irregular menstruation and infertility).

How it works: Blocks ovulation and changes the properties of cervical mucus and endometrium.

Contraindications (reasons you shouldn't take it): Hypersensitivity to drug or class, pregnancy, liver carcinoma, being a smoker and over the age of 35, undiagnosed vaginal bleeding, breast cancer, endometrial cancer, coronary artery disease, stroke, history of liver dysfunction, history of cholestatic jaundice with other oral contraceptives.

Possible side effects and warnings: Can cause blood clots, heart attack, stroke, high blood pressure, jaundice, benign liver tumors, nausea, vomiting, abdominal pain, bloating, altered menstrual flow, cessation of menstruation, breakthrough bleeding, breast tenderness, swelling, migraine, weight changes, cervical secretion changes, mood swings, headache, vaginal yeast infection, acne, rash, and glucose intolerance.

Should be used with caution in women with liver dysfunction, diabetes, high cholesterol and triglycerides, depression, migraines, or who are breast-feeding.

How it can affect pregnant women: Mestranol is a synthetic estrogen chemically related to ethinyl estradiol. Oral contraceptives containing mestranol are linked to an increased incidence of benign liver tumors and a decreased incidence of benign breast disease. These liver tumors are not worsened by pregnancy. Estrogens are implicated as human carcinogens (substances that can cause cancer), and there is sufficient evidence in experimental animals to conclude that mestranol is a potential carcinogen. There is no indication for mestranol during pregnancy.

How it can affect a developing embryo or fetus: There are no adequate reports or well-controlled studies in human fetuses. Limited rodent studies are reassuring, revealing no evidence of birth defects after early pregnancy exposure. However, animal studies are not necessarily good indicators of how a drug will behave in humans.

Breast-feeding: There are no adequate reports or well-controlled studies in nursing women. Mestranol enters human breast milk, and breast milk and infant weight gain are reduced when mestranol is given after delivery in the initial postpartum period. It is generally considered incompatible with breast-feeding until the milk reflex is well established. There are alternative contraceptives to mestranol while breast-feeding.

Potential drug interactions: Interaction between the following medications or substances and mestranol has the potential to impact the effect of one or more of the drugs. In some instances the interaction can be dangerous or life-threatening and must be avoided: St. John's wort, phenobarbital, carbamazepine, rifampin, erythromycin, clarithromycin, ketoconazole, itraconazole, ritonavir, grapefruit and grapefruit juice.

What the FDA says about use in pregnancy: Category X (see Appendix).

What the available evidence suggests about breast-feeding safety: Not safe.

The bottom line for you:

- Mestranol is an effective contraceptive when combined with a progestational agent.
- There are no indications for its use during pregnancy or while breast-feeding.

METAPROTERENOL

Brand names: Alupent, Arm-A-Med, Dey-Dose, Metaprel, Prometa

Drug classes: Adrenergic agonist; Beta-2 agonist; Bronchodilator

Indications (what it is used for): Asthma.

How it works: Activates the beta-2 adrenergic receptors to eliminate the symptoms.

Contraindications (reasons you shouldn't take it): Hypersensitivity to drug or class, abnormal heart rate, hyperthyroidism, seizure disorder.

Possible side effects and warnings: Can cause palpitations, rapid heart rate, tremor, cardiac arrest, nervousness, headache, nausea, vomiting, dizziness, worsening of asthma, sleeplessness, and diarrhea. Should be used with caution in women with high blood pressure, low potassium levels, heart disease, diabetes, or liver cirrhosis.

How it can affect pregnant women: Metaproterenol is a bronchodilator used for the treatment of asthma. Asthma is a common disease in life and in pregnancy. Approximately one-third of pregnant women with asthma get worse during pregnancy, one-third get better, and one-third remain clinically unchanged. When asthma is well controlled it does not affect pregnancy outcome, but poorly controlled asthma may increase the risk of preterm birth (before 37 weeks) or low birth weight. Inhaled corticosteroids are considered the preventative medication of choice for pregnant women with persistent asthma unless their condition is well controlled by cromolyn or nedocromil. Budesonide and beclomethasone are considered the first-line treatments. Metaproterenol is a second- or third-line treatment. The inhalation format has been discontinued in the U.S.; tablets and syrup are available.

Like other beta-mimetic agents, metaproterenol increases the pulse and lowers blood pressure. There are no adequate reports or well-controlled studies of metaproterenol in pregnant women. It has been used to treat preterm labor, but there is no evidence that it provides any advantage over other medications such as terbutaline.

How it can affect a developing embryo or fetus: There are no adequate reports or well-controlled studies in human fetuses. Although it is unknown whether metaproterenol crosses the human placenta, other beta-mimetic agents do cross. In rabbits, metaproterenol caused birth defects when given at doses more than 50 times the maximum recommended clinical dose; there were no adverse effects on other rodents. Studies in animals and humans revealed no evidence that beta-2 adrenergic agonists pose a cardiovascular risk for the fetus and newborn. However, animal studies are not necessarily good indicators of how a drug will behave in humans.

Breast-feeding: There is no published data in nursing women. It is unknown whether metaproterenol enters human breast milk. Considering the pattern of use, it is unlikely that a breast-feeding baby would be affected by occasional maternal use.

Potential drug interactions: Interaction between the following medications and metaproterenol has the potential to impact the effect of one or more of the drugs. In some instances the interaction can be dangerous or life-threatening and must be avoided: other beta-adrenergic bronchodilators, monoamine oxidase inhibitors (MAOIs), tricyclic antidepressants (TCAs).

What the FDA says about use in pregnancy: Category C (see Appendix).

What the available evidence suggests about breast-feeding safety: Unknown, but likely safe.

The bottom line for you:

- Metaproterenol is an effective and reasonably safe bronchodilator for pregnant and breast-feeding women with bronchial asthma and reversible bronchospasm.

METARAMINOL

Brand name: Aramine

Drug classes: Adrenergic agonist; Alpha- and beta-agonist

Indications (what it is used for): Circulatory shock.

How it works: Raises blood pressure by activating alpha- and beta-1 adrenergic receptors, causing constriction of the blood vessels.

Contraindications (reasons you shouldn't take it): Hypersensitivity to drug or class, general anesthesia with halothane or cyclopropane.

Possible side effects and warnings: Can cause cardiac arrest, fluid in the lungs, high blood pressure, seizures, irregular heart rate, cerebral hemorrhage, anxiety, restlessness, dizziness, headache, nausea, vomiting, flushing, pallor, and sweating. Should be used with caution in women with cardiovascular disease, thyroid disease, diabetes, or a history of malaria.

How it can affect pregnant women: Metaraminol increases both systolic and diastolic blood pressure. There are no adequate reports or well-controlled studies of metaraminol in pregnant women. It has been used during pregnancy to maintain blood pressure immediately after spinal anesthesia before a cesarean delivery, and for cardiovascular support in women with septic shock (an overwhelming infection leading to life-threatening low blood pressure). As metaraminol is a strong constrictor of the uterine arteries, many doctors prefer ephedrine prior to placing spinal anesthesia.

How it can affect a developing embryo or fetus: There are no adequate reports or well-controlled studies in human fetuses. It is unknown whether metaraminol crosses the human placenta. Rodent birth defect studies have not been performed. Both a slow fetal heart rate or a heart rate deceleration after a contraction are well-recognized complications of spinal/epidural analgesia and are caused by low blood pressure. Metaraminol-treated pregnancies have a lower incidence of low blood pressure and, as a direct result, a lower risk of increased acid levels in the newborn. It is unclear whether metaraminol is better than ephedrine for this indication.

Breast-feeding: There is no published data in nursing women. It is unknown whether metaraminol enters human breast milk. However, considering the limited exposure long before breast-feeding begins, it is unlikely that a breast-feeding baby would ingest clinically relevant amounts.

Potential drug interactions: Interaction between the following medications and metaraminol has the potential to impact the effect of one or more of the drugs. In some instances the interaction can be dangerous or life-threatening and must be avoided: digitalis, monoamine oxidase inhibitors (MAOIs), tricyclic antidepressants (TCAs).

What the FDA says about use in pregnancy: Category C (see Appendix).

What the available evidence suggests about breast-feeding safety: Likely safe.

The bottom line for you:

- Metaraminol effectively maintains arterial pressure and blood flow to the uterus during spinal/epidural analgesia.
- Its use during labor and delivery is unlikely to have any effect on breast-feeding.

METFORMIN

Brand names: Glucophage, Glucophage XR

Drug classes: Biguanide; Hypoglycemic

Indications (what it is used for): Type II diabetes, polycystic ovary syndrome (PCOS [multiple cysts inside the ovary leading to irregular menstruation and infertility]).

How it works: Increases insulin sensitivity, thus decreasing liver glucose production and intestinal glucose absorption; also decreases serum insulin and androgen levels.

Contraindications (reasons you shouldn't take it): Hypersensitivity to drug or class, kidney or liver dysfunction, metabolic acidosis (too much acid in the blood despite normal respirations), congestive heart failure, recent heart attack, use of iodinated contrast.

Possible side effects and warnings: Can cause flatulence, diarrhea, nausea, vomiting, weakness, indigestion, abdominal discomfort, headache, anemia due to a folate or B12 deficiency, loss of appetite, altered taste, and rash. Should be used with caution in women with lung disease or liver dysfunction.

How it can affect pregnant women: Metformin is an insulin-sensitizing agent effective in women with metabolic syndrome (includes obesity, high blood pressure, diabetes, high lipid levels) or polycystic ovary syndrome who have significant insulin resistance. More than 25% of U.S. women have metabolic syndrome and another 5% of women have PCOS and have difficulty conceiving. Seventy percent of women with PCOS who ovulate while taking only metformin conceive within 6 months. Metformin also improves the outcome of in vitro fertilization in women with clomiphene-resistant PCOS. There are no adequate reports or well-controlled studies of metformin in pregnant women. Metformin use is associated with a decreased rate of miscarriage and a tenfold reduction in gestational diabetes. Metformin, glyburide, and acarbose are alternatives to insulin for the treatment of high glucose levels in women with gestational or type II diabetes.

How it can affect a developing embryo or fetus: There are no adequate reports or well-controlled studies in human fetuses. Metformin crosses the human placenta. It does not block placental glucose uptake and transport. In clinical study, metformin was not associated with birth defects, nor did it adversely affect birth weight or height, weight, or motor and social development at 3 and 6 months. Newborns of women whose serum glucose levels were controlled by metformin do not develop hypoglycemic episodes more frequently than newborns delivered to women treated by insulin alone. Rodent studies are reassuring, revealing no evidence of birth defects or low birth weight despite the use of doses higher than those used clinically. However, animal studies are not necessarily good indicators of how a drug will behave in humans.

Breast-feeding: Less than 1% of the maternal dose of metformin enters human breast milk, an amount too small to have a clinically significant effect on a breast-feeding baby.

Potential drug interactions: Interaction between the following medications and metformin has the potential to impact the effect of one or more of the drugs. In some instances the interaction can be dangerous or life-threatening and must be avoided: furosemide, nifedipine, cationic drugs (e.g., amiloride, digoxin, morphine, procainamide, quinidine, quinine, ranitidine, triamterene, trimethoprim, vancomycin), cimetidine, thiazides and other diuretics, corticosteroids, phenothiazines, thyroid products, estrogens, oral contraceptives, phenytoin, nicotinic acid, sympathomimetics, calcium channel blockers, isoniazid.

What the FDA says about use in pregnancy: Category B (see Appendix).

What the available evidence suggests about breast-feeding safety: Safe.

The bottom line for you:

- Metformin therapy throughout pregnancy and while breast-feeding is safe and effective for the treatment of metabolic disorders associated with insulin resistance.
- It is a useful adjunct for the treatment of gestational and type II diabetes when glyburide alone fails to achieve normal glucose levels.

METHADONE

Brand names: Dolophine, Dolophine HCL, Methadone HCl, Methadose, Tussol, Westadone

Drug class: Analgesic, narcotic

Indications (what it is used for): Pain, opiate addiction.

How it works: Partially activates the opiate receptors and avoids the elevated mood opiates usually produce.

Contraindications (reasons you shouldn't take it): Hypersensitivity to drug or class.

Possible side effects and warnings: Can cause elevated mood, depressed mood, weakness, sleeplessness, agitation, visual disturbances, headache, disorientation, seizures, shock, cardiac arrest, respiratory depression or arrest, dizziness, sedation, nausea, vomiting, sweating, dry mouth, flushing, urinary retention, rash, and low platelet count. Should be used with caution in women with kidney or liver dysfunction; low levels of thyroid hormone; Addison's disease (deficiency of adrenal gland hormones); or sudden abdominal pain; or who are taking rifampin, pentazocine, desipramine, or monoamine oxidase inhibitors (MAOIs).

How it can affect pregnant women: Methadone is a synthetic narcotic with many actions similar to morphine except it does not cause intense euphoria. Methadone is nonsedating. Methadone is a first-line treatment of heroin addiction. Drug use during pregnancy is a major perinatal health issue worldwide. Some 200,000 addicted infants are born each year in the U.S. The goal of methadone maintenance is to relieve the narcotic craving in the mother, suppress withdrawal, and block the euphoric effects associated with heroin. Treatment continues for an indefinite period of time. Because drug-addicted women often use more than one illicit agent, the impact of methadone alone is difficult to ascertain. Its use throughout pregnancy is associated with less illicit drug use and does not increase the rates of newborn withdrawal compared with women who begin methadone in the second or third trimester. Addicted women should seek help early in pregnancy.

Postoperative pain management is a challenge with opiate-addicted women. Women on a stable dose of methadone who experience physical trauma, postoperative pain, or other acute pain do not obtain pain relief from their methadone and require larger doses of pain medication during labor. It is generally recommended that methadone treatment be continued while short-acting narcotics are given to relieve the pain as necessary. Sometimes methadone-treated women experience anxiety during pregnancy or after delivery (just as any woman can) and their doctors may increase the methadone dose. However, methadone is not effective for treating anxiety, and other medications should be considered.

How it can affect a developing embryo or fetus: Women who continue heroin use throughout pregnancy have a greater likelihood of preterm birth and an undergrown newborn than women who go on methadone instead. Methadone crosses the human placenta, but fetal levels decline as pregnancy advances. Daily maternal treatment does alter the behavior of the fetus, with a decrease in breathing and movement. Infants of women on methadone maintenance have higher mean birth weights. Although infants experiencing withdrawal from the medication after they are born have a more intense withdrawal compared to heroin-exposed babies without methadone treatment, this is offset by the fact that women who use heroin (and therefore their fetuses) tend to experience withdrawal several times during the pregnancy as opposed to just once with methadone. In one study of selected pregnancies, lowering the maternal methadone dose several weeks before delivery was associated with decreased incidence and severity of newborn withdrawal. Methadone does not appear detrimental for fetal brain development. Some reports suggest an increased incidence of SIDS (sudden infant death syndrome) in newborns delivered to mothers who use methadone during pregnancy.

Breast-feeding: Only small quantities of methadone are excreted into human breast milk, too small to reliably prevent newborn withdrawal. The risk of an adverse event with either breast-feeding or weaning is low. Pregnant women on methadone maintenance therapy are encouraged to nurse if they are HIV negative.

Potential drug interactions: Interaction between the following medications and methadone has the potential to impact the effect of one or more of the drugs. In some instances the interaction can be dangerous or life-threatening and must be avoided: antagonists or partial antagonists (e.g., buprenorphine, butorphanol, nalbuphine, naloxone, naltrexone, pentazocine); abacavir; amprenavir; efavirenz; nelfinavir; nevirapine; ritonavir; lopinavir-ritonavir combination; didanosine; stavudine; zidovudine; rifampin; phenytoin; strong CYP3A4 inhibitors, such as azole antifungal agents (e.g., ketoconazole); selective serotonin reuptake inhibitors (SSRIs) (e.g., fluvoxamine, sertraline); monoamine oxidase inhibitors (MAOIs); desipramine; arrhythmogenic agents such as class I and III antiarrhythmics; neuroleptics, trycyclic antidepressants (TCAs); calcium channel blockers; drugs capable of inducing electrolyte disturbances (including diuretics, laxatives, and mineralocorticoid hormones); ethanol; alcohol; other opioids or central nervous system depressants (both legal and illicit); benzodiazepines.

What the FDA says about use in pregnancy: Category C (see Appendix).

What the available evidence suggests about breast-feeding safety: Safe.

The bottom line for you:

- Methadone is itself addictive to the mother and her fetus, but is considered safe and effective during pregnancy and while breast-feeding for the treatment of substance abuse.

- Methadone maintenance is not a curative treatment for heroin addiction and should be undertaken only in specialized centers.

- Methadone maintenance reduces and/or eliminates the use of heroin, reduces the maternal death rates and criminality associated with heroin use, and allows patients to improve their health and social productivity.

- Pregnant women on methadone maintenance therapy are encouraged to nurse if they are HIV negative.

- Enrollment in a methadone maintenance program has the potential to reduce the transmission of infectious diseases associated with heroin injection.

METHAMPHETAMINE

Brand names: Desoxyn, Methampex

Drug classes: Amphetamine; Anorexiant; CNS stimulant

Indications (what it is used for): Attention deficit disorder (ADD), weight loss, narcolepsy.

How it works: Appetite suppression and central nervous system stimulation.

Contraindications (reasons you shouldn't take it): Hypersensitivity to drug or class, glaucoma, arteriosclerosis, cardiovascular disease, severe high blood pressure, hyperthyroidism, agitation, drug abuse.

Possible side effects and warnings: Can cause rapid or irregular heart rate, palpitations, dizziness, depressed mood, overstimulation, elevated mood, sleeplessness, tremor, restlessness, headache, diarrhea, constipation, dry mouth, unpleasant taste, hives, decreased sex drive, stroke, stomach cramps, shaking, anxiety, paranoia, hallucinations, structural changes in the brain, and growth suppression. Should be used with caution in women with high blood pressure.

How it can affect pregnant women: Methamphetamine is a central nervous system stimulant that has no medical indications during pregnancy. The illicit use of methamphetamine, also called crystal meth or speed, is a major health-care problem in some regions of the U.S. It is injected, smoked, snorted, or ingested orally. Addiction is common. The use of a variant, Ecstasy (3,4-methylenedioxymethamphetamine; MDMA), is also becoming more common during pregnancy. Maternal death can occur with usage. Ecstasy users tend to be young and single and have a higher rate of unplanned pregnancies and a higher likelihood of using other potentially harmful substances (smoking, heavy alcohol intake, and the use of multiple illicit drugs).

How it can affect a developing embryo or fetus: There are no adequate reports or well-controlled studies in human fetuses. Methamphetamine crosses the human placenta and produces significant and long-lasting maternal and fetal cardiovascular effects, including a decrease in fetal oxygen and changes in fetal blood pressure. Children who were exposed to methamphetamine during pregnancy have smaller brain sizes, lower birth weights, and more neurocognitive deficits compared with a control group. Children of dependent women are at risk for low birth weight, preterm birth (before 37 weeks), and neglect and abuse after delivery. Increased frequencies of cleft lip and palate and cardiac anomalies are reported in humans. Rodent studies showed that methamphetamine use can cause damage to embryos and is associated with an increased incidence of birth defects such as small head, open spine defects, incomplete rotation of the body axis, and spinal cord abnormalities. However, animal studies are not necessarily good indicators of how a drug will behave in humans.

Breast-feeding: There is no published data in nursing women. It is unknown whether methamphetamine enters human breast milk.

Potential drug interactions: Interaction between the following medications and methamphetamine has the potential to impact the effect of one or more of the drugs. In some instances the interaction can be dangerous or life-threatening and must be avoided: insulin, guanethidine, monoamine oxidase inhibitors (MAOIs), trycyclic antidepressants (TCAs), amphetamines, phenothiazines.

What the FDA says about use in pregnancy: Category C (see Appendix).

What the available evidence suggests about breast-feeding safety: Unknown.

The bottom line for you:
- There is no medical indication for legally prescribed methamphetamine during pregnancy.
- Methamphetamine is the most common illicitly abused amphetamine and is a teratogen (substance that can cause birth defects). It increases the risk of adverse pregnancy outcomes and congenital malformations (birth defects).
- More and more pregnant women report use of the related compound MDMA during pregnancy. It may well have the same risks.

- Dependent women who become pregnant should seek help immediately and the fetus should be screened for structural defects.
- Methamphetamine is likely to have a negative effect on breast-feeding because increased caloric intake is necessary for lactation, and methamphetamine decreases appetite.

METHENAMINE
Brand names: Hexydal, Lemandine, Mandameth, Mandelamine, Metanamin, Methenamine
Drug classes: Antibiotic; Urologic
Indications (what it is used for): Urinary tract infections due to susceptible bacteria.
How it works: Bactericidal; converted into both ammonia and the bactericidal formaldehyde.
Contraindications (reasons you shouldn't take it): Hypersensitivity to drug or class, kidney insufficiency, low intravascular volume, sulfonamide use.
Possible side effects and warnings: Can cause swelling, lung disease, nausea, vomiting, cramps, bladder irritation, painful urination, urinary urgency, protein and/or blood in the urine, headache, stomatitis (inflammation of the lining of the mouth), and loss of appetite.
How it can affect pregnant women: There are no adequate reports or well-controlled studies of methenamine in pregnant women. Methenamine is used for chronic suppressive treatment of asymptomatic bacteria growing in the urine during pregnancy. Methenamine may be successful after other medications fail.
How it can affect a developing embryo or fetus: There are no adequate reports or well-controlled studies in human fetuses. Methenamine crosses the human placenta. The concentrations of methenamine in umbilical cord plasma and amniotic fluid are low. Rodent studies of birth defects have not been conducted.
Breast-feeding: Methenamine enters human breast milk at a concentration similar to that in the mother's

blood. It is generally considered compatible with breast-feeding.

Potential drug interactions: Should not be given with sulfamethizole.

What the FDA says about use in pregnancy: Category C (see Appendix).

What the available evidence suggests about breast-feeding safety: Safe.

The bottom line for you:

- Methenamine is safe and effective for the treatment of urinary tract infections during pregnancy and while breast-feeding. It may succeed in curing the infection when other medications have failed.

METHICILLIN

Brand name: Staphcillin

Drug classes: Antibiotic; Penicillin

Indications (what it is used for): Bacterial infections with penicillinase-resistant staphylococci.

How it works: Kills bacteria by inhibiting cell wall synthesis.

Contraindications (reasons you shouldn't take it): Hypersensitivity to drug or class.

Possible side effects and warnings: Can cause a life-threatening allergic reaction, rapid swelling of tissue layers under the skin, laryngospasm, bronchospasm, low blood pressure, vascular collapse, serum sickness–like symptoms (fever, malaise, hives, muscle pain, joint pain, abdominal pain), nausea, vomiting, diarrhea, stomatitis (inflammation of the lining of the mouth), hairy tongue, kidney damage, bone marrow depression, and death. It should be used with caution in women with kidney or liver dysfunction.

How it can affect pregnant women: Although methicillin has been largely replaced by cloxacillin and dicloxacillin, the phrase "methicillin resistant *Staphylococcus aureus*" (MRSA) continues to be used to describe *S. aureus* strains resistant to all penicillins. Pregnant women often have mixed vaginal flora of both sensitive and resistant *S. aureus*,

with the latter being a major cause of hospital-acquired infection. There are no adequate reports or well-controlled studies of methicillin in pregnant women.

How it can affect a developing embryo or fetus: There are no adequate reports or well-controlled studies in human fetuses. Methicillin crosses the human placenta, achieving fetal levels similar to those of the mother. Clinical experience does not suggest an increase in birth defects or low birth weight. Rodent studies are reassuring, revealing no evidence of birth defects or low birth weight despite the use of doses higher than those used clinically. However, animal studies are not necessarily good indicators of how a drug will behave in humans.

Breast-feeding: There are no adequate reports or well-controlled studies in nursing women. Methicillin enters human breast milk, but it is generally considered compatible with breast-feeding based on clinical experience.

Potential drug interactions: May reduce the efficacy of oral contraceptives. Disulfiram and probenecid may increase penicillin levels. Methicillin may increase the effect of oral anticoagulants.

What the FDA says about use in pregnancy: Category B (see Appendix).

What the available evidence suggests about breast-feeding safety: Safe.

The bottom line for you:

- Methicillin is safe for use during pregnancy and while breast-feeding for bacterial infections due to methicillin-sensitive strains.

METHIMAZOLE

Brand names: Antitroide-GW, Favistan, Mercaptizol, Mercazole, Tapazole

Drug classes: Antithyroid agent; Hormone

Indications (what it is used for): Hyperthyroidism secondary to thyroid-stimulating immunoglobulin.

How it works: Inhibits thyroid hormone synthesis.

Contraindications (reasons you shouldn't take it): Hypersensitivity to drug or class, breast-feeding.

Possible side effects and warnings: Can cause bone marrow suppression; kidney disease; low levels of prothrombin, a key clotting protein; and inflammation surrounding arteries. It should be used with caution in women with bone marrow suppression or who are pregnant.

How it can affect pregnant women: The most common cause of excess thyroid hormone levels (hyperthyroidism) during pregnancy is Graves' disease, in which the mother makes an antibody that stimulates her thyroid as well as the fetal thyroid. Definitive treatment is the ingestion of a radioactive iodine cocktail that destroys the thyroid. This treatment should not be used in pregnancy. The palliative treatment (which treats the symptoms but does not cure the condition) is either propylthiouracil or methimazole. During a 12-week study of Graves' disease, a single daily dose of 15 mg methimazole was much more effective in producing normal thyroid function than a single daily dose of 150 mg propylthiouracil. Thyroid function tests should be obtained during pregnancy in women suffering from hyperthyroidism and the dose of methimazole adjusted until the hormone level is within the upper normal range. The lowest effective dose is recommended. Women previously treated with either a radioactive cocktail or thyroidectomy may still be producing thyroid-stimulating immunoglobulin even though they are no longer hyperthyroid. If the level of thyroid-stimulating immunoglobulin is elevated, the fetus is at risk for hyperthyroidism and should be referred to a fetal center for evaluation (see propylthiouracil).

How it can affect a developing embryo or fetus: There are no adequate reports or well-controlled studies in human fetuses. Methimazole crosses the human placenta and is an alternative to propylthiouracil for the treatment of fetal hyperthyroidism. The fetal response to a given dose of drug is often different from the maternal response, and some doctors recommend that the fetal thyroid activity be tested directly. Excess methimazole can cause fetal thyroid enlargement and mental retardation due to a very low thyroid hormone level. Recent studies of children exposed to methimazole in utero who were followed until ages 3 to 11 years reveal no negative effects on either thyroid function or physical and intellectual development. However, rare instances of congenital methimazole syndrome (skin missing in small patches, defects in the esophagus and/or trachea and nose combined with absent or underdeveloped nipples) were reported in the past, suggesting that methimazole is a weak human teratogen (substance that can cause birth defects). More recent studies were unable to confirm a difference in the potential to cause birth defects between methimazole and propylthiouracil.

Breast-feeding: Methimazole is excreted in human breast milk, but the quantities are small (2–3%) and newborn thyroid function unaffected. Recent studies showed no adverse effects on newborn thyroid function or on physical and intellectual development of the breast-fed infants of treated mothers.

Potential drug interactions: Interaction between the following medications and methimazole has the potential to impact the effect of one or more of the drugs. In some instances the interaction can be dangerous or life-threatening and must be avoided: anticoagulants, beta-adrenergic blockers, digoxin, theophylline.

What the FDA says about use in pregnancy: Category D (see Appendix).

What the available evidence suggests about breast-feeding safety: Safe.

The bottom line for you:

- Methimazole may be a weak human teratogen and should be avoided during the first trimester.
- Methimazole is a safe and effective alternative to propylthiouracil for the management of maternal Graves' disease or fetal hyperthyroidism after the first trimester if propylthiouracil cannot be used.
- Methimazole is safe for use while breast-feeding.

METHOHEXITAL

Brand name: Brevital

Drug classes: Anesthetic, general; Barbiturate

Indications (what it is used for): Anesthesia induction and maintenance.

How it works: Alters sensory cortex, cerebellar, and motor activities.

Contraindications (reasons you shouldn't take it): Hypersensitivity to drug or class, porphyria (a rare group of blood disorders).

Possible side effects and warnings: Can cause slow, rapid, or irregular heart rate; sudden cardiovascular collapse; low blood pressure, shortness of breath; respiratory depression; and blood clots. It should be used with caution in women with severe cardiovascular disease, low blood pressure, or liver or kidney dysfunction.

How it can affect pregnant women: Methohexital is a very potent but short-acting barbiturate. Cumulative effects are fewer and recovery is more rapid compared to thiobarbiturates. It is used for first-trimester suction abortion, where it is similar in effect to propofol. It is inferior to propofol for cesarean delivery.

How it can affect a developing embryo or fetus: There are no adequate reports or well-controlled studies in human fetuses. Methohexital rapidly crosses the placenta. Rodent studies are reassuring, revealing no evidence of birth defects or low birth weight despite the use of doses higher than those used clinically. However, animal studies are not necessarily good indicators of how a drug will behave in humans.

Breast-feeding: There is no published data in nursing women. It is unknown whether methohexital enters human breast milk. Considering its rapid clearance (how fast it is eliminated from the body), it is unlikely that a clinically significant amount would enter the breast milk.

Potential drug interactions: Interaction between the following medications and methohexital has the potential to impact the effect of one or more of the drugs. In some instances the interaction can be dangerous or life-threatening and must be avoided: phenytoin, halothane, anticoagulants, corticosteroids, ethanol.

What the FDA says about use in pregnancy: Category B (see Appendix).

What the available evidence suggests about breast-feeding safety: Likely safe.

The bottom line for you:

- Methohexital is safe and effective during pregnancy and while breast-feeding.

METHOTREXATE

Brand names: Abitrexate, Emtexate, Folex, Mexate, Rheumatrex, Tremetex

Drug classes: Antineoplastic, antimetabolite; Antirheumatic; Abortificant

Indications (what it is used for): Ectopic pregnancy, trophoblastic disease (tumors that develop from the placenta), rheumatoid arthritis, psoriasis, mycosis fungoides (T cell lymphoma), chemotherapy.

How it works: Inhibits the regeneration of folic acid, which is essential for growth in rapidly growing cells; immunosuppressant.

Contraindications (reasons you shouldn't take it): Hypersensitivity to drug or class, alcohol consumption, liver failure, infection, water in the chest cavity, immunodeficiency syndrome.

Possible side effects and warnings: Can cause low platelet, white blood cell, or red blood cell counts; liver and kidney dysfunction; immunosuppression; opportunistic infection; seizures; neurotoxicity, brain inflammation; spinal cord damage; Stevens-Johnson syndrome or erythema multiforme (both skin disorders); pulmonary fibrosis; nausea; vomiting; exfoliative dermatitis; fever; dizziness; diarrhea; itching; hair loss; and sensitivity to light. Should be used with caution in women with kidney or liver dysfunction, bone marrow depression, ulcerative colitis, or peptic ulcer.

How it can affect pregnant women: Methotrexate has multiple uses in reproductive-age women.

Ectopic pregnancy: Ectopic pregnancy (a pregnancy that establishes itself outside the uterus, often in the fallopian tube) is a major cause of maternal illness and death. Although treatment is often surgical, treatment with methotrexate is becoming routine for appropriate women in many centers. With this approach, 80–90% of women can avoid surgery.

Trophoblastic disease: Trophoblastic disease is a group of pregnancy-related tumors that occur when cells comprising the placenta called trophoblasts start to grow out of control. Methotrexate is a first choice for uncomplicated malignant trophoblastic disease. Low-risk patients are treated by methotrexate alone. Medium- to high-risk women are given multidrug regimens that may include methotrexate. Resistance can occur, requiring the use of alternative drug regimens. After treatment, women should avoid pregnancy until their pregnancy hormone (hCG; human chorionic gonadotropin) level has been normal for 1 year.

Medical abortion: Methotrexate is used to induce a medical abortion of an intrauterine pregnancy. It is more effective combined with misoprostol than when used alone. As it is not 100% effective, women must be followed clinically until their serum hCG is negative.

How it can affect a developing embryo or fetus: Methotrexate attacks rapidly growing cells, so it makes sense that it would pose a risk to an embryo in the first trimester. There are no adequate reports or well-controlled studies in human fetuses of continuing pregnancies. It is unknown whether methotrexate crosses the human placenta. Methotrexate is rapidly taken up by placental cells and then excreted. First-trimester exposure results in an increased risk of birth defects affecting the skull, head, heart, lungs, bowels, and skin. The potential to cause birth defects is increased by the addition of misoprostol. Although most pregnancies exposed to low doses are successful, methotrexate is also associated with developmental delay. There is no link between pregnancy exposure after the first trimester and birth defects.

Breast-feeding: There are no adequate reports or well-controlled studies in nursing women. Despite the fact that it is unknown whether methotrexate enters human breast milk, it is generally considered contraindicated (should not be used) in nursing mothers.

Potential drug interactions: Interaction between the following medications and methotrexate has the potential to impact the effect of one or more of the drugs. In some instances the interaction can be dangerous or life-threatening and must be avoided: nonsteroidal anti-inflammatory drugs (NSAIDs), phenylbutazone, phenytoin, salicylates, sulfonamides, probenecid, oral antibiotics (e.g., chloramphenicol, tetracycline, nonabsorbable broad-spectrum antibiotics), penicillins.

What the FDA says about use in pregnancy: Category X (see Appendix).

What the available evidence suggests about breast-feeding safety: Possibly unsafe.

The bottom line for you:

- Methotrexate is a known teratogen (substance that can cause birth defects) and damages placental growth and function. It should not be used for a continuing pregnancy at any dose in the first trimester (and only at low doses thereafter) unless required to treat a potentially life-threatening illness.

- It is effective for medical abortion in the first trimester and as a treatment of ectopic pregnancy.

- Methotrexate is the drug of choice for low-risk malignant trophoblastic disease.

- The safest course is not to breast-feed while taking methotrexate since it interferes with rapidly growing cells.

METHOXAMINE

Brand name: Vasoxyl

Drug classes: Adrenergic agonist; Dermatologic

Indications (what it is used for): Low blood pressure.

How it works: Activates the a-adrenergic receptors that narrow blood vessels to raise the blood pressure.

Contraindications (reasons you shouldn't take it): Hypersensitivity to drug or class, high blood pressure.

Possible side effects and warnings: Can cause increased uterine contractions, slow fetal heart rate, high blood pressure, nausea, vomiting, headache, anxiety, sweating, and urinary urgency. Should be used with caution in women who are taking tricyclic antidepressants or oxytocic agents or who have taken monoamine oxidase inhibitors (MAOIs) within 14 days, or who have heart block, high thyroid hormone levels, slow heart rate, heart disease, or hardening of the arteries.

How it can affect pregnant women: Spinal or epidural analgesia may cause low blood pressure, and if untreated can cause adverse maternal and fetal effects. The low blood pressure may be corrected by methoxamine if ephedrine fails. There are no adequate reports or well-controlled studies of methoxamine in pregnant women. It decreased uterine blood flow in pregnant sheep and monkeys at doses similar to those used clinically. In rats, methoxamine increased the number of uterine contractions. It is unclear whether the same occurs in humans. In contrast, methoxamine may cause high blood pressure if given with drugs that cause contractions, such as ergonovine, ergotamine, methylergonovine, and vasopressin, and may cause severe high blood pressure.

How it can affect a developing embryo or fetus: There are no adequate reports or well-controlled studies in human fetuses. It is unknown whether methoxamine crosses the human placenta. It decreases uterine blood flow and, as a result, causes a slow fetal heart rate with an accumulation of acid in the fetus.

Breast-feeding: There is no published data in nursing women. It is unknown whether methoxamine enters human breast milk.

Potential drug interactions: Interaction between the following medications and methoxamine has the potential to impact the effect of one or more of the drugs. In some instances the interaction can be dangerous or life-threatening and must be avoided: use of a monoamine oxidase inhibitor (MAOI) within 21 days, tricyclic antidepressants (TCAs).

What the FDA says about use in pregnancy: Category C (see Appendix).

What the available evidence suggests about breast-feeding safety: Unknown.

The bottom line for you:

- Ephedrine remains the drug of choice for the treatment of low blood pressure associated with spinal or epidural anesthesia, because of its wide safety profile. Methoxamine may be used if ephedrine fails to correct the mother's blood pressure.

- There is not enough information currently to determine whether methoxamine is safe for use while breast-feeding.

METHOXSALEN

Brand names: Deltasoralen, Houva-Caps, 8-MOP, Oxsoralen

Drug classes: Photosensitizer; Psoralen

Indications (what it is used for): Severe psoriasis.

How it works: Sensitizes the skin to ultraviolet light, which (probably by DNA damage) decreases cell proliferation.

Contraindications (reasons you shouldn't take it): Hypersensitivity to drug or class, invasive skin cell carcinomas, melanoma.

Possible side effects and warnings: Can cause eye damage, skin aging, skin cancer, skin burn, nervousness, sleeplessness, depression, nausea, vomiting, itching, skin redness, swelling, dizziness, headache, malaise, hypopigmentation, blisters, rash, hives, folliculitis (inflammation of hair follicles), bowel disturbances, leg cramps, low blood pressure, and worsening of psoriasis. Should be used with caution in women with systemic lupus, several types of porphyria (a rare group of blood disorders), xeroderma pigmentosum (extreme sensitivity to UV light), or albinism.

How it can affect pregnant women: There are no adequate reports or well-controlled studies of methoxsalen in pregnant women. Absorption of the topically applied drug is likely low.

How it can affect a developing embryo or fetus: There are no adequate reports or well-controlled studies in human fetuses. It is unknown whether methoxsalen crosses the human placenta. Rodent birth defect studies have not been performed. In one limited rodent study, it may have damaged the embryo. However, animal studies are not necessarily good indicators of how a drug will behave in humans.

Breast-feeding: There is no published data in nursing women. It is unknown whether methoxsalen enters human breast milk, but the concentration is likely low.

Potential drug interactions: Interaction between the following medications and methoxsalen has the potential to impact the effect of one or more of the drugs. In some instances the interaction can be dangerous or life-threatening and must be avoided: anthralin; coal tar or coal tar derivatives; griseofulvin; phenothiazines; nalidixic acid; halogenated salicylanilides (antibacterial soaps); sulfonamides; tetracyclines; thiazides; certain organic staining dyes such as methylene blue, toluidine blue, rose bengal, and methyl orange.

What the FDA says about use in pregnancy: Category C (see Appendix).

What the available evidence suggests about breast-feeding safety: Unknown.

The bottom line for you:

- Methoxsalen should be used during pregnancy and breast-feeding only if the benefit to the woman justifies the potential risk to the embryo, fetus, or newborn.

METHSUXIMIDE

Brand name: Celontin
Drug classes: Anticonvulsant; Succinimide

Indications (what it is used for): Seizures (petit mal).

How it works: Depresses the motor cortex and elevates the level a stimulus must reach to cause a convulsion.

Contraindications (reasons you shouldn't take it): Hypersensitivity to drug or class.

Possible side effects and warnings: Can cause nausea, vomiting, loss of appetite, weight loss, diarrhea, abdominal pain, constipation, abnormal blood counts, bone marrow suppression, irritability, nervousness, headache, blurred vision, light sensitivity, hiccups, sleeplessness, drowsiness, lack of gross-muscle control, dizziness, hives, Stevens-Johnson syndrome (a rare but serious skin reaction to medication), protein in the urine, and puffiness around the eyes. Should be used with caution in women with blood dyscrasias (abnormal blood cells or cells in abnormal quantities) or liver dysfunction.

How it can affect pregnant women: Women on medication for a seizure disorder should (when possible) plan their pregnancies, discuss the optimal medication with their neurologist, and begin appropriate supplemental folate therapy before conception (4 mg per day) to minimize the risk of birth defects. The risks of birth defects associated with antiseizure medications must be weighed against the risks of continued seizures to both the mother and fetus. Women who become pregnant during treatment should not stop treatment on their own but rather meet quickly with their doctor before making a decision.

Methsuximide is indicated for the control of absence (petit mal) seizures resistant to other drugs. There is no published data during pregnancy.

How it can affect a developing embryo or fetus: There are no adequate reports or well-controlled studies in human fetuses. It is unknown whether methsuximide crosses the human placenta. Rodent birth defect studies have not been conducted. Many anticonvulsants are associated with an increased risk of birth defects. The limited experience with methsuximide does not provide enough information to judge its risks other than that it is likely no more than a weak teratogen (substance that can cause birth defects). As with most anticonvulsants, using only one drug and the lowest effective quantity given in divided doses to minimize fetal exposure can reduce the risks.

Breast-feeding: There is no published data in nursing women. It is unknown whether methsuximide enters human breast milk.

Potential drug interactions: May interact with other antiepileptic drugs such as phenytoin and phenobarbital.

What the FDA says about use in pregnancy: No assigned category (see Appendix).

What the available evidence suggests about breast-feeding safety: Unknown.

The bottom line for you:

- Although there are alternative agents with which there is more experience during pregnancy and while breast-feeding, methsuximide may be useful and preferable to control a petit mal seizure.

METHYLCELLULOSE

Brand name: None
Drug class: Laxative
Indications (what it is used for): Constipation.
How it works: Increases stool bulk.
Contraindications (reasons you shouldn't take it): Hypersensitivity to drug or class, appendicitis, fecal impaction, acute abdomen.
Possible side effects and warnings: Can cause nausea, diarrhea, and abdominal cramps.
How it can affect pregnant women: There are no adequate reports or well-controlled studies of methylcellulose in pregnant women. It is neither digestible, toxic, nor allergenic, and as a result, little if any makes its way to the mother's bloodstream.
How it can affect a developing embryo or fetus: There are no adequate reports or well-controlled studies in human fetuses. Based on molecular size, it is unlikely methylcellulose would cross the hu-

man placenta even if it reached the mother's bloodstream. Rodent studies are reassuring, revealing no evidence of birth defects or low birth weight. However, animal studies are not necessarily good indicators of how a drug will behave in humans.

Breast-feeding: There are no adequate reports or well-controlled studies in nursing women. It is unknown whether methylcellulose enters human breast milk. Considering maternal absorption, it is likely safe.

Potential drug interactions: No clinically relevant interactions identified.

What the FDA says about use in pregnancy: No assigned category (see Appendix).

What the available evidence suggests about breast-feeding safety: Safe.

The bottom line for you:

- Methylcellulose is safe for use during pregnancy and while breast-feeding.

METHYLDOPA

Brand names: Aldomet, Alfametildopa, Dimal, Elanpres, Highprepin, Hypermet, Medomet, Methyldopum, Modepres, Prodop, Scandopa
Drug classes: Adrenergic antagonist, central; Antihypertensive
Indications (what it is used for): High blood pressure.
How it works: Activates a-2 adrenergic receptors in the brain that stimulate dilation of the peripheral blood vessels.
Contraindications (reasons you shouldn't take it): Hypersensitivity to drug or class, acute hepatitis, cirrhosis.
Possible side effects and warnings: Can cause hemolytic anemia; heart, liver, or pancreas inflammation; bone marrow suppression; slow heart rate; headache, sedation; chest pain; weakness; congestive heart failure; nausea; vomiting; diarrhea; black tongue; joint pain; muscle pain; jaundice; absent menstruation; breast enlargement; decreased sex drive; and liver dysfunction. It should be used with caution

in women who are taking another antihypertensive or levodopa, have used a monoamine oxidase inhibitor (MAOI) in the last 14 days, or who have kidney dysfunction, positive Coombs' test (presence of antibodies that can destroy red blood cells), or hemolytic anemia.

How it can affect pregnant women: Around 6% of young women (under the age of 30) have chronically high blood pressure. Methyldopa is perhaps the best-studied antihypertensive (blood-pressure-lowering) agent during pregnancy and remains commonly used during pregnancy (if only out of habit; there are superior agents of equal safety in pregnancy). In women with mild to moderate high blood pressure, antihypertensive therapy improves the maternal but apparently not the fetal outcome. In such patients, methyldopa prolongs pregnancy by about 10 days compared to placebo, but it does not decrease the prevalence of superimposed preeclampsia (severe high blood pressure due to a combination of chronic high blood pressure and preeclampsia). Methyldopa is less effective than metoprolol, but with adequate time it is as effective as nifedipine, labetalol, and ketanserin in decreasing both systolic and diastolic blood pressure in women with chronic high blood pressure. Neither short- nor long-term use of methyldopa is associated with adverse maternal effects.

How it can affect a developing embryo or fetus: Most blood-pressure-lowering medications cross the placenta. Neither short- nor long-term effects on the fetus or newborn are reported after long-term methyldopa use. A potentially beneficial effect of methyldopa is that it appears to increase placental blood flow and thus the amount of oxygen delivered to the fetus. Longitudinal studies revealed no developmental disturbances in children at 3 years of age who were exposed to methyldopa in the uterus.

Breast-feeding: The small amount of methyldopa that enters human breast milk appears to be clinically insignificant.

Potential drug interactions: Interaction between the following medications and methyldopa has the potential to impact the effect of one or more of the drugs. In some instances the interaction can be dangerous or life-threatening and must be avoided: other blood-pressure-lowering medications, ferrous sulfate, ferrous gluconate.

What the FDA says about use in pregnancy: Category B (see Appendix).

What the available evidence suggests about breast-feeding safety: Safe.

The bottom line for you:

- Methyldopa is considered safe for the treatment of high blood pressure during pregnancy and while breast-feeding.

METHYLERGONOVINE

Brand name: Methergine

Drug classes: Ergot alkaloid; Oxytocic; Uterine stimulant

Indications (what it is used for): Postpartum bleeding.

How it works: Acts directly on uterine muscle to strengthen the contractions.

Contraindications (reasons you shouldn't take it): Hypersensitivity to drug or class, high blood pressure, preeclampsia/toxemia, pregnancy.

Possible side effects and warnings: Can cause heart attack, nausea, vomiting, diarrhea, headache, hallucinations, high blood pressure, chest pain, ringing in the ears, nasal congestion, blood in the urine, shortness of breath, blood clots, and dizziness. It should be used with caution in women with sepsis (chemicals released into the bloodstream to fight infection trigger inflammation throughout the body).

How it can affect pregnant women: Postpartum hemorrhage remains a leading cause of maternal death and morbidity. Oxytocin, methylergonovine, and several prostaglandins are the pharmacologic agents most frequently used to prevent or treat postpartum hemorrhage. There is a long clinical experience with methylergonovine. It is for the most part safe, effective, and inexpensive. Unfortunately, its shelf life is short in tropical climates, where miso-prostol may be preferable. Methylergonovine is typically administered immediately after delivery when oxytocin alone fails to treat a floppy uterus associated with maternal hemorrhage. The combination of oxytocin and methylergonovine is more effective than oxytocin and misoprostol and has fewer side effects. A combination of misoprostol and methylergonovine is effective for medical termination of pregnancy in the second trimester.

How it can affect a developing embryo or fetus: There are no adequate reports or well-controlled studies in human fetuses. It is unknown whether methylergonovine crosses the human placenta. Rodent birth defect studies have not been performed. Inadvertent administration during pregnancy is followed by strong, unremitting contractions and a slow fetal heart rate.

Breast-feeding: There are no adequate reports or well-controlled studies in nursing women. The concentrations of methylergonovine in human breast milk are clinically insignificant. It has been used for decades for as long as a week after delivery to prevent postpartum hemorrhage without adverse effects on either breast-feeding or the newborn.

Potential drug interactions: Interaction between the following medications or substances and methylergonovine has the potential to impact the effect of one or more of the drugs. In some instances the interaction can be dangerous or life-threatening and must be avoided: certain ergot alkaloids (e.g., dihydroergotamine, ergotamine), potent CYP3A4 inhibitors (e.g., clarithromycin, erythromycin, troleandomycin), HIV protease or reverse transcriptase inhibitors (e.g., delavirdine, indinavir, nelfinavir, ritonavir), azole antifungals (e.g., itraconazole, ketoconazole, voriconazole), less potent CYP3A4 inhibitors (e.g., clotrimazole, fluconazole, fluoxetine, fluvoxamine, grapefruit and grapefruit juice, nefazodone, saquinavir, zileuton).

What the FDA says about use in pregnancy: Category C (see Appendix).

What the available evidence suggests about breast-feeding safety: Safe.

The bottom line for you:

- There are no indications for methylergonovine during a continuing pregnancy.
- Although oxytocin remains the drug of first choice to prevent and treat postpartum uterine atony, methylergonovine rapidly treats most women if oxytocin fails.
- In those instances, it should not have any adverse effects on either breast-feeding or the newborn.

METHYLPHENIDATE

Brand names: Concerta, Metadate CD, Metadate ER, Ritalin, Ritalin LA, Ritalin-SR

Drug classes: Amphetamine; Central nervous system (CNS) stimulant

Indications (what it is used for): Attention deficit/hyperactivity disorder, narcolepsy.

How it works: Stimulates the central nervous system.

Contraindications (reasons you shouldn't take it): Hypersensitivity to drug or class, glaucoma, Tourette's syndrome (involuntary movements and vocalizations), anxiety, use of a monoamine oxidase inhibitor (MAOI) within 14 days.

Possible side effects and warnings: Can cause seizures, growth suppression, psychosis, low white blood cell and/or platelet counts, thrombocytopenic purpura (a serious clotting disorder), Tourette's syndrome, exfoliative dermatitis, drug dependency, abnormal heart rate, erythema multiforme (skin disorder), inflammation in arteries of the brain, liver dysfunction, nervousness, sleeplessness, abdominal pain, nausea, vomiting, blurred vision, rapid heart rate, motor tics, weight loss, chest pain, rash, fever, hives, drowsiness, and involuntary movements similar to tics. It should be used with caution in women with high blood pressure, seizure disorder, psychosis, cardiovascular disease, or alcohol or drug abuse.

How it can affect pregnant women: There are no adequate reports or well-controlled studies of methylphenidate in pregnant women. The clinical experience is limited to case reports of narcolepsy and substance abuse.

How it can affect a developing embryo or fetus: There are no adequate reports or well-controlled studies in human fetuses. Although it is unknown whether methylphenidate crosses the human placenta, the limited human data does not indicate a significant risk of structural abnormalities. However, maternal abuse of methylphenidate plus pentazocine (Ts and Blues) is associated with preterm birth (before 37 weeks), low birth weight, and newborn withdrawal. Skeletal abnormalities were seen in rabbits treated with 40 times the maximum recommended clinical dose. However, animal studies are not necessarily good indicators of how a drug will behave in humans.

Breast-feeding: There is no published data in nursing women. The quantity of methylphenidate that enters human breast milk is unknown.

Potential drug interactions: Interaction between the following medications and methylphenidate has the potential to impact the effect of one or more of the drugs. In some instances the interaction can be dangerous or life-threatening and must be avoided: pressor agents (e.g., guanethidine), coumarin anticoagulants, anticonvulsants (e.g., phenobarbital, phenytoin, primidone), tricyclic (TCA) and selective serotonin reuptake inhibitor (SSRI) antidepressants, clonidine, monoamine oxidase inhibitors (MAOIs).

What the FDA says about use in pregnancy: Category C (see Appendix).

What the available evidence suggests about breast-feeding safety: Unknown.

The bottom line for you:

- Methylphenidate use during pregnancy and while breast-feeding should be restricted to women who have difficulty functioning safely without it.

METHYLPREDNISOLONE

Brand names: Medlone, Medrol, Metrocort Summicort

Drug class: Corticosteroid

Indications (what it is used for): Inflammatory disorders, congenital adrenal hyperplasia (the fetus makes excess male hormones), arthritis, collagen vascular diseases (diseases of the connective tissue), allergy, respiratory diseases, hematologic disorders, worsening multiple sclerosis (autoimmune disease affecting the brain and spinal cord).

How it works: Unknown.

Contraindications (reasons you shouldn't take it): Hypersensitivity to drug or class, systemic fungal infection.

Possible side effects and warnings: Can cause immunosuppression, menstrual irregularities, high blood pressure, peptic ulcer, congestive heart failure, adrenal insufficiency, steroid psychosis (psychotic reactions to steroid use; aka roid rage), pancreatic inflammation, pseudotumor cerebri (increased pressure in the brain unrelated to a tumor), nausea, vomiting, headache, dizziness, heartburn, mood swings, sleeplessness, anxiety, low potassium levels, swelling, appetite changes, skin changes, acne, high blood glucose, and bruising. It should be used with caution in women with congestive heart failure, seizure disorder, diabetes, high blood pressure, osteoporosis, tuberculosis, or liver dysfunction.

How it can affect pregnant women: Methylprednisolone effectively treats a wide range of disorders that may occur during pregnancy, including acute asthma, lupus erythematosus (a chronic inflammatory disease in which the immune system attacks the body's own tissues and organs), nephrotic syndrome (kidney disorder causing protein loss in the urine) due to connective tissue disease, immune glomerulonephritis (inflammation of the kidneys), alloimmune low platelet count, immune low platelet count, inflammatory bowel disease, Bell's palsy (facial paralysis), and herpes gestationis (a rare blistering skin disorder of pregnancy), and is used for a "stress" dose during labor to supplement women who have been taking steroids for more than several weeks. It does not help women with severe morning sickness, as sometimes thought. Steroids may also help reduce the severity and speed the recovery of women with atypical severe preeclampsia (high blood pressure and protein in the urine during pregnancy and complications associated with it). Methylprednisolone can also reduce the risk of ovarian hyperstimulation during ovulation induction for in vitro fertilization (IVF).

How it can affect a developing embryo or fetus: There are no adequate reports or well-controlled studies in human fetuses. Methylprednisolone does not cross the placenta. However, a recent well-designed control trial concluded that high-dose methylprednisolone reduces fetal risks from maternal fever and inflammation but increases the risk of bacteria in the newborn's bloodstream. The effect on the fetus of a large one-time dose is unknown. Although there is evidence that some corticosteroids may be weak teratogens (substances that cause birth defects) when taken in the first trimester, there is no such information for methylprednisolone. There is no increase in risk of anomalies when any steroids are begun after organ formation (after 11 weeks). A few small studies suggested a possible relationship between long-term steroid use during pregnancy and poor fetal growth; however, it is hard to tell if that was the result of the medication or the disease it was being used to treat.

Breast-feeding: There are no adequate reports or well-controlled studies in nursing women. It is unknown whether methylprednisolone enters human breast milk. What little evidence exists suggests that the quantity of corticosteroid excreted into breast milk is not clinically relevant for the newborn.

Potential drug interactions: Interaction between the following medications and methylprednisolone has the potential to impact the effect of one or more of the drugs. In some instances the interaction can be dangerous or life-threatening and must be avoided: cyclosporine, phenobarbital, phenytoin, rifampin, troleandomycin, ketoconazole, high-dose aspirin, oral anticoagulants.

What the FDA says about use in pregnancy: No assigned category (see Appendix).

What the available evidence suggests about breast-feeding safety: Likely safe.

The bottom line for you:

- Methylprednisolone is generally considered safe and effective during pregnancy and while breast-feeding.

METHYSERGIDE

Brand names: Deseril, Sansert
Drug class: Ergot alkaloid
Indications (what it is used for): Migraine headache, diarrhea as a result of carcinoid (a slow-growing cancer, usually in the gastrointestinal tract).
How it works: Blocks serotonin receptors, whose activation causes the symptoms of the disease.
Contraindications (reasons you shouldn't take it): Hypersensitivity to drug or class, arteriosclerosis, kidney or liver dysfunction, high blood pressure, coronary artery disease, collagen (connective tissue) disease, valvular heart disease.
Possible side effects and warnings: Can cause retroperitoneal, pleural, pulmonary, or cardiac fibrosis (scar tissue formation); thickening of the aortic root; aortic and mitral valve thickening; nausea and vomiting; diarrhea; heartburn; abdominal pain; sleeplessness; drowsiness; mild euphoria; dizziness; lack of gross-muscle control; light-headedness; increased sensitivity to touch; facial flushing; nests of superficial blood vessels; increased hair loss; peripheral swelling; low white blood cell count; high eosinophil (type of white blood cell) count; and joint and muscle pain. It should be used with caution in women with retroperitoneal space fibrosis (affecting the kidneys, aorta, renal tract, and other structures) or pulmonary insufficiency.
How it can affect pregnant women: Methysergide constricts cranial and peripheral blood vessels. In doing so, it can prevent or treat migraine headache. There are no adequate reports or well-controlled studies of methysergide in pregnant women. Despite the limited clinical experience, methysergide

is generally considered contraindicated (should not be used) during pregnancy because by constricting blood vessels it could decrease blood flow to the uterus.

How it can affect a developing embryo or fetus: There are no adequate reports or well-controlled studies in human fetuses. It is unknown whether methysergide crosses the human placenta. Rodent studies revealed evidence of damage to embryos and a slow fetal heart rate when administered at high doses, presumably by decreasing uterine blood flow. However, animal studies are not necessarily good indicators of how a drug will behave in humans.

Breast-feeding: There is no published data in nursing women. It is unknown whether methysergide enters human breast milk.

Potential drug interactions: Interaction between the following medications and methysergide has the potential to impact the effect of one or more of the drugs. In some instances the interaction can be dangerous or life-threatening and must be avoided: narcotic analgesics, vasoconstrictor agents (e.g., ergot alkaloids, sumatriptan, nicotine).

What the FDA says about use in pregnancy: Category X (see Appendix).

What the available evidence suggests about breast-feeding safety: Unknown.

The bottom line for you:
- Methysergide generally should not be used during pregnancy and while breast-feeding.
- There are alternative agents with which there is more experience.

METOCLOPRAMIDE

Brand name: Reglan

Drug classes: Antiemetic; Antivertigo agent; Gastrointestinal

Indications (what it is used for): Nausea and vomiting (with or without chemotherapy), gastroesophageal reflux disease (GERD), slow bowel motility due to diabetes.

How it works: Stimulates rhythmic movement of the bowels.

Contraindications (reasons you shouldn't take it): Hypersensitivity to drug or class, pheochromocytoma (adrenal gland tumor), seizure disorder, bowel bleeding or obstruction.

Possible side effects and warnings: Can cause thoughts of suicide, seizures, low white blood cell count, bronchospasm, movement disorders, no menstruation, low or high blood pressure, changes in sex drive, congestive heart failure, abnormal heart rate, porphyria (a rare group of blood disorders), methemoglobinemia (blood disorder that produces too much oxidized hemoglobin), diarrhea, irritability, urinary frequency, anxiety, rash, dizziness, hives, sleeplessness, headache, and confusion. It should be used with caution in women with cirrhosis, congestive heart failure, kidney or liver dysfunction, Parkinson's disease (disorder of the brain that affects movement and coordination), high blood pressure, depression, or breast cancer.

How it can affect pregnant women: Nausea and vomiting are common during the first trimester. Metoclopramide effectively reduces the incidence and severity. Some reports suggest an increased risk of preterm birth (before 37 weeks) with metoclopramide use, but it is unclear whether this is related to metoclopramide or to the underlying disease. Metoclopramide is a second-line medication for the treatment of severe morning sickness or gastroesophageal reflux. Metoclopramide is highly effective for controlling nausea and vomiting during cesarean delivery. Metoclopramide is also helpful for the treatment of migraine.

How it can affect a developing embryo or fetus: There are no adequate reports or well-controlled studies in human fetuses. Metoclopramide crosses the human placenta. Its use in the first trimester has not been associated with an increased risk of malformations, miscarriage, or decreased birth weight. Rodent studies are reassuring, revealing no evidence of birth defects or low birth weight despite the use of doses higher than those used clinically. However, animal studies are not necessarily good indicators of how a drug will behave in humans.

Breast-feeding: Metoclopramide is concentrated in breast milk, but the amount absorbed by a breast-fed baby is considerably less than the dose recommended for infants. Metoclopramide probably does not increase breast milk volume as was once thought.

Potential drug interactions: Interaction between the following medications and metoclopramide has the potential to impact the effect of one or more of the drugs. In some instances the interaction can be dangerous or life-threatening and must be avoided: alcohol, sedatives, hypnotics, narcotics, tranquilizers, monoamine oxidase inhibitors (MAOIs), digoxin, acetaminophen, cyclosporine, ethanol, levodopa, tetracycline.

What the FDA says about use in pregnancy: Category B (see Appendix).

What the available evidence suggests about breast-feeding safety: Safe.

The bottom line for you:

- Metoclopramide complements other antiemetic drugs for the management of nausea and vomiting during pregnancy and while breast-feeding.

METOPROLOL

Brand names: Betalor, Bloxan, Cardoxone, Lopressor, Metolar, Seloxen, Toprol XL

Drug classes: Adrenergic antagonist; Beta-blocker

Indications (what it is used for): High blood pressure, heart attack, angina.

How it works: Blocks the beta-1 adrenergic receptors, whose activation causes the symptoms.

Contraindications (reasons you shouldn't take it): Hypersensitivity to drug or class, bronchospasm, abnormal heart rates or rhythms, congestive heart failure, low blood pressure, depressed respiratory function.

Possible side effects and warnings: Can cause slow heart rate, congestive heart failure, bronchospasm, depression, shortness of breath, fatigue, dizziness, abdominal pain, dry mouth, low white blood cell count, platelet disorders, nausea, vomiting, heartburn, flatulence, constipation, diarrhea, itching, headache, sleepiness, nightmares, sleeplessness, musculoskeletal pain, blurred vision, decreased sex drive, and ringing in the ears. It should be used with caution in women with asthma, diabetes, or hyperthyroidism, or who have recently had major surgery.

How it can affect pregnant women: Metoprolol has been extensively tested during pregnancy and deemed safe. Metoprolol is more effective than methyldopa in decreasing both systolic and diastolic blood pressure in women with chronic high blood pressure, but it is less effective than nicardipine. Metoprolol is an effective treatment for mild to moderate chronic high blood pressure, stable angina, and abnormal heart rate, and for patients recovering from a heart attack. Its clearance from the blood is increased during pregnancy, and as a result the dose may need to be increased each trimester. In principle, the management of an abnormal heart rate is similar whether the patient is pregnant or not.

How it can affect a developing embryo or fetus: Although metoprolol is used extensively, there are no adequate reports or well-controlled studies in human fetuses. Metoprolol crosses the human placenta but does not adversely affect the fetal heart rate. Some beta-blockers (e.g., atenolol and propranolol) are associated with an increased risk of low birth weight, but this has not been noted with metoprolol. Rodent studies are reassuring, revealing no evidence of birth defects or low birth weight despite the use of doses higher than those used clinically. However, animal studies are not necessarily good indicators of how a drug will behave in humans.

Breast-feeding: Small quantities of metoprolol are excreted into human breast milk, but levels in breast-feeding newborns are very low or undetectable between breast-feeding periods.

Potential drug interactions: Interaction between the following medications and metoprolol has the potential to impact the effect of one or more of the drugs. In some instances the interaction can be dangerous or life-threatening and must be avoided: catecholamine-depleting drugs (e.g., MAOIs, reserpine), CYP2D6 inhibitors (e.g., fluoxetine, paroxetine, propafenone, quinidine), clonidine.

What the FDA says about use in pregnancy: Category C (see Appendix).

What the available evidence suggests about breast-feeding safety: Safe.

The bottom line for you:

- Metoprolol is generally considered safe and effective during pregnancy and while breast-feeding.

METRONIDAZOLE

Brand name: Flagyl

Drug classes: Antibiotic; Antiprotozoal; Dermatologic

Indications (what it is used for): Infection due to sensitive bacteria and certain parasites.

How it works: Inhibits DNA synthesis.

Contraindications (reasons you shouldn't take it): Hypersensitivity to drug or class, alcohol consumption.

Possible side effects and warnings: Can cause seizures, nerve damage, metallic taste, mouth or tongue sores, low white blood cell count, vaginal yeast infection, dizziness, vertigo, decreased coordination, lack of gross-muscle control, confusion, irritability, depression, weakness, sleeplessness, red rash, flushing, nasal congestion, dry mucous membranes, fever, painful and/or frequent urination, incontinence, painful intercourse, decreased sex drive, nervous distress, nausea, vomiting, and headache. It should be used with caution in women with liver dysfunction, blood dyscrasias (abnormal blood cells or cells in abnormal quantities), seizures, or neuropathies (nerve damage outside the brain and spinal cord).

How it can affect pregnant women: Metronidazole is used widely during pregnancy for the treatment of bacterial vaginosis (BV). Bacterial vaginosis is associated with preterm premature rupture of membranes

(water breaking before 37 weeks), preterm labor and delivery, and postpartum endometritis. Systemic and local therapy with metronidazole effectively treats BV. However, treatment does not clearly improve pregnancy outcome. Women who deliver preterm with symptomatic BV have a lower risk of preterm birth in a subsequent pregnancy if treated with metronidazole. Unfortunately, the treatment of women with asymptomatic BV and no prior preterm birth does not alter their preterm delivery rate. Further, women in several studies treated with metronidazole before 26 weeks for asymptomatic BV actually had a higher rate of preterm labor than the untreated group. In a study of women in the second trimester with a risk factor for preterm birth (fetal fibronectin, a protein, detected in the cervical mucus), metronidazole was associated with a near doubling of the preterm birth rate. These studies indicate that metronidazole should not be prescribed for asymptomatic vaginitis in the first and second trimesters.

High-risk conditions that require treatment of BV with metronidazole include women with prior preterm birth, low body mass, and evidence of endometritis (inflammation of the lining of the uterus) before pregnancy. Metronidazole also decreases the risk of upper genital tract infection after first-trimester abortion. Symptomatic trichomoniasis (a sexually transmitted disease caused by a parasite) is associated with an increased incidence of adverse outcomes of pregnancy. A single dose of metronidazole cures 90% of trichomoniasis; the cure rate is higher if both partners are treated. Unfortunately, the treatment of pregnant women with asymptomatic trichomoniasis does not prevent preterm delivery. Other diseases, such as inflammatory bowel disease, *C. difficile* colitis (diarrhea caused by a bacterial infection related to the use of antibiotics), and anaerobic and protozoal infections, are successfully treated during pregnancy with a short-term course of metronidazole.

How it can affect a developing embryo or fetus: Metronidazole crosses the human placenta. Although it achieves levels in the fetus similar to those in the mother, there is no evidence that metronidazole is a major cause of birth defects when used in the recommended doses.

Metronidazole appears safe if used for short durations. The possible adverse fetal effects related to the long-term exposure necessary to treat inflammatory bowel disease remain unknown. Rodent studies are reassuring, revealing no evidence of birth defects or low birth weight despite the use of doses higher than those used clinically. However, animal studies are not necessarily good indicators of how a drug will behave in humans.

Breast-feeding: Metronidazole is concentrated in human breast milk but is not associated with adverse effects in breast-fed newborns.

Potential drug interactions: Interaction between the following medications and metronidazole has the potential to impact the effect of one or more of the drugs. In some instances the interaction can be dangerous or life-threatening and must be avoided: coumarin anticoagulants, drugs that induce microsomal liver enzymes (e.g., phenobarbital, phenytoin), alcohol, disulfiram, lithium.

What the FDA says about use in pregnancy: Category B (see Appendix).

What the available evidence suggests about breast-feeding safety: Safe.

The bottom line for you:

- Metronidazole is a first-line treatment for symptomatic bacterial vaginosis during pregnancy.
- However, it is unclear whether such treatment improves pregnancy outcome in asymptomatic women, and in some instances, treatment may actually increase the risk of preterm birth. It should be used only when clearly indicated.
- Metronidazole is considered safe for use while breast-feeding.

MEZLOCILLIN

Brand name: Mezlin

Drug classes: Antibiotic; Penicillin

Indications (what it is used for): Infections due to sensitive bacteria.

How it works: Inhibits bacterial wall mucopeptide synthesis, leading to death of the bacteria.

Contraindications (reasons you shouldn't take it): Hypersensitivity to drug or class.

Possible side effects and warnings: Can cause rash, itching, hives, drug fever, unpleasant taste, seizures, bone marrow suppression, hemolytic anemia, infection of the colon, pain, blood clots, nausea, vomiting, fever, and liver dysfunction. It should be used with caution in women experiencing bleeding, renal failure, or low potassium levels.

How it can affect pregnant women: Mezlocillin is effective as treatment or prevention for a variety of diseases during pregnancy, including pyelonephritis (a bacterial infection of the kidneys), preterm premature rupture of the membranes (PPROM, water breaking before 37 weeks), and postpartum uterine infection, and for prevention of infection after cesarean section. In several small trials, mezlocillin prolonged the time from membrane rupture until delivery.

How it can affect a developing embryo or fetus: There are no adequate reports or well-controlled studies in human fetuses. Mezlocillin crosses the placenta and is found in fetal blood and amniotic fluid at low levels. Rodent studies are reassuring, revealing no evidence of birth defects or low birth weight despite the use of doses higher than those used clinically. However, animal studies are not necessarily good indicators of how a drug will behave in humans.

Breast-feeding: There are no adequate reports or well-controlled studies in nursing women. The levels of mezlocillin found in human breast milk are too low to achieve a clinically relevant level in a newborn.

Potential drug interactions: Interaction between the following medications and mezlocillin has the potential to impact the effect of one or more of the drugs. In some instances the interaction can be dangerous or life-threatening and must be avoided:

vecuronium; nondepolarizing muscle relaxants; probenecid; heparin, oral anticoagulants, or other drugs that may affect the blood coagulation system or thrombocyte function.

What the FDA says about use in pregnancy: Category B (see Appendix).

What the available evidence suggests about breast-feeding safety: Safe.

The bottom line for you:

- Mezlocillin is safe and effective as treatment and prevention for a variety of bacterial infections during pregnancy and while breast-feeding.

MICONAZOLE

Brand names: Fungoid, Monistat, Ony-Clear, Tara

Drug classes: Antifungal; Dermatologic

Indications (what it is used for): Yeast, mold, and fungal infections.

How it works: Prevents fungal cell wall synthesis.

Contraindications (reasons you shouldn't take it): Hypersensitivity to drug or class.

Possible side effects and warnings: Can cause a life-threatening allergic reaction, low platelet count, cardiac arrest, vulvovaginal burning, itching, hives, rash, irritation, blood clots, itching, nausea, vomiting, fever, drowsiness, diarrhea, loss of appetite, and flushing.

How it can affect pregnant women: Yeast vaginitis is the most common female genital tract infection. The vaginal environment during pregnancy can encourage the overgrowth of *C. albicans,* which causes yeast infections. There are no adequate reports or well-controlled studies of miconazole in pregnant women. Studies conducted immediately after miconazole was released suggested that it was significantly better than nystatin, clotrimazole, and butoconazole for the treatment of vaginal yeast infection during pregnancy. However, there is no real difference in cure rates after 7 to 14 days of therapy, although more patients relapsed after being cured with nystatin or clotrimazole than with miconazole. Miconazole is as effective as oral therapy with flu-

conazole for vaginal yeast infection. About 25–30% of the oral dose, but less than 0.1% of the vaginal dose, is absorbed into the bloodstream. Although women frequently prefer oral medication, it is not recommended during pregnancy.

How it can affect a developing embryo or fetus: There are no adequate reports or well-controlled studies in human fetuses. It is unknown whether miconazole crosses the human placenta, but it has been used successfully in yeast infections (thrush) of the newborn mouth. Only a small amount of miconazole is absorbed into the mother's blood after vaginal application. Postmarketing studies (studies done by a drug's manufacturer after the drug is on the market) reveal no excess rates of adverse outcomes. Rodent studies are reassuring, revealing no evidence of birth defects or low birth weight despite the use of doses higher than those used clinically. However, animal studies are not necessarily good indicators of how a drug will behave in humans.

Breast-feeding: There is no published data in nursing women. It is unknown whether miconazole enters human breast milk. However, when used vaginally, it is unlikely that a breast-fed newborn would ingest clinically relevant amounts.

Potential drug interactions: Interaction between the following medications and miconazole has the potential to impact the effect of one or more of the drugs. In some instances the interaction can be dangerous or life-threatening and must be avoided: drugs containing cremophor-type vehicles (a chemical used to promote the absorption of a drug), coumarins, hypoglycemic agents, rifampin, ketoconazole, central nervous system–active drugs (e.g., carbamazepine, phenytoin).

What the FDA says about use in pregnancy: Category C (see Appendix).

What the available evidence suggests about breast-feeding safety: Unknown; likely safe after vaginal administration.

The bottom line for you:

- Miconazole is effective treatment of confirmed vaginal yeast infections during pregnancy and while breast-feeding, but its use should be confined to topical or vaginal (not oral) applications.

MIDAZOLAM

Brand names: Midolam, Versed

Drug classes: Anxiolytic; Benzodiazepine; Sedative

Indications (what it is used for): Sedation.

How it works: Decreases anxiety by activating benzodiazepine receptors and enhances GABA effects.

Contraindications (reasons you shouldn't take it): Hypersensitivity to drug or class, glaucoma, shock, central nervous system depression.

Possible side effects and warnings: Can cause respiratory and/or cardiac arrest, withdrawal, addiction, nausea, vomiting, confusion, euphoria, involuntary movements, low blood pressure, sedation, agitation, amnesia for events preceding use of the drug, hallucinations, marked aggressiveness, lack of gross-muscle control, hives, rash, dizziness, metallic taste, dry mouth, and constipation. It should be used with caution in women with chronic obstructive pulmonary disease (COPD), congestive heart failure, or kidney or liver dysfunction, or who have a history of substance abuse.

How it can affect pregnant women: Midazolam is one of the most frequently used benzodiazepines for short surgical procedures and is especially useful in patients who are particularly anxious. Conscious sedation with midazolam and fentanyl significantly improves patient satisfaction with first-trimester abortion performed under local anesthesia. Similar results are obtained in women undergoing outpatient procedures such as retrieving eggs for an IVF (in vitro fertilization) cycle. Women undergoing cesarean delivery also express higher satisfaction with their epidural or spinal block when supplemented with midazolam.

How it can affect a developing embryo or fetus: There are no adequate reports or well-controlled studies in human fetuses. Midazolam crosses the human placenta somewhat more slowly than diazepam, but it eventually reaches the same concentration as that of the mother. The reported effects of benzodiazepines on development are inconsistent. Studies in the 1970s suggested that first-trimester exposure to benzodiazepines increased the risk of facial clefts, cardiac malformations, and other multiple malformations, yet no specific syndrome could be described. Diazepam and chlordiazepoxide were most frequently implicated. However, an increased risk has not been confirmed in recent studies. Midazolam use during the third trimester or labor may be associated with floppy baby syndrome (a laxness to muscles when lying down) or symptoms of newborn withdrawal after birth. These symptoms can include mild sedation, low muscle tone, episodes where the newborn stops breathing, blue tinge to skin from low oxygen, impaired metabolic responses to cold stress, and reluctance to suck, all of which may persist for hours to months after birth.

Breast-feeding: Midazolam is excreted at low concentrations into human breast milk. It is unlikely that a breast-feeding newborn would ingest clinically relevant amounts.

Potential drug interactions: Interaction between the following medications and midazolam has the potential to impact the effect of one or more of the drugs. In some instances the interaction can be dangerous or life-threatening and must be avoided: CYP3A4 inhibitors (e.g., cimetidine [but not ranitidine], diltiazem, erythromycin, ketoconazole, itraconazole, saquinavir, verapamil), CYP3A4 inducers (e.g., carbamazepine, phenytoin, rifampin), phenobarbitol, thiopental, halothane.

What the FDA says about use in pregnancy: Category D (see Appendix).

What the available evidence suggests about breast-feeding safety: Safe.

The bottom line for you:

- Midazolam reduces anxiety associated with surgery performed during pregnancy or while breast-feeding.

• It is unlikely that midazolam is a significant cause of birth defects.

MIFEPRISTONE

Brand names: Mifeprex, RU-486
Drug classes: Abortifacient; Stimulans, uterine
Indications (what it is used for): Abortion/pregnancy termination.
How it works: Progesterone receptor antagonist.
Contraindications (reasons you shouldn't take it): Hypersensitivity to drug, class, or prostaglandins; ectopic pregnancy (implantation outside the uterus); IUD in place; anticoagulation; corticosteroid use; chronic adrenal failure; bleeding disorder; porphyria (a rare group of blood disorders); no access to emergency health care; inability to comply with the treatment.
Possible side effects and warnings: Can cause vaginal bleeding, abdominal cramps, incomplete abortion, birth defects, hemorrhage, nausea, vomiting, anxiety, fever, chills, heartburn, fainting, vaginitis, weakness, vaginal discharge, and sleeplessness.
How it can affect pregnant women: Progesterone is essential for an ongoing pregnancy, and mifepristone blocks progesterone. It is a useful emergency contraceptive after unprotected intercourse for up to 6 days after exposure. In 1996, the FDA Advisory Committee for Reproductive Health Drugs concluded that mifepristone was safe and effective for early pregnancy termination. In 2000, the FDA approved mifepristone to induce abortion in pregnancies that were fewer than 49 days from the last menstrual period. Treated women should expect some bleeding for 9 to 16 days afterward. Eight percent of treated women bleed 30 days or more. The duration of bleeding increases with the gestational age at termination. The duration of bleeding, degree of blood loss, and frequency of uterine pain, vomiting, and diarrhea are all greater with mifepristone abortion compared to surgical termination of pregnancy. The incidence of major complications such as blood transfusion and pelvic infection does not differ between the two. Surgical complications, such as uterine perforation and cervical tears, are less common in women who choose medical abortion (pregnancy termination with drugs such as mifepristone). Termination can be performed later in pregnancy when mifepristone is coupled with misoprostil, a prostaglandin. Mifepristone helps preserve fertility and avoid major maternal complications (death, hysterectomy) in women with ectopic pregnancies that establish themselves in the cervix or in uterine scar tissue.
How it can affect a developing embryo or fetus: There are no adequate reports or well-controlled studies in human fetuses. Mifepristone is contraindicated in women who are planning to continue their pregnancies. It does cross the primate placenta. The human experience with continued pregnancy after failed medical termination is limited. Normal outcomes are reported.
Breast-feeding: There are no adequate reports or well-controlled studies in nursing women. It is unknown whether mifepristone enters human breast milk. Rodent studies suggested that mifepristone enhances milk production.
Potential drug interactions: Interaction between the following medications and mifepristone has the potential to impact the effect of one or more of the drugs. In some instances the interaction can be dangerous or life-threatening and must be avoided: CYP3A4 inducers, including dexamethasone, rifampin, St. John's wort, and certain anticonvulsants (e.g., carbamazepine, phenobarbital, phenytoin).
What the FDA says about use in pregnancy: Category X (see Appendix).
What the available evidence suggests about breast-feeding safety: Unknown.
The bottom line for you:
• Mifepristone is an effective medication for pregnancy termination either alone or in combination with a prostaglandin analog.
• Mifepristone appears to be an effective emergency contraceptive with a good safety profile.
• Mifepristone is contraindicated in women planning to continue pregnancy. The fetal impact of

continuing the pregnancy after a failed medical termination remains unclear.

- There is no information for mifepristone and breast-feeding because there is no use for it during breast-feeding.

MINOCYCLINE

Brand names: Arestin, Dynacin, Lederderm, Minocin, Vectrin

Drug classes: Antibiotic; Tetracycline

Indications (what it is used for): Infection due to susceptible bacteria and parasites.

How it works: Inhibits protein synthesis and slows the rate of growth.

Contraindications (reasons you shouldn't take it): Hypersensitivity to drug or class.

Possible side effects and warnings: Can cause low platelet and/or white blood cell counts, liver toxicity, Jarisch-Herxheimer reaction (fever, chills, headache, and muscle pain caused by large quantities of toxins released into the body as bacteria die during treatment), inflammation of the colon and small intestine, fatty liver disease, infection of the colon, hemolytic anemia, liver or kidney dysfunction, blisters on the tongue, lack of gross-muscle control, dizziness, ringing in the ears, increased pressure in the brain without presence of a tumor, and vaginal yeast infection. It should be used with caution in women with kidney or liver dysfunction.

How it can affect pregnant women: There are no adequate reports or well-controlled studies of minocycline in pregnant women. It is often applied topically to minimize acne development. Case reports note its use for the treatment of recurrent pemphigoid (a group of rare skin diseases with large blisters). As with other tetracyclines, concern has been raised that it might lower the effectiveness of low-dose oral contraceptive agents (see tetracycline).

How it can affect a developing embryo or fetus: There are no adequate reports or well-controlled studies in human fetuses. It is unknown whether minocycline crosses the human placenta. There is

no evidence to suggest that minocycline is a cause of birth defects when exposure occurs in the first trimester. It is unlikely that the maternal systemic concentration reaches a clinically relevant level if applied topically for acne. Later in pregnancy, other tetracyclines cross the human placenta and are associated with tooth discoloration. In rodents, tetracycline use has been associated with higher death rates of the early embryo (see tetracycline). However, animal studies are not necessarily good indicators of how a drug will behave in humans.

Breast-feeding: There are no adequate reports or well-controlled studies in nursing women. It is unknown whether minocycline enters human breast milk. The concentrations of other tetracyclines are very low and have not been reported to cause tooth discoloration (see tetracycline).

Potential drug interactions: Interaction between the following medications and minocycline has the potential to impact the effect of one or more of the drugs. In some instances the interaction can be dangerous or life-threatening and must be avoided: anticoagulants, penicillin, isotretinoin, ergot alkaloids. Minocycline may make oral contraceptives less effective.

What the FDA says about use in pregnancy: Category D (see Appendix).

What the available evidence suggests about breast-feeding safety: Unknown.

The bottom line for you:

- The tetracyclines are generally contraindicated during pregnancy because of the potential for fetal tooth discoloration, although topical minocycline likely poses little to no risk. However, there are alternative agents for use during pregnancy for almost all indications.
- Minocycline is probably safe for use while breast-feeding, although there are other agents with which there is more experience. Topical minocycline is likely safe for use while breast-feeding.

MINOXIDIL

Brand names: Alopexil, Alostil, Loniten, Lonolax, Mintop, Modil, Rogaine

Drug classes: Antihypertensive; Vasodilator

Indications (what it is used for): High blood pressure, baldness.

How it works: Peripheral vessel vasodilator.

Contraindications (reasons you shouldn't take it): Hypersensitivity to drug or class, pheochromocytoma (adrenal gland tumor), fluid around the heart.

Possible side effects and warnings: Can cause congestive heart failure, rapid heart rate, fluid around the heart, substernal (chest) pain, Stevens-Johnson syndrome (a rare but serious skin reaction to medication), swelling, abnormal facial hair growth, tingling, headache, breast tenderness, weight gain, low platelet and/or white blood cell counts, contact dermatitis, itching, and skin irritation. It should be used with caution in women with kidney or liver dysfunction or a prior heart attack.

How it can affect pregnant women: There are no adequate reports or well-controlled studies of minoxidil in pregnant women. Minoxidil is not often used for the treatment of high blood pressure but rather for the treatment of balding, which can typically be delayed until after delivery. Balding is a normal physiologic occurrence in women after delivery or while taking oral contraceptives. It can be treated with either progesterone or minoxidil. Less than 2% of the topical dose is absorbed systemically.

How it can affect a developing embryo or fetus: There are no adequate reports or well-controlled studies in human fetuses. It is unknown whether minoxidil crosses the human placenta, although excess fetal facial hair has been reported after mothers used minoxidil topically throughout pregnancy, which suggests both absorption and placental transfer. There is one report of failure of the legs and lower spine to develop in the fetus of a mother taking minoxidil long before and during pregnancy. Rodent studies are reassuring, revealing no evidence of birth defects or low birth weight despite the use of doses higher than those used clinically. However, animal studies are not necessarily good indicators of how a drug will behave in humans.

Breast-feeding: There are no adequate reports or well-controlled studies in nursing women. Minoxidil enters human breast milk. However, it is unlikely that topically administered drug would result in a clinically relevant milk concentration.

Potential drug interactions: Interaction between the following medications and minoxidil has the potential to impact the effect of one or more of the drugs. In some instances the interaction can be dangerous or life-threatening and must be avoided: guanethidine.

What the FDA says about use in pregnancy: Category C (see Appendix).

What the available evidence suggests about breast-feeding safety: Safe for topical use; unknown for oral use.

The bottom line for you:

- Minoxidil is used for the treatment of pregnancy-associated hair loss, which typically can be delayed until after delivery and breast-feeding has ended.

MISOPROSTOL

Brand name: Cytotec

Drug classes: Abortifacient; Gastrointestinal; Oxytocic; Prostaglandin; Stimulant, uterine

Indications (what it is used for): NSAID-induced gastric ulcer, constipation, cervical ripening, induction of labor, pregnancy termination.

How it works: Inhibits gastric acid secretions; protects gastric mucosa; stimulates uterine contractions.

Contraindications (reasons you shouldn't take it): Hypersensitivity to drug or class, pregnancy (for gastrointestinal indications).

Possible side effects and warnings: Can cause unintended abortion, uterine rupture, uterine hyperstimulation, diarrhea, constipation, abdominal pain, nausea, vomiting, flatulence, heartburn, heavy and/

or painful menses, and earache. It should be used with caution in women of reproductive age when the reason for treatment is gastrointestinal or who have had prior cesarean section; myomectomy (removal of fibroids) or other uterine surgery; a very large fetus; or five or more pregnancies.

How it can affect pregnant women: Misoprostol is a prostaglandin E analog. Its only FDA-approved indication is the treatment and prevention of stomach ulcer disease caused by nonsteroidal anti-inflammatory drugs (NSAIDs). However, misoprostol is well studied and widely used for cervical ripening and the induction of labor during the second and third trimesters. The drug can be given orally, vaginally, or rectally, but the vaginal route is preferred for cervical ripening or the induction of labor. Side effects are highest when given by mouth.

Early to mid-pregnancy termination: Combined with mifepristone, misoprostol is safe and effective for medical termination of pregnancy.

Term pregnancy: Misoprostol is commonly used to induce cervical ripening and labor at term (when pregnancy is completed). However, clinical trials report increased frequencies of meconium passage (a fetal bowel movement prior to birth), an increase in newborn acid levels, and cesarean delivery due to fetal distress when high doses are used. Misoprostol is effective for the induction of labor in women with premature rupture of the membranes (PROM; breaking of the water before the onset of labor), preeclampsia (high blood pressure and protein in the urine during pregnancy and complications associated with it) and after fetal death. In 2002, the American Congress of Obstetricians and Gynecologists concluded that the risk of uterine rupture during VBAC (vaginal birth after cesarean section) is increased by the use of various prostaglandin cervical-ripening agents. Mechanical methods are preferred in women who have previously had a cesarean delivery.

Postpartum hemorrhage: Misoprostol is effective for the prevention and treatment of maternal hemorrhage after delivery and is often used routinely. Rectal or oral misoprostol is less effective than oxytocin plus methylergonovine.

How it can affect a developing embryo or fetus: There are no adequate reports or well-controlled studies in human fetuses. Misoprostol is associated with fetal heart rate decelerations and, with higher doses, a higher rate of meconium (bowel movement before birth that could be inhaled by the fetus or newborn). However, there is no increase in cesarean section for fetal distress or fetal acid levels compared to oxytocin (another popular agent for inducing labor). Congenital defects after unsuccessful medical abortions have been reported, but it has not been determined whether misoprostol is responsible. Several reports associate misoprostol in the first trimester with skull defects, cranial nerve palsies, facial malformations, and limb defects. However, it is important to keep in mind that the goal of its administration was to end pregnancy and it is unfortunate that the process was not completed in those instances.

Breast-feeding: Orally administered misoprostol is secreted in colostrum within 1 hour, but it is essentially undetectable by 5 hours after ingestion. The level achieved is low and likely does not pose a risk to the breast-fed newborn.

Potential drug interactions: No clinically relevant interactions identified.

What the FDA says about use in pregnancy: Category X (see Appendix).

What the available evidence suggests about breast-feeding safety: Likely safe.

The bottom line for you:

- Misoprostol is a safe and effective adjunct to mifepristone for medical abortion.
- Misoprostol can induce cervical ripening and labor. Oral misoprostol is more convenient than vaginal but may increase the risk of frequent contractions and chills.
- Misoprostol should not be used for ripening or labor induction in women after a prior cesarean delivery.

- Misoprostol is likely safe for a breast-fed newborn.

MITOXANTRONE
Brand name: Novantrone
Drug class: Antineoplastic
Indications (what it is used for): Acute myeloid leukemia (AML; cancer that starts in the bone marrow), multiple sclerosis (autoimmune disease affecting the brain and spinal cord).
How it works: Multiple actions that disturb DNA synthesis, leading to cell death.
Contraindications (reasons you shouldn't take it): Hypersensitivity to drug or class, prior doxorubicin exposure, congestive heart failure, myelosuppression (decreased bone marrow activity).
Possible side effects and warnings: Can cause seizures, abnormal heart rate, heart toxicity, congestive heart failure, bone marrow suppression, kidney failure, nausea, vomiting, fever, abdominal pain, gastrointestinal bleeding, hair loss, diarrhea, bacterial infection in the blood, blisters in the mouth, conjunctivitis, pneumonia, urinary tract infection, headache, cough, and fungal infection.
How it can affect pregnant women: There are no adequate reports or well-controlled studies of mitoxantrone in pregnant women. Mitoxantrone has been advocated as a treatment for MS, and there are several published case reports of its use during pregnancy noting no adverse effects.
How it can affect a developing embryo or fetus: There are no adequate reports or well-controlled studies in human fetuses. It is unknown whether mitoxantrone crosses the human placenta. Low birth weight was noted in one report; another observed the Pierre Robin sequence (a rare grouping of birth defects including a very small jaw, retraction of the tongue, and an obstructed airway). Rodent studies are reassuring, revealing no evidence of birth defects, but the doses studied were too low, and animal studies are not necessarily good indicators of how a drug will behave in humans.

Breast-feeding: There is no published data in nursing women. Mitoxantrone enters human breast milk, reaching a significant concentration. It should probably be considered incompatible with breast-feeding until there is additional study.
Potential drug interactions: No clinically relevant interactions identified.
What the FDA says about use in pregnancy: Category D (see Appendix).
What the available evidence suggests about breast-feeding safety: Possibly unsafe.
The bottom line for you:
- There is inadequate information to conclude whether or not mitoxantrone causes birth defects. Although successful pregnancies occur after exposure, it should probably be avoided until there are new research findings.
- Until there is new information, breast-feeding is best avoided while using mitoxantrone.

MODAFINIL
Brand name: Provigil
Drug classes: Analeptic; Central nervous system (CNS) stimulant
Indications (what it is used for): Narcolepsy, multiple sclerosis (autoimmune disease affecting the brain and spinal cord).
How it works: Unknown.
Contraindications (reasons you shouldn't take it): Hypersensitivity to drug or class, left ventricular hypertrophy.
Possible side effects and warnings: Can cause abnormal or rapid heart rate, chest pain, heart attack, headache, nausea, vomiting, palpitations, sleeplessness, anxiety, euphoria, runny nose, sore throat, and nosebleed. It should be used with caution in women with coronary artery disease, high blood pressure, kidney or liver dysfunction, history of psychosis, or alcohol use.
How it can affect pregnant women: Although MS is fairly common in reproductive-age women, the published data with modafinil during pregnancy is

limited to one case report. Modafinil may reduce the effectiveness of oral contraceptives during treatment and up to 1 month after discontinuation of modafinil.

How it can affect a developing embryo or fetus: There are no adequate reports or well-controlled studies in human fetuses. It is unknown whether modafinil crosses the human placenta. Adequate rodent birth defect studies have not been performed. The manufacturer reports fewer than a dozen exposures during pregnancy without apparent adverse effects.

Breast-feeding: There is no published data in nursing women. It is unknown whether modafinil enters human breast milk.

Potential drug interactions: Interaction between the following medications and modafinil has the potential to impact the effect of one or more of the drugs. In some instances the interaction can be dangerous or life-threatening and must be avoided: methylphenidate, dextroamphetamine, ethinyl estradiol, triazolam, cyclosporine, modafinil sulfone, drugs that are largely eliminated via CYP2C19 metabolism (e.g., diazepam, propranolol, phenytoin), certain trycyclic antidepressants (e.g., clomipramine, desipramine), potent CYP3A4 inducers (e.g., carbamazepine, phenobarbital, rifampin), CYP3A4 inhibitors (e.g., itraconazole, ketoconazole).

What the FDA says about use in pregnancy: Category C (see Appendix).

What the available evidence suggests about breast-feeding safety: Unknown.

The bottom line for you:
- Modafinil is best avoided during pregnancy and breast-feeding unless the benefit to the woman justifies the potential risk to the embryo, fetus, or newborn.

MOMETASONE

Brand names: Elocon, Nasonex
Drug classes: Corticosteroid; Dermatologic
Indications (what it is used for): Allergic runny nose, dermatitis.

How it works: Anti-inflammatory.

Contraindications (reasons you shouldn't take it): Hypersensitivity to drug or class.

Possible side effects and warnings: Can cause adrenal suppression; thinning of the skin; dryness, irritation, and burning of the nose; inflammation of hair follicles; itching of the face, tongue, or throat.

How it can affect pregnant women: Allergic runny nose affects 1 in 3 women of childbearing age. There are no adequate reports or well-controlled studies of mometasone in pregnant women. This product offers the potential advantage of once-daily dosing. However, budesonide is generally considered the preferred medication during pregnancy.

How it can affect a developing embryo or fetus: There are no adequate reports or well-controlled studies in human fetuses. It is unknown whether mometasone crosses the human placenta. There are no documented epidemiologic studies with intranasal corticosteroids (e.g., budesonide, fluticasone, mometasone) during pregnancy. However, inhaled corticosteroids (e.g., beclomethasone) are not considered a cause of birth defects; it is unlikely that the maternal systemic concentration would reach a clinically relevant level that could damage the fetus after intranasal use.

Breast-feeding: There is no published data in nursing women. It is unknown whether mometasone enters human breast milk. Considering the occasional intranasal use, it is unlikely that a breast-feeding baby would ingest clinically relevant amounts.

Potential drug interactions: Should be used with caution with ketoconazole.

What the FDA says about use in pregnancy: Category C (see Appendix).

What the available evidence suggests about breast-feeding safety: Likely safe.

The bottom line for you:
- Mometasone may be used during pregnancy and while breast-feeding if other medications with which we have more experience such as budesonide and fluticasone fail.

MORPHINE

Brand names: Avinza, Kadian, MS Contin, MSIR, Oramorph, Roxanol

Drug class: Analgesic, narcotic

Indications (what it is used for): Severe pain.

How it works: Binds to opiate receptor to relieve pain.

Contraindications (reasons you shouldn't take it): Hypersensitivity to drug or class, respiratory depression, asthma, loss of bowel motility.

Possible side effects and warnings: Can cause addiction, seizures, respiratory depression or cessation, low blood pressure, shock, cardiac arrest, slow heart rate, extreme dilation of the colon, intestinal obstruction, abdominal pain, narrow pupils, itching, dry mouth, decreased libido, gallbladder pain, tingling, itching, flushing, urinary retention, and weakness. It should be used with caution in women with chronic obstructive pulmonary disease (COPD), head injury, central nervous system depression, seizure disorder, acute pancreatitis, infection of the colon, low blood pressure, liver or kidney dysfunction, biliary disease (damaged bile ducts in the liver), or alcoholism.

How it can affect pregnant women: Morphine is one of the most frequently used opioids for pain control during childbirth. The elimination of morphine from the body is faster during pregnancy and the dosing may need to be adjusted. Morphine as part of an epidural or patient-controlled infusion is common. It is also given by epidural after cesarean section for relief of postoperative pain for the first 48 hours. The addition of a small dose of morphine to the spinal component of a continuous spinal epidural improves the effectiveness of labor analgesia and reduces the need for pain medications over 24 hours after delivery. Epidural morphine reduces the chance of headache and the need for a blood patch after dural puncture (a rare complication of epidural injections). There is a long clinical experience supporting the relative safety of morphine for the listed indications.

How it can affect a developing embryo or fetus: Morphine readily crosses the human placenta, although the drug is quickly cleared from the mother's bloodstream, shortening the fetal exposure. The higher the level of free morphine in umbilical venous blood, the greater the chance a newborn will need extensive stimulation after delivery. Morphine exposure may reduce the fetal biophysical profile score (a test for fetal well-being), since morphine slows fetal breathing and decreases the variability of the fetal heart rate. This can give the false impression that the fetus is in trouble and in need of urgent delivery.

Morphine has been combined with benzodiazepines (e.g., diazepam) for the relief of pain and anxiety during fetal surgical procedures. Although there is no evidence that morphine is a human teratogen (substance that can cause birth defects), a long clinical experience with newborns chronically exposed to other opioids suggests an association with reduced brain volume at birth that normalizes during the first month of life. Infants born to opioid-abusing mothers more often have low birth weight and an increased risk of sudden infant death. Newborn withdrawal syndrome due to opiate exposure during pregnancy produces sleep and feeding difficulties, weight loss, and seizures. Exposure during labor has no long-term effect on the newborn.

Breast-feeding: Morphine is concentrated in human breast milk. In general, morphine is preferred to meperidine in breast-feeding women. Spinal or epidural morphine does not produce a clinically relevant level in breast milk. The colostrum concentration of morphine and its active metabolites in women using PCA (patient-controlled analgesia) after cesarean delivery is also small, supporting the safety of breast-feeding in those instances.

Potential drug interactions: Interaction between the following medications and morphine has the potential to impact the effect of one or more of the drugs. In some instances the interaction can be dangerous or life-threatening and must be avoided: other central nervous system (CNS) depressants (including sedatives, hypnotics, general anesthetics, droperidol, phenothiazines or other tranquilizers, and ethanol/alcohol), monoamine oxidase inhibitors (MAOIs), neuromuscular-blocking agents, cimetidine.

What the FDA says about use in pregnancy: Category C (see Appendix).

What the available evidence suggests about breast-feeding safety: Safe.

The bottom line for you:

- Morphine provides safe and effective pain relief for pregnant and breast-feeding women.

MOXIFLOXACIN

Brand name: Avelox

Drug classes: Antibiotic; Quinolone

Indications (what it is used for): Infection due to susceptible bacteria.

How it works: Inhibits DNA synthesis, leading to bacterial death.

Contraindications (reasons you shouldn't take it): Hypersensitivity to drug or class, electrocardiogram abnormalities, use with an antiarrhythmic medication (class IA, sodium channel blockers; class III, potassium channel blockers), being under the age of 18.

Possible side effects and warnings: Can cause vaginitis, sensitivity to light, infection of the colon, seizures, increased intracranial pressure, headache, psychosis, nausea, vomiting, diarrhea, abdominal pain, heartburn, dizziness, sleeplessness, agitation, tendonitis, and joint pain. It should be used with caution in women older than 45 years, or who have seizure disorder or central nervous system disorder, or are dehydrated.

How it can affect pregnant women: Its use during pregnancy is limited to predominantly case reports.

How it can affect a developing embryo or fetus: There are no adequate reports or well-controlled studies in human fetuses. Moxifloxacin crosses the human placenta more efficiently than ciprofloxacin; both cross poorly compared to a penicillin class agent. Studies in rodents and dogs revealed that fetal exposure to quinolone antibiotics is associated

with damage to weight-bearing joints. Although damage has only rarely been observed in humans, the toxicity observed in immature animals has led to the restricted use of quinolones in pregnant women. There was no evidence of birth defects in monkeys fed 2½ times the maximum recommended clinical dose. However, animal studies are not necessarily good indicators of how a drug will behave in humans.

Breast-feeding: There is no published data in nursing women. It is unknown whether moxifloxacin enters human breast milk. It is excreted into rodent milk.

Potential drug interactions: Interaction between the following medications and moxifloxacin has the potential to impact the effect of one or more of the drugs. In some instances the interaction can be dangerous or life-threatening and must be avoided: nonsteroidal anti-inflammatory drugs (NSAIDs).

What the FDA says about use in pregnancy: Category C (see Appendix).

What the available evidence suggests about breast-feeding safety: Unknown.

The bottom line for you:

- Moxifloxacin is an option for intrauterine bacterial infection sensitive only to quinolone antibiotics, however, overall transport across the placenta is relatively low. There are alternative agents with which there is more experience during pregnancy and while breast-feeding.

NADOLOL

Brand name: Corgard

Drug classes: Adrenergic antagonist; Beta-blocker

Indications (what it is used for): High blood pressure, chest pain, irregular heart rate, headache prevention (vascular).

How it works: Blocks the beta-adrenergic receptors, whose activation causes the symptoms.

Contraindications (reasons you shouldn't take it): Hypersensitivity to drug or class, asthma, abnormally slow heart rate.

Possible side effects and warnings: Can cause fatigue, dizziness, slurred speech, slow heart rate, rash, congestive heart failure, bronchospasm, constipation, dry mouth, nausea, diarrhea, weight gain, cough, nasal stuffiness, sweating, ringing in the ears, facial swelling, and blurred vision. Should be used with caution in women with diabetes, liver failure, or congestive heart failure.

How it can affect pregnant women: Nadolol is a nonselective beta-blocker offering the advantage of once-daily dosing. There are no adequate reports or well-controlled studies of nadolol in pregnant women. The published literature is limited to scattered case reports.

How it can affect a developing embryo or fetus: There are no adequate reports or well-controlled studies in human fetuses. It is unknown whether nadolol crosses the human placenta; other drugs in this class do cross. Scattered case reports suggest that fetal exposure may increase the risk of respiratory depression at birth, low blood glucose, and low birth weight. The long-lasting nature of nadolol makes it less desirable during pregnancy than other beta-blockers, such as propranolol. Rodent studies are generally reassuring, revealing no evidence of birth defects despite the use of doses higher than those used clinically. There is evidence of increased embryo loss and low birth weight. However, animal studies are not necessarily good indicators of how a drug will behave in humans.

Breast-feeding: Although the amount of nadolol excreted into human breast milk is small, it has the potential to affect the newborn. Breast-fed newborns should be observed for evidence of beta blockade (possibly leading to a slowed heart rate and other symptoms).

Potential drug interactions: Nadolol may increase the low blood pressure caused by general anesthesia and enhance the glucose-lowering (or -increasing) effect of antidiabetic drugs; dosages need to be adjusted accordingly.

What the FDA says about use in pregnancy: Category C (see Appendix).

What the available evidence suggests about breast-feeding safety: Likely safe.

The bottom line for you:

- There are many alternative medications with which there is more experience during pregnancy and while breast-feeding.
- Nadolol should be used during pregnancy and breast-feeding only if other medications are ineffective.

NAFCILLIN

Brand names: Nafcil, Nallpen, Unipen
Drug classes: Antibiotic; Penicillin
Indications (what it is used for): Bacterial infections, especially penicillinase-producing *Staphylococcus*.
How it works: Kills bacteria by inhibiting the synthesis of cell walls.
Contraindications (reasons you shouldn't take it): Hypersensitivity to drug or class.
Possible side effects and warnings: Can cause pain, swelling, inflammation, kidney inflammation, bowel infection, liver toxicity, seizures, tissue death, nausea, vomiting, diarrhea, yeast infection, hives, blood clots, bone marrow suppression, low potassium level, and rash. Should be used with caution in women with cephalosporin allergy or kidney or liver dysfunction.
How it can affect pregnant women: There are no adequate reports or well-controlled studies of nafcillin in pregnant women. Nafcillin is a penicillinase-resistant penicillin eliminated primarily by the liver, whereas most penicillins are eliminated by the kidneys. The published literature consists of scattered case reports. Other penicillins have proved safe for use during pregnancy.
How it can affect a developing embryo or fetus: There are no adequate reports or well-controlled studies in human fetuses. It is unknown whether nafcillin crosses the human placenta. Rodent studies are reassuring, revealing no evidence of birth defects or low birth weight despite the use of doses higher than those used clinically. However, animal studies are not necessarily good indicators of how a drug will behave in humans.

Breast-feeding: There is no published data in nursing women. It is unknown whether nafcillin enters human breast milk. Penicillins are generally considered compatible with breast-feeding.

Potential drug interactions: Interaction between the following medications and nafcillin has the potential to impact the effect of one or more of the drugs. In some instances the interaction can be dangerous or life-threatening and must be avoided: warfarin, cyclosporine, tetracycline.

What the FDA says about use in pregnancy: Category B (see Appendix).

What the available evidence suggests about breast-feeding safety: Likely safe.

The bottom line for you:

- There are alternative medications if necessary during pregnancy for almost all indications.
- Nafcillin is one of several drugs useful for the treatment of mastitis (infection of breast tissue) while breast-feeding.

NALBUPHINE

Not available in the U.S.

Brand name: Nubain

Drug classes: Analeptic; Narcotic agonist-antagonist

Indications (what it is used for): Pain, an aid for anesthesia.

How it works: Activates the opiate receptors to blunt the sensation of pain.

Contraindications (reasons you shouldn't take it): Hypersensitivity to drug or class.

Possible side effects and warnings: Can cause headache, nervousness, depression, restlessness, crying, feeling of floating, hostility, unusual dreams, confusion, euphoria, depressed mood, hallucinations, faintness, feeling of heaviness, numbness, tingling, dizziness, slow heart rate, low blood pressure, respiratory depression, heartburn, nausea, vomiting, sweating, dry mouth, hives, cramps, shortness of breath, asthma, bitter taste, speech difficulty, urgent need to urinate, blurred vision, itching, and substance abuse.

Should be used with caution in women who have an opiate dependency; kidney, liver, or lung dysfunction; a history of gallbladder surgery; or sulfite allergy.

How it can affect pregnant women: There are no well-controlled studies of nalbuphine in pregnant women. It is, however, a popular agent for analgesia during labor. Its potency is essentially equivalent to that of morphine. The manufacturer was concerned about fetal safety and no longer sells nalbuphine in the U.S. However, there is insufficient information to support their concerns. Intravenous nalbuphine is sometimes used for the treatment of epidural morphine-induced itching after cesarean delivery.

How it can affect a developing embryo or fetus: There are no adequate reports or well-controlled studies in human fetuses. Nalbuphine crosses the human placenta, reaching about three-quarters of the maternal level. Like other opiates, it decreases fetal activity and, as a result, decreases the number of fetal heart rate accelerations that are used by the obstetrician as a measure of fetal well-being. Nalbuphine can cause respiratory depression and should be used with caution in women delivering prematurely. Rodent studies are reassuring, revealing no evidence of birth defects or low birth weight despite the use of doses higher than those used clinically. However, animal studies are not necessarily good indicators of how a drug will behave in humans.

Breast-feeding: The concentration of nalbuphine excreted into human breast milk is clinically insignificant.

Potential drug interactions: No clinically relevant interactions identified.

What the FDA says about use in pregnancy: Category B (see Appendix).

What the available evidence suggests about breast-feeding safety: Safe.

The bottom line for you:

- Nalbuphine is a safe and popular labor analgesic on its own and an effective treatment of side effects of epidural morphine.
- Nalbuphine is safe for use while breast-feeding.

NALIDIXIC ACID

Brand names: Enexina, Faril, Nalidixio, Nalydixine, NegGram, Nevigramon, Notricel, Urodic, Winlomylon

Drug classes: Antibiotic; Quinolone

Indications (what it is used for): Bacterial infections.

How it works: Kills bacteria by inhibiting DNA synthesis.

Contraindications (reasons you shouldn't take it): Hypersensitivity to drug or class, seizures.

Possible side effects and warnings: Can cause vaginitis, light sensitivity, bowel infection, seizures, increased pressure in the brain, headache, psychosis, nausea, vomiting, diarrhea, abdominal pain, heartburn, dizziness, sleeplessness, agitation, tendonitis, joint pain, and liver dysfunction. Should be used with caution in women with kidney or liver dysfunction, impaired lung function, or cardiovascular disease, or who are exposed to excessive sunlight.

How it can affect pregnant women: The presence of bacteria in the urine is common during pregnancy. About 1 in 3 affected women will develop a bladder or kidney infection if untreated. Nalidixic acid is an effective treatment for asymptomatic bacteria in the urine (bacteria with no symptoms of infection) and reduces the chance of symptomatic infection later in pregnancy.

How it can affect a developing embryo or fetus: There are no adequate reports or well-controlled studies in human fetuses. Nalidixic acid crosses the human placenta, although how much is unclear. In rodent and canine birth defect studies, the older quinolones, such as nalidixic acid, flumequine, and pipemidic acid were associated with inflammation of the weight-bearing joints in the fetus. Although this joint problem is rare in adult humans, toxicity has been observed in immature animals, leading to the restricted use of these medications during pregnancy. More recent studies conclude that nalidixic acid is not associated with any increased risks of miscarriage, prematurity, low birth weight, or newborn disorders. A small increase in the risk of a repairable bowel problem (pyloric stenosis) has been suggested.

Breast-feeding: The amount of nalidixic acid excreted into human breast milk is clinically insignificant.

Potential drug interactions: Interaction between the following medications and nalidixic has the potential to impact the effect of one or more of the drugs. In some instances the interaction can be dangerous or life-threatening and must be avoided: nitrofurantoin, oxolinic acid, oral anticoagulants.

What the FDA says about use in pregnancy: Category C (see Appendix).

What the available evidence suggests about breast-feeding safety: Safe.

The bottom line for you:

- Nalidixic acid is a reasonable first-line drug for the treatment of asymptomatic bacteriuria during the second and third trimesters.
- Nalidixic acid is safe for use while breast-feeding.

NALOXONE

Brand name: Narcan

Drug classes: Antidote; Narcotic agonist-antagonist

Indications (what it is used for): Opiate overdose, postoperative opiate reversal.

How it works: Blocks various opiate receptors.

Contraindications (reasons you shouldn't take it): Hypersensitivity to drug or class.

Possible side effects and warnings: Can cause cardiac arrest, rapid heart rate, high or low blood pressure, seizures, nausea, vomiting, tremor, profuse sweating, excess lung fluid, and withdrawal symptoms. Should be used with caution in women who have an opiate addiction or kidney or liver dysfunction, or are taking heart toxic drugs.

How it can affect pregnant women: Naloxone is often used to treat epidural or spinal-injected morphine-associated itching. It has been used more recently to help pregnant women stop using heroin, which is associated with poor maternal and newborn outcomes. Medically supervised heroin withdrawal is generally discouraged during pregnancy because of the fetal risk and a high likelihood of failure with return to regular illicit heroin use. But a number of withdrawal procedures developed using naloxone or naltrexone have met with some success in users who continue the medications throughout pregnancy.

How it can affect a developing embryo or fetus: There are no adequate reports or well-controlled studies in human fetuses. It is unknown whether naloxone crosses the human placenta. Newborns of women given opioids during labor who are born with respiratory depression are given naloxone. Naloxone blocks morphine from decreasing fetal movement, heart rate variation, and respiration, three things obstetricians monitor as a sign of fetal well-being. Rodent studies are reassuring, revealing no evidence of birth defects or low birth weight despite the use of doses higher than those used clinically. However, animal studies are not necessarily good indicators of how a drug will behave in humans.

Breast-feeding: There are no adequate reports or well-controlled studies in nursing women. It is unknown whether naloxone enters human breast milk. However, considering the typical indication and dose, one-time naloxone use is unlikely to pose a clinically significant risk to a breast-feeding newborn.

Potential drug interactions: No clinically relevant interactions identified.

What the FDA says about use in pregnancy: Category C (see Appendix).

What the available evidence suggests about breast-feeding safety: Likely safe.

The bottom line for you:
- Naloxone reverses the effect of narcotics on the fetus and newborn. It should be given within minutes of delivery if there is neonatal respiratory depression associated with narcotic administration.
- Naloxone has no impact on breast-feeding.

NALTREXONE

Brand names: ReVia, Trexan

Drug classes: Antidote; Narcotic agonist-antagonist

Indications (what it is used for): Opiate addiction, alcohol dependence.

How it works: Blocks the opioid receptors.

Contraindications (reasons you shouldn't take it): Hypersensitivity to drug or class, hepatitis, liver failure, opiate use, failed naloxone or naltrexone challenge, recent opiate dependence or recent opiate withdrawal.

Possible side effects and warnings: Can cause thoughts of suicide; opiate withdrawal symptoms; sleeplessness; nausea; vomiting; headache; anxiety; chills; loss of appetite; sleepiness; constipation; abdominal pain; muscle aches; rash; dizziness; fatigue; restlessness; muscle, bone, or joint pain; and nosebleeds.

How it can affect pregnant women: There are no adequate reports or well-controlled studies of naltrexone in pregnant women. Naltrexone is effective after cesarean section to treat itching and vomiting from epidural or spinal morphine, but it shortens the period of pain relief those agents provide. It has been used to help pregnant women stop using heroin, which is associated with poor maternal and newborn outcomes. However, medically supervised heroin withdrawal is generally discouraged during pregnancy because of the fetal risk and a high likelihood of failure with return to regular illicit heroin use. But a number of withdrawal procedures developed using naloxone or naltrexone have met with some success in users who continue the medication throughout pregnancy. Naltrexone administration to women with ovarian failure of hypothalamic origin can lead to ovulation and pregnancy.

How it can affect a developing embryo or fetus: There are no adequate reports or well-controlled studies in human fetuses. Naltrexone crosses the human and rodent placenta. Rodent studies are generally reassuring, revealing no evidence of birth defects or low birth weight despite the use of doses higher than those used clinically. There is evidence of increased miscarriage and early fetal toxicity. However, animal studies are not necessarily good indicators of how a drug will behave in humans.

Breast-feeding: Based on limited study, the excretion of naltrexone in breast milk is clinically insignificant.

Potential drug interactions: Naltrexone may precipitate opiate withdrawal in patients taking the XR (extended release) form of the medication.

What the FDA says about use in pregnancy: Category C (see Appendix).

What the available evidence suggests about breast-feeding safety: Likely safe.

The bottom line for you:

- Naltrexone reduces the adverse symptoms associated with morphine analgesia but shortens the duration of pain relief it provides.
- Naltrexone should be used during pregnancy only if the benefit to the woman justifies the potential risk to the embryo or fetus.
- Naltrexone is safe for use while breast-feeding.

NAPHAZOLINE

Brand names: Ak-Con, Albalon, Allersol, I-Naphline, Murine, Muro's Opcon, Nafazair, Naphacel, Naphazole, Naphcon Forte, Nazil, Ocu-Zoline, Opcon, Spectro-Con, Vasocon

Drug classes: Decongestant; Sympathomimetic

Indications (what it is used for): Bloodshot eyes.

How it works: Stimulates a-adrenergic receptors to constrict the dilated vessels.

Contraindications (reasons you shouldn't take it): Hypersensitivity to drug or class, glaucoma.

Possible side effects and warnings: Can cause hyperemia (redness in the skin or eyes because of increased blood flow), headache, dizziness, blurred vision, large pupils, increased sweating, weakness, and nervousness. Should be used with caution in women with cardiovascular disease, diabetes, low thyroid hormone level, or high blood pressure.

How it can affect pregnant women: There are no adequate reports or well-controlled studies of naphazoline in pregnant women.

How it can affect a developing embryo or fetus: There are no adequate reports or well-controlled studies in human fetuses. It is unknown whether naphazoline crosses the human placenta. Considering the dose and how it is administered, it is unlikely that the maternal systemic level will be clinically relevant and therefore it is unlikely to present a risk to the embryo or fetus.

Breast-feeding: There is no published data in nursing women. It is unknown whether naphazoline enters human breast milk. However, considering the indication and dosing, occasional naphazoline use is unlikely to pose a clinically significant risk to the breast-feeding newborn.

Potential drug interactions: No clinically relevant interactions identified.

What the FDA says about use in pregnancy: Category C (see Appendix).

What the available evidence suggests about breast-feeding safety: Likely safe.

The bottom line for you:

- Naphazoline appears safe and effective for use during pregnancy and while breast-feeding.

NAPROXEN

Brand names: Aleve, EC-Naprosyn, Ec-Naprosyn, Flexipen, Napoton, Napren, Naprosyn, Sutony

Drug classes: Analgesic, nonnarcotic; NSAID (nonsteroidal anti-inflammatory drug)

Indications (what it is used for): Osteoarthritis or rheumatoid arthritis, painful menstruation, pain, ankylosing spondylitis (inflammation of joints and spine), inflammation.

How it works: Inhibits the enzymes cyclooxygenase and lipoxygenase, which produce the prostaglandin that causes pain and inflammation.

Contraindications (reasons you shouldn't take it): Hypersensitivity to drug or class, NSAID-induced asthma, kidney or liver dysfunction.

Possible side effects and warnings: Can cause headache, shortness of breath, dizziness, drowsiness, light-headedness, skin eruption and blotches, bruising, sweating, swelling, palpitations, ringing in the ears or other hearing disturbances, visual disturbances, kidney failure, bronchospasm, Stevens-Johnson syndrome (a rare but serious skin reaction to medication), kidney or liver dysfunction, low white blood cell or platelet counts, constipation, rash, hives, and fluid retention. Should be used with caution in women with bowel bleeding, high blood pressure, congestive heart failure, nasal polyps, chronic alcoholic liver disease, or anemia.

How it can affect pregnant women: About 5% of women report the use of ibuprofen or naproxen near conception or during pregnancy. Naproxen may be combined with sumatriptan for the treatment of acute migraine. Findings from a recent prospective case-control study (a study that follows a group of individuals for a period of time), suggest the first trimester use of naproxen almost doubles the risk of miscarriage. The association was stronger if the initial use was around conception or if the use lasted more than 1 week. Naproxen offers no distinct clinical advantage after the first trimester over other NSAIDs. It provides analgesic relief similar to acetaminophen after vaginal delivery.

How it can affect a developing embryo or fetus: Naproxen crosses the human placenta, achieving a level similar to that of the mother. NSAID use has been associated with gastroschisis (a birth defect where the bowel pokes out through the abdominal wall). Most NSAIDs are associated, late in pregnancy, with narrowing or (rarely) closure of the ductus arteriosus (a critical fetal blood vessel directing blood away from the lungs). Its closure leads to heart failure and high blood pressure in the lungs, all of which can cause long-term damage. Stopping the drug appears to reverse the process. It is best to avoid repeated dosing of NSAIDs after 32 weeks. Rodent studies are reassuring, revealing no evidence of birth defects or low birth weight despite the use of doses higher than those used clinically. However, animal studies are not necessarily good indicators of how a drug will behave in humans.

Breast-feeding: The amount of naproxen excreted into human breast milk is clinically insignificant.

Potential drug interactions: Interaction between the following medications and naproxen has the potential to impact the effect of one or more of the drugs. In some instances the interaction can be dangerous or life-threatening and must be avoided: aspirin, furosemide, thiazide diuretics, lithium, warfarin, coumarin-type anticoagulants, beta-blockers, probenicid.

What the FDA says about use in pregnancy: Category C (see Appendix).

What the available evidence suggests about breast-feeding safety: Safe.

The bottom line for you:

- Acetaminophen is the pain-reliever of choice in the first trimester.
- Naproxen (and possibly other NSAIDs) may increase the risk of miscarriage and gastroschisis. First-trimester exposure should be avoided until there is better information on safety.
- Naproxen should be used during pregnancy and while breast-feeding only if the benefit to the woman justifies the potential risk to the embryo or fetus. Naproxen probably poses minimal risk when taken occasionally after the first trimester but before 32 weeks' gestation.
- Naproxen is safe for use while breast-feeding.

NARATRIPTAN

Brand name: Amerge

Drug class: Serotonin receptor agonist

Indications (what it is used for): Migraine headache.

How it works: Stimulates the 5-HT1B/1D receptors to constrict the dilated blood vessels in the brain to stop the migraine.

Contraindications (reasons you shouldn't take

it): Hypersensitivity to drug or class, high blood pressure, coronary artery disease, liver failure or significant kidney or liver dysfunction, use of monoamine oxidase inhibitors (MAOIs) within 14 days or ergot derivatives within 24 hours.

Possible side effects and warnings: Can cause tiredness; fatigue; heart attack; stroke; coronary vasospasm; cardiac arrest; palpitations; rapid heart rate; severe high blood pressure; colonic ischemia (decreased blood flow to the intestines); dry mouth; vomiting; sore throat; asthma; inflamed lining of the lungs; tremors; cognitive function disorders; sleep disorders; balance disorders; anxiety; depression; hallucinations; panic; frequent urination; and inflammation of the breast, vagina, or bladder. Should be used with caution in women with cerebrovascular disease (narrowing of blood vessels that supply the brain) or mild liver dysfunction.

How it can affect pregnant women: Migraine headaches are a frequent complaint during pregnancy, and the mainstay of treatment outside of pregnancy, ergot compounds, are generally considered contraindicated (should not be used) during pregnancy. So patients and physicians have to look for other options. From 50% to 90% of pregnant women experience an improvement in headache symptoms during the second and third trimesters; this is especially true for women with menstrual migraine. There are no adequate reports or well-controlled studies of naratriptan in pregnant women. A post-marketing study of 52 first-trimester women failed to find any increase in pregnancy losses. Triptans, as a group, may be associated with preterm birth and are best avoided at the extremes of prematurity (before 28 weeks) until more data is available.

How it can affect a developing embryo or fetus: There are no adequate reports or well-controlled studies in human fetuses. It is unknown whether naratriptan crosses the human placenta. Population studies (studies of a large group of people taken from the larger population) performed after the drug was on the market are limited but reassuring.

There is, however, more experience during pregnancy with the related compound sumatriptan. Rodent studies revealed an increase in miscarriage and skeletal abnormalities at doses higher than the maximum recommended clinical dose. The frequencies of these adverse outcomes are not dose-dependent (meaning their frequency does not increase with increasing dosage), suggesting that they are not necessarily related to the medication. However, animal studies are not necessarily good indicators of how a drug will behave in humans.

Breast-feeding: There is no published data in nursing women. It is unknown whether naratriptan enters human breast milk; it does enter rodent milk. Considering the limited dosing, it is unlikely to pose a significant risk to a breast-feeding newborn. Women may choose to pump their milk for 24 hours after treatment for added safety.

Potential drug interactions: Interaction between the following medications and naratriptan has the potential to impact the effect of one or more of the drugs. In some instances the interaction can be dangerous or life-threatening and must be avoided: ergotamine-containing or ergot-type medications (e.g., dihydroergotamine, methysergide), selective serotonin reuptake inhibitors (SSRIs; e.g., fluoxetine, fluvoxamine, paroxetine, sertraline).

What the FDA says about use in pregnancy: Category C (see Appendix).

What the available evidence suggests about breast-feeding safety: Probably safe.

The bottom line for you:

- Naratriptan should be used during pregnancy and while breast-feeding only if the benefit to the woman justifies the potential risk to the embryo, fetus, or newborn. There are alternative agents with which there is more experience.

- Triptans, as a group, may be associated with preterm birth and are best avoided at the extremes of prematurity (before 28 weeks) until more data is available.

NATEGLINIDE

Brand name: Starlex

Drug class: Antidiabetic agent; Biguanide

Indications (what it is used for): Type II diabetes.

How it works: Stimulates pancreatic beta cells to release insulin.

Contraindications (reasons you shouldn't take it): Hypersensitivity to drug or class, type I diabetes, diabetic ketoacidosis (lack of insulin prevents body using sugar as a fuel).

Possible side effects and warnings: Can cause upper respiratory infection, joint inflammation, bronchitis, low blood glucose, diarrhea, and dizziness. Should be used with caution in women with liver dysfunction.

How it can affect pregnant women: Oral hypoglycemic agents such as glyburide, acarbose, and metformin are increasingly being used as insulin alternatives during pregnancy in women with type II diabetes. Nateglinide is a phenylalanine derivative that helps reduce high glucose levels after meals. There is no published data with it during pregnancy.

How it can affect a developing embryo or fetus: There is no published data in human fetuses. It is unknown whether nateglinide crosses the human placenta. Rodent studies are generally reassuring, although an increase in congenital (existing at birth) absence of the gallbladder was reported when doses 40 times the maximum recommended clinical dose were given. However, animal studies are not necessarily good indicators of how a drug will behave in humans.

Breast-feeding: There is no published data in nursing women. It is unknown whether nateglinide enters human breast milk. It is excreted into rodent milk, and administration of high doses to a breast-feeding rat mother slowed the weight gain of her pups. It is unknown whether the reduced growth was a result of the medication or the lowered blood glucose in the mother. Animal studies are not necessarily good indicators of how a drug will behave in humans.

Potential drug interactions: Interaction between the following medications and nateglinide has the potential to impact the effect of one or more of the drugs. In some instances the interaction can be dangerous or life-threatening and must be avoided: nonsteroidal anti-inflammatory drugs (NSAIDs), salicylates, monoamine oxidase inhibitors (MAOIs), nonselective beta-adrenergic blocking agents, thiazides, corticosteroids, thyroid products, sympathomimetics.

What the FDA says about use in pregnancy: Category C (see Appendix).

What the available evidence suggests about breast-feeding safety: Unknown.

The bottom line for you:

- Until there is new information, nateglinide should not be used during pregnancy and while breast-feeding.
- There are other oral hypoglycemic agents for use in women with gestational diabetes or type II diabetes during pregnancy and while breast-feeding that are considered safe and effective.

NEDOCROMIL

Brand names: Alocril, Tilade

Drug classes: Allergy; Mast cell stabilizer

Indications (what it is used for): Chronic asthma, allergic bloodshot eyes.

How it works: Inhibits release of cell proteins that cause the inflammation.

Contraindications (reasons you shouldn't take it): Hypersensitivity to drug or class, acute asthma attack.

Possible side effects and warnings: Can cause bronchospasm, headache, bitter taste, cough, pharyngitis, runny nose, bronchitis, shortness of breath, nausea, vomiting, dry mouth, heartburn, and fatigue.

How it can affect pregnant women: Nedocromil is effective long-term maintenance therapy for bronchial asthma. Asthma is a common disease in life and in pregnancy. Approximately one-third of pregnant women with asthma get worse during pregnancy, one-third get better, and one-third remain clinically unchanged. Well-controlled asthma does not affect pregnancy outcome, but poorly controlled asthma may increase the risk of preterm birth (before 37 weeks) or low birth weight. Inhaled corticosteroids are the preventative medication of choice for pregnant women with persistent asthma unless their condition is well controlled by cromolyn or nedocromil. There is no published data with nedocromil during pregnancy.

Certain medications used during labor and delivery have the potential to worsen asthma, including nonselective beta-blockers, some prostaglandins (used to induce labor), and ergonovine (used to control blood loss after delivery).

How it can affect a developing embryo or fetus: There are no adequate reports or well-controlled studies in human fetuses. It is unknown whether nedocromil crosses the human placenta. Considering the dose and how it is administered, it is unlikely that the maternal blood level would be clinically relevant to the fetus. Rodent studies are reassuring, revealing no evidence of birth defects or low birth weight despite the use of doses higher than those used clinically. However, animal studies are not necessarily good indicators of how a drug will behave in humans.

Breast-feeding: There is no published data in nursing women. It is unknown whether nedocromil enters human breast milk. However, considering the indication and dosing, occasional nedocromil use is unlikely to pose a clinically significant risk to a breast-feeding newborn.

Potential drug interactions: No clinically relevant interactions identified.

What the FDA says about use in pregnancy: Category B (see Appendix).

What the available evidence suggests about breast-feeding safety: Likely safe.

The bottom line for you:
● There are alternative agents with which there is more experience during pregnancy and while breast-feeding.
● Nedocromil should be used during pregnancy or while breast-feeding only when the alternative agents have failed.

NELFINAVIR

Brand name: Viracept
Drug classes: Antiviral; Protease inhibitor
Indications (what it is used for): HIV infection.
How it works: Blocks the action of an enzyme that breaks down other proteins that allow the virus to replicate.
Contraindications (reasons you shouldn't take it): Hypersensitivity to drug or class; use of amiodarone, astemizole, ergot derivatives, midazolam, pimozide, quinidine, or rifampin; phenylketonuria (an inherited amino acid disorder).
Possible side effects and warnings: Can cause nausea, vomiting, gas, diarrhea, hepatitis, seizures, rash, weakness, abdominal pain, joint pain, muscle ache, muscle disorders, abnormal lipid profiles, high glucose levels, low white blood cell or platelet counts, and itching. Should be used with caution in women with liver dysfunction.
How it can affect pregnant women: Highly active antiretroviral therapy (HAART), which consists of 3–5 drugs (the so-called cocktail), is the current standard of care for the management of HIV infection during pregnancy. Some HAART protocols use nelfinavir as the protease inhibitor. Treatment of HIV which reduces the number of viral particles circulating in the mother's blood dramatically reduces the risk of transmitting the virus to her child. Pregnancy increases clearance (how fast the drug is eliminated from the body) of nelfinavir, and women in the later stages of pregnancy may require an increase in dose to maintain effectiveness. This increased clearance lasts for at least a week after delivery.

Careful monitoring for liver toxicity during therapy with nelfinavir is recommended. Side effects possible with nelfinavir such as bowel symptoms and high glucose levels may be more common during pregnancy.

How it can affect a developing embryo or fetus: There are no adequate reports or well-controlled studies in human fetuses. Like most protease inhibitors, nelfinavir crosses the human placenta but reaches a level approximating 25% of the mother, too low to treat fetal infection. Combination antiviral therapy with protease inhibitors may increase the risk of very low birth weight. This may be either a drug effect or result from the severity of the mother's illness. Rodent studies are reassuring, revealing no evidence of birth defects or low birth weight despite the use of doses higher than those used clinically. However, animal studies are not necessarily good indicators of how a drug will behave in humans.

Breast-feeding: Nelfinavir enters human breast milk, but the level is too low to provide any benefit to a newborn. If infant formula is available, breast-feeding is usually not recommended when a mother is HIV positive because HIV can be transmitted to the newborn in the breast milk.

Potential drug interactions: Interaction between the following medications and nelfinavir has the potential to impact the effect of one or more of the drugs. In some instances the interaction can be dangerous or life-threatening and must be avoided: drugs primarily metabolized by CYP3A (e.g., dihydropyridine calcium channel blockers, HMG-CoA reductase inhibitors, immunosuppressants, sildenafil), lovastatin, simvastatin, atorvastatin, rifampin, St. John's wort, indinavir, ritonavir, saquinavir, delavirdine, nevirapine, carbamazepine, phenobarbital, phenytoin, methadone, ethinyl estradiol, azithromycin, fluticasone. Alternative or additional contraceptive measures should be used when women taking oral contraceptives go on nelfinavir.

What the FDA says about use in pregnancy: Category B (see Appendix).

What the available evidence suggests about breast-feeding safety: Not safe.

The bottom line for you:

- Treatment regimens consisting of 3–5 drugs are the current standard of care for the management of HIV infection during pregnancy and may include nelfinavir.
- The clearance of nelfinavir increases significantly during pregnancy, and blood levels of the medication should be monitored.
- Pregnant women require careful monitoring for liver toxicity during antiretroviral therapy.
- If infant formula is available, breast-feeding is not recommended when a mother is HIV positive because HIV can be transmitted to the newborn in the breast milk.
- Women taking nelfinavir during pregnancy are encouraged to register with the Antiretroviral Pregnancy Registry (1-800-258-4263) to help increase the available information about the effect of nelfinavir on pregnancy. The registry can also be a resource for information for pregnant women considering nelfinavir treatment.

NEOMYCIN

Brand names: Mycifradin, Myciguent, Neo-Rx, Qrp

Drug classes: Aminoglycoside; Antibiotic

Indications (what it is used for): Liver coma (loss of conscious due to liver failure), bacterial infections caused by sensitive bacteria.

How it works: Blocks protein synthesis, reducing ammonia-forming bacteria in the gut and leading to their death.

Contraindications (reasons you shouldn't take it): Hypersensitivity to drug or class, bowel obstruction, inflammatory and ulcerative GI disease, severe dermatologic diseases.

Possible side effects and warnings: Can cause nausea, vomiting, diarrhea, malabsorption syndrome (small intestine cannot absorb nutrients from food), kidney and/or ear toxicity, and neuromuscular blockage. Should be used with caution in women with liver dysfunction.

How it can affect pregnant women: There are no adequate reports or well-controlled studies of neomycin in pregnant women. Neomycin is poorly absorbed from both the skin (where it is used as part of triple antibiotic ointment) and the bowel when taken by mouth.

How it can affect a developing embryo or fetus: There are no adequate reports or well-controlled studies in human fetuses. It is unknown whether neomycin crosses the human placenta. Although there is no evidence that it causes birth defects, some aminoglycosides (e.g., streptomycin) have been associated with irreversible deafness after exposure in the uterus. Considering that it is applied to the skin and how little is absorbed systemically, it is unlikely that the maternal systemic concentration would reach a clinically relevant level for an embryo or fetus. Rodent birth defect studies have not been performed. Neomycin is used for the prevention of newborn eye infection, but it has not been tested in clinical trials.

Breast-feeding: There are no adequate reports or well-controlled studies in nursing women. It is unknown whether neomycin enters human breast milk. Neomycin is excreted into both sheep and rat breast milk. Considering the indication, dose, and its topical application, occasional use is unlikely to pose a clinically significant risk to a breast-feeding newborn.

Potential drug interactions: Interaction between the following medications and neomycin has the potential to impact the effect of one or more of the drugs. In some instances the interaction can be dangerous or life-threatening and must be avoided: other neurotoxic and/or nephrotoxic drugs, aminoglycosides, polymyxins, penicillin V, oral vitamin B_{12}, methotrexate, 5-fluorouracil, digoxin, coumarins.

What the FDA says about use in pregnancy: Category D (see Appendix).

What the available evidence suggests about breast-feeding safety: Safe (topical); likely safe (oral).

The bottom line for you:

● Topical neomycin is probably safe and effective during pregnancy and while breast-feeding.

NETILMICIN

Brand name: Netromycin

Drug classes: Aminoglycoside; Antibiotic

Indications (what it is used for): Bacterial infections of the skin and respiratory tract, sepsis, intra-abdominal infections caused by sensitive bacteria.

How it works: Inhibits protein synthesis, leading to bacterial death.

Contraindications (reasons you shouldn't take it): Hypersensitivity to drug or class.

Possible side effects and warnings: Can cause kidney and/or ear toxicity, hearing loss, ringing in the ears, rash, neuromuscular blockade, low magnesium levels, high platelet count, pain at injection site, and involuntary eye movement.

How it can affect pregnant women: There are no adequate reports or well-controlled studies of netilmicin in pregnant women. It is the first alternative to gentamicin for the treatment of brucellosis (a highly infectious disease that can be transmitted from animals to humans) during pregnancy. There are case reports of its use for listeriosis (infection by *Listeria* bacteria, usually caused by eating contaminated food) during pregnancy.

How it can affect a developing embryo or fetus: There are no adequate reports or well-controlled studies in human fetuses. It is unknown whether netilmicin crosses the human placenta. Although there is no evidence that netilmicin causes birth defects in humans, some aminoglycosides (e.g., streptomycin) have been associated with irreversible deafness after exposure in the uterus. Rodent birth defect studies have not been performed. Transfer across the rat placenta appears low. Its effect on hearing varies among rodent species.

Breast-feeding: There is no published data in nursing women. It appears that the amount of netilmicin that enters human breast milk is clinically insignificant.

Potential drug interactions: No clinically relevant interactions identified.

What the FDA says about use in pregnancy: Category D (see Appendix).

What the available evidence suggests about breast-feeding safety: Probably safe.

The bottom line for you:

- There are alternative agents with which there is more experience during pregnancy and while breast-feeding.
- Netilmicin should be used only if the benefit to the woman justifies the potential risk to the embryo, fetus, or newborn.

NEVIRAPINE

Brand name: Viramune

Drug classes: Antiviral; Nonnucleoside reverse transcriptase inhibitor

Indications (what it is used for): HIV.

How it works: Inhibits reverse transcriptase, an enzyme necessary for the virus to replicate.

Contraindications (reasons you shouldn't take it): Hypersensitivity to drug or class.

Possible side effects and warnings: Can cause Stevens-Johnson syndrome (a rare but serious skin reaction to medication), fever, liver toxicity, hepatitis, low white blood cell count, peripheral neuropathy (nerve damage causing numbness, tingling or pain in the hands and feet), nausea, vomiting, abdominal pain, diarrhea, rash, muscle ache, headache, joint pain, and mouth ulcers. Should be used with caution in women with kidney or liver dysfunction.

How it can affect pregnant women: Treatment of HIV is rapidly improving. Triple (e.g., zidovudine, lamivudine, nevirapine) or quadruple therapy is still a standard for the management of HIV infection in adults because of the high efficacy. Nevirapine-based highly active antiretroviral therapy (HAART) (compared mainly with nelfinavir-based HAART), is probably the regimen of choice during pregnancy because of its effectiveness.

In women who are not on antiretroviral therapy during pregnancy, a single dose of nevirapine given at the onset of labor dramatically reduces the transmission of HIV from mother to child. It is more effective than zidovudine if given to both the mother at the onset of labor and her newborn within 72 hours of birth. Nevirapine resistance does occur from this approach. However, combining a single dose of tenofovir and emtricitabine at delivery reduces resistance; this treatment should be considered as an adjuvant to nevirapine during labor. Women who receive a single dose of nevirapine to prevent transmission of HIV-1 to their babies have higher rates of failure with subsequent nevirapine-based antiretroviral therapy if the therapy is initiated within 6 months after the single dose in labor. If, however, women have been receiving antiretroviral therapy during pregnancy, the addition of nevirapine during labor does not further reduce HIV transmission to the baby if cesarean section is available. Liver toxicity usually does not appear before 5 months of therapy.

Women who for any medical reason are not eligible for antiretroviral treatment should receive zidovudine from 28 weeks of pregnancy; zidovudine, lamivudine, and a single dose of nevirapine during delivery; and zidovudine and lamivudine for 7 days after delivery—to reduce the development of nevirapine resistance. Newborns should receive a single dose of nevirapine at birth and 1–4 weeks of zidovudine, depending on the duration of the regimen received by the mother.

How it can affect a developing embryo or fetus: There are no adequate reports or well-controlled studies in human fetuses. The safety of many approved antiretroviral agents during pregnancy is not established. In contrast to most protease inhibitors, nevirapine rapidly crosses the human placenta, reaching a level in the fetus similar to that in the mother. The limited regimen described is well tolerated and reduces the risk of a mother passing the virus to her child by nearly 50% in women and infants receiving no other antiretrovirals. Infants born less than 2 hours after maternal nevirapine during labor should receive a dose immediately after birth in addition to the standard dose at 48–72 hours to ensure therapeutic levels.

Breast-feeding: There are no adequate reports or well-controlled studies in nursing women. Nevirapine is excreted into human breast milk. Breast-feeding is contraindicated (not recommended) in HIV-infected women when formula is available to reduce the risk of transmitting the virus to the newborn. However, breast-feeding is essential in some countries where formula is not available. In those instances, nevirapine during labor and after delivery lowers HIV-1 transmission risk in breast-feeding women more effectively than zidovudine. This simple, inexpensive, well-tolerated regimen has the potential to significantly decrease mother-to-child transmission of HIV-1 worldwide.

Potential drug interactions: Interaction between the following medications and nevirapine has the potential to impact the effect of one or more of the drugs. In some instances the interaction can be dangerous or life-threatening and must be avoided: drugs metabolized by CYP3A4 and 2B6, warfarin, clarithromycin, efavirenz, ethinyl estradiol/norethindrone, indinavir, ketoconazole, lopinavir/ritonavir combination, methadone, nelfinavir, saquinavir, amiodarone, carbamazepine, cisapride, clonazepam, cyclophosphamide, cyclosporine, diltiazem, disopyramide, ergotamine, ethosuximide, fentanyl, itraconazole, lidocaine, nifedipine, sirolimus, tacrolimus, and verapamil. Hormonal methods of birth control should not be used as the sole method of contraception in women taking nevirapine. An alternative or additional method of contraception is recommended.

What the FDA says about use in pregnancy: Category B (see Appendix).

What the available evidence suggests about breast-feeding safety: It is not recommended for an HIV-positive woman to breast-feed if formula is available.

The bottom line for you:

- Nevirapine in combination with other antiretrovirals (e.g., HAART) is the preferred regimen for most HIV-positive women during pregnancy.
- Nevirapine given at the onset of labor and to newborns within 72 hours of birth is more effective than zidovudine for women who have not received the regular antiretroviral therapy during pregnancy.
- Women taking nevirapine during pregnancy are encouraged to register with the Antiretroviral Pregnancy Registry (1-800-258-4263) to increase the available information about nevirapine use during pregnancy. The registry can also be a resource for pregnant women considering (or already under) treatment.
- Although breast-feeding is not recommended in HIV-positive women when formula is available, nevirapine is a drug of choice when an HIV-positive woman must breast-feed.

NIACIN

Brand names: Acido Nicotinico, Akotin, Niaspan, Nicolar, Niconacid, Nicotinic Acid, Nikacid, Nikotime, Novo-Niacin, Slo Niacin, Span Niacin, Vitaplex, Wampocap

Drug classes: Antihyperlipidemic; Vitamin/mineral

Indications (what it is used for): High cholesterol, high triglycerides, pellagra (disease caused by niacin deficiency).

How it works: Decreases cholesterol and lipids through multiple effects on the liver.

Contraindications (reasons you shouldn't take it): Hypersensitivity to drug or class, bleeding, low blood pressure, active ulcer disease, severe liver dysfunction.

Possible side effects and warnings: Can cause muscle breakdown, abnormal heart rates, low blood pressure when standing or sitting, heartburn, vomiting, peptic ulceration, liver dysfunction, diarrhea, flushing, dry skin, decreased glucose tolerance, high uric acid levels, gout, fluid and protein deposits on or under the macula of the eye, lazy eye, and headache. Should be used with caution in women with gout, mild liver dysfunction, diabetes, coronary artery disease, or low blood pressure.

How it can affect pregnant women: Niacin is a water-soluble B-complex vitamin with essential roles in lipid and glucose metabolism and in tissue respiration. Women with pellagra are more likely than men to die because of an interaction with estrogen, and pregnancy increases estrogen levels. It also imposes metabolic demands on the mother due to the growing fetus that necessitate additional niacin. The recommended dose of niacinamide (a by-product of niacin) varies between 15 and 17 mg per day, and it is usually found in prenatal vitamins. There are no adequate reports or well-controlled studies of niacin in pregnant women. Despite routine vitamin supplementation, a high percentage of pregnant women are deficient in vitamins A, B₆, B₁₂, niacin, and thiamine. Niacin deficiency is particularly common during the first trimester. However, there is no evidence that supplementation changes pregnancy outcome.

How it can affect a developing embryo or fetus: There are no adequate reports or well-controlled studies in human fetuses. Niacin crosses the human placenta. Rodent birth defect studies have not been conducted.

Breast-feeding: There are no adequate reports or well-controlled studies in nursing women. Niacin is excreted into human breast milk. It is not known whether supplementation increases niacin concentrations in breast milk or in breast-fed newborns. Niacin is generally considered compatible with breast-feeding.

Potential drug interactions: Interaction between the following medications and niacin has the potential to impact the effect of one or more of the drugs. In some instances the interaction can be dangerous or life-threatening and must be avoided: bile acid–binding resins, vitamins or other nutritional supplements containing large doses of niacin or related compounds such as nicotinamide.

What the FDA says about use in pregnancy: Category C (see Appendix).

What the available evidence suggests about breast-feeding safety: Safe.

The bottom line for you:

- Niacin is a component of most prenatal vitamins. Many pregnant women are deficient despite supplementation.
- Niacin is safe for use while breast-feeding.

NICARDIPINE

Brand name: Cardene

Drug classes: Antiarrhythmic; Antihypertensive; Calcium channel blocker

Indications (what it is used for): High blood pressure, chest pain.

How it works: Inhibits the flow of calcium into vascular smooth muscle and myocardium (heart wall) cells, which is required for them to contract.

Contraindications (reasons you shouldn't take it): Hypersensitivity to drug or class, aortic stenosis.

Possible side effects and warnings: Can cause swelling, flushing, weakness, tiredness, nausea, vomiting, shortness of breath, palpitations, rapid heart rate, dizziness, dry mouth, constipation, nervousness, urination at night, ECG abnormalities, and low blood pressure when standing or sitting. Should be used with caution in women with kidney or liver dysfunction, congestive heart failure, or cardiac conduction disease.

How it can affect pregnant women: There are several uses for nicardipine during pregnancy.

High blood pressure during pregnancy: High blood pressure remains a significant cause of maternal and fetal illness and death. Severe high blood pressure during pregnancy should be treated immediately to improve both maternal and fetal outcome. Treatment of sudden high blood pressure is more complicated during pregnancy since a rapid decrease in blood pressure may adversely affect the fetus as well; it may also lead to coma, stroke, heart attack, sudden kidney failure, and death in the mother. The goal is not just to decrease the pressure but also to do so safely and limit any adverse effects and preserve organ function.

Quality studies reveal that nicardipine is safe and effective for this purpose. It is more efficient than metoprolol and similar to labetalol. Although the definitive treatment for severe preeclampsia (high blood pressure and protein in the urine during pregnancy and complications associated with it) remains delivering the fetus, some practitioners try to avoid prematurity by treating aggressively until delivery is mandatory. Preliminary study indicates that long-term treatment with nicardipine for severe preeclampsia is safe as long as the woman remains responsive to therapy.

Premature labor at or before 34 weeks: One quality study concluded that nicardipine is an effective, safe, and well-tolerated tocolytic agent (medication to delay preterm labor and delivery). It causes a modest decline in blood pressure in women who have otherwise normal blood pressure. Women treated with nicardipine have fewer adverse medication effects and episodes of recurrent preterm labor compared to those treated with the ineffective magnesium sulfate. Treatment-related maternal low blood pressure is not associated with fetal distress. In another study, nicardipine allowed a greater percentage of women to delay delivery more than 7 days compared to salbutamol, and there were fewer maternal side effects. Nicardipine seems especially helpful to women with high blood pressure, diabetes, or maternal heart disease. A relationship between oral nicardipine and sudden cardiac death was reported in patients also receiving strong inhibitors of CYP3A (such as erythromycin). This is important, since pregnant women often receive antibiotics (including erythromycin) to decrease the risk of infection from preterm premature rupture of membranes (water breaking before 37 weeks).

How it can affect a developing embryo or fetus: There are no adequate reports or well-controlled studies in human fetuses. One study documented placental transport low enough to predict that the fetal level is likely clinically insignificant. Transfer across the nonhuman primate placenta is also poor, and there is no negative cardiovascular effect on fetuses after maternal administration. Rodent studies are reassuring, revealing no evidence of birth defects or low birth weight despite the use of doses higher than those used clinically. However, animal studies are not necessarily good indicators of how a drug will behave in humans.

Breast-feeding: The amount of nicardipine excreted into breast milk is clinically insignificant.

Potential drug interactions: Interaction between the following medications and nicardipine has the potential to impact the effect of one or more of the drugs. In some instances the interaction can be dangerous or life-threatening and must be avoided: cimetidine, digitalis, cyclosporine.

What the FDA says about use in pregnancy: Category C (see Appendix).

What the available evidence suggests about breast-feeding safety: Safe.

The bottom line for you:

- Calcium channel blockers have excellent safety profiles and a high degree of efficacy for the treatment of acute and chronic high blood pressure during pregnancy.

- Calcium channel blockers are among the agents of choice for delaying preterm birth. There is more experience with nifedipine than nicardipine for that purpose.

- Oral erythromycin should probably be avoided in women receiving a calcium channel blocker as a tocolytic agent. Ampicillin plus sulbactam is preferred.

- Nicardipine is safe for use while breast-feeding.

NICOTINE

Brand names: Habitrol, NicoDerm, Nicotrol, Pro-Step, Quit Spray, Stubit

Drug class: Central nervous system stimulant

Indications (what it is used for): Smoking cessation.

How it works: Stimulates nicotinic-cholinergic receptors.

Contraindications (reasons you shouldn't take it): Hypersensitivity to drug or class, nonsmoker, recent history of heart attack, irregular heart rate, chest pain, allergy to menthol, Buerger's disease (blood clots in the hands and feet), Prinzmetal's variant angina (cycles of chest pain), Raynaud's disease (disorder in which blood vessels are prone to spasm, which causes discoloration of the fingers, toes, and occasionally other areas often triggered by cold), high levels of thyroid hormone, pheochromocytoma (adrenal gland tumor), type I diabetes.

Possible side effects and warnings: Can cause life-threatening irregular heart rates, heart attack, inflammation of the blood vessels, dependence, local erythema (redness of the skin), local itching, nausea, vomiting, diarrhea, sleeplessness, headache, nervousness, abnormal dreams, dizziness, and rash. Should be used with caution in women with coronary artery disease or peptic ulcer disease.

How it can affect pregnant women: Cigarette smoking is directly linked to an array of health problems. Active and secondhand maternal smoking (inhaling near someone who is smoking) have damaging effects in each trimester. It is the single largest modifiable risk for pregnancy-related morbidity and death in the U.S. Cigarette smoke contains numerous toxins that have a direct effect on placental and fetal cell proliferation and differentiation. Cigarette smoking increases the rate of subfertility and failed in vitro fertilization.

Nicotine replacement helps people quit by relieving the physiologic symptoms of withdrawal. Nicotine delivery systems include gum, patch, nasal spray, and vapor inhaler. Because nicotine medications do not include the toxins and carcinogens delivered by cigarettes, they are safer than smoking during pregnancy if used as directed. Women should stop smoking completely during pregnancy since simply reducing the number of cigarettes smoked, or switching to so-called low-tar or low-nicotine concentration cigarettes does not significantly reduce the risks to the embryo or fetus. The nicotine patch may help some pregnant smokers, but the success rate during pregnancy is low. Despite the failure of large numbers of treated women to quit, the average birth weight of their babies is increased by therapy. The success rate is increased by the addition of a selective serotonin reuptake inhibitor (SSRI) and formal counseling. Social support systems also enhance the likelihood of long-term success in women who do quit smoking during pregnancy. The starting dose of nicotine should approximate the amount of nicotine being inhaled. Intermittent-use formulations of nicotine (gum, spray, inhaler) are preferred, as the total dose of nicotine delivered to the fetus is less than with the skin patch.

How it can affect a developing embryo or fetus: Cigarette smoke contains thousands of chemicals, many of which are well-documented reproductive toxins (e.g., nicotine, carbon monoxide, lead). Nicotine rapidly crosses the placenta, and the fetuses of mothers who smoke are actually exposed to higher concentrations than their mothers. Smoking during pregnancy is a major risk factor for miscarriage, preterm placental abruption (the placenta separating from the uterus), low birth weight, late fetal death, a dangerously high number of red blood cells, and SIDS (sudden infant death syndrome). The mean reduction in birth weight in infants of smokers is almost half a pound. There may also be a higher rate of facial clefts in the offspring of smokers. Quality studies suggest that prenatal exposure to nicotine increases the risks for cognitive deficits, attention deficit disorder, conduct disorder, criminality in adulthood, and a predisposition of the offspring to abuse tobacco and alcohol. Prenatal nicotine affects the fetal defenses for low oxygen and has long-term effects on a newborn's breathing pattern. Nicotine-exposed newborns are unable to maximize the amount of blood the heart pumps during times of stress and are, as a result, at increased risk for illness and possible death. Human newborn nicotine withdrawal does occur. Rodent studies showed that nicotine exposure compromises nerve maturation, leading to long-lasting structural alterations in key brain regions associated with thinking, learning, and memory.

Breast-feeding: Nicotine is excreted in human breast milk at low concentrations. Milk cotinine (a by-product of nicotine) levels do not correlate with the number of cigarettes smoked. Newborns breast-fed by smoking women are exposed not only to environmental ("passive") smoke but also by ingesting nicotine metabolites and toxic by-products present in the milk. Smoking around children increases their risk for respiratory diseases. If a woman continues to smoke she should do so well away from her child, but breastfeeding will provide antibodies to her baby to help lower that risk. Maternal smoking cessation with the nicotine patch is a safer option than continued smoking while breast-feeding.

Potential drug interactions: Interaction between the following medications and nicotine has the potential to impact the effect of one or more of the drugs. In some instances the interaction can be dangerous or life-threatening and must be avoided: acetaminophen, caffeine, imipramine, oxazepam, pentazocine, propranolol, other beta-blockers, theophylline, nasal vasoconstrictors such as xylometazoline, adrenergic agonists (e.g., isoproterenol, phenylephrine).

What the FDA says about use in pregnancy: Category D (see Appendix).

What the available evidence suggests about breast-feeding safety: Safe.

The bottom line for you:
- If you smoke, stop. It causes long-term damage to you and your unborn child. Pregnant smokers unable to stop smoking without medical treatment should seek nicotine replacement therapy.
- Cigarette smoking during pregnancy subjects the child to increased risks of low birth weight, perinatal mortality, and behavior problems (increased activity, decreased attention), as well as diminished intellectual abilities and school failure.
- If you smoke and wish to breast-feed, stop smoking. Breast-feeding smokers unable to stop smoking should be offered nicotine replacement therapy.

NIFEDIPINE
Brand names: Adalat, Adalat CC, Alonix, Corinfar, Ecodipin-E, Procardia, Procardia XL
Drug classes: Antiarrhythmic; Antihypertensive; Calcium channel blocker
Indications (what it is used for): High blood pressure, chest pain.
How it works: Inhibits Ca^{2+} (calcium ion) flow into vascular smooth muscle and heart cells, which is responsible for triggering the muscle contraction.
Contraindications (reasons you shouldn't take it): Hypersensitivity to drug or class.
Possible side effects and warnings: Can cause flushing, congestive heart failure, excess water in the lungs, shortness of breath, heart attack, headache, nausea, vomiting, dizziness, peripheral edema, nervousness, weakness, wheezing, nasal congestion, itching, and muscle cramps. Should be used with caution in women with congestive heart failure.
How it can affect pregnant women: There are several uses for nifedipine during pregnancy.

High blood pressure: High blood pressure remains a significant cause of maternal and fetal illness and death. Severe high blood pressure during pregnancy should be treated immediately to improve both maternal and fetal outcome. Treatment of sudden high blood pressure is more complicated during pregnancy since a rapid and uncontrolled decrease in blood pressure may adversely affect the fetus as well; it may also lead to coma, stroke, heart attack, sudden kidney failure, and death in the mother. The goal is not just to decrease the pressure, but also to do so safely and limit any adverse effects and preserve organ function.

Nifedipine is proven safe and effective for the treatment of sudden or chronically high blood pressure during pregnancy.

Preterm labor: Nifedipine is used to slow preterm labor (tocolysis). No tocolytic agents actually stop preterm labor or alone improve perinatal outcome, but they can improve the baby's outcome by keeping the fetus inside the uterus long enough for the administration of corticosteroids that can help the fetus's lungs mature. Compared to placebo and any other tocolytic agent, calcium channel blockers, and specifically nifedipine, reduce the number of women giving birth within 2–7 days of a preterm labor diagnosis. There are also fewer instances of women having to stop nifedipine therapy because of adverse effects compared to other tocolytic medications. The use of nifedipine with magnesium sulfate to reduce the risk of cerebral palsy is potentially dangerous; the combination is more frequently associated with severe low blood pressure, muscle weakness, and cardiac weakness. A relationship between oral erythromycin and sudden cardiac death was reported in patients also receiving strong CYP3A inhibitors (such as erythromycin). This is important, since pregnant women often receive antibiotics (including erythromycin) to reduce the risk of infection from preterm premature rupture of membranes (water breaking before 37 weeks).

Pulmonary high blood pressure: The treatment of high blood pressure in the lungs during pregnancy remains controversial in part because of its rarity and complexity. Nifedipine is sometimes used.

How it can affect a developing embryo or fetus: There are no adequate reports or well-controlled studies in human fetuses. Nifedipine crosses the human placenta, reaching about three-quarters of the level in the mother. Newborns exposed to nifedipine to treat preterm labor have lower admission rates to the neonatal intensive care unit and lower incidences of respiratory distress syndrome (surfactin insufficiency), bleeding into the brain, and jaundice (turning yellow). Part of the benefit stems from the fact that nifedipine prolongs pregnancy. In rodents, nifedipine increased rates of skeletal abnormalities, cleft palate, and low birth weight. However, animal studies are not necessarily good indicators of how a drug will behave in humans.

Breast-feeding: Although nifedipine is excreted into human breast milk, the amount is clinically insignificant.

Potential drug interactions: Interaction between the following medications or substances and nifedipine has the potential to impact the effect of one or more of the drugs. In some instances the interaction can be dangerous or life-threatening and must be avoided: beta-blockers, digoxin, cimetidine. Use of nifedipine with grapefruit and grapefruit juice should be avoided.

What the FDA says about use in pregnancy: Category C (see Appendix).

What the available evidence suggests about breast-feeding safety: Likely safe.

The bottom line for you:

- Nifedipine is safe and effective during pregnancy for controlling blood pressure in women with severe preeclampsia or chronic high blood pressure.

- Current evidence indicates that calcium channel blockers, and nifedipine specifically, are among the most effective agents to slow preterm birth with the highest maternal/fetal safety profile.

- Nifedipine should be considered a first-line tocolytic agent for the treatment of preterm labor before 34 weeks. Oral erythromycin should probably be avoided in women receiving a calcium channel blocker as a tocolytic agent. Ampicillin plus sulbactam is preferred.

- Nifedipine is safe for use while breast-feeding.

NIMODIPINE

Brand name: Nimotop
Drug class: Calcium channel blocker
Indications (what it is used for): Subarachnoid hemorrhage with vasospasm.
How it works: Inhibits Ca^{2+} (calcium ion) flow into vascular smooth muscle and heart cells, which is responsible for triggering the muscle contraction.
Contraindications (reasons you shouldn't take it): Hypersensitivity to drug or class.
Possible side effects and warnings: Can cause low blood pressure; rapid, slow, or irregular heart rates; bowel bleeding; low platelet count; blood clots; liver dysfunction; diarrhea; swelling; shortness of breath; headache; rash; heartburn; anemia; acne; muscle aches; and flushing. Should be used with caution in women with liver dysfunction.
How it can affect pregnant women: Nimodipine is a calcium channel blocker used for several indications during pregnancy, although often there are better choices for these same conditions.

High blood pressure: High blood pressure remains a significant cause of maternal and fetal illness and death. Severe high blood pressure during pregnancy should be treated immediately to improve both maternal and fetal outcome. Treatment of sudden high blood pressure is more complicated during pregnancy since a rapid and uncontrolled decrease in blood pressure may adversely affect the fetus as well; it may also lead to coma, stroke, heart attack, sudden kidney failure, and death in the mother. The goal is not just to decrease the pressure, but also to do so safely and limit any adverse effects and preserve organ function.

A recent review of the world's experience concluded that nimodipine should not be used to treat preeclamptic high blood pressure, as it was associated with twice the risk of eclampsia.

Preterm labor: Calcium channel blockers reduce the number of women giving birth within 2–7 days of a diagnosis of preterm labor. Calcium channel blockers are also a tocolytic (medication to delay preterm labor) of choice because as a group they have lower risks of adverse effects compared to all other agents available in the U.S. However, there are no adequate reports or well-controlled studies specifically of nimodipine for tocolysis in pregnant women. Nifedipine or nicardipine is preferable.

Psychiatric disorders: Nimodipine may be an alternative to lithium in pregnant women with bipolar disorder.

How it can affect a developing embryo or fetus: There are no adequate reports or well-controlled studies in human fetuses. Nimodipine crosses the human placenta, reaching the same level as that of the mother within hours. It dilates blood vessels in the fetal brain, which is often used as a sign of decreased oxygen. Rodent studies were somewhat conflicting. Placental transfer is inefficient. Early embryo loss, birth defects, and low birth weight were reported in some studies, but they occur independent of what dose is given, which makes it difficult to say that the drug is responsible. However, animal studies are not necessarily good indicators of how a drug will behave in humans.
Breast-feeding: There are no adequate reports or well-controlled studies in nursing women. Nimodipine enters human breast milk. In one case report, the amount of nimodipine was clinically insignificant.
Potential drug interactions: Interaction between the following medications and nimodipine has the potential to impact the effect of one or more of the drugs. In some instances the interaction can be dangerous or life-threatening and must be avoided: cimetidine.
What the FDA says about use in pregnancy: Category C (see Appendix).
What the available evidence suggests about breast-feeding safety: Likely safe.
The bottom line for you:
- There are alternative agents with which there is more experience during pregnancy and while breast-feeding.

- Nimodipine should be used during pregnancy only if the benefit to the woman justifies the potential risk to the embryo or fetus.
- It is probably safe for use while breast-feeding if needed.

NITROFURANTOIN

Brand names: Furadantin, Furalan, Furan, Furanite, Furantoina, Furatoin, Macrobid, Macrodantin, Nitrofan, Nitrofuracot

Drug classes: Antibiotic; Nitrofuran

Indications (what it is used for): Urinary tract infection (UTI).

How it works: Inhibits protein and cell wall synthesis, resulting in the death of the bacteria.

Contraindications (reasons you shouldn't take it): Hypersensitivity to drug or class, kidney function less than half of normal.

Possible side effects and warnings: Can cause sudden lung hypersensitivity, hepatitis, pancreatitis, cholestatic jaundice, nausea, vomiting, gas, peripheral neuropathy, exfoliative dermatitis, erythema multiforme and Stevens-Johnson syndrome (skin disorders), lupuslike syndrome, swelling underneath the skin, hives, rash, bone marrow suppression, hemolytic anemia, interstitial pneumonitis (a lung disease), and joint pain. It should be used with caution in women with asthma, anemia, or G6PD deficiency.

How it can affect pregnant women: Urinary tract infection is common during pregnancy, and all pregnant women should be screened. Some 30% of pregnant women will have a bladder infection without symptoms, and about 25% of these women will go on to develop symptomatic disease. The treatment of bladder infection without symptoms reduces the risk of an infection developing to the point of having symptoms. Symptomatic bladder and/or kidney infection is life-threatening. Ampicillin should not be used anymore because of the high prevalence of resistant *E. coli* bacteria. Nitrofurantoin is safe and effective during pregnancy for the treatment of asymptomatic bacteriuria (bacteria in the urine without symptoms of urinary tract infection) as well as new and persistent UTIs. Kidney infection occurs in 7% of women despite adequate treatment. In women with recurrent urinary tract infections, doctors may consider using nitrofurantoin long term to prevent recurrence. During labor, the amount of nitrofurantoin excreted by the kidneys is reduced, making it a poor choice to treat bladder or kidney infection at that time. Acute lung reactions to nitrofurantoin are uncommon but may be life-threatening. Symptoms include fever, chills, cough, pain with inhaling, shortness of breath, free fluid in the chest, and lung hemorrhage. The drug should be discontinued and corticosteroids initiated for severe reactions; otherwise irreversible lung damage can occur. Patients with G6PD deficiency may experience breakdown of red blood cells leading to anemia.

How it can affect a developing embryo or fetus: There are no adequate reports or well-controlled studies in human fetuses. It is unknown whether nitrofurantoin crosses the human placenta. There is no evidence that nitrofurantoin causes birth defects. Although contraindicated (should not be used) in labor and in infants less than 1 month old (because of the potential for breakdown of red blood cells), there are no well-documented cases of this happening in newborns. Rodent studies are reassuring, revealing no evidence of birth defects or low birth weight despite the use of doses higher than those used clinically. However, animal studies are not necessarily good indicators of how a drug will behave in humans.

Breast-feeding: The long clinical experience is reassuring, although the literature is conflicting. One study concluded that a nursing newborn could ingest 6% of the maternal dose. Another study concluded that the likelihood of a nursing newborn ingesting a clinically relevant amount of nitrofurantoin was low. This is more consistent with clinical experience. Concern remains for breast-feeding women treated therapeutically with nitrofurantoin if they have a family history of G6PD deficiency or sensitivity to nitrofurantoin.

Potential drug interactions: Interaction between the following medications and nitrofurantoin has the potential to impact the effect of one or more of the drugs. In some instances the interaction can be dangerous or life-threatening and must be avoided: antacids containing magnesium trisilicate, uricosuric drugs (e.g., probenecid, sulfinpyrazone).

What the FDA says about use in pregnancy: Category B (see Appendix).

What the available evidence suggests about breast-feeding safety: Likely safe.

The bottom line for you:

- Nitrofurantoin is a first-line medication for the treatment of UTI and prevention of UTI recurrence.
- For most women, nitrofurantoin is probably safe for use while breast-feeding, although concern remains for women with a family history of G6PD deficiency or sensitivity to nitrofurantoin.

NITROGLYCERIN

Brand names: Deponit, Glyceryl, Minitran, Mi-Trates, Natirose, Nitrek, Nitro, Nitro-Bid, Nitrocap T.D., Nitrocine, Nitrocot, Nitrodisc, Nitro-Dur, Nitrogard, Nitroglyn, Nitrol, Nitrolin, Nitrolingual, Nitronal, Nitrong, Nitro-Par, Nitrorex, Nitrospan, Nitrostat, Nitro-Time, NTG, NTS, Transderm-Nitro, Transiderm, Tridil

Drug class: Vasodilator

Indications (what it is used for): Chest pain.

How it works: A nitric oxide donor; nitric oxide is a potent relaxer of all smooth muscle.

Contraindications (reasons you shouldn't take it): Hypersensitivity to drug or class, anemia, methemoglobinemia ('reduced' hemoglobin that cannot carry oxygen), increased intracranial pressure, head trauma, cerebral hemorrhage.

Possible side effects and warnings: Can cause low blood pressure, methemoglobinemia, severe allergic reaction, slow or rapid heart rate, headache, tolerance/dependence, light-headedness, burning/tingling oral sensation, low blood pressure when standing or sitting, dizziness, flushing, and swelling. Should be used with caution in women with low blood pressure, hypovolemia (decreased blood volume), chronic heart failure, or recent heart attack.

How it can affect pregnant women: There are several indications for nitroglycerin during pregnancy.

High blood pressure: High blood pressure remains a significant cause of maternal and fetal illness and death. Severe high blood pressure during pregnancy should be treated immediately to improve both maternal and fetal outcome. Treatment of sudden high blood pressure is more complicated during pregnancy since a rapid decrease in blood pressure may adversely affect the fetus as well; it may also lead to coma, stroke, heart attack, sudden kidney failure, and death in the mother. The goal is not just to decrease the pressure, but also to do so safely and limit any adverse effects and preserve organ function. Nitroglycerin dilates the uterine arteries, increasing blood flow to the uterus and potentially the placenta.

Cervical ripening and tocolysis: Nitroglycerin may have a role in preparing the cervix for labor. High doses of sublingual or IV nitroglycerin have been used to relax the uterus during fetal surgery, fetal extraction at cesarean section, external version (turning a breech fetus so it is head-first), internal intrapartum podalic version of the second twin (turning the second twin so it can be delivered vaginally as a breech), manual exploration of the uterus to remove a retained placenta, and replacement of an inverted uterus. Yet high-quality studies demonstrate that nitroglycerin is no better than placebo for fetal extraction at C-section and external version. Swelling of the lungs with water is the most common complication of using nitroglycerin during pregnancy. Although nitroglycerin is sometimes used to soften the cervix before first-trimester abortion, it is less effective than prostaglandins for that purpose. Nitroglycerin has also proved a poor tocolytic (medication to delay preterm labor) with a high rate of maternal adverse effects.

How it can affect a developing embryo or fetus: There are no adequate reports or well-controlled studies in human fetuses. Low levels of nitroglycerin cross the placenta, as it is found in the fetus after its use to facilitate an obstetric procedure. Nitroglycerin appears to dilate the placental blood vessels, potentially increasing blood flow to them when given to women with mild preeclampsia (high blood pressure and protein in the urine during pregnancy and complications associated with it). Rodent birth defect studies are reassuring but limited. However, animal studies are not necessarily good indicators of how a drug will behave in humans.

Breast-feeding: There is no published data in nursing women. It is unknown whether nitroglycerin enters human breast milk. However, considering how it is used, the typical dose, and how quickly it is cleared from the body, short-term nitroglycerin use is unlikely to pose a clinically significant risk to a breast-feeding newborn.

Potential drug interactions: Interaction between the following medications and nitroglycerin has the potential to impact the effect of one or more of the drugs. In some instances the interaction can be dangerous or life-threatening and must be avoided: ethanol, vasodilators, calcium channel blockers.

What the FDA says about use in pregnancy: Category C (see Appendix).

What the available evidence suggests about breast-feeding safety: Likely safe.

The bottom line for you:

- Nitroglycerin should be used during pregnancy only if the benefit to the woman justifies the potential risk to the embryo or fetus.
- In emergencies associated with uterine contractions, IV nitroglycerin may provide short-term uterine relaxation. There are superior options for cervical ripening.
- Nitroglycerin is a poor drug for slowing preterm birth.

- Nitroglycerin use appears safe while breast-feeding.

NITROPRUSSIDE

Brand names: Nipride, Nitropress
Drug class: Vasodilator
Indications (what it is used for): High blood pressure, heart failure.
How it works: A nitric oxide donor; nitric oxide is a potent relaxer of all smooth muscle.
Contraindications (reasons you shouldn't take it): Hypersensitivity to drug or class, poor cerebral or coronary perfusion (blood flow), optic atrophy (deterioration of optic nerve), tobacco-induced amblyopia (loss of vision).
Possible side effects and warnings: Can cause increased pressure in the brain, dizziness, nausea, vomiting, cyanide or thiocyanate toxicity, slow or rapid heart rate, ileus (intestinal obstruction), profuse sweating, abdominal pain, headache, muscle twitching, acidosis (too much acid in body fluids), and flushing. Should be used with caution in women with increased intracranial pressure.
How it can affect pregnant women: Nitroprusside has several potential uses during pregnancy. When nitroprusside breaks down within the body, it releases a low level of cyanide that if continued for a long period could accumulate.

High blood pressure: High blood pressure remains a significant cause of maternal and fetal illness and death. Severe high blood pressure during pregnancy must be treated immediately to improve both maternal and fetal outcome. Treatment of sudden high blood pressure during pregnancy is further complicated, because a rapid decrease in blood pressure may adversely affect the fetus; it may also lead to coma, stroke, heart attack, sudden kidney failure, and death in the mother. The goal is not just to decrease the blood pressure, but to do so safely and limit any adverse effects and preserve organ function. Intravenous nitroprusside is an excellent medication for the controlled reduction of severe high blood pressure.

Cervical ripening: Nitroprusside softens the cervix and reduces the force necessary to dilate the cervix for a first-trimester pregnancy termination.

How it can affect a developing embryo or fetus: There are no adequate reports or well-controlled studies in human fetuses. It is unknown whether nitroprusside crosses the human placenta. Fetal cyanide toxicity occurred in sheep after maternal administration. Rodent birth defect studies have not been performed. Animal studies are not necessarily a good indicator of how a drug will behave in humans.

Breast-feeding: There is no published data in nursing women. It is unknown whether nitroprusside enters human breast milk. However, considering how it is used, the typical dose, and how fast it is cleared from the body, limited nitroprusside use is unlikely to pose a clinically significant risk to a breast-feeding newborn.

Potential drug interactions: The blood-pressure-lowering effect of nitroprusside is increased by most other blood-pressure-lowering medications, including ganglionic blocking agents, negative inotropic agents, and inhaled anesthetics.

What the FDA says about use in pregnancy: Category C (see Appendix).

What the available evidence suggests about breast-feeding safety: Likely safe.

The bottom line for you:

- The prudent use of nitroprusside is excellent for the rapid treatment of severe high blood pressure during pregnancy.
- There are superior options for cervical ripening.
- Short-term nitroprusside use to control maternal blood pressure around delivery should have no impact on breast-feeding.

NIZATIDINE

Brand name: Axid

Drug classes: Antihistamine, H2; Gastrointestinal

Indications (what it is used for): Gastroesophageal reflux disease (GERD), duodenal ulcer.

How it works: Blocks the peripheral H2 receptor, whose activation causes the symptoms.

Contraindications (reasons you shouldn't take it): Hypersensitivity to drug or class.

Possible side effects and warnings: Can cause hepatitis, thrombocytopenic purpura (a serious clotting disorder), exfoliative dermatitis (skin disease with redness and scaling), runny nose, headache, nausea, vomiting, loss of appetite, heartburn, abdominal pain, constipation, liver dysfunction, sore throat, agitation, confusion, sleepiness, sleeplessness, sinusitis, dry mouth, low white blood cell and/or red blood cell counts. Should be used with caution in women with kidney dysfunction.

How it can affect pregnant women: Gastroesophageal reflux disease and/or heartburn occurs in 45–85% of pregnant women in part because of high progesterone and estrogen levels. The treatment for GERD consists of reducing gastric acidity starting with lifestyle and dietary changes. If these fail, antacids or sucralfate are first-line medical therapies, followed by histamine receptor blockers.

There are no adequate reports or well-controlled studies of nizatidine in pregnant women. Nizatidine should be reserved for patients with severe symptoms.

How it can affect a developing embryo or fetus: There are no adequate reports or well-controlled studies in human fetuses. Nizatidine crosses the human placenta. A collaborative study by the European Network of Teratology Information Services of H2 blockers noted an excess of spontaneous preterm deliveries (before 37 weeks) in women who had used a drug in this group. Rodent studies are reassuring, revealing no evidence of birth defects or low birth weight despite the use of doses higher than those used clinically. However, animal studies are not necessarily good indicators of how a drug will behave in humans.

Breast-feeding: There are no adequate reports or well-controlled studies in nursing women. The amount of nizatidine excreted into human breast milk is clinically insignificant.

Potential drug interactions: No clinically relevant interactions identified.

What the FDA says about use in pregnancy: Category B (see Appendix).

What the available evidence suggests about breast-feeding safety: Likely safe.

The bottom line for you:

- Increased severity of nausea and vomiting in pregnancy is associated with the presence of heartburn and acid reflux.
- Antacids, some histamine H2 receptor antagonists, and proton pump inhibitors can be used safely during pregnancy, as large studies have shown no evidence of birth defects.
- However, nizatidine should be reserved for women who fail to respond to better-studied drugs, as nizatidine may be associated with preterm birth.
- Nizatidine is safe for use while breast-feeding.

NORETHINDRONE

Brand names: Dianor, Micronor, Norethisterone, Norlutin, Nor-QD, Primulut

Drug classes: Contraceptive; Hormone; Progestin

Indications (what it is used for): Contraception, dysmenorrhea, dysfunctional uterine bleeding, endometriosis (the endometrium grows outside the uterus), polycystic ovary syndrome (PCOS; multiple cysts inside the ovary leading to irregular menstruation and infertility).

How it works: Prevents pregnancy by preventing ovulation, by converting proliferative endometrium (which is needed for implantation) into secretory endometrium (which is hostile to implantation), and by thickening the cervical mucus so the sperm cannot penetrate.

Contraindications (reasons you shouldn't take it): Hypersensitivity to drug or class, pregnancy, breast or liver disease or liver cancer, coronary artery disease, and abnormal vaginal bleeding.

Possible side effects and warnings: Can cause irregular vaginal bleeding, altered menstrual bleeding, absent menstruation, acne, facial hair growth, weight gain, headache, breast tenderness, nausea, vomiting, blood clots, heart attack, high blood pressure, liver tumor, swelling, facial pigmentation, rash, and dizziness. Should be used with caution in women who smoke.

How it can affect pregnant women: Norethindrone is the synthetic progesterone in several popular oral contraceptives. The use of oral contraceptives containing norethindrone is associated with an increased rate of breakthrough bleeding. The rate of ectopic pregnancy (implantation of the embryo outside the uterus, usually in the fallopian tubes) may be slightly increased when used as a progesterone-only contraceptive. There is no indication for norethindrone during pregnancy and while breast-feeding.

How it can affect a developing embryo or fetus: There are no adequate reports or well-controlled studies in human fetuses. Norethindrone is structurally related to testosterone and likely crosses the placenta, and there are scattered reports of newborn girls delivered with an enlarged clitoris after exposure to norethindrone. It is recommended after a first-trimester exposure that the fetus undergo a detailed anatomic ultrasound by a skilled sonographer between 18 and 22 weeks. Norethindrone did not cause birth defects in rodents. However, animal studies are not necessarily good indicators of how a drug will behave in humans.

Breast-feeding: The small amounts of norethindrone found in breast milk are clinically insignificant.

Potential drug interactions: Interaction between the following medications and norethindrone has the potential to impact one or more of the drugs. In some instances, the interaction can be dangerous or life-threatening and must be avoided: liver enzyme–

inducing drugs such as phenytoin, carbamazepine, barbiturates, and rifampin.

What the FDA says about use in pregnancy: Category X (see Appendix).

What the available evidence suggests about breast-feeding safety: Safe.

The bottom line for you:

- Norethindrone is an effective contraceptive. There are no indications for its use during pregnancy.
- Women exposed to it inadvertently during the first trimester should undergo a detailed second trimester ultrasound by a skilled perinatologist to look for any possible genital abnormalities.
- Norethindrone is safe for use while breast-feeding.

NORFLOXACIN

Brand names: Chibroxin, Floxenor, Norofin, Noroxin, Norxacin, Oroflox

Drug classes: Antibiotic; Ophthalmic; Quinolone

Indications (what it is used for): Bacterial infections due to susceptible bacteria, gastroenteritis, traveler's diarrhea.

How it works: Kills bacteria by blocking the synthesis of DNA.

Contraindications (reasons you shouldn't take it): Hypersensitivity to drug or class.

Possible side effects and warnings: Can cause light sensitivity, bowel infection, vaginitis, seizures, increased pressure in the brain, headache, psychosis, nausea, vomiting, diarrhea, abdominal pain, heartburn, dizziness, sleeplessness, agitation, tendonitis, joint pain, tendon rupture, restlessness, and liver dysfunction. Should be used with caution in women with kidney, liver, or lung dysfunction; cardiovascular disease; central nervous system disorder; seizures; diabetes; G6PD deficiency; myasthenia gravis (an autoimmune disease causing muscle weakness).

How it can affect pregnant women: There are no adequate reports or well-controlled studies of norfloxacin in pregnant women. Norfloxacin is a fluo-roquinolone antibiotic. Fluoroquinolone therapy is widely used as a treatment for gonorrhea in pregnant (and nonpregnant) women because it is relatively inexpensive and requires only one dose administered orally. However, gonorrhea is becoming increasingly resistant to some fluroquinolones (e.g. ciprofloxacin), and they are no longer recommended for this indication.

How it can affect a developing embryo or fetus: There are no adequate reports or well-controlled studies in human fetuses. It is unknown whether norfloxacin crosses the human placenta. The limited human experience is reassuring, as first-trimester exposure does not appear associated with an increased risk of malformations or musculoskeletal problems. Rodent and monkey studies are reassuring, revealing no evidence of birth defects or low birth weight despite the use of doses 6–50 times higher than those used clinically. However, animal studies are not necessarily good indicators of how a drug will behave in humans.

Breast-feeding: There is no published data in nursing women. It is unknown whether norfloxacin enters human breast milk.

Potential drug interactions: Interaction between the following medications and norfloxacin has the potential to impact the effect of one or more of the drugs. In some instances the interaction can be dangerous or life-threatening and must be avoided: oral anticoagulants, including warfarin or its derivatives or similar agents; glyburide; probenecid; nitrofurantoin. Multivitamins or other products containing iron or zinc, antacids, and sucralfate should not be used with, or within 2 hours of, norfloxacin because they may interfere with absorption of norfloxacin.

What the FDA says about use in pregnancy: Category C (see Appendix).

What the available evidence suggests about breast-feeding safety: Unknown.

The bottom line for you:

- There are alternative medications with which there is more experience during pregnancy and while breast-feeding.

- Fluroquinolones are no longer recommended for the treatment of gonorrhea.
- Norfloxacin should be used only if the benefit to the woman justifies the potential risk to the embryo, fetus, or newborn.

NORGESTREL

Brand names: Norplant, Ovrette

Drug classes: Contraceptive; Hormone; Progestin

Indications (what it is used for): Contraception, painful menstruation or abnormal bleeding, endometriosis (the endometrium grows outside the uterus), polycystic ovary syndrome (PCOS; multiple cysts inside the ovary leading to irregular menstruation and infertility).

How it works: Prevents pregnancy by preventing ovulation, by converting proliferative endometrium (which is needed for implantation) into secretory endometrium (which is hostile to implantation), and by thickening the cervical mucus so the sperm cannot penetrate.

Contraindications (reasons you shouldn't take it): Hypersensitivity to drug or class, pregnancy, breast cancer, liver cancer, coronary artery disease, abnormal vaginal bleeding, recent liver disease.

Possible side effects and warnings: Can cause acne, facial hair increase, weight gain, headache, breast tenderness, nausea, vomiting, blood clots, heart attack, high blood pressure, liver tumors, swelling, breakthrough bleeding, altered menstrual bleeding, absent menstruation, increased facial pigmentation, rash, and dizziness. Should be used with caution in women who smoke.

How it can affect pregnant women: Norgestrel is a synthetic progestogen that, alone or in combination with estrogen, is used in several popular oral, sustained-release (e.g., vaginal ring), and local (IUD) forms of contraception. It is pharmacologically similar to levonorgestrel. There is no indication for norgestrel during pregnancy. Progestin-only emergency contraception ("morning-after" pills) is available as a prepackaged product with or without a prescription. The levonorgestrel-only regimen prevents 85% of unintended pregnancies compared with 57% for the Yuzpe regimen, which uses a low-dose oral contraceptive containing both an estrogen and a progestin. Though the implantable form (Norplant) is effective, up to 65% of women report menstrual abnormalities, and 7.5% discontinue use in less than 4 years because of increased bleeding. Other side effects reported include headache, weight gain, sore breasts, decreased sex drive, abdominal pain, and high blood pressure. Implants are contraindicated (should not be used) in women with a history of seizures. The effectiveness of the IUD is excellent—one of the most effective forms of contraception. Contrary to popular belief, the IUD does not increase the risk of pelvic inflammatory disease or infertility in women who have had or have not had children, and it may be protective against infection. There are no indications for norgestrel during pregnancy.

How it can affect a developing embryo or fetus: There are no adequate reports or well-controlled studies of norgestrel in human fetuses. Exposure of male fetuses to progestational agents such as norgestrel may double their risk of hypospadias (the opening of the urethra is on the underside of the penis). Although there is insufficient data to quantify the risk for a female fetus, some progestational agents may cause an enlarged clitoris. Defects outside the external genitalia were not reported in either humans or rodents. Fetuses who have been exposed in the first trimester exposure should undergo a detailed anatomic ultrasound between 18 and 22 weeks.

Breast-feeding: Norgestrel is excreted into maternal milk. Long-term follow-up studies reveal that progestogen-only contraceptives do not adversely affect breast-feeding and infant development.

Potential drug interactions: Interaction between the following medications and norgestrel has the potential to impact the effect of one or more of the drugs. In some instances the interaction can be dangerous or life-threatening and must be avoided: carbamazepine, oxcarbazepine, phenobarbital, phenytoin, liver enzyme inducers, rifampicin, St. John's wort.

What the FDA says about use in pregnancy: Category X (see Appendix).

What the available evidence suggests about breast-feeding safety: Safe.

The bottom line for you:

- Norgestrel is an effective contraceptive. There are no indications for its use during pregnancy.
- A pregnant woman who is inadvertently exposed to norgestrel during the first trimester should undergo a detailed second-trimester ultrasound by a skilled perinatologist.
- Norgestrel is safe for use while breast-feeding.

NORTRIPTYLINE

Brand names: Allergron, Lisunim, Pamelor
Drug class: Antidepressant, tricyclic
Indications (what it is used for): Depression.
How it works: Alters mood by inhibiting the reuptake of norepinephrine and serotonin by nerve endings.
Contraindications (reasons you shouldn't take it): Hypersensitivity to drug or class, a recent heart attack, use of monoamine oxidase inhibitors (MAOIs) within 14 days.
Possible side effects and warnings: Can cause seizures, heart attack, stroke, low platelet and/or white blood cell count, confusion, disorientation, constipation, rapid heart rate, dizziness, increased appetite, blurred vision, drowsiness, and dry mouth. Should be used with caution in women with liver dysfunction, coronary artery disease, suicide risk, thyroid disease, glaucoma, or seizures.
How it can affect pregnant women: Depression is common during and after pregnancy but often goes unrecognized and untreated. Depression can be made worse by pregnancy or delivery, and suicide is

a not uncommon cause of maternal death. Pregnancy is not a reason to discontinue antidepressant drugs if the medication is effective and needed. A woman being treated for depression who becomes pregnant should not discontinue medication abruptly on her own but rather discuss her treatment and condition with her medical provider. Pregnancy may require an increased dose to remain effective, and women with a history of depression have a higher rate of recurrence after delivery.

There are no adequate reports or well-controlled studies of nortriptyline in pregnant women. Women who experienced one episode of postpartum depression are at high risk for recurrence after a subsequent pregnancy. Unfortunately, nortriptyline does not prevent recurrent postpartum depression in high-risk women. Recent population-based studies have revealed the use of tricyclic antidepressants may increase the risk of preeclampsia by 2 to 3 times. Nortriptyline can be helpful for women who are trying to quit smoking. Cigarette smoking during pregnancy is the single largest modifiable risk factor for pregnancy-related illness and death in the U.S. Nicotine replacement therapy (gum, patch, nasal spray, and inhaler) combined with bupropion has the highest rate of success, but nortriptyline can be a useful supplement. Smoking is a far greater risk to mother and fetus than any of the therapies used to help a woman quit smoking. Nortriptyline is also used for the treatment of nerve pain, chronic pain, and panic disorder. Its use for these indications may be avoidable during pregnancy.

How it can affect a developing embryo or fetus: There are no adequate reports or well-controlled studies in human fetuses. Nortriptyline does cross the placenta, reaching about half the maternal level in the fetus. There is a single report suggesting an association between nortriptyline and limb abnormalities. There is no other support for this possibility. Rodent birth defect studies yielded conflicting results.

Breast-feeding: The amount of nortriptyline excreted into breast milk is considered clinically insignificant. Nortriptyline is generally the drug of choice for breast-feeding women suffering from depression.

Potential drug interactions: Interaction between the following medications and nortriptyline has the potential to impact the effect of one or more of the drugs. In some instances the interaction can be dangerous or life-threatening and must be avoided: reserpine, other anticholinergic and sympathomimetic drugs, cimetidine, ethanol, chlorpropamide.

What the FDA says about use in pregnancy: No assigned category (see Appendix).

What the available evidence suggests about breast-feeding safety: Safe.

The bottom line for you:

- Nortriptyline should be used during pregnancy and while breast-feeding only if the benefit to the woman justifies the potential risk to the embryo or fetus.
- If you become pregnant, do not discontinue your medication until speaking to your physician.
- Nortriptyline is generally considered a drug of choice for breast-feeding women suffering from depression.

NYSTATIN

Brand names: Barstatin, Bio-Statin, Candex, Candio-Hermal, Korostatin, Mycostatin, Mykinac, Nilstat, Nysert, Nystex, Nystop, O-V Statin, Pedi-Dry, Statin, Vagistat

Drug classes: Antifungal; Dermatologic

Indications (what it is used for): Yeast infection (*C. albicans*).

How it works: Inhibits biosynthesis of ergosterol (a sterol found in fungi) and thus weakens the fungal cell wall.

Contraindications (reasons you shouldn't take it): Hypersensitivity to drug or class.

Possible side effects and warnings: Can cause Stevens-Johnson syndrome (a rare but serious skin reaction to medication), local irritation, nausea, vomiting, and diarrhea.

How it can affect pregnant women: *Candida* vaginitis is the most common female genital tract infection. Nystatin is an antifungal antibiotic that both slows growth and kills a wide variety of yeasts and yeastlike fungi. The vaginal environment during pregnancy predisposes it to *C. albicans* overgrowth. Nystatin is effective against about 80% of *C. albicans.* There are no adequate reports or well-controlled studies of nystatin in pregnant women. It is not clear whether related drugs differ in their effectiveness for mycotic vaginitis. Nystatin is considered less effective than miconazole for the treatment of vaginal candidiasis during pregnancy, although there are no randomized trials to substantiate this conclusion. There is no significant difference in the cure rates achieved after 7 days or 14 days of therapy. However, more women relapsed after a cure with nystatin than with miconazole.

How it can affect a developing embryo or fetus: There are no adequate reports or well-controlled studies in human fetuses. It is unknown whether nystatin crosses the human placenta. First-trimester use of nystatin (and other imidazole agents) is not associated with an increased prevalence of miscarriage or birth defects. Yeast infection of the newborn's skin is rare and nystatin is used to treat this infection. Rodent birth defect studies are limited to a single report where fetal loss was associated with maternal toxicity from the medication. However, animal studies are not necessarily good indicators of how a drug will behave in humans.

Breast-feeding: There are no adequate reports or well-controlled studies in nursing women. It is unknown whether nystatin enters human breast milk. However, considering the indication and typical dose, limited nystatin use is unlikely to pose a clinically significant risk to a breast-feeding newborn. Nystatin is not an effective treatment of nipple candidiasis, which may occur while breast-feeding.

Potential drug interactions: No clinically relevant interactions identified.

What the FDA says about use in pregnancy: Category C (see Appendix).

What the available evidence suggests about breast-feeding safety: Safe.

The bottom line for you:

- Nystatin is effective for the treatment of yeast infection during pregnancy and while breast-feeding.
- Topical imidazole agents may be more effective than nystatin for treating symptomatic vaginal yeast in pregnancy.
- A 7-day treatment regimen may be necessary during pregnancy rather than the shorter courses more commonly used in nonpregnant women.

OATMEAL

Brand name: Aveeno

Drug class: Dermatologic

Indications (what it is used for): Contact dermatitis (e.g., poison ivy/oak).

How it works: Forms a moisturizing, colloidal suspension that soothes the skin.

Contraindications (reasons you shouldn't take it): Hypersensitivity to drug or class.

Possible side effects and warnings: None reported.

How it can affect pregnant women: There is no published data with topical oatmeal during pregnancy.

How it can affect a developing embryo or fetus: There are no adequate reports or well-controlled studies of topical oatmeal in human fetuses. Absorption into the maternal bloodstream is likely insignificant, indicating that it cannot directly affect the fetus.

Breast-feeding: There are no adequate reports or well-controlled studies in nursing women. As it is a traditional food substance, oatmeal is unlikely to pose a clinically significant risk to a nursing infant.

Potential drug interactions: No clinically relevant interactions identified.

What the FDA says about use in pregnancy: No assigned category (see Appendix).

What the available evidence suggests about breast-feeding safety: Safe.

The bottom line for you:

- Oatmeal is safe and effective for symptomatic relief of contact dermatitis during pregnancy and while breast-feeding.

OFLOXACIN

Brand name: Floxin

Drug classes: Antibiotic; Ophthalmic; Quinolone

Indications (what it is used for): Bacterial infection, chlamydia, conjunctivitis, corneal ulcer, otitis externa (inflammation of the outer ear and ear canal).

How it works: Kills bacteria by interfering with DNA synthesis.

Contraindications (reasons you shouldn't take it): Hypersensitivity to drug or class.

Possible side effects and warnings: Can cause vaginitis, light sensitivity, bowel infection, seizures, increased pressure in the skull, headache, psychosis, nausea, vomiting, diarrhea, abdominal pain, heartburn, dizziness, sleeplessness, agitation, tendonitis, joint pain, and liver dysfunction. Should be used with caution in women with liver or kidney dysfunction, seizure disorder, central nervous system abnormalities, diabetes, dehydration, or sun exposure.

How it can affect pregnant women: There are no adequate reports or well-controlled studies in pregnant women. Ofloxacin achieves high tissue penetration. The FDA has added a black box warning covering the potential for tendon rupture, which is a rare event in adults. Fluroquinolones are no longer recommended for the treatment of gonorrhea because of widespread resistance.

How it can affect a developing embryo or fetus: There are no adequate reports or well-controlled studies in human fetuses. Less than 4% of maternal ofloxacin crosses the human placenta. But it is removed from the fetus's system slowly and reaches a high enough level in the fetal blood to possibly treat an infection. Fluoroquinolones such as ofloxacin are not associated with an increased risk of birth defects in humans. Neither eye nor ear use results in significant levels of the drug in the system. In general, rodent studies are reassuring, although some studies where the drug was applied to the mother's ears revealed minor fetal skeletal abnormalities and low birth weight. The use of very high multiples of the maximum recommended clinical dose has been associated with damage to the fetus. However, animal studies are not necessarily good indicators of how a drug will behave in humans.

Breast-feeding: There are no adequate reports or well-controlled studies in nursing women. Ofloxacin is excreted into breast milk, but even if 100% were absorbed by a breast-fed newborn, he or she would still have lower levels than what is needed for treatment.

Potential drug interactions: Interaction between the following medications and ofloxacin has the potential to impact the effect of one or more of the drugs. In some instances the interaction can be dangerous or life-threatening and must be avoided: antacids containing calcium, magnesium, or aluminum; sucralfate; divalent or trivalent cations such as iron; multivitamins containing zinc; didanosine chewable/buffered tablets or the pediatric powder for oral solution; drugs metabolized by the CYP system (e.g., cyclosporine, theophylline/methylxanthines, warfarin); nonsteroidal anti-inflammatory drugs (NSAIDs); probenicid; theophylline; antidiabetic agents.

What the FDA says about use in pregnancy: Category C (see Appendix).

What the available evidence suggests about breast-feeding safety: Likely safe.

The bottom line for you:

- Ofloxacin should be used during pregnancy only if the benefit to the woman justifies the potential risk to the embryo or fetus.
- Although the fetal risk may not be as great as once thought, there are alternative agents during pregnancy for almost all indications.
- Ofloxacin is likely safe for use while breast-feeding.

OLANZAPINE

Brand name: Zyprexa

Drug class: Antipsychotic

Indications (what it is used for): Bipolar disorder, psychosis.

How it works: May work by binding 5-HT2A/2C and dopamine receptors to cause a mood change.

Contraindications (reasons you shouldn't take it): Hypersensitivity to drug or class.

Possible side effects and warnings: Can cause low blood pressure, fast heart rate, menstrual irregularities, high prolactin levels, involuntary and repetitive body movements, a variety of movement disorders, diabetes, high glucose levels, drowsiness, weight gain, constipation, dry mouth, heartburn, runny nose, fever, and liver dysfunction. Should be used with caution in women with seizures, narrow-angle glaucoma, paralytic ileus (bowel paralysis), low blood pressure, hypovolemia (decreased blood volume), liver dysfunction, or cardiovascular or cerebrovascular disease (narrowing of blood vessels that supply the brain).

How it can affect pregnant women: Although there are no adequate reports or well-controlled studies in pregnant women, the growing body of clinical experience with olanzapine during pregnancy is reassuring. Olanzapine is an atypical antipsychotic agent whose clearance (how fast it is removed from the body) is 30% lower in women than men. Patients treated with olanzapine for schizophrenia have less inability to sit still but gain more weight than patients treated with haloperidol. Side effects and overall quality of life are similar for the two drugs.

How it can affect a developing embryo or fetus: There are no adequate reports or well-controlled studies in human fetuses. Fetal levels have ranged from one-third to three-quarters of the maternal level. Early experience with pregnancies exposed to olanzapine found no increased risk of miscarriage, stillbirth, prematurity, or any major malformation (birth defect) in comparison to the general population. There were tendencies toward higher rates of low birth weight and admission to the neonatal intensive care unit (30% increase each). As with most psychotropic drugs, using only one drug and at the lowest effective quantity given in divided doses to minimize the peaks can reduce any risks to the developing embryo or fetus. Rodent studies are reassuring, revealing no evidence of birth defects despite the use of doses higher than those used clinically. There was no effect of intrauterine exposure on learning after birth in rodent studies. However, animal studies are not necessarily good indicators of how a drug will behave in humans.

Breast-feeding: There are no adequate reports or well-controlled studies in nursing women. Olanzapine enters human breast milk, but initial studies suggest that the amount ingested by a breast-fed newborn will not be clinically relevant. Mothers who want to minimize infant exposure can avoid feeding when the milk concentration peaks (about 5 hours after a dose).

Potential drug interactions: Interaction between the following medications and olanzapine has the potential to impact the effect of one or more of the drugs. In some instances the interaction can be dangerous or life-threatening and must be avoided: drugs that affect the central nervous system, including ethanol (alcohol); blood-pressure-lowering medications; levodopa; dopamine agonists; drugs that induce CYP1A2 or glucuronyl transferase enzymes, such as omeprazole and rifampin; CYP1A2 inhibitors; carbamazepine; fluvoxamine.

What the FDA says about use in pregnancy: Category C (see Appendix).

What the available evidence suggests about breast-feeding safety: Likely safe.

The bottom line for you:

- Olanzapine may be used during pregnancy if necessary.
- The data supports olanzapine use while breast-feeding. However, breast-fed infants must be monitored closely for evidence of a drug effect.

OLOPATADINE

Brand names: Pataday, Patanol

Drug classes: Allergy; Antihistamine, H1; Ophthalmic

Indications (what it is used for): Allergic conjunctivitis.

How it works: Selectively blocks the H1 receptor and inhibits mast cell release of histamine, both of which lead to the red, itchy eyes.

Contraindications (reasons you shouldn't take it): Hypersensitivity to drug or class.

Possible side effects and warnings: Can cause dry eyes, headache, red or burning eyes, eyelid swelling, runny nose, and sinusitis.

How it can affect pregnant women: There is no published data with olopatadine during pregnancy. Considering the dose and opthalmic application, it seems unlikely maternal blood levels will be high.

How it can affect a developing embryo or fetus: There are no adequate reports or well-controlled studies in human fetuses. It is unknown whether olopatadine crosses the human placenta. Rodent studies are reassuring, revealing no evidence of birth defects or low birth weight despite the use of doses higher than those used clinically. However, animal studies are not necessarily good indicators of how a drug will behave in humans.

Breast-feeding: There is no published data in nursing women. It is unknown whether olopatadine enters human breast milk, although it has been found in rodent milk. However, considering the dose and the fact that it is administered topically to the eye, it is unlikely that nursing could result in a clinically significant level in a newborn.

Potential drug interactions: No current relevant references are available.

What the FDA says about use in pregnancy: Category C (see Appendix).

What the available evidence suggests about breast-feeding safety: Likely safe.

The bottom line for you:

- Olopatadine should be used during pregnancy

and while breast-feeding only if the benefit to the woman justifies the potential risk to the embryo, fetus, or newborn.

OLSALAZINE

Brand name: Dipentum
Drug classes: Gastrointestinal; Inflammatory bowel disease agent; Salicylate
Indications (what it is used for): Ulcerative colitis.
How it works: Appears to work directly on the gut.
Contraindications (reasons you shouldn't take it): Hypersensitivity to drug or class, hypersensitivity to salicylates.
Possible side effects and warnings: Can cause liver toxicity, inflammation of the kidney or pancreas, bone marrow suppression, nausea, vomiting, heartburn, diarrhea, abdominal pain, joint pain, bloating, loss of appetite, itching, fatigue, depression, and dizziness. Should be used with caution in women with kidney dysfunction.
How it can affect pregnant women: There are no adequate reports or well-controlled studies of olsalazine in pregnant women. Limited experience consists predominantly of case reports and small series. These reports suggest that olsalazine is effective during pregnancy.
How it can affect a developing embryo or fetus: There are no adequate reports or well-controlled studies in human fetuses. Less than 5% of the olsalazine ingested is absorbed into the mother's bloodstream. Limited quantities of olsalazine and its metabolites (substances it is broken down into) cross the human placenta. Large studies are reassuring, revealing no evidence of increased adverse pregnancy outcomes. Rodent studies using multiples of the maximum recommended clinical dose revealed low birth weight and delayed skeletal and organ maturation. However, animal studies are not necessarily good indicators of how a drug will behave in humans.
Breast-feeding: There are no adequate reports or well-controlled studies in nursing women. The mother absorbs little of the drug systemically. In a single study, only a low concentration of its active metabolite was detected in breast milk up to 48 hours after ingestion. Olsalazine is likely safe for use while breast-feeding. Exposed infants should be observed for diarrhea.
Potential drug interactions: Interaction between the following medications and olsalazine has the potential to impact the effect of one or more of the drugs. In some instances the interaction can be dangerous or life-threatening and must be avoided: warfarin.
What the FDA says about use in pregnancy: Category C (see Appendix).
What the available evidence suggests about breast-feeding safety: Likely safe.
The bottom line for you:

- Olsalazine is probably safe for use during pregnancy if the benefit to the woman justifies the potential risk to the embryo or newborn.
- Olsalazine is likely safe for use while breast-feeding, although the infant should be observed for diarrhea.

OMEPRAZOLE

Brand names: Losec, Omid, Prilosec, Roweprazol
Drug classes: Antiulcer; Gastrointestinal; Proton pump inhibitor
Indications (what it is used for): Gastroesophageal reflux disease (GERD), stomach ulcer, erosive esophagitis, *H. pylori* infection.
How it works: Inhibits the production of acid by the stomach.
Contraindications (reasons you shouldn't take it): Hypersensitivity to drug or class.
Possible side effects and warnings: Can cause headache, diarrhea, liver dysfunction, Stevens-Johnson syndrome (a rare but serious skin reaction to medication), and various blood disorders. Should be used with caution in women with liver dysfunction or who require long-term use.
How it can affect pregnant women: Heartburn occurs in 45–85% of pregnant women, in part because of high progesterone and estrogen levels. Proton

pump inhibitors are popular for the treatment of GERD during pregnancy, but they should be used only if diet changes and antacids fail to cure the problem. Although there are no adequate reports or well-controlled studies in pregnant women, omeprazole appears to be safe during pregnancy. Omeprazole has long been used to treat a number of stomach disorders and to reduce the damage caused by inhalation of stomach acid if vomiting occurs after general anesthesia. Although there are no adequate reports or well-controlled studies in pregnant women, omeprazole appears to be safe to use. Heartburn occurs in 45–85% of pregnant women, in part because of high progesterone and estrogen levels. Proton pump inhibitors are popular for the treatment of GERD during pregnancy, but they should be used only if diet changes and antacids fail to cure the problem.

How it can affect a developing embryo or fetus: There are no adequate reports or well-controlled studies in human fetuses. It is unknown whether omeprazole crosses the human placenta. Proton pump inhibitors in general, and omeprazole specifically, are not associated with an increased risk of birth defects in postmarketing studies (studies done by a drug's manufacturer after the drug is on the market). Rodent studies are reassuring, revealing no evidence of birth defects despite the use of doses higher than those used clinically. However, animal studies are not necessarily good indicators of how a drug will behave in humans.

Breast-feeding: There are no adequate reports or well-controlled studies in nursing women. The amount of omeprazole excreted in human breast milk is clinically insignificant.

Potential drug interactions: Interaction between the following medications and omeprazole has the potential to impact the effect of one or more of the drugs. In some instances the interaction can be dangerous or life-threatening and must be avoided: diazepam, warfarin, phenytoin, other drugs metabolized via liver CYPs (e.g., benzodiazepines, cyclosporine, disulfiram), drugs that depend on stomach acid for

absorption (e.g., ampicillin, iron salts, ketoconazole), clarithromycin.

What the FDA says about use in pregnancy: Category C (see Appendix).

What the available evidence suggests about breast-feeding safety: Likely safe.

The bottom line for you:

● Omeprazole appears safe and effective during pregnancy. However, antacids are the drug of choice to treat heartburn or GERD during pregnancy.

● Omeprazole is safe for use while breast-feeding.

ONDANSETRON

Brand name: Zofran

Drug classes: Antiemetic; Serotonin receptor antagonist

Indications (what it is used for): Severe nausea and vomiting.

How it works: Selectively blocks the 5-HT3 receptors, whose activation leads to the nausea.

Contraindications (reasons you shouldn't take it): Hypersensitivity to drug or class.

Possible side effects and warnings: Can cause bronchospasm, various movement disorders that are usually the result of taking dopamine antagonists like antipsychotic drugs used to control psychosis, extreme and sustained upward deviation of the eyeballs, headache, fatigue, constipation, diarrhea, agitation, itching, and dizziness. Should be used with caution in women with liver dysfunction.

How it can affect pregnant women: Ondansetron is effective for nausea and vomiting related to pregnancy. A single IV dose reduces the nausea and vomiting after cesarean delivery. Ondansetron significantly reduces the itching associated with epidural or spinal morphine or fentanyl. Recent study indicates that epidural ondansetron is more effective than intravenous ondansetron at preventing nausea and itching after a C-section. It is no better than metoclopramide to prevent nausea and vomiting after minor gynecologic surgery, but it is superior to it for patients undergoing chemotherapy.

How it can affect a developing embryo or fetus: There are no adequate reports or well-controlled studies in human fetuses. Despite being widely used, it is not known whether ondansetron crosses the human placenta. Rodent studies are reassuring, revealing no evidence of birth defects or low birth weight despite the use of doses higher than those used clinically. However, animal studies are not necessarily good indicators of how a drug will behave in humans.

Breast-feeding: There is no published data in nursing women. It is unknown whether ondansetron enters human breast milk. It is detectable in rat milk.

Potential drug interactions: Interaction between the following medications and ondansetron has the potential to impact the effect of one or more of the drugs. In some instances the interaction can be dangerous or life-threatening and must be avoided: Potent CYP3A4 inducers (i.e., carbamazepine, phenytoin, rifampicin).

What the FDA says about use in pregnancy: Category B (see Appendix).

What the available evidence suggests about breast-feeding safety: Unknown.

The bottom line for you:

- Ondansetron is a reasonable medication for the prevention of postoperative nausea and vomiting.
- It is widely used for morning sickness but should be used only if other cheaper primary measures fail (pyridoxine and Unisom, prochlorperazine).
- There is not enough information to comment on the safety of ondansetron while breast-feeding.

ORLISTAT

Brand name: Xenical
Drug classes: Gastrointestinal; Lipase inhibitor
Indications (what it is used for): Obesity.

How it works: Inhibits gastric and pancreatic lipases so that fats are not absorbed.

Contraindications (reasons you shouldn't take it): Hypersensitivity to drug or class, cholestasis (slow or blocked flow of bile from the liver), chronic malabsorption syndromes (small intestine cannot absorb nutrients from food).

Possible side effects and warnings: Can cause diarrhea, flatulence, greasy fat in the stool, fecal incontinence, and nausea and vomiting. Should be used with caution in women with a history of kidney stones.

How it can affect pregnant women: Orlistat is a reversible lipase inhibitor for obesity management that acts by inhibiting the absorption of dietary fats. There is no published experience with it during pregnancy. It has been suggested (but unproved) that orlistat might interfere with the absorption of oral contraceptives and lower their effectiveness.

How it can affect a developing embryo or fetus: There are no adequate reports or well-controlled studies in human fetuses. It is unknown whether orlistat crosses the human placenta. However, the mother absorbs little of the drug systemically, which means it cannot directly affect the fetus. Rodent studies are reassuring, revealing no evidence of birth defects or low birth weight despite the use of doses higher than those used clinically. However, animal studies are not necessarily good indicators of how a drug will behave in humans.

Breast-feeding: There is no published data in nursing women. Considering that the maternal systemic level is low, it is unlikely that a clinically relevant concentration of orlistat enters human breast milk. It is not known whether orlistat alters the components of breast milk.

Potential drug interactions: Interaction between the following medications and orlistat has the potential to impact the effect of one or more of the drugs. In some instances the interaction can be dangerous or life-threatening and must be avoided: cyclosporine, beta-carotene, and vitamin E.

What the FDA says about use in pregnancy: Category X (see Appendix).

What the available evidence suggests about breast-feeding safety: Likely safe.

The bottom line for you:

- Although there are no clear reasons to avoid orlistat during pregnancy, weight loss is rarely recommended during pregnancy.
- Orlistat is likely safe for use while breast-feeding since the mother absorbs little of the drug.

ORPHENADRINE

Brand names: Banflex, Flexoject, Flexon, Flexor, Marflex, Mio-Rel, Myolin, Myophen, Myotrol, Neocyten, Noradex, Norflex, O'Flex, Orflagen, Orfro, Orphenate, Qualaflex, Tega-Flex

Drug class: Muscle relaxant

Indications (what it is used for): Muscle spasm.

How it works: Unknown.

Contraindications (reasons you shouldn't take it): Hypersensitivity to drug or class, glaucoma, pyloric or duodenal obstruction, myasthenia gravis (an autoimmune disease causing muscle weakness).

Possible side effects and warnings: Can cause drowsiness, nausea, vomiting, dry mouth, aplastic anemia, light-headedness, and headache. Should be used with caution in women with cardiovascular disease, sulfite allergy, or arrhythmia (irregular heartbeat).

How it can affect pregnant women: There is no published data with orphenadrine during pregnancy.

How it can affect a developing embryo or fetus: There are no adequate reports or well-controlled studies in human fetuses. It is unknown whether orphenadrine crosses the human placenta. There is some passage across the sheep placenta. Rodent birth defect studies have not been conducted.

Breast-feeding: There is no published data in nursing women. It is unknown whether orphenadrine enters human breast milk.

Potential drug interactions: No clinically relevant interactions identified.

What the FDA says about use in pregnancy: Category C (see Appendix).

What the available evidence suggests about breast-feeding safety: Unknown.

The bottom line for you:

- Orphenadrine should be used during pregnancy and while breast-feeding only if the benefit to the woman justifies the potential risk to the embryo, fetus, or newborn.
- There are other agents with which there is more experience.

OSELTAMIVIR

Brand name: Tamiflu

Drug class: Antiviral

Indications (what it is used for): Influenza A and B virus prevention and treatment.

How it works: Blocks influenza neuraminidase, altering the ability of the virus to replicate.

Contraindications (reasons you shouldn't take it): Hypersensitivity to drug or class.

Possible side effects and warnings: Can cause nausea, vomiting, bronchitis, sleeplessness, and dizziness. Should be used with caution in women with liver dysfunction.

How it can affect pregnant women: Published data with oseltamivir during pregnancy is limited mostly to case reports. Influenza places pregnant women and their fetuses at risk for serious illness and can be fatal. All pregnant women should be vaccinated for influenza. There is evidence of emerging viral resistance to the medication.

How it can affect a developing embryo or fetus: There are no adequate reports or well-controlled studies in human fetuses. Oseltamivir apparently crosses the human placenta achieving a level of about half that of the mother's within 4 hours. Rodent studies are reassuring, revealing no evidence of birth defects despite the use of doses higher than those used clinically. However, animal studies are not necessarily good indicators of how a drug will behave in humans.

Breast-feeding: There is no published data in nursing women. It is unknown whether oseltamivir enters human breast milk.

Potential drug interactions: Clinically significant drug interactions are unlikely.

What the FDA says about use in pregnancy: Category C (see Appendix).

What the available evidence suggests about breast-feeding safety: Unknown.

The bottom line for you:

- Oseltamivir is considered safe for use during pregnancy and while breast-feeding. However, it should not be used as a replacement for annual vaccination, which is the mainstay of influenza prevention.

OXACILLIN

Brand names: Bactocill, Dicloxal OX, Prostaphlin, Staphaloxin, Wydox

Drug classes: Antibiotic; Penicillin

Indications (what it is used for): Bacterial infection, especially with penicillinase-producing *Staphylococcus*.

How it works: Kills the bacteria by inhibiting their cell wall synthesis.

Contraindications (reasons you shouldn't take it): Hypersensitivity to drug or class.

Possible side effects and warnings: Can cause bone marrow suppression, hemolytic anemia, nausea, vomiting, diarrhea, bowel infection, oral sores, fever, chills, rash, lethargy, hives, kidney inflammation, and liver dysfunction.

How it can affect pregnant women: There is a long clinical experience with oxacillin during pregnancy demonstrating its safety.

How it can affect a developing embryo or fetus: There are no adequate reports or well-controlled studies in human fetuses. Most penicillin com-

pounds cross the human placenta. There is no evidence that oxacillin causes birth defects. Rodent studies are reassuring, revealing no evidence of birth defects or low birth weight despite the use of doses higher than those used clinically. However, animal studies are not necessarily good indicators of how a drug will behave in humans.

Breast-feeding: There are no adequate reports or well-controlled studies in nursing women. Oxacillin is concentrated in human breast milk, reaching high enough levels to treat bacterial infection of the breasts. Unfortunately, many staphylococci are now resistant. Although oxacillin is compatible with breast-feeding, clindamycin is a better choice.

Potential drug interactions: Interaction between the following medications and oxacillin has the potential to impact the effect of one or more of the drugs. In some instances the interaction can be dangerous or life-threatening and must be avoided: tetracyclines and bacteriostatic antibiotics, probenecid.

What the FDA says about use in pregnancy: Category B (see Appendix).

What the available evidence suggests about breast-feeding safety: Safe.

The bottom line for you:

- Oxacillin is safe and effective for use during pregnancy.
- It is an alternative for the treatment of infected breasts, although an increasing number of bacteria have developed resistance to the drug. Alternative agents should be used for almost all indications.

OXAZEPAM

Brand names: Murelax, Serax, Wakezepam

Drug classes: Anxiolytic; Benzodiazepine

Indications (what it is used for): Anxiety, alcohol withdrawal.

How it works: Reduces the impact of withdrawal by binding to benzodiazepine receptors and increasing responses of the neurotransmitter GABA, which leads to mood alteration.

Contraindications (reasons you shouldn't take it): Hypersensitivity to drug or class, psychosis.

Possible side effects and warnings: Can cause nausea, liver dysfunction, jaundice, low white blood cell count, dizziness, fainting, perception that the room is spinning, headache, swelling, tremor, rash, and lethargy.

How it can affect pregnant women: There are no adequate reports or well-controlled studies in pregnant women. Alcoholism is an often unrecognized problem during pregnancy that poses a clear hazard to mother and child. Oxazepam may be helpful in quitting. It has a wide safety range compared to other benzodiazepines. Some also consider oxazepam a second-line choice for the treatment of itching during pregnancy, despite the lack of study for this indication. It is highly effective for the short-term relief of anxiety. Dependency is possible after long-term use.

How it can affect a developing embryo or fetus: There are no adequate reports or well-controlled studies in human fetuses. Oxazepam crosses the human placenta, reaching a level of about half of the mother's within 4 hours. Long-term follow-up studies are for the most part reassuring. Exposure to the fetus is minimized by taking more frequent but smaller doses to avoid peak drug levels. Rodent studies found subtle behavioral effects among offspring that were exposed in the uterus. However, animal studies are not necessarily good indicators of how a drug will behave in humans.

Breast-feeding: There are no adequate reports or well-controlled studies in nursing women. The amount of oxazepam excreted into human breast milk is likely clinically insignificant.

Potential drug interactions: No clinically relevant interactions identified.

What the FDA says about use in pregnancy: Category D (see Appendix).

What the available evidence suggests about breast-feeding safety: Likely safe.

The bottom line for you:
- Oxazepam should be safe and effective during pregnancy. Although unnecessary treatment should be avoided, appropriate candidates should not be denied therapy solely because they are pregnant.
- Oxazepam is likely safe for use while breast-feeding.

OXCARBAZEPINE

Brand name: Trileptal

Drug class: Anticonvulsant

Indications (what it is used for): Seizure disorder.

How it works: Alters the seizure threshold by blocking the voltage-sensitive sodium channels.

Contraindications (reasons you shouldn't take it): Hypersensitivity to drug or class.

Possible side effects and warnings: Can cause low blood levels of sodium, low white blood cell and/or platelet counts, Stevens-Johnson syndrome and toxic epidermal necrolysis (both rare but serious skin disorders), nausea, vomiting, heartburn, abdominal pain, drowsiness, dizziness, double vision, fatigue, wandering eye, acne, hair loss, and liver dysfunction. Should be used with caution in women with kidney dysfunction.

How it can affect pregnant women: For women taking oxcarbazepine and a hormonal contraceptive (pill, patch, ring), either a higher-dose contraceptive or a second method of contraception is recommended, because oxcarbazepine decreases the efficacy of the contraceptive. Women on medication for a seizure disorder should plan their pregnancies (when possible), discuss the optimal medication with their neurologist, and begin appropriate supplemental folate therapy before conception (4 mg per day) to minimize the risk of birth defects. The risks of birth defects associated with antiseizure medications must be weighed against the risks of continued seizures to both the mother and fetus. Women who become pregnant during treatment should not stop treatment on their own but rather meet quickly with their doctor before making a decision.

There are no adequate reports or well-controlled studies of oxcarbazepine in pregnant women. Maternal levels decline with advancing pregnancy, suggesting the need for a dose adjustment.

How it can affect a developing embryo or fetus: There are no adequate reports or well-controlled studies in human fetuses. Oxcarbazepine crosses the human placenta, reaching a level similar to that of the mother. Vitamin K has been recommended during the last month of pregnancy in women taking some enzyme-inducing agents such as oxcarbazepine, carbamazepine, phenobarbital, phenytoin, and topiramate under the theory it will reduce the risk of newborn bleeding. However, there is not good evidence that the risk is increased and the incidence of newborn bleeding does not appear to be decreased by maternal treatment with vitamin K. The frequency of newborn bleeding complications is not increased after oxcarbazepine. Carbamazepine is structurally similar to some anticonvulsants that are known teratogens (substances that can cause birth defects) and may be a weak cause of birth defects in humans. Its use in combination with other medications increases the risk of birth defects. If feasible, the number of medications used during pregnancy should be reduced. Rodent studies performed at doses comparable to those used clinically demonstrated an increased rate of miscarriage, low birth weight, and a variety of malformations (predominantly face, heart and skeleton). However, animal studies are not necessarily good indicators of how a drug will behave in humans.

Breast-feeding: There are no adequate reports or well-controlled studies in nursing women. The levels of oxcarbazepine and its major metabolites (products the body breaks it down into) in human breast milk are low, and newborn concentrations decline over time, suggesting that the risk is low, though not nonexistent.

Potential drug interactions: Interaction between the following medications and oxcarbazepine has the potential to impact the effect of one or more of the drugs. In some instances the interaction can be dangerous or life-threatening and must be avoided: dihydropyridine calcium antagonists; several antiepileptic drugs that are strong CYP inducers (i.e., carbamazepine, phenobarbital, phenytoin); ethinyl estradiol (EE); levonorgestrel (LNG). Use of oxcarbazepine with hormonal contraceptives may render them less effective; a secondary method should be used.

What the FDA says about use in pregnancy: Category C (see Appendix).

What the available evidence suggests about breast-feeding safety: Likely safe.

The bottom line for you:

- Oxcarbazepine may be a weak teratogen, but it may be used during pregnancy when the benefit of the medication is clear. As with most psychotropic drugs, using only one medication at the lowest effective quantity, given in divided doses to minimize the peaks, can reduce the risks.
- Oxcarbazepine is likely safe for use while breast-feeding.

OXYBUTYNIN

Brand name: Ditropan

Drug classes: Anticholinergic; Antispasmodic

Indications (what it is used for): Bladder spasm.

How it works: Direct antispasmodic effect.

Contraindications (reasons you shouldn't take it): Hypersensitivity to drug or class, glaucoma, ulcerative colitis, bowel or intestinal paralysis (ileus), myasthenia gravis (an autoimmune disease causing muscle weakness).

Possible side effects and warnings: Can cause fast heart rate, blood vessel dilation, rash, constipation, decreased sweating, dry mouth, drowsiness, hallucinations, restlessness, cycloplegia (inability of the pupil of the eye to constrict), and sleeplessness.

Should be used with caution in women with liver or kidney dysfunction.

How it can affect pregnant women: There is no published data with oxybutynin during pregnancy.

How it can affect a developing embryo or fetus: There are no adequate reports or well-controlled studies in human fetuses. It is not known whether oxybutynin crosses the human placenta. Rodent studies revealed a slight increase in the incidence of fetal malformations at dosages that caused maternal toxicity. It had no effect on embryonic or fetal development in rats and rabbits at lower dosages. However, animal studies are not necessarily good indicators of how a drug will behave in humans.

Breast-feeding: There is no published data in nursing women. It is unknown whether oxybutynin enters human breast milk.

Potential drug interactions: Interaction between the following medications and oxybutynin has the potential to impact the effect of one or more of the drugs. In some instances the interaction can be dangerous or life-threatening and must be avoided: other anticholinergic drugs; ketoconazole; other CYP3A4 inhibitors, such as antimycotic agents (e.g., itraconazole, miconazole); macrolide antibiotics (e.g., clarithromycin, erythromycin).

What the FDA says about use in pregnancy: Category B (see Appendix).

What the available evidence suggests about breast-feeding safety: Unknown.

The bottom line for you:

- Oxybutynin should be used during pregnancy and while breast-feeding only if the benefit to the woman justifies the potential risk to the embryo, fetus, or newborn.

OXYCODONE

Brand names: OxyContin [slow release]; Roxicodone [immediate release]

Drug class: Analgesic, narcotic

Indications (what it is used for): Moderate to severe pain.

How it works: Binds to opiate receptors to dull the sense of pain.

Contraindications (reasons you shouldn't take it): Hypersensitivity to drug or class.

Possible side effects and warnings: Can cause dependency, liver toxicity, seizures, respiratory depression, dizziness, sedation, nausea, vomiting, itching, rash, depressed mood, and constipation. Should be used with caution in women with a history of opiate abuse, liver dysfunction, acute abdominal pain, bowel or intestinal paralysis (ileus).

How it can affect pregnant women: Oxycodone has about a third of the strength of morphine. Women have higher plasma oxycodone concentrations than men (up to 25%). In one high-quality trial, the combination of oxycodone and acetaminophen after cesarean delivery controlled pain better and with fewer side effects than morphine given by a patient-controlled device.

How it can affect a developing embryo or fetus: There are no adequate reports or well-controlled studies of oxycodone in human fetuses. Other drugs in its class readily cross the human placenta. Oxycodone abuse during pregnancy may be associated with newborn withdrawal.

Breast-feeding: Oxycodone is excreted into human breast milk. However, oxycodone taken up to 72 hours after C-section poses only minimal risk to a breast-feeding infant because the volume of breast milk ingested is low during this period.

Potential drug interactions: Interaction between the following medications and oxycodone has the potential to impact the effect of one or more of the drugs. In some instances the interaction can be dangerous or life-threatening and must be avoided: skeletal muscle relaxants; other central nervous system depressants, including sedatives and hypnotics, general anesthetics, phenothiazines, centrally acting antiemetics, tranquilizers, and ethanol (alcohol).

What the FDA says about use in pregnancy: Category C; Category D if combined with ibuprofen from 30 weeks on (see Appendix).

What the available evidence suggests about breast-feeding safety: Likely safe.

The bottom line for you:
- Oxycodone is a reasonable choice for postcesarean pain. There are alternative agents with which there is more experience during pregnancy and while breast-feeding.
- Oxycodone is likely safe for use during the first 72 hours of breast-feeding. Thereafter, a nonnarcotic agent such as a nonsteroidal anti-inflammatory drug (NSAID) is preferred.

OXYMETAZOLINE

Brand names: Afrin, Nasivion, Vicks Sinex, Visine

Drug class: Nasal or ophthalmic spray

Indications (what it is used for): Congestion.

How it works: a2-adrenergic agonist that narrows the blood vessels, relieving swelling of the nasal passages or blood-shot eyes.

Contraindications (reasons you shouldn't take it): Hypersensitivity to drug or class, glaucoma.

Possible side effects and warnings: Can cause high blood pressure, cardiovascular collapse, rebound runny nose, nasal irritation, burning, and sneezing. Should be used with caution in women with preeclampsia (high blood pressure and protein in the urine during pregnancy and complications associated with it), high blood pressure, excess thyroid hormone, diabetes, or eye injury.

How it can affect pregnant women: Allergic runny nose affects about 1 in 3 women of reproductive age. The eyes are also often affected. Oxymetazoline is available over the counter, and the prevalence of its use during pregnancy and while breast-feeding is unknown. Chronic abuse may lead to rebound runny nose. Because there are no adequate reports or well-controlled studies in pregnant women, it should be considered a second-line choice behind first-generation antihistamines such as chlorpheniramine. Oxymetazoline can, at least in the laboratory, cause the uterine muscle to contract. Preeclamptic women may experience an acute rise in blood pressure after administration.

How it can affect a developing embryo or fetus: There are no adequate reports or well-controlled studies in human fetuses. It is suggested that some vasoactive decongestants including oxymetazoline may be associated with gastroschisis, a birth defect in which the bowel protrudes through an opening in the fetal abdomen (it can be repaired with surgery). Some but not all studies suggest that it can constrict the umbilical artery and cause an abnormal fetal heart rate.

Breast-feeding: There are no adequate reports or well-controlled studies in nursing women. It is unknown whether oxymetazoline enters human breast milk. However, considering the dose, method of administration, and frequency of dosing, it is unlikely that a breast-feeding newborn would absorb clinically relevant quantities.

Potential drug interactions: No clinically relevant interactions identified.

What the FDA says about use in pregnancy: Category C (see Appendix).

What the available evidence suggests about breast-feeding safety: Likely safe.

The bottom line for you:
- Oxymetazoline probably should be avoided during the first trimester and in women with preeclampsia. There are alternative agents with which there is more experience during pregnancy.
- It is probably safe for use while breast-feeding.

OXYMORPHONE

Brand names: Numorphan, Opana

Drug class: Analgesic, narcotic

Indications (what it is used for): Moderate to severe pain, labor analgesia.

How it works: Binds opiate receptors to dull the perception of pain.

Contraindications (reasons you shouldn't take it): Hypersensitivity to drug or class.

Possible side effects and warnings: Can cause abuse or addiction, constipation, low blood pressure, respiratory depression, sedation, confusion, nausea, vomiting, dizziness, sweating, nervousness, and hallucinations. Should be used with caution in women with lung, liver, or kidney dysfunction; head trauma; seizure disorder; or a history of substance abuse.

How it can affect pregnant women: Oxymorphone was once popular for labor analgesia. It provides similar pain relief with less itching compared to morphine when used in an epidural. Oxymorphone is an alternative to morphine administered by a patient-controlled device after cesarean section but may be associated with increased nausea. The level of sedation is similar.

How it can affect a developing embryo or fetus: There are no adequate reports or well-controlled studies of oxymorphone in human fetuses. It readily crosses the human placenta, although the drug is quickly cleared from the mother's bloodstream, shortening the fetal exposure. The higher the level of free morphine in umbilical venous blood, the greater the chance a newborn will need extensive stimulation after delivery. Morphine exposure may reduce the fetal biophysical profile score (a test for fetal well-being), since morphine slows fetal breathing and heart rate. This can give the false impression that the fetus is in trouble and in need of urgent delivery.

Although there is no evidence that morphine is a human teratogen (substance that causes birth defects), a long clinical experience with newborns chronically exposed to other opioids suggests an association with reduced brain volume at birth that normalizes during the first month of life. Infants born to opioid-abusing mothers more often have low birth weight and an increased risk of sudden infant death. Newborn withdrawal syndrome due to opiate exposure during pregnancy produces sleep and feeding difficulties, weight loss, and seizures. Exposure during labor has no detectable long-term effect on the newborn.

Breast-feeding: There is no published data in nursing women. It is unknown whether oxymorphone enters human breast milk. Only limited quantities of morphine enter breast milk.

Potential drug interactions: Interaction between the following medications and oxymorphone has the potential to impact the effect of one or more of the drugs. In some instances the interaction can be dangerous or life-threatening and must be avoided: other central nervous system depressants, including sedatives, hypnotics, tranquilizers, general anesthetics, phenothiazines, other opioids, tricyclic antidepressants (TCAs), monoamine oxidase inhibitors (MAOIs), and ethanol (alcohol); anticholinergics; propofol; cimetidine; agonist-antagonist analgesics (e.g., buprenorphine, butorphanol, nalbuphine, pentazocine).

What the FDA says about use in pregnancy: Category C (see Appendix).

What the available evidence suggests about breast-feeding safety: Safe.

The bottom line for you:

- Oxymorphone is a useful analgesic after cesarean delivery.
- Oxymorphone, like morphine, is safe for use while breast-feeding.
- There are other agents with which there is more experience during pregnancy and while breast-feeding.

OXYTETRACYCLINE

Brand names: Clinmycin, E.P. Mycin, Oxy-Kesso-Tetra, Terramycin, Tija, Uri-Tet

Drug classes: Antibiotic; Tetracycline

Indications (what it is used for): Bacterial infections with sensitive bacteria, including *Mycoplasma pneumoniae, Borrelia recurrentis* (relapsing fever), *H. influenzae* (respiratory), *H. ducreyi* (chancroid), *Bacteroides* species (intestinal), *Shigella* species (dysentery), *Klebsiella* species (respiratory and urinary), the agents of psittacosis and ornithosis (infections spread by birds), lymphogranuloma venereum (an infection of lymphatics and lymph nodes caused by Chlamydia), and granuloma inguinale (genital ulcers).

How it works: Slows the growth of bacteria and allows the natural body defenses to remove them.

Contraindications (reasons you shouldn't take it): Hypersensitivity to drug or class.

Possible side effects and warnings: Can cause nausea, vomiting, diarrhea, inflamed tongue, rash, sensitivity to light, kidney toxicity, hives, rapid swelling of the skin layers, hemolytic anemia, low white blood cell and/or platelet counts. Should be used with caution in women also taking anticoagulants or penicillin.

How it can affect pregnant women: When penicillin is contraindicated (cannot be used), tetracyclines are alternative drugs for the treatment of *N. gonorrhoeae*, *T. pallidum* and *T. pertenue* (syphilis and yaws), *Listeria monocytogenes* (listeria, usually caused by eating contaminated food), *Clostridium* species, *B. anthracis* (anthrax), *Fusobacterium fusiforme* (Vincent's infection, trench mouth), and *Actinomyces* species (mouth infections). There are no adequate reports or well-controlled studies of oxytetracycline in pregnant women. Tetracyclines generally should not be used during pregnancy because of their effect on the fetal teeth (See "How it can affect a developing embryo or fetus").

How it can affect a developing embryo or fetus: There are no adequate reports or well-controlled studies in human fetuses. Oxytetracycline rapidly crosses the placenta and blood-brain barrier. Large studies of exposed pregnancies link first-trimester use of oxytetracycline with defects of the fetal spine such as spina bifida, cleft palate, and cardiovascular malformations. Tetracyclines in general are known to cause tooth discoloration when given in the second half of pregnancy and during the newborn period. Rodent studies revealed no evidence of birth defects despite the use of doses higher than those used clinically. However, animal studies are not necessarily good indicators of how a drug will behave in humans.

Breast-feeding: There is no published data in nursing women. It is unknown whether oxytetracycline enters human breast milk. Other tetracyclines are excreted in breast milk.

Potential drug interactions: Interaction between the following medications and tetracyclines has the potential to impact the effect of one or more of the drugs. In some instances the interaction can be dangerous or life-threatening and must be avoided: bactericidal antibiotics, anticoagulant medications, methoxyflurane. Absorption of tetracyclines is impaired by antacids containing aluminum, calcium, or magnesium, and preparations containing iron, zinc, or sodium bicarbonate. Tetracyclines may make low-estradiol oral contraceptives less effective.

What the FDA says about use in pregnancy: Category D (see Appendix).

What the available evidence suggests about breast-feeding safety: Unknown.

The bottom line for you:

- There is reason to suspect that oxytetracycline is a weak teratogen (substance that can cause birth defects) in humans; it should be avoided, especially in the first trimester.

- There are alternative agents with which there is more experience during pregnancy and while breast-feeding.

OXYTOCIN

Brand names: Pitocin, Syntocinon, Xitocin

Drug classes: Hormone/hormone modifier; Oxytocic; Stimulant, uterine

Indications (what it is used for): Labor induction, postpartum bleeding, lactation aid.

How it works: Binds oxytocin receptors to cause the uterus to contract.

Contraindications (reasons you shouldn't take it): Hypersensitivity to drug or class; contraindications to vaginal delivery including abnormal fetal position, fetus too large to fit through the pelvis, fetal distress, placenta previa (the placenta covering the cervix), vasa previa (fetal blood vessels blocking the cervical opening), umbilical cord prolapse, slow fetal heart rate.

Possible side effects and warnings: Can cause uterine tetany (sustained contraction), irregular heart rate, uterine rupture, placental abruption (placenta separating from the wall of the uterus), fetal distress, and nausea and vomiting. Should be used with caution in women with prior uterine scarring or whose babies are in a breech presentation.

How it can affect pregnant women: Oxytocin is produced in the pituitary gland. The physiologic role of oxytocin in the stimulation and maintenance of human labor remains unclear. Oxytocin (given as a drug, as opposed to the oxytocin produced naturally in the body) is usually effective for stimulating rhythmic uterine contractions and is the current drug of choice for helping labor along. Higher-dose oxytocin produces shorter labors without adverse fetal or newborn effects compared to lower-dose oxytocin. However, caution is indicated at the higher doses of oxytocin during an attempt at a VBAC delivery (a vaginal birth after having had a cesarean section in the prior pregnancy). Low-dose oxytocin is equivalent to misoprostol for cervical ripening. Oxytocin is also important for the management of postpartum bleeding. It reduces the need for additional uterotonic agents after cesarean delivery.

How it can affect a developing embryo or fetus: Oxytocin is used only to stimulate or strengthen labor, and as such poses only labor-associated risks to the fetus. There are no indications for its use in the first trimester. Animal birth defect studies have not been conducted. Electronic fetal heart rate monitoring is indicated whenever oxytocin is used during labor.

Breast-feeding: There are no adequate reports or well-controlled studies in nursing women. Naturally occurring oxytocin is essential for the initiation of lactation, and synthetic oxytocin can aid the establishment of a milk reflex.

Potential drug interactions: Interaction between the following medications and oxytocin has the po-

tential to impact the effect of one or more of the drugs. In some instances the interaction can be dangerous or life-threatening and must be avoided: vasoconstrictor in conjunction with caudal block anesthesia, cyclopropane anesthesia.

What the FDA says about use in pregnancy: Category X (see Appendix).

What the available evidence suggests about breast-feeding safety: Safe.

The bottom line for you:

- Oxytocin is the drug of choice for labor augmentation.
- It remains a first-line medication for the stimulation/strengthening of labor and the treatment of heavy bleeding from the uterus after delivery.
- Oxytocin is safe for use while breast feeding.

PACLITAXEL

Brand names: Onxol, Taxol

Drug class: Antineoplastic, antimitotic

Indications (what it is used for): Malignancy, metastatic ovarian or breast cancer, lung (non–small cell) cancer, HIV-related Kaposi's sarcoma (cancer that causes patches of abnormal tissue to grow under the skin).

How it works: Prevents cell replication by inhibiting mitosis.

Contraindications (reasons you shouldn't take it): Hypersensitivity to drug or class, hypersensitivity to castor oil, low white blood cell count.

Possible side effects and warnings: Can cause hair loss, bone marrow suppression, nausea, vomiting, diarrhea, joint pain, muscle pain, peripheral nerve pain, infection, liver dysfunction, and injection site reactions. Should be used with caution in women undergoing radiation therapy or who are pregnant.

How it can affect pregnant women: Paclitaxel is a natural product usually combined with cisplatin as first-line therapy for a variety of cancers. Numerous women have been treated effectively with paclitaxel during pregnancy. No matter which trimester treatment began, the offspring seemed healthy with a median follow-up of 16 months (the range of follow-up ages was 3–36 months).

How it can affect a developing embryo or fetus: There are no adequate reports or well-controlled studies in human fetuses. It is unknown whether paclitaxel crosses the human placenta. However, several case reports note the development of low amniotic fluid during paclitaxel treatment although the final newborn outcome was unaffected. Rodent studies revealed increased embryo loss and low birth weight but no increase in birth defects. However, animal studies are not necessarily good indicators of how a drug will behave in humans.

Breast-feeding: There is no published data in nursing women. It is unknown whether paclitaxel enters human breast milk. It is concentrated in rat milk.

Potential drug interactions: Interaction between the following medications and paclitaxel has the potential to impact the effect of one or more of the drugs. In some instances the interaction can be dangerous or life-threatening and must be avoided: known substrates or inhibitors of CYP2C8 and CYP3A4, protease inhibitors, cisplatin.

What the FDA says about use in pregnancy: Category D (see Appendix).

What the available evidence suggests about breast-feeding safety: Unknown.

The bottom line for you:

- Paclitaxel is used during pregnancy for the treatment of life-threatening maternal disease.
- There is not enough information to conclude whether or not paclitaxel is safe while breast-feeding.

PANCRELIPASE

Brand names: Amylase, Amylase Lipase Protease, Cotazym-S, Creon, Creon 5, Donnazyme, Encron 10, Entolase, Enzymase 16, Festalan, Ilozyme, Ku-Zyme HP, Lipase, Panase, Pancote, Pancrease, Pancreatic Enzyme, Pancreatin 10, Pancrelipase 10000, Pancrelipase Mt-16, Pancron 10, Panokase, Promylin, Protease, Protilase, Protilase Mt 16, Ultrase, Ultrase Mt, Vio-Moore, Zymase

Drug classes: Digestive enzyme; Gastrointestinal

Indications (what it is used for): Pancreatic insufficiency, most often in women with cystic fibrosis.

How it works: Replaces natural enzymes missing in women with cystic fibrosis (life-threatening lung and pancreatic disease).

Contraindications (reasons you shouldn't take it): Hypersensitivity to drug or class, allergy to pork, acute pancreatitis.

Possible side effects and warnings: Can cause nausea, vomiting, diarrhea, sores on the mouth and/or tongue, rash, high uric acid levels, and anal soreness.

How it can affect pregnant women: The enzymes in pancrelipase act locally in the bowel, where they are either digested or partially absorbed and then excreted in the urine. Undigested enzymes are excreted in the feces. There is no published data in pregnancy, although pancrelipase is commonly used in pregnant women with cystic fibrosis.

How it can affect a developing embryo or fetus: There are no adequate reports or well-controlled studies of pancrelipase in human fetuses. The enzymes are not intact and functional when absorbed out of the gut and pose no risk to the fetus. Rodent studies are reassuring, revealing no evidence of birth defects or low birth weight despite the use of doses higher than those used clinically. However, animal studies are not necessarily good indicators of how a drug will behave in humans.

Breast-feeding: There is no published data with pancrelipase in nursing women. However, the enzymes are not absorbed systemically and are unlikely to enter human breast milk.

Potential drug interactions: Antacids containing calcium carbonate and magnesium hydroxide should not be taken at the same time as pancrelipase.

What the FDA says about use in pregnancy: Category C (see Appendix).

What the available evidence suggests about breast-feeding safety: Safe.

The bottom line for you:
- Clinical experience indicates that pancrelipase is safe and effective during pregnancy and while breast-feeding.

PANCURONIUM
Brand name: Pavulon
Drug class: Neuromuscular blocker, nondepolarizing
Indications (what it is used for): Anesthesia, paralysis.
How it works: Blocks the motor nerve endings so that the muscles cannot contract.
Contraindications (reasons you shouldn't take it): Hypersensitivity to drug or class.
Possible side effects and warnings: Can cause irregular or rapid heart rate, high blood pressure, rash, increased salivation, and itching. Should be used with caution in women with blood loss due to hemorrhage or dehydration or liver dysfunction.
How it can affect pregnant women: There are no adequate reports or well-controlled studies of pancuronium in pregnant women. However, there is a long clinical experience with its use during cesarean delivery. The paralysis produced by pancuronium is reversed by anticholinesterase agents such as edrophonium, neostigmine, and pyridostigmine. Magnesium sulfate prolongs the effect of pancuronium.
How it can affect a developing embryo or fetus: There are no adequate reports or well-controlled studies of pancuronium in human fetuses. There is minimal transport across the human placenta. Pancuronium is used for fetal paralysis to facilitate fetal surgical procedures.
Breast-feeding: There is no published data in nursing women. It is unknown whether pancuronium enters human breast milk. However, it is unlikely that a significant amount of pancuronium would enter the breast milk if it is given once for the described indications.
Potential drug interactions: Interaction between the following medications and pancuronium has the potential to impact the effect of one or more of the drugs. In some instances the interaction can be dangerous or life-threatening and must be avoided: succinylcholine, other nondepolarizing neuromuscular blocking agents (e.g., atracurium, d-tubocurarine, gallamine, metocurine, vecuronium), volatile inhalational anesthetics (e.g., enflurane, isoflurane, halothane), tricyclic antidepressants (TCAs), certain antibiotics (e.g., aminoglycosides such as dihydrostreptomycin, gentamicin, kanamycin, neomycin, and streptomycin; tetracyclines; bacitracin; polymyxin B; colistin; colistimethate), quinidine, magnesium sulfate.
What the FDA says about use in pregnancy: Category C (see Appendix).
What the available evidence suggests about breast-feeding safety: Probably safe.
The bottom line for you:
- Pancuronium is safe for use during pregnancy and while breast-feeding.

PANTOPRAZOLE
Brand names: Protonix, Somac
Drug classes: Antiulcer; Gastrointestinal; Proton pump inhibitor
Indications (what it is used for): Erosive esophagitis, hypersecretory conditions.
How it works: Inhibits the production of acid by the stomach.
Contraindications (reasons you shouldn't take it): Hypersensitivity to drug or class.
Possible side effects and warnings: Can cause headache, diarrhea, pancreatitis, various blood disorders, liver dysfunction, toxic epidermal necrolysis and erythema multiforme (skin disorders). Should be used with caution for long-term use.
How it can affect pregnant women: There are fewer than 100 reported cases of pantoprazole use during pregnancy. It seems effective for the approved indications.
How it can affect a developing embryo or fetus: There are no adequate reports or well-controlled

studies in human fetuses. It is unknown whether pantoprazole crosses the human placenta. The limited published data does not raise an alarm. Rodent studies are reassuring, revealing no evidence of birth defects or low birth weight despite the use of doses higher than those used clinically. However, animal studies are not necessarily good indicators of how a drug will behave in humans.

Breast-feeding: There is no published data during breast-feeding. It is unknown whether pantoprazole enters human breast milk; it is excreted into rodent milk.

Potential drug interactions: Interaction between the following medications and pantoprazole has the potential to impact the effect of one or more of the drugs. In some instances the interaction can be dangerous or life-threatening and must be avoided: warfarin, ampicillin esters, iron salts, and ketoconazole.

What the FDA says about use in pregnancy: Category B (see Appendix).

What the available evidence suggests about breast-feeding safety: Unknown.

The bottom line for you:

- There are alternative agents with which there is more experience during pregnancy and while breast-feeding.
- Pantoprazole may be used if other alternatives fail.

PANTOTHENIC ACID (VITAMIN B₅)

Brand name: Vilantae
Drug class: Vitamins/minerals
Indications (what it is used for): Supplementation.
How it works: Unknown.
Contraindications (reasons you shouldn't take it): Hypersensitivity to drug or class.
Possible side effects and warnings: None reported.
How it can affect pregnant women: Pantothenic acid (vitamin B₅) is a water-soluble B vitamin that is contained in most prenatal vitamins. There are no adequate reports or well-controlled studies of pan-

tothenic acid in pregnant women. Maternal blood levels may decline slightly during pregnancy.

How it can affect a developing embryo or fetus: There are no adequate reports or well-controlled studies in human fetuses. Pantothenic acid is actively transported across the placenta. Maternal consumption of pantothenic acid correlates directly with newborn size—higher levels result in larger newborns. However, it is not known whether maternal supplementation with pantothenic acid increases the fetal concentration. Supplementation did reduce the incidence of spina bifida (an opening in the spine) and related birth defects in mice that were also treated with valproate (a medication which can cause birth defects).

Breast-feeding: There are no adequate reports or well-controlled studies in nursing women. Pantothenic acid enters human breast milk. Maternal blood levels may decline slightly during breast-feeding without supplementation.

Potential drug interactions: No clinically relevant interactions identified.

What the FDA says about use in pregnancy: Category A (see Appendix).

What the available evidence suggests about breast-feeding safety: Safe.

The bottom line for you:

- Pantothenic acid is a common component of prenatal vitamins. At those levels, it appears safe for use during pregnancy. However, it is unclear whether its consumption improves pregnancy outcome.
- Pantothenic acid is safe and effective while breast-feeding. Supplementation increases levels in milk and prevents a decline in the mother's blood.

PAREGORIC

Brand name: None
Drug classes: Antidiarrheal; Narcotic
Indications (what it is used for): Diarrhea.
How it works: Binds opioid receptors.

Contraindications (reasons you shouldn't take it): Hypersensitivity to drug or class, increased sensitivity to morphine, diarrhea caused by toxic metal poisoning.

Possible side effects and warnings: Can cause low blood pressure, convulsions, and rapid heart rate. Should be used with caution in women with head injury or abdominal pain of unknown origin.

How it can affect pregnant women: Paregoric is a mixture of opium powder (morphine) and alcohol with a touch of anise oil. It blocks normal bowel motility to control severe diarrhea. It is also a cough suppressant. Paregoric is often confused with laudanum, because their chemical names are similar: camphorated tincture of opium (paregoric) vs. tincture of opium (laudanum). However, laudanum contains 25 times more morphine than paregoric. There are no adequate reports or well-controlled studies of paregoric in pregnant women. Morphine, however, is one of the most frequently used opioids for pain control during childbirth. The elimination of morphine from the body is faster during pregnancy and the dosing may need to be adjusted. Morphine as part of an epidural or patient-controlled infusion is common. It is also given by epidural after cesarean section for relief of postoperative pain for the first 48 hours. The addition of a small dose of morphine to the spinal component of a continuous spinal epidural improves the effectiveness of labor analgesia and reduces the need for pain medications over 24 hours after delivery. Epidural morphine reduces the chance of headache and the need for a blood patch after dural puncture (a rare complication of epidural injections). There is a long clinical experience supporting the relative safety of morphine for the listed indications.

How it can affect a developing embryo or fetus: There are no adequate reports or well-controlled studies of paregoric in human fetuses, although the long clinical experience during pregnancy is reassuring. Paregoric is used after delivery to treat newborns undergoing withdrawal from maternal drug addiction. Rodent birth defects studies have not been conducted.

Morphine readily crosses the human placenta, although the drug is quickly cleared from the mother's bloodstream, shortening the fetal exposure. The higher the level of free morphine in umbilical venous blood, the greater the chance a newborn will need extensive stimulation after delivery. Morphine exposure may reduce the fetal biophysical profile score (a test for fetal well-being), since morphine slows fetal breathing and decreases the variability of the fetal heart rate. This can give the false impression that the fetus is in trouble and in need of urgent delivery.

Morphine has been combined with benzodiazepines (e.g., diazepam) for the relief of pain and anxiety during fetal surgical procedures. Although there is no evidence that morphine is a human teratogen (substance that can cause birth defects), a long clinical experience with newborns chronically exposed to other opioids suggests an association with reduced brain volume at birth that normalizes during the first month of life. Infants born to opioid-abusing mothers more often have low birth weight and an increased risk of sudden infant death. Newborn withdrawal syndrome due to opiate exposure during pregnancy produces sleep and feeding difficulties, weight loss, and seizures. Exposure during labor has no long-term effect on the newborn.

Breast-feeding: There are no adequate reports or well-controlled studies of paregoric in nursing women. Morphine is concentrated in human breast milk. In general, morphine is preferred to meperidine in breast-feeding women. Spinal or epidural morphine does not produce a clinically relevant level in breast milk. The colostrum concentration of morphine and its active metabolites in women using PCA (patient-controlled analgesia) after cesarean delivery is also small, supporting the safety of breast-feeding in those instances.

Potential drug interactions: Interaction between the following medications and paregoric has the potential to impact the effect of one or more of the drugs. In some instances the interaction can be dangerous or life-threatening and must be avoided: other central nervous system (CNS) depressants (including sedatives, hypnotics, general anesthetics, droperidol, phenothiazines or other tranquilizers, and ethanol/alcohol), monoamine oxidase inhibitors (MAOIs), neuromuscular-blocking agents, cimetidine.

What the FDA says about use in pregnancy: Category C (see Appendix).

What the available evidence suggests about breast-feeding safety: Safe.

The bottom line for you:

● Paregoric may be used during pregnancy and while breast-feeding if necessary, although there are alternative agents with which there is more experience.

PAROXETINE

Brand name: Paxil

Drug classes: Antidepressant; SSRI

Indications (what it is used for): Depression, postpartum depression, obsessive-compulsive disorder, panic disorder, anxietal disorders, post-traumatic stress, chronic headache, diabetic neuropathy.

How it works: Selectively inhibits the reuptake of serotonin, a neurotransmitter involved in mood.

Contraindications (reasons you shouldn't take it): Hypersensitivity to drug or class, monoamine oxidase inhibitor (MAOI) use within 14 days, thioridazine use.

Possible side effects and warnings: Can cause serotonin or withdrawal syndromes; movement disorders that result from taking dopamine antagonists, usually antipsychotic drugs; mania; seizures; nausea; diarrhea; headache; drowsiness; dizziness; weakness; constipation; tremor; gas; anxiety; sweating; decreased sex drive; blurred vision; appetite changes; and flushing. Should be used with caution in women with mania, history of seizures, liver or kidney dysfunction, narrow-angle glaucoma, a history of suicide attempts or who have serious thoughts of suicide. The medication should not be withdrawn abruptly.

How it can affect pregnant women: Depression is common during and after pregnancy but often goes unrecognized and untreated. Depression can be made worse by pregnancy or delivery, and suicide is a not uncommon cause of maternal death. Pregnancy is not a reason to discontinue antidepressant drugs if the medication is effective and needed. A woman being treated for depression who becomes pregnant should not discontinue medication abruptly on her own but rather discuss her treatment and condition with her medical provider. Pregnancy may increase the dose needed to be effective, and women with a history of depression have a higher rate of recurrence after delivery. About two-thirds of the women with major depression taking paroxetine or similar drugs during pregnancy must increase their dose to maintain its effect. If, after consultation with their doctors, they decide to stop, paroxetine should be tapered gradually to avoid an abrupt discontinuation syndrome. Recent population-based studies indicate depression and the use of paroxetine is associated with an increased risk of preeclampsia. There is growing clinical experience with the use of paroxetine for the treatment of postpartum depression. Paroxetine is also effective for the treatment of menopause-associated hot flashes.

How it can affect a developing embryo or fetus: There are no adequate reports or well-controlled studies in human fetuses. Paroxetine crosses the human placenta, reaching a level approximating half that of the mother, a value lower than that with citalopram and fluoxetine. Some studies have shown a small increase in the risk of heart defects in embryos exposed to SSRIs in the first trimester (the strongest link was found with paroxetine) but current studies indicate it is not dose dependent (the risk does not increase or decrease as the dose does, suggesting other factors may play a role in creating the defect). The safest approach for all SSRIs is probably to avoid them in the first trimester. Women with moderate to severe depression responsive to their medication, however, should continue treatment during pregnancy as the benefit outweighs the possible risks to mother and child.

SSRI use late in pregnancy may double the risk of persistent pulmonary hypertension (high blood pressure affecting the lungs) during the newborn period (which, at 2 in 1000 births, is low to begin with). SSRI exposure during the third trimester and until delivery may also lead to a withdrawal syndrome during the first few days of life, requiring extra care. Symptoms in the newborn may include problems breathing, jitteriness, increased muscle tone, irritability, altered sleep patterns, tremors, and poor eating. In most cases, these symptoms are mild and disappear within 2 weeks with no treatment. These symptoms can occur in up to 30% of exposed newborns, and, although they can can occur at all doses, may occur more often with higher doses. The risk does not outweigh the benefit of needed therapy. Rodent studies are reassuring, revealing no evidence of birth defects or low birth weight despite the use of doses higher than those used clinically. However, animal studies are not necessarily good indicators of how a drug will behave in humans.

Breast-feeding: There are no adequate reports or well-controlled studies in nursing women. Paroxetine is excreted into human breast milk, with the highest concentrations in the milk released at the end of the feeding. However, the levels are variable, and no breast-fed child studied to date has had clinically relevant levels detected, suggesting that paroxetine is a good selection for breast-feeding women.

Potential drug interactions: Interaction between the following medications and paroxetine has the potential to impact the effect of one or more of the drugs. In some instances the interaction can be dangerous or life-threatening and must be avoided: pimozide; other drugs or agents that may affect the serotonergic neurotransmitter systems (e.g., tryptophan, triptans, other SSRIs, linezolid, lithium, tramadol, St. John's wort), warfarin, sumatriptan; drugs that are metabolized by CYP2D6 (e.g., amitriptyline, fluoxetine, imipramine, nortriptyline), phenothiazines, class 1C antiarrhythmics (e.g., encainide, flecainide, propafenone), desipramine, risperidone, atomoxetine, thioridazine, tricyclic antidepressants (TCAs), procyclidine, fosamprenavir-ritonavir.

What the FDA says about use in pregnancy: Category D (see Appendix).

What the available evidence suggests about breast-feeding safety: Likely safe.

The bottom line for you:

- Paroxetine may be used during pregnancy when the maternal benefit justifies the potential risk to the embryo or fetus.
- There may be a small increase in the risk of cardiac malformations with first-trimester exposure; women should have a fetal echocardiogram at 20–22 weeks. Pulmonary hypertension in the newborn is a second concern.
- Paroxetine appears safe for use while breast-feeding.

PEGINTERFERON ALFA-2B

Brand names: PEG-Intron, Rebetol, Roferon-A
Drug classes: Antiviral; Immunomodulator
Indications (what it is used for): Hepatitis C infection.
How it works: Blocks viral replication via multiple actions.
Contraindications (reasons you shouldn't take it): Hypersensitivity to drug or class, autoimmune hepatitis, decompensated liver disease.
Possible side effects and warnings: Can cause psychosis, thoughts of suicide, anemia, low white blood cell or platelet counts, cardiomyopathy (disease of the heart muscle), irregular heart rate, heart attack, pancreatitis, bleeding or clotting in the retina of the eye, headache, nausea, vomiting, fatigue, shaking, fever, depression, abdominal pain, diarrhea, and injection site reactions. Should be used with caution in women with bone marrow suppression, diabetes, psychiatric disorders, thyroid disease, colitis, heart or lung disease, or eye disorders.
How it can affect pregnant women: There is no published data in pregnancy. In nonpregnant patients, alfa interferons like peginterferon alfa-2b can cause or aggravate life-threatening or fatal neuropsychiatric, autoimmune, ischemic, and infectious disor-

ders. Anyone taking peginterferon alfa-2b should be monitored closely with periodic clinical and laboratory evaluations. Therapy should be discontinued in women with persistently severe or worsening signs or symptoms. In many, but not all, instances, these adverse effects resolve after discontinuing the medication. Irregular menstrual cycles were seen in monkeys treated with doses that were multiples of the maximum recommended human dose.

How it can affect a developing embryo or fetus: There are no adequate reports or well-controlled studies in human fetuses. It is unknown whether peginterferon alfa-2b crosses the human placenta. High doses of native interferon alfa-2b (from which peginterferon is modeled) were associated with miscarriage in monkeys. However, animal studies are not necessarily good indicators of how a drug will behave in humans.

Breast-feeding: There is no published data during breast-feeding. It is unknown whether peginterferon alfa-2b enters human breast milk. Breast-feeding is not contraindicated just because a woman has hepatitis C.

Potential drug interactions: No clinically relevant interactions identified.

What the FDA says about use in pregnancy: Category C (see Appendix).

What the available evidence suggests about breast-feeding safety: Unknown.

The bottom line for you:

- Peginterferon alfa-2b should be used during pregnancy and while breast-feeding only if the benefit to the woman justifies the potential risk to the embryo, fetus, or newborn.

PEMIROLAST OPHTHALMIC

Brand name: Alamast

Drug classes: Allergy; Mast cell stabilizer; Ophthalmic

Indications (what it is used for): Allergic conjunctivitis.

How it works: Blocks the release of granules in mast cells that cause the allergic reaction.

Contraindications (reasons you shouldn't take it): Hypersensitivity to drug or class.

Possible side effects and warnings: Can cause headache, dry eyes, burning or other eye discomfort, and breathing difficulties.

How it can affect pregnant women: There is no published data with pemirolast in pregnancy.

How it can affect a developing embryo or fetus: There are no adequate reports or well-controlled studies in human fetuses. It is unknown whether pemirolast crosses the human placenta. However, considering the dose and the fact that it is administered to the eye, it is unlikely that the maternal blood concentration would achieve a clinically relevant level for an embryo or fetus. Rodent studies revealed skeletal abnormalities when doses more than 20,000 times the maximum recommended clinical dose were used. However, animal studies are not necessarily good indicators of how a drug will behave in humans.

Breast-feeding: There is no published data during breast-feeding. It is unknown whether pemirolast enters human breast milk. However, considering the dose and the fact that it is administered to the eye, it is unlikely that a breast-fed newborn will ingest clinically relevant amounts. It is concentrated in rodent milk.

Potential drug interactions: No clinically relevant interactions identified.

What the FDA says about use in pregnancy: Category C (see Appendix).

What the available evidence suggests about breast-feeding safety: Likely safe.

The bottom line for you:

- Pemirolast may be used during pregnancy.
- Pemirolast is likely safe while breast-feeding.

PEMOLINE

Brand name: Cylert

Drug classes: Anorexiant; CNS stimulant

Indications (what it is used for): Attention deficit/hyperactivity disorder, narcolepsy.

How it works: Stimulates the brain by unknown mechanisms.

Contraindications (reasons you shouldn't take it): Hypersensitivity to drug or class, liver dysfunction, Tourette's syndrome (involuntary movements and vocalizations), dependency.

Possible side effects and warnings: Can cause seizures, aplastic anemia, hearing damage, nausea, vomiting, abdominal pain, headache, rash, sleeplessness, drowsiness, irritability, Tourette's syndrome, involuntary movements like tics, and liver damage. Should be used with caution in women with a seizure disorder or kidney dysfunction.

How it can affect pregnant women: There are no adequate reports or well-controlled studies in pregnant women. It has been used to treat narcolepsy during pregnancy.

How it can affect a developing embryo or fetus: There are no adequate reports or well-controlled studies in human fetuses. It is unknown whether pemoline crosses the human placenta. Rodent studies are reassuring, revealing no evidence of birth defects or low birth weight despite the use of doses higher than those used clinically. However, animal studies are not necessarily good indicators of how a drug will behave in humans.

Breast-feeding: There is no published data in nursing women. It is unknown whether pemoline enters human breast milk.

Potential drug interactions: Pemoline decreases the seizure threshold in patients also receiving anti-epileptic drugs.

What the FDA says about use in pregnancy: Category B (see Appendix).

What the available evidence suggests about breast-feeding safety: Unknown.

The bottom line for you:

- Pemoline should be used during pregnancy and while breast-feeding only if the benefit to the woman justifies the potential risk to the embryo, fetus, or newborn.

PENCICLOVIR TOPICAL

Brand name: Denavir

Drug classes: Antiviral; Dermatologic

Indications (what it is used for): Genital herpes.

How it works: Inhibits an enzyme necessary for viral replication.

Contraindications (reasons you shouldn't take it): Hypersensitivity to drug or class.

Possible side effects and warnings: Can cause headache, itching, taste changes, and redness. Should be used with caution in women with an immune deficiency.

How it can affect pregnant women: There is no published data with penciclovir in pregnancy. Little of the medication is absorbed into the body after topical application.

How it can affect a developing embryo or fetus: There are no adequate reports or well-controlled studies in human fetuses. It is unknown whether penciclovir crosses the human placenta; it does apparently cross the rodent placenta. However, considering that little of the drug is absorbed into the maternal bloodstream when it is used topically, it is unlikely that the maternal blood concentration would reach clinically relevant levels for the embryo or fetus. Rodent studies are reassuring, revealing no evidence of birth defects or low birth weight despite the use of doses higher than those used clinically. However, animal studies are not necessarily good indicators of how a drug will behave in humans.

Breast-feeding: There is no published data in nursing women. It is unknown whether penciclovir enters human breast milk. However, considering the dose and that low amounts are absorbed when used topically, it is unlikely that a breast-fed newborn would ingest clinically relevant amounts.

Potential drug interactions: No clinically relevant interactions identified.

What the FDA says about use in pregnancy: Category B (see Appendix).

What the available evidence suggests about breast-feeding safety: Likely safe.

The bottom line for you:
- Penciclovir appears to be safe for use for the topical treatment of herpes during pregnancy and while breast-feeding.

PENICILLIN G, AQUEOUS

Brand name: None

Drug classes: Antibiotic; Penicillin

Indications (what it is used for): Moderate to severe systemic infection, anthrax, syphilis.

How it works: Kills bacteria by blocking cell wall synthesis.

Contraindications (reasons you shouldn't take it): Hypersensitivity to drug or class.

Possible side effects and warnings: Can cause low platelet and/or white blood cell counts, seizures, Stevens-Johnson syndrome (a rare but serious skin reaction to medication), hemolytic anemia, kidney inflammation, nausea, vomiting, abdominal pain, diarrhea, rash, fever, and blood clots. Should be used with caution in women with kidney dysfunction, cephalosporin allergy, or seizure disorder.

How it can affect pregnant women: There is a long clinical experience with penicillin G during pregnancy that is reassuring. About a third of all pregnant women have group B streptococcus bacteria in their vagina, which can infect and damage the newborn either after rupture of membranes (water breaking) or during vaginal delivery. As a result, women are routinely tested for the presence of group B streptococcus before delivery. Vaginal group B streptococcus levels rapidly decline after penicillin G is given during labor. It is as effective as cephalothin for the prevention of post–cesarean section infection.

How it can affect a developing embryo or fetus: There are no adequate reports or well-controlled studies in human fetuses. Most penicillins cross the human placenta to some extent. Rodent studies are reassuring, revealing no evidence of birth defects or low birth weight despite the use of doses higher than those used clinically. However, animal studies are not necessarily good indicators of how a drug will behave in humans.

Breast-feeding: There are no adequate reports or well-controlled studies in nursing women. Only trace amounts of penicillin G enter human breast milk. It is generally considered compatible with breast-feeding.

Potential drug interactions: Interaction between the following medications and penicillin G has the potential to impact the effect of one or more of the drugs. In some instances the interaction can be dangerous or life-threatening and must be avoided: tetracycline, probenecid.

What the FDA says about use in pregnancy: Category B (see Appendix).

What the available evidence suggests about breast-feeding safety: Safe.

The bottom line for you:
- Penicillin G has been used for decades during pregnancy and while breast-feeding. Although there is little objective study, it is generally considered safe.
- Penicillin resistance, however, is a growing concern.

PENICILLIN G, BENZATHINE

Brand names: Bicillin LA, Pen-Di-Ben, Permapen

Drug classes: Antibiotic; Penicillin

Indications (what it is used for): Syphilis, group A streptococcus infection.

How it works: Kills bacteria by blocking cell wall synthesis.

Contraindications (reasons you shouldn't take it): Hypersensitivity to drug or class.

Possible side effects and warnings: Can cause low platelet and/or white blood cell counts, seizures, rash, Stevens-Johnson syndrome (a rare but serious skin reaction to medication), Jarisch-Herxheimer reaction (fever, chills, headache, muscle pain, and worsening of skin lesions caused by large quantities of toxins released into the body as bacteria die during treatment), fever, hemolytic anemia, kidney inflammation, nausea, vomiting, abdominal pain, diarrhea, and blood clots. Should be used with caution in women with kidney dysfunction, cephalosporin allergy, or seizure disorder.

How it can affect pregnant women: Benzathine penicillin G is the drug of choice when prolonged low levels of penicillin are required. It is given intramuscular only. There are no adequate reports or well-controlled studies in pregnant women. Benzathine penicillin G remains the drug of choice for syphilis during pregnancy. There is some concern that benzathine penicillin G may not prevent a late stage of syphilis when the brain is infected, but the overall risk appears low. If you have syphilis, it is important that your partner be treated to prevent spread of the disease. About 40% of patients experience a Jarisch-Herxheimer reaction after treatment. It is seen in 50% of treated patients with primary syphilis and about 90% of patients with secondary syphilis, and they should be watched closely during the first 48 hours.

How it can affect a developing embryo or fetus: There are no adequate reports or well-controlled studies in human fetuses. Most penicillins cross the human placenta to some extent. The currently recommended dose of benzathine penicillin G is effective for preventing or curing fetal syphilis. Azithromycin and ceftriaxone are potential alternatives for treating penicillin-allergic women, but there is insufficient information on their effectiveness in preventing fetal infection. Rodent studies of benzathine penicillin G are reassuring, revealing no evidence of birth defects or low birth weight despite the use of doses higher than those used clinically. However, animal studies are not necessarily good indicators of how a drug will behave in humans.

Breast-feeding: There are no adequate reports or well-controlled studies in nursing women. Only trace amounts of benzathine penicillin G enter human breast milk. It is generally considered compatible with breast-feeding.

Potential drug interactions: Interaction between the following medications and benzathine penicillin G has the potential to impact the effect of one or more of the drugs. In some instances the interaction can be dangerous or life-threatening and must be avoided: tetracycline, probenecid.

What the FDA says about use in pregnancy: Category B (see Appendix).

What the available evidence suggests about breast-feeding safety: Safe.

The bottom line for you:

- Benzathine penicillin G has been used for decades during pregnancy and while breast-feeding. Although there is little objective study, it is generally considered safe.
- Benzathine penicillin G remains the drug of choice for the treatment of syphilis before, during, and after pregnancy.

PENICILLIN G, PROCAINE

Brand names: Crysticillin AS, Duracillin AS, Pfizerpen AS, Provaine Penicillin, Wycillin

Drug classes: Antibiotic; Penicillin

Indications (what it is used for): Bacterial infection in the blood (moderate to severe), pneumococcal pneumonia, gonorrhea, syphilis.

How it works: Kills bacteria by blocking cell wall synthesis.

Contraindications (reasons you shouldn't take it): Hypersensitivity to drug or class.

Possible side effects and warnings: Can cause low platelet and/or low white blood cell counts, seizures, rash, Stevens-Johnson syndrome (a rare but serious skin reaction to medication), Jarisch-Herxheimer reaction (fever, chills, headache, muscle pain, and worsening of skin lesions caused by large quantities of toxins released into the body as bacteria die during treatment), poor heart function, hemolytic anemia, low kidney inflammation, nausea, vomiting, abdominal pain, diarrhea, fever, sterile abscess, and blood clots. Should be used with caution in women with kidney dysfunction, cephalosporin allergy, or seizure disorder. The medication should be administered only by intramuscular injection, not intravenously.

How it can affect pregnant women: Procaine penicillin G is a combination of benzylpenicillin and procaine, a local anesthetic. It is slowly absorbed after intramuscular injection and provides prolonged but low concentrations of benzylpenicillin. The addition of procaine reduces the pain and discomfort of a large intramuscular injection of penicillin. There are no adequate reports or well-controlled studies in pregnant women. Procaine penicillin G may be used in place of benzathine penicillin G for the treatment of syphilis, but it has no medical advantage.

How it can affect a developing embryo or fetus: There are no adequate reports or well-controlled studies in human fetuses. Most penicillins cross the human placenta to some extent. Procaine penicillin G should behave the same as benzathine penicillin G. The large clinical experience in humans is reassuring, as are rodent studies, which reveal no evidence of birth defects or low birth weight despite the use of doses higher than those used clinically. However, animal studies are not necessarily good indicators of how a drug will behave in humans.

Breast-feeding: There are no adequate reports or well-controlled studies in nursing women. Only trace amounts of procaine penicillin G enter human breast milk. It is generally considered compatible with breast-feeding.

Potential drug interactions: Interaction between the following medications and procaine penicillin G has the potential to impact the effect of one or more of the drugs. In some instances the interaction can be dangerous or life-threatening and must be avoided: bacteriostatic antibiotics (e.g., erythromycin, tetracycline), probenecid.

What the FDA says about use in pregnancy: Category B (see Appendix).

What the available evidence suggests about breast-feeding safety: Safe.

The bottom line for you:
- Procaine penicillin G has been used for decades during pregnancy and while breast-feeding. Although there is little objective study, it is generally considered safe.
- Penicillin resistance is a growing concern.

PENICILLIN VK
Brand names: Pen-Vee K, Veetids
Drug classes: Antibiotic; Penicillin
Indications (what it is used for): Group A streptococcus infection, pneumococcal pneumonia or rheumatic fever prophylaxis (prevention).
How it works: Kills bacteria by blocking cell wall synthesis.
Contraindications (reasons you shouldn't take it): Hypersensitivity to drug or class.
Possible side effects and warnings: Can cause low platelet and/or white blood cell counts, seizures, rash, Stevens-Johnson syndrome (a rare but serious skin reaction to medication), hemolytic anemia, kidney inflammation, nausea, vomiting, abdominal pain, diarrhea, bowel infection, and fever. Should be used with caution in women with kidney dysfunction, cephalosporin allergy, seizure disorder, or phenylketonuria (an inherited amino acid disorder).
How it can affect pregnant women: Penicillin VK is the oral form of penicillin. It is less active than benzylpenicillin and is used only when high tissue concentrations are unnecessary. There are no adequate reports or well-controlled studies in pregnant women. However, the long clinical experience is reassuring.
How it can affect a developing embryo or fetus: There are no adequate reports or well-controlled studies of penicillin VK in human fetuses. Most penicillins cross the human placenta to some extent. The large clinical experience is reassuring, as are rodent studies, which revealed no evidence of birth defects or low birth weight despite the use of doses

higher than those used clinically. However, animal studies are not necessarily good indicators of how a drug will behave in humans.

Breast-feeding: There are no adequate reports or well-controlled studies in nursing women. Only trace amounts of penicillin VK enter human breast milk. It is generally considered compatible with breast-feeding.

Potential drug interactions: Interaction between the following medications and penicillin VK has the potential to impact the effect of one or more of the drugs. In some instances the interaction can be dangerous or life-threatening and must be avoided: bacteriostatic antibiotics (e.g., erythromycin, tetracycline), probenecid.

What the FDA says about use in pregnancy: Category B (see Appendix).

What the available evidence suggests about breast-feeding safety: Safe.

The bottom line for you:

- Penicillin VK has been used for decades during pregnancy and while breast-feeding. Although there is little objective study, it is generally considered safe.
- Penicillin resistance is a growing concern.

PENTAMIDINE

Brand names: Nebupent, Pentam
Drug class: Antiprotozoal
Indications (what it is used for): *Pneumocystis carinii* pneumonia (PCP) prevention and treatment.
How it works: Unknown.
Contraindications (reasons you shouldn't take it): Hypersensitivity to drug or class.
Possible side effects and warnings: Can cause kidney failure, low platelet and/or white blood cell counts, low blood glucose, Stevens-Johnson syndrome (a rare but serious skin reaction to medication), bronchospasm, fatigue, nausea, heartburn, decreased appetite, fever, rash, cough, and dizziness. Should be used with caution in women with liver or kidney dysfunction, high or low blood pressure, low white blood cell count, or low blood glucose.

How it can affect pregnant women: There are no adequate reports or well-controlled studies of pentamidine in pregnant women. PCP is a rare type of pneumonia found typically in immunocompromised individuals with cancer or HIV and is resistant to common antibiotic agents. PCP during pregnancy can have a more aggressive course, with increased severity of illness and risk of death. Withholding appropriate PCP preventative treatment may adversely affect maternal and fetal outcomes.

How it can affect a developing embryo or fetus: There are no adequate reports or well-controlled studies in human fetuses. There are no published human reports of concern, and human placental transport of pentamidine is limited. Rodent studies are, in general, reassuring, revealing increased miscarriage but no birth defects or low birth weight. However, animal studies are not necessarily good indicators of how a drug will behave in humans.

Breast-feeding: There is no published data in nursing women. It is unknown whether pentamidine enters human breast milk. If infant formula is available, breast-feeding is usually not recommended when a mother is HIV positive because HIV can be transmitted to the newborn in the breast milk.

Potential drug interactions: No clinically relevant interactions identified.

What the FDA says about use in pregnancy: Category C (see Appendix).

What the available evidence suggests about breast-feeding safety: Not safe.

The bottom line for you:

- Pentamidine can be used during pregnancy. Withholding appropriate PCP prophylaxis can adversely affect maternal and fetal outcomes.
- If infant formula is available, breast-feeding is usually not recommended when a mother is HIV positive because HIV can be transmitted to the newborn in the breast milk.

PENTAZOCINE

Brand name: Talwin

Drug classes: Analgesic, narcotic; Narcotic agonist-antagonist

Indications (what it is used for): Moderate to severe pain, obstetric analgesia, anesthesia adjunct.

How it works: Binds opiate receptors, reducing the perception of pain.

Contraindications (reasons you shouldn't take it): Hypersensitivity to drug or class.

Possible side effects and warnings: Can cause addiction, respiratory depression, low blood pressure, seizures, low white blood cell count, nausea, vomiting, dizziness, euphoria, hallucinations, sedation, headache, constipation, blurred vision, pinpoint pupils, tremor, irritability, flushing, and itching. Should be used with caution in women with opiate dependence; head injury; liver, kidney, or lung dysfunction; or prior heart attack.

How it can affect pregnant women: Pentazocine is a potent painkiller comparable to morphine and meperidine. There are no adequate reports or well-controlled studies in pregnant women. Pentazocine is a poor choice for labor analgesia because it causes greater depression of breathing in laboring women than the alternatives. Some patients also receiving narcotics, including methadone, may experience withdrawal symptoms when given pentazocine, since it is a weak blocker of the opioid receptor.

How it can affect a developing embryo or fetus: There are no adequate reports or well-controlled studies in human fetuses. Pentazocine crosses the human placenta. The addictive combination of pentazocine and tripelennamine (Ts and Blues) remains a popular recreational drug. Newborns of women who use Ts and Blues throughout pregnancy have behavioral changes and withdrawal similar to those seen in methadone-addicted newborns. In general, rodent studies are reassuring, revealing no evidence of birth defects or low birth weight despite the use of doses higher than those used clinically. However, animal studies are not necessarily good indicators of how a drug will behave in humans.

Breast-feeding: There is no published data in nursing women. Although it is unknown whether pentazocine enters human breast milk, the clinical experience is reassuring.

Potential drug interactions: Ethanol (alcohol) should be avoided because of the potential for increasing central nervous system depressant effects.

What the FDA says about use in pregnancy: Category C (see Appendix).

What the available evidence suggests about breast-feeding safety: Unknown.

The bottom line for you:

- There are less-addictive but equally effective analgesics available for most indications during pregnancy and while breast-feeding.

PENTOBARBITAL

Brand names: Carbrital, Nembutal

Drug classes: Anticonvulsant; Anxiolytic; Barbiturate; Sedative

Indications (what it is used for): Sedation, sleeplessness, barbiturate coma.

How it works: Depresses the sensory and motor brain function.

Contraindications (reasons you shouldn't take it): Hypersensitivity to drug or class, decreased lung function, porphyria (a rare group of blood disorders).

Possible side effects and warnings: Can cause addiction, respiratory depression, suspension of breathing, Stevens-Johnson syndrome (a rare but serious skin reaction to medication), confusion, agitation, restlessness, lack of gross-muscle control, central nervous system depression, hallucinations, dizziness, slow heart rate, low blood pressure, headache, fainting, nausea, vomiting, constipation, and systemic lupus erythematosus (a chronic inflammatory disease in which the immune system attacks the body's own tissues and organs). Should be used with caution in women with liver dysfunction or a history of substance abuse or serious thoughts of suicide.

How it can affect pregnant women: Barbiturates produce mood alteration ranging from excitation to sedation to hypnosis and deep coma. Barbiturates are of limited value as a sleep aid since they lose effectiveness after 1–2 weeks. There are superior agents that have less effect on the sleep cycle. There are no adequate reports or well-controlled studies of pentobarbital in pregnant women.

How it can affect a developing embryo or fetus: There are no adequate reports or well-controlled studies in human fetuses. Pentobarbital rapidly crosses the human placenta. Its use during labor can cause breathing depression in the newborn. Preterm infants are particularly susceptible to this, and resuscitation equipment should be available. Chronic use during the third trimester can result in addicted newborns who have an extended withdrawal syndrome. Some studies suggest a connection between barbiturates and an increased risk of fetal abnormalities, although there are no such reports specifically for pentobarbital. The rodent studies are reassuring; however, animal studies are not necessarily good indicators of how a drug will behave in humans.

Breast-feeding: There are no adequate reports or well-controlled studies in nursing women. Only small amounts of pentobarbital enter human breast milk, and it is generally considered compatible with breast-feeding.

Potential drug interactions: Interaction between the following medications and pentobarbital has the potential to impact the effect of one or more of the drugs. In some instances the interaction can be dangerous or life-threatening and must be avoided: oral anticoagulants (e.g., acenocoumarol, dicumarol, phenprocoumon, warfarin); corticosteroids; griseofulvin; doxycycline; valproate and valproic acid; central nervous system depressants, including other sedatives or hypnotics, antihistamines, tranquilizers, or ethanol (alcohol); monamine oxidase inhibitors (MAOIs). Pretreatment with or concurrent use of phenobarbital may decrease the effect of estradiol by increasing its breakdown and clearance by the body. There are reports of women treated with antiepileptic drugs (e.g., phenobarbital) becoming pregnant while taking oral contraceptives; another form of contraception should be considered.

What the FDA says about use in pregnancy: Category D (see Appendix).

What the available evidence suggests about breast-feeding safety: Safe.

The bottom line for you:

- There are few indications for the use of pentobarbital during pregnancy or while breast-feeding. For all but an induced coma after brain trauma, there are other agents with superior safety profiles during pregnancy.
- Pentobarbital is safe for use while breast-feeding.

PERMETHRIN TOPICAL

Brand names: Acticin, Elimite, Nix

Drug classes: Antiparasitic; Dermatologic; Scabicide/pediculicide

Indications (what it is used for): Scabies (mites), body lice.

How it works: Disrupts nerve cells in the parasite.

Contraindications (reasons you shouldn't take it): Hypersensitivity to drug or class.

Possible side effects and warnings: Can cause burning, numbness, tingling, itching, and redness.

How it can affect pregnant women: Permethrin is applied topically, and the amount absorbed after a single application appears to be less than 2%. What is absorbed is rapidly metabolized to inactive metabolites (breakdown products) that are excreted primarily in urine. There are no adequate reports or well-controlled studies in pregnant women. Permethrin improves maternal outcomes in less-developed countries where infection is more common, especially when used as part of a broad strategy such as insecticide-incorporating nets.

How it can affect a developing embryo or fetus: There are no adequate reports or well-controlled studies in human fetuses. It is unknown whether

permethrin crosses the human placenta. Recent large case series of patients are reassuring. It is unlikely that the maternal blood concentration reaches a clinically relevant level for the embryo or fetus. Rodent studies are reassuring, revealing no evidence of birth defects or growth restriction despite the use of doses higher than those used clinically. However, animal studies are not necessarily good indicators of how a drug will behave in humans.

Breast-feeding: There are no adequate reports or well-controlled studies in nursing women. Permethrin is excreted into human breast milk, but considering that the medication is applied topically and little is absorbed into the mother's blood, it is unlikely that a clinically relevant blood concentration would reach the newborn.

Potential drug interactions: No clinically relevant interactions identified.

What the FDA says about use in pregnancy: Category B (see Appendix).

What the available evidence suggests about breast-feeding safety: Likely safe.

The bottom line for you:

- Permethrin appears safe and effective for use during pregnancy and while breast-feeding.

PERPHENAZINE

Brand names: Trilifan, Trilafon

Drug classes: Antiemetic; Antipsychotic; Antivertigo agent; Phenothiazine

Indications (what it is used for): Psychosis, severe nausea and vomiting.

How it works: Unknown.

Contraindications (reasons you shouldn't take it): Hypersensitivity to drug or class, central nervous system depression, blood disorders, bone marrow depression, liver disease, coma, brain damage.

Possible side effects and warnings: Can cause cardiac arrest, rapid heart rate, seizures, liver toxicity, hemolytic anemia, low platelet and/or white blood cell counts, neuroleptic malignant syndrome (life-threatening muscle rigidity, fever, vital sign insta-

bility, and cognitive changes such as delirium), extrapyramidal effects (various movement disorders, usually the result of taking dopamine antagonists like antipsychotic drugs), involuntary movements like tics, sedation, drowsiness, dry mouth, blurred vision, nausea, vomiting, rash, and loss of appetite.

How it can affect pregnant women: Perphenazine is commonly combined in the U.S. with amitriptyline (Triavil, Etrafon). It is a first-generation antipsychotic agent, and there may be more effective alternatives with similar or better safety profiles for use during pregnancy. There are no adequate reports or well-controlled studies in pregnant women.

How it can affect a developing embryo or fetus: There are no adequate reports or well-controlled studies in human fetuses. It is unknown whether perphenazine crosses the human placenta. Some researchers have noted subtle behavioral abnormalities in newborns exposed to perphenazine. Rodent birth defects studies apparently have not been conducted.

Breast-feeding: There are no adequate reports or well-controlled studies in nursing women. Perphenazine is excreted into human breast milk at levels too low to be clinically significant.

Potential drug interactions: Some 10% of the Caucasian population are so-called poor metabolizers. They have higher plasma concentrations of antipsychotic drugs at usual doses, which may leave them more susceptible to side effects and toxicity. Use of other drugs that inhibit CYP2D6 may acutely increase plasma concentrations of antipsychotics, which is of particular concern with poor metabolizers. Among these are tricyclic antidepressants (TCAs) and selective serotonin reuptake inhibitors (SSRIs) (e.g., fluoxetine, paroxetine, sertraline).

What the FDA says about use in pregnancy: Category C (see Appendix).

What the available evidence suggests about breast-feeding safety: Probably safe.

The bottom line for you:

- There are alternative agents with which there is more experience during pregnancy.

- Perphenazine is probably safe for use while breast-feeding.

PHENDIMETRAZINE

Brand names: Adipost, Anorex, Appecon, Bontril, Cam-Metrazine, Dital, Melfiat, Metra, Obalan, Obezine, P.D.M., Phenazine, Phendiet, Phendimetrazine Bitartrate, Plegine, Prelu-2, PT 105, Statobex, X-Trozine

Drug classes: Anorexiant; Central nervous system (CNS) stimulant

Indications (what it is used for): Obesity.

How it works: Stimulates the brain to diminish appetite.

Contraindications (reasons you shouldn't take it): Hypersensitivity to drug or class, substance abuse, advanced hardening of the arteries, symptomatic cardiovascular disease, moderate or severe high blood pressure, high thyroid hormone levels, glaucoma, use of other central nervous system stimulants, agitation.

Possible side effects and warnings: Can cause restlessness, sleeplessness, agitation, flushing, tremor, sweating, dizziness, headache, psychosis, blurred vision, rapid heart rate, high blood pressure, dry mouth, nausea, diarrhea, constipation, stomach pain, urinary frequency, painful or difficult urination, and changes in sex drive. Should be used with caution in women with mild high blood pressure or diabetes.

How it can affect pregnant women: Phendimetrazine is similar to amphetamine. Obese adults given dietary instruction and treated with "anorectic" drugs lost a fraction of a pound more in short-term trials compared to those treated with placebo and diet. Addiction is a risk with phendimetrazine. There is no published data with phendimetrazine in pregnancy and no indications for its use.

How it can affect a developing embryo or fetus: There are no adequate reports or well-controlled studies in human fetuses. It is unknown whether phendimetrazine crosses the human placenta; simi-

lar compounds do. Rodent birth defects studies have apparently not been performed.

Breast-feeding: There are no published studies in nursing women. It is unknown whether phendimetrazine enters human breast milk.

Potential drug interactions: Interaction between the following medications and phendimetrazine has the potential to impact the effect of one or more of the drugs. In some instances the interaction can be dangerous or life-threatening and must be avoided: monoamine oxidase inhibitors (MAOIs), central nervous system depressants.

What the FDA says about use in pregnancy: Category C (see Appendix).

What the available evidence suggests about breast-feeding safety: Unknown.

The bottom line for you:
- There are no indications for the use of phendimetrazine during pregnancy or while breast-feeding.
- Phendimetrazine is of limited value for the treatment of obesity.

PHENELZINE

Brand name: Nardil

Drug classes: Antidepressant; Monamine inhibitor antidepressant

Indications (what it is used for): Depression, binging and purging.

How it works: Inhibits monoamine oxidase (an enzyme involved with neurotransmitter breakdown) to alter mood.

Contraindications (reasons you shouldn't take it): Hypersensitivity to drug or class, congestive heart failure, high blood pressure, pheochromocytoma (adrenal gland tumor), liver disease, general anesthesia or cocaine use within 10 days, bupropion use.

Possible side effects and warnings: Can cause life-threatening high blood pressure, bleeding in the brain, seizures, depressed mood, respiratory or central nervous system depression, coma, low white blood cell count, lupuslike syndrome, headache, dizziness, weakness, tremor, constipation, dry mouth, heartburn, liver dysfunction, weight gain, low blood pressure when upright, and swelling.

How it can affect pregnant women: Depression is common during and after pregnancy but often goes unrecognized and untreated. Depression can be made worse by pregnancy or delivery, and suicide is a not uncommon cause of maternal death. Pregnancy is not a reason to discontinue antidepressant drugs if the medication is effective and needed. A woman being treated for depression who becomes pregnant should not discontinue medication abruptly on her own but rather discuss her treatment and condition with her medical provider. Pregnancy may increase the dose needed to be effective, and women with a history of depression have a higher rate of recurrence after delivery. Phenelzine is often effective in treating depression characterized as atypical or neurotic. People with this condition frequently have anxiety and depression mixed with phobic or hypochondriacal features. There are no adequate reports or well-controlled studies of phenelzine in pregnant women. Most publications consist of case reports or small series of patients. Well-documented and potentially fatal interactions between monoamine oxidase inhibitors (MAOIs) such as phenelzine and opioids, notably meperidine, require that labor analgesia be well planned in advance for anyone being treated with phenelzine.

How it can affect a developing embryo or fetus: There are no adequate reports or well-controlled studies in human fetuses. It is unknown whether phenelzine crosses the human placenta. As for most psychotropic drugs, using one medication at the smallest effective quantity given in divided doses to reduce peak blood levels may minimize any potential risk. Rodent birth defects studies have apparently not been performed.

Breast-feeding: There is no published data in nursing women. It is unknown whether phenelzine enters human breast milk.

Potential drug interactions: Nonselective MAOIs such as phenelzine may cause serious, sometimes fatal, reactions if combined with serotonergic agents (e.g., citalopram, dexfenfluramine, fluoxetine, fluvoxamine, paroxetine, sertraline, venlafaxine).

What the FDA says about use in pregnancy: Category C (see Appendix).

What the available evidence suggests about breast-feeding safety: Unknown.

The bottom line for you:

- Phenelzine should be used during pregnancy and breast-feeding only if required for the mother's health and safety.

PHENOBARBITAL

Brand names: Barbita, Dormiral, Luminaletten, Luminal Sodium, Phenobarbital Sodium, Phenobarbitone, Sedofen, Solfoton

Drug classes: Anticonvulsant; Barbiturate; Preanesthetic; Sedative/hypnotic

Indications (what it is used for): Seizure disorder, status epilepticus (constant or near-constant seizures), sedation.

How it works: Nonselectively depresses brain's sensory and motor activities.

Contraindications (reasons you shouldn't take it): Hypersensitivity to drug or class, history of porphyria (a rare group of blood disorders) or liver or respiratory dysfunction.

Possible side effects and warnings: Can cause respiratory depression, addiction, erythema multiforme and Stevens-Johnson syndrome (both skin disorders), hepatitis, angioedema (sudden swelling of the skin layers), megaloblastic anemia, various blood diseases, thrombotic thrombocytopenia (a serious clotting disorder), drowsiness, lethargy, nausea, vomiting, rash, pain, blood clots, swelling, and tissue death. Should be used with caution in women with kidney failure, depression, or serious thoughts of suicide.

How it can affect pregnant women: Less time is spent in dream (REM) sleep during barbiturate-induced sleep compared to normal sleep. Stopping the drug abruptly can trigger increased dreaming, nightmares, and/or sleeplessness. There are no adequate reports or well-controlled studies of phenobarbital in pregnant women. Several investigations indicate that clearance (how rapidly the body processes the drug) is increased during pregnancy and that periodic dose increases are necessary to maintain the same level of effectiveness.

Most pregnancies are uneventful in women with epilepsy, and most babies are delivered healthy. However, women on medication for a seizure disorder should plan their pregnancies, discuss the optimal medication with their neurologist, and begin appropriate supplemental folate therapy before conception (4 mg per day) to minimize the risk of birth defects. The risks of birth defects associated with antiseizure medications must be weighed against the risks of continued seizures to both the mother and fetus. Women who become pregnant during treatment should not stop treatment on their own but rather meet quickly with their doctor before making a decision.

How it can affect a developing embryo or fetus: There are no adequate reports or well-controlled studies of phenobarbital in human fetuses. Barbiturates readily cross the human placental barrier and are distributed throughout fetal tissues, with levels approximately equal to those of the mother. Withdrawal symptoms can occur in newborns exposed to barbiturates throughout the third trimester. Reports of healthy women who did not attempt to withdraw from barbiturates (and were probably taking them for sedation) showed no increase in adverse pregnancy outcomes. It is not clear whether barbiturate use is associated with a higher than expected incidence of birth defects (e.g., cleft lip or palate, heart malformations) as some anticonvulsants are. Phenobarbital exposure during pregnancy does not alter the neurodevelopmental outcome of preterm infants when tested at 18–22 months of age. Vitamin K has been recommended during the last month of pregnancy in women taking some enzyme-inducing agents such as oxcarbazepine, carbamazepine, phenobarbital, phenytoin, and topiramate under the theory it will reduce the risk of newborn bleeding. However, there is not good evidence that the risk is increased and the incidence of newborn bleeding does not appear to be decreased by maternal treatment with vitamin K.

Breast-feeding: Phenobarbital enters human breast milk, and the amount is altered when multiple drugs are used at the same time, especially early in breast-feeding. The use of phenobarbital while breast-feeding is controversial because of the potential for newborns to take a long time to eliminate the drug from their systems. Infant sedation is possible, and the child should be observed closely. Monitoring the blood levels of the drug in the newborn may be advisable if phenobarbital is continued during breast-feeding.

Potential drug interactions: Interaction between the following medications and phenobarbital has the potential to impact the effect of one or more of the drugs. In some instances the interaction can be dangerous or life-threatening and must be avoided: oral anticoagulants (e.g., acenocoumarol, dicumarol, phenprocoumon, warfarin); corticosteroids; griseofulvin; doxycycline; phenytoin; valproate and valproic acid; other central nervous system depressants, including other sedatives or hypnotics, antihistamines, tranquilizers, or ethanol (alcohol). There are reports of patients treated with antiepileptic drugs (e.g., phenobarbital) who became pregnant using oral contraceptives. An alternate contraceptive method should be considered.

What the FDA says about use in pregnancy: Category D (see Appendix).

What the available evidence suggests about breast-feeding safety: Safe with close observation of the newborn.

The bottom line for you:

- Phenobarbital may be used during pregnancy and while breast-feeding when the maternal benefit justifies the potential risk to the embryo, fetus, or newborn.

PHENSUXIMIDE

Brand name: Milontin
Drug classes: Anorexiant; Anticonvulsant
Indications (what it is used for): Absence (petit mal) seizures.
How it works: Unknown.
Contraindications (reasons you shouldn't take it): Hypersensitivity to drug or class.
Possible side effects and warnings: Can cause itching, various blood diseases, bone marrow suppression, sore throat, fever, liver dysfunction, muscle weakness, nausea, vomiting, loss of appetite, drowsiness, dizziness, lack of gross-muscle control, headache, dreamlike state, lethargy, skin eruptions, erythema multiforme and Stevens-Johnson syndrome (both skin disorders), red rashes, and hair loss. Should be used with caution in women with liver or kidney dysfunction, or systemic lupus erythematosus (a chronic inflammatory disease in which the immune system attacks the body's own tissues and organs).
How it can affect pregnant women: Women on medication for a seizure disorder should plan their pregnancies (when possible), discuss the optimal medication with their neurologist, and begin appropriate supplemental folate therapy before conception (4 mg per day) to minimize the risk of birth defects. The risks of birth defects associated with antiseizure medications must be weighed against the risks of continued seizures to both the mother and fetus. Women who become pregnant during treatment should not stop treatment on their own but rather meet quickly with their doctor before making a decision.

Phensuximide suppresses the lapse of consciousness common in petit mal seizures. There is no published data with phensuximide during pregnancy. There is more experience with ethosuximide, which is probably the drug of first choice for the treatment of absence seizures. It may be possible to stop phensuximide use during pregnancy if the severity of the seizures is mild and the frequency rare. However, even minor seizures pose some hazard to the embryo and fetus.

How it can affect a developing embryo or fetus: There are no adequate reports or well-controlled studies in human fetuses. It is unknown whether phensuximide crosses the human placenta. It is difficult to separate the impact of phensuximide from other medications usually used with it as well as the impact of the seizures themselves on the embryo or fetus. The best estimate is that the risk is similar to that of ethosuximide. Limited rodent studies are reassuring.
Breast-feeding: There is no published data in nursing women. It is unknown whether phensuximide enters human breast milk.
Potential drug interactions: May interact with other antiepileptic drugs.
What the FDA says about use in pregnancy: Category D (see Appendix).
What the available evidence suggests about breast-feeding safety: Unknown.
The bottom line for you:
- Phensuximide should be used during pregnancy and while breast-feeding only when the maternal benefit justifies the potential risk to the fetus, embryo, or newborn.
- Ethosuximide is probably the drug of first choice for treating absence seizures.

PHENTERMINE

Brand names: Adipex-P, Dapex-37.5, Fastin, Obe-Nix, Oby-Cap, Oby-Trim, Ona-Mast, Panbesyl, Phentercot, Phentride, T-Diet, Teramine, Tora, Umi-Pex 30, Zantryl
Drug classes: Anorexiant; Central nervous system stimulant
Indications (what it is used for): Obesity.
How it works: Activates sympathomimetic nervous system receptors.
Contraindications (reasons you shouldn't take it): Hypersensitivity to drug or class, severe high

blood pressure, symptomatic cardiovascular disease, use of monoamine oxidase inhibitors (MAOIs) within 14 days, glaucoma, agitated states, or a history of substance abuse.

Possible side effects and warnings: Can cause high blood pressure, sleeplessness, palpitations, dry mouth, headache, dizziness, excitation, constipation, diarrhea, and hives.

How it can affect pregnant women: Phentermine is similar to amphetamine. It is used only for short-term therapy, and the associated weight loss is typically modest. Resistance develops to the effects of phentermine and all related drugs. Serious heart valve disease developed in some women taking a combination of phentermine and fenfluramine (Fen-Phen). The latter drug was withdrawn from the U.S. market, but it is not definitive which drug was at fault. There are no adequate reports or well-controlled studies of phentermine in pregnant women, and there is probably no indication for its use during either pregnancy or while breast-feeding. In one lower-quality study, the rate of gestational diabetes was greater in the women who took phentermine and fenfluramine during the first trimester.

How it can affect a developing embryo or fetus: There are no adequate reports or well-controlled studies in human fetuses. It is unknown whether phentermine crosses the human placenta, although similar medications do. There was no significant increase in miscarriage or major birth defects in almost 100 women who took phentermine and fenfluramine during pregnancy. Rodent birth defects studies have not been performed. Altered nerve function and thickening of a particular heart valve were observed in the pups of rats exposed to the combination during gestation. However, animal studies are not necessarily good indicators of how a drug will behave in humans.

Breast-feeding: There is no published data in nursing women. It is unknown whether phentermine enters human breast milk.

Potential drug interactions: Use with ethanol (alcohol) may result in an adverse drug interaction.

What the FDA says about use in pregnancy: Category X (see Appendix).

What the available evidence suggests about breast-feeding safety: Unknown.

The bottom line for you:

- There are no legitimate indications for phentermine use during pregnancy or while breast-feeding.

PHENYLEPHRINE

Brand names: Ah-Chew D, Ak-Dilate, Dilatair, Efrin, Fenilefrina, I-Phrine, Minims, Mydfrin, Neo-Synephrine, Neofrin, Ocu-Phrin, Phenylephrine HCl, Pupiletto-Forte, Ricobid-D, Spectro-Dilate, Spectro-Nephrine, Storz-Fen, Sudafed PE

Drug classes: Adrenergic agonist; Alpha-agonist; Inotrope; Pressor; Sympathomimetic

Indications (what it is used for): Shock, nasal congestion, low blood pressure after spinal or epidural anesthesia.

How it works: Activates the alpha-adrenergic receptors, causing the blood vessels to constrict.

Contraindications (reasons you shouldn't take it): Hypersensitivity to drug or class, high blood pressure, ventricular rapid heart rate.

Possible side effects and warnings: Can cause palpitations, irregular heart rate, heart attack, asthma exacerbation, high blood pressure, headache, tissue death, and excitability. Should be used with caution in women with diabetes or thyroid disease.

How it can affect pregnant women: Allergic runny nose affects about 1 in 3 of reproductive-age women. Almost 200 over-the-counter preparations in the U.S. contain a sympathomimetic agent such as phenylephrine as their active ingredient. Phenylephrine should be considered a second-line agent behind first- and second-generation antihistamines for the treatment of a stuffy nose during pregnancy. It is popular for the prevention of low blood pressure after epidural or spinal anesthesia, especially when ephedrine is contraindicated (cannot be used) (e.g., if there is maternal heart disease).

How it can affect a developing embryo or fetus: There are no adequate reports or well-controlled studies in human fetuses. It is unknown whether phenylephrine crosses the human placenta. Pseudoephedrine is associated with bowel blockage, but the same has yet to be reported for phenylephrine. The combination of pseudoephedrine, phenylephrine, and phenylpropanolamine (sometimes sold together though no longer available in the US) may be associated with distal limb reduction (poor development of the hands or feet) and should be avoided in the first half of pregnancy.

Breast-feeding: There is no published data in breast-feeding women. It is unknown whether phenylephrine enters human breast milk. However, considering the frequency of use and dose, it seems unlikely that breast-feeding newborns would ingest a clinically relevant amount.

Potential drug interactions: Interaction between the following medications and phenylephrine has the potential to impact the effect of one or more of the drugs. In some instances the interaction can be dangerous or life-threatening and must be avoided: use of a monoamine oxidase inhibitor (MAOI) within 21 days, tricyclic antidepressants (TCAs).

What the FDA says about use in pregnancy: Category C (see Appendix).

What the available evidence suggests about breast-feeding safety: Likely safe.

The bottom line for you:

- A first- or second-generation antihistamine is preferred for the relief of nasal congestion during pregnancy.
- Alone or in combination, pseudoephedrine, phenylephrine, and phenylpropanolamine should be avoided in the first half of pregnancy.
- Phenylephrine is likely safe to use while breast-feeding.

PHENYLPROPANOLAMINE
Not available in the U.S.

Brand names: Kleer, Propan, Rhindecon
Drug classes: Adrenergic agonist; Decongestant
Indications (what it is used for): Nasal decongestant.

How it works: Activates the alpha-adrenergic receptors, causing the blood vessels to constrict.

Contraindications (reasons you shouldn't take it): Severe hypersensitivity to drug or class, severe high blood pressure, severe coronary artery disease, concurrent use of monoamine oxidase inhibitors (MAOIs).

Possible side effects and warnings: Can cause rapid heart rate, irregular heart rate, palpitations, headache, dizziness, nausea, vomiting, fear, anxiety, weakness, pallor, sleeplessness, hallucinations, central nervous system depression, stroke, and cardiovascular collapse. Should be used with caution in women with high blood pressure, diabetes, ischemic heart disease (reduced blood supply to the coronary arteries of the heart), increased eye pressure, high thyroid hormone levels, or hyperreactivity to ephedrine.

How it can affect pregnant women: More than 170 over-the-counter medications contain a sympathomimetic agent such as phenylpropanolamine as their active ingredient. An estimated 5 billion doses of phenylpropanolamine are taken each year. There are no adequate reports or well-controlled studies in pregnant women. The authors of one small but high-quality study concluded that phenylpropanolamine was effective during pregnancy for the treatment of allergic runny nose. However, irregular heart rate has been reported during pregnancy and intracranial hemorrhage has been reported after delivery. In 2005, the FDA required the removal of phenylpropanolamine from over-the-counter products because of an increased risk of stroke. The agency estimated that it caused 200–500 strokes annually among users age 18 to 49.

How it can affect a developing embryo or fetus: There are no adequate reports or well-controlled studies in human fetuses. It is unknown whether

phenylpropanolamine crosses the human placenta. Large population studies are reassuring, finding no increased rate of adverse pregnancy outcome. Rodent reproduction and birth defects studies have not been conducted. A similar medication, pseudoephedrine, is associated with intestinal blockages that require surgical repair after birth, but similar findings have not been reported for phenylpropanolamine. Other studies suggest a relationship between first-trimester use and gastroschisis (the infant's intestines stick out of a hole in the abdominal wall), which requires surgical repair after birth. The combination of pseudo-ephedrine, phenylephrine, and phenylpropanolamine (sometimes sold together though no longer available in the US) may be associated with distal limb reduction (poor development of the hands or feet) and should be avoided in the first half of pregnancy.

Breast-feeding: There are no adequate reports or well-controlled studies in nursing women. It is unknown whether phenylpropanolamine enters human breast milk.

Potential drug interactions: Interaction between the following medications and phenylpropanol-amine has the potential to impact the effect of one or more of the drugs. In some instances the interaction can be dangerous or life-threatening and must be avoided: monoamine oxidase inhibitors (MAOIs), blood-pressure-lowering medications.

What the FDA says about use in pregnancy: Category C (see Appendix).

What the available evidence suggests about breast-feeding safety: Unknown.

The bottom line for you:

- Phenylpropanolamine is no longer available in the U.S. because of its possible risks to mother and fetus, but it is widely sold in other countries.
- A first- or second-generation antihistamine is preferred for the relief of nasal congestion during pregnancy and while breast-feeding.
- There is not enough information to make a judgment on safety while breast-feeding.

PHENYTOIN

Brand names: Aladdin, Aleviatin, Dantoin, Decatona, Dilantin, Ditoin, Ditomed, Epilantin-E, Eptoin, Hidantoina, Hydantol, Neosidantoina, Phenilep, Zentropil

Drug classes: Anticonvulsant; Hydantoin

Indications (what it is used for): Seizure disorder, status epilepticus (constant or near-constant seizures).

How it works: Regulates motor nerve activity to make it more difficult for seizures to occur.

Contraindications (reasons you shouldn't take it): Hypersensitivity to drug or class, heart conduction abnormalities (with IV administration), Stokes-Adams syndrome (insufficient blood flow to the brain due to an abnormal heart rate causing fainting) (with IV administration).

Possible side effects and warnings: When administered orally for a long period of time, can cause liver toxicity, hepatitis, overgrowth of the gums, bone marrow suppression, megaloblastic anemia, exfoliative dermatitis, Stevens-Johnson syndrome and toxic epidermal necrolysis (rare but serious skin disorders), hypersensitivity syndrome (acute, potentially life-threatening reaction to the medication), lymphoma, systemic lupus erythematosus (a chronic inflammatory disease in which the immune system attacks the body's own tissues and organs), bone breakdown, nausea, vomiting, rash, lack of gross-muscle control, slurred speech, dizziness, confusion, drowsiness, constipation, headache, sleeplessness, tremor, high blood glucose, and coarse facial features. When administered intravenously, can cause fibrillation, low blood pressure, cardiovascular collapse, and tissue necrosis. Should be used with caution in women with liver or kidney dysfunction, low blood pressure, cardiovascular disease, diabetes, or thyroid disease, or who use alcohol.

How it can affect pregnant women: Women on medication for a seizure disorder should (when possible) plan their pregnancies, discuss the optimal

398 | The Complete Guide to Medications During Pregnancy and Breast-feeding

medication with their neurologist, and begin appropriate supplemental folate therapy before conception (4 mg per day) to minimize the risk of birth defects. The risks of birth defects associated with antiseizure medications must be weighed against the risks of continued seizures to both the mother and fetus. Women who become pregnant during treatment should not stop treatment on their own but rather meet quickly with their doctor before making a decision.

Phenytoin is a first-generation enzyme-inducing anticonvulsant. Drug clearance (how fast the medication is processed and eliminated by the body) is increased during pregnancy, with levels declining to half that of prepregnancy if the dose is not adjusted. Phenytoin may interfere with the effect of corticosteroids, coumarin, digitoxin, doxycycline, furosemide, quinidine, rifampin, theophylline, and vitamin D. Phenytoin may decrease the effect of estrogen and oral contraceptives. Either a higher-dose oral contraceptive or a second contraceptive method is recommended for women on phenytoin.

How it can affect a developing embryo or fetus: There are no adequate reports or well-controlled studies in human fetuses. Phenytoin crosses the human placenta, and the risk of major birth defects in children of women taking enzyme-inducing anticonvulsants is double that of women not taking such drugs. The risk increases with rising doses of phenytoin and when multiple medications are used together. Associated birth defects include congenital heart defects, cleft palate, and underdevelopment of either the face or digits (both of which correlate with neurodevelopmental damage). Vitamin K has been recommended during the last month of pregnancy in women taking some enzyme-inducing agents such as oxcarbazepine, carbamazepine, phenobarbital, phenytoin, and topiramate under the theory it will reduce the risk of newborn bleeding. However, there is not good evidence that the risk is increased and the incidence of newborn bleeding does not appear to be decreased by maternal treatment with vitamin K. As with most psychotropic drugs, the risks may be minimized by using one drug at the smallest effective quantity given in divided doses to reduce the peaks of medication in the blood.

Breast-feeding: There are no adequate reports or well-controlled studies in nursing women. The transfer of phenytoin into human breast milk appears relatively low, and it is generally considered safe for breast-feeding.

Potential drug interactions: Interaction between the following medications and phenytoin has the potential to impact the effect of one or more of the drugs. In some instances the interaction can be dangerous or life-threatening and must be avoided: amiodarone, chloramphenicol, chlordiazepoxide, diazepam, dicumarol, disulfiram, estrogens, ethanol, H2 antagonists, halothane, isoniazide, methylphenidate, phenothiazines, phenylbutazone, salicylates, succinimides, sulfonamides, tolbutamide, trazodone, carbamazepine, chronic ethanol (alcohol) abuse, reserpine, sucralfate, phenobarbital, valproate and valproic acid, corticosteroids, coumarin anticoagulants, digitoxin, doxycycline, furosemide, oral contraceptives, quinidine, rifampin, theophylline, vitamin D.

What the FDA says about use in pregnancy: Category D (see Appendix).

What the available evidence suggests about breast-feeding safety: Safe.

The bottom line for you:

- Phenytoin may be used during pregnancy when the maternal benefit justifies the potential risk to the embryo or newborn.
- As with most psychotropic drugs, the risks may be minimized by using only one medication and the smallest effective quantity given in divided doses.
- The risk of birth defects may be decreased by folate supplementation.
- Phenytoin is considered safe for use while breast-feeding.

PHYTONADIONE

Brand names: Aqua-Mephyton, Konakion, Mephyton, Vitamin K$_1$

Drug classes: Bleeding disorder; Vitamin/mineral

Indications (what it is used for): Low levels of prothrombin (a crucial clotting factor) and vitamin K deficiency.

How it works: Essential for liver production of the clotting factors II, VII, IX, X.

Contraindications (reasons you shouldn't take it): Hypersensitivity to drug or class, congenitally low prothrombin.

Possible side effects and warnings: Can cause resistance to anticoagulants, low blood pressure, taste changes, flushing, sweating, shortness of breath, swelling, and injection site hematoma (bruise) or pain. Should be used with caution in women anticoagulated with heparin.

How it can affect pregnant women: A low prothrombin level causes poor blood clotting and as a result easy or excess bleeding. Vitamin K production requires normal bacteria in the gut, and broad-spectrum antibiotic therapy or bowel disease can destroy the normal bacteria. The vitamin K products listed are not identical and have some pharmacologic differences. There are no adequate reports or well-controlled studies of phytonadione in pregnant women.

How it can affect a developing embryo or fetus: There are no adequate reports or well-controlled studies in human fetuses. Although phytonadione crosses the human placenta, the amount is likely too small to dramatically alter the fetal level of vitamin K. Birth defects studies apparently have not been conducted. Phytonadione is often given to newborns in hopes of preventing brain hemorrhage associated with some anticonvulsants, although there is little evidence that it is effective.

Breast-feeding: Phytonadione is concentrated in human breast milk and may be useful as a supplement for a preterm breast-feeding newborn who is at increased risk of brain bleeding. It is generally considered compatible with breast-feeding.

Potential drug interactions: No clinically relevant interactions identified.

What the FDA says about use in pregnancy: Category C (see Appendix).

What the available evidence suggests about breast-feeding safety: Safe.

The bottom line for you:

- Phytonadione is considered safe for use during pregnancy and while breast-feeding.

PILOCARPINE

Brand names: Adsorbocarpine, Akarpine, I-Pilopine, Isopto Carpine, Ocu-Carpine, Pilokair, Pilopine HS, Pilosol, Pilostat, Salagen, Spectro-Pilo, Storzine

Drug classes: Cholinergic; Miotic; Ophthalmic

Indications (what it is used for): Dry mouth due to Sjögren's syndrome (immune system disorder characterized by dry eyes and mouth) or head/neck cancer, glaucoma (open-angle and acute angle-closure).

How it works: Blocks the activation of cholinergic nerves, which normally release saliva or if placed in the eye, constricts the pupil.

Contraindications (reasons you shouldn't take it): Hypersensitivity to drug or class, acute asthma, narrow-angle glaucoma, inflammation of the iris, severe liver dysfunction.

Possible side effects and warnings: When ingested, can cause fluid in the lungs, visual impairment, impaired fertility, slow or rapid heart rate, low or high blood pressure, gallbladder inflammation or spasm, shock, sweating, chills, nausea, vomiting, flushing, runny nose, dizziness, weakness, diarrhea, headache, heartburn, swelling, tremor, difficulty swallowing, and voice changes. Should be used with caution in women with moderate liver dysfunction, asthma, chronic obstructive lung disease (COPD), chronic bronchitis, gallbladder disease, kidney stones, or psychiatric illness.

How it can affect pregnant women: There is no published data with pilocarpine in pregnancy, probably because it is used at low concentrations on the eye. It is unlikely application to the eye results in measurable levels in the mother's blood.

How it can affect a developing embryo or fetus: There are no adequate reports or well-controlled studies in human fetuses. It is unknown whether pilocarpine crosses the human placenta. It is unlikely application to the eye results in measurable levels in the mother's blood. Only scant amounts cross the rat placenta.

Breast-feeding: There is no published data during breast-feeding. It is unknown whether pilocarpine enters human breast milk. It is unlikely application to the eye results in measurable levels in the mother's blood or breast milk.

Potential drug interactions: Interaction between the following medications and pilocarpine has the potential to impact the effect of one or more of the drugs. In some instances the interaction can be dangerous or life-threatening and must be avoided: beta-adrenergic antagonists, drugs with parasympathomimetic effects, drugs with anticholinergic effects, atropine, inhaled ipratropium.

What the FDA says about use in pregnancy: Category C (see Appendix).

What the available evidence suggests about breast-feeding safety: Safe for opthalamic use; unknown when taken orally.

The bottom line for you:
- Pilocarpine is considered safe during pregnancy and while breast-feeding when applied to the eyes; there is no data to determine safety when used orally.

PIMECROLIMUS, TOPICAL

Brand name: Elidel
Drug classes: Dermatologic; Immunosuppressant
Indications (what it is used for): Allergic dermatitis.
How it works: Inhibits the activation of the white blood cell type that causes the inflammation.
Contraindications (reasons you shouldn't take it): Hypersensitivity to drug or class, local infection, Netherton syndrome (A genetic skin disease that causes fishlike scales).

Possible side effects and warnings: Can cause viral reactivation (e.g., herpes or varicella viruses that can live silently in nerves), swollen lymph nodes, burning skin, headache, cough, sore throat, skin redness and itching. Should be used with caution in women with HIV, varicella (chickenpox) virus, or herpes virus infections, or who have frequent sun exposure.

How it can affect pregnant women: There is no published data with pimecrolimus in pregnancy. However, a low concentration is applied topically, suggesting that any maternal blood level will be low.

How it can affect a developing embryo or fetus: There are no adequate reports or well-controlled studies in human fetuses. It is unknown whether pimecrolimus crosses the human placenta. Considering the dose and that it is applied topically to a small surface area, it is unlikely that the maternal systemic concentration reaches a clinically relevant level. Rodent studies are reassuring, revealing no evidence of toxicity, birth defects, or low birth weight despite the use of doses higher than those used clinically. However, animal studies are not necessarily good indicators of how a drug will behave in humans.

Breast-feeding: There are no published reports of pimecrolimus use during breast-feeding. It is unknown whether it enters human breast milk. Considering the dose and that it is applied topically to a small surface area, it is unlikely that the medication would reach a clinically relevant level in the breast milk.

Potential drug interactions: Interaction between the following medications and pimecrolimus has the potential to impact the effect of one or more of the drugs. In some instances the interaction can be dangerous or life-threatening and must be avoided: CYP3A inhibitors (e.g., calcium channel blockers, cimetidine, erythromycin, fluconazole, itraconazole, ketoconazole).

What the FDA says about use in pregnancy: Category C (see Appendix).

What the available evidence suggests about breast-feeding safety: Likely safe.

The bottom line for you:

- Pimecrolimus may be used with relative safety during pregnancy and while breast-feeding if alternative agents with which there is more experience fail.

PIOGLITAZONE

Brand name: Actos

Drug classes: Antidiabetic agent; Thiazolidinedione

Indications (what it is used for): Type II diabetes

How it works: Makes insulin more effective at lowering blood glucose.

Contraindications (reasons you shouldn't take it): Hypersensitivity to drug or class, type I diabetes, diabetic ketoacidosis (lack of insulin prevents body using sugar as a fuel), severe congestive heart failure.

Possible side effects and warnings: Can cause liver toxicity, congestive heart failure, anemia, fluid retention, swelling, weight gain, upper respiratory infection, headache, sinusitis, muscle pain, sore throat, heartburn, and low blood sugar. Should be used with caution in women with mild congestive heart failure, liver dysfunction, high blood pressure, or swelling.

How it can affect pregnant women: Pioglitazone improves glucose control, and when used alone it is slightly less effective than sulfonylureas and metformin. Drug clearance (how fast the drug is processed and eliminated by the body) is faster in nonpregnant women than men, suggesting that it would be further altered by pregnancy. There is no published data in pregnancy.

How it can affect a developing embryo or fetus: There are no adequate reports or well-controlled studies in human fetuses. It is unknown whether pioglitazone crosses the human placenta. Rodent studies are for the most part reassuring, revealing no evidence of birth defects or functional or behavioral abnormalities despite the use of doses higher than those used clinically. However, animal studies are not necessarily good indicators of how a drug will behave in humans.

Breast-feeding: There is no published data with pioglitazone during breast-feeding. It is unknown whether it enters human breast milk. Pioglitazone is excreted into rat breast milk.

Potential drug interactions: None significant.

What the FDA says about use in pregnancy: Category C (see Appendix).

What the available evidence suggests about breast-feeding safety: Unknown.

Bottom line for you:

- There are alternative agents (e.g., glyburide, metformin, acarbose) with which there is more experience during pregnancy and while breast-feeding.

PIPERACILLIN

Brand name: Pipracil

Drug classes: Antibiotic; Penicillin

Indications (what it is used for): Susceptible bacterial infections, including intra-abdominal, gonorrhea, lower respiratory and urinary tracts, skin, and bone.

How it works: Kills bacteria by blocking cell wall synthesis.

Contraindications (reasons you shouldn't take it): Hypersensitivity to drug or class.

Possible side effects and warnings: Can cause low platelet and/or white blood cell counts, seizures, fever, bowel infection, kidney inflammation, hemolytic anemia, rash, bleeding, slow clotting, low potassium levels, headache, dizziness, fatigue, phlebitis (blood clot in a vein), high bilirubin levels, and liver dysfunction. Should be used with caution in women with cephalosporin allergy, kidney failure, low potassium levels, seizure disorder, or kidney dysfunction, or who are on sodium restriction or taking medications that are toxic to the kidneys.

How it can affect pregnant women: Piperacillin is best studied during pregnancy for the treatment of gonorrhea, preterm premature rupture of the membranes (PPROM, water breaking before 37 weeks), and for the prevention of infection after cesarean section. Piperacillin has a higher clearance rate (how fast the medication is processed and eliminated by the body) during pregnancy, suggesting that the dose must be increased to successfully treat serious infections in pregnant women near term or postpartum. No single antibiotic proven effective for the prevention of infection after cesarean delivery is superior to the other; cost and convenience are the deciding factors. Several studies conclude that piperacillin increases the time between PPROM and labor.

How it can affect a developing embryo or fetus: There are no adequate reports or well-controlled studies of piperacillin in human fetuses. Piperacillin crosses the placenta, reaching a level in the fetus that is about one quarter of that of the mother. Rodent studies are reassuring, revealing no evidence of birth defects or low birth weight despite the use of doses higher than those used clinically. However, animal studies are not necessarily good indicators of how a drug will behave in humans.

Breast-feeding: There are no adequate reports or well-controlled studies in nursing women. The small amount of piperacillin excreted into human breast milk and its poor oral absorption indicates that any newborn level will be clinically insignificant.

Potential drug interactions: Interaction between the following medications and piperacillin has the potential to impact the effect of one or more of the drugs. In some instances the interaction can be dangerous or life-threatening and must be avoided: vecuronium, nondepolarizing muscle relaxants, probenecid, heparin, oral anticoagulants, other drugs that may affect the blood coagulation system or thrombocyte function.

What the FDA says about use in pregnancy: Category B (see Appendix).

What the available evidence suggests about breast-feeding safety: Safe.

Bottom line for you:

- Piperacillin is safe and effective during pregnancy and while breast-feeding.

PIPERACILLIN-TAZOBACTAM

Brand names: Tazosyn, Zosyn

Drug classes: Antibiotic; Penicillin

Indications (what it is used for): Susceptible bacterial infections, including intra-abdominal, gonorrhea, lower respiratory and urinary tracts, skin, and bone.

How it works: Kills bacteria by blocking cell wall synthesis.

Contraindications (reasons you shouldn't take it): Hypersensitivity to drug or class.

Possible side effects and warnings: Can cause low platelet and/or white blood cell counts, seizures, fever, erythema multiforme (skin disorder), bowel infection, kidney inflammation, hemolytic anemia, rash, bleeding, prolonged bleeding time, low potassium level, headache, dizziness, fatigue, phlebitis (an inflamed, clotted vein), jaundice, high bilirubin, and liver dysfunction. Should be used with caution in women with cephalosporin allergy, kidney dysfunction or failure, low potassium level, or seizure disorder, or who are on sodium restriction or taking medications toxic to the kidneys.

How it can affect pregnant women: Tazobactam is a beta-lactamase inhibitor that expands the antibacterial spectrum of piperacillin. Piperacillin-tazobactam is active against most strains of piperacillin-resistant b-lactamase-producing bacteria. Clearance (how fast the medication is processed and eliminated by the body) of the combination appears to increase during pregnancy. Piperacillin is best studied during pregnancy for the treatment of gonorrhea, preterm premature rupture of the membranes (PPROM, water breaking before 37 weeks), and for the prevention of infection after cesarean section. Piperacillin has a higher clearance rate (how fast the medication is processed and eliminated by the body) during pregnancy, suggesting that the dose must be increased to successfully treat serious infections in pregnant women near term or postpartum. No single antibiotic proven effective for the prevention of infection after cesarean delivery is superior to the other; cost and convenience are the deciding factors. Several studies conclude that piperacillin increases the time between PPROM and labor.

How it can affect a developing embryo or fetus: There are no adequate reports or well-controlled studies of piperacillin-tazobactam in human fetuses. Piperacillin-tazobactam crosses the placenta, reaching a level of tazobactam in the fetus that is about one quarter that of the mother. Rodent studies at doses up to 4 times the maximum recommended clinical dose are reassuring, showing no evidence of impaired fertility or birth defects. However, animal studies are not necessarily good indicators of how a drug will behave in humans.

Breast-feeding: There are no adequate reports or well-controlled studies in nursing women. The small amount of piperacillin excreted into human breast milk and its poor oral absorption indicates that any newborn level will be clinically insignificant. It is not known whether tazobactam enters human breast milk. It is usually considered compatible with breast-feeding.

Potential drug interactions: Interaction between the following medications and piperacillin-tazobactam has the potential to impact the effect of one or more of the drugs. In some instances the interaction can be dangerous or life-threatening and must be avoided: aminoglycosides, probenecid, heparin, oral anticoagulants and other drugs that affect coagulation, vecuronium.

What the FDA says about use in pregnancy: Category B (see Appendix).

What the available evidence suggests about breast-feeding safety: Likely safe.

Bottom line for you:
- Piperacillin-tazobactam is safe and effective during pregnancy and while breast-feeding.

PIPERAZINE

Brand names: Aloxin, Antcucs, Antepar, Ascalix, Expellin, Multifuge, Rotape, Vermidol, Vermizine, Worm-Away

Drug classes: Adrenergic agonist; Anthelmintic

Indications (what it is used for): Treatment of intestinal roundworms and pinworms.

How it works: Paralyzes the worm, allowing the body to eliminate it.

Contraindications (reasons you shouldn't take it): Hypersensitivity to drug or class, kidney dysfunction, convulsive disorders.

Possible side effects and warnings: Can cause nausea, vomiting, abdominal cramps, diarrhea, hives, erythema multiforme (skin disorder), reddish or purple discoloration of the skin, fever, joint pain, headache, dizziness, lack of gross-muscle control, tremors, assorted movement disorders, muscular weakness, decreased reflexes, skin numbness, blurred vision, convulsions, and memory deficit. Should be used with caution in women with liver dysfunction, malnutrition, or anemia.

How it can affect pregnant women: There are no adequate reports or well-controlled studies of piperazine in pregnant women. The long clinical experience is reassuring.

How it can affect a developing embryo or fetus: There are no adequate reports or well-controlled studies in human fetuses. It is unknown whether piperazine crosses the human placenta.

Breast-feeding: There is no published data in nursing women. It is unknown whether piperazine enters human breast milk. However, it has been widely used by women while breast-feeding in some countries.

Potential drug interactions: No clinically relevant interactions identified.

What the FDA says about use in pregnancy: Category B (see Appendix).
What the available evidence suggests about breast-feeding safety: Unknown.
Bottom line for you:

- There is a long experience with piperazine that indicates it is safe for use during pregnancy and while breast-feeding.

PIRBUTEROL

Brand name: Maxair
Drug classes: Bronchodilator; Sympathomimetic
Indications (what it is used for): Bronchospasm.
How it works: Activates the beta-2 adrenergic receptor, causing the bronchioles to dilate.
Contraindications (reasons you shouldn't take it): Hypersensitivity to drug or class.
Possible side effects and warnings: Can cause irregular heart rate, chest pain, loss of appetite, severe high blood pressure, tremor, nervousness, nausea, vomiting, diarrhea, headache, dizziness, and taste changes. Should be used with caution in women with diabetes, high thyroid hormone levels, seizures, cardiovascular disease, or low potassium levels.
How it can affect pregnant women: Asthma is a common disease in life and in pregnancy. Approximately one-third of pregnant women with asthma get worse during pregnancy, one-third get better, and one-third remain clinically unchanged. When asthma is well controlled, it does not affect pregnancy outcome, but poorly controlled asthma may increase the risk of preterm birth (before 37 weeks) or low birth weight. Inhaled corticosteroids are considered the preventative medication of choice for pregnant women with persistent asthma unless their condition is well controlled by cromolyn or nedocromil. Budesonide and beclomethasone are considered the first-line treatments. There is no published experience with pirbuterol in pregnancy.

Certain medications used during labor and delivery have the potential to worsen asthma, including nonselective beta-blockers, some prostaglandins (used to induce labor), and ergonovine (used to control blood loss after delivery).
How it can affect a developing embryo or fetus: There are no adequate reports or well-controlled studies of pirbuterol in human fetuses. Rodent studies, both inhalational and oral, are reassuring, revealing no evidence of birth defects or low birth weight despite the use of doses higher than those used clinically. Toxicity to the fetus was noted at the higher doses tested. However, animal studies are not necessarily good indicators of how a drug will behave in humans.
Breast-feeding: There is no published data during breast-feeding. It is unknown whether pirbuterol enters human breast milk.
Potential drug interactions: Interaction between the following medications and pirbuterol has the potential to impact the effect of one or more of the drugs. In some instances the interaction can be dangerous or life-threatening and must be avoided: other beta-adrenergic aerosol bronchodilators, monoamine oxidase inhibitors (MAOIs), tricyclic antidepressants (TCAs).
What the FDA says about use in pregnancy: Category C (see Appendix).
What the available evidence suggests about breast-feeding safety: Unknown.
Bottom line for you:

- Inhaled corticosteroids are considered the preventative medication of choice for pregnant women with persistent asthma unless their condition is well controlled by cromolyn or nedocromil.
- There are alternative agents with which there is more experience during pregnancy and while breast-feeding. If these fail, pirbuterol may be used if the maternal benefit justifies the potential risk to the embryo, fetus, or newborn.

PIROXICAM

Brand names: Brexicam, Feldene

Drug classes: Analgesic, nonnarcotic; NSAID; Oxicam

Indications (what it is used for): Bone and rheumatoid arthritis, mild to moderate pain, painful menses.

How it works: Blocks the synthesis of prostaglandins that trigger the inflammation and pain.

Contraindications (reasons you shouldn't take it): Hypersensitivity to drug or class, aspirin- or NSAID-induced asthma.

Possible side effects and warnings: Can cause bowel bleeding, sudden kidney failure, bronchospasm, low platelet and/or white blood cell counts, Stevens-Johnson syndrome (a rare but serious skin reaction to medication), kidney inflammation, liver toxicity, heartburn, nausea, abdominal pain, constipation, headache, dizziness, rash, drowsiness, ringing in the ears, and fluid retention. Should be used with caution in women with bowel bleeding, nasal polyps, high blood pressure, or congestive heart failure.

How it can affect pregnant women: Piroxicam has anti-inflammatory, pain-relieving, and fever-reducing properties. There are no adequate reports or well-controlled studies in pregnant women. In one high-quality study, piroxicam increased implantation and pregnancy rates after embryo transfer in both fresh and frozen-thawed cycles during IVF. The beneficial effect seemed more pronounced in patients who were older than 40 years, whose infertility was related to the man, and who had problems in the fallopian tubes or endometriosis (the endometrium grows outside the uterus). In rodents, piroxicam decreased the effectiveness of hormone-containing IUDs.

How it can affect a developing embryo or fetus: There are no adequate reports or well-controlled studies in human fetuses. Like other NSAIDs, piroxicam crosses the human placenta and is associated with very low levels of amniotic fluid. NSAIDS like piroxicam probably should be avoided in the first trimester because they have been associated with gastroschisis (a birth defect where loops of bowel poke through the fetal abdominal wall), which is repairable with surgery. Piroxicam is also likely to trigger closure of the ductus arteriousus (a critical fetal blood vessel directing blood away from the lungs) when given for prolonged periods of time after 32 weeks. Its closure leads to tricuspid valve incompetence, heart failure, and high blood pressure in the lungs, all of which can cause long-term damage. Stopping the medication appears to reverse this process.

Breast-feeding: There are no adequate reports or well-controlled studies in nursing women. The small quantity of piroxicam excreted into human breast milk is not clinically relevant.

Potential drug interactions: Interaction between the following medications and piroxicam has the potential to impact the effect of one or more of the drugs. In some instances the interaction can be dangerous or life-threatening and must be avoided: aspirin, methotrexate, ACE inhibitors, furosemide, thiazides, warfarin.

What the FDA says about use in pregnancy: Category C, first trimester; D, third trimester (see Appendix).

What the available evidence suggests about breast-feeding safety: Safe.

The bottom line for you:

- There are alternative agents with which there is more experience.
- If these fail, limited use of piroxicam is considered safe for use during pregnancy after 12 weeks and before 32 weeks and while breast-feeding.

PNEUMOCOCCAL VACCINE

Brand names: Pneumovax 23, Pnu-Imune 23

Drug class: Vaccine

Indications (what it is used for): Enhanced susceptibility to pneumococcus.

How it works: Prompts the body to make protective antibodies against the bacteria.

Contraindications (reasons you shouldn't take it): Hypersensitivity to any component of the vaccine, Hodgkin's disease (a type of cancer of the lymphatic system) treated with immunosuppressive therapy or radiation.

Possible side effects and warnings: Can cause local injection site soreness, redness and swelling, rash, hives, arthritis, joint pain, serum sickness (a reaction to proteins in antiserum derived from an animal source), swollen lymph nodes, and fever.

How it can affect pregnant women: Pneumococcal infection is a leading cause of death and a major cause of pneumonia, meningitis (inflammation of the membranes covering the brain and spinal cord), and otitis media (middle ear infection). The antibody induced by the vaccine can persist as long as 5 years. HIV-positive women are considered at increased risk and should be vaccinated.

How it can affect a developing embryo or fetus: There are no adequate reports or well-controlled studies of pneumococcal vaccine in human fetuses. Stimulated antibodies are transferred across the placenta, and newborns of treated women have higher antibody levels during the first 6 months to 1 year of life than children of nonvaccinated mothers. However, it is unclear whether maternal pneumococcal vaccination reduces the risk of infant infection. Rodent birth defects studies have not been performed, although there is no reason to expect an adverse fetal effect. Vaccinated rodents transfer enough antibody to their offspring to protect against otitis media. However, animal studies are not necessarily good indicators of how a drug will behave in humans.

Breast-feeding: There are no adequate reports or well-controlled studies in nursing women. It is unknown whether pneumococcal vaccine enters human breast milk. The antibodies produced will.

Potential drug interactions: Immunosuppressive agents (e.g., corticosteroids, antimetabolites, alkylating agents, cytotoxic agents) may render the vaccine less effective.

What the FDA says about use in pregnancy: Category C (see Appendix).

What the available evidence suggests about breast-feeding safety: Safe.

Bottom line for you:

- Pneumococcal vaccine is safe and effective during pregnancy and while breast-feeding.

PODOFILOX

Brand name: Condylox

Drug classes: Antiviral; Dermatologic

Indications (what it is used for): Genital or perianal warts.

How it works: Unknown; interferes with cell division.

Contraindications (reasons you shouldn't take it): Hypersensitivity to drug or class.

Possible side effects and warnings: Can cause burning and inflammation.

How it can affect pregnant women: There are no adequate reports or well-controlled studies in pregnant women. Podofilox should not be used to treat large lesions during pregnancy. Toxicity with overuse is reported, but systemic absorption of doses up to 1.5 mL is low. Although podofilox is an effective medication, there are other therapies, such as laser and cryotherapy, that pose fewer risks.

How it can affect a developing embryo or fetus: There are no adequate reports or well-controlled studies of podofilox in human fetuses. Topical application of less than 1.5 mL results in a very low blood level in a pregnant woman and it is rapidly eliminated by her body. Thus, it is unlikely that a pregnant woman's systemic concentration after the treatment of small warts would reach a level that presents a risk to the embryo or fetus. Limited rodent studies are reassuring, revealing no evidence of birth defects or low birth weight despite the use of doses higher than those used clinically. However, animal studies are not necessarily good indicators of how a drug will behave in humans.

Breast-feeding: There are no adequate reports or

well-controlled studies in nursing women. It is unknown whether podofilox enters human breast milk. However, considering the indication and dosing, podofilox use is unlikely to pose a clinically significant risk to a breast-feeding newborn.

Potential drug interactions: No clinically relevant interactions identified.

What the FDA says about use in pregnancy: Category C (see Appendix).

What the available evidence suggests about breast-feeding safety: Likely safe.

The bottom line for you:

- Laser and cryotherapy pose fewer risks.
- Podofilox may be used topically during pregnancy and while breast-feeding for the treatment of small venereal warts.

PODOPHYLLUM RESIN

Brand names: Podoben, Podocon-25, Pododerm, Podofin

Drug classes: Antiviral; Dermatologic

Indications (what it is used for): Genital or perianal warts.

How it works: Unknown; interferes with cell division.

Contraindications (reasons you shouldn't take it): Hypersensitivity to drug or class, diabetes, chronically receiving corticosteroids.

Possible side effects and warnings: Can cause skin numbness, polyneuritis (damage to peripheral nerves, those outside the brain and spinal cord), temporarily paralyzed bowel, fever, low platelet and/or white blood cell counts, coma, and death.

How it can affect pregnant women: Podophyllum resin is a mixture of resins from the mandrake, a plant of the northern and middle U.S. There are no adequate reports or well-controlled studies in pregnant women. Although systemic absorption of doses up to 1.5 mL is low, toxicity has been reported with overuse. Thus, podophyllum resin should not be used during pregnancy for large lesions. Though it is an effective medication, there

are other therapies, such as laser and cryotherapy, that pose fewer risks.

How it can affect a developing embryo or fetus: There are no adequate reports or well-controlled studies in human fetuses. It is unknown whether podophyllum resin crosses the human placenta. Topical application of less than 1.5 mL results in a very low blood level in a pregnant woman and it is rapidly eliminated by her body. Thus it is unlikely that her systemic concentration after the treatment of small warts would reach a level that presents a risk to the embryo or fetus. Although there are reports of complications associated with the topical use of podophyllum on genital warts of pregnant patients, including birth defects, fetal death, and stillbirth, it is unclear whether these were caused by the podophyllum resin.

Breast-feeding: There are no adequate reports or well-controlled studies in nursing women. It is unknown whether podophyllum resin enters human breast milk. However, considering the indications and dosing, podophyllum resin use is unlikely to pose a clinically significant risk to a breast-feeding newborn.

Potential drug interactions: No clinically relevant interactions identified.

What the FDA says about use in pregnancy: Category X (see Appendix).

What the available evidence suggests about breast-feeding safety: Likely safe.

The bottom line for you:

- Laser and cryotherapy pose fewer risks.
- Podophyllum resin is probably safe for use during pregnancy and while breast-feeding if confined to small venereal warts.

POLIOVIRUS VACCINE, INACTIVATED

Brand names: Ipol, Poliovax b

Drug class: Vaccine

Indications (what it is used for): Prevention of polio.

How it works: Stimulates the production of protective antipolio antibodies.

Contraindications (reasons you shouldn't take it): Hypersensitivity to drug or class; hypersensitivity to neomycin, streptomycin, or polymyxin B; recent fever.

Possible side effects and warnings: This is the injected Salk vaccine. Can cause redness at the injection site, fever, and temporary decreased appetite.

How it can affect pregnant women: Inactivated poliovirus vaccine is a sterile suspension of three types of polio virus grown in culture and then inactivated so it cannot cause disease. Paralytic poliomyelitis has not been reported after vaccination. Routine primary poliovirus vaccination of adults (older than 18 years) living in the U.S. is not recommended. Adults at increased risk of exposure but not previously immunized should be vaccinated. This group includes travelers to regions where poliomyelitis is endemic or epidemic (parts of Africa, Afghanistan, and Pakistan), health-care workers in close contact with patients who may be excreting polioviruses, laboratory workers handling specimens that may contain polioviruses, members of groups with disease caused by wild polioviruses, and incompletely vaccinated or unvaccinated adults in contact with children given live oral poliovirus vaccine. Vaccination during pregnancy is safe and effective, and the antibodies are detectable in the fetus.

How it can affect a developing embryo or fetus: There are no adequate reports or well-controlled studies of inactivated poliovirus vaccine in human fetuses. Poliovirus antibodies cross the human placenta and may offer some protection to a newborn, but is not a replacement for vaccination.

Breast-feeding: There are no adequate reports or well-controlled studies in nursing women. Although it is unknown whether inactivated poliovirus vaccine enters human breast milk, the stimulated antibodies might.

Potential drug interactions: No clinically relevant interactions identified.

What the FDA says about use in pregnancy: Category C (see Appendix).

What the available evidence suggests about breast-feeding safety: Safe.

Bottom line for you:

- Inactivated poliovirus vaccine is safe and effective during pregnancy and while breast-feeding.

POLIOVIRUS VACCINE, ORAL LIVE

Brand name: Orimune

Drug class: Vaccine

Indications (what it is used for): Prevention of polio.

How it works: Stimulates the production of antipolio antibodies, which create immunity.

Contraindications (reasons you shouldn't take it): Hypersensitivity to drug or class; hypersensitivity to neomycin, streptomycin, or polymyxin B; immune deficiency states or altered immunity due to disease or therapy; recent fever.

Possible side effects and warnings: Can cause paralysis and Guillain-Barré syndrome (the body's immune system attacks the nerves).

How it can affect pregnant women: Oral poliovirus vaccine (the Sabin vaccine) is a live, trivalent mixture of three types of modified polioviruses not capable of producing the symptoms of polio. Oral vaccine simulates natural infection, inducing a robust and wide-ranging immunity without symptoms of disease. Live virus vaccines are generally contraindicated (should not be used) in pregnancy, but the oral polio vaccine has proved safe and effective in pregnancy if exposure is imminent and immediate protection is needed.

Oral poliovirus vaccine is used for epidemic control, and under these circumstances, vaccination during pregnancy is effective and does not increase the risk of a complication. Routine primary poliovirus vaccination of adults (over the age of 18) living in the U.S. is not recommended. Adults who are at increased risk of exposure and who have not been adequately immunized should receive poliovirus vaccination. This group includes travelers to regions where poliomyelitis is endemic or epidemic (parts of African, Pakistan, and Afghanistan), health-care workers in close contact with patients who may be excreting polioviruses, laboratory workers handling specimens that may contain polioviruses, and members of groups with disease caused by wild polioviruses.

How it can affect a developing embryo or fetus: There are no adequate reports or well-controlled studies of oral poliovirus vaccine in human fetuses. Maternal vaccination results in a level of passive immunity for the newborn, but is not a substitute for vaccination. There is no evidence of birth defects or fetal toxicity. Rodent birth defects studies have not been performed.

Breast-feeding: There are no adequate reports or well-controlled studies in nursing women. Antibodies are found in breast milk. Although it is unknown whether oral poliovirus vaccine enters human breast milk, the resulting IgA (immunoglobulin A) antibodies do and may offer a level of protection for the newborn, but is not a substitute for vaccination. It is generally considered compatible with breast-feeding.

Potential drug interactions: No clinically relevant interactions identified.

What the FDA says about use in pregnancy: Category C (see Appendix).

What the available evidence suggests about breast-feeding safety: Safe.

The bottom line for you:

- Although live virus vaccines are generally considered to be contraindicated during pregnancy, live oral poliovirus is safe and effective for use during pregnancy and while breast-feeding when necessary. Otherwise, inactivated polio vaccine may be used for protection.

POLYETHYLENE GLYCOL
Brand name: MiraLAX
Drug class: Laxative

Indications (what it is used for): Constipation.

How it works: Causes water retention in stool.

Contraindications (reasons you shouldn't take it): Hypersensitivity to drug or class, bowel obstruction.

Possible side effects and warnings: Can cause nausea, abdominal bloating, cramping, gas, diarrhea, hives, and electrolyte disorders. Should be used with caution in women who are elderly.

How it can affect pregnant women: There is little if any systemic absorption of polyethylene glycol. There are no adequate reports or well-controlled studies in pregnant women. It is used successfully for the treatment of constipation during pregnancy and after delivery.

How it can affect a developing embryo or fetus: There are no adequate reports or well-controlled studies in human fetuses. It is unknown whether polyethylene glycol crosses the human placenta. However, it is unlikely that a clinically significant quantity is absorbed into the mother's blood.

Breast-feeding: There are no adequate reports or well-controlled studies in nursing women. It is unknown whether polyethylene glycol enters human breast milk. Considering the lack of systemic absorption, polyethylene glycol is unlikely to achieve clinically relevant levels in milk.

Potential drug interactions: No clinically relevant interactions identified.

What the FDA says about use in pregnancy: Category C (see Appendix).

What the available evidence suggests about breast-feeding safety: Safe.

The bottom line for you:

- Polyethylene glycol is safe and effective for use during pregnancy and while breast-feeding, although there are alternative medications with which there is more experience.

POTASSIUM CHLORIDE
Brand names: Cena-K, Chloropotassuril, Durules, K-10, Kadalex, Kaochlor, Kaon Cl, Kay Ciel, K-Care,

K-Dur, K-Lease, K-Lor, Klor-Con, Klorvess, Klotrix, K-Lyte Cl, K-Norm, Kolyum, K-Sol, K Tab, Micro-K, Rum-K, Slow-K, Ten-K, Ultra-K-Chlor

Drug class: Electrolyte replacement

Indications (what it is used for): Low potassium level, treatment and prevention.

How it works: Electrolyte replacement.

Contraindications (reasons you shouldn't take it): Hypersensitivity to drug or class, untreated Addison's disease (deficiency of adrenal gland hormones), high potassium level, kidney failure.

Possible side effects and warnings: Can cause irregular heart rate, heartburn, nausea, vomiting, diarrhea, rash, and bleeding. Should be used with caution in women with kidney dysfunction or cardiovascular disease.

How it can affect pregnant women: There are no adequate reports or well-controlled studies of potassium chloride in pregnant women. Potassium is a natural and important element in the body. The most common cause of low potassium during pregnancy is the administration of B-mimetic agents for the treatment of preterm labor. Routine treatment is not necessary.

How it can affect a developing embryo or fetus: There are no adequate reports or well-controlled studies in human fetuses. Potassium chloride readily crosses the human placenta. It is unlikely that potassium supplementation would have an adverse effect on the fetus unless the mother's level reached the toxic range.

Breast-feeding: There are no adequate reports or well-controlled studies in nursing women. Potassium chloride enters human breast milk; supplementation is considered safe while breast-feeding.

Potential drug interactions: Potassium-sparing diuretics and angiotensinogen-converting enzyme inhibitors may lead to a high potassium level.

What the FDA says about use in pregnancy: Category C (see Appendix).

What the available evidence suggests about breast-feeding safety: Safe.

The bottom line for you:

- Potassium chloride is safe and effective for use during pregnancy and while breast-feeding.

POTASSIUM IODIDE

Brand name: SSKI

Drug classes: Electrolyte; Thyroid agent; Vitamin/mineral

Indications (what it is used for): Dangerously high thyroid hormone levels, to prepare the thyroid for surgical removal, expectorant, to protect the thyroid from radiation during cancer treatment.

How it works: Inhibits thyroid hormone synthesis.

Contraindications (reasons you shouldn't take it): Hypersensitivity to drug or class, hyperkalemia (excess potassium in the blood), severe volume depletion (loss of water and salts from cells), Addison's disease (deficiency of adrenal gland hormones), low level of thyroid hormone, sudden bronchitis, tuberculosis.

Possible side effects and warnings: Can cause irregular heart rate, bowel bleeding, angioedema (swelling beneath the skin), swollen parotid (salivary) gland, enlarged lymph nodes, enlarged thyroid gland, thyroid tumors, metallic taste, heartburn, hives, headache, acne, fever, runny nose, joint pain, confusion, and skin numbness. Should be used with caution in women with kidney dysfunction, cardiovascular disease, or cystic fibrosis (life-threatening lung disease).

How it can affect pregnant women: Potassium iodide effectively reduces the uptake of radioactive iodide by the thyroid and is used as an adjunct in both nonpregnant and pregnant women with high thyroid hormone levels due to Graves' disease (immune system disorder with overproduction of thyroid hormones). There are no adequate reports or well-controlled studies in pregnant women. Potassium iodide replacement is effective during pregnancy for the treatment of mild to moderate iodine deficiency.

How it can affect a developing embryo or fetus: There are no adequate reports or well-controlled

studies in human fetuses. Potassium iodide crosses the human placenta and if used in excess can cause fetal goiter and hypothyroidism.

Breast-feeding: There are no adequate reports or well-controlled studies in nursing women. Supplementation with potassium iodide has little effect on the iodine concentration of human breast milk.

Potential drug interactions: Potassium-sparing diuretics and angiotensinogen-converting enzyme inhibitors may lead to a high potassium level.

What the FDA says about use in pregnancy: Category D (see Appendix).

What the available evidence suggests about breast-feeding safety: Safe.

The bottom line for you:

- Potassium iodide is safe and effective for use during pregnancy and while breast-feeding.
- Unindicated supplementation can harm the fetus by causing severe hypothyroidism.

PRAVASTATIN

Brand name: Pravachol

Drug classes: Antihyperlipidemic; HMG-CoA reductase inhibitor

Indications (what it is used for): Hypercholesterolemia (high cholesterol and lipids/triglycerides).

How it works: Blocks the action of an enzyme necessary for cholesterol synthesis.

Contraindications (reasons you shouldn't take it): Hypersensitivity to drug or class, active liver disease.

Possible side effects and warnings: Can cause muscle breakdown, liver toxicity, gallbladder inflammation, heartburn, abdominal pain, gas, constipation, rash, muscle pain, and weakness. Should be used with caution in women who abuse alcohol or have liver or kidney dysfunction.

How it can affect pregnant women: Pravastatin lowers lipids in two ways. First, it reduces the available pool of the main building block, cholesterol. Second, pravastatin inhibits bad lipid production by blocking its synthesis by the liver. There are no adequate reports or well-controlled studies in preg-

nant women. Since atherosclerosis develops over a prolonged period of time; discontinuation of pravastatin during pregnancy should have little impact on long-term maternal outcome.

How it can affect a developing embryo or fetus: Cholesterol and related substances are building blocks for the placenta and fetus, which is why there might be concern about using drugs to block their production during pregnancy. There are no adequate reports or well-controlled studies of pravastatin in human fetuses. It is unknown whether it crosses the human placenta. In a review of 214 pregnant women exposed to pravastatin or a related drug, there were 31 adverse outcomes, including 22 fetuses with structural defects and 5 fetal deaths. There were 2 principal categories of recurrent structural defects: cerivastatin and lovastatin were associated with 4 severe midline brain and spine problems; simvastatin, lovastatin, and atorvastatin were associated with limb abnormalities, including 2 similar complex lower limb defects after simvastatin exposure. No adverse outcomes were reported after exposure to pravastatin.

Breast-feeding: There are no adequate reports or well-controlled studies in nursing women. It is unknown whether pravastatin enters human breast milk. Certainly cholesterol and its by-products are important components of breast milk. In the absence of further study, pravastatin should be considered incompatible with breast-feeding.

Potential drug interactions: Interaction between the following medications and pravastatin has the potential to impact the effect of one or more of the drugs. In some instances the interaction can be dangerous or life-threatening and must be avoided: itraconazole, gemfibrozil.

What the FDA says about use in pregnancy: Category X (see Appendix).

What the available evidence suggests about breast-feeding safety: Possibly unsafe.

The bottom line for you:

- Pravastatin decreases cholesterol synthesis and potentially other biologically active substances derived from cholesterol. It should not be used during pregnancy and while breast-feeding until additional study has been completed.

- Atherosclerosis is a chronic process; discontinuation of pravastatin during pregnancy should have little impact on long-term outcome for most patients.

PRAZOSIN

Brand names: Hypovase, Lopres, Minipress
Drug classes: Adrenergic antagonist; Alpha-blocker; Antihypertensive
Indications (what it is used for): High blood pressure.
How it works: Blocks alpha-adrenergic receptors on blood vessels, which dilates the blood aterioles and lowers blood pressure.
Contraindications (reasons you shouldn't take it): Hypersensitivity to drug or class.
Possible side effects and warnings: Can cause fainting after the first dose, low blood pressure when you stand up, dizziness, palpitations, edema, nausea, vomiting, diarrhea, headache, skin numbness and tingling, blurred vision, drowsiness, malaise, dry mouth, joint pain, fever, and itching. Should be used with caution in women with liver or kidney dysfunction.
How it can affect pregnant women: Prazosin is a secondary medication (i.e., not the first choice) for the treatment of severe high blood pressure and associated complications of pregnancy (preeclampsia).
How it can affect a developing embryo or fetus: There are no adequate reports or well-controlled studies in human fetuses. Prazosin crosses the human placenta, reaching less than a quarter of the mother's blood level. Although prazosin is as effective as nifedipine, the associated fetal death rate from prazosin is higher for unknown reasons. Rodent studies are reassuring, revealing no evidence of birth defects or low birth weight despite the use of doses higher than those used clinically. However,

animal studies are not necessarily good indicators of how a drug will behave in humans.
Breast-feeding: There are no adequate reports or well-controlled studies in nursing women. Small quantities of prazosin enter human breast milk; however, it is generally considered compatible with breast-feeding.
Potential drug interactions: Interaction between the following medications and prazosin has the potential to impact the effect of one or more of the drugs. In some instances the interaction can be dangerous or life-threatening and must be avoided: diuretics, other blood-pressure-lowering medications.
What the FDA says about use in pregnancy: Category C (see Appendix).
What the available evidence suggests about breast-feeding safety: Safe.
The bottom line for you:
- Prazosin is one of many backup alternatives for the treatment of chronic high blood pressure during pregnancy.
- For unknown reasons, prazosin is associated with an increase in the fetal death rate when used to treat women with severe high blood pressure due to preeclampsia. An alternative agent should be used.
- Prazosin is safe for use while breast-feeding.

PREDNISOLONE

Brand names: Adnisolone, Cortalone, Delta-Cortef, Orapred, Prelone, Ultracortenol
Drug class: Corticosteroid
Indications (what it is used for): Inflammatory disorders, multiple sclerosis (autoimmune disease affecting the brain and spinal cord), asthma (sudden onset or persistent severe), adrenal insufficiency.
How it works: Unknown.
Contraindications (reasons you shouldn't take it): Hypersensitivity to drug or class, fungal infection in the bloodstream.
Possible side effects and warnings: Can cause adrenal insufficiency, steroid psychosis (psychotic

reactions to steroid use; aka 'roid rage), immuno-suppression, peptic ulcer, congestive heart failure, osteoporosis, increased intracranial pressure, nausea, vomiting, heartburn, edema, headache, dizziness, mood swings, sleeplessness, anxiety, menstrual irregularities, bruises, acne, skin atrophy, impaired wound healing, high blood pressure, low potassium level, and high blood glucose. Should be used with caution in women with a seizure disorder, diabetes, high blood pressure, tuberculosis, thin fragile bones, or liver dysfunction.

How it can affect pregnant women: Prednisolone is a metabolite of prednisone (a form the medication prednisone is broken down into). It provides effective relief of severe vomiting during pregnancy that is unresponsive to first-line therapy and associated with at least a 10% weight loss. Prednisolone is used widely for the treatment of inflammatory/autoimmune disorders that are common in reproductive-age women. Although prednisolone was once used for the treatment antiphospholipid syndrome (the immune system mistakenly produces antibodies against normal blood proteins) during pregnancy, several studies have documented a higher miscarriage rate with prednisolone and aspirin than with heparin and aspirin (currently the standard). Similarly, the combination of prednisone, aspirin, and progesterone is no better than enoxaparin alone for the treatment of idiopathic recurrent miscarriage (miscarriage with no known cause).

How it can affect a developing embryo or fetus: There are no adequate reports or well-controlled studies in human fetuses. The human placenta metabolizes prednisone, reducing fetal exposure to perhaps 10% of the maternal level. Prednisone is often used as salvage therapy for the treatment of fetal low platelet count (alloimmune thrombocytopenia) when the fetus is unresponsive to immune globulin infusion.

The best evidence is that corticosteroids are weak teratogens (substance that can cause birth defects) when taken in the first trimester when the rates of both cleft lip and palate are increased. There is no increase in risk of anomalies when steroids are begun after organ formation (after 11 weeks) or if given only topically. A few small studies suggested a possible relationship between long-term steroid use during pregnancy and poor fetal growth; however, it is hard to tell if that was the result of the medication or the disease it was being used to treat.

Breast-feeding: There are no adequate reports or well-controlled studies in nursing women. It is unknown whether prednisolone enters human breast milk. However, long clinical experience suggests that prednisolone therapy is compatible with breast-feeding.

Potential drug interactions: Interaction between the following medications and prednisolone has the potential to impact the effect of one or more of the drugs. In some instances the interaction can be dangerous or life-threatening and must be avoided: drugs that induce liver enzymes (e.g., phenobarbital, phenytoin, rifampin), troleandomycin, ketoconazole, estrogens, warfarin, aspirin or other nonsteroidal anti-inflammatory drugs (NSAIDs), salicylate, anticholinesterase agents, toxoids, live or inactivated vaccines, hypoglycemic agents.

What the FDA says about use in pregnancy: Category D, first trimester; C, otherwise (see Appendix).

What the available evidence suggests about breast-feeding safety: Likely safe.

The bottom line for you:
- Prednisolone may be a cause of cleft lip and palate, and should be avoided in the first trimester.
- Otherwise, it is safe and effective for use during pregnancy and while breast-feeding.

PREDNISONE

Brand names: Adasone, Cartancyl, Colisone, Cordrol, Cortan, Dacortin, Deltasone, Orasone, Paracort, Prednicot, Sterapred, Sterapred DS

Drug class: Corticosteroid

Indications (what it is used for): Inflammatory disorder, multiple sclerosis (autoimmune disease affecting the brain and spinal cord), *Pneumocystis* pneumonia, adrenal insufficiency.

How it works: Unknown.

Contraindications (reasons you shouldn't take it): Hypersensitivity to drug or class, systemic fungal infection.

Possible side effects and warnings: Can cause adrenal insufficiency, steroid psychosis (psychotic reactions to steroid use; aka 'roid rage), immunosuppression, peptic ulcer, congestive heart failure, thin and fragile bones, increased intracranial pressure, nausea, vomiting, heartburn, edema, headache, dizziness, mood swings, sleeplessness, anxiety, menstrual irregularities, bruises, acne, skin atrophy, impaired wound healing, high blood pressure, low potassium level, and high blood glucose. Should be used with caution in women with seizure disorder, diabetes, high blood pressure, tuberculosis, thin and fragile bones, or liver dysfunction.

How it can affect pregnant women: There are no adequate reports or well-controlled studies of prednisone in pregnant women. Crohn's disease and other chronic inflammatory diseases often affect reproductive-age women. The available data shows that women with Crohn's disease can expect to conceive successfully, carry to term, and deliver a healthy baby. Control of disease activity before conception and during pregnancy is critical to optimize both maternal and fetal outcomes. Pregnancy does not affect the treatment of Crohn's disease. Patients in remission should continue their drug regimen during pregnancy. Although prednisone was previously used for the treatment of antiphospholipid syndrome (the immune system mistakenly produces antibodies against normal blood proteins), several trials reported that the miscarriage rate is higher with prednisone and aspirin versus heparin and aspirin.

How it can affect a developing embryo or fetus: There are no adequate reports or well-controlled studies in human fetuses. The placenta metabolizes prednisone, reducing fetal exposure to perhaps 10% of the maternal level. Prednisone is often used as salvage therapy for the treatment of fetal low platelet count (alloimmune thrombocytopenia) when the fetus is unresponsive to immune globulin infusion.

The best evidence is that corticosteroids are weak teratogens (substances that can cause birth defects) when taken in the first trimester when the rates of both cleft lip and palate are increased. There is no increase in risk of anomalies when steroids are begun after organ formation (after 11 weeks) or if given only topically. A few small studies suggested a possible relationship between long-term steroid use during pregnancy and poor fetal growth; however, it is hard to tell if that was the result of the medication or the disease it was being used to treat.

Breast-feeding: There are no adequate reports or well-controlled studies in nursing women. It is unknown whether prednisone enters human breast milk. The long clinical experience is reassuring.

Potential drug interactions: Interaction between the following medications and prednisone has the potential to impact the effect of one or more of the drugs. In some instances the interaction can be dangerous or life-threatening and must be avoided: drugs that induce liver enzymes (e.g., phenobarbital, phenytoin, rifampin), troleandomycin, ketoconazole, aspirin.

What the FDA says about use in pregnancy: Category D, first trimester; C, otherwise (see Appendix).

What the available evidence suggests about breast-feeding safety: Safe.

The bottom line for you:

- Prednisone may be a cause of cleft lip and palate, and should be avoided in the first trimester.
- Otherwise, it is safe and effective for use during pregnancy and while breast-feeding.

PRILOCAINE

Brand name: Citanest

Drug class: Anesthetic, local

Indications (what it is used for): Dental nerve block.

How it works: Prevents the sensation of pain by blocking the nerve impulse.

Contraindications (reasons you shouldn't take it): Hypersensitivity to drug or class, congenital or idiopathic methemoglobinemia (hemoglobin does not release oxygen to the tissues).

Possible side effects and warnings: Can cause light-headedness; nervousness; apprehension; euphoria; confusion; dizziness; drowsiness; ringing in the ears; blurred or double vision; vomiting; twitching; tremors; convulsions; unconsciousness; respiratory depression or arrest; and sensations of heat, cold, or numbness. Should be used with caution in women with severe liver dysfunction.

How it can affect pregnant women: There are no adequate reports or well-controlled studies in pregnant women. Prilocaine is sometimes used for a local anesthetic at delivery. Because prilocaine causes vascular smooth-muscle contraction, it should not be used for a paracervical block (given near the main arteries to the uterus), since it could increase the risk of a slow fetal heart rate due to a decrease in blood supply. Prilocaine/lidocaine cream is a local anesthetic, but the combination is not appropriate for obstetric procedures.

How it can affect a developing embryo or fetus: There are no adequate reports or well-controlled studies in human fetuses. Prilocaine crosses the human placenta, and after a local injection for delivery, it reaches the same level in the fetus as it does in the mother. There are several reports of newborn methemoglobinemia after prilocaine administration. Rodent studies are reassuring, revealing no evidence of birth defects or low birth weight despite the use of doses higher than those used clinically. However, animal studies are not necessarily good indicators of how a drug will behave in humans.

Breast-feeding: There are no adequate reports or well-controlled studies in nursing women. It is unknown whether prilocaine enters human breast milk. However, considering the indication and dosing, one-time prilocaine use is unlikely to pose a clinically significant risk to a breast-feeding newborn.

Potential drug interactions: Interaction between the following medications and prilocaine has the potential to impact the effect of one or more of the drugs. In some instances the interaction can be dangerous or life-threatening and must be avoided: monoamine oxidase inhibitors (MAOIs), tricyclic antidepressants (TCAs), phenothiazine.

What the FDA says about use in pregnancy: Category B (see Appendix).

What the available evidence suggests about breast-feeding safety: Safe.

The bottom line for you:

- Although prilocaine is generally considered safe for use during pregnancy and while breast-feeding, there are superior alternatives for labor analgesia. It should not be used for a paracervical block.

PRIMAQUINE
Not available in the U.S. or U.K.

Brand name: Primaquine

Drug classes: Antimalarial; Antiprotozoal

Indications (what it is used for): Malaria, *Pneumocystis carinii* pneumonia.

How it works: Unknown.

Contraindications (reasons you shouldn't take it): Hypersensitivity to drug or class, bone marrow suppression, rheumatoid arthritis, systemic lupus erythematosus (a chronic inflammatory disease in which the immune system attacks the body's own tissues and organs), recent quinacrine use.

Possible side effects and warnings: Can cause hemolytic anemia, methemoglobinemia (a hemoglobin form that does not release oxygen to the tissues), low white blood cell count, damage to the retina, nausea, vomiting, abdominal pain, headache, itching, and vision disturbances. Should be used with caution in women with G6PD deficiency (favism; an inherited red blood cell enzyme defect).

How it can affect pregnant women: There are no adequate reports or well-controlled studies in pregnant women. Primaquine is mainly used to treat the

P. vivax or *P. ovale* malaria. Primaquine is considered by some to be contraindicated (should not be used) in pregnancy since the G6PD status of the fetus will be unknown, which means it is not clear how it could affect it (see "How it can affect a developing embryo or fetus" below). Pregnant women should take weekly chloroquine prophylaxis until after delivery, when eradication of the immature parasites can be undertaken. Primaquine is used to prevent malaria only in travelers when no other alternatives are available. It is not licensed for this use in the U.S. or U.K. Primaquine causes methemoglobinemia in all patients, but this seldom causes symptoms and is always self-repairing. Dangerous levels of methemoglobinemia occur only in patients with G6PD deficiency.

How it can affect a developing embryo or fetus: There are no adequate reports or well-controlled studies in human fetuses. Primaquine likely crosses the human placenta, as rupture of red blood cells has been reported in a fetus with G6PD deficiency. Except for the tetracyclines, there is no evidence that at recommended doses any of the antimalarial drugs can cause birth defects. However, primaquine is generally not recommended because of the potential to cause fetal hemolytic anemia.

Breast-feeding: There are no adequate reports or well-controlled studies in nursing women. It is unknown whether primaquine enters human breast milk.

Potential drug interactions: No clinically relevant interactions identified.

What the FDA says about use in pregnancy: Category C (see Appendix).

What the available evidence suggests about breast-feeding safety: Unknown.

The bottom line for you:

• Primaquine may be used with relative safety during pregnancy and while breast-feeding when either there are no other options or the patient is not likely to have a G6PD deficiency.

PROBENECID

Brand names: Benemid, Panuric, Probalan, Solpurin, Urocid

Drug classes: Antigout; Uricosuric

Indications (what it is used for): To prolong the life of penicillin, to treat gout.

How it works: Inhibits penicillin secretion by the kidneys while blocking the resorption of urate by the kidneys.

Contraindications (reasons you shouldn't take it): Hypersensitivity to drug or class, poor kidney function, urate kidney stones, ongoing gout attack.

Possible side effects and warnings: Can cause hemolytic or aplastic anemia, liver destruction, headache, dizziness, loss of appetite, nausea, vomiting, sore gums, kidney damage, kidney obstruction, itching, flushing, and fever. Should not be used for gout until 2 or 3 weeks after attack has subsided. Should be used with caution in women who have hypersensitivity to sulfa drugs, peptic ulcer disease, or kidney dysfunction.

How it can affect pregnant women: Probenecid is used during pregnancy with penicillin almost exclusively for the treatment of sexually transmitted diseases that require a prolonged level of penicillin in the mother's blood, such as gonorrhea and syphilis.

How it can affect a developing embryo or fetus: There are no adequate reports or well-controlled studies in human fetuses. Probenecid crosses the human placenta but is not associated with adverse effects on a fetus. Rodent studies are reassuring, revealing no evidence of birth defects or low birth weight despite the use of doses higher than those used clinically. However, animal studies are not necessarily good indicators of how a drug will behave in humans.

Breast-feeding: Experience is limited, but it appears that the amount of probenecid a breast-fed newborn would consume and absorb is clinically insignificant.

Potential drug interactions: Probenecid decreases the kidneys' clearance of many drugs, so it is important for a prescribing doctor and the pharmacist know all they drugs you are taking. Salicylates and pyrazinamide decrease the effectiveness of probenecid. Probenecid increases the effect of oral sulfonylureas.

What the FDA says about use in pregnancy: Category B (see Appendix).

What the available evidence suggests about breast-feeding safety: Safe.

The bottom line for you:

- Probenecid is considered safe and effective for use during pregnancy and while breast-feeding.

PROCAINAMIDE

Brand names: Biocoryl, Procanbid, Procan SR, Promine, Pronestyl, Ritmocam

Drug class: Antiarrhythmics, class IA

Indications (what it is used for): Irregular heart rate.

How it works: Depresses the transmission of nerve signals that trigger the heartbeat.

Contraindications (reasons you shouldn't take it): Hypersensitivity to drug or class, blockade of the heart pacemaker impulse, myasthenia gravis, systemic lupus erythematosus (a chronic inflammatory disease in which the immune system attacks the body's own tissues and organs).

Possible side effects and warnings: Can cause cardiac arrest, dangerous heart rate rhythms, seizures, lupuslike syndrome, hemolytic anemia, low platelet and/or white blood cell counts, low blood pressure, flushing, hives, itching, swelling under the skin, rash, fever, nausea, vomiting, bitter taste, hallucinations, confusion, depression, diarrhea, dizziness, and liver dysfunction. Should be used with caution in women with bone marrow depression, congestive heart failure, or kidney dysfunction.

How it can affect pregnant women: There are no adequate reports or well-controlled studies in pregnant women. Procainamide is well tolerated and is a first-choice treatment of acute undiagnosed wide-complex rapid heart rates. It may be used alone or in combination with digoxin. All such drugs must be given in the hospital under continuous cardiac monitoring. Electrical heart shock is necessary in all women who are unstable with life-threatening fast heart rates originating in the ventricles. Electrical shocking will not harm the fetus.

How it can affect a developing embryo or fetus: There are no adequate reports or well-controlled studies in human fetuses. Procainamide crosses the human placenta to reach the fetal bloodstream. There are numerous case reports of its use to treat an irregular fetal heart rate.

Breast-feeding: There are no adequate reports or well-controlled studies in nursing women. Clinically insignificant amounts of procainamide and its main metabolite (product that it is broken down into) are excreted into human breast milk and absorbed by a breast-feeding newborn.

Potential drug interactions: Procainamide should not be used with other antiarrhythmic drugs.

What the FDA says about use in pregnancy: Category C (see Appendix).

What the available evidence suggests about breast-feeding safety: Safe.

The bottom line for you:

- Procainamide is considered safe for use during pregnancy and while breast-feeding for the treatment of dangerous heart rhythms in the mother.

PROCAINE

Brand name: Novocain

Drug class: Anesthetic, local

Indications (what it is used for): Local and regional anesthesia.

How it works: Prevents the sensation of pain and the ability to move by blocking the nerve impulse necessary to transmit the information to the brain.

Contraindications (reasons you shouldn't take it): Hypersensitivity to drug or class, infection at site.

Possible side effects and warnings: Can cause brain toxicity; irregular heart rate, heart block or stoppage; convulsions; adult respiratory distress syndrome (acute lung dysfunction); unconsciousness; low blood pressure; drowsiness; nervousness; blurred vision; tremors; nausea; vomiting; pupil constriction; ringing in the ears; chills; and itching. Should be used with caution in women with heart block, low blood pressure, cholinesterase deficiency, sulfite allergy, kidney disease, or impaired heart function.

How it can affect pregnant women: There are no adequate reports or well-controlled studies in pregnant women. Procaine has been used for decades during labor to create spinal, epidural, and local anesthesia.

How it can affect a developing embryo or fetus: There are no adequate reports or well-controlled studies of procaine in human fetuses. Local anesthetics rapidly cross the placenta. However, the long clinical experience is reassuring.

Breast-feeding: There is no published data in nursing women. It is unknown whether procaine enters human breast milk. However, considering the indication and dosing, one-time procaine use is unlikely to pose a clinically significant risk to a breast-feeding newborn.

Potential drug interactions: Interaction between the following medications and procaine has the potential to impact the effect of one or more of the drugs. In some instances the interaction can be dangerous or life-threatening and must be avoided: monoamine oxidase inhibitors (MAOIs), tricyclic antidepressants (TCAs), vasopressor or ergot-type oxytocic drugs (medications used to stimulate labor).

What the FDA says about use in pregnancy: Category C (see Appendix).

What the available evidence suggests about breast-feeding safety: Safe.

The bottom line for you:

- Procaine is safe and effective for use during pregnancy and while breast-feeding.

PROCHLORPERAZINE

Brand names: Buccastem, Compa-Z, Compazine, Cotranzine, Nautisol, Novomit, Prochlorperazine Edisylate, Prochlorperazine Maleate, Steremal, Tementil, Ultrazine-10, Vertigon

Drug classes: Antiemetic; Antipsychotic; Antivertigo; Phenothiazine

Indications (what it is used for): Nausea, vomiting, anxiety, psychosis.

How it works: Blocks the zone in the brain that is responsible for causing severe nausea and vomiting.

Contraindications (reasons you shouldn't take it): Hypersensitivity to drug or class, brain depression, adrenergic blockade, phenothiazine use, various blood disorders.

Possible side effects and warnings: Can cause low platelet and/or white blood cell counts, hemolytic anemia, electrocardiogram abnormalities, exfoliative dermatitis (an inflammatory skin disease with redness and scaling), involuntary movements like tics, liver toxicity, drowsiness, absent menstruation, blurred vision, rash, low blood pressure on sitting or standing, jaundice, dry mouth, constipation, sensitivity to light, anxiety, and extrapyramidal effects (movement disorders due to taking dopamine-blocking drugs such as those to treat psychosis). Should be used with caution in women with glaucoma, epilepsy, heart disease, or bone marrow depression.

How it can affect pregnant women: Prochlorperazine is most often used for the short-term treatment of nausea and vomiting, or dizziness. There are no adequate reports or well-controlled studies in pregnant women. In the U.K., an oral form is used for the treatment of migraine; its use is limited to 2 days because of the drug's potentially severe side effects. Long clinical experience confirms its effectiveness for the treatment of severe vomiting in pregnancy when combined with hydration and rest.

How it can affect a developing embryo or fetus: There are no adequate reports or well-controlled studies in human fetuses. It is unknown whether prochlorperazine crosses the human placenta. The extensive clinical experience during pregnancy is reassuring, with no substantial evidence of birth defects.

Breast-feeding: There are no adequate reports or well-controlled studies in nursing women. Prochlorperazine enters human breast milk, but the amount is unclear.

Potential drug interactions: No clinically relevant interactions identified.

What the FDA says about use in pregnancy: Category C (see Appendix).

What the available evidence suggests about breast-feeding safety: Unknown.

The bottom line for you:

- Prochlorperazine is a commonly used medication for the treatment of severe nausea and vomiting during pregnancy. It is considered safe.
- There is not enough information at present to determine whether prochloperazine is safe for use while breast-feeding.

PROGESTERONE

Brand names: Crinone, Gesterol 50, Lutolin-S, Progestaject-50, Prometrium

Drug classes: Contraceptive; Hormone; Progestin

Indications (what it is used for): Absent menses (no period), hormone replacement, infertility, prevention of spontaneous preterm birth (before 37 weeks).

How it works: Makes the endometrium hostile to implantation of the embryo; withdrawal of progesterone leads to menses.

Contraindications (reasons you shouldn't take it): Hypersensitivity to drug or class, peanut allergy, fetal death, miscarriage.

Possible side effects and warnings: Can cause menstrual irregularities, absent menstruation, breast tenderness, weight gain, stroke, blood clots, heart attack, breast cancer, gallbladder disease, jaundice, high blood pressure, headache, fluid retention, depression, rash, itching, changes in sex drive, acne, facial hair, leaky breasts, and hair loss. Should be used with caution in women with congestive heart failure or liver dysfunction, or who are breast-feeding.

How it can affect pregnant women: Progesterone is central for reproduction. This entry applies only to natural hormone and not synthetic compounds that may differ significantly (see megestrol, norethindrone, norgestrel).

Pregnancy Support: Progesterone is used throughout the first trimester to provide support for a pregnancy resulting from ovulation induction or in vitro fertilization (IVF) until the placenta takes over. Other than those, there are no proven indications for its use during pregnancy. Progesterone administration does not prevent pregnancy loss in women with a clinically recognized pregnancy greater than 7 weeks, after which the placenta is hormonally functional.

Preterm Delivery: A short cervix as measured by transvaginal ultrasound between 18 and 22 weeks is associated with an increase in the spontaneous preterm birth rate. Micronized progesterone vaginal gel or cream reduces that risk by about 40%. Pregnant women with a prior spontaneous preterm birth but a normal sonographic cervical length in their current pregnancy are not at greatly increased risk for recurrent preterm birth and probably do not need treatment.

How it can affect a developing embryo or fetus: The various types of progesterone compounds differ in their hormonal effects. There are no adequate reports or well-controlled studies of progesterone in human fetuses. Although masculinization of the female fetus has been attributed to some progestogens, there is no substantive evidence that natural progesterone is a cause of birth defects.

Breast-feeding: There are no adequate reports or well-controlled studies in nursing women. Progesterone is excreted into human breast milk, and the quantity of milk produced correlates with the predelivery progesterone level.

Potential drug interactions: No clinically relevant interactions identified.

What the FDA says about use in pregnancy: Category B (see Appendix).
What the available evidence suggests about breast-feeding safety: Safe.
The bottom line for you:

- There is no sound evidence that native progesterone is a cause of birth defects. Progesterone appears safe for use during pregnancy to support placental function after ovulation induction or IVF.
- Women with a sonographically short cervix are at increased risk for spontaneous preterm birth. The administration of micronized progesterone vaginal gel/cream reduces that risk by 40% regardless of their past obstetric history. There appears to be no benefit in selecting patients for progesterone treatment based on history alone.
- Progesterone is considered safe while breast-feeding.

PROMAZINE

Brand names: Liranol, Prazine, Primazine, Protactyl, Prozine-50, Savamine, Sparine, Talofen
Drug classes: Antipsychotic; Phenothiazine
Indications (what it is used for): Psychotic disorder.
How it works: Unknown.
Contraindications (reasons you shouldn't take it): Hypersensitivity to drug or class, drug-induced brain depression, intra-arterial injection, bone marrow suppression.
Possible side effects and warnings: Can cause involuntary movements like tics, drowsiness, jaundice, bone marrow suppression, hemolytic anemia, thrombocytopenic purpura (a serious clotting disorder), fever, decreased appetite, paradoxical increasing of psychotic symptoms, seizures, swelling of the brain, absent menstruation, leaky breasts, and dry mouth. Should be used with caution in women who have hardening of the arteries or severe low blood pressure. The medication should not be stopped abruptly but should be tapered off according to doctor's instructions.

How it can affect pregnant women: Promazine is a prototype phenothiazine used with varying success in the treatment of depressive neurosis, alcohol withdrawal, nausea, vomiting, symptoms of dementia, Tourette's syndrome (involuntary movements and vocalizations), Huntington's disease (a genetic disease causing breakdown of nerves in the brain), and Reye's syndrome (swelling in the liver and brain). Previously used to treat schizophrenia, promazine's use has largely been replaced by newer medications. Although promazine has been used in obstetrics for almost three decades, there are no adequate reports or well-controlled studies in pregnant women.
How it can affect a developing embryo or fetus: There are no adequate reports or well-controlled studies in human fetuses. It is unknown whether promazine crosses the human placenta. Older reports suggest a relationship between exposure to promazine during pregnancy and jaundice in the newborn.
Breast-feeding: There are no adequate reports or well-controlled studies in nursing women. It is unknown whether promazine enters human breast milk.
Potential drug interactions: No clinically relevant interactions identified.
What the FDA says about use in pregnancy: Category C (see Appendix).
What the available evidence suggests about breast-feeding safety: Unknown.
The bottom line for you:

- Promazine should be used during pregnancy and breast-feeding only if the benefit to the woman justifies the potential risk to the embryo, fetus, or newborn.

PROMETHAZINE

Brand names: Anergan, Antiallersin, Camergan, Fargan, Metaryl, Pentazine, Phenergan, Phenerzine, Promethacon, Prozine, Sayomol, Xepagan

Drug classes: Antiemetic; Antihistamine; Phenothiazine

Indications (what it is used for): Nausea, vomiting, motion sickness, sedation, allergic runny nose.

How it works: Blocks both central and peripheral histamine 1 receptors, which are responsible for the symptoms.

Contraindications (reasons you shouldn't take it): Hypersensitivity to drug or class, narrow-angle glaucoma.

Possible side effects and warnings: Can cause involuntary movements like tics, extrapyramidal effects (various movement disorders due to taking dopamine-blocking drugs such as those to treat psychosis), respiratory depression, low blood pressure, slow or rapid heart rate, low platelet and/or white blood cell counts, dry mouth, sedation, drowsiness, nausea, vomiting, rash, and thickened bronchial secretions. Should be used with caution in women with a seizure disorder, asthma, liver dysfunction, or bone marrow suppression.

How it can affect pregnant women: Promethazine has been used for decades in obstetrics to treat nausea and vomiting and to provide sedation or help relieve apprehension. It is often combined with a narcotic such as meperidine. Promethazine is similar to ondansetron but inferior to a short course of methylprednisolone for the relief of nausea and vomiting during pregnancy. It is not effective for the relief of nausea following thiopentone anesthesia for pregnancy termination.

How it can affect a developing embryo or fetus: There are no adequate reports or well-controlled studies in human fetuses. It is unknown whether promethazine crosses the human placenta. Large-scale human studies are reassuring, revealing no evidence of an increased rate of birth defects even when large doses have been taken for an attempted suicide.

Breast-feeding: There is no published data in nursing women. It is unknown whether promethazine enters human breast milk. The long clinical experience is reassuring.

Potential drug interactions: Interaction between the following medications and promethazine has the potential to impact the effect of one or more of the drugs. In some instances the interaction can be dangerous or life-threatening and must be avoided: central nervous system depressants, such as ethanol (alcohol), sedative-hypnotics (including barbiturates), general anesthetics, narcotics, narcotic analgesics, and tranquilizers; medications with anticholinergic properties.

What the FDA says about use in pregnancy: Category C (see Appendix).

What the available evidence suggests about breast-feeding safety: Unknown.

The bottom line for you:

- Promethazine is considered safe and effective for use during pregnancy and while breast-feeding as a treatment of nausea.

PROPANTHELINE

Brand names: Bropantil, Corrigast, Ercoril, Norproban, Pantheline, Pro-Banthine

Drug classes: Antispasmodic; Antiulcer agent; Gastrointestinal

Indications (what it is used for): Peptic ulcer.

How it works: Cholinergic antagonist.

Contraindications (reasons you shouldn't take it): Hypersensitivity to drug or class, bowel obstruction, myasthenia gravis (autoimmune disorder causing muscle weakness), angle-closure glaucoma, bleeding, stomach reflux.

Possible side effects and warnings: Can cause dry mouth, blurred vision, confusion, palpitations, headache, low blood pressure when standing or sitting, sleeplessness, drowsiness, rapid heart rate, narrow or dilated pupils, constipation, nausea, bloating, hives, decreased sweat, and respiratory distress. Should be used with caution in women with coronary artery disease or ulcerative colitis.

How it can affect pregnant women: There is no published data with propantheline in pregnancy.

How it can affect a developing embryo or fetus: There are no adequate reports or well-controlled studies in human fetuses. It is unknown whether

propantheline crosses the human placenta. Rodent birth defects studies apparently have not been performed.

Breast-feeding: There is no published experience during breast-feeding. It is unknown whether propantheline enters human breast milk.

Potential drug interactions: Interaction between the following medications and propantheline has the potential to impact the effect of one or more of the drugs. In some instances the interaction can be dangerous or life-threatening and must be avoided: anticholinergics, belladonna alkaloids, synthetic or semisynthetic anticholinergic medications, narcotic analgesics such as meperidine, class I antiarrhythmic drugs (e.g., disopyramide, procainamide, quinidine), antihistamines, phenothiazines, tricyclic antidepressants (TCAs), other psychoactive drugs, corticosteroids.

What the FDA says about use in pregnancy: Category C (see Appendix).

What the available evidence suggests about breast-feeding safety: Unknown.

The bottom line for you:

- There are alternative medications with which there is more experience during pregnancy and while breastfeeding.
- Propantheline should be used during pregnancy and breast-feeding only if the benefit to the mother justifies the potential risk to the embryo, fetus, or newborn.

PROPOFOL

Brand name: Diprivan

Drug class: Anesthesia, induction/maintenance

Indications (what it is used for): Anesthesia induction and maintenance, sedation for ventilated patients.

How it works: Unknown.

Contraindications (reasons you shouldn't take it): Hypersensitivity to drug or class; allergy to soybean, egg lecithin, or glycerol.

Possible side effects and warnings: Can cause fluid in the lungs; inflammation of the pancreas; severe hyperextension and spasticity of the head, neck and spine; suspension of breathing; slow heart rate; low blood pressure; involuntary movements; nausea; vomiting; and injection site reactions. Should be used with caution in women with a lipid metabolism disorder or increased intracranial pressure.

How it can affect pregnant women: Propofol is popular for a variety of procedures including egg retrieval during in vitro fertilization (IVF) and surgical pregnancy termination. Its use after cord clamping at cesarean delivery under general anesthesia to reduce postoperative nausea and vomiting. In addition, a small IV dose decreases the itching associated with epidural or spinal morphine. In small series of women whose anesthesia for cesarean delivery was induced and maintained with propofol, there were no differences in newborn outcome as compared to more commonly administered anesthetic agents.

How it can affect a developing embryo or fetus: There are no adequate reports or well-controlled studies in human fetuses. Propofol crosses the human placenta, reaching the same level in the fetus as in the mother. There are no adverse effects from using propofol for conscious sedation during C-section under either a spinal or an epidural anesthetic.

Breast-feeding: A small amount of propofol is excreted in human breast milk. However, considering the indications, prior exposure to propofol is not likely to pose a significant risk to a breast-feeding newborn.

Potential drug interactions: The central nervous system depressant effect of propofol is increased by the use of other central nervous system depressants, including ethanol (alcohol).

What the FDA says about use in pregnancy: Category B (see Appendix).

What the available evidence suggests about breast-feeding safety: Likely safe.

The bottom line for you:

- Propofol is an excellent anesthetic agent during pregnancy and while breast-feeding.

PROPOXYPHENE

Not available in the U.S.

Brand names: Abalgin, Darvon, Deprancol, Develin, Dolotard, Dolpoxene, Margesic, Parvon

Drug class: Analgesic, narcotic

Indications (what it is used for): Mild to moderate pain.

How it works: Stimulates the opioid receptors to block the perception of pain.

Contraindications (reasons you shouldn't take it): Hypersensitivity to drug or class.

Possible side effects and warnings: Can cause slow, shallow breathing; dependency; drowsiness; dizziness; hallucinations; dysphoria (intense depression); constipation; liver dysfunction; and painful muscles. Should be used with caution in women with a history of substance abuse, depression, serious thoughts of suicide, or liver or kidney dysfunction.

How it can affect pregnant women: Propoxyphene is a synthetic narcotic. There are no adequate reports or well-controlled studies in pregnant women. Once frequently prescribed, propoxyphene was removed from the U.S. market because it was a popular agent for attempting suicide.

How it can affect a developing embryo or fetus: There are no adequate reports or well-controlled studies in human fetuses. Both propoxyphene and norpropoxyphene, its principal active metabolite (product the body breaks it down into), cross the human placenta and reach the same level in the fetus as in the mother. Newborn addiction and withdrawal occur. Although there are scattered case reports of miscellaneous birth defects, no pattern has emerged.

Breast-feeding: There are no adequate reports or well-controlled studies in nursing women. Although low levels of propoxyphene are excreted into human breast milk, its use as directed is generally considered compatible with breast-feeding.

Potential drug interactions: Propoxyphene is a narcotic and its effect is increased when combined with other central nervous system depressants, including ethanol (alcohol).

What the FDA says about use in pregnancy: Category C (see Appendix).

What the available evidence suggests about breast-feeding safety: Safe.

The bottom line for you:

- There are nonnarcotic alternatives that provide similar or superior analgesia for most indications.

PROPRANOLOL

Brand name: Inderal

Drug classes: Adrenergic antagonist; Antiarrhythmic, class II; Beta-blocker

Indications (what it is used for): High blood pressure, prevention of migraine headache, supraventricular tachycardia (rapid heart rhythm originating in the large pumping chambers), angina.

How it works: Blocks all types of beta-adrenoceptors responsible for at least some of the symptoms.

Contraindications (reasons you shouldn't take it): Hypersensitivity to drug or class, asthma, congestive heart failure, slow heart rate.

Possible side effects and warnings: Can cause congestive heart failure, irregular or slow heart rate, bronchospasm, dizziness, sleeplessness, weakness, fatigue, hallucinations, nausea, vomiting, abdominal pain, diarrhea, constipation, sore throat, rash, hair loss, and a low white blood cell count. Should be used with caution in women with diabetes or with liver or kidney dysfunction.

How it can affect pregnant women: Propranolol is used extensively during pregnancy for the treatment of high blood pressure, irregular heart rate, and migraine headache, and is generally considered safe. It is also used to provide relief of symptoms from an overactive thyroid (production of excess thyroid hormone. Graves' disease is one cause.) and from pheochromocytoma (adrenal gland tumor). Propranolol appears as effective as alpha-methyldopa in treating high blood pressure and is often coupled with other blood-pressure-lowering medications such as hydralazine.

How it can affect a developing embryo or fetus: There are no adequate reports or well-controlled studies in human fetuses. Propranolol crosses the human placenta but has no effect on placental blood flows in women with chronically high blood pressure. There are case reports of its use, usually with digoxin, for the treatment of a fetal abnormal rapid heart rate, although there are superior medications for that purpose. The impact of propranolol on the fetuses of women with chronic high blood pressure is unclear. When combined with other antihypertensive medications, the risk of low birth weight is apparently increased. However, low birth weight is more common when maternal blood pressure control requires high doses and the low birth weight is a result of a dose high enough to actually decrease the amount of blood the mother's heart pumps to the uterus. Other reported newborn effects of exposure during pregnancy include slow heart rate and low blood glucose.

Breast-feeding: The amount of propranolol in human breast milk is thought to be clinically insignificant.

Potential drug interactions: Interaction between the following medications and propranolol has the potential to impact the effect of one or more of the drugs. In some instances the interaction can be dangerous or life-threatening and must be avoided: ACE inhibitors, clonidine, prazosin, propafenone, quinidine, disopyramid, amiodarone, lidocaine, calcium channel blockers, catecholamine-depleting drugs such as reserpine, monoamine oxidase inhibitors (MAOIs), tricyclic antidepressants (TCAs), haloperidol, nonsteroidal anti-inflammatory drugs (NSAIDs), warfarin, theophylline. Propranolol may also worsen depression.

What the FDA says about use in pregnancy: Category C (see Appendix).

What the available evidence suggests about breast-feeding safety: Safe.

The bottom line for you:

- Propranolol is an effective drug for the control of chronic high blood pressure during pregnancy. High doses increase the risk of a low-birth-weight newborn.
- Propranolol is considered safe for use while breast-feeding.

PROPYLTHIOURACIL

Brand name: PTU

Drug classes: Antithyroid agent; Hormone modifier; Hormone

Indications (what it is used for): Excess thyroid hormone.

How it works: Blocks the production of thyroid hormone by the thyroid.

Contraindications (reasons you shouldn't take it): Hypersensitivity to drug or class.

Possible side effects and warnings: Can cause bone marrow suppression, liver toxicity, exfoliative dermatitis (inflammatory skin disease with redness and scaling), hives, inflamed blood vessels, lung inflammation, nausea, vomiting, rash, drowsiness, dizziness, headache, joint pain, swollen lymph nodes, tingling of the skin, hyperpigmentation, jaundice, hair loss, and inflammation of nerves. Should be used with caution in women who are pregnant, who have kidney dysfunction or bone marrow suppression, or who are taking drugs that are toxic to the liver or suppress white blood cell counts.

How it can affect pregnant women: Hyperthyroidism (overactive thyroid) occurs in 1 out of every 1,000–2,000 pregnancies. Graves' disease is the result of an antibody the mother produces that stimulates her thyroid to produce excess thyroid hormone. This antibody also crosses the placenta and stimulates the fetal thyroid. Propylthiouracil remains the popular choice for the treatment of Graves' disease during pregnancy because it is believed to have a lower potential than methimazole or carbimazole to overly suppress the fetal or newborn thyroid by crossing the placenta or entering the breast milk. However, recent studies have not confirmed that concern, and it is likely that methimazole is equally effective. There are no adequate reports or well-controlled studies in pregnant women. It is generally recommended that the minimum dose of propylthiouracil necessary to control the maternal thyroid be used. However, this is a poor approach since the mother's dose is not necessarily indicative of the effect it will have on the thyroid activity in the fetus/newborn. Instead, dosing should be individualized—by testing the thyroid hormone levels of both mother and fetus—to achieve the optimal maternal and fetal outcomes. Women with a history of Graves' disease should be screened for the continued presence of thyroid-stimulating antibody even if they no longer require treatment, since fetal hyperthyroidism is still likely if they have significant levels of the stimulating antibody.

How it can affect a developing embryo or fetus: There are no adequate reports or well-controlled studies in human fetuses. Several studies suggest that either too much or too little fetal thyroid hormone can affect brain development. Heart failure and death are rare complications of fetal hypothyroidism. Propylthiouracil crosses the human placenta. The fetuses of mothers treated with propylthiouracil rarely have normal thyroid function and many experts suggest that the fetus should be tested directly and maternal therapy altered to optimize the fetal thyroid function.

Breast-feeding: There are no adequate reports or well-controlled studies in nursing women. Small quantities of propylthiouracil are excreted into human breast milk, but thyroid function of breast-fed newborns is unaffected.

Potential drug interactions: The activity of anticoagulants may be increased by propylthiouracil.

What the FDA says about use in pregnancy: Category D (see Appendix).

What the available evidence suggests about breast-feeding safety: Probably safe.

The bottom line for you:

- Propylthiouracil is safe and effective for use during pregnancy when supervised by an expert in fetal medicine.

- Propylthiouracil is probably safe for use while breast-feeding.

PROTAMINE

Brand name: None

Drug class: Antidote, bleeding disorders

Indications (what it is used for): Heparin reversal.

How it works: Prevents anticoagulation from heparin by binding to it.

Contraindications (reasons you shouldn't take it): Hypersensitivity to drug or class.

Possible side effects and warnings: Can cause life-threatening allergic reaction, bronchospasm, fatigue, swelling under the skin, circulatory collapse, slow heart rate, bleeding, paradoxical hemorrhage, low platelet and/or white blood cell counts, shortness of breath, flushing, hives, and nausea and vomiting. Should be used with extreme caution in women who have a fish allergy or prior exposure to various protamine insulins.

How it can affect pregnant women: There are no adequate reports or well-controlled studies of protamine in pregnant women. Case reports note sudden low blood pressure, slow heart rate, and life-threatening allergic reactions in pregnant women treated with it. Protamine does not reverse anticoagulation caused by low-molecular-weight heparins such as enoxaparin.

How it can affect a developing embryo or fetus: There are no adequate reports or well-controlled studies in human fetuses. It is unknown whether protamine crosses the human placenta. Rodent birth defect studies have not been conducted. However, protamine combined with insulin taken by diabetic pregnant women has a long safety record.

Breast-feeding: There is no published data in nursing women. It is unknown whether protamine enters human breast milk. However, insulin coupled with protamine has a long safety record in breast-feeding.

Potential drug interactions: Protamine is incompatible with certain antibiotics, including several of the cephalosporins and penicillins.

What the FDA says about use in pregnancy: Category C (see Appendix).
What the available evidence suggests about breast-feeding safety: Probably safe.
The bottom line for you:
- Protamine is indicated only for rare occasions in pregnancy when heparinization must be reversed for the health of the mother.
- Protamine is probably safe for use while breast-feeding.

PSEUDOEPHEDRINE

Brand names: Bronalin, Cenafed, Chlordrine, Novafed, Sudafed, Sufedrin
Drug classes: Decongestant; Sympathomimetic
Indications (what it is used for): Nasal decongestion.
How it works: Stimulates the alpha-adrenergic receptors, constricting blood vessels and reducing congestion.
Contraindications (reasons you shouldn't take it): Hypersensitivity to drug or class, monoamine oxidase inhibitor (MAOI) use within 14 days, narrow-angle glaucoma, severe high blood pressure, severe coronary artery disease.
Possible side effects and warnings: Can cause high blood pressure, irregular heart rate, palpitations, nausea, vomiting, headache, dizziness, nervousness, excitability, agitation, anxiety, weakness, and tremor. Should be used with caution in women with high blood pressure, diabetes, mild to moderate coronary artery disease, high thyroid hormone level, kidney dysfunction, or phenylketonuria (an inherited amino acid disorder).
How it can affect pregnant women: Pseudoephedrine is a second choice during pregnancy behind first- and second-generation antihistamines. There are no adequate reports or well-controlled studies in pregnant women. Pseudoephedrine has been observed to worsen high blood pressure in women with preeclampsia (high blood pressure and protein

in the urine during pregnancy and complications associated with it). For almost a decade, readily accessible over-the-counter products in the U.S. have not contained pseudoephedrine out of concern that they where being used to manufacture methamphetamine. Pseudoephedrine is still available at the pharmacist counter.
How it can affect a developing embryo or fetus: There are no adequate reports or well-controlled studies in human fetuses. The chemical structure of pseudoephedrine suggests that it crosses the human placenta. Population studies (studies of a large group of people taken from the larger population) suggest that exposed fetuses are 4 times more likely to develop gastroschisis (the bowel protrudes through the abdomen, which must be surgically repaired after birth). They are also at increased risk of blockages of the small intestine that must be repaired surgically after delivery compared to women who did not take pseudoephedrine. The risk appears increased by tobacco use. The combination of pseudoephedrine, phenylephrine, and phenylpropanolamine (sometimes sold together, though no longer available in the U.S.) may be associated with distal limb reduction (poor development of the hands or feet) and should be avoided in the first half of pregnancy.
Breast-feeding: There are no adequate reports or well-controlled studies in nursing women. The amount of pseudoephedrine excreted into human breast milk is not clinically relevant. However, one study reported that a single 60 mg dose of pseudoephedrine reduced milk volume by 25%. Thus, women with low milk production should consider another decongestant.
Potential drug interactions: Interaction between the following medications and pseudoephedrine has the potential to impact the effect of one or more of the drugs. In some instances the interaction can be dangerous or life-threatening and must be avoided: monoamine oxidase inhibitors (MAOIs), beta-blockers, mecamylamine, methyldopa, reserpine, veratrum alkaloids.

What the FDA says about use in pregnancy: Category C (see Appendix).

What the available evidence suggests about breast-feeding safety: Safe.

The bottom line for you:

- Antihistamines are the drugs of choice for the treatment of nasal congestion during pregnancy.
- Alone or in combination, pseudoephedrine, phenylephrine, and phenylpropanolamine should be avoided in the first half of pregnancy.
- Pseudoephedrine is safe to use while breast-feeding but may reduce milk volume. Women with low production should avoid it.

PSYLLIUM

Brand name: Metamucil

Drug class: Laxative

Indications (what it is used for): Constipation.

How it works: Increases stool bulk.

Contraindications (reasons you shouldn't take it): Hypersensitivity to drug or class, suspected appendicitis, intestinal obstruction.

Possible side effects and warnings: Can cause esophageal or bowel obstruction, constipation, diarrhea, abdominal cramps, bronchospasm, runny nose, and conjunctivitis.

How it can affect pregnant women: There are no adequate reports or well-controlled studies in pregnant women. Psyllium is not absorbed systemically.

How it can affect a developing embryo or fetus: There are no adequate reports or well-controlled studies in human fetuses. Psyllium is not absorbed systemically and poses no direct threat to the fetus.

Breast-feeding: There is no published data in nursing women. As psyllium is not absorbed systemically, it is unlikely to be excreted into human breast milk.

Potential drug interactions: No clinically relevant interactions identified.

What the FDA says about use in pregnancy: Category B (see Appendix).

What the available evidence suggests about breast-feeding safety: Safe.

The bottom line for you:

- Psyllium is safe and effective during pregnancy and while breast-feeding.

PYRANTEL PAMOATE

Brand name: Antiminth

Drug class: Antiparasitic

Indications (what it is used for): Pinworm, roundworm, hookworm, whipworm.

How it works: Paralyzes the worm so that it is passed in the bowel movement.

Contraindications (reasons you shouldn't take it): Hypersensitivity to drug or class.

Possible side effects and warnings: Can cause loss of appetite, nausea, vomiting, abdominal cramps, diarrhea, dizziness, drowsiness, sleeplessness, tenesmus (feeling of constantly needing to pass stools), rash, weakness, and liver dysfunction. Should be used with caution in women with liver dysfunction or malnutrition.

How it can affect pregnant women: There are no published reports of pyrantel pamoate use during pregnancy.

How it can affect a developing embryo or fetus: There are no adequate reports or well-controlled studies in human fetuses. It is unknown whether pyrantel pamoate crosses the human placenta.

Breast-feeding: There is no published data in nursing women. It is unknown whether pyrantel pamoate enters human breast milk.

Potential drug interactions: No clinically relevant interactions identified.

What the FDA says about use in pregnancy: Category C (see Appendix).

What the available evidence suggests about breast-feeding safety: Unknown.

The bottom line for you:

- The effect of pyrantel pamoate on pregnancy and breast-feeding is unknown. There are

428 | The Complete Guide to Medications During Pregnancy and Breast-feeding

alternative drugs with which there is more experience.

PYRIDOSTIGMINE

Brand name: Mestinon

Drug classes: Cholinesterase inhibitor; Musculoskeletal agent

Indications (what it is used for): Myasthenia gravis (an autoimmune disease causing muscle weakness).

How it works: Cholinesterase inhibitor.

Contraindications (reasons you shouldn't take it): Hypersensitivity to drug or class, mechanical bowel obstruction.

Possible side effects and warnings: Can cause bronchospasm, slow heart rate, high blood pressure, cholinergic crisis (paralysis, respiratory failure, increased sweating, salivation, bronchial secretions, small pupils), heart block, irregular heart rate, cardiac or respiratory arrest, nausea, vomiting, diarrhea, heartburn, abdominal pain, weakness, rash, muscle cramps, increased bronchial secretions or salivation, narrow pupils, and tearing. Should be used with caution in women with asthma, peptic ulcer disease, irregular or slow heart rate, seizures, or kidney dysfunction.

How it can affect pregnant women: There are no adequate reports or well-controlled studies of pyridostigmine in pregnant women. The published literature consists of small series of patients and case reports. Myasthenia gravis is a potentially life-threatening disease if not treated, although symptoms can wax and wane. The impact of pregnancy on myasthenia is variable: a third of women stay the same, a third get better, and a third become worse.

How it can affect a developing embryo or fetus: There are no adequate reports or well-controlled studies in human fetuses. It is unknown whether pyridostigmine crosses the human placenta. Several case reports suggest a relationship between pyridostigmine and neurologic abnormalities, including multiple and severe joint contractures (muscles

or tendons that have tightened, thus becoming shorter) and very small heads. Rodent birth defects studies have not been conducted.

Breast-feeding: There are no adequate reports or well-controlled studies in nursing women. The amount of pyridostigmine excreted into human breast milk is clinically insignificant.

Potential drug interactions: No clinically relevant interactions identified.

What the FDA says about use in pregnancy: Category C (see Appendix).

What the available evidence suggests about breast-feeding safety: Safe.

The bottom line for you:

- Pyridostigmine is used during pregnancy with women who have myasthenia gravis, a life-threatening disease. Although the actual risk of birth defects appears quite low, it is safest to avoid using the drug in the first trimester if the severity of the disease allows.

- Pyridostigmine is safe for use while breast-feeding.

PYRIDOXINE

Brand names: Beesix, Hexa-Betalin, Rodex, Vitamin B_6

Drug class: Vitamins/minerals

Indications (what it is used for): Morning sickness, pyridoxine deficiency or supplementation, premenstrual syndrome, isoniazid adjunct.

How it works: Replacement

Contraindications (reasons you shouldn't take it): Hypersensitivity to drug or class, levodopa therapy.

Possible side effects and warnings: Can cause unsteady gait and numbness and tingling of the skin.

How it can affect pregnant women: Pyridoxine is a protein necessary for the function of several important enzymes. It reduces nausea and vomiting of pregnancy. Recent study suggests that the preventative use of pyridoxine early in pregnancy also decreases the risk of severe nausea and vomiting in at-risk women. It also appears effective in reducing postoperative nausea after laparoscopy. Pyridoxine is used in combination with the antituberculosis drug isoniazid to reduce the risk of nerve damage associated with treatment with isoniazid alone. There is not enough evidence to confirm the benefits of routine supplementation during pregnancy other than one trial suggesting that it may protect against maternal dental decay.

How it can affect a developing embryo or fetus: Pyridoxine crosses the human placenta; it is not a cause of birth defects. Pyridoxine supplementation during pregnancy increases the pyridoxine stores in the newborn.

Breast-feeding: Pyridoxine requirements are thought to increase during breast-feeding. Maternal supplementation increases the content of pyridoxine in human breast milk.

Potential drug interactions: Pyridoxine blocks the action of levodopa used to treat the tremors of Parkinson's disease.

What the FDA says about use in pregnancy: Category A (see Appendix).

What the available evidence suggests about breast-feeding safety: Safe.

The bottom line for you:

- Pyridoxine is safe and effective during pregnancy for the treatment of nausea and vomiting.

- Routine supplementation during pregnancy and breast-feeding is generally recommended, but the evidence that it improves outcome is scant.

PYRIMETHAMINE

Brand names: Daraprim, Eraprelina, Malocide
Drug class: Antiprotozoal
Indications (what it is used for): Malaria treatment and prevention, toxoplasmosis (infection caused by the parasite *Toxoplasma gondii*), cystoisosporiasis (intestinal disease caused by the parasite *Cystoisospora belli*).

How it works: Blocks an enzyme in the parasite that is essential for its synthesis of folate, without which the parasite dies.

Contraindications (reasons you shouldn't take it): Hypersensitivity to drug or class, folate deficiency.

Possible side effects and warnings: Can cause bone marrow suppression, Stevens-Johnson syndrome and erythema multiforme (skin disorders), megaloblastic anemia, seizures, nausea, vomiting, abdominal pain, dizziness, malaise, diarrhea, rash, fever, dry mouth, and increased skin pigmentation. Should be used with caution in women with liver or kidney dysfunction or G6PD deficiency.

How it can affect pregnant women: Parasitic disease is a major contributor to maternal illness in many areas of the world. Severe anemia is one side effect. Pyrimethamine has a long history of use during pregnancy, especially for the treatment of primary toxoplasmosis and malaria. HIV infection during pregnancy is also associated with an increased risk of malaria. Recent study suggests that the use of intermittent preventative treatment with pyrimethamine in areas of widespread infection improves pregnancy outcomes.

How it can affect a developing embryo or fetus: Pyrimethamine crosses the human placenta, reaching about a third of the mother's level. Although it has been long used for the treatment of toxoplasmosis during pregnancy, several recent studies have concluded that therapy during pregnancy does not alter neonatal outcome, perhaps because fetal infection has already occurred. Other studies suggest that pyrimethamine does not reduce transmission from mother to fetus but rather lessens the impact of the infection. Further research is required to define the role of prenatal screening and therapy for congenital toxoplasmosis. The treatment of pregnant women with a combination of pyrimethamine with sulfadoxine in malaria-endemic areas reduces the risk of prematurity and low birth weight due to malaria.

Breast-feeding: There are no adequate reports or

well-controlled studies in nursing women. Pyrimethamine is excreted into human breast milk in low concentrations that will not result in a clinically relevant level in a breast-feeding newborn.

Potential drug interactions: Interaction between the following medications and pyrimethamine has the potential to impact the effect of one or more of the drugs. In some instances the interaction can be dangerous or life-threatening and must be avoided: other antifolic drugs or medications associated with myelosuppression, including sulfonamides or trimethoprimsulfamethoxazole combinations; proguanil; zidovudine; cytostatic agents (e.g., methotrexate). If signs of folate deficiency develop, pyrimethamine should be discontinued.

What the FDA says about use in pregnancy: Category C (see Appendix).

What the available evidence suggests about breast-feeding safety: Safe.

The bottom line for you:

- Pyrimethamine is safe for use during pregnancy and while breast-feeding.

QUETIAPINE

Brand name: Seroquel
Drug class: Antipsychotic
Indications (what it is used for): Psychosis.
How it works: Unknown.
Contraindications (reasons you shouldn't take it): Hypersensitivity to drug or class.
Possible side effects and warnings: Can cause low blood pressure, involuntary repetitive body movements, menstrual irregularities, high prolactin levels, low thyroid hormone level, diabetes, life-threatening muscle rigidity, fever, and mental changes such as delirium; low white blood cell count, headache, sleepiness, dizziness, constipation, rapid heart rate, dry mouth, weakness, rash, high cholesterol and/or high triglycerides, liver dysfunction, heartburn, abdominal pain, runny nose, weight gain, and fever. Should be used with caution in women with liver dysfunction, heart disease, cerebrovascular disease

(narrowing of blood vessels that supply the brain), seizures, low blood pressure, or hypovolemia (decreased blood volume).

How it can affect pregnant women: Quetiapine is a dibenzothiazepine derivative. The published data during pregnancy is limited to case reports of individual patients. A single report suggested that drug clearance (how fast the drug is eliminated by the body) during pregnancy is increased by 25–30%, suggesting that the dose may need to be increased in order to remain effective as pregnancy advances.

How it can affect a developing embryo or fetus: There are no adequate reports or well-controlled studies in human fetuses. Quetiapine crosses the human placenta, achieving levels in the fetus that are about one-quarter of those of the mother. The pregnancy outcomes of 36 women who contacted a teratogen information service (an information service on possible causes of birth defects) after exposure to quetiapine during pregnancy appear normal. This suggests that quetiapine is not a major cause of birth defects. Rodent studies are mostly reassuring, revealing no evidence of birth defects despite the use of doses higher than those used clinically. Embryo loss and low birth weight were noted at the highest doses. However, animal studies are not necessarily good indicators of how a drug will behave in humans.

Breast-feeding: There are no adequate reports or well-controlled studies in nursing women. The small amounts of quetiapine excreted into human breast milk are likely clinically insignificant, since levels in newborn plasma reach only 6% of the mother's level. No adverse effects have been reported.

Potential drug interactions: Interaction between the following medications and quetiapine has the potential to impact the effect of one or more of the drugs. In some instances the interaction can be dangerous or life-threatening and must be avoided: ethanol (alcohol), blood-pressure-lowering medications, phenytoin, other hepatic enzyme inducers (e.g., barbiturates, carbamazepine, glucocorticoids, rifampin), thioridazine, ketoconazole, other CYP3A inhibitors (e.g., erythromycin, fluconazole, itraconazole), lorazepam.

What the FDA says about use in pregnancy: Category C (see Appendix).

What the available evidence suggests about breast-feeding safety: Likely safe.

The bottom line for you:

- There are alternative agents with which there is more experience. However, based on limited study, quetiapine appears safe during pregnancy and while breast-feeding in women for whom treatment is necessary.

QUINAPRIL

Brand name: Accupril

Drug classes: ACEI/A2R-antagonist; Antihypertensive

Indications (what it is used for): High blood pressure, congestive heart failure.

How it works: Blocks angiotensinogen-converting enzyme (ACE), resulting in lower blood pressure.

Contraindications (reasons you shouldn't take it): Hypersensitivity to drug or class, angioedema (rapid swelling of the layers of the skin).

Possible side effects and warnings: Can cause rapid swelling of the layers of the skin, low blood pressure, kidney failure, cough, dizziness, fatigue, nausea, vomiting, coldlike symptoms, muscle pain, joint pain, high potassium level, low white blood cell count, and kidney dysfunction. Should be used with caution in women with kidney dysfunction, narrowing of the renal artery, collagen vascular disease (disease of the connective tissue), or low sodium levels.

How it can affect pregnant women: There are no adequate reports or well-controlled studies of quinapril in pregnant women. In general, ACE inhibitors should be avoided during pregnancy. The lowest effective dose should be used if quinapril is required for the treatment of life-threatening maternal high blood pressure.

How it can affect a developing embryo or fetus: There is no published data in human fetuses. Quinapril likely crosses the human placenta like other ACE inhibitors do. Adverse fetal effects can occur after exposure to ACE inhibitors (as a group) at any time in pregnancy. Abnormalities that can happen after exposure in the first trimester include cardiovascular and brain/spine disorders. Later pregnancy exposure is associated with an underdeveloped skull, reversible or irreversible kidney failure, low amniotic fluid, prematurity, low birth weight, failure of the ductus arteriosus (fetal blood vessel that directs blood away from the lungs) to close after birth, and death.

The medication likely causes fetal kidney damage by decreasing the blood flow to the kidneys. Fetuses of women taking quinapril should be monitored regularly by ultrasound. If low amniotic fluid is detected, quinapril should be discontinued immediately unless continuation is lifesaving for the mother. However, low amniotic fluid may not occur until after the fetus has experienced irreversible injury. Newborns exposed in the womb to ACE inhibitors should be observed closely for low blood pressure, low urine production, and high potassium. The drug may need to be washed out of a newborn's system if low urine production occurs despite adequate blood pressure and blood flow to the kidneys.

Breast-feeding: There are no adequate reports or well-controlled studies in nursing women. The amount of quinapril excreted into human breast milk is likely clinically insignificant.

Potential drug interactions: Interaction between the following medications and quinapril has the potential to impact the effect of one or more of the drugs. In some instances the interaction can be dangerous or life-threatening and must be avoided: diuretics, lithium.

What the FDA says about use in pregnancy: Category D (see Appendix).

What the available evidence suggests about breast-feeding safety: Likely safe.

The bottom line for you:

- Quinapril is likely a significant human teratogen (substance that can cause birth defects). Along with other ACE inhibitors, it should be avoided during pregnancy.
- If a pregnant woman's disease requires treatment with quinapril, the lowest dose should be used, accompanied by close monitoring of the fetus.
- Quinapril is likely safe for use while breast-feeding.

QUININE

Brand names: Qm-260, Quin-Amino, Quinaminoph, Quinamm, Quinasul, Quindan, Quinite, Quiphile

Drug classes: Antimalarial; Antiprotozoal

Indications (what it is used for): Malaria.

How it works: Unknown.

Contraindications (reasons you shouldn't take it): Hypersensitivity to drug, class, or mefloquine or quinidine; G6PD deficiency; inflammation of the optic nerve; ringing in the ears; thrombocytopenia (a low platelet count), thrombotic thrombocytopenic purpura or hemolytic uremic suyndrome (both life threatening clotting disorders); low blood glucose; myasthenia gravis (autoimmune disorder causing muscle weakness).

Possible side effects and warnings: Can cause fracture of red blood cells, low blood sugar, low platelet and/or white blood cell count, optic nerve damage, nausea, vomiting, diarrhea, headache, confusion, low blood pressure, altered color perception, sensitivity to light, rash, itching, delirium, ringing in the ears, and dilated pupils. Should be used with caution in women with irregular heart rate.

How it can affect pregnant women: Malaria is a major cause of maternal, fetal, and newborn illness and death in some regions of the world. Treatment dramatically reduces those risks. Quinine is used extensively in developing countries for the treatment of malaria during pregnancy. It is one of a limited number of drugs used where drug-resistant malaria is endemic. However, quinine has a higher treatment failure rate than chloroquine. High levels of quinine are associated with miscarriage.

How it can affect a developing embryo or fetus: There are no adequate reports or well-controlled studies in human fetuses. Quinine crosses the placenta, reaching a level that is about one-third of the mother's level. Rates of miscarriage, low birth weight, or birth defects are not increased by first-trimester exposure for treatment for malaria. Birth defects were reported after women took unusually large doses in an attempt to end their pregnancy. In about half of those cases, the resulting abnormality was deafness. Other abnormalities reported included limb defects, a variety of organ defects, and visual changes. Birth defects were seen in rabbits and guinea pigs but not mice, rats, dogs, and monkeys. However, animal studies are not necessarily good indicators of how a drug will behave in humans. Considering how poorly it crosses the placenta, fetal toxicity seems a low probability at recommended doses. Quinine is used for the treatment of newborn malaria.

Breast-feeding: There are no adequate reports or well-controlled studies in nursing women. Quinine enters human breast milk, achieving a level about one-third that of the mother. Despite widespread use, there are no reports of toxicity in breast-fed newborns.

Potential drug interactions: Interaction between the following medications and quinine has the potential to impact the effect of one or more of the drugs. In some instances the interaction can be dangerous or life-threatening and must be avoided: antacids containing aluminum and/or magnesium, cimetidine, ketoconazole, erythromycin, rifampin, tetracycline, troleandomycin, urinary alkalinizing agents, drugs that are cleared from the body by the enzymes CYP3A4 and CYP2D6, digoxin, carbamazepine, phenobarbital, astemizole, cisapride, halofantrine, pimozide, quinidine, terfenadine, mefloquine, warfarin and other oral anticoagulants, heparin.

What the FDA says about use in pregnancy: Category C (see Appendix).

What the available evidence suggests about breast-feeding safety: Likely safe.

The bottom line for you:

- Malaria is a major maternal, fetal, and newborn illness. Quinine is effective treatment of malaria. Except for the tetracyclines, there is no evidence that quinine or any other antimalarial drugs in use cause birth defects at the recommended doses.

- Quinine appears safe for use while breast-feeding.

RABEPRAZOLE

Brand name: Aciphex

Drug classes: Antiulcer agent; Gastrointestinal; Proton pump inhibitor.

Indications (what it is used for): GERD (gastroesophageal reflux), prevention and treatment of stomach ulcer, increased stomach acid secretion, stress ulcer.

How it works: Lowers the production of acid by inhibiting hydrogen-potassium ATPase in the stomach wall.

Contraindications (reasons you shouldn't take it): Hypersensitivity to drug or class.

Possible side effects and warnings: Can cause liver failure, various blood disorders, headache, and diarrhea. Should be used with caution in women with liver dysfunction or who require long-term use.

How it can affect pregnant women: Gastroesophageal reflux and/or heartburn occurs in 45–85% of pregnant women in part because of high progesterone and estrogen levels. Treatment for GERD begins with reducing gastric acidity with lifestyle and dietary changes. If these fail, antacids or sucralfate

are first-line medical therapies, followed by histamine receptor blockers.

There is no published data with rabeprazole during pregnancy. Other proton pump inhibitors are generally considered effective treatment for GERD during pregnancy. There are no reported adverse effects. Proton pump inhibitors are first-choice medications for the prevention of lung damage from breathing in vomit after or during general anesthesia.

How it can affect a developing embryo or fetus: There are no adequate reports or well-controlled studies in human fetuses. It is unknown whether rabeprazole crosses the human placenta. Rodent studies are reassuring, revealing no evidence of birth defects or low birth weight despite the use of doses higher than those used clinically. However, animal studies are not necessarily good indicators of how a drug will behave in humans.

Breast-feeding: There is no published data in nursing women. It is unknown whether rabeprazole enters human breast milk. It is concentrated in rodent breast milk.

Potential drug interactions: Interaction between the following medications and rabeprazole has the potential to impact the effect of one or more of the drugs. In some instances the interaction can be dangerous or life-threatening and must be avoided: warfarin; drugs that depend on stomach acid for absorption, including ketoconazole and digoxin; amoxicillin; clarithromycin; pimozide.

What the FDA says about use in pregnancy: Category B (see Appendix).

What the available evidence suggests about breast-feeding safety: Unknown.

The bottom line for you:

- There are alternative agents with which there is more experience during pregnancy and while breast-feeding.

- Safety data during pregnancy is limited to animal studies and manufacturer's case reports. As a result, proton pump inhibitors are recommended during pregnancy only for the treatment of severe GERD that is unresponsive to lifestyle changes or other medications.

RABIES IMMUNE GLOBULIN, HUMAN

Brand names: BayRab, Hyperab, Imogam rabies

Drug classes: Antiviral; Immune globulin

Indications (what it is used for): Rabies exposure.

How it works: Provides antibodies needed to prevent rabies after exposure.

Contraindications (reasons you shouldn't take it): None known.

Possible side effects and warnings: Can cause injection site reaction and mild fever. Should be used with caution in women who have a hypersensitivity to the drug or class or who have asthma.

How it can affect pregnant women: More than 50% of the rabies cases in the U.S. result from exposure to dogs outside the U.S. Rabies that is left untreated is almost universally fatal. Administering rabies immunoglobulin (IgG) as soon as possible (preferably immediately) after a bite from an infected animal can prevent the development of the disease. Rabies vaccine and rabies immune globulin should be given to anyone suspected of rabies exposure unless he or she has been previously immunized with rabies vaccine (see "rabies vaccine" entry below). Rabies immune globulin has been used successfully without complications during pregnancy. The reported adverse reaction rate is similar in pregnant and nonpregnant women.

How it can affect a developing embryo or fetus: A fetus can become infected with rabies if the pregnant mother becomes infected. There are no adequate reports or well-controlled studies of (IgG) in human fetuses. Antirabies IgG likely crosses the human placenta. It is not known whether maternal treatment provides any level of protection to a fetus. Animal reproduction studies have not been performed.

Breast-feeding: There is no published data in nursing women. It is unknown whether rabies immune globulin enters human breast milk. However, other IgG antibodies are excreted into breast milk.

Potential drug interactions: Repeated doses of rabies immune globulin should not be administered after vaccine treatment has been initiated. Other antibodies in the rabies immune globulin preparation may interfere with the response to live vaccines for polio and for measles, mumps, and rubella. Immunization with live vaccines should not be given within 3 months after rabies immune globulin administration.

What the FDA says about use in pregnancy: Category C (see Appendix).

What the available evidence suggests about breast-feeding safety: Likely safe.

The bottom line for you:

- Rabies immune globulin is safe and effective for use during pregnancy and while breast-feeding.

RABIES VACCINE

Brand names: Imovax Rabies; RabAvert

Drug class: Vaccine

Indications (what it is used for): Rabies exposure.

How it works: Stimulates protective immunity by exposing the patient to inactivated rabies virus.

Contraindications (reasons you shouldn't take it): None known.

Possible side effects and warnings: Can cause life-threatening allergic reaction and paralysis. Should be used with caution in women who have a hypersensitivity to bovine gelatin, chicken protein, neomycin, chlortetracycline, or amphotericin B.

How it can affect pregnant women: More than 50% of the rabies cases in the U.S. result from exposure to dogs outside the U.S. Rabies that is left untreated is almost universally fatal. Administering rabies immunoglobulin as soon as possible (preferably immediately) after a bite from an infected animal can prevent the development of the disease. Rabies vaccine is an inactivated vaccine grown in chicken cells. Rabies vaccine and rabies immune globulin should be given to anyone suspected of rabies exposure. The vaccine has been used successfully during pregnancy, and pregnant women respond immunologically at least as well as nonpregnant women. The reported adverse reaction rate is similar in pregnant and nonpregnant women.

How it can affect a developing embryo or fetus: A fetus can become infected with rabies if the pregnant mother becomes infected. There are no adequate reports or well-controlled studies of rabies vaccine in human fetuses. It is likely that the IgG antibody produced in response to the vaccine crosses the placenta, but it is not known whether it provides any protection to the fetus. There were no adverse vaccine effects reported in more 250 treated pregnancies; all outcomes were normal.

Breast-feeding: There is no published data in nursing women. It is unknown whether rabies vaccine enters human breast milk. It is likely that the antibodies produced in response to the vaccine are excreted into the milk. Avoid breast-feeding until the vaccination series has begun, at which time it is considered safe.

Potential drug interactions: Interaction between the following medications and rabies vaccine has the potential to impact the effect of one or more of the drugs or of the vaccine. In some instances the interaction can be dangerous or life-threatening and must be avoided: corticosteroids, other immunosuppressive agents, antimalarials.

What the FDA says about use in pregnancy: Category C (see Appendix).

What the available evidence suggests about breast-feeding safety: Likely safe.

The bottom line for you:

- Rabies vaccine is safe and effective during pregnancy and while breast-feeding.

RAMIPRIL

Brand name: Altace
Drug class: ACEI/A2R-antagonist
Indications (what it is used for): High blood pressure, congestive heart failure after a heart attack, reducing the risk of cardiovascular disease.

How it works: Inhibits the production and action of angiotensin, which dilates arteries and lowers blood pressure.

Contraindications (reasons you shouldn't take it): Hypersensitivity to drug or class, angioedema (rapid swelling of the layers of the skin).

Possible side effects and warnings: Can cause rapid swelling of the layers of the skin, severe low blood pressure, high potassium level, liver toxicity, inflammation of the pancreas, low white blood cell count, cough, dizziness, fatigue, nausea, vomiting, muscle pain, joint pain, and cold symptoms. Should be used with caution in women with severe congestive heart failure, kidney dysfunction, renal artery stenosis, collagen vascular disease (disease of the connective tissue), low sodium level, or volume depletion (loss of water and salts from cells).

How it can affect pregnant women: There are no adequate reports or well-controlled studies of ramipril in pregnant women. In general, ACE inhibitors must be avoided during pregnancy because of risk to the fetus (see "How it can affect a developing embryo or fetus" below). The lowest effective dose should be used if ramipril is required for the control of life-threatening high blood pressure during pregnancy.

How it can affect a developing embryo or fetus: There is no published data in human fetuses. Ramipril likely crosses the human placenta since similar medications do. Adverse fetal effects occur after exposure to ACE inhibitors anytime during pregnancy. First-trimester exposure to ACE inhibitors almost triples the risk of cardiovascular and brain/spine disorders. No such increase is seen with other types of blood-pressure-lowering drugs. Exposure later in pregnancy can cause an underdeveloped skull, reversible or irreversible kidney failure, low blood pressure, preterm birth, low birth weight, a persistently open ductus arteriosus (fetal vessel that diverts blood away from the lungs) after birth, and death.

ACE inhibitors cause kidney damage probably

by causing a prolonged lack of adequate blood flow to the kidneys due to low blood pressure. There is not enough information to determine whether ramipril produces these effects as other ACE inhibitors do. Fetuses of women taking ramipril should be monitored regularly by ultrasound. If low amniotic fluid volume is detected, ramipril should be discontinued immediately unless it is lifesaving for the mother. However, low amniotic fluid may not appear until after the fetus has irreversible injury. Newborns exposed during pregnancy to ACE inhibitors should be watched closely for low blood pressure, low urine production, and a high potassium level. It may be necessary to wash the drug out of a newborn's system if low urine production continues despite adequate blood pressure and kidney blood flow.

Breast-feeding: There is no published data in nursing women. It is unknown whether ramipril enters human breast milk. It is described as low in rodents.

Potential drug interactions: Interaction between the following medications and ramipril has the potential to impact the effect of one or more of the drugs. In some instances the interaction can be dangerous or life-threatening and must be avoided: nonsteroidal anti-inflammatory drugs (NSAIDs), thiazide diuretics, potassium-sparing diuretics (e.g., amiloride, spironolactone, triamterene), potassium supplements, lithium.

What the FDA says about use in pregnancy: Category D (see Appendix).

What the available evidence suggests about breast-feeding safety: Unknown.

The bottom line for you:
- Ramipril and other ACE inhibitors are teratogens (substances that can cause birth defects) and should be avoided throughout pregnancy.
- When the mother's disease requires treatment with ramipril, the lowest doses should be used accompanied by close monitoring of the fetus.
- Until there is new information, it is best to avoid ramipril while breast-feeding.

RANITIDINE

Brand names: Ranitiget, Zantac
Drug classes: Antihistamine, H2; Antiulcer agent; Gastrointestinal
Indications (what it is used for): Duodenal or gastric ulcer, GERD (gastroesophageal reflux), heartburn.
How it works: H2 antagonist.
Contraindications (reasons you shouldn't take it): Hypersensitivity to drug or class, porphyria (a rare group of blood disorders).
Possible side effects and warnings: Can cause liver toxicity, low platelet count, muscle pain, headache, nausea, vomiting, diarrhea, constipation, dizziness, tiredness, dry skin, rash, and confusion. Should be used with caution in women with liver or kidney dysfunction.
How it can affect pregnant women: Gastroesophageal reflux disease and/or heartburn occurs in 45–85% of pregnant women in part because of high progesterone and estrogen levels. The treatment for GERD consists of reducing gastric acidity starting with lifestyle and dietary changes. If these fail, antacids or sucralfate are first-line medical therapies, followed by histamine receptor blockers. If these don't work, ranitidine and cimetidine are second-line options that are effective during pregnancy. Ranitidine is used in labor wards every 6 hours to reduce the risk of acid aspiration (inhaling vomit) during labor or delivery.
How it can affect a developing embryo or fetus: There are no adequate reports or well-controlled studies in human fetuses. Ranitidine crosses the human placenta, reaching a level in the fetus that is about 40% of the mother's level. Population-based studies reveal no increase in the rate of adverse fetal outcomes after first-trimester exposure. Rodent studies are reassuring, noting no evidence of birth defects or low birth weight despite the use of doses higher than those used clinically. However, animal studies are not necessarily good indicators of how a drug will behave in humans.
Breast-feeding: There is no published data in nursing women. Although ranitidine is concentrated in

human breast milk, no adverse effects are reported. Ranitidine is approved for use in pediatric practice.

Potential drug interactions: None that is clinically relevant.

What the FDA says about use in pregnancy: Category B (see Appendix).

What the available evidence suggests about breast-feeding safety: Likely safe.

The bottom line for you:

- GERD is common during pregnancy. First-line treatments include lifestyle modification and antacids.
- If first-line treatments fail, ranitidine appears safe and effective during pregnancy.
- Ranitidine is generally considered safe for use while breast-feeding.

REMIFENTANIL

Brand name: Ultiva

Drug class: Analgesic, narcotic

Indications (what it is used for): Anesthesia.

How it works: Binds opiate receptors to reduce the perception of pain.

Contraindications (reasons you shouldn't take it): Hypersensitivity to drug or class, epidural or intrathecal (An injection into a portion of the spinal canal, the sub-arachnoid space; useful in pain management [spinal anesthesia] or chemotherapy) anesthetic use.

Possible side effects and warnings: Can cause suspension of breathing, chest wall rigidity, rapid or slow heart rate, low blood pressure, dependency, seizures, nausea, vomiting, shivering, fever, dizziness, constipation, headache, blurred vision, itching, low urine production, confusion, agitation, anxiety, and biliary spasm. Should be used with caution in women who have respiratory depression.

How it can affect pregnant women: Remifentanil is an opiate that takes effect quickly and lasts only a short period of time. In a pilot study, remifentanil provided superior pain relief to women during labor when given by a patient-controlled device compared to intramuscular injection of meperidine. However, the difference between a safe dose of remifentanil and one that produces high levels of sedation and slow maternal breathing is small, limiting its safe use. It is more often used as a supplement to epidural/spinal anesthesia during cesarean delivery.

How it can affect a developing embryo or fetus: Remifentanil crosses the human placenta, reaching a level in the fetus that is half the level of the mother. It is rapidly cleared (eliminated from the body) by the fetus, although newborns have been sedated after its use during delivery. Rodent studies are reassuring, revealing no evidence of birth defects or low birth weight despite the use of doses higher than those used clinically. However, animal studies are not necessarily good indicators of how a drug will behave in humans.

Breast-feeding: There is no published data in nursing women. It is unknown whether remifentanil enters human breast milk; it is excreted into rodent breast milk. Considering what it is used for and how quickly the body breaks it down, one-time remifentanil use is unlikely to pose a clinically significant risk to a breast-feeding newborn.

Potential drug interactions: Remifentanil may increase the effect of other central nervous system depressants.

What the FDA says about use in pregnancy: Category C (see Appendix).

What the available evidence suggests about breast-feeding safety: Likely safe.

The bottom line for you:

- There are alternative agents with a higher safety profile with which there is more experience during pregnancy.
- Limited use of remifentanil will have no effect on a breast-feeding newborn.

REPAGLINIDE

Brand name: Prandin

Drug classes: Adrenergic antagonist; Antidiabetic agent

Indications (what it is used for): Type II diabetes

How it works: Stimulates pancreatic islet cell insulin release in response to the level of glucose.

Contraindications (reasons you shouldn't take it): Hypersensitivity to drug or class, type I diabetes, ketoacidosis (high blood levels of acids called ketones).

Possible side effects and warnings: Can cause low blood glucose, inflammation of the pancreas, Stevens-Johnson syndrome (a rare but serious skin reaction to medication), hemolytic anemia, liver dysfunction, headache, cold symptoms, nausea, vomiting, constipation, diarrhea, heartburn, muscle pain, and chest pain. Should be used with caution in women who have severe kidney disease.

How it can affect pregnant women: The published data during pregnancy with repaglinide is limited to isolated case reports. Women eliminate it from the body more slowly than men. While a growing body of research indicates that some oral hypoglycemic agents such as glyburide may be equally effective and safe as insulin to control glucose in women with diabetes, that information does not yet exist for repaglinide.

How it can affect a developing embryo or fetus: There are no adequate reports or well-controlled studies in human fetuses. It is unknown whether repaglinide crosses the human placenta. Rodent studies are reassuring, revealing no evidence of birth defects. An increased risk of low birth weight was seen, perhaps the result of chronically low blood glucose in the mother. However, animal studies are not necessarily good indicators of how a drug will behave in humans.

Breast-feeding: There is no published data in nursing women. It is unknown whether repaglinide enters human breast milk. It does enter rat milk and is associated with skeletal deformities in the feeding pups.

Potential drug interactions: Interaction between the following medications and repaglinide has the potential to impact the effect of one or more of the drugs. In some instances the interaction can be dangerous or life-threatening and must be avoided: CYP3A4 inhibitors (e.g., ketoconazole, miconazole), antibacterial agents (e.g., clarithromycin, erythromycin), CYP3A4 inducers (e.g., barbiturates, carbamezapine, rifampin), gemfibrozil, b-adrenergic blocking agents, chloramphenicol, coumarins, monoamine oxidase inhibitors (MAOIs), nonsteroidal antiinflammatory drugs (NSAIDs), other drugs that are highly protein bound, probenecid, salicylates, sulfonamides.

What the FDA says about use in pregnancy: Category C (see Appendix).

What the available evidence suggests about breast-feeding safety: Unknown.

The bottom line for you:

- There are alternative agents with which there is more experience during pregnancy and while breast-feeding.

RESERPINE

Brand names: Reserpaneed, Serpalan, Serpasil, Serpatabs, Serpate, Serpivite

Drug classes: Adrenergic antagonist, other; Antihypertensive

Indications (what it is used for): High blood pressure, adjunct for psychosis.

How it works: Depletes catecholamine (e.g. epinephrine) and 5-HT (an amino acid) stores from nerve endings, decreasing nerve transmission and lowering blood pressure.

Contraindications (reasons you shouldn't take it): Hypersensitivity to drug or class, electroconvulsive therapy.

Possible side effects and warnings: Can cause nausea, vomiting, diarrhea, loss of appetite, mouth dryness, excess saliva and mucus production, irregular or slow heart rate, fainting, chest pain, skin swelling, shortness of breath, nosebleeds, nasal congestion, dizziness, headache, paradoxical anxiety, depression, nervousness, nightmares, drowsiness, muscle pain, weight gain, deafness, and itching.

Should be used with caution in women with a history of peptic ulcer or ulcerative colitis, gallstones, kidney insufficiency; who are about to receive or recently received a general anesthetic drug; or who are taking digoxin, quinidine, or other blood-pressure-lowering medications.

How it can affect pregnant women: Reserpine is a second-line choice for the treatment of high blood pressure. It is also used for the treatment of constriction of arteries in the brain, migraines, Raynaud's disease (disorder in which blood vessels are prone to spasm, which causes discoloration of the fingers, toes, and occasionally other areas often triggered by cold), refractory depression, involuntary repetitive body movements that have a slow onset, and severely elevated thyroid hormone levels. There is only limited study during pregnancy.

How it can affect a developing embryo or fetus: There are no adequate reports or well-controlled studies in human fetuses. Reserpine crosses the human placenta. It can increase newborn mucus secretions in the lungs and cause nasal congestion, blue skin from a lack of oxygen, and poor appetite. Although it is unclear whether reserpine is a human teratogen (substance that can cause birth defects), rodent studies revealed an increased risk of birth defects and miscarriage. However, animal studies are not necessarily good indicators of how a drug will behave in humans.

Breast-feeding: Reserpine is excreted in human breast milk. Increased respiratory tract secretions that plug up the affected passageways may cause blue skin from a lack of oxygen and poor appetite in breast-fed infants.

Potential drug interactions: Interaction between the following medications and reserpine has the potential to impact the effect of one or more of the drugs. In some instances the interaction can be dangerous or life-threatening and must be avoided: monoamine oxidase inhibitors (MAOIs), digitalis, quinidine, since cardiac arrhythmias have occurred; direct-acting amines (e.g., epinephrine, isoprotere-

nol, metaraminol, phenylephrine); indirect-acting amines (e.g., amphetamines, ephedrine, tyramine).

What the FDA says about use in pregnancy: Category C (see Appendix).

What the available evidence suggests about breast-feeding safety: Not safe.

The bottom line for you:

- There are alternative agents with which there is more experience during pregnancy and while breast-feeding.
- Reserpine should be used during pregnancy and while breast-feeding only if there is no other option.

RHO(D) IMMUNE GLOBULIN

Brand names: Gamulin Rh, HypRho-D, Mini-Gamulin Rh, Rhesonativ, WinRho SDF

Drug class: Immune globulin

Indications (what it is used for): Prevention of at risk of Rh-negative women developing Rh antibodies that would attack the red blood cells of their Rh-positive fetuses.

How it works: Prevents stimulation of Rh-positive antibodies.

Contraindications (reasons you shouldn't take it): Hypersensitivity to drug or class, Rh-positive women.

Possible side effects and warnings: Can cause injection site reaction and fever.

How it can affect pregnant women: The Rh factor is a part of your red blood cell that is either present (Rh positive) or missing (Rh negative). Rh disease occurs when an Rh-negative woman is exposed to Rh-positive red blood cells from her fetus and develops antibodies to the Rh-positive red blood cells. This response can occur anytime in pregnancy after about 10 weeks. These antibodies cross the placenta and coat the fetal red blood cells leading to their breakdown. When antibody levels are high, the fetus becomes anemic. Severe anemia can cause heart failure and fetal death.

Anti-D human (Rho[D]) immunoglobulin has been used to prevent this from happening for more than 30 years. It is estimated to have reduced the number of perinatal deaths by about 10,000 cases a year in the U.S. alone. It is recommended that Rho(D) immune globulin be given to all nonsensitized Rh-negative women at the following times: 28 weeks of pregnancy; at delivery after confirming that the newborn is Rh positive; after spontaneous or induced abortion, ruptured tubal pregnancy, chorionic villus sampling (to test for chromosomal abnormalities such as Down syndrome and Tay-Sachs disease), amniocentesis, abdominal trauma, or any occurrence of transplacental hemorrhage to reduce the risk of the woman developing anti-D antibodies that will threaten the health of this or subsequent pregnancies. There is minimal evidence that giving RhoD immune globulin for first-trimester vaginal bleeding is needed. If there is no doubt in paternity and the father is Rh negative, Rho(D) immune globulin is unnecessary.

How it can affect a developing embryo or fetus: There has been no evidence of fetal harm after extensive clinical experience. There has been some media coverage linking Rho(D) immune globulin to autism, but there is no credible evidence to support this.

Breast-feeding: There are no adequate reports or well-controlled studies in nursing women. Rho(D) immune globulin is excreted into human breast milk, but the amount of intact antibody detected in the breast-fed newborn is clinically insignificant.

Potential drug interactions: Other antibodies contained in Rho(D) immune globulin may interfere with the response to live virus vaccines such as polio and measles, mumps, and rubella for up to 3 months after birth.

What the FDA says about use in pregnancy: Category C (see Appendix).

What the available evidence suggests about breast-feeding safety: Safe.

The bottom line for you:

- Rho(D) immune globulin is safe and effective during pregnancy and while breast-feeding.

RIBAVIRIN
Brand names: Rebetol, Viramid, Virazid, Virazole
Drug class: Antiviral
Indications (what it is used for): Chronic hepatitis C viral infection.
How it works: Unknown.
Contraindications (reasons you shouldn't take it): Hypersensitivity to drug or class, male partner of a pregnant woman, significant cardiac disease, autoimmune hepatitis, genetic defects of hemoglobin, moderate kidney dysfunction.
Possible side effects and warnings: Can cause hemolytic anemia, low platelet and/or white blood cell counts, bone marrow suppression, heart attack, serious thoughts of suicide, nausea, vomiting, autoimmune disorders, lung toxicity, inflammation of the pancreas, diabetes, headache, fatigue, muscle pain, joint pain, fever, sleeplessness, depression, hair loss, irritability, loss of appetite, rash, itching, shortness of breath, heartburn, and loss of concentration. Should be used with caution in women with a psychiatric disorder, myelosuppression (decreased bone marrow activity), lung or heart disease, or diabetes.
How it can affect pregnant women: Hepatitis C is a growing problem worldwide. Perhaps 1 in 3 patients with HIV also have hepatitis C. Liver disease due to chronic hepatitis C virus infection is now the second leading cause of death in some HIV-infected populations. It is the most common cause of chronic liver disease and liver transplantation. While transmission of virus to newborn is now one of the leading causes of perinatal Hepatitis C infection, it accounts for only about 2–3% of the cases. HIV-positive women are 2 to 4 times more likely to transmit hepatitis C to their newborn than those who have hepatitis C but not HIV.

Cesarean delivery does not appear to decrease the chance that a woman will pass hepatitis C to her child. Although no adverse effects have been reported, the published data with ribavirin during pregnancy is limited to case reports of small numbers of patients. The CDC does not recommend that ribavirin be used to prevent hepatitis C infection after a known exposure (e.g., with an infected sex partner) if the person does not develop symptoms. The treatment of women with chronic hepatitis can be delayed until after pregnancy and should not be undertaken until controlled studies of use during pregnancy are available. However, inadvertent exposure to ribavirin during pregnancy is not a medical reason to terminate a pregnancy. Pregnant women treated with ribavirin for new-onset hepatitis C are encouraged to register with the Ribavirin Pregnancy Registry.

How it can affect a developing embryo or fetus: Transmission from a pregnant woman to her fetus is now the leading cause of hepatitis C transmission in developed countries. There are no adequate reports or well-controlled studies in human fetuses. It is unknown whether ribavirin crosses the human placenta. There are only limited case reports of its use during pregnancy, and they do not suggest an increase in adverse pregnancy outcomes. Preliminary results from the Ribavirin Pregnancy Registry including 131 pregnancies do not suggest an increase in birth defects. Rodent studies revealed an increased risk of limb, eye, and brain defects. Birth defects were not seen at doses approximating the recommended clinical dose. However, animal studies are not necessarily good indicators of how a drug will behave in humans. Ribavirin is often used by pediatricians for the treatment of RSV (respiratory syncytial virus, which is mild in adults but can be life-threatening in young children).

Breast-feeding: There is no published data in nursing women. It is unknown whether ribavirin enters human breast milk. Ribavirin is toxic to lactating rats and their offspring.

Potential drug interactions: Interaction between the following medications and ribavirin has the potential to impact the effect of one or more of the drugs. In some instances the interaction can be dangerous or life-threatening and must be avoided: didanosine, stavudine, zidovudine.

What the FDA says about use in pregnancy: Category X (see Appendix).

What the available evidence suggests about breast-feeding safety: Unknown.

The bottom line for you:

- Early human studies suggest that ribavirin is not a teratogen (substance that can cause birth defects).
- Ribavirin should be used during pregnancy only if the maternal benefit justifies the potential risk to the fetus or newborn. Women who take ribavirin during pregnancy are encouraged to register with the Ribavirin Pregnancy Registry (1-800-593-2214) to help increase the available information about the effect of ribavirin on pregnancy. The registry can also be a source of information for women taking, or considering taking, ribavirin during pregnancy.
- There is not enough information to conclude whether ribavirin is safe to use while breast-feeding.

RIBOFLAVIN

Brand name: None

Drug class: Vitamin/mineral

Indications (what it is used for): Replacement, supplementation.

How it works: Unknown.

Contraindications (reasons you shouldn't take it): Hypersensitivity to drug or class.

Possible side effects and warnings: Can cause bright yellow urine.

How it can affect pregnant women: Riboflavin (vitamin B_2) is an important nutrient contained in virtually all multivitamin supplements. Most prenatal vitamins contain about 3 mg, roughly twice the recommended daily intake while pregnant or breast-feeding. Additional supplementation beyond what is contained in prenatal vitamins is probably unneeded for most healthy pregnant women. Riboflavin does not decline during normal, unsupplemented pregnancy, and supplementation produces levels well above normal. Population studies (studies of a large group of people taken from the larger population) suggest that multivitamin supplementation for pregnant HIV-positive women improves maternal weight gain.

How it can affect a developing embryo or fetus: There are no adequate reports or well-controlled studies in human fetuses. Riboflavin is pumped across the human placenta. Some poorly designed studies suggest that the higher the maternal riboflavin level, the larger the fetus. There is no substantive evidence that riboflavin causes birth defects, and studies of whole regions of women suggest that a low intake of riboflavin may actually be associated with congenital heart disease in the newborn. Further study is warranted.

Breast-feeding: Riboflavin is excreted into human breast milk, and the concentration is similar to that in the mother's blood. Women who do not drink milk are more likely to have low concentrations of riboflavin in their breast milk.

Potential drug interactions: No clinically relevant interactions identified.

What the FDA says about use in pregnancy: Category A (see Appendix).

What the available evidence suggests about breast-feeding safety: Safe.

The bottom line for you:

- Riboflavin is safe for use during pregnancy and while breast-feeding. Prenatal vitamins typically provide about 3 mg of riboflavin and increase the maternal levels.

RIFABUTIN

Brand names: Ansamycin, Mycobutin

Drug class: Antimycobacterial

Indications (what it is used for): Prevention of disseminated *Mycobacterium avium* (a serious infection affecting the lymph nodes, central nervous system, and bone marrow), which can infect people with HIV.

How it works: Causes mycobacterium death by blocking the action of a mycobacterial DNA-dependent RNA polymerase.

Contraindications (reasons you shouldn't take it): Hypersensitivity to drug or class, active tuberculosis.

Possible side effects and warnings: Can cause low platelet and/or white blood cell counts, inflammation of the middle layer of the eye, rash, nausea, vomiting, abdominal pain, headache, heartburn, diarrhea, belching, discolored urine, taste changes, fever, loss of appetite, muscle pain, weakness, gas, chest pain, and sleeplessness. Should be used with caution in women with low platelet and/or white blood cell counts.

How it can affect pregnant women: Rifabutin is an alternative to rifampin for the treatment of tuberculosis in HIV-positive women taking certain antiretroviral medications. It is also recommended by the U.S. Public Health Service as an alternative to rifampin for the preventative treatment of tuberculosis. There is no data with rifabutin during pregnancy. In healthy nonpregnant women, rifabutin and rifampin significantly increase how fast the body eliminates ethinyl estradiol, suggesting that women who use low-estrogen oral contraceptives should switch to a higher dose or use a backup contraceptive method while taking rifabutin.

How it can affect a developing embryo or fetus: There are no adequate reports or well-controlled studies in human fetuses. It is unknown whether rifabutin crosses the human placenta. Rodent studies are reassuring, revealing no evidence of birth defects or low birth weight despite the use of doses higher than those used clinically. However, animal studies are not necessarily good indicators of how a drug will behave in humans.

Breast-feeding: There are no adequate reports or well-controlled studies in nursing women. It is unknown whether rifabutin enters human breast milk.

If infant formula is available, breast-feeding is not recommended when a mother is HIV positive because HIV can be transmitted to the newborn in the breast milk.

Potential drug interactions: Interaction between the following medications and rifabutin has the potential to impact the effect of one or more of the drugs. In some instances the interaction can be dangerous or life-threatening and must be avoided: zidovudine, analgesics, anticoagulants, cardiac glycoside preparations, corticosteroids, cyclosporine, dapsone, narcotics (including methadone), oral contraceptives, oral hypoglycemic agents (sulfonylureas), quinidine, anticonvulsants, barbiturates, beta-adrenergic blockers, chloramphenicol, clofibrate, diazepam, disopyramide, ketoconazole, mexiletine, progestins, theophylline, verapamil. Patients using oral contraceptives should consider changing to nonhormonal methods of birth control.

What the FDA says about use in pregnancy: Category B (see Appendix).

What the available evidence suggests about breast-feeding safety: Unknown.

The bottom line for you:

- Rifabutin should be used during pregnancy and while breast-feeding only if the benefit to the woman justifies the potential risk to the embryo, fetus, or newborn.
- If infant formula is available, breast-feeding is not recommended when a mother is HIV positive because HIV can be transmitted to the newborn in the breast milk.

RIFAMPIN

Brand names: Abrifam, Aptecin, Corifam, Fenampicin, Rifadin, Rifamate, Rifamed, Rifampicin, Rifamycin, Rifarad, Rifocina, Rifumycin, Rimactane, Rimpacin, Syntaxil, Syntoren, Tibirim, Visedan
Drug class: Antimycobacterial
Indications (what it is used for): Tuberculosis (TB), prevention of meningococcal meningitis (bacterial infection of the membranes covering the brain and spinal cord).
How it works: Causes bacterial death by blocking the action of a bacterial DNA-dependent RNA polymerase.
Contraindications (reasons you shouldn't take it): Hypersensitivity to drug or class.
Possible side effects and warnings: Can cause kidney inflammation or failure, shock, liver toxicity, hemolytic anemia, low platelet and/or white blood cell counts, nausea, vomiting, diarrhea, loss of appetite, headache, fatigue, dizziness, abdominal pain, itching, rash, shortness of breath, lack of gross-muscle control, visual changes, and hives. Should be used with caution in women with liver dysfunction or who are using a medication that induces liver enzymes.
How it can affect pregnant women: Untreated tuberculosis poses a significant threat to a mother, fetus, and family. A 3-drug regimen of rifampin, isoniazid, and pyrazinamide is recommended for the initial 2-month treatment phase of TB. All pregnant women taking isoniazid should also take pyridoxine to reduce the risk of developing a "chemical" hepatitis. The CDC recommends that either streptomycin or ethambutol be added during the initial treatment unless the likelihood of isoniazid resistance is low. However, streptomycin is contraindicated (should not be used) in pregnancy. Ciprofloxacin has the best safety profile of second-line drugs for the treatment of drug-resistant tuberculosis. After the initial phase, treatment is continued with rifampin and isoniazid for 4 months or longer. There are no adequate reports or well-controlled studies of rifampin in pregnant women. A long clinical experience suggests that pregnancy does not increase the risk of an adverse effect. Rifampin may cause hemorrhage in the mother and newborn when administered during the third trimester; treatment with vitamin K may help reduce that risk. Rifampin decreases the effectiveness of oral contraceptives. Women using a low-dose oral contraceptive should

444 | The Complete Guide to Medications During Pregnancy and Breast-feeding

consider a higher dose contraceptive or a backup method of contraception.

How it can affect a developing embryo or fetus: There are no adequate reports or well-controlled studies in human fetuses. Rifampin crosses the human placenta, but there is no substantive evidence that it causes birth defects in humans. Rifampin does cross the rodent placenta and causes birth defects affecting the bone, spine, and palate when oral doses 15–25 times the maximum recommended clinical dose are used. However, animal studies are not necessarily good indicators of how a drug will behave in humans. Congenital TB (a baby born with TB) does occur on occasion when the mother has widespread TB. Rifampin is used to treat newborns infected with tuberculosis.

Breast-feeding: There are no adequate reports or well-controlled studies in nursing women. The trace amounts of rifampin excreted into human breast milk are likely clinically insignificant.

Potential drug interactions: Interaction between the following medications and rifampin has the potential to impact the effect of one or more of the drugs. In some instances the interaction can be dangerous or life-threatening and must be avoided: antiarrhythmics (e.g., disopyramide, mexiletine, quinidine, tocainide), anticonvulsants (e.g., phenytoin), antifungals (e.g., fluconazole, itraconazole, ketoconazole), barbiturates, beta-blockers, calcium channel blockers (e.g., diltiazem, nifedipine, verapamil), cardiac glycoside preparations, chloramphenicol, clofibrate, corticosteroids, cyclosporine, dapsone, diazepam, doxycycline, fluoroquinolones (e.g., ciprofloxacin), haloperidol, levothyroxine, methadone, narcotic analgesics, nortriptyline, oral anticoagulants, oral hypoglycemic agents (sulfonylureas), hormonal contraceptives, progestins, quinine, tacrolimus, tricyclic antidepressants (TCAs; e.g., amitriptyline, nortriptyline), theophylline, zidovudine, coumarin-type anticoagulants, halothane, isoniazid. Women using oral or other systemic hormonal contraceptives should change to nonhormonal methods of birth control. The daily dose of rifampin should be given at least 1 hour before any antacids.

What the FDA says about use in pregnancy: Category C (see Appendix).

What the available evidence suggests about breast-feeding safety: Safe.

The bottom line for you:

- Rifampin and most of the core group of antituberculosis drugs appear safe and effective during pregnancy and while breast-feeding.

RITONAVIR

Brand name: Norvir

Drug classes: Antiviral; Protease inhibitor

Indications (what it is used for): HIV infection.

How it works: Binds and blocks the action of enzymes (proteases) needed to replicate new virus.

Contraindications (reasons you shouldn't take it): Hypersensitivity to drug or class, use of a potent CYP3A4 inhibitor.

Possible side effects and warnings: Can cause seizures, diabetes, low platelet and/or white blood cell counts, high lipid levels, liver damage, nausea, vomiting, diarrhea, weakness, taste changes, tingling or numbness of the skin, blood vessel dilation, anxiety, loss of appetite, sore throat, abdominal pain, muscle pain, nerve pain, and rash. Should be used with caution in women with liver dysfunction.

How it can affect pregnant women: There are few well-controlled studies of ritonavir in pregnant women. Those that are available suggest no increased risk of an adverse outcome during pregnancy. Many commonly used drugs alter the way the body eliminates ritonavir.

How it can affect a developing embryo or fetus: There are no adequate reports or well-controlled studies in human fetuses. Very little if any ritonavir crosses the placenta; most umbilical cord samples studied are below the level of detection. Rodent studies are generally reassuring, revealing no evidence of birth defects or low birth weight despite the use of doses higher than those used clinically.

However, animal studies are not necessarily good indicators of how a drug will behave in humans. Combination therapy (treatment with other drugs at the same time) may increase the chance of a mother developing toxicity to ritonavir (see "Potential drug interactions" below). Maternal toxicity from high doses in animals can damage embryos.

Breast-feeding: There are no adequate reports or well-controlled studies in nursing women. It is unknown whether ritonavir enters human breast milk. If infant formula is available, breast-feeding is not recommended when a mother is HIV positive because HIV can be transmitted to the newborn in the breast milk.

Potential drug interactions: It is important your physician and pharmacist know all medications you are taking (prescription and over-the-counter). Interaction between the following medications and ritonavir has the potential to impact the effect of one or more of the drugs. In some instances the interaction can be dangerous or life-threatening and must be avoided: a-adrenergic antagonists such as alfuzosin; antiarrhythmics (e.g., amiodarone, bepridil, flecainide, propafenone, quinidine); antihistamines (e.g., astemizole, terfenadine); cisapride; pimozide; antifungals such as voriconazole; ergot derivatives (e.g., dihydroergotamine, ergonovine, ergotamine, methylergonovine); herbal products similar to St. John's wort; HMG-CoA reductase inhibitors such as lovastatin and simvastatin; atorvastatin; sedative-hypnotics such as midazolam and triazolam; buspirone; clorazepate; diazepam; estazolam; flurazepam; zolpidem; didanosine; carbamazepine; clonazepam; ethosuximide; divalproex; lamotrigine; phenytoin; bupropion; nefazodone; selective serotonin reuptake inhibitors (SSRIs); tricyclic antidepressants (TCAs); desipramine; trazodone; dronabinol; ketoconazole, itraconazole; clarithromycin; rifabutin and rifabutin metabolites; atovaquone; quinine; the beta-blockers metoprolol and timolol; the calcium channel blockers diltiazem, nifedipine, and verapamil; theophylline; digoxin; cyclosporine; tacrolimus; sirolimus; fluticasone; methadone; perphenazine; risperidone; thioridazine; prednisone, dexamethasone. May decrease the effectiveness of oral contraceptives. Alternate methods of contraception should be considered.

What the FDA says about use in pregnancy: Category B (see Appendix).

What the available evidence suggests about breast-feeding safety: Not safe.

The bottom line for you:

- Ritonavir is a protease inhibitor widely used during pregnancy as part of several HIV treatment "cocktails."

- If infant formula is available, breast-feeding is not recommended when a mother is HIV positive because HIV can be transmitted to the newborn in the breast milk.

- Women taking ritonavir during pregnancy are encouraged to register with the Antiretroviral Pregnancy Registry (1-800-258-4263) to help increase the available information about ritonavir use during pregnancy. The registry can also be a resource for women considering, or undergoing, ritonavir treatment during pregnancy.

RIZATRIPTAN

Brand names: Maxalt, Rizalt

Drug classes: Migraine; Serotonin receptor agonist

Indications (what it is used for): Migraine headache.

How it works: Activates the 5-HT1 receptor, contracting arteries in the brain, which stops the headache.

Contraindications (reasons you shouldn't take it): Hypersensitivity to drug or class, coronary artery disease, heart attack, uncontrolled high blood pressure, use of a 5-HT1 agonist within 24 hours, use of a monoamine oxidase inhibitor (MAOI) within 14 days, use of an ergot derivative within 24 hours, basilar migraine, hemiplegic migraine.

Possible side effects and warnings: Can cause acute heart attack, irregular heart rate, coronary spasm, palpitations, severe high blood pressure, cerebral hemorrhage, stroke, poor blood flow to the bowel or to the hands and feet, rapid swelling of the layers of the skin, sleepiness, chest pain, neck tightness, dizziness, tingling or numbness of the skin, flushing, nausea, vomiting, diarrhea, shortness of breath, decreased mental acuity, tremor, and euphoria. Should be used with caution in women with peripheral vascular or cerebrovascular disease (reduced blood flow to the limbs or brain), cardiac risk factors, or liver dysfunction.

How it can affect pregnant women: There is no published data with rizatriptan during pregnancy. Triptans, as a group, may be associated with preterm birth and are best avoided at the extremes of prematurity (before 28 weeks) until more data is available.

How it can affect a developing embryo or fetus: There are no adequate reports or well-controlled studies in human fetuses. It is unknown whether rizatriptan crosses the human placenta. A review of the outcomes of 25 reports supplied to the manufacturer's pregnancy registry and other sources does not suggest that rizatriptan dramatically increases the risk of miscarriage or birth defects. Rodent studies are generally reassuring, revealing no evidence of birth defects, but embryo toxicity and low birth weight were reported. However, animal studies are not necessarily good indicators of how a drug will behave in humans.

Breast-feeding: There is no published data in nursing women. It is unknown whether rizatriptan enters human breast milk.

Potential drug interactions: Interaction between the following medications and rizatriptan has the potential to impact the effect of one or more of the drugs. In some instances the interaction can be dangerous or life-threatening and must be avoided: propranolol, ergotamine-containing or ergot-type medications (e.g., dihydroergotamine, methysergide), other 5-HT1 agonists, selective serotonin reuptake inhibitors (SSRIs; e.g., fluoxetine, fluvoxamine, paroxetine, sertraline), the enzyme monoamine oxidase A (MAO-A), inhibitors and non-

selective monoamine oxidase inhibitors (MAOIs), moclobemide.

What the FDA says about use in pregnancy: Category C (see Appendix).

What the available evidence suggests about breast-feeding safety: Unknown.

The bottom line for you:

- There are alternative agents with which there is more experience. Rizatriptan should be used during pregnancy and while breast-feeding only if the maternal benefit justifies the potential risk to the embryo, fetus, or newborn.

- Triptans, as a group, are best avoided at the extremes of prematurity (before 28 weeks) until more data is available.

- Women who are exposed to rizatriptan during pregnancy are encouraged to register with the manufacturer's pregnancy registry (1-800-986-8999) to help increase the available information about the effect of rizatriptan on pregnancy outcomes. The registry can also be a source of information for women exposed to rizatriptan during pregnancy.

ROCURONIUM

Brand name: Zemuron

Drug class: Neuromuscular blocker, nondepolarizing

Indications (what it is used for): Anesthetic paralysis.

How it works: Blocks the ability of the motor nerves to conduct a signal.

Contraindications (reasons you shouldn't take it): Hypersensitivity to drug or class.

Possible side effects and warnings: Can cause irregular heart rate, bronchospasm, low or high blood pressure, and injection site pain. Should be used with caution in women who are obese, or who have difficulties breathing or liver dysfunction.

How it can affect pregnant women: There are no adequate reports or well-controlled studies of rocuronium in pregnant women, although it has been used for cesarean delivery as part of general anesthesia in patients who cannot use succinylcholine. However, the manufacturer does not recommend replacing succinylcholine with rocuronium for induction of general anesthesia for cesarean delivery. Rocuronium may be prolonged by magnesium sulfate infusion used in women with preeclampsia (high blood pressure and protein in the urine during pregnancy and complications associated with it) or who are about to deliver prematurely (see magnesium sulfate).

How it can affect a developing embryo or fetus: There are no adequate reports or well-controlled studies in human fetuses. Rocuronium crosses the human placenta. In women who are being rapidly put to sleep for cesarean delivery, the fetal levels are about one-fifth that of the mother. No clinical problems have been noted. Rodent studies are reassuring, revealing no evidence of birth defects or low birth weight despite the use of doses higher than those used clinically. However, animal studies are not necessarily good indicators of how a drug will behave in humans.

Breast-feeding: There is no published data in nursing women. However, limited use of rocuronium during surgery is unlikely to pose a clinically significant risk to a breast-feeding newborn.

Potential drug interactions: Interaction between the following medications and rocuronium has the potential to impact the effect of one or more of the drugs. In some instances the interaction can be dangerous or life-threatening and must be avoided: other neuromuscular blocking agents (enflurane, isoflurane, halothane), carbamazepine, phenytoin, certain antibiotics (e.g., aminoglycosides, bacitracin, colistin, polymyxins, sodium colistimethate, tetracyclines, vancomycin), quinidine, magnesium sulfate.

What the FDA says about use in pregnancy: Category C (see Appendix).

What the available evidence suggests about breast-feeding safety: Safe.

The bottom line for you:
- There are alternative agents with which there is more experience. When necessary, rocuronium can be used safely during pregnancy.
- Rocuronium is safe for use if breast-feeding is planned after delivery.

ROSIGLITAZONE
Brand name: Avandia
Drug classes: Antidiabetic agent; Thiazolidinedione
Indications (what it is used for): Type II diabetes
How it works: Increases insulin sensitivity.
Contraindications (reasons you shouldn't take it): Hypersensitivity to drug or class, type I diabetes, diabetic ketoacidosis (lack of insulin prevents body using sugar as a fuel), concurrent insulin use, moderate to severe congestive heart failure.
Possible side effects and warnings: Can cause liver toxicity, hepatitis, anemia, congestive heart failure, cold symptoms, fluid retention, skin swelling, headache, weight gain, and low blood glucose. Should be used with caution in women with minimal to mild congestive heart failure, high blood pressure, liver dysfunction, or edema (swelling).
How it can affect pregnant women: Rosiglitazone can be used either alone or in combination with metformin or a sulfonylurea. The short-term use of rosiglitazone and clomiphene is more effective than metformin and clomiphene to induce ovulation in women with clomiphene-resistant polycystic ovary syndrome (PCOS; multiple cysts inside the ovary leading to irregular menstruation and infertility). Improved glucose control can restore ovulation in premenopausal nonovulating women and increase the risk of an unplanned pregnancy. Paradoxically, it can also interfere with ovulation each month. There are reports that rosiglitazone may increase the risk of heart attack and stroke; until this relationship is being clarified, caution is advised. The published data with rosiglitazone during pregnancy is limited

to case reports and small studies of patients reporting success.

How it can affect a developing embryo or fetus: There are no adequate reports or well-controlled studies in human fetuses. Rosiglitazone crosses the human placenta. Drug transfer rises as a pregnancy advances, ultimately reaching approximately half the level of the mother's. Rodent studies are generally reassuring, revealing no evidence of birth defects despite the use of doses higher than those used clinically. However, high doses were associated with miscarriage and low birth weight, possibly as a result of sustained low blood glucose in the mother or fetus. Animal studies are not necessarily good indicators of how a drug will behave in humans.

Breast-feeding: There is no published data in nursing women. It is unknown whether rosiglitazone enters human breast milk. It is excreted into rat milk.

Potential drug interactions: Interaction between the following medications and rosiglitazone has the potential to impact the effect of one or more of the drugs. In some instances the interaction can be dangerous or life-threatening and must be avoided: CYP2C8 inhibitors (e.g., gemfibrozil), CYP2C8 inducers (e.g., rifampin).

What the FDA says about use in pregnancy: Category C (see Appendix).

What the available evidence suggests about breast-feeding safety: Unknown.

The bottom line for you:

- Rosiglitazone should be used during pregnancy and while breast-feeding only if the benefit to the woman justifies the potential risk to the embryo, fetus, or newborn. There are alternative agents with which there is more experience.
- It is perhaps wise to reserve rosiglitazone for patients who are unsuccessful with ovulation induction using metformin and clomiphene.

RUBELLA VIRUS VACCINE, LIVE

Brand name: Meruvax II
Drug class: Vaccine

Indications (what it is used for): Rubella (German measles) susceptibility.

How it works: A genetically modified virus causes immunity without illness.

Contraindications (reasons you shouldn't take it): Hypersensitivity to drug or class, allergy to neomycin, any active infection that causes a fever, untreated tuberculosis, immunosuppressive therapy (except replacement corticosteroids), various blood disorders, lymphoma, primary or acquired immunodeficiency (including AIDS).

Possible side effects and warnings: Can cause injection site reaction, swollen lymph nodes, hives, rash, tiredness, sore throat, fever, headache, nausea, vomiting, diarrhea, fainting, and low platelet count. Should not be used with immunoglobulin.

How it can affect pregnant women: The rubella virus vaccine produces a modified rubella infection in susceptible persons that cannot be transmitted. The resulting immunity to the virus persists for at least 10 years. Women who are vaccinated before conception have only minimal risk of contracting rubella during pregnancy and thereby effectively protect their fetus from rubella infection. Yet only about half the world's countries vaccinate for rubella. Outbreaks continue to occur in countries with national immunization programs, typically involving women born in other countries or who are suspicious of vaccines. Before a woman is vaccinated for rubella, her blood should be tested to confirm that she is susceptible to infection. Women planning their first pregnancy should be tested and vaccinated if they are found to be susceptible. Following vaccination, they should delay conception for at least a month.

How it can affect a developing embryo or fetus: Rubella virus (the kind found in nature, not the kind used to create vaccines) is a major cause of birth defects when a pregnant women develops rubella in the first or second trimester. Those defects include deafness, eye abnormalities (especially retinopathy [disease of the retina], cataract [clouded lens of the eye], and microphthalmia [one or both eyeballs are abnormally small]), and congenital heart disease.

Other possible abnormalities include problems with the spleen, liver, or bone marrow; mental retardation; small head size (microcephaly); low birth weight; low platelet counts causing a characteristic blueberry muffin rash; and small chin. Children who were exposed to rubella in the womb should be watched closely as they age for any indication of developmental delay, autism disorders, schizophrenia, learning disabilities, diabetes, and glaucoma.

Rubella vaccination of the woman does not cause fetal disease. The manufacturer reports that in more than 700 women inadvertently vaccinated within 3 months before or after conception, no newborn had any findings consistent with congenital rubella (rubella that is acquired before birth). Pregnancy termination is not necessary in the case of vaccination.

Breast-feeding: Rubella vaccine virus is excreted into human breast milk, and there have been rare instances of newborns developing a mild case of rubella that does not cause damage. However, the risk is considered small, and immunization is not a reason to avoid breast-feeding.

Potential drug interactions: Use with immune globulins may interfere with the expected immune response of rubella vaccine.

What the FDA says about use in pregnancy: Category C (see Appendix).

What the available evidence suggests about breast-feeding safety: Safe.

The bottom line for you:

- Rubella virus vaccination of susceptible women prevents their babies from being born with rubella.
- Women planning their first pregnancy should be tested and vaccinated if they are found to be susceptible. After vaccination, they should delay conception for at least a month.
- Inadvertent vaccination during pregnancy is not associated with an adverse outcome.
- Women vaccinated for rubella during pregnancy or immediately after delivery can safely breast-feed.

SALMETEROL, INHALED

Brand names: Serevent, Serevent Diskus
Drug classes: Adrenergic agonist; Beta-agonist; Bronchodilator
Indications (what it is used for): Prevention of an asthma attack, exercise-induced asthma, chronic obstructive pulmonary disease (COPD).
How it works: Stimulates the beta-2 adrenergic receptors to dilate the lung passages.
Contraindications (reasons you shouldn't take it): Hypersensitivity to drug or class, acute asthma, irregular heart rate.
Possible side effects and warnings: Can cause rapid swelling of the layers of the skin, paradoxical bronchospasm and/or laryngospasm, irregular or rapid heart rate, high blood pressure, headache, nasal congestion, runny nose, sore throat, hives, palpitations, tremor, and nervousness. Should be used with caution in women with high blood pressure, cardiovascular disease, diabetes, seizures, high thyroid hormone level, or a low potassium level.
How it can affect pregnant women: Asthma is a common disease in life and in pregnancy. Approximately one-third of pregnant women with asthma get worse during pregnancy, one-third get better, and one-third remain clinically unchanged. When asthma is well controlled it does not affect pregnancy outcome, but poorly controlled asthma may increase the risk of preterm birth (delivery before 37 weeks) or low birth weight. Inhaled corticosteroids are considered the preventative medication of choice for pregnant women with persistent asthma unless their condition is well controlled by cromolyn or nedocromil. Budesonide and beclomethasone are considered the first-line treatments.

Certain medications used during labor and delivery have the potential to worsen asthma, including nonselective beta-blockers, some prostaglandins (used to induce labor), and ergonovine (used to control blood loss after delivery).

Salmeterol is a long-acting beta-adrenergic receptor activator that inhibits the release of chemicals that cause the bronchospasm. There are no published trials of its use during pregnancy. Salmeterol is typically used as a secondary agent after a first-line treatment has failed. Maternal blood levels of salmeterol are low or undetectable after inhalation. It also has been used for the treatment of altitude sickness in pregnant and nonpregnant women.

How it can affect a developing embryo or fetus: There are no adequate reports or well-controlled studies in human fetuses. It is unknown whether salmeterol crosses the human placenta. Transfer across the rat placenta is low. Considering the low blood levels in the mother and the poor transport across the placenta, it is unlikely that a fetus is exposed to a clinically relevant concentration.

Breast-feeding: There is no published data with salmeterol in breast-feeding women. However, considering that the maternal blood level is low, it is unlikely a breast-fed newborn would ingest clinically relevant amounts.

Potential drug interactions: Interaction between the following medications and salmeterol has the potential to impact the effect of one or more of the drugs. In some instances the interaction can be dangerous or life-threatening and must be avoided: monoamine oxidase inhibitors (MAOIs), tricyclic antidepressants (TCAs), beta-adrenergic receptor blocking agents, beta-blockers.

What the FDA says about use in pregnancy: Category C (see Appendix).

What the available evidence suggests about breast-feeding safety: Safe.

The bottom line for you:

- Salmeterol is likely safe and effective for use during pregnancy and while breast-feeding.

SAQUINAVIR

Brand names: Fortovase, Invirase
Drug classes: Antiviral; Protease inhibitor
Indications (what it is used for): Secondary treatment for HIV when primary drugs are no longer effective.

How it works: Binds and blocks the action of enzymes (proteases) needed to replicate new virus.

Contraindications (reasons you shouldn't take it): Hypersensitivity to drug or class; astemizole, cisapride, ergot, midazolam, terfenadine, or triazolam use.

Possible side effects and warnings: Can cause nausea, vomiting, diarrhea, diabetes, high glucose level, nerve damage, headache, ulcers in the mouth, rash, heartburn, abdominal pain, and eczema. Should be used with caution in women with liver dysfunction or who are taking lovastatin or simvastatin.

How it can affect pregnant women: Treating HIV during pregnancy significantly reduces the risk of a mother transmitting the virus to her child. Combination therapy (lamivudine, nevirapine, zidovudine) remains the standard treatment during pregnancy due to its high efficacy. Ideally, infected women remain on the drug cocktail throughout pregnancy, reaching a point where the virus is no longer detectable in their blood. At that time, the risk of transmitting the infection to the child is minimal.

Saquinavir is well tolerated during pregnancy and is part of several HIV treatment regimens. Its clearance (how fast the body processes and eliminates the drug) is increased by pregnancy, and the usually recommended dose may have to be increased to retain effectiveness. Ritonavir significantly increases the saquinavir level, and the combination of the two medications during pregnancy may have some advantage.

How it can affect a developing embryo or fetus: There are no adequate reports or well-controlled studies in human fetuses. Saquinavir, like many protease inhibitors, does not significantly cross the human placenta; it is unlikely to pose a risk to the fetus. Rodent studies are reassuring, revealing no evidence of birth defects or low birth weight. However, animal studies are not necessarily good indicators of how a drug will behave in humans.

Breast-feeding: There is no published data in nursing women. It is unknown whether saquinavir enters human breast milk. If infant formula is available, breast-feeding is not recommended when a mother is HIV positive because HIV can be transmitted to the newborn in the breast milk.

Potential drug interactions: Antiarrhythmics (e.g., amiodarone, bepridil, flecainide, propafenone, quinidine) and antihistamines (e.g., astemizole, terfenadine) should not be used with saquinavir because of the risk of serious and/or life-threatening interactions. Interaction between the following medications and saquinavir has the potential to impact the effect of one or more of the drugs. In some instances the interaction can be dangerous or life-threatening and must be avoided: ergot derivatives (e.g., dihydroergotamine, ergonovine, ergotamine, methylergonovine), garlic capsules, cisapride, rifampin, herbal products such as St. John's wort, other HIV protease inhibitors (e.g., indinavir, nelfinavir, ritonavir), warfarin, anticonvulsant drugs (e.g., carbamazepine, phenobarbital, phenytoin), benzodiazepines (e.g., alprazolam, clorazepate, diazepam, flurazepam), calcium channel blockers (e.g., amlodipine, diltiazem, felodipine, isradipine, nicardipine, nifedipine, nimodipine, nisoldipine, verapamil), dexamethasone, tricyclic antidepressants (TCAs) such as amitriptyline and imipramine. Alternative or additional contraceptive measures should be used when estrogen-based oral contraceptives and saquinavir are taken at the same time.

What the FDA says about use in pregnancy: Category B (see Appendix).

What the available evidence suggests about breast-feeding safety: Not safe.

The bottom line for you:

- Saquinavir is a safe and effective protease inhibitor during pregnancy when used in conjunction with other retroviral agents.
- If infant formula is available, breast-feeding is not recommended when a mother is HIV positive because HIV can be transmitted to the newborn in the breast milk.
- Women who are taking saquinavir during pregnancy are encouraged to register with the Anti-

retroviral Pregnancy Registry (1-800-258-4263) to help increase the information available about saquinavir use during pregnancy. The registry can also be a resource for women considering, or undergoing, treatment with saquinavir during pregnancy.

SCOPOLAMINE

Brand names: Isopto Hyoscine, Minims Hyoscine Hydrobromide, Scopoderm, Transderm Scop

Drug classes: Anesthetic, adjunct; Anticholinergic; Antiemetic; Cycloplegic; Gastrointestinal; Motion sickness agent; Mydriatic; Ophthalmic; Vertigo agent

Indications (what it is used for): Motion sickness, obstetric amnesia, preoperative sedation, intraoperative amnesia.

How it works: Blocks cholinergic nerve endings to eliminate motion sickness and prevent memory formation.

Contraindications (reasons you shouldn't take it): Hypersensitivity to drug or class, narrow-angle glaucoma.

Possible side effects and warnings: Can cause narrow-angle glaucoma, drowsiness, blurred vision, disorientation, dizziness, dilated pupils, hallucinations, confusion, psychosis, bronchospasm, respiratory depression, rash, muscle weakness, and red eyes. Should be used with caution in women who have an intestinal obstruction or a history of seizures or psychosis, impaired metabolic function, or liver or kidney dysfunction.

How it can affect pregnant women: Scopolamine is similar to atropine. It was at one time popular for "twilight sleep" during labor but has appropriately fallen out of favor. A recent study suggests that it is effective in reducing the duration of the first stage of labor without adverse outcomes. Scopolamine may reduce the post–cesarean section nausea/vomiting associated with epidural morphine.

How it can affect a developing embryo or fetus: There are no adequate reports or well-controlled

studies in human fetuses. Scopolamine rapidly crosses the human placenta and may cause a rapid fetal heart rate with decreased variation (an indicator used to assess the fetus's oxygen level). Rodent studies are reassuring, revealing no evidence of birth defects or low birth weight despite the use of doses higher than those used clinically. However, animal studies are not necessarily good indicators of how a drug will behave in humans.

Breast-feeding: There are no adequate reports or well-controlled studies in nursing women. Scopolamine enters human breast milk, but the long clinical experience is reassuring.

Potential drug interactions: Interaction between the following medications and scopolamine has the potential to impact the effect of one or more of the drugs. In some instances the interaction can be dangerous or life-threatening and must be avoided: other drugs that have weak antimuscarinic activity (e.g., certain antihistamines, meperidine, phenothiazines, tricyclic antidepressants); drugs (including alcohol) that can suppress the central nervous system; drugs with anticholinergic (acetylcholine-blocking) properties, such as belladonna alkaloids, antihistamines (including meclizine), and antidepressants. Scopolamine may decrease the absorption of oral medications.

What the FDA says about use in pregnancy: Category C (see Appendix).

What the available evidence suggests about breast-feeding safety: Likely safe.

The bottom line for you:

- Scopolamine appears safe for use during pregnancy for motion sickness and will have no effect on subsequent breast-feeding.
- Its other historical uses (e.g., obstetrical anesthesia) are no longer considered appropriate.

SECOBARBITAL

Brand names: Immenoctal, Novosecobarb, Secanal, Seconal

Drug classes: Anesthetic, adjunct; Anxiolytic; Barbiturate; Hypnotic

Indications (what it is used for): Short-term insomnia.

How it works: Depresses brain function.

Contraindications (reasons you shouldn't take it): Hypersensitivity to drug or class, respiratory depression, porphyria (a rare group of blood disorders).

Possible side effects and warnings: Can cause respiratory depression, dependency, liver toxicity, Stevens-Johnson syndrome (a rare but serious skin reaction to medication), rapid swelling of the skin layers, lethargy, and drowsiness.

How it can affect pregnant women: Barbiturates are dangerous drugs, with a narrow range of safety between a dose that is required for sedation and a dose that can cause coma and death. Secobarbital is used by patients to self-treat the unpleasant effects of illegal stimulants, to reduce anxiety, and to get high. It is physiologically addicting when taken in high doses, and withdrawal can be life-threatening. There are no adequate reports or well-controlled studies of secobarbital in pregnant women. Secobarbital was used for decades as a short-term sleeping aid for pregnant women. However, the sleep produced was not restful, and new alternative drugs have replaced it.

How it can affect a developing embryo or fetus: There are no adequate reports or well-controlled studies in human fetuses. It is likely that secobarbital rapidly crosses the human placenta. There is no substantive evidence that secobarbital causes birth defects. Administration during labor may cause respiratory depression in the newborn. Premature infants are particularly susceptible to the depressant effects of barbiturates. Withdrawal symptoms occur in infants of women who receive secobarbital throughout the third trimester.

Breast-feeding: There is no published data in nursing women. Small amounts of secobarbital are excreted into human breast milk, but its occasional use is generally considered compatible with breast-feeding.

Potential drug interactions: Interaction between the following medications and secobarbital has the potential to impact the effect of one or more of the drugs. In some instances the interaction can be dangerous or life-threatening and must be avoided: oral anticoagulants (e.g., acenocoumarol, dicumarol, phenprocoumon, warfarin); exogenous corticosteroids; oral griseofulvin; doxycycline; sodium valproate and valproic acid; other central nervous system depressants, including other sedatives or hypnotics, antihistamines, tranquilizers, or ethanol (alcohol); monoamine oxidase inhibitors (MAOIs). There have been reports of patients treated with AEDs (e.g. phenobarbital) who became pregnant while taking oral contraceptives. An alternative contraceptive method should be considered.

What the FDA says about use in pregnancy: Category D (see Appendix).

What the available evidence suggests about breast-feeding safety: Safe.

The bottom line for you:

- There are alternative agents with greater safety and efficacy for the same indications during pregnancy and while breast-feeding.

SELENIUM SULFIDE TOPICAL

Brand names: Abbottselsun, Exsel, Glo-Sel, Lenium, Micalon, Sebo-Lenium, Sel-Pen, Selsum, Selsun, Selukos, Versel

Drug classes: Antidermatophyte; Antifungal; Dermatologic

Indications (what it is used for): Dandruff, seborrhea, tinea versicolor (fungal skin infection).

How it works: Reduces the shedding of the superficial layer of skin.

Contraindications (reasons you shouldn't take it): Hypersensitivity to drug or class, inflamed skin.

Possible side effects and warnings: Can cause skin irritation, hair discoloration or loss, and oily or dry scalp.

How it can affect pregnant women: There is no published data with selenium sulfide during pregnancy. There is little systemic absorption whether measured after shampooing or lotion application.

How it can affect a developing embryo or fetus: There are no adequate reports or well-controlled studies in human fetuses. It is unknown whether selenium sulfide crosses the human placenta. Elemental selenium does cross the placenta to keep the concentrations equal in mother and fetus. Considering the dose and how it is applied, it is unlikely that the maternal level will be clinically relevant for the fetus.

Breast-feeding: There is no published data in nursing women. It is unknown whether selenium sulfide enters human breast milk. Considering the indication and dosing, any effect of selenium sulfide on breast milk is likely clinically insignificant.

Potential drug interactions: No clinically relevant interactions identified.

What the FDA says about use in pregnancy: Category C (see Appendix).

What the available evidence suggests about breast-feeding safety: Safe.

The bottom line for you:

- Selenium sulfide is safe and effective for use during pregnancy and while breast-feeding.

SENNA

Brand names: ex-lax, Senna-Gen, Senokot

Drug class: Laxative

Indications (what it is used for): Constipation.

How it works: Increases bowel motility.

Contraindications (reasons you shouldn't take it): Hypersensitivity to drug or class, bowel obstruction, undiagnosed abdominal pain.

Possible side effects and warnings: Can cause laxative abuse, nausea, bloating, cramps, gas, diarrhea, and discolored urine.

How it can affect pregnant women: Despite a long clinical experience, there are no adequate reports or well-controlled studies of senna in pregnant women. Only a small amount is absorbed across the bowel wall. Some doctors consider senna the laxative of choice during pregnancy and breast-feeding if one must be used. It is also effective for postpartum constipation.

How it can affect a developing embryo or fetus: There are no adequate reports or well-controlled studies in human fetuses. It is unknown whether senna crosses the human placenta. However, the maternal level is so low it would not have a direct fetal effect.

Breast-feeding: Less than 1% of the maternal dose of senna enters human breast milk. This amount is clinically insignificant.

Potential drug interactions: No clinically relevant interactions identified.

What the FDA says about use in pregnancy: Category C (see Appendix).

What the available evidence suggests about breast-feeding safety: Safe.

The bottom line for you:

● Senna is safe and effective for use during pregnancy and while breast-feeding when used occasionally.

SERTRALINE

Brand names: Lustral, Zoloft

Drug classes: Antidepressant; SSRI, type 1

Indications (what it is used for): Depression, postpartum depression, obsessive-compulsive disorder, premenopausal dysphoric disorder, post-traumatic stress disorder, panic disorder.

How it works: Selectively prevents nerve reuptake of serotonin to alter mood.

Contraindications (reasons you shouldn't take it): Hypersensitivity to drug or class, monoamine oxidase inhibitor (MAOI) use within 14 days.

Possible side effects and warnings: Can cause serotonin withdrawal syndrome, nausea, vomiting, diarrhea, insomnia, headache, dry mouth, sleepiness, dizziness, fatigue, tremor, heartburn, constipation, decreased sex drive, sweating, loss of appetite, nervousness, agitation, anxiety, and visual disturbances. Should be used with caution in women with kidney dysfunction.

How it can affect pregnant women: Depression is common during and after pregnancy but often goes unrecognized and untreated. Depression can be made worse by pregnancy or delivery, and suicide is a not uncommon cause of maternal death. Pregnancy is not a reason to discontinue antidepressant drugs if the medication is effective and needed. A woman being treated for depression who becomes pregnant should not discontinue medication abruptly on her own but rather discuss her treatment and condition with her medical provider. Pregnancy may increase the dose needed to be effective, and women with a history of depression have a higher rate of recurrence after delivery.

There are no adequate reports or well-controlled studies of sertraline in pregnant women, although there is growing experience with its use for the treatment of postpartum depression. Sertraline is not recommended for the prevention of depression, only for the treatment of it. In general, women taking SSRIs during pregnancy for depression require an increased dose to maintain effectiveness.

How it can affect a developing embryo or fetus: There are no adequate reports or well-controlled studies in human fetuses. Sertraline crosses the human placenta. Limited study suggests that the fetal levels range from one- to two-thirds of the maternal level, lower than citalopram, fluoxetine, and paroxetine. Some studies have shown a small increase in the risk of heart defects in embryos exposed to SSRIs in the first trimester but current study suggests it is not dose dependent (the risk does not increase or decrease as the dose does, suggesting other factors may play a role in creating the defect). The safest approach for all SSRIs is probably to avoid them in the first trimester. Women with moderate to severe depression responsive to their medication, however, should continue treatment during pregnancy as the benefit outweighs the possible risks to mother and child.

SSRI use late in pregnancy may double the risk of persistent pulmonary hypertension (high blood pressure in the lungs) during the newborn period (which, at 2 in 1,000 births, is low to begin with). SSRI exposure during the third trimester and until delivery may also lead to a withdrawal syndrome during the first few days of life, requiring extra care. Symptoms in the newborn may include problems breathing, jitteriness, increased muscle tone, irritability, altered sleep patterns, tremors, and poor eating. In most cases, these symptoms are mild and disappear within 2 weeks with no treatment. These symptoms can occur in up to 30% of exposed newborns, and, although they can can occur at all doses, occur more often with higher doses. The risk does not outweigh the benefit of needed therapy. Children born to women taking sertraline have higher average birth weights than those born to women taking citalopram, paroxetine, or fluoxetine. The same is true for newborn length. Rodent studies are generally reassuring, showing no increase in birth defects or low birth weight. However, animal studies are not necessarily good indicators of how a drug will behave in humans.

Breast-feeding: Sertraline and desmethylsertraline are present in human breast milk, but the amount in the newborn blood is usually below a detectable level. As a precaution, breast-fed infants should be monitored for possible adverse effects.

Potential drug interactions: Interaction between the following medications and sertraline has the potential to impact the effect of one or more of the drugs. In some instances the interaction can be dangerous or life-threatening and must be avoided: drugs that are metabolized by CYP2D6 (e.g., tricyclic antidepressants and the class 1C antiarrhythmics flecainide and propafenone), sumatriptan.

What the FDA says about use in pregnancy: Category C (see Appendix).

What the available evidence suggests about breast-feeding safety: Likely safe.

The bottom line for you:
- Sertraline is a good choice for the treatment of significant depression during pregnancy and while breast-feeding.

SEVOFLURANE

Brand names: Sevorane, Ultane
Drug class: Anesthesia, general
Indications (what it is used for): Induction and maintenance of anesthesia.
How it works: Unknown.
Contraindications (reasons you shouldn't take it): Hypersensitivity to drug or class, malignant hyperthermia.
Possible side effects and warnings: Can cause malignant hyperthermia (a rare life-threatening rise in body temperature, usually triggered by exposure to some general anesthetics), irregular, slow, or rapid heart rate, hepatitis, increased pressure within the brain, nausea, vomiting, agitation, cough, low or high blood pressure, shivering, laryngospasm, breath holding, increased salivation, dizziness, and apnea. Should be used with caution in women with hepatitis, liver or kidney dysfunction, heart valve disease, head injury, myasthenia gravis (autoimmune disorder causing muscle weakness), or increased intracranial pressure.
How it can affect pregnant women: There are no adequate reports or well-controlled studies of sevoflurane in pregnant women. It is a popular general anesthetic for cesarean delivery, resulting in outcomes similar to spinal anesthesia. Like the other volatile anesthetics (halothane and isoflurane), sevoflurane is thought to cause uterine relaxation and may be useful for the treatment of some obstetric complications. A limited number of case reports of patients in the first trimester do not report adverse outcomes.
How it can affect a developing embryo or fetus: Sevoflurane rapidly crosses the human placenta. It has been used for fetal anesthesia for procedures

performed before or during birth. Rodent studies are reassuring, revealing no evidence of birth defects or low birth weight. However, animal studies are not necessarily good indicators of how a drug will behave in humans.

Breast-feeding: There are no adequate reports or well-controlled studies in nursing women. It is unknown whether sevoflurane enters human breast milk. However, one-time sevoflurane use is unlikely to pose a clinically significant risk to a breast-feeding newborn.

Potential drug interactions: Interaction between the following medications and sevoflurane has the potential to impact the effect of one or more of the drugs. In some instances the interaction can be dangerous or life-threatening and must be avoided: nitrous oxide, nondepolarizing muscle relaxants, atracurium, pancuronium, vecuronium.

What the FDA says about use in pregnancy: Category B (see Appendix).

What the available evidence suggests about breast-feeding safety: Safe.

The bottom line for you:

- Sevoflurane is considered safe and effective for general anesthesia during pregnancy and while breast-feeding.

SIBUTRAMINE

Brand name: Meridia

Drug class: Anorexiant; central nervous system stimulant

Indications (what it is used for): Obesity.

How it works: Inhibits the uptake of multiple neurotransmitters to alter appetite.

Contraindications (reasons you shouldn't take it): Hypersensitivity to drug or class, monoamine oxidase inhibitor (MAOI) use within 14 days, coronary artery disease, congestive heart failure, irregular heart rate, stroke, severe liver or kidney dysfunction, anorexia nervosa.

Possible side effects and warnings: Can cause menstrual irregularities, painful menstruation, rapid heart rate, severe high blood pressure, seizures, headache, dry mouth, insomnia, runny nose, loss of/or increased appetite, constipation, dizziness, anxiety, heartburn, nausea, rash, and sinusitis.

How it can affect pregnant women: Obesity is a major epidemic in industrialized countries. Research confirms a relationship between obesity and cardiovascular disease, type II diabetes, certain forms of cancer, gallstones, certain respiratory disorders, and an increase in overall mortality rate. Sibutramine leads to weight loss, which if sustained may produce health benefits for patients with chronic obesity. Maintenance therapy increases the likelihood of maintaining the loss. The published data during pregnancy is limited to case reports and small series. Until there is additional study, there is no indication for its use during pregnancy.

How it can affect a developing embryo or fetus: There are no adequate reports or well-controlled studies in human fetuses. It is unknown whether sibutramine crosses the human placenta. Case reports and small series of patients are reassuring. Rodent studies are generally reassuring, with developmental abnormalities noted only at the highest doses that produced maternal toxicity and only in rabbits. Transport across the rodent placenta is limited. However, animal studies are not necessarily good indicators of how a drug will behave in humans.

Breast-feeding: There is no published data in nursing women. It is unknown whether sibutramine enters human breast milk.

Potential drug interactions: Interaction between the following medications and sibutramine has the potential to impact the effect of one or more of the drugs. In some instances the interaction can be dangerous or life-threatening and must be avoided: monoamine oxidase inhibitors (MAOIs; e.g., phenelzine, selegiline), drugs used for migraine therapy (e.g., dihydroergotamine, sumatriptan), certain opioids (e.g., dextromethorphan, fentanyl, meperidine, pentazocine), lithium, tryptophan.

What the FDA says about use in pregnancy: Category C (see Appendix).
What the available evidence suggests about breast-feeding safety: Unknown.
The bottom line for you:

- There are no indications for sibutramine during pregnancy and while breast-feeding.

SILDENAFIL

Brand name: Viagra
Drug class: PDE inhibitor
Indications (what it is used for): Pulmonary hypertension, sexual dysfunction.
How it works: Increases blood flow throughout the body by dilating essentially all blood vessels.
Contraindications (reasons you shouldn't take it): Hypersensitivity to drug or class, nitrate use.
Possible side effects and warnings: Can cause severe low blood pressure, heart attack, irregular heart rate, sudden death, stroke, transient ischemic attack (ministroke), increased eye pressure, headache, flushing, heartburn, nasal congestion, urinary track burning, blurred or blue-tinted vision, diarrhea, dizziness, rash, and photophobia (eye discomfort in bright light). Should be used with caution in women with coronary artery disease, liver dysfunction, severe kidney disease, or low blood pressure.
How it can affect pregnant women: Sildenafil appears effective in postmenopausal women for the treatment of sexual arousal disorder and is suggested as a treatment for sexual arousal disorder in premenopausal women. Although there are no adequate reports or well-controlled studies of sildenafil in pregnant women, it is a potentially attractive medication because it increases levels of nitric oxide, a potent dilator of blood vessels normally produced by the lining of the vessel. There are several reports of its use to treat pulmonary artery high blood pressure during pregnancy, a potentially lethal disease. Sildenafil has also been tested as a medication to increase uterine blood flow and endometrial development in women undergoing in vitro fertilization (IVF).

How it can affect a developing embryo or fetus: There are no adequate reports or well-controlled studies in human fetuses. It is unknown whether sildenafil crosses the human placenta. Rodent studies are reassuring, revealing no evidence of birth defects or low birth weight despite the use of doses higher than those used clinically. However, animal studies are not necessarily good indicators of how a drug will behave in humans. It is being studied to see if it can minimize the impact of sudden loss of oxygen during birth.
Breast-feeding: There is no published data in nursing women. It is unknown whether sildenafil enters human breast milk.
Potential drug interactions: Interaction between the following medications and sildenafil has the potential to impact the effect of one or more of the drugs. In some instances the interaction can be dangerous or life-threatening and must be avoided: cimetidine, erythromycin, saquinavir, ritonavir, bosentan, doxazosin, amlodipine.
What the FDA says about use in pregnancy: Category B (see Appendix).
What the available evidence suggests about breast-feeding safety: Unknown.
The bottom line for you:

- There are currently no indications for sildenafil during pregnancy or while breast-feeding.
- Sildenafil appears effective for the treatment of female sexual arousal disorder in postmenopausal women.

SILVER NITRATE

Brand name: None
Drug classes: Antibacterial; Ophthalmic
Indications (what it is used for): Prevention of gonorrheal ophthalmia neonatorum (serious eye infection, conjunctivitis, in newborns).
How it works: Binds bacterial proteins, causing the bacteria to die.
Contraindications (reasons you shouldn't take it): Hypersensitivity to drug or class.

Possible side effects and warnings: Can cause chemical conjunctivitis.

How it can affect pregnant women: Pregnant women who have gonorrhea or chlamydia can pass the infection on to their children during vaginal delivery, causing conjunctivitis. Silver nitrate was used routinely for decades to prevent gonorrheal infections. Unfortunately, silver nitrate eye drops do not prevent infection with chlamydia and have been largely replaced with erythromycin ointment.

How it can affect a developing embryo or fetus: Not relevant.

Breast-feeding: Not relevant.

Potential drug interactions: No clinically relevant interactions identified.

What the FDA says about use in pregnancy: Category B (see Appendix).

What the available evidence suggests about breast-feeding safety: Safe.

The bottom line for you:
- Silver nitrate is effective for preventing gonorrheal conjunctivitis in newborns but is not effective at preventing chlamydia.
- Use of silver nitrate has no impact on breast-feeding.

SILVER SULFADIAZINE TOPICAL

Brand names: Canflame, Dermazin, Flamazine, Flammazine, Geben, Sildimac, Silvadene, Silvazine, Silverderma, Silverol, Silvirin, Sofargen, SSD, Thermazene

Drug classes: Antibacterial; Dermatologic

Indications (what it is used for): Second- or third-degree burns.

How it works: Slows the growth of bacteria so the body can eliminate them.

Contraindications (reasons you shouldn't take it): Hypersensitivity to drug or class.

Possible side effects and warnings: Can cause low white blood cell count, erythema multiforme (skin disorder), burning, pain, itching, skin death, and rash.

How it can affect pregnant women: There is little medical literature on burn injuries to pregnant women. There are no adequate reports or well-controlled studies of silver sulfadiazine in pregnant women. Absorption of silver sulfadiazine varies depending on the percent of body surface area involved and the severity of the tissue damage.

How it can affect a developing embryo or fetus: There are no adequate reports or well-controlled studies in human fetuses. It is unknown whether silver sulfadiazine crosses the human placenta. Considering the topical application and low concentration, it is unlikely that the maternal systemic concentration will reach a clinically relevant level for an embryo or fetus. Rodent studies are reassuring, revealing no evidence of birth defects or low birth weight despite the use of doses higher than those used clinically. However, animal studies are not necessarily good indicators of how a drug will behave in humans.

Breast-feeding: There are no adequate reports or well-controlled studies in nursing women. It is unknown whether silver sulfadiazine enters human breast milk. Considering the topical application and low concentration, it is unlikely a breast-fed newborn will ingest a clinically relevant amount.

Potential drug interactions: No clinically relevant interactions identified.

What the FDA says about use in pregnancy: Category B (see Appendix).

What the available evidence suggests about breast-feeding safety: Likely safe.

The bottom line for you:
- Silver sulfadiazine is effective and likely safe for the treatment of significant thermal burns during pregnancy and while breast-feeding.

SIMETHICONE

Brand name: Mylicon

Drug class: Gastrointestinal

Indications (what it is used for): Flatulence.

How it works: Allows the gas to dissolve in fluid.

Contraindications (reasons you shouldn't take it): Hypersensitivity to drug or class, intestinal perforation, bowel obstruction.

Possible side effects and warnings: Can cause nausea and diarrhea.

How it can affect pregnant women: Simethicone significantly reduces vomiting, stomach discomfort, and abdominal pain after cesarean delivery. Bowel function appears to return more rapidly after C-section when simethicone is used.

How it can affect a developing embryo or fetus: There are no adequate reports or well-controlled studies in human fetuses. Although it is unknown whether simethicone crosses the human placenta, it is unlikely that the maternal blood level would be clinically relevant. Rodent birth defect studies have not been conducted.

Breast-feeding: There are no adequate reports or well-controlled studies in nursing women. Although it is unknown whether simethicone enters human breast milk, it is unlikely that the maternal blood level is clinically relevant. It is generally considered compatible with breast-feeding.

Potential drug interactions: No clinically relevant interactions identified.

What the FDA says about use in pregnancy: No assigned category (see Appendix).

What the available evidence suggests about breast-feeding safety: Safe.

The bottom line for you:

- Simethicone is effective for the relief of flatulence and abdominal distention during pregnancy and after cesarean delivery.
- Simethicone is safe for use while breast-feeding.

SIMVASTATIN

Brand name: Zocor

Drug classes: Antihyperlipidemic; HMG-CoA reductase inhibitor

Indications (what it is used for): Hypercholesterolemia, hypertriglyceridemia, dysbetalipoproteinemia, and familial hypercholesterolemia (all conditions involving high cholesterol, lipids, and/or triglycerides in the blood); secondary prevention of cardiovascular events.

How it works: Blocks the action of HMG-CoA reductase, an enzyme needed for cholesterol synthesis.

Contraindications (reasons you shouldn't take it): Hypersensitivity to drug or class, active liver disease, unexplained elevated liver function tests.

Possible side effects and warnings: Can cause muscle breakdown, liver toxicity, constipation, diarrhea, gas, heartburn, nausea, gallstones, weakness, muscle aches, and rash. Should be used with caution in women with liver dysfunction, alcohol abuse, or severe kidney disease.

How it can affect pregnant women: Simvastatin is a synthetic statin that reduces the overall lipid level and the associated risk of adverse cardiovascular events. It may modestly increase the risk of gallstones. There are no adequate reports or well-controlled studies of simvastatin in pregnant women. Postmarketing studies (studies done by a drug's manufacturer after the drug is on the market) do not suggest an increase in adverse outcomes. However, since atherosclerosis is a chronic disease, discontinuation of treatment during pregnancy should have little impact on the long-term outcome of high cholesterol levels in most women.

How it can affect a developing embryo or fetus: Cholesterol and related substances are building blocks for the placenta and fetus, which is why there might be concern about using drugs to block their production during pregnancy. There are no adequate reports or well-controlled studies of simvastatin human fetuses. It is unknown whether it crosses the human placenta. Postmarketing studies in humans are reassuring, though most statins associated with birth defects are not soluble in water as is the case for simvastatin. Rodent studies revealed no evidence of birth defects despite using doses that were multiples of the maximum recommended clinical dose. However, animal studies are not necessarily good indicators of how a drug will behave in humans. Inadvertent exposure during pregnancy is not a medical indication for pregnancy termination.

Breast-feeding: There are no adequate reports or well-controlled studies in nursing women. It is unknown whether simvastatin enters human breast milk.

Potential drug interactions: Interaction between the following medications or substances and simvastatin has the potential to impact the effect of one or more of the drugs. In some instances the interaction can be dangerous or life-threatening and must be avoided: potent CYP3A4 inhibitors, including clarithromycin, cyclosporine, erythromycin, HIV protease inhibitors, itraconazole, ketoconazole, nefazodone; grapefruit or grapefruit juice; amiodarone; verapamil; digoxin; coumarin anticoagulants.

What the FDA says about use in pregnancy: Category X (see Appendix).

What the available evidence suggests about breast-feeding safety: Unknown; generally considered unsafe.

The bottom line for you:
- Simvastatin is best avoided during pregnancy and while breast-feeding until additional safety data becomes available.
- Inadvertent exposure is not a reason to end a pregnancy.

SIROLIMUS

Brand name: None
Drug class: Immunosuppressant
Indications (what it is used for): To prevent rejection of a transplanted kidney.
How it works: Inhibits cell-based immunity.
Contraindications (reasons you shouldn't take it): Hypersensitivity to drug or class, acute infection.
Possible side effects and warnings: Can cause high lipid and/or cholesterol levels, kidney or liver dysfunction, opportunistic infection, nosebleeds, leakage of lymph fluid, sleeplessness, hemolytic-uremic syndrome (hemolytic anemia, sudden kidney failure, and a low platelet count), shingles (painful skin rash due to the virus that causes chickenpox), malaise, skin ulcer, low blood pressure, diabetes, ringing in the ears, deafness, facial swelling, rapid heart rate, atrial fibrillation, congestive heart failure, hemorrhage, palpitations, fainting, blood clots, loss of appetite, problems swallowing, belching, acid reflux, flatulence, gastritis, gastroenteritis, bleeding gums, poor bowel motility, mouth ulceration, oral yeast infection (thrush), skin cancer, and lymphoma. Women taking sirolimus should avoid exposure to the sun.

How it can affect pregnant women: A growing number of obstetric patients have benefited from organ transplant. Pregnancy after transplant is considered reasonably safe if a woman is 2 years post-transplantation and has good organ function, well-controlled blood pressure, and no evidence of ongoing organ rejection. However, these women remain at high risk for adverse pregnancy outcomes and should be followed at a large, full-service multidisciplinary medical center by a perinatologist. There are no adequate reports or well-controlled studies of sirolimus in pregnant women. The published data is limited to case reports and moderate-sized series of patients. Sirolimus is generally avoided during pregnancy in favor of tacrolimus or azathioprine with or without steroids.

How it can affect a developing embryo or fetus: There are no adequate reports or well-controlled studies in human fetuses. It is unknown whether sirolimus crosses the human placenta. Early pregnancy exposure has not been associated with an increased risk of birth defects. Sirolimus increased the rate of miscarriage in rodents. However, animal studies are not necessarily good indicators of how a drug will behave in humans.

Breast-feeding: There are no adequate reports or well-controlled studies in nursing women. It is unknown whether sirolimus enters human breast milk. Trace amounts were found in rat milk, and laboratory experiments suggest that it may inhibit milk production.

Potential drug interactions: Interaction between the following medications and sirolimus has the potential to impact the effect of one or more of the drugs. In some instances the interaction can be dangerous or life-threatening and must be avoided: cyclosporine, diltiazem, erythromycin, ketoconazole, itraconazole, voriconazole, rifampin, rifabutin, verapamil, bromocriptine, cimetidine, cisapride, clotrimazole, danazol, fluconazole, HIV-protease inhibitors (e.g., indinavir, ritonavir), metoclopramide, troleandomycin, carbamazepine, phenobarbital, phenytoin, rifapentine. Immunosuppressants such as sirolimus may affect response to vaccination; the use of live vaccines should be avoided during treatment.

What the FDA says about use in pregnancy: Category C (see Appendix).

What the available evidence suggests about breast-feeding safety: Unknown.

The bottom line for you:

- There are alternative medications with which there is more experience.
- Sirolimus should be used during pregnancy and breast-feeding only if the benefit to the woman justifies the potential risk to the embryo, fetus, or newborn.

SODIUM FERRIC GLUCONATE

Brand name: Ferrlecit

Drug classes: Replacement; Vitamin/mineral

Indications (what it is used for): Iron deficiency in patients undergoing dialysis.

How it works: Provides an essential component for red blood cell production.

Contraindications (reasons you shouldn't take it): Hypersensitivity to drug or class, non–iron deficiency anemia, iron overload.

Possible side effects and warnings: Can cause a life-threatening allergic reaction, iron toxicity, low blood pressure, flushing, headache, nausea, vomiting, diarrhea, weakness, fatigue, injection site reactions, pain, fever, shortness of breath, itching, and rash.

How it can affect pregnant women: Sodium ferric gluconate is a stable iron complex in a sugar injection. There is no adequate published data with sodium ferric gluconate complex during pregnancy. Life-threatening allergic reactions have been reported during pregnancy.

How it can affect a developing embryo or fetus: There are no adequate reports or well-controlled studies in human fetuses. It is unknown whether sodium ferric gluconate complex crosses the human placenta. Iron is transported across the placenta. There is no physiologic reason to expect an adverse effect from iron supplementation during pregnancy as long as the resulting maternal iron content is in the normal range.

Breast-feeding: There is no published data in nursing women. It is unknown whether sodium ferric gluconate complex enters human breast milk. However, iron is a normal component of breast milk, and other iron supplements increase the concentration of iron in milk.

Potential drug interactions: No clinically relevant interactions identified.

What the FDA says about use in pregnancy: Category B (see Appendix).

What the available evidence suggests about breast-feeding safety: Safe.

The bottom line for you:

- Sodium ferric gluconate complex may be used during pregnancy and while breast-feeding.
- It should be used in a medical facility equipped to respond rapidly to an allergic reaction.

SOTALOL

Brand names: Sorine

Drug classes: Anti-adrenergic; Antiarrhythmic, class III

Indications (what it is used for): Ventricular irregular heart rate.

How it works: Blocks the beta-receptor to correct the irregular heart rate.

Contraindications (reasons you shouldn't take it): Hypersensitivity to drug or class, slow but regular heart rate, heart block, abnormal heart conduction, uncontrolled congestive heart failure, asthma, low potassium and/or magnesium level.

Possible side effects and warnings: Can cause irregular, rapid, or slow heart rate that may be severe; congestive heart failure; palpitations; shortness of breath; fatigue; dizziness; chest pain; weakness; low blood pressure; headache; nausea; vomiting; diarrhea; swelling; sweating; and heartburn. Should be used with caution in women with kidney dysfunction, sick heart pacemaker, compensated congestive heart failure, diabetes, diuretic use, or electrolyte abnormalities.

How it can affect pregnant women: There are no adequate reports or well-controlled studies of sotalol in pregnant women. The published literature is limited to case reports of individual patients. Sotalol reduces blood pressure in women with chronic high blood pressure, but its reported use during pregnancy has been for heart rate abnormalities.

How it can affect a developing embryo or fetus: There are no adequate reports or well-controlled studies in human fetuses. Sotalol crosses the human placenta, reaching levels in the fetus that are similar to those in the mother. It has been used to treat an abnormally high fetal heart rate. Rodent studies are reassuring, revealing no evidence of birth defects or low birth weight despite the use of doses higher than those used clinically. In rabbits, high doses were associated with miscarriage, most likely due to an irregular embryonic heart rate. However, animal studies are not necessarily good indicators of how a drug will behave in humans.

Breast-feeding: There are no adequate reports or well-controlled studies in nursing women. Sotalol is concentrated in human breast milk, and it has been calculated that an infant would ingest 20–23% of the maternal dose. Although this dose is not associated with a slow heart rate, the infant should be closely observed for a slow heart rate, low blood pressure, respiratory distress, and low blood glucoses.

Potential drug interactions: Interaction between the following medications and sotalol has the potential to impact the effect of one or more of the drugs. In some instances the interaction can be dangerous or life-threatening and must be avoided: class 1a antiarrhythmic drugs (e.g., disopyramide, procainamide, quinidine) and other class III antiarrhythmic drugs (e.g., amiodarone), calcium channel blockers, catecholamine-depleting drugs (e.g., guanethidine, reserpine), b-agonists (e.g., isopkidneyine, salbutamol, terbutaline), antacids containing aluminum oxide and magnesium hydroxide, phenothiazines, tricyclic antidepressants (TCAs), astemizole, bepridil, some oral macrolides, some quinolone antibiotics, digoxin.

What the FDA says about use in pregnancy: Category B (see Appendix).

What the available evidence suggests about breast-feeding safety: Possibly safe.

The bottom line for you:

- Sotalol has been used effectively during pregnancy and while breast-feeding.
- Efficient transport across the placenta makes sotalol one of the medications of choice for the treatment of an abnormally high fetal heart rate.

SPECTINOMYCIN

Brand name: Trobicin

Drug classes: Aminoglycoside; Antibiotic

Indications (what it is used for): Gonorrhea.

How it works: Kills bacteria by blocking protein synthesis.

Contraindications (reasons you shouldn't take it): Hypersensitivity to drug or class.

Possible side effects and warnings: Can cause hives, dizziness, nausea, chills, fever, injection site pain, sleeplessness, anemia, and kidney or liver dysfunction.

How it can affect pregnant women: There are no adequate reports or well-controlled studies of spectinomycin in pregnant women. All pregnant (and nonpregnant) women with gonorrhea should have their blood tested for syphilis and again 3 months later. Spectinomycin (which is used to treat gonorrhea) is not effective for the treatment of syphilis and may in fact mask or delay the symptoms of syphilis. Sexual partners should be tested and, if necessary, treated.

How it can affect a developing embryo or fetus: There are no adequate reports or well-controlled studies in human fetuses. It is unknown whether spectinomycin crosses the human placenta. Rodent studies are reassuring, revealing no evidence of birth defects or low birth weight despite the use of doses higher than those used clinically. However, animal studies are not necessarily good indicators of how drug will behave in humans.

Breast-feeding: There is no published data in nursing women. It is unknown whether spectinomycin enters human breast milk. Considering the likely dosage and that other aminoglycosides are considered safe for breast-feeding, the same should be true for spectinomycin.

Potential drug interactions: No clinically relevant interactions identified.

What the FDA says about use in pregnancy: No assigned category (see Appendix).

What the available evidence suggests about breast-feeding safety: Likely safe.

The bottom line for you:

● Spectinomycin is one of several safe and effective medications for the treatment of gonorrhea during pregnancy and while breast-feeding.

ST. JOHN'S WORT

Brand name: None
Drug class: Herb
Indications (what it is used for): Depression.
How it works: Unknown.
Contraindications (reasons you shouldn't take it): Hypersensitivity to drug or class, HIV.
Possible side effects and warnings: Can cause early-onset cataracts, dry mouth, dizziness, sexual dysfunction, bowel symptoms, increased sensitivity to sunlight, fatigue, and reduction in the effectiveness of several drugs. Should be used with caution in women with cataracts.

How it can affect pregnant women: St. John's wort is an herb that has been used for centuries. It contains multiple drug compounds with highly variable concentrations and effects. There are no adequate reports or well-controlled studies of St. John's wort during pregnancy. Multiple studies suggest that St. John's wort is of no benefit treating major depression. HIV-infected women being treated with indinavir should avoid St. John's wort because it substantially decreases indinavir plasma levels, compromising their care. St. John's wort is best avoided during pregnancy, as it has no valid medicinal purpose.

How it can affect a developing embryo or fetus: There are no adequate reports or well-controlled studies in human fetuses. It is unknown whether St. John's wort crosses the human placenta. One rodent study suggested that maternal administration before and throughout pregnancy does not affect long-term growth and physical maturation of the exposed offspring. However, animal studies are not necessarily good indicators of how a drug will behave in humans.

Breast-feeding: There are no adequate reports or well-controlled studies of St. John's wort in breast-feeding women. One poorly controlled study suggested an increased rate of drowsiness in the breast-fed newborns of women taking St. John's Wort compared to a group that was not taking the herb. In another study, no side effects were seen in the mothers or infants.

Potential drug interactions: Interaction between the following medications and St. John's Wort has the potential to impact the effect of one or more of the drugs or of St. John's Wort. In some instances the interaction can be dangerous or life-threatening and must be avoided: drugs metabolized by CYP3A4 (e.g., indinavir).

What the FDA says about use in pregnancy: No assigned category (see Appendix).

What the available evidence suggests about breast-feeding safety: Unknown.

The bottom line for you:

- There are superior agents for the treatment of depression with which there is more experience during pregnancy and breast-feeding.
- The FDA recommends that health-care providers alert their patients that St. John's wort might reduce the effectiveness of their other medications.

STREPTOKINASE

Brand names: Kabikinase, K-Nase, Streptase, Zykinase

Drug class: Thrombolytic

Indications (what it is used for): Heart attack, pulmonary embolus (blood clot in the lung), deep-vein thrombosis.

How it works: Activates plasmin, a natural enzyme that breaks down blood clots.

Contraindications (reasons you shouldn't take it): Hypersensitivity to drug or class, recent stroke, active bleeding, recent trauma, brain tumor, ulcerative colitis, severe high blood pressure, rheumatic heart disease, a diagnostic arterial procedure within 10 days.

Possible side effects and warnings: Can cause life-threatening allergic reaction, cholesterol embolism (cholesterol blockage of a blood vessel), irregular heart rate, severe bleeding, stroke, low or high blood pressure, fever, and bronchospasm. Should be used with caution in women who have delivered within the past three weeks or who have had recent bowel bleeding, left-sided heart blood clot, diabetic retinopathy, or bacterial endocarditis.

How it can affect pregnant women: Streptokinase is a natural product purified from a strain of streptococcus bacteria. Streptokinase is superior to heparin in promoting the clearance of a blood clot from an obstructed vessel. In addition, streptokinase treatment preserves the function of the valves found in veins, decreasing the chance of chronic leg pain (postphlebitic syndrome) that occurs in 90% of those treated with heparin alone. There are no adequate reports or well-controlled studies of streptokinase in pregnant women, though numerous case reports of patients suggest relative safety compared to alternative medications.

How it can affect a developing embryo or fetus: There are no adequate reports or well-controlled studies in human fetuses. It is unknown whether streptokinase crosses the human placenta. The published case reports suggest that it can be used safely, with bleeding being the most common complication. Rodent birth defect studies have not been conducted.

Breast-feeding: There is no published data in nursing women. It is unknown whether streptokinase enters human breast milk.

Potential drug interactions: Use with aspirin or other anticoagulants (e.g., heparin, coumarins) increases the risk of bleeding complications.

What the FDA says about use in pregnancy: Category C (see Appendix).

What the available evidence suggests about breast-feeding safety: Unknown.

The bottom line for you:

- Streptokinase should be used during pregnancy and breast-feeding only if the benefit to the woman justifies the potential risk to the embryo, fetus, or newborn.

SUCCINYLCHOLINE

Brand names: Anectine, Celocurin, Quelicin, Sucostrin, Suxamethonium, Sux-Cert

Drug classes: Musculoskeletal agent; Neuromuscular blocker, depolarizing

Indications (what it is used for): Paralysis, anesthesia.

How it works: Activates nerve endings so that they cannot transmit a motor impulse.

Contraindications (reasons you shouldn't take it): Hypersensitivity to drug or class, pseudocholinesterase deficiency (increased sensitivity to certain muscle relaxant drugs used during anesthesia), narrow-angle glaucoma, penetrating eye injury, history of malignant hyperthermia (a rare life-threatening rise in body temperature, usually triggered by exposure to some general anesthetics), slow heart rate, severe burns, high potassium level, neuromuscular disorders, history of muscle breakdown.

Possible side effects and warnings: Can cause irregular, slow, or rapid heart rate; respiratory depression; cardiovascular collapse; malignant hyperthermia; stoppage of breathing; high potassium level; muscle breakdown; muscle twitching; postoperative muscle aches and stiffness; excess salivation; and increased intraocular pressure. Should be used with caution in women with stroke, severe liver disease, or myasthenia gravis (an autoimmune disease causing muscle weakness).

How it can affect pregnant women: There are no adequate reports or well-controlled studies of succinylcholine in pregnant women. It is routinely used for cesarean delivery during induction of general anesthesia to help with tracheal intubation. The large clinical experience supports the safety of the drug.

How it can affect a developing embryo or fetus: There are no adequate reports or well-controlled studies in human fetuses. Small amounts of succinylcholine are known to cross the placenta, but under normal conditions the amount of drug does not endanger the fetus. However, the higher the level of succinylcholine in the mother, the greater the amount that reaches the fetus. So over a long surgery, where a pregnant woman receives multiples doses of succinylcholine, it is possible for it to have an effect on the fetus, including possibly temporary paralysis or weakness as a newborn. Rodent birth defect studies have not been conducted.

Breast-feeding: There are no adequate reports or well-controlled studies in nursing women. It is unknown whether succinylcholine enters human breast milk. However, considering the one-time use for surgery, succinylcholine is unlikely to pose a clinically significant risk to a breast-feeding newborn.

Potential drug interactions: Interaction between the following medications and succinylcholine has the potential to impact the effect of one or more of the drugs. In some instances the interaction can be dangerous or life-threatening and must be avoided: aprotinin, beta-adrenergic blockers, chloroquine, desflurane, diethylether, isoflurane, lidocaine, lithium, magnesium salts, metoclopramide, some nonpenicillin antibiotics, oxytocin, procainamide, promazine, quinidine, quinine, terbutaline, trimethaphan, drugs that reduce plasma cholinesterase activity (e.g., chronically administered oral contraceptives, glucocorticoids, or certain monoamine oxidase inhibitors [MAOIs]), drugs that irreversibly inhibit plasma cholinesterase.

What the FDA says about use in pregnancy: Category C (see Appendix).

What the available evidence suggests about breast-feeding safety: Safe.

The bottom line for you:

- The extensive clinical experience during pregnancy and while breast-feeding indicates that the use of succinylcholine for cesarean delivery is safe.

SUCRALFATE

Brand names: Calmidan, Carafate, Scrat, Sucafate, Sucrace, Ulcona, Ulcumaag, Ulsidex, Yuwan-S

Drug classes: Antiulcer agent; Cytoprotective; Gastrointestinal

Indications (what it is used for): Duodenal ulcer.

How it works: Coats the ulcer to help it heal.

Contraindications (reasons you shouldn't take it): Hypersensitivity to drug or class, poor swallowing, bowel obstruction.

Possible side effects and warnings: Can cause diarrhea, nausea, vomiting, gas, constipation, rash, dizziness, and sleeplessness. Should be used with caution in women with kidney dysfunction.

How it can affect pregnant women: Gastroesophageal reflux disease (GERD) and/or heartburn occurs in 45–85% of pregnant women in part because of high progesterone and estrogen levels. The treatment for GERD consists of reducing gastric acidity starting with lifestyle and dietary changes. If these fail, antacids or sucralfate are first-line medical therapies, followed by histamine receptor blockers. There are no adequate reports or well-controlled studies of sucralfate in pregnant women.

How it can affect a developing embryo or fetus: There are no adequate reports or well-controlled studies of sucralfate in human fetuses. It is only minimally absorbed across the bowel wall and thus should pose no risk to the fetus.

Breast-feeding: There are no adequate reports or well-controlled studies in nursing women. Although it is unknown whether sucralfate enters human breast milk, it is only minimally absorbed by the mother and should pose no risk to a breast-feeding newborn.

Potential drug interactions: The following medications should not be taken within 2 hours of taking sucralfate: cimetidine, digoxin, fluoroquinolone antibiotics, ketoconazole, phenytoin, quinidine, ranitidine, tetracycline, theophylline, thyroxine.

What the FDA says about use in pregnancy: Category B (see Appendix).

What the available evidence suggests about breast-feeding safety: Safe.

The bottom line for you:

- Sucralfate is a first-line drug for the treatment of GERD during pregnancy and while breast-feeding.

SUFENTANIL

Brand name: Sufenta

Drug classes: Analgesic, narcotic; Anesthesia, general

Indications (what it is used for): General anesthesia, neuraxial (spinal) anesthesia.

How it works: Activates multiple opiate receptors, which lessens concern for pain.

Contraindications (reasons you shouldn't take it): Hypersensitivity to drug or class.

Possible side effects and warnings: Can cause spasm of the voice box, respiratory depression, chest stiffness, irregular or slow heart rate, bronchospasm, low blood pressure, itching, nausea, vomiting, chills, postoperative confusion, biliary (bile duct) spasm, constipation, severe kidney-type pain, and blurred vision. Should be used with caution in women with respiratory depression or liver or kidney dysfunction.

How it can affect pregnant women: Sufentanil is a potent opioid. When used in balanced general anesthesia, sufentanil has perhaps 10 times the potency of fentanyl. Sufentanil is a useful drug for labor epidural analgesia, allowing the amount of local anesthetic to be decreased and thus preserving the ability of the mother to move. However, sufentanil costs more and has a greater risk of dosing error than fentanyl because of its higher potency.

How it can affect a developing embryo or fetus: There are no adequate reports or well-controlled studies in human fetuses. Sufentanil crosses the human placenta, achieving the same level in the fetus as it does in the mother. The amount transferred is even higher if the fetus has an excess level of acid in its blood. Sufentanil is used for fetal analgesia during a variety of surgeries. Rodent studies are generally reassuring, revealing no evidence of birth defects or low birth weight despite the use of doses higher than those used clinically. Miscarriage was seen when twice the maximum recommended clinical dose was used. However, animal studies are not necessarily good indicators of how a drug will behave in humans.

Breast-feeding: There are no adequate reports or well-controlled studies in nursing women. However, considering the one-time use and rapid clearance (how fast it is eliminated by the body), sufentanil is unlikely to pose a clinically significant risk to a breast-feeding newborn.

Potential drug interactions: Interaction between the following medications and sufentanil has the potential to impact the effect of one or more of the drugs. In some instances the interaction can be dangerous or life-threatening and must be avoided: calcium channel blockers, beta-blockers, benzodiazepines.

What the FDA says about use in pregnancy: Category C (see Appendix).

What the available evidence suggests about breast-feeding safety: Safe.

The bottom line for you:

- Sufentanil is a useful drug for labor epidural analgesia.
- Use of sufentanil during medical procedures will have no effect on breast-feeding.

SULFADIAZINE

Brand name: Microsulfon

Drug classes: Antibiotic; Sulfonamide

Indications (what it is used for): Toxoplasmosis (infection caused by the parasite *Toxoplasma gondii*).

How it works: Blocks folate synthesis the parasite needs for survival.

Contraindications (reasons you shouldn't take it): Hypersensitivity to drug or class, various inherited or acquired blood disorders.

Possible side effects and warnings: Can cause hemolytic anemia, Stevens-Johnson syndrome (a rare but serious skin reaction to medication), low platelet and/or white blood cell counts, hepatitis, acute kidney failure, newborn jaundice fever, dizziness, headache, nausea, vomiting, diarrhea, sensitivity to light, rash, and blood in the urine. Should be used with caution in women with liver or kidney dysfunction, G6PD deficiency, or low blood volume.

How it can affect pregnant women: Toxoplasmosis is one of the most common parasitic infections in humans, and there are often few or no symptoms of infection. There are no adequate reports or well-controlled studies of sulfadiazine in infected women during pregnancy. Sulfadiazine is also marketed as a silver-based cream used as an adjunct for the prevention and treatment of wound infections in patients with second- and third-degree burns.

How it can affect a developing embryo or fetus: There are no adequate reports or well-controlled studies in human fetuses. A fetus can become infected with toxoplasmosis if its mother is infected with the parasite. Fetal toxoplasmosis is associated with a range of adverse effects, including hydrocephalus (water on the brain), mental retardation, and blindness. Sulfadiazine crosses the human placenta and has been used in combination with pyrimethamin to treat toxoplasmosis during pregnancy (although it is unclear whether such treatment prevents or reduces the disease in fetuses). Because the moment of maternal infection is rarely if ever known, the diagnosis is usually made after routine blood screening that is performed in countries with high rates of toxoplasmosis infection. The inevitable delay initiating treatment until the disease is discovered in the mother may explain the unclear impact of treatment on the development or the severity of disease in the fetus. Rodent birth defect studies have not been performed. Sulfadiazine is also standard for the treatment of congenital toxoplasmosis after birth. The drug can cause newborn jaundice.

Breast-feeding: There is no published data in nursing women. Although it is unknown whether sulfadiazine enters human breast milk, there are no adverse effects reported in numerous children who have been breast-fed by women who were treated earlier for toxoplasmosis.

Potential drug interactions: No clinically relevant interactions identified.

What the FDA says about use in pregnancy: Category C (see Appendix).

What the available evidence suggests about breast-feeding safety: Safe.

The bottom line for you:

- Sulfadiazine is safe to use during pregnancy and while breast-feeding to treat burns or toxoplasmosis infection.

SULFAMETHOXAZOLE
Brand names: Gamazole, Gantanol, Sinomin, Urobak
Drug classes: Antibiotic; Sulfonamide
Indications (what it is used for): Bacterial infection, including pyelonephritis (kidneys), cystitis (bladder), meningitis (inflammation of the membranes covering the brain and spinal cord), otitis media (middle ear).
How it works: Slows the growth of bacteria by blocking folate availability.
Contraindications (reasons you shouldn't take it): Hypersensitivity to drug or class.
Possible side effects and warnings: Can cause bone marrow suppression, hemolytic anemia, seizures, erythema multiforme (skin disorder), low blood glucose, exfoliative dermatitis (skin disease with redness and scaling), rash, liver damage, and various allergic reactions. Should be used with caution in women who have G6PD deficiency.
How it can affect pregnant women: When combined with trimethoprim, sulfamethoxazole is effective for the treatment of Q fever (infection with the bacterium *Coxiella burnetii,* transmitted by farm animals) and for the treatment or prevention of *pneumocystis carinii* pneumonia (a type of pneumonia most common in HIV-infected patients). There are no adequate reports or well-controlled studies of sulfamethoxazole in pregnant women. Trimethoprim sulfamethoxazole is an alternative to high-dose penicillin for the treatment of listeriosis (infection by *Listeria* bacteria, usually caused by eating contaminated food) during pregnancy. It is also used to treat cystitis during pregnancy, although there is concern about growing bacterial resistance.
How it can affect a developing embryo or fetus: There are no adequate reports or well-controlled studies in human fetuses. Sulfamethoxazole readily crosses the human placenta. One study noted a small increase in the rate of birth defects affecting the heart after treatment with trimethoprim sulfamethoxazole in the second and third trimesters. However, since that period is well after the heart has formed, it seems unlikely that the increase in defects is due to the medication. Rodent studies performed using high multiples of the maximum recommended clinical dose revealed an increased prevalence of cleft palate. However, animal studies are not necessarily good indicators of how a drug will behave in humans. It is probably best to avoid sulfamethoxazole during the first trimester, as it inhibits the synthesis of folate, which is important to organ development.
Breast-feeding: There are no adequate reports or well-controlled studies in nursing women. It is unknown whether sulfamethoxazole enters human breast milk.
Potential drug interactions: Interaction between the following medications and sulfamethoxazole has the potential to impact the effect of one or more of the drugs. In some instances the interaction can be dangerous or life-threatening and must be avoided: thiazides, warfarin, phenytoin.
What the FDA says about use in pregnancy: Category C (see Appendix).
What the available evidence suggests about breast-feeding safety: Unknown.
The bottom line for you:
- Sulfamethoxazole should be used during pregnancy and while breast-feeding only if the benefit to the woman justifies the potential risk to the embryo, fetus, or newborn.
- It should be avoided in the first trimester whenever possible.

SULFASALAZINE
Brand names: Azaline, Azaline EC, Azulfidine
Drug classes: Inflammatory bowel disease agent; Salicylate
Indications (what it is used for): Ulcerative colitis, rheumatoid arthritis, Crohn's disease (an inflammatory bowel disease).
How it works: Unknown.

Contraindications (reasons you shouldn't take it): Hypersensitivity to drug or class, hypersensitivity to salicylates, liver or kidney dysfunction, various inherited or acquired blood disorders, intestinal or urinary obstruction.

Possible side effects and warnings: Can cause Stevens-Johnson syndrome, epidermal necrolysis, and exfoliative dermatitis (skin disorders); hepatitis; peripheral neuropathy (nerve damage causing numbness, tingling or pain in the hands and feet), hemolytic anemia, headache; depression; hives; rash; itching; nausea; vomiting; diarrhea; abdominal pain; loss of appetite; blood in the urine; low white blood cell count; jaundice; and fever. Should be used with caution in women with a G6PD deficiency.

How it can affect pregnant women: Bacteria in the bowel break down sulfasalazine into its active compounds—aminosalicylic acid and sulfapyridine. There are no adequate reports or well-controlled studies of sulfasalazine in pregnant women.

How it can affect a developing embryo or fetus: There are no adequate reports or well-controlled studies in human fetuses. Sulfasalazine and sulfapyridine cross the human placenta, reaching levels in the fetus that are similar to those in the mother. High-quality studies reveal no evidence that it causes either birth defects or low birth weight. Rodent studies are likewise reassuring, although animal studies are not necessarily good indicators of how a drug will behave in humans.

Breast-feeding: There are no adequate reports or well-controlled studies in nursing women. Sulfasalazine is generally considered safe while breast-feeding, as the amounts of sulfasalazine and aminosalicylic acid found in breast milk are clinically insignificant, and the sulfapyridine levels are about 30–60% of the maternal blood level.

Potential drug interactions: May reduce the absorption of folate and digoxin.

What the FDA says about use in pregnancy: Category B (see Appendix).

What the available evidence suggests about breast-feeding safety: Safe.

The bottom line for you:
- Sulfasalazine is safe and effective as first-line treatment of inflammatory bowel disease during pregnancy and while breast-feeding.

SULFISOXAZOLE

Brand names: Gantrisin, Gulfasin, Isoxazine, Lipo Gantrisin, Novosoxazole, Oxazole, Sosol, Soxa, Sulfalar, Sulfazin, Sulfazole, Sulphafurazole, Sulsoxin, Thiasin, Truxazole, Urazole

Drug classes: Antibiotic; Sulfonamide

Indications (what it is used for): Acute, recurrent, or chronic bacterial urinary tract infections; meningococcal meningitis (bacterial infection of the membranes covering the brain and spinal cord); otitis media (middle ear infection).

How it works: Slows the growth of bacteria by blocking folate availability.

Contraindications (reasons you shouldn't take it): Hypersensitivity to drug or class, various inherited or acquired blood disorders.

Possible side effects and warnings: Can cause Stevens-Johnson syndrome (a rare but serious skin reaction to medication), jaundice, bone marrow suppression, infection of the colon, stomatitis (inflammation of the lining of the mouth), hepatitis, inflammation-mediated destruction of blood vessels, sensitivity to light, loss of appetite, nausea, vomiting, rash, headache, and dizziness. Should be used with caution in women with liver or kidney dysfunction.

How it can affect pregnant women: There are no adequate reports or well-controlled studies of sulfisoxazole in pregnant women. Sulfisoxazole is an alternative to ampicillin, which some doctors say should no longer be used in the treatment of asymptomatic bacteriuria (bacteria in the urine without the usual symptoms of urinary tract infection) because of high rates of bacterial resistance. It has been used as an alternative for the treatment of chlamydia in erythromycin-allergic women.

How it can affect a developing embryo or fetus: There are no adequate reports or well-controlled

studies in human fetuses. It is unknown whether sulfisoxazole crosses the human placenta. The large human experience is reassuring, with no reports suggesting that it causes birth defects. Rodent studies performed at multiples of the maximum recommended clinical dose were associated with cleft palate and bone abnormalities. However, animal studies are not necessarily good indicators of how a drug will behave in humans.

Breast-feeding: There are no adequate reports or well-controlled studies in nursing women. Only small amounts of sulfisoxazole enter human breast milk, and it is generally considered compatible with breast-feeding.

Potential drug interactions: Coumarins used with sulfisoxazole can increase the risk of bleeding. Sulfonylureas used with sulfisoxazole can lead to low blood sugar.

What the FDA says about use in pregnancy: Category C (see Appendix).

What the available evidence suggests about breast-feeding safety: Safe.

The bottom line for you:

- Sulfisoxazole is probably safe and effective during pregnancy and while breast-feeding.

SUMATRIPTAN

Brand names: Imigran, Imitrex

Drug classes: Migraine; Serotonin receptor agonist

Indications (what it is used for): Migraine headache.

How it works: Activates the 5-HT1 receptor, causing blood vessels to contract, curing the headache.

Contraindications (reasons you shouldn't take it): Hypersensitivity to drug or class, uncontrolled high blood pressure, coronary artery disease, basilar or hemiplegic migraine, use of monoamine oxidase inhibitors (MAOIs) within 14 days.

Possible side effects and warnings: IV administration can cause palpitations, angina, heart attack, rapid or irregular heart rate, life-threatening high blood pressure, stroke, bowel or peripheral vascular disease, weakness, chest pain, neck tightness, dizziness, flushing, tingling, rash, itching, hives, muscle aches, sleepiness, sweating, and death. The nasal spray can cause runny nose, taste changes, and ringing in the ears. Should be used with caution in women with peripheral or cerebrovascular disease (reduced blood flow to the limbs or brain), liver dysfunction, or cardiac risk factors, or who have used a 5-HT1 activator or ergot derivative within 24 hours.

How it can affect pregnant women: There are no adequate reports or well-controlled studies of sumatriptan in pregnant women. The best study available looked at 1,394 women who used either an ergot or a triptanlike drug after the first trimester. Women using drugs for migraine were older and more likely to be overweight and hence at greater risk for pregnancy complications to begin with. There was a 40% increased risk for preeclampsia (high blood pressure and protein in the urine during pregnancy and complications associated with it) and a 50% increased risk for preterm birth when the drugs were used to treat migraine later in pregnancy. There was no increased risk for stillbirth or early newborn death.

How it can affect a developing embryo or fetus: There are no adequate reports or well-controlled studies in human fetuses. Less than 5% of sumatriptan crosses the human placenta, posing minimal risk to the fetus. Population studies (studies of a large group of people taken from the larger population) are likewise reassuring, revealing no increase in adverse pregnancy outcomes. The best study available looked at 3,286 women who used either an ergot or a triptanlike drug during the first trimester. There was no evidence of increased miscarriage or birth defects. Rodent studies conducted at doses at least 6 times the maximum recommended clinical dose were associated with miscarriage and vascular and skeletal abnormalities; no adverse effects were seen at lower doses. However, animal studies are not necessarily good indicators of how a drug will behave in humans.

Breast-feeding: There are no adequate reports or well-controlled studies in nursing women. A small amount of sumatriptan enters human breast milk, but the quantity absorbed by a breast-feeding newborn will be negligible.

Potential drug interactions: Interaction between the following medications and sumatriptan has the potential to impact the effect of one or more of the drugs. In some instances the interaction can be dangerous or life-threatening and must be avoided: ergotamine-containing or ergot-type medications (e.g., dihydroergotamine, methysergide), monamine oxidase inhibitors (MAOIs), selective serotonin reuptake inhibitors (SSRIs; e.g., fluoxetine, fluvoxamine, paroxetine, sertraline).

What the FDA says about use in pregnancy: Category C (see Appendix).

What the available evidence suggests about breast-feeding safety: Likely safe.

The bottom line for you:

- Triptans, as a group, may be associated with preterm birth and are best avoided at the extremes of prematurity (before 28 weeks) until more data is available.

- After that time, sumatriptan is likely safe and effective for use during pregnancy and while breast-feeding.

TACROLIMUS

Brand names: FK 506, Prograf, Protopic

Drug classes: Immunosuppressant; Transplantation agent; Eczema agent

Indications (what it is used for): Prevention of liver or kidney transplant rejection.

How it works: Blocks cell-mediated immunity.

Contraindications (reasons you shouldn't take it): Hypersensitivity to drug or class.

Possible side effects and warnings: Can cause low platelet count, kidney toxicity, liver dysfunction, high blood pressure, high potassium level, seizures, diabetes, immunosuppression, increased risk of malignancy, nausea, diarrhea, headache, sleeplessness, abdominal pain, tremor, weakness, fever, high blood glucose, anemia, itching, and loss of appetite. Should be used with caution in women with liver or kidney dysfunction.

How it can affect pregnant women: A growing number of obstetric patients have benefited from organ transplantation before pregnancy. As a rule, pregnancy after transplant is reasonably safe if a woman is 2 years past transplantation and has good organ function, no uncontrolled high blood pressure, and no evidence of active organ rejection. However, these women remain at high risk for adverse pregnancy outcomes and should be followed at a large, full-service multidisciplinary medical center by a perinatologist. There are no adequate reports or well-controlled studies of tacrolimus in pregnant women. Although it has been used widely during pregnancy without obvious adverse effect, the published data is limited to case series of individual patients.

How it can affect a developing embryo or fetus: There are no adequate reports or well-controlled studies in human fetuses, and little animal research. It is unknown whether tacrolimus crosses the placenta. Available human studies do not indicate an obvious increase in birth defects.

Breast-feeding: There are no adequate reports or well-controlled studies in nursing women. Tacrolimus does enter human breast milk, but the amount absorbed by the breast-fed baby appears clinically insignificant.

Potential drug interactions: Interaction between the following medications or substances and tacrolimus has the potential to impact the effect of one or more of the drugs. In some instances the interaction can be dangerous or life-threatening and must be avoided: drugs associated with kidney dysfunction (including but not limited to aminoglycosides, amphotericin B, cisplatin, and possibly cyclosporine); calcium channel blockers (e.g., diltiazem, nicardipine, nifedipine, verapamil); antifungal agents (e.g., clotrimazole, fluconazole, itraconazole, ketoconazole, voriconazole); macrolide antibiotics (e.g., clarithromycin, erythromycin, troleandomycin); gastrointestinal prokinetic drugs (e.g., cisapride, metoclopramide); bromocriptine; chloramphenicol; cimetidine; danazol, ethinyl estradiol; lansoprazole; magnesium-aluminum hydroxide; methylprednisolone; nefazodone; omeprazole; protease inhibitors; anticonvulsants (e.g., carbamazepine, phenol barbital, phenytoin); antimicrobials (e.g., caspofungin, rifabutin, rifampin); St. John's wort; sirolimus; phenytoin; CYP3A4 inhibitors such as calcium channel blockers; cimetidine; erythromycin; fluconazole; itraconazole; ketoconazole. Grapefruit juice should be avoided. The use of live vaccines should be avoided, including but not limited to measles, mumps, rubella, oral polio, BCG (tuberculosis), yellow fever, and Ty21a typhoid.

What the FDA says about use in pregnancy: Category C (see Appendix).

What the available evidence suggests about breast-feeding safety: Likely safe.

The bottom line for you:

- The little information available indicates that tacrolimus is safe and effective for preventing transplant rejection during pregnancy and while breast-feeding.

TAMOXIFEN

Brand names: Dignotamoxi, Nolvadex, Valodex

Drug classes: Antineoplastic; Antineoplastic, antiestrogen; SERM (selective estrogen receptor modulator)

Indications (what it is used for): Breast cancer, breast pain, ovulation induction.

How it works: Partial estrogen receptor activator and blocker.

Contraindications (reasons you shouldn't take it): Hypersensitivity to drug or class, undiagnosed genital bleeding, history of blood clots, taking coumarin anticoagulation.

Possible side effects and warnings: Can cause blood clots, cerebrovascular disease (narrowing of blood vessels that supply the brain), endometrial cancer, thickened lining of the uterus, hot flashes, vaginal discharge, irregular menstruation, increased bone or tumor pain, high calcium level, low platelet and/or white blood cell count, fibroids, ovarian cysts, retinopathy, cataracts, dizziness, swelling of feet and hands, fatigue, headache, visual changes, vulvar itching, hair loss, loss of appetite, and liver dysfunction. Should be used with caution in women with bone metastases or low platelet or white blood cell count.

How it can affect pregnant women: Tamoxifen is one of several selective estrogen receptor modulators. SERMs act differently in different parts of the body, which enables doctors to use them to inhibit or stimulate estrogenlike action in specific tissues. Tamoxifen blocks estrogen in the breast, where some cancers are dependent on estrogen for growth. The role of tamoxifen in the prevention of breast cancer is unclear, but it appears to reduce the number of estrogen receptor positive invasive and noninvasive cancers. Currently, tamoxifen is used only to prevent breast cancer in women who are at high risk. In contrast to its actions in the breast, tamoxifen is an estrogen receptor activator in the uterus, which increases the risk of endometrial cancer and other tumors. It is also associated with an increased risk of blood clots. There are no adequate reports or well-controlled studies of tamoxifen in pregnant women. Breast cancers diagnosed during pregnancy and breast-feeding are typically aggressive and present at an advanced stage. The timing of treatment in pregnant women is complex and requires the input of multiple specialists, including a perinatologist, a breast surgeon, and a medical oncologist. Alternatives to tamoxifen that are relatively safe for mother and fetus are available, although it is possible that they carry unforeseen risks. The published literature includes numerous cases of breast cancer diagnosed during pregnancy and treated with surgery followed by tamoxifen usually after the first trimester. There were no obvious drug-related complications.

How it can affect a developing embryo or fetus: There are no adequate reports or well-controlled

studies in human fetuses. It is unknown whether tamoxifen crosses the human placenta. Several reports suggest an association between first-trimester exposure and skull and face abnormalities. In rodents, tamoxifen decreased placental and fetal weights and, as a consequence, increased the risk of fetal death. However, animal studies are not necessarily good indicators of how a drug will behave in humans.

Breast-feeding: There are no adequate reports or well-controlled studies in nursing women. It is unknown whether tamoxifen enters human breast milk. It is generally recommended that women not breast-feed while taking tamoxifen.

Potential drug interactions: Interaction between the following medications and tamoxifen has the potential to impact the effect of one or more of the drugs. In some instances the interaction can be dangerous or life-threatening and must be avoided: warfarin, other cytotoxic agents, phenobarbital.

What the FDA says about use in pregnancy: Category D (see Appendix).

What the available evidence suggests about breast-feeding safety: Unknown.

The bottom line for you:

- Tamoxifen should be avoided during pregnancy and while breast-feeding unless maternal survival requires it.

TAZAROTENE TOPICAL

Brand name: Tazorac

Drug classes: Dermatologic; Retinoid

Indications (what it is used for): Psoriasis, acne vulgaris.

How it works: Unknown.

Contraindications (reasons you shouldn't take it): Hypersensitivity to drug or class, pregnancy.

Possible side effects and warnings: Can cause birth defects, itching, burning, redness, and irritation. Women taking tazarotene should avoid sun exposure.

How it can affect pregnant women: There is no published data with tazarotene during pregnancy. The maternal systemic concentration is reportedly low. Tazarotene, however, is a retinoid, a class of medication that is known to cause birth defects (see "How it can affect a developing embryo or fetus"). As a precaution, women should have a negative blood pregnancy test within 2 weeks of beginning treatment.

How it can affect a developing embryo or fetus: There are no adequate reports or well-controlled studies in human fetuses. Tazarotene is a retinoid, and other retinoids are known causes of birth defects, so tazarotene is treated the same way. However, it is unknown whether tazarotene crosses the human placenta. The maternal systemic concentration is reportedly low, and 6 women accidentally exposed to the drug during pregnancy in clinical tests gave birth to healthy babies. It is not known what level of exposure would be required to cause birth defects There may be less drug absorption in the treatment of the face alone, due to less surface area for application. Rodent studies revealed no increase in birth defects after topical application. However, animals treated with related drugs with doses covering about 20% of their skin area had a greater risk of miscarriage and fetal malformation, including neural tube and heart defects. Animal studies are not necessarily good indicators of how a drug will behave in humans.

Breast-feeding: There is no published data in nursing women. It is unknown whether tazarotene enters human breast milk. However, considering the dose and the fact that it is applied topically, it is unlikely that a breast-feeding newborn would have a clinically relevant level.

Potential drug interactions: Avoid use with other dermatologic medications and cosmetics with a strong drying effect.

What the FDA says about use in pregnancy: Category X (see Appendix).

What the available evidence suggests about breast-feeding safety: Possibly safe.

The bottom line for you:

- Tazarotene and related drugs are considered causes of birth defects and should be avoided during pregnancy until there are additional quality studies determining that it is safe.
- Exposure to tazarotene is not, however, an indication for pregnancy termination since it has not yet been shown to cause birth defects in humans after topical application. Instead, women should be seen by a perinatologist skilled in diagnostic ultrasound to screen for any potential birth defects.
- Tazarotene may be safe for use while breast-feeding, but the studies are few and incomplete.

TECHNETIUM-99M (99MTC)

Brand names: Cardiolite, Cardiotec, Cardiotech, Ceretec, Miraluma, Neurolite, NeoTect, RBC-Scan, Ultratag

Drug class: Diagnostic, radiopharmaceutical

Indications (what it is used for): Diagnostic imaging.

How it works: Radioactive label attaches to proteins, allowing parts of the body to be seen in diagnostic-imaging tests.

Contraindications (reasons you shouldn't take it): Hypersensitivity to drug or class.

Possible side effects and warnings: Can cause metallic taste, burning at the injection site, facial swelling, numbness of hand and arm, low blood pressure, and nausea.

How it can affect pregnant women: The clearance (how fast it is eliminated by the body) of technetium-99m is reduced in women. There are no adequate reports or well-controlled studies of technetium-99m during pregnancy, although a long clinical experience supports its use when medically indicated. A diagnostically indicated test should not be withheld simply because of pregnancy.

How it can affect a developing embryo or fetus: There are no adequate reports or well-controlled studies in human fetuses. Technetium-99m crosses the human placenta but delivers a maximal total fetal radiation dose well below that considered the threshold for concern. Rodent birth defect studies have not been performed.

Breast-feeding: There are no adequate reports or well-controlled studies in nursing women. Technetium-99m is excreted in human milk for about 24 hours after administration. Although formula feedings for at least 24 hours may seem wise, a single case report suggests that this may not be necessary.

Potential drug interactions: No clinically relevant interactions identified.

What the FDA says about use in pregnancy: Category C (see Appendix).

What the available evidence suggests about breast-feeding safety: Likely safe.

The bottom line for you:

- Technetium-99m should be used during pregnancy and breast-feeding when the benefit to the woman justifies the potential risk to the embryo, fetus, or newborn.
- Pregnancy is not a valid reason to withhold a diagnostically indicated test.

TEGASEROD

Brand name: Zelnorm

Drug classes: Gastrointestinal; Serotonin receptor agonist

Indications (what it is used for): Irritable bowel syndrome characterized by constipation.

How it works: Activates 5-HT4 receptor to stimulate bowel motility.

Contraindications (reasons you shouldn't take it): Hypersensitivity to drug or class, severe kidney dysfunction, moderate to severe liver disease, history of bowel obstruction, abdominal adhesions, symptomatic gallbladder disease, diarrhea.

Possible side effects and warnings: Can cause gallbladder inflammation, headache, nausea, abdominal pain, gas, diarrhea, and dizziness. Should be used with caution in women with mild liver dysfunction.

How it can affect pregnant women: There are no published reports of tegaserod use during pregnancy.

How it can affect a developing embryo or fetus: There are no adequate reports or well-controlled studies in human fetuses. It is unknown whether tegaserod crosses the human placenta. Rodent studies are reassuring, revealing no evidence of birth defects or low birth weight despite the use of doses higher than those used clinically. However, animal studies are not necessarily good indicators of how a drug will behave in humans.

Breast-feeding: There is no published data in nursing women. Tegaserod is excreted at high levels into human breast milk. Its impact on a breast-feeding newborn is unknown.

Potential drug interactions: No clinically relevant interactions identified.

What the FDA says about use in pregnancy: Category B (see Appendix).

What the available evidence suggests about breast-feeding safety: Unknown.

The bottom line for you:

- There are alternative agents with which there is more experience during pregnancy and breast-feeding that may be as effective in the short term.

TELMISARTAN

Brand name: Micardis

Drug class: ACEI/A2R-antagonist

Indications (what it is used for): High blood pressure.

How it works: Blocks the AT-1 receptor, whose activation can cause high blood pressure.

Contraindications (reasons you shouldn't take it): Hypersensitivity to drug or class, pregnancy.

Possible side effects and warnings: Can cause rapid swelling of the skin layers, low blood pressure, dizziness, upper respiratory infection symptoms, back pain, diarrhea, fatigue, heartburn, low white blood cell count, and high potassium level. Should be used with caution in women with a history of ACE inhibitor–related rapid swelling of the skin layers, kidney artery stenosis, liver or kidney dysfunction, congestive heart failure, or low sodium level.

How it can affect pregnant women: The plasma concentration of telmisartan is 2–3 times higher in females than in males, suggesting that the dose may need to be altered during pregnancy. There is no published data with telmisartan during pregnancy. However, all inhibitors of the renin-angiotensin system such as telmisartan should be avoided during pregnancy for fetal reasons (see "How it can affect a developing embryo or fetus"). The lowest effective dose should be used when telmisartan is absolutely required during pregnancy for blood pressure control.

How it can affect a developing embryo or fetus: There are no adequate reports or well-controlled studies in human fetuses. It is unknown whether telmisartan crosses the human placenta. Inhibitors of the renin-angiotensin system such as telmisartan are considered contraindicated (should not be used) throughout pregnancy. Their use has been associated with underdevelopment of the skull, low urine production, low amniotic fluid, reversible or irreversible kidney failure, prematurity, low birth weight, and death. If treatment with telmisartan is absolutely necessary during pregnancy, close observation of the fetus using ultrasound may be appropriate. If low amniotic fluid occurs, telmisartan should be discontinued unless considered lifesaving for the mother. Low amniotic fluid may not appear until after irreversible injury has occurred in the fetus. Newborns who were exposed during pregnancy should be closely observed for low blood pressure, low urine output, and high potassium level.

Breast-feeding: There is no published data in nursing women. It is unknown whether telmisartan enters human breast milk. It is excreted into rodent milk.

Potential drug interactions: Telmisartan may increase the blood level of digoxin.

What the FDA says about use in pregnancy: Category D (see Appendix).

What the available evidence suggests about breast-feeding safety: Unknown.

The bottom line for you:

- Renin angiotensin-inhibiting drugs such as Telmisartan are teratogens (substances that can cause birth defects), may cause fetal damage at any time during pregnancy after the mid-first trimester, and should be avoided.
- There are numerous alternative medications with a superior safety profile with which there is more experience during pregnancy and breast-feeding.
- The lowest effective dose should be used when telmisartan is required during pregnancy for blood pressure control.

TEMAZEPAM

Brand names: Euhypnos, Levanxol, Normison, Planum, Restoril

Drug classes: Benzodiazepine; Hypnotic; Sedative

Indications (what it is used for): Sleeplessness.

How it works: Activates benzodiazepine and possibly GABA receptors to stimulate the associated mood change.

Contraindications (reasons you shouldn't take it): Hypersensitivity to drug or class.

Possible side effects and warnings: Can cause respiratory depression, seizures, coma, drowsiness, headache, fatigue, nervousness, lethargy, weakness, dizziness, nausea, vomiting, anxiety, depression, dry mouth, diarrhea, abdominal pain, euphoria, blurred vision, nightmares, and dizziness.

How it can affect pregnant women: There are no adequate reports or well-controlled studies of temazepam in pregnant women. There are alternative agents with which there is more experience.

How it can affect a developing embryo or fetus: There are no adequate reports or well-controlled studies in human fetuses. Temazepam crosses the second-trimester human placenta, achieving a level in the fetus about a third of that of the mother. Several studies suggest an increased prevalence of fetal birth defects after first-trimester use of the related drug diazepam. Decreased fetal movement frequently follows IV diazepam administration, and prolonged central nervous system depression may occur in newborns due to their inability to metabolize the drug. It is unknown whether the effect of temazepam is similar. Rodent birth defect studies revealed an increased prevalence of skeletal abnormalities and miscarriage. However, animal studies are not necessarily good indicators of how a drug will behave in humans.

Breast-feeding: Temazepam is excreted into breast milk. Benzodiazepines in general enter human breast milk and may cause lethargy, sedation, and weight loss in infants.

Potential drug interactions: No clinically relevant interactions identified.

What the FDA says about use in pregnancy: Category X (see Appendix).

What the available evidence suggests about breast-feeding safety: Unknown.

The bottom line for you:

- There are alternative medications with which there is more experience.
- Although it is unlikely that a one-time use would cause harm, continuous use should be avoided during pregnancy and while breast-feeding.

TENOFOVIR

Brand name: Viread

Drug classes: Antiviral; Nucleotide reverse transcriptase inhibitor (NRTI)

Indications (what it is used for): HIV infection.

How it works: Inhibits an enzyme that changes RNA into DNA, a conversion needed for HIV to replicate.

Contraindications (reasons you shouldn't take it): Hypersensitivity to drug or class, kidney insufficiency, high lactate levels.

Possible side effects and warnings: Can cause a buildup of lactate, fatty liver enlargement, nausea, vomiting, diarrhea, loss of appetite, and gas. Should be used with caution in women with alcoholism or liver dysfunction.

How it can affect pregnant women: There are few high-quality studies of tenofovir in pregnant women. The current standard in areas where HIV screening and treatment during pregnancy are not widespread is to give nevirapine to the woman during labor and then to the newborn. Unfortunately, such limited use can lead to viral resistance. In contrast to nevirapine, a single dose of tenofovir and emtricitabine at delivery reduces the chance of resistance by 50% while still protecting the newborn.

How it can affect a developing embryo or fetus: There are no adequate reports or well-controlled studies in human fetuses. It is unknown whether tenofovir crosses the human placenta. Small case series of patients are reassuring to date. Tenofovir crossed the rhesus monkey placenta well enough to lower the amount of virus in the blood of an infected fetus. However, treatment was associated with delayed bone growth, and in humans, HIV infection of the fetus before birth is rare. Rodent studies are reassuring, revealing no evidence of birth defects or low birth weight despite the use of doses higher than those used clinically. However, animal studies are not necessarily good indicators of how a drug will behave in humans.

Breast-feeding: There is no published data in nursing women. It is unknown whether tenofovir enters human breast milk. If infant formula is available, breast-feeding is not recommended when a mother is HIV positive because HIV can be transmitted to the newborn in the breast milk.

Potential drug interactions: Interaction between the following medications and tenofovir has the potential to impact the effect of one or more of the drugs. In some instances the interaction can be dangerous or life-threatening and must be avoided: didanosine, drugs that reduce kidney function.

What the FDA says about use in pregnancy: Category B (see Appendix).

What the available evidence suggests about breast-feeding safety: Not safe.

The bottom line for you:

- There are alternative medications with which there is more experience during pregnancy and breast-feeding.
- If infant formula is available, breast-feeding is not recommended when a mother is HIV positive because HIV can be transmitted to the newborn in the breast milk.
- Women who take tenofovir during pregnancy are encouraged to register with the Antiretroviral Pregnancy Registry (1-800-258-4263) to help increase the available information about tenofovir use during pregnancy. The registry can also be a source of information for women considering, or undergoing, tenofovir treatment during pregnancy.

TERBINAFINE

Brand name: Lamisil

Drug classes: Antifungal; Dermatologic

Indications (what it is used for): Onychomycosis (fungal infection of fingernails and/or toenails), ringworm.

How it works: Weakens the cell membrane of the fungus.

Contraindications (reasons you shouldn't take it): Hypersensitivity to drug or class.

Possible side effects and warnings: Can cause liver toxicity or failure, Stevens-Johnson syndrome and toxic epidermal necrolysis (rare but serious skin disorders), rash, redness, itching, low white blood cell count, headache, diarrhea, heartburn, nausea, abdominal pain, constipation, gas, and hives. Should be used with caution in women with liver or kidney dysfunction.

How it can affect pregnant women: There is no published data with terbinafine during pregnancy.

How it can affect a developing embryo or fetus: There are no adequate reports or well-controlled studies in human fetuses. It is unknown whether terbinafine crosses the human placenta. Rodent studies are reassuring, revealing no evidence of birth defects or low birth weight despite the use of doses higher than those used clinically. However, animal studies are not necessarily good indicators of how a drug will behave in humans.

Breast-feeding: There is no published data in nursing women. The manufacturer reports that terbinafine is concentrated in breast milk. Until data to the contrary becomes available, breast-feeding should be avoided.

Potential drug interactions: Interaction between the following medications and terbinafine has the potential to impact the effect of one or more of the drugs. In some instances the interaction can be dangerous or life-threatening and must be avoided: rifampin, cimetidine.

What the FDA says about use in pregnancy: Category B (see Appendix).

What the available evidence suggests about breast-feeding safety: Not safe.

The bottom line for you:

- There are alternative medications with which there is more experience during pregnancy. Terbinafine should be used during pregnancy only if the benefit to the woman justifies the potential risk to the embryo, fetus, or newborn.
- Terbinafine should probably be avoided while breast-feeding until more information is available.

TERBUTALINE

Brand names: Brethaire, Brethancer, Brethine, Bricanyl, Monovent, Syntovent

Drug classes: Adrenergic agonist; Beta-agonist; Bronchodilator

Indications (what it is used for): Asthma, tocolysis (postponement of preterm labor).

How it works: Activates the beta-2 adrenoreceptor, causing relaxation of smooth muscle.

Contraindications (reasons you shouldn't take it): Hypersensitivity to drug or class.

Possible side effects and warnings: Can cause swelling in the lungs, low blood pressure, rapid or irregular heart rate, palpitations, nervousness, tremor, headache, nausea, vomiting, drowsiness, sweating, muscle cramps, and high blood sugar. Should be used with caution in women with diabetes, infection (when used to slow preterm labor), high blood pressure, high thyroid hormone levels, irregular heart rate, seizures, or low potassium level.

How it can affect pregnant women: Asthma is a common disease in life and in pregnancy. Approximately one-third of pregnant women with asthma get worse during pregnancy, one-third get better, and one-third remain clinically unchanged. When asthma is well controlled it does not affect pregnancy outcome, but poorly controlled asthma may increase the risk of preterm birth (delivery before 37 weeks) or low birth weight. Inhaled corticosteroids are considered the preventative medication of choice for pregnant women with persistent asthma unless their condition is well controlled by cromolyn or nedocromil. Budesonide and beclomethasone are considered the first-line treatments. Terbutaline is also an effective agent for the treatment of asthma during pregnancy if first line treatments fail.

Certain medications used during labor and delivery have the potential to worsen asthma, including nonselective beta-blockers, some prostaglandins (used to induce labor), and ergonovine (used to control blood loss after delivery).

When used to slow preterm labor, terbutaline is similar to other effective medications and delays delivery about 48 hours. This allows the time necessary to give corticosteroid (e.g., betamethasone) to help the fetus's lungs mature. Maternal side effects are common. Serious adverse reactions, including pulmonary edema (fluid in the lungs) and maternal death, have been reported with terbutaline. Several large analyses conclude that of the currently available medications, nifedipine is the drug of choice to delay preterm delivery. Terbutaline has also been used when the fetal heart rate is abnormal because of uterine contractions that are too frequent.

How it can affect a developing embryo or fetus: Terbutaline crosses the human placenta, after several hours reaching a level in the fetus that is similar to that in the mother. Multiple case reports suggest that it can speed the heart rate of fetuses with an abnormally slow rate. A series of rodent studies from one laboratory concluded that terbutaline use during pregnancy could cause autism. However, the research is not likely relevant since the dose of terbutaline used was much higher than what is normally used and there is no evidence that terbutaline can reach the fetal brain in order to directly affect brain development. Otherwise, rodent studies are reassuring, showing no evidence of birth defects or low birth weight despite the use of doses higher than those used clinically. However, animal studies are not necessarily good indicators of how a drug will behave in humans.

Breast-feeding: Terbutaline is excreted into human breast milk, although its level in a breast-fed newborn is undetectable.

Potential drug interactions: Interaction between the following medications and terbutaline has the potential to impact the effect of one or more of the drugs. In some instances the interaction can be dangerous or life-threatening and must be avoided: other sympathomimetic agents, monoamine oxidase inhibitors (MAOIs), tricyclic antidepressants (TCAs), beta-adrenergic blocking agents.

What the FDA says about use in pregnancy: Category B (see Appendix).

What the available evidence suggests about breast-feeding safety: Safe.

The bottom line for you:
- Terbutaline is a second-line treatment of asthma during pregnancy and while breast-feeding.

- There are alternative agents for slowing preterm labor, such as nifedipine, that are more effective and have a superior safety profile.

TERCONAZOLE
Brand name: Terazol
Drug classes: Antifungal; Dermatologic
Indications (what it is used for): Vulvovaginal yeast infection.
How it works: Unknown.
Contraindications (reasons you shouldn't take it): Hypersensitivity to drug or class.
Possible side effects and warnings: Can cause local irritation, headache, and itching.
How it can affect pregnant women: There are no adequate reports or well-controlled studies of terconazole in pregnant women. Topical terconazole may be more effective than nystatin for treating yeast infections during pregnancy. Treatment periods of 7 days may be necessary during pregnancy rather than the shorter courses typically recommended.
How it can affect a developing embryo or fetus: There are no adequate reports or well-controlled studies in human fetuses. It is unknown whether terconazole crosses the human placenta. Rodent studies are generally reassuring, revealing no evidence of birth defects or low birth weight until the dose exceeds 20 times the maximum recommended clinical dose.
Breast-feeding: There is no published data in nursing women. It is unknown whether terconazole enters human breast milk.
Potential drug interactions: No clinically relevant interactions identified.
What the FDA says about use in pregnancy: Category C (see Appendix).
What the available evidence suggests about breast-feeding safety: Unknown.
The bottom line for you:
- There are alternative medications with which there is more experience.

- Terconazole should be used during pregnancy and while breast-feeding only if the benefit to the woman justifies the potential risk to the embryo, fetus, or newborn.

TETANUS IMMUNE GLOBULIN
Brand names: HyperTET, Hypertet
Drug class: Immune globulin
Indications (what it is used for): Prevention of tetanus after injury with an unknown/uncertain vaccination history, active tetanus.
How it works: Provides antibodies to fight tetanus.
Contraindications (reasons you shouldn't take it): Hypersensitivity to drug or class.
Possible side effects and warnings: Can cause injection site soreness, fever, rapid swelling of the layers of the skin, and renal disease. Should be used with caution in women with a low platelet count or bleeding disorder.
How it can affect pregnant women: Tetanus is a highly lethal disease and a significant cause of maternal death in some parts of the world. Tetanus immune globulin provides a level of immunity to the tetanus toxin. In the U.S., there is universal primary vaccination, with subsequent timed boosters to maintain antitoxin levels. There are no adequate reports or well-controlled studies of tetanus immune globulin in pregnant women. During pregnancy, it appears that the antibodies produced in response to tetanus toxoid provide incomplete protection. So even previously vaccinated women should be given tetanus immunoglobulin if they are exposed to tetanus during pregnancy. A long clinical experience suggests safety.
How it can affect a developing embryo or fetus: There are no adequate reports or well-controlled studies in human fetuses. The antibodies in tetanus immune globulin cross the human placenta and provide at least partial protection from tetanus for the newborn. Maternal immunization will not interfere with a newborn's response to the standard DPT vac-cination series. Rodent birth defect studies have not been performed.
Breast-feeding: There are no adequate reports or well-controlled studies in nursing women. It is unknown whether tetanus immune globulin enters human breast milk, but likely.
Potential drug interactions: Antibodies in immunoglobulin preparations may interfere with the response to live viral vaccines such as polio, measles, mumps, and rubella (German measles). Use of such vaccines should be delayed approximately 3 months after tetanus immune globulin.
What the FDA says about use in pregnancy: Category C (see Appendix).
What the available evidence suggests about breast-feeding safety: Safe.
The bottom line for you:
- Tetanus immune globulin is considered safe and effective during pregnancy and while breast-feeding.

TETANUS TOXOID
Brand name: Tetanus toxoid adsorbed
Drug class: Vaccine
Indications (what it is used for): Tetanus susceptibility.
How it works: Stimulates the production of antibodies that prevent tetanus.
Contraindications (reasons you shouldn't take it): Hypersensitivity to drug or class, acute respiratory infection or other active infection (unless emergency), use of immunosuppressive agents.
Possible side effects and warnings: Can cause injection site soreness, fever, malaise, enlarged lymph nodes, generalized aches, low blood pressure, and itching.
How it can affect pregnant women: Tetanus is a highly lethal disease and a significant cause of maternal death in some parts of the world. Tetanus immune globulin provides a level of immunity to the tetanus toxin. In the U.S., there is universal primary vaccination, with subsequent timed boosters to

maintain antitoxin levels. A completed primary series of vaccinations creates protection that lasts 10 years or more. During pregnancy, it appears that the antibodies produced in response to tetanus toxoid provide incomplete protection. So even previously vaccinated women should be given tetanus immunoglobulin if they are exposed to tetanus during pregnancy. A long clinical experience suggests safety.

How it can affect a developing embryo or fetus: There are no adequate reports or well-controlled studies in human fetuses. The antibodies generated in response to tetanus toxoid appear to cross the human placenta and are capable of stimulating active immunity in a fetus at full term. The long clinical experience with immunization during pregnancy is reassuring.

Breast-feeding: There are no adequate reports or well-controlled studies in nursing women. It is unknown whether tetanus toxoid enters human breast milk.

Potential drug interactions: No clinically relevant interactions identified.

What the FDA says about use in pregnancy: Category C (see Appendix).

What the available evidence suggests about breast-feeding safety: Safe.

The bottom line for you:

- Tetanus toxoid is considered safe and effective during pregnancy and while breast-feeding.

TETRACAINE

Brand names: Ak-T-Caine, Dermacaine, Pontocaine, Tetocain

Drug class: Anesthetic, local

Indications (what it is used for): Spinal anesthetic.

How it works: Blocks sodium-potassium channels, inhibiting the transmission of nerve impulses.

Contraindications (reasons you shouldn't take it): Hypersensitivity to drug or class, conditions that increase the risk of spinal anesthesia.

Possible side effects and warnings: Spinal anesthesia can cause side effects related to systemic low blood pressure, including unconsciousness, respiratory/cardiac arrest, and nausea and vomiting, as well as those related to leaking of spinal fluid after puncture (e.g., ringing in the ears, blurry vision, headache). Should be used with caution in women with an irregular heart rate, low blood pressure, hypovolemia (decreased blood volume), or shock.

How it can affect pregnant women: Tetracaine produces 2–3 hours of surgical anesthesia depending on the site of surgery. There are no adequate reports or well-controlled studies of tetracaine in pregnant women. Although once routinely used for spinal anesthesia for cesarean delivery, tetracaine has been replaced by bupivacaine as the spinal agent of choice for C-section.

How it can affect a developing embryo or fetus: There are no adequate reports or well-controlled studies in human fetuses. It is unknown whether tetracaine crosses the human placenta. Considering the dose and administration into the spinal canal, it is unlikely that the maternal blood level will be clinically relevant level to the fetus.

Breast-feeding: There is no published data in nursing women. It is unknown whether tetracaine enters human breast milk. Other local anesthetics are excreted into breast milk. One-time tetracaine for a spinal anesthetic is unlikely to pose a clinically significant risk to a breast-feeding newborn.

Potential drug interactions: Should not be used with a sulfonamide.

What the FDA says about use in pregnancy: Category C (see Appendix).

What the available evidence suggests about breast-feeding safety: Safe.

The bottom line for you:

- Although it has been replaced by bupivacaine for cesarean delivery, tetracaine is still used during pregnancy for spinal anesthesia for surgical procedures longer than C-section.
- Tetracaine is safe for use while breast-feeding.

TETRACYCLINE

Brand names: Achromycin, Acrimicina, Actisite, Ala-Tet, Alphacycline, Ambramycin, Austramycin, Bekatetracyn, Biocycline, Bristacycline, Brodspec, Cofarcilina, Cyclopar, Emtet-500, Hydracycline, Maviciclina, Nelmicyn, Nor-Tet, Panmycin, Polfamycine, Robitet, Sarocycline, Sumycin, Supramycin, Tega-Cycline, Teline, Telmycin, Tetocyn, Tetracap, Tetrachel, Tetraciclina, Tetracitro-S, Tetracon, Tetracyn, Tetralan, Tetram, Tetramed, Topicycline, Upcyclin, Wesmycin, Wintellin, Wintrex, Xepacycline

Drug classes: Antibiotic; Dermatologic; Ophthalmic; Tetracycline

Indications (what it is used for): Bacterial infection, chlamydia infection, acne vulgaris.

How it works: Slows bacterial growth by blocking protein synthesis.

Contraindications (reasons you shouldn't take it): Hypersensitivity to drug or class, pregnancy.

Possible side effects and warnings: Can cause increased intracranial pressure not due to a detectable disease, liver toxicity, Jarisch-Herxheimer reaction (fever, chills, headache, muscle pain, and worsening of skin lesions caused by large quantities of toxins released into the body as bacteria die during treatment), inflammation of the colon or heart sac, tooth discoloration in the fetus, nausea, vomiting, heartburn, loss of appetite, diarrhea, light sensitivity, sores in the mouth, mouth and/or vaginal yeast, hives, light-headedness, dizziness, uncontrolled movements, ringing in the ears, headache, blurred vision, and low white blood cell and/or platelet count. Should be used with caution in women with liver or kidney dysfunction.

How it can affect pregnant women: Tetracycline is a broad-spectrum antibiotic. When penicillin is contraindicated (cannot be used), tetracycline-class antibiotics are alternatives for the treatment of gonorrhea, syphilis, Vincent's infection (trench mouth), and *Actinomyces* species, which can cause infection and abscesses in the mouth. Tetracycline may be more damaging than doxycycline to the liver. There are no adequate reports or well-controlled studies of tetracycline in pregnant women. It is generally avoided during pregnancy because of fetal considerations.

How it can affect a developing embryo or fetus: There are no adequate reports or well-controlled studies in human fetuses. Tetracycline crosses the human placenta and may cause a yellow-gray-brown tooth discoloration in adults after they were exposed during pregnancy or as children. It is unlikely that topically applied tetracycline during pregnancy achieves a blood level high enough to cause this effect. Another tetracycline, oxytetracycline (but not doxycycline) is associated with an increased risk of neural tube defects, cleft palate, and defects in the cardiovascular system. There are no similar studies for tetracycline. Rodent studies are generally reassuring, revealing no evidence of birth defects, but there is some increase in miscarriage at high doses. However, animal studies are not necessarily good indicators of how a drug will behave in humans.

Breast-feeding: There are no adequate reports or well-controlled studies in nursing women. Tetracycline enters human breast milk, although clinical experience suggests that it is compatible with breast-feeding.

Potential drug interactions: Interaction between the following medications and tetracycline has the potential to impact the effect of one or more of the drugs. In some instances the interaction can be dangerous or life-threatening and must be avoided: bactericidal antibiotics, anticoagulant medications, methoxyflurane. Absorption of tetracycline is impaired by antacids containing aluminum, calcium, or magnesium, and preparations containing iron, zinc, or sodium bicarbonate. Tetracycline may make low-estradiol oral contraceptives less effective.

What the FDA says about use in pregnancy: Category D (see Appendix).

What the available evidence suggests about breast-feeding safety: Safe.

The bottom line for you:

- Intravenous, intramuscular, and oral tetracycline should be avoided during pregnancy because of their effect on the fetal tooth coloration.

- Tetracycline is likely safe for use while breast-feeding.

THALIDOMIDE

Brand name: Thalomid

Drug classes: Dermatologic; Immunomodulator

Indications (what it is used for): Red nodules, HIV wasting, canker sore.

How it works: Unknown.

Contraindications (reasons you shouldn't take it): Hypersensitivity to drug or class, pregnancy, moderate/severe neuritis.

Possible side effects and warnings: Can cause severe birth defects, peripheral nerve damage, toxic epidermal necrolysis and Stevens-Johnson syndrome (rare but serious skin disorders), seizures, slow heart rate, high blood pressure, low blood pressure when standing or sitting, headache, drowsiness, dizziness, rash, diarrhea, fever, chills, increased appetite, weight gain, confusion, amnesia, mood changes, light sensitivity, low white blood cell count, and increased HIV viral load. Should be used with caution in women who are of reproductive age or have a history of seizure disorder or cardiovascular disease.

How it can affect pregnant women: Thalidomide is a known human teratogen (substance that can cause birth defects) and is contraindicated (should not be used) during pregnancy. It is excreted in semen, and treated males should wear a condom during intercourse. Initially banned in the U.S. (after the discovery of birth defects in the children of women who took thalidomide during their pregnancies), it has since proved to be a superb drug for the treatment of several formerly resistant diseases. The potential uses for thalidomide are growing, which means there is an increasing chance that a pregnant woman could be inadvertently exposed to the medication. Anyone taking thalidomide should use effective contraception. There are no adequate reports or well-controlled studies of thalidomide in pregnant women.

How it can affect a developing embryo or fetus: There are no adequate reports or well-controlled studies in human fetuses. Thalidomide crosses the human placenta and is a potent human teratogen, causing limb abnormalities after first-trimester exposure. Even a single low dose can cause defects. If pregnancy occurs, the drug should be discontinued and the patient referred to a fetal medicine expert for evaluation and counseling. Any suspected fetal exposure to thalidomide must be reported to the FDA via the MedWatch program at 1-800-FDA-1088 and also to the Celgene Corporation.

Breast-feeding: There is no published data in nursing women. It is unknown whether thalidomide enters human breast milk.

Potential drug interactions: Interaction between the following medications and thalidomide has the potential to impact the effect of one or more of the drugs. In some instances the interaction can be dangerous or life-threatening and must be avoided: barbiturates, chlorpromazine, ethanol, reserpine. Use of thalidomide at the same time as carbamazepine, griseofulvin, certain herbal supplements such as St. John's wort, HIV protease inhibitors, modafinil, penicillins, phenytoin, rifabutin, or rifampin may reduce the effectiveness of oral contraception during and up to 1 month after discontinuation of any of these drugs. Therefore, women requiring treatment with one or more of these drugs must use two highly effective methods of contraception or abstain from heterosexual sexual contact while taking thalidomide.

What the FDA says about use in pregnancy: Category X (see Appendix).

What the available evidence suggests about breast-feeding safety: Unknown.

The bottom line for you:

- Thalidomide is a potent human teratogen (substance that can cause birth defects). It should be avoided during pregnancy.

- Any woman exposed to thalidomide during pregnancy should consult with a fetal medicine expert, and pregnancy termination should be discussed.
- Any suspected fetal exposure to thalidomide must be reported to the FDA via the MedWatch program at 1-800-FDA-1088 and also to Celgene Corporation.
- Though occasionally used in pediatric populations, it is best to avoid breast feeding while taking thalidomide.

THEOPHYLLINE

Brand names: Accurbron, Aerolate, Aloefilina, Aminomal, Aquaphyllin, Asmalix, Asperal, Bilordyl, Bronkodyl, Bykofilin, Constant-T, Elixicon, Elixomin, Elixophyllin, Hydro-Spec, Labid, Lanophyllin, Lixolin, Neulin-SA, Phyllocontin, Provent, Pulmo, Respbid, Slo-Bid, Slo-Phyllin, Solu-Phyllin, Somophyllin, Sustaire, Talofren, Teofilina, Teophyllin, Theo-24, Theobid, Theochron, Theoclear, Theocontin, Theocot, Theo-Dur, Theolair, Theomar, Theophyl, Theophylline Anhydrous, Theosol-80, Theospan Sr, Theostat 80, Theo-Time, Theovent, Theox, T-Phyl, Truxophyllin, Uni-Dur, Unifyl, Uniphyl

Drug classes: Bronchodilator; Xanthine derivative

Indications (what it is used for): Chronic asthma, maintenance of chronic obstructive pulmonary disease (COPD).

How it works: Increases cAMP, necessary for smooth-muscle relaxation.

Contraindications (reasons you shouldn't take it): Hypersensitivity to drug or class, irregular heart rate, seizures, peptic ulcer disease.

Possible side effects and warnings: Can cause irregular or rapid heart rate, palpitations, seizures, respiratory arrest, nausea, vomiting, headache, sleeplessness, rash, hair loss, flushing, fever, nervousness, agitation, and tremor. Should be used with caution in women with liver or kidney dysfunction or low thyroid hormone.

How it can affect pregnant women: Asthma is a common disease in life and in pregnancy. Approximately one-third of women with asthma get worse during pregnancy, one-third get better, and one-third remain clinically unchanged. When asthma is well controlled, it does not affect pregnancy outcome, but poorly controlled asthma increases the risk of preterm birth (before 37 weeks) or low birth weight. Inhaled corticosteroids are considered the preventative medication of choice for pregnant women with persistent asthma unless their condition is well controlled by cromolyn or nedocromil. Budesonide and beclomethasone are considered the first-line treatments. Theophylline is considered a second-choice treatment for asthma during pregnancy. The clearance (how fast the body processes and eliminates the medication) of theophylline is significantly decreased in the third trimester and immediately after delivery, often requiring a decrease in the dose needed.

Certain medications used during labor and delivery have the potential to worsen asthma, including nonselective beta-blockers, some prostaglandins (used to induce labor), and ergonovine (used to control blood loss after delivery).

How it can affect a developing embryo or fetus: There are no adequate reports or well-controlled studies in human fetuses. Theophylline crosses the human placenta, quickly reaching the same level in the fetus as in the mother. In the laboratory, theophylline can dilate placental arteries, indicating that it may actually improve blood flow. In rabbits, theophylline used at more than 5 times the recommended clinical dose caused fetal toxicity, cleft palate, and skeletal defects. In studies using chicks theophylline increased the rate of cardiovascular defects. However, animal studies are not necessarily good indicators of how a drug will behave in humans.

Breast-feeding: Theophylline enters human breast milk and can reportedly cause irritability in a nursing newborn. However, newborn toxicity is unlikely. Women who choose to breast-feed should monitor their children's behavior closely.

Potential drug interactions: Theophyline can alter the response to numerous drugs, some of which are listed below. It is important your pharmacist and doctor know all the drugs you are taking (prescription and over the counter) before adding theophylline. In some instances, their interaction can be dangerous or life-threatening and must be avoided: alcohol, aminoglutethimide, carbamazepine, phenobarbital, cimetidine, ciprofloxacin, fluvoxamine, propranolol, tacrine, enoxacin, clarithromycin, erythromycin, benzodiazepines (e.g., diazepam, flurazepam, lorazepam), disulfiram, mexiletine, verapamil, estrogen-containing oral contraceptives, human recombinant interferon alfa-2a, isoproterenol (IV), lithium, pentoxifylline, propafenone, thiabendazole, ticlopidine, phenytoin, rifampin, sulfinpyrazone.

What the FDA says about use in pregnancy: Category C (see Appendix).

What the available evidence suggests about breast-feeding safety: Likely safe.

The bottom line for you:

- Theophylline is typically considered a second-choice medication for the treatment of asthma during pregnancy. Although the long clinical experience is reassuring, the results from animal studies suggest that we can't rule out the possibility that it is a weak human teratogen (substance that can cause birth defects).

- Newborn effects while breast-feeding are rare but should be watched for.

THIAMINE

Brand names: Actamin, Alivio, Anacrodyne, Benerva, Beneuril, Beneuron, Betabion, Betalin S, Betamin, Betatabs, Betaxin, Bevitine, Bewon, Biamine, Dumovit, Invite, Metabolin, Oryzanin, Ottovit, Tiamina, Vitamin B$_1$, Vitanon, Vitantial

Drug class: Vitamin/mineral

Indications (what it is used for): Dietary supplement, beriberi and wet beriberi (thiamine deficiency affecting the peripheral nervous system and cardio-vascular system, respectively) and Wernicke encephalopathy.

How it works: Replacement for vitamin deficiency.

Contraindications (reasons you shouldn't take it): Hypersensitivity to drug or class.

Possible side effects and warnings: Can cause blue lips and skin, rapid swelling of the layers of the skin, itching, hives, warmth, and injection site reaction.

How it can affect pregnant women: Pure thiamine deficiency is rare; it is usually associated with poor nutrition, often a result of alcoholism. There are no adequate reports or well-controlled studies of thiamine in pregnant women. Despite thiamine's inclusion in prenatal vitamins, deficiency still occurs commonly during pregnancy. Wernicke encephalopathy (degenerative brain disorder due to thiamine deficiency, causing lack of gross-muscle control, paralysis of eye muscles, confusion, and poor short-term memory), is reported during pregnancy, often in association with severe nausea and vomiting. When given as part of a multivitamin prenatal supplement, thiamine improves weight gain among HIV-infected women.

How it can affect a developing embryo or fetus: There are no adequate reports or well-controlled studies in human fetuses. Thiamine is actively transported across the human placenta; thus, the fetus is likely to have adequate thiamine even if the mother is deficient.

Breast-feeding: There are no adequate reports or well-controlled studies in nursing women. Thiamine enters human breast milk, and maternal supplementation increases the thiamine level in milk.

Potential drug interactions: No clinically relevant interactions identified.

What the FDA says about use in pregnancy: Category A (see Appendix).

What the available evidence suggests about breast-feeding safety: Safe.

The bottom line for you:

- Thiamine deficiency is not unusual during pregnancy and often is associated with nausea and vomiting. Thiamine is a standard component of prenatal vitamins.

- Thiamine is safe for use while breast-feeding.

THIOPENTAL

Brand name: Pentothal

Drug classes: Anesthesia, induction/maintenance; Barbiturate

Indications (what it is used for): Induction and maintenance of anesthesia, increased intracranial pressure.

How it works: Central nervous system depressant.

Contraindications (reasons you shouldn't take it): Hypersensitivity to drug or class, a variety of red blood cell diseases.

Possible side effects and warnings: Can cause dependency; respiratory depression; cardiovascular collapse; irregular, fast, or slow heart rate; low blood pressure; blood clots; and shortness of breath. Should be used with caution in women with liver or kidney dysfunction, severe cardiovascular disease, low blood pressure, increased brain pressure, myasthenia gravis (an autoimmune disease causing muscle weakness), and severe asthma.

How it can affect pregnant women: Thiopental is a very short-acting central nervous system depressant that has been used for more than 60 years. It induces hypnosis and anesthesia but not pain relief. Recovery after a small dose is rapid, with some sleepiness and amnesia for events that happened recently. There are no adequate reports or well-controlled studies of thiopental in pregnant women. It remains a popular agent to initiate general anesthesia for cesarean delivery. Low blood pressure and awareness during surgery are more common when thiopental is used compared to ketamine.

How it can affect a developing embryo or fetus: There are no adequate reports or well-controlled studies in human fetuses. Thiopental rapidly crosses the human placenta, achieving a level in the fetus equal to the mother's. The long clinical history of use in pregnant women is reassuring. Rodent birth defect studies have not been performed.

Breast-feeding: There are no adequate reports or well-controlled studies in nursing women. Thiopental enters human breast milk, but when it is used during delivery, the concentrations in breast milk are negligible by the time the milk comes in (typically 36 hours after delivery).

Potential drug interactions: Interaction between the following medications and thiopental has the potential to impact the effect of one or more of the drugs. In some instances the interaction can be dangerous or life-threatening and must be avoided: probenecid, aminophylline, zimelidine.

What the FDA says about use in pregnancy: Category C (see Appendix).

What the available evidence suggests about breast-feeding safety: Safe.

The bottom line for you:

- Thiopental has been used to initiate general anesthesia for decades without obvious pregnancy-specific risk.
- Its one-time use for delivery anesthesia will have no effect on breast-feeding.

THIORIDAZINE

Brand names: Dazine, Meleretten, Mellaril, Mellaril-S, Novoridazine, Sonapex, Thinin, Winleril

Drug classes: Antipsychotic; Phenothiazine

Indications (what it is used for): Refractory schizophrenia.

How it works: Unknown.

Contraindications (reasons you shouldn't take it): Hypersensitivity to drug or class, severe high or low blood pressure, irregular heart rate, central nervous system (CNS) depression, coma, narrow-angle glaucoma, electrolyte imbalance, decreased bowel motility, bowel obstruction, and bone marrow depression.

Possible side effects and warnings: Can cause bowel obstruction, neuroleptic malignant syndrome (life-threatening muscle rigidity, fever, vital sign instability, and cognitive changes such as delirium), involuntary and repetitive body movements that can have a slow or belated onset, rapid or irregular heart rate, menstrual irregularities, jaundice, various blood disorders, seizures, drowsiness, dry mouth, constipation, nausea, blurred vision, anxiety, tremor, weight gain, swelling, leaky breasts, low white blood cell count, and skin or eye pigmentation. Should be used with caution in women with liver dysfunction, cardiovascular disease, seizures, or Parkinson's disease (disorder of the brain that affects movement and coordination), or who are taking CNS depressants.

How it can affect pregnant women: There are no adequate reports or well-controlled studies of thioridazine in pregnant women.

How it can affect a developing embryo or fetus: There are no adequate reports or well-controlled studies in human fetuses. It is unknown whether thioridazine crosses the human placenta.

Breast-feeding: There is no published data in nursing women. It is unknown whether thioridazine enters human breast milk.

Potential drug interactions: Thioridazine is contraindicated (should not be used) with any of the following medications or in patients who have a genetic defect leading to reduced levels of CYP2D6 (about 7% of the normal population): drugs that inhibit CYP2D6 (e.g., fluoxetine, paroxetine), fluvoxamine, pindolol, propranolol.

What the FDA says about use in pregnancy: No assigned category (see Appendix).

What the available evidence suggests about breast-feeding safety: Unknown.

The bottom line for you:

- Thioridazine should be used during pregnancy and while breast-feeding only if the benefit to the woman justifies the potential risk to the embryo, fetus, or newborn.

THIOTHIXENE

Brand name: Navane
Drug class: Antipsychotic
Indications (what it is used for): Schizophrenia.
How it works: Unknown.
Contraindications (reasons you shouldn't take it): Hypersensitivity to drug or class, coma, central nervous system depression, various blood disorders.

Possible side effects and warnings: Can cause neuroleptic malignant syndrome (life-threatening muscle rigidity, fever, vital sign instability and cognitive changes such as delirium), seizures, involuntary and repetitive body movements that can have a slow or belated onset, low white blood cell count, drowsiness, restlessness, agitation, sleeplessness, low blood pressure, blurred vision, dry mouth, rapid heart rate, light sensitivity, and liver dysfunction. Should be used with caution in women with seizures, glaucoma, or coronary artery disease, or who are withdrawing from alcohol.

How it can affect pregnant women: There are no adequate reports or well-controlled studies of thiothixene in pregnant women.

How it can affect a developing embryo or fetus: There are no adequate reports or well-controlled studies in human fetuses. It is unknown whether thiothixene crosses the human placenta. Rodent studies are reassuring, revealing no evidence of birth defects or low birth weight despite the use of doses higher than those used clinically. However, animal studies are not necessarily good indicators of how a drug will behave in humans.

Breast-feeding: There is no published data in nursing women. It is unknown whether thiothixene enters human breast milk.

Potential drug interactions: No clinically relevant interactions identified.

What the FDA says about use in pregnancy: No assigned category (see Appendix).

What the available evidence suggests about breast-feeding safety: Unknown.

The bottom line for you:

- Thiothixene should be used during pregnancy and while breast-feeding only if the benefit to the woman justifies the potential risk to the embryo, fetus, or newborn.

TIAGABINE

Brand name: Gabitril

Drug class: Anticonvulsant

Indications (what it is used for): Complex partial seizures.

How it works: Unknown.

Contraindications (reasons you shouldn't take it): Hypersensitivity to drug or class.

Possible side effects and warnings: Can cause central nervous system depression, withdrawal seizures, dizziness, weakness, sleepiness, nausea, vomiting, impaired memory, and nervousness. It should be used with caution in women with liver dysfunction or whose EEG test shows a spike/wave.

How it can affect pregnant women: Women on medication for a seizure disorder should (when possible) plan their pregnancies, discuss the optimal medication with their neurologist, and begin appropriate supplemental folate therapy before conception (4 mg per day) to minimize the risk of birth defects. The risks of birth defects associated with antiseizure medications must be weighed against the risks of continued seizures to both the mother and fetus. Women who become pregnant during treatment should not stop treatment on their own but rather meet quickly with their doctor before making a decision. Tiagabine is a newer anticonvulsant more often used with another agent rather than alone. In contrast to some older anticonvulsants, there is no interaction between tiagabine and oral contraceptives. There are no adequate reports or well-controlled studies of tiagabine in pregnant women. If required during pregnancy to maintain seizure control, maternal levels of the drug should be measured periodically.

How it can affect a developing embryo or fetus: There are no adequate reports or well-controlled studies in human fetuses. It is unknown whether tiagabine crosses the human placenta. In rodents, tiagabine caused face and skull defects, limb defects, and multiple organ defects as well as low birth weight. However, animal studies are not necessarily good indicators of how a drug will behave in humans.

Breast-feeding: There is no published data in nursing women. It is unknown whether tiagabine enters human breast milk.

Potential drug interactions: Interaction between the following medications and tiagabine has the potential to impact the effect of one or more of the drugs. In some instances the interaction can be dangerous or life-threatening and must be avoided: carbamazepine, phenytoin, phenobarbital, primidone, valproate.

What the FDA says about use in pregnancy: Category C (see Appendix).

What the available evidence suggests about breast-feeding safety: Unknown.

The bottom line for you:

- Until there is additional information indicating safety, tiagabine should probably be avoided during pregnancy and while breast-feeding unless there is no other acceptable option.

TICARCILLIN

Brand names: Ticar, Timentin

Drug classes: Antibiotic; Penicillin

Indications (what it is used for): Bacterial infection, skin and soft tissue infection, acute and chronic respiratory infection.

How it works: Kills bacteria by blocking the synthesis of cell wall mucopeptide.

Contraindications (reasons you shouldn't take it): Hypersensitivity to drug or class.

Possible side effects and warnings: Can cause seizures, low white blood cell and/or platelet counts, Stevens-Johnson syndrome (a rare but serious skin reaction to medication), rash, hives, bleeding, headache, dizziness, low potassium or high sodium level, fatigue, fever, bowel infection, gas, blood clots, and liver dysfunction. Should be used with caution in women who have cephalosporin allergy, kidney dysfunction, seizures, sodium restriction, or a bleeding disorder.

How it can affect pregnant women: Ticarcillin is an extended-spectrum penicillin primarily used for gram-negative infections and is often combined with an aminoglycoside. Clavulanic acid (a component of ticarcillin) inhibits the beta-lactamase enzyme found in bacteria that breaks down penicillins and cephalosporins and renders the bacteria resistant to these antibiotics. There are no adequate reports or well-controlled studies of ticarcillin in pregnant women. Like other antibiotics, it reduces the risk of an infection in the uterus in women with preterm premature rupture of the membranes (PPROM, water breaking before 37 weeks) but may also increase the number of newborns with an infection from ampicillin-resistant bacteria.

How it can affect a developing embryo or fetus: There are no adequate reports or well-controlled studies in human fetuses. Transfer of ticarcillin across the human placenta is slow, but it does accumulate in the fetus over time. Rodent studies are reassuring, revealing no evidence of birth defects or low birth weight despite the use of doses higher than those used clinically. However, animal studies are not necessarily good indicators of how a drug will behave in humans.

Breast-feeding: There are no adequate reports or well-controlled studies in nursing women. The levels of ticarcillin excreted into human breast milk are not clinically relevant.

Potential drug interactions: No clinically relevant interactions identified.

What the FDA says about use in pregnancy: Category B (see Appendix).

What the available evidence suggests about breast-feeding safety: Safe.

The bottom line for you:
- Ticarcillin is generally considered safe for use during pregnancy and while breast-feeding.

TIMOLOL

Brand names: Aquanil, Blocadren, Cusimolol, Dispatim, Equiton, Glauco-Opu, Glucolol, Glucomol, Nyolol, Ocupres, Optimol, Tiloptic, Timoptic, Timoptic-Xe, Timoptol, Timpotic

Drug classes: Adrenergic antagonist; Beta-blocker

Indications (what it is used for): High blood pressure, angina, very recent heart attack, migraine prevention, glaucoma.

How it works: Blocks the beta-adrenoreceptors to relieve the symptoms.

Contraindications (reasons you shouldn't take it): Hypersensitivity to drug or class, congestive heart failure, slow or irregular heart rate, asthma, cardiogenic shock.

Possible side effects and warnings: Can cause congestive heart failure, slow heart rate, low blood pressure, bronchospasm, fatigue, dizziness, headache, shortness of breath, itching, and nightmares. Should be used with caution in women with liver or kidney dysfunction or diabetes.

How it can affect pregnant women: There are no adequate reports or well-controlled studies of timolol in pregnant women. Timolol is superior to a-methyldopa for the treatment of high blood pressure after delivery. It is unclear whether timolol offers a therapeutic advantage over any other beta-blocker during pregnancy.

How it can affect a developing embryo or fetus: There are no adequate reports or well-controlled studies in human fetuses. Timolol crosses the human placenta, although how much is unclear. Rodent studies are reassuring, revealing no evidence of birth defects or low birth weight despite the use of doses higher than those used clinically. However, animal studies are not necessarily good indicators of how a drug will behave in humans.

Breast-feeding: There are no adequate reports or well-controlled studies in nursing women. Timolol is excreted into human milk when taken orally, although the effect on a newborn is unknown. The amount of timolol in breast milk originating in eyedrops used to treat glaucoma would not be clinically relevant.

Potential drug interactions: Interaction between the following medications and timolol has the potential to impact the effect of one or more of the drugs. In some instances the interaction can be dangerous or life-threatening and must be avoided: epinephrine; calcium channel antagonists (e.g., nifedipine, verapamil, diltiazem); catecholamine-depleting drugs such as reserpine, digitalis, calcium antagonists, quinidine, clonidine.

What the FDA says about use in pregnancy: Category C (see Appendix).

What the available evidence suggests about breast-feeding safety: Safe (eye drops); unknown (pills).

The bottom line for you:

- There are alternative medications with which there is more experience during pregnancy and while breast-feeding.

TINZAPARIN

Brand name: Innohep

Drug classes: Anticoagulant; Antithrombotic; LMWH (low-molecular-weight heparin)

Indications (what it is used for): Blood clots and pulmonary embolus (blood clot in the lung).

How it works: Blocks a key point in the clotting sequence

Contraindications (reasons you shouldn't take it): Hypersensitivity to drug or class, hypersensitivity to pork products, active or recent bleeding, epidural or spinal anesthesia, low platelet count, history of heparin-associated low platelet count.

Possible side effects and warnings: Can cause hemorrhage, hematoma, skin necrosis and Stevens-Johnson syndrome (both rare but serious skin disorders), injection site reaction, and liver dysfunction. Should be used with caution in women with bleeding tendency, recent surgery, bacterial endocarditis (infection of a heart valve), uncontrolled high blood

pressure, diabetic retinopathy, platelet inhibitors, or kidney dysfunction.

How it can affect pregnant women: Pregnant women are at greater risk for blood clots during pregnancy, because estrogen increases the blood's ability to clot in arteries and veins. Tinzaparin is a low-molecular-weight heparin extracted from pigs that is at least as effective as regular heparin for the treatment and prevention of blood clots. It appears to be more effective than enoxaparin after cesarean section. Because the clearance (how fast the body processes and eliminates the medication) of tinzaparin and all other LMWHs are increased by pregnancy, a woman taking one of these medications must have her blood level of the medication monitored at least once per trimester.

How it can affect a developing embryo or fetus: There are no adequate reports or well-controlled studies in human fetuses. Tinzaparin does not cross the human placenta and thus cannot have a direct effect on the fetus.

Breast-feeding: There are no adequate reports or well-controlled studies in nursing women. It is unknown whether tinzaparin enters human breast milk.

Potential drug interactions: Interaction between the following medications and tinzaparin has the potential to impact the effect of one or more of the drugs. In some instances the interaction can be dangerous or life-threatening and must be avoided: oral anticoagulants, platelet inhibitors (e.g., dextran, dipyridamole, nonsteroidal anti-inflammatory drugs [NSAIDs], salicylates, sulfinpyrazone), thrombolytics.

What the FDA says about use in pregnancy: Category B (see Appendix).

What the available evidence suggests about breast-feeding safety: Unknown.

The bottom line for you:

- Tinzaparin is an alternative to heparin and other low-molecular-weight heparins during pregnancy but has no clear advantage over them.

• Tinzaparin is effective and safe for use while breast-feeding.

TOBRAMYCIN

Brand names: Aktob, Nebcin, Tobradistin, Tobrasix, Tobrex, Toround, Trazil

Drug classes: Aminoglycoside; Antibiotic; Ophthalmic

Indications (what it is used for): Bacterial infection, prevention of bacterial endocarditis (infection of a heart valve), treatment of lung infection associated with cystic fibrosis (inherited life-threatening lung disease), ocular infection.

How it works: Kills bacteria by inhibiting protein synthesis.

Contraindications (reasons you shouldn't take it): Hypersensitivity to drug or class.

Possible side effects and warnings: Can cause kidney, ear, or nerve toxicity; increased pressure in the brain unassociated with other diseases; inflammation of the colon and small intestine; diarrhea; nausea; vomiting; itching; rash; weakness; tremor; muscle cramps; loss of appetite; headache; swelling; increased salivation; ringing in the ears; vertigo; low white blood cell and/or platelet counts; and muscle weakness. Should be used with caution in women with myasthenia gravis (an autoimmune disease causing muscle weakness), vestibular/cochlear implant, or kidney dysfunction, or who are taking medications that can be toxic to the kidneys.

How it can affect pregnant women: There are no adequate reports or well-controlled studies of tobramycin in pregnant women. During pregnancy, and after delivery, the clearance (how fast the drug is processed and eliminated by the body) of tobramycin is increased, requiring a higher dose to obtain adequate levels.

How it can affect a developing embryo or fetus: There are no adequate reports or well-controlled studies in human fetuses. It is unknown whether tobramycin crosses the human placenta. Other aminoglycoside antibiotics do cross, and there are reports of irreversible congenital deafness after the use of streptomycin. Serious side effects to mother, fetus, or newborn are not reported after treatment with other aminoglycosides. Tobramycin (like gentimicin) likely causes little or no damage to the fetus. Systemic levels are much lower after administration through a nebulizer or eyedrops compared to an injection. Rodent studies are reassuring, revealing no evidence of birth defects or low birth weight despite higher doses than those used clinically. However, animal studies are not necessarily good indicators of how a drug will behave in humans.

Breast-feeding: There are no adequate reports or well-controlled studies in nursing women. The small amounts of tobramycin excreted into human breast milk are likely clinically insignificant.

Potential drug interactions: Interaction between the following medications and tobramycin has the potential to impact the effect of one or more of the drugs. In some instances the interaction can be dangerous or life-threatening and must be avoided: other drugs that can cause nerve or ear damage, diuretics, ethacrynic acid, furosemide, mannitol, urea.

What the FDA says about use in pregnancy: Category D; B for ophthalmic applications (see Appendix).

What the available evidence suggests about breast-feeding safety: Safe.

The bottom line for you:

• There are alternative medications with which there is more experience.

• Tobramycin should be used during pregnancy and breast-feeding only if the benefit to the woman justifies the potential risk to the embryo, fetus, or newborn.

TOLAZAMIDE

Brand names: Tolinase, Tolisan

Drug classes: Hypoglycemic; Sulfonylurea

Indications (what it is used for): Type II diabetes

How it works: Stimulates insulin release from pancreatic islet cells.

Contraindications (reasons you shouldn't take it): Hypersensitivity to drug or class, or to sulfonamides.

Possible side effects and warnings: Can cause low blood glucose, nausea, feeling of fullness in the stomach, heartburn, low white blood cell and/or platelet count, hemolytic anemia, aplastic anemia, bone marrow suppression, itching, redness, and hives.

How it can affect pregnant women: Diet remains the first-line treatment of type II diabetes in people who are not pregnant. Caloric restriction and weight loss are essential in anyone with diabetes who is obese and may by themselves be effective for controlling blood glucose and symptoms. Regular physical activity is also important, as well as identifying and improving any cardiovascular risk factors (e.g. high cholesterol, inflammation in the blood). If this approach fails, oral hypoglycemic agents may be indicated.

Tolazamide is a first-generation sulfonylurea (a medication that stimulates the pancreas to release insulin). However, sulfonylureas may be associated with an excess of cardiovascular deaths in the diabetic population. There are no adequate reports or well-controlled studies of tolazamide in pregnant women; additional study is necessary. If oral medications such as glyburide or metformin are ineffective, insulin becomes the drug of choice during pregnancy.

How it can affect a developing embryo or fetus: There are no adequate reports or well-controlled studies in human fetuses. It is unknown whether tolazamide crosses the human placenta. However, prolonged severe low blood glucose has been reported in newborns delivered to women receiving a sulfonylurea at the time of delivery. Tolazamide should be discontinued at least 2 weeks before the due date. Rodent studies are reassuring, revealing no evidence of birth defects or low birth weight despite the use of doses higher than those used clini-

cally. Only with doses more than 100 times the maximum recommended clinical dose was miscarriage noted. However, animal studies are not necessarily good indicators of how a drug will behave in humans.

Breast-feeding: There are no adequate reports or well-controlled studies in nursing women. It is unknown whether tolazamide enters human breast milk. Other sulfonylurea drugs are excreted into breast milk.

Potential drug interactions: Interaction between the following medications and tolazamide has the potential to impact the effect of one or more of the drugs. In some instances the interaction can be dangerous or life-threatening and must be avoided: beta-adrenergic blocking agents, chloramphenicol, coumarins, monoamine oxidase inhibitors (MAOIs), nonsteroidal anti-inflammatory drugs (NSAIDs), drugs that are highly protein bound, probenecid, salicylates, sulfonamides, miconazole.

What the FDA says about use in pregnancy: Category C (see Appendix).

What the available evidence suggests about breast-feeding safety: Unknown.

The bottom line for you:

- There are alternative medications with which there is more experience during pregnancy and while breast-feeding.
- Oral medications for diabetes are selected based on low transfer across the placenta. Glyburide is preferred for this reason.

TOLBUTAMIDE

Brand names: Aglicem, Aglycid, Ansulin, Diabecid-R, Dolipol, Fordex, Glucosulfa, Guabeta, Mobenol, Noglucor, Novobutamide, Orabet, Orinase, Orinase Diagnostic, Raston, Tolbusal, Tolbutamida Valdecases

Drug classes: Hypoglycemic; Sulfonylurea

Indications (what it is used for): Type II diabetes

How it works: Stimulates insulin release from pancreatic islet cells.

Contraindications (reasons you shouldn't take it): Hypersensitivity to drug or class, sole therapy for type I diabetes, diabetic ketoacidosis (lack of insulin prevents body using sugar as a fuel).

Possible side effects and warnings: Can cause low platelet and/or white blood cell count, aplastic anemia, bone marrow suppression, low blood glucose, jaundice, severe vomiting, headache, constipation, diarrhea, heartburn, loss of appetite, dizziness, rash, and light sensitivity. Should be used with caution in women with a hypersensitivity to sulfonamides.

How it can affect pregnant women: Diet remains the first-line treatment of type II diabetes in people who are not pregnant. Caloric restriction and weight loss are essential in anyone with diabetes who is obese and may by themselves be effective controlling blood glucose and symptoms. Regular physical activity is also important, as well as identifying and improving any cardiovascular risk factors (e.g., high cholesterol, evidence of inflammation in the blood). If this approach fails, oral hypoglycemic agents may be indicated.

There are no adequate reports or well-controlled studies of tolbutamide, which is a sulfonylurea (medication that stimulates the pancreas to release insulin) in pregnant women; additional study is necessary. If oral medications such as glyburide or metformin are ineffective, insulin becomes the drug of choice.

How it can affect a developing embryo or fetus: There are no adequate reports or well-controlled studies in human fetuses. Tolbutamide crosses the human placenta to a greater extent than glyburide, which makes the fetus more likely to develop very low blood glucose levels. Prolonged severe low blood glucose is reported in newborns of mothers who received a sulfonylurea at the time of delivery. If tolbutamide is used during pregnancy, it should be discontinued at least 2 weeks before the expected delivery date. Tolbutamide caused birth defects in rats. It was associated with an increased prevalence of eye and bone abnormalities at doses 25–100 times the maximum recommended clinical dose. However, animal studies are not necessarily good indicators of how a drug will behave in humans.

Breast-feeding: There are no adequate reports or well-controlled studies in nursing women. Tolbutamide enters human breast milk, although the amount and impact are not known.

Potential drug interactions: Interaction between the following medications and tolbutamide has the potential to impact the effect of one or more of the drugs. In some instances the interaction can be dangerous or life-threatening and must be avoided: beta-adrenergic blocking agents, chloramphenicol, coumarins, monoamine oxidase inhibitors (MAOIs), nonsteroidal anti-inflammatory drugs (NSAIDs), drugs that are highly protein bound, probenecid, salicylates, sulfonamides, miconazole.

What the FDA says about use in pregnancy: Category C (see Appendix).

What the available evidence suggests about breast-feeding safety: Safe.

The bottom line for you:

- There are alternative medications with which there is more experience during pregnancy and while breast-feeding.
- Oral medications for diabetes are selected based on low transfer across the placenta. Glyburide is preferred for this reason.

TOLTERODINE

Brand name: Detrol

Drug classes: Antispasmodic; Urologic

Indications (what it is used for): Overactive bladder.

How it works: Blocks cholinergic receptors, whose activation causes the symptoms.

Contraindications (reasons you shouldn't take it): Hypersensitivity to drug or class, narrow-angle glaucoma, stomach obstruction.

Possible side effects and warnings: Can cause psychosis, dry mouth, headache, heartburn, constipation, dry eyes, dizziness, blurred vision, sleepiness, chest pain, cough, rapid heart rate, and swelling. Should be used with caution in women with liver or kidney dysfunction.

How it can affect pregnant women: There is no published experience with tolterodine during pregnancy. There is also probably no indication for its use during pregnancy.

How it can affect a developing embryo or fetus: There are no adequate reports or well-controlled studies in human fetuses. It is unknown whether tolterodine crosses the human placenta. It crosses the rodent placenta, and studies using 20–25 times the maximum recommended clinical dose resulted in miscarriage, low birth weight, and birth defects including cleft palate and skeletal malformations. However, animal studies are not necessarily good indicators of how a drug will behave in humans.

Breast-feeding: There is no published data in nursing women. It is unknown whether tolterodine enters human breast milk. It is excreted at low levels into rodent milk.

Potential drug interactions: Interaction between the following medications and tolterodine has the potential to impact the effect of one or more of the drugs. In some instances the interaction can be dangerous or life-threatening and must be avoided: ketoconazole, other potent CYP3A4 inhibitors, azole antifungals (e.g., itraconazole, miconazole), macrolide antibiotics (e.g., clarithromycin, erythromycin), cyclosporine, vinblastine.

What the FDA says about use in pregnancy: Category C (see Appendix).

What the available evidence suggests about breast-feeding safety: Unknown.

The bottom line for you:

- Tolterodine should be avoided during pregnancy as it is used to treat a condition that is not life-threatening, and animal studies suggest a risk of birth defects.
- There is not enough information to determine the safety of tolterodine during breast-feeding.

TOPIRAMATE

Brand name: Topamax

Drug class: Anticonvulsant

Indications (what it is used for): Tonic-clonic seizures (also called grand mal seizures; include loss of consciousness and violent muscle contractions), adjunct therapy.

How it works: Unknown.

Contraindications (reasons you shouldn't take it): Hypersensitivity to drug or class, liver dysfunction.

Possible side effects and warnings: Can cause kidney stones, nearsightedness, secondary angle-closure glaucoma, dizziness, sleepiness, fatigue, difficulty speaking and expressing oneself verbally, memory difficulty, nervousness, lack of gross-muscle control, involuntary eye movement, depression, double vision, mood disturbances, tingling, tremor, weight loss, confusion, abdominal pain, agitation, and upper respiratory symptoms.

How it can affect pregnant women: Topiramate increases the metabolism of ethinyl estradiol and progestogens, which are both common components of oral contraceptives. If a women being treated with topiramate wishes to take oral contraceptives, the preparation should contain at least 50 mcg of ethinyl estradiol. Levonorgestrel implants are contraindicated (should not be used) if a woman is taking topiramate, because of the increased risk of contraceptive failure. It is also recommended that medroxyprogesterone injections for contraception be given every 10 weeks rather than every 12 weeks.

There are no adequate reports or well-controlled studies of topiramate in pregnant women. Women on medication for a seizure disorder should (when possible) plan their pregnancies, discuss the optimal medication with their neurologist, and begin appropriate supplemental folate therapy before conception (4 mg per day) to minimize the risk of birth defects. The risks of birth defects associated with antiseizure medications must be weighed against the risks of continued seizures to both the mother and fetus. Women who become pregnant during treatment should not stop treatment on their own but rather meet quickly with their doctor before making a decision.

How it can affect a developing embryo or fetus: There are no adequate reports or well-controlled studies in human fetuses. Topiramate readily crosses the human placenta, reaching the same level in the fetus as in the mother. Preliminary study done after the drug went on the market suggests that topiramate use during pregnancy may increase the risk of major birth defects, especially cleft lip and/or palate. In rodents the higher the dose, the greater the increase in rates of skull, face, and limb defects, even with doses that represent a fraction of the maximum recommended clinical dose. However, animal studies are not necessarily good indicators of how a drug will behave in humans. Vitamin K has been recommended during the last month of pregnancy in women taking some enzyme-inducing agents such as oxcarbazepine, carbamazepine, phenobarbital, phenytoin, and topiramate under the theory it will reduce the risk of newborn bleeding. However, there is not good evidence that the risk is increased and the incidence of newborn bleeding does not appear to be decreased by maternal treatment with vitamin K.

Breast-feeding: There are no adequate reports or well-controlled studies in nursing women. Topiramate enters human breast milk at low concentrations, but breast-feeding newborns have levels that are clinically insignificant.

Potential drug interactions: Interaction between the following medications and topiramate has the potential to impact the effect of one or more of the drugs. In some instances the interaction can be dangerous or life-threatening and must be avoided: carbamazepine, phenytoin, lamotrigine, hydrochlorothiazide, lithium, amitriptyline, risperidone, and other carbonic anhydrase inhibitors (e.g., acetazolamide, dichlorphenamide). The possibility of decreased contraceptive efficacy and increased breakthrough bleeding should be considered when topiramate and hormonal contraceptive products are taken at the same time.

What the FDA says about use in pregnancy: Category D (see Appendix).

What the available evidence suggests about breast-feeding safety: Likely safe.

The bottom line for you:

- Topiramate appears to be a human teratogen (substance that can cause birth defects), increasing the risk of cleft lip and/or palate.
- Topiramate should be used during pregnancy only if alternative therapy fails to provide adequate seizure control. As for most psychotropic drugs, using one medication and the lowest effective quantity given in divided doses to minimize the peaks of medication in the maternal system can reduce the risks.
- Topiramate appears a good choice for breast-feeding women.

TRAMADOL

Brand names: Adamon, Ultram

Drug class: Analgesic, narcoticlike

Indications (what it is used for): Moderate to severe pain.

How it works: Unknown.

Contraindications (reasons you shouldn't take it): Hypersensitivity to drug or class, alcohol or drug use.

Possible side effects and warnings: Can cause dependency, seizures, rapid swelling of the layers of the skin, bronchospasm, respiratory depression, Stevens-Johnson syndrome and toxic epidermal necrolysis (both rare but serious skin disorders), low blood pressure when upright, serotonin syndrome, hallucinations, serious thoughts of suicide, dizziness, nausea, vomiting, sleepiness, itching, nervousness, anxiety, agitation, euphoria, tremor, spasticity, visual disturbances, loss of appetite, and rash. Should be used with caution in women who have a history of substance abuse, respiratory depression, seizures, head injury, increased intracranial pressure, sudden abdominal pain, or liver or kidney dysfunction, or who are taking a central nervous or respiratory system depressant.

How it can affect pregnant women: There are no adequate reports or well-controlled studies of tramadol in pregnant women. A single study comparing it with meperidine for labor analgesia concluded that tramadol created less maternal sedation and fetal respiratory depression. Tramadol reduces postanesthetic shivering and lowers the frequency of sleepiness compared to meperidine. It is an excellent oral agent for the relief of significant postoperative pain.

How it can affect a developing embryo or fetus: There are no adequate reports or well-controlled studies in human fetuses. Tramadol crosses the human placenta, achieving a fetal level approaching that of the mother. Chronic use during pregnancy may lead to physical dependence and postpartum withdrawal symptoms in the newborn. Rodent studies are generally reassuring, revealing embryo and maternal toxicity only at high concentrations. However, animal studies are not necessarily good indicators of how a drug will behave in humans.

Breast-feeding: It is unlikely that a clinically significant amount of tramadol enters human breast milk.

Potential drug interactions: Interaction between the following medications and tramadol has the potential to impact the effect of one or more of the drugs. In some instances the interaction can be dangerous or life-threatening and must be avoided: carbamazepine; quinidine; other CYP2D6 inhibitors including amitriptyline, fluoxetine, and paroxetine; monoamine oxidase inhibitors (MAOIs); CYP3A4 inhibitors (e.g., erythromycin, ketoconazole) or inducers (e.g., rifampin, St. John's wort).

What the FDA says about use in pregnancy: Category C (see Appendix).

What the available evidence suggests about breast-feeding safety: Likely safe.

The bottom line for you:
- Tramadol is a reasonable oral agent for the management of postoperative pain during or after pregnancy. However, there are other medications with which there is more experience during pregnancy.
- Tramadol is likely safe for use while breast-feeding.

TRAZODONE
Brand names: Desyrel, Sideril, Trazalon, Trazonil
Drug class: Antidepressant, type 4
Indications (what it is used for): Depression.
How it works: Unknown.
Contraindications (reasons you shouldn't take it): Hypersensitivity to drug or class, recent acute heart attack.
Possible side effects and warnings: Can cause low blood pressure, fainting, drowsiness, bitter taste, dry mouth, nausea, vomiting, headache, blurred vision, fatigue, joint pain, lack of coordination, and tremor. Should be used with caution in women with an irregular heart rate, who are taking central nervous system depressants or blood-pressure-lowering medication, or who are undergoing electroconvulsive therapy.

How it can affect pregnant women: Depression is common during and after pregnancy but often goes unrecognized and untreated. Depression can be made worse by pregnancy or delivery, and suicide is a not uncommon cause of maternal death. Pregnancy is not a reason to discontinue antidepressant drugs if the medication is effective and needed. A woman being treated for depression who becomes pregnant should not discontinue medication abruptly on her own but rather discuss her treatment and condition with her medical provider. Pregnancy may increase the dose needed to be effective, and women with a history of depression have a higher rate of recurrence after delivery.

The published data with trazodone during pregnancy is limited but reassuring. In one report, levels of the medication were lower in the first and second trimesters compared to the third trimester, suggesting that a dose adjustment may be needed.

How it can affect a developing embryo or fetus: There are no adequate reports or well-controlled studies in human fetuses. It is unknown whether trazodone crosses the human placenta. Available studies are reassuring, revealing no increase in the prevalence of adverse outcomes, including birth defects or low birth weight. Trazodone crosses the rat placenta, and rodent birth defect studies found an increased risk of miscarriage at doses that are multiples of the maximum recommended clinical dose. However, animal studies are not necessarily good indicators of how a drug will behave in humans.

Breast-feeding: The amount of trazodone ingested by a breast-feeding newborn is not clinically relevant.

Potential drug interactions: Interaction between the following medications and trazodone has the potential to impact the effect of one or more of the drugs. In some instances the interaction can be dangerous or life-threatening and must be avoided: digoxin, phenytoin, monoamine oxidase inhibitors (MAOIs).

What the FDA says about use in pregnancy: Category C (see Appendix).

What the available evidence suggests about breast-feeding safety: Safe.

The bottom line for you:

- There are alternative medications with which there is more experience during pregnancy.
- As for most psychotropic drugs, using one medication, at the lowest effective quantity and given in divided doses, will lower the peaks of the medication in the mother's system and minimize any risks.
- Trazodone is safe for use while breast-feeding.

TREPROSTINIL

Brand name: Remodulin
Drug classes: Platelet inhibitor; Prostaglandin; Vasodilator

Indications (what it is used for): Pulmonary high blood pressure, symptoms of heart failure.

How it works: Inhibits platelet clumping and dilates blood vessels.

Contraindications (reasons you shouldn't take it): Hypersensitivity to drug or class.

Possible side effects and warnings: Can cause pulmonary high blood pressure, infusion site reaction, headache, diarrhea, nausea, rash, jaw pain, dizziness, swelling, itching, and low blood pressure. Should be used with caution in women with liver or kidney dysfunction. The medication should not be withdrawn abruptly.

How it can affect pregnant women: Significant high blood pressure in the lungs is a serious condition that can be fatal, especially during pregnancy. Treprostinil is one of the few effective drug treatments. It is a synthetic version of a natural substance, prostacyclin. Although there is no published data with treprostinil during pregnancy, the critical nature of the disease makes its use reasonable.

How it can affect a developing embryo or fetus: There are no adequate reports or well-controlled studies in human fetuses. It is unknown whether treprostinil crosses the human placenta. Rodent studies are reassuring, revealing no evidence of birth defects or low birth weight despite using doses higher than those used clinically. However, animal studies are not necessarily good indicators of how a drug will behave in humans.

Breast-feeding: There is no published data in nursing women. It is unknown whether treprostinil enters human breast milk.

Potential drug interactions: Low blood pressure may be exacerbated by drugs that alter blood pressure (e.g., antihypertensive agents, diuretics, vasodilators). Treprostinil may increase the risk of bleeding, particularly in people who are taking anticoagulants.

What the FDA says about use in pregnancy: Category B (see Appendix).

What the available evidence suggests about breast-feeding safety: Unknown.

The bottom line for you:
- Treprostinil is probably safe for use during pregnancy and while breast-feeding for the treatment of a life-threatening condition.

TRETINOIN

Brand names: Acnavit, Avita, Avitoin, Cordes-Vas, Dermojuventus, Kerlocal, Relief, Renova, Retin-A, Retin-A Micro, Retinoic Acid, SteiVAA, Vesanoid

Drug classes: Acne; Antineoplastic; Dermatologic; Retinoid

Indications (what it is used for): Acne, acute promyelocytic leukemia.

How it works: Unknown.

Contraindications (reasons you shouldn't take it): Hypersensitivity to drug or class.

Possible side effects and warnings: Can cause peeling, redness, and blistering after topical therapy; high cholesterol and/or triglyceride levels; increased intracranial pressure unrelated to an identifiable disease; and liver dysfunction.

How it can affect pregnant women: There are no adequate reports or well-controlled studies of tretinoin in pregnant women, but some retinoid agents are highly toxic to the fetus. Therefore, women should have a pregnancy test in their doctor's office within the week prior to starting tretinoin therapy and wait until a negative result is documented before beginning the medication. Women on tretinoin therapy should use two reliable forms of contraception during treatment and should take a pregnancy test monthly.

How it can affect a developing embryo or fetus: There are no adequate reports or well-controlled studies in human fetuses. Tretinoin is a teratogen (substance that can cause birth defects) in rodents and primates when given orally. Tretinoin crosses the human placenta. However, 106 pregnant women with first-trimester exposure to topical tretinoin were reported between 1983 and 2003 and then followed. Their birth outcomes were similar to 389 similarly followed women who had not used the medication. Fewer than 10 children have been born to women treated with oral tretinoin during pregnancy (always for acute promyelocytic leukemia and all after the first trimester); they too had normal outcomes. However, the experience is too small to conclude that tretinoin is safe after oral administration during the first trimester. Rodent and primate studies have associated tretinoin with abnormalities of the central nervous system, musculoskeletal system, ear, eye, thymus, and the blood vessel connections of the heart, as well as abnormal facial development and cleft palate. However, animal studies are not necessarily good indicators of how a drug will behave in humans.

Breast-feeding: There is no published data in nursing women. It is unknown whether tretinoin enters human breast milk.

Potential drug interactions: Interaction between the following medications and tretinoin has the potential to impact the effect of one or more of the drugs. In some instances the interaction can be dangerous or life-threatening and must be avoided: drugs that induce liver CYP450 enzymes (e.g., glucocorticoids, pentobarbital, phenobarbital, rifampicin) and medications that inhibit liver CYP450 enzymes (e.g., cimetidine, cyclosporine, diltiazem, erythromycin, ketoconazole, verapamil). Caution should be exercised when the topical form is used with topical over-the-counter acne preparations containing benzoyl peroxide, resorcinol, salicylic acid, or sulfur.

What the FDA says about use in pregnancy: Category D (oral); C (topical) (see Appendix).

What the available evidence suggests about breast-feeding safety: Unknown.

The bottom line for you:
- Oral tretinoin should be avoided during pregnancy and while breast-feeding unless maternal risk dictates it and there are no alternatives. The fetal risk appears low following topical exposure.

TRIAMCINOLONE

Brand names: Acetocot, Amcort, Aricin, Arist-cort, Aristocort, Aristocort Forte, Aristocort Suspension, Aristocort Topical, Aristogel, Aristo-Pak, Aristospan Intralesional, Aristospan Parenteral, Articulose-L.A., Azmacort, Cenocort A-40, Cenocort Forte, Cinalog, Cinolar, Cinonide 40, Delta-Tritex, Extracort, Flutex, Kenac, Kenacort, Kenaject-40, Kenalog, Kenalog-10, Kenalone, Kena-Plex 40, Kenonel, Nasacort, Oracort, Oralone, Oricort, Sholog A, Sholog K, Tac, Tramacort 40, Tramacort-D, Triacet, Triacort, Triam-A, Triamcinair, Triamcot, Triam-Forte, Triaminoral, Triamolone 40, Triamonide 40, Trianide, Triatex, Triderm, Tri-Kort, Trilog, Trilone, Tri-Med, Tristoject, Tristo-Plex, Trylone A, Trylone D, Trymex, U-Tri-Lone

Drug class: Corticosteroid

Indications (what it is used for): Adrenal insufficiency, inflammatory disorders, chronic asthma, allergic runny nose, steroid-responsive dermatitis.

How it works: Anti-inflammatory; replacement of corticosteroid deficiency.

Contraindications (reasons you shouldn't take it): Hypersensitivity to drug or class, systemic fungal infection.

Possible side effects and warnings: The potential side effects depend upon how the medication is administered (injection, nasal spray, tablet, topical gel/cream) but can include inadequate cortisol production (when used long term), psychosis, poor immune response to infection, menstrual irregularities, peptic ulcer, congestive heart failure, bone thinning, cataracts, nausea, vomiting, heartburn, appetite change, edema, headache, dizziness, mood swings, sleeplessness, anxiety, sinusitis, high blood pressure, sore throat, oral yeast (thrush), eczema, high blood glucose, low potassium level, bruising, acne, dry skin, skin atrophy, and impaired wound healing. Should be used with caution in women with congestive heart failure, seizures, diabetes, high blood pressure, tuberculosis, osteoporosis, liver dysfunction, respiratory infection, history of nasal surgery, or herpes infection.

How it can affect pregnant women: Asthma is a common disease in life and in pregnancy. Approximately one-third of pregnant women with asthma get worse during pregnancy, one-third get better, and one-third remain clinically unchanged. When asthma is well controlled it does not affect pregnancy outcome, but poorly controlled asthma may increase the risk of preterm birth (before 37 weeks) or low birth weight. Inhaled corticosteroids are considered the preventative medication of choice for pregnant women with persistent asthma unless their condition is well controlled by cromolyn or nedocromil. Budesonide and beclomethasone are considered the first-line treatments.

Certain medications used during labor and delivery have the potential to worsen asthma, including nonselective beta-blockers, some prostaglandins (used to induce labor), and ergonovine (used to control blood loss after delivery).

There are no adequate reports or well-controlled studies of triamcinolone in pregnant women. Triamcinolone appears to be at least as effective as beclomethasone for the treatment of asthma during pregnancy. Some unconfirmed research suggested that extended topical use might be associated with low fetal birth weight.

How it can affect a developing embryo or fetus: There are no adequate reports or well-controlled studies in human fetuses. It is unknown whether triamcinolone crosses the human placenta. However, it does cross the nonhuman primate placenta and is relatively resistant to breakdown by the placenta. Large quality human studies are reassuring, having found no increase in birth defects or low birth weight. Its administration to nonhuman primates at doses 5–60 times the maximum recommended clinical dose revealed an increased rate of low birth weight and skull and face birth defects. In several rodent models, triamcinolone caused cleft lip and palate, whereas cortisol did not. Although there is no epidemiologic evidence suggesting that oral triamcinolone causes birth defects in humans, it is best to avoid it in the first trimester. It is less likely that the maternal systemic concentration will reach a clinically relevant level after topical use or inhalation.

Breast-feeding: There is no published data in nursing women. It is unknown whether triamcinolone enters human breast milk. The topically applied drug likely poses little risk to a nursing newborn.

Potential drug interactions: No clinically relevant interactions identified.

What the FDA says about use in pregnancy: Category C (see Appendix).

What the available evidence suggests about breast-feeding safety: Unknown. The bottom line for you:

- Although there is no evidence to suggest that oral triamcinolone is a human teratogen (substance that can cause birth defects), it is probably best to avoid using it in the first trimester.
- Inhaled corticosteroids are considered the preventative medication of choice for pregnant women with persistent asthma unless their condition is well controlled by cromolyn or nedocromil.
- The impact of oral triamcinolone on a breast-fed newborn is unknown.

TRIFLUOPERAZINE

Brand names: Calmazine, Flupazine, Novoflurazine, Stelazine, Suprazine, TFP

Drug classes: Antipsychotic; Phenothiazine

Indications (what it is used for): Schizophrenia, anxiety.

How it works: Unknown.

Contraindications (reasons you shouldn't take it): Hypersensitivity to drug or class, coma, central nervous system depression, liver disease, bone marrow depression.

Possible side effects and warnings: Can cause dry mouth, constipation, low blood pressure when standing, dizziness, blurred vision, involuntary repetitive body movements that have a slow onset, light sensitivity, rash, nausea, rapid heart rate, fatigue, headache, weight gain, low white blood cell count, jaundice, and neuroleptic malignant syndrome (life-threatening muscle rigidity, fever, vital sign instability, and cognitive changes such as delirium).

How it can affect pregnant women: There are no adequate reports or well-controlled studies of trifluoperazine in pregnant women. Like other phenothiazines, trifluoperazine decreases the feeling of nausea. The published literature consists of scattered uninformative case reports.

How it can affect a developing embryo or fetus: There are no adequate reports or well-controlled studies in human fetuses. Trifluoperazine apparently crosses the human placenta, but the amount is unknown. Rodent studies are generally reassuring, revealing no evidence of birth defects or low birth weight despite the use of doses higher than those used clinically. However, animal studies are not necessarily good indicators of how a drug will behave in humans.

Breast-feeding: There are no adequate reports or well-controlled studies in nursing women. Trifluoperazine is excreted into human breast milk but at lower levels than the similar medications haloperidol and chlorpromazine. Using only one medication and the lowest effective quantity given in divided doses will minimize the medication peaks in the mother's system and may reduce any risks.

Potential drug interactions: No clinically relevant interactions identified.

What the FDA says about use in pregnancy: No assigned category (see Appendix).

What the available evidence suggests about breast-feeding safety: Likely safe.

The bottom line for you:

- There are alternative medications with which there is more experience during pregnancy.
- Trifluoperazine should be used during pregnancy only when the benefit to the woman justifies the potential risk to the embryo or fetus.
- As for most psychotropic drugs, using one medication and the lowest effective quantity given in

- divided doses to minimize medication peaks in the mother's system may reduce any risks.
- Trifluoperazine is likely safe for use while breast-feeding.

TRIMETHOPRIM-SULFAMETHOXAZOLE

Brand names: Bactrim DS/SS, Cotrim DS/SS, Septra DS/SS/IV

Drug classes: Folate antagonist; Sulfonamide

Indications (what it is used for): Bacterial infection, *Pneumocystis carinii* treatment and prevention, middle ear infection, shigellosis (bacterial infection of the intestinal lining).

How it works: Each inhibits a different enzyme needed for the synthesis of active folate in the bacteria, blocking growth.

Contraindications (reasons you shouldn't take it): Hypersensitivity to drug or class, hypersensitivity to sulfonamides, megaloblastic anemia (anemia with larger than normal red blood cells), folate deficiency, G6PD deficiency.

Possible side effects and warnings: Can cause bone marrow suppression, blood dyscrasias (abnormal blood cells or cells in abnormal quantities), Stevens-Johnson syndrome and toxic epidermal necrolysis (rare but serious skin disorders), overwhelming liver necrosis, hepatitis, liver and/or kidney toxicity, kidney inflammation, colon infection, meningitis (inflammation of the membranes covering the brain and spinal cord), high potassium level, enlarged thyroid, lupus erythematosus (a chronic inflammatory disease in which the immune system attacks the body's own tissues and organs), nausea, vomiting, diarrhea, rash, hives, light sensitivity, dizziness, stomach upset, headache, and lethargy. Should be used with caution in women with bone marrow suppression or liver or kidney dysfunction.

How it can affect pregnant women: Bacteria in the urine is common during pregnancy with or without symptoms. If left untreated, 20–30% of patients go on to develop a severe kidney infection, which in turn increases the risk of preterm labor and low-birth-weight infants. Unfortunately, established first-line drugs such as amoxicillin, ampicillin, and trimethoprim-sulfamethoxazole are associated with a high rate of resistance in *E. coli,* the most common infecting bacteria, limiting the number of antibiotics for treatment. There are no adequate reports or well-controlled studies of trimethoprim-sulfamethoxazole in pregnant women. Nitrofurantoin and beta-lactam agents are other first-line agents for the treatment of asymptomatic bacteriuria.

There are no adequate reports or well-controlled studies of trimethoprim-sulfamethoxazole in pregnant women. However, the best study to date showed an increased rate of adverse events when trimethoprim was given, including preeclampsia (high blood pressure and protein in the urine during pregnancy and complications associated with it), placental abruption (the placenta separating from the uterus before delivery, often in association with high blood pressure), low birth weight, and even fetal death. A growing number of women are treated with trimethoprim in combination with an array of antivirals for HIV-related complications. The impacts of these combinations are poorly studied.

How it can affect a developing embryo or fetus: There are no adequate reports or well-controlled studies in human fetuses. Transfer of trimethoprim across the human placenta is limited. Although there is no solid evidence of resulting birth defects in humans, there is a possibility that trimethoprim is a weak human teratogen (substance that can cause birth defects) due to the way it acts. Sulfamethoxazole readily crosses the placenta, reaching a level in the fetus that is similar to that of the mother. The combination has been associated with an increased risk of low birth weight, as well as cardiovascular, neural tube, and urinary tract malformations.

Breast-feeding: There are no adequate reports or well-controlled studies in nursing women. Trimethoprim enters human breast milk, but the extent is unknown. It is unknown whether sulfamethoxazole enters human breast milk. If infant formula is available, breast-feeding is not recommended when a mother is HIV positive because HIV can be transmitted to the newborn in the breast milk.

Potential drug interactions: Interaction between the following medications and trimethoprim-sulfamethoxazole has the potential to impact the effect of one or more of the drugs. In some instances the interaction can be dangerous or life-threatening and must be avoided: phenytoin, warfarin, methotrexate, cyclosporine, digoxin, indomethacin, pyrimethamine, tricyclic antidepressants (TCAs), oral hypoglycemics.

What the FDA says about use in pregnancy: Category C (see Appendix).

What the available evidence suggests about breast-feeding safety: Unknown.

The bottom line for you:

- Studies suggest that trimethoprim-sulfamethoxazole should be avoided during pregnancy because of the risk of adverse effects to the embryo or fetus.
- There is not enough information to judge its effect on breast-feeding.
- If infant formula is available, breast-feeding is not recommended when a mother is HIV positive because HIV can be transmitted to the newborn in the breast milk.

TROVAFLOXACIN

Brand name: Trovan

Drug classes: Antibiotic; Quinolone

Indications (what it is used for): A wide range of bacterial infections.

How it works: Kills bacteria by interfering with DNA.

Contraindications (reasons you shouldn't take it): Hypersensitivity to drug or class.

Possible side effects and warnings: Can cause fatal liver toxicity, colon infection, increased intracranial pressure, seizures, psychosis, tendon rupture, pancreatic inflammation, nausea, vomiting, diarrhea, abdominal pain, headache, heartburn, restlessness, light-headedness, vaginitis, joint pain, sleeplessness, itching, anxiety, rash, and light sensitivity. Should be used with caution in women with liver or kidney dysfunction, seizures, central nervous system disorder, dehydration, or diabetes. Women taking trovafloxacin should avoid sun exposure.

How it can affect pregnant women: There is no published data with trovafloxacin during pregnancy.

How it can affect a developing embryo or fetus: There are no adequate reports or well-controlled studies in human fetuses. Trovafloxacin crosses the human placenta but is not concentrated in the fetus. Rodent studies using more than 10 times the maximum recommended clinical dose found that it was damaging to the fetus and increased the rate of birth defects such as skeletal malformations. However, animal studies are not necessarily good indicators of how a drug will behave in humans.

Breast-feeding: There is no published data in nursing women. The manufacturer reports that the levels of trovafloxacin excreted into human breast milk are clinically insignificant.

Potential drug interactions: Absorption of trovafloxacin is significantly reduced by use with antacids containing magnesium, aluminum, citric acid, sodium citrate, and/or sucralfate and iron (ferrous ions). These agents as well as formulations containing divalent and trivalent cations (e.g., didanosine) should be taken at least 2 hours before or 2 hours after trovafloxacin. IV morphine significantly reduces the absorption of oral trovafloxacin and should be administered at least 2 hours after trovafloxacin if taken while fasting, or at least 4 hours after if taken with food.

What the FDA says about use in pregnancy: Category C (see Appendix).

What the available evidence suggests about breast-feeding safety: Likely safe.

The bottom line for you:

- There are alternative medications with which there is more experience.
- Trovafloxacin should be used during pregnancy and breast-feeding only if the benefit to the

woman justifies the potential risk to the embryo, fetus, or newborn.

UREA

Brand name: Ureaphil

Drug classes: Antihypertensive; Cerebral edema

Indications (what it is used for): Increased intracranial or intraocular pressure, syndrome of inappropriate antidiuretic hormone secretion (excess release of a hypothalamus produced hormone stored in the pituitary gland that decreases urination), pregnancy termination, nail removal (topical).

How it works: Diuretic.

Contraindications (reasons you shouldn't take it): Hypersensitivity to drug or class, dehydration, liver failure, intracranial hemorrhage, kidney dysfunction, lower extremity itching or burning.

Possible side effects and warnings: Can cause headache, nausea, vomiting, fainting, disorientation, and injection site reaction. Should be used with caution in women with cardiovascular disease.

How it can affect pregnant women: There are no adequate reports or well-controlled studies of urea in pregnant women. Urea injected into the amniotic cavity effectively stimulates labor for pregnancy termination at 18–22 weeks when used with a prostaglandin. There is no published experience in pregnant women for the remaining listed indications.

How it can affect a developing embryo or fetus: There are no adequate reports or well-controlled studies in human fetuses. Urea crosses the human placenta. Urea injected into the amniotic cavity effectively stimulates labor for pregnancy termination at 18–22 weeks when used with a prostaglandin. Urea is typically lethal to the fetus when given prior to 24 weeks.

Breast-feeding: There is no published data in nursing women.

Potential drug interactions: No clinically relevant interactions identified.

What the FDA says about use in pregnancy: Category C (see Appendix).

What the available evidence suggests about breast-feeding safety: Safe.

The bottom line for you:

- The published data demonstrates that intra-amniotic urea is a valuable aid for pregnancy termination at 18–22 weeks.
- Topical urea is safe for use during pregnancy and while breast feeding.

UROKINASE

Brand name: Abbokinase

Drug classes: Anticoagulant; Thrombolytic

Indications (what it is used for): Pulmonary embolus (blood clot in the lung), coronary artery thrombosis.

How it works: Activates plasmin, a natural enzyme that breaks down clots.

Contraindications (reasons you shouldn't take it): Hypersensitivity to drug or class, stroke history, active bleeding, aneurysm, arteriovenous malformation (abnormal connection between veins and arteries), recent trauma, intracranial malignancy, ulcerative colitis, severe uncontrolled high blood pressure.

Possible side effects and warnings: Can cause bleeding, irregular heart rate, rash, bronchospasm, and injection site blood clot. Should be used with caution in women who have diabetic retinopathy, cerebrovascular disease (narrowing of blood vessels that supply the brain), or severe liver dysfunction, or who have undergone surgery or delivery within 10 days or are bleeding from a needle puncture or in the muscle from an intramuscular injection.

How it can affect pregnant women: There are no adequate reports or well-controlled studies of urokinase in pregnant women. The published literature consists of case reports of patients using urokinase to treat heart attack or blood clots in the arteries of the lungs, the brain, or the vein of the ovary either during pregnancy or after delivery. Hemorrhage from the placenta or placental bed is common when urokinase is given during pregnancy. In one series of 8 pregnant women with a blood clot in a brain artery, 2 suffered bleeding outside the brain and 2 bleeding in the brain cause by the medication.

How it can affect a developing embryo or fetus: There are no adequate reports or well-controlled studies in human fetuses. It is unknown whether urokinase crosses the human placenta. Rodent studies are reassuring, revealing no evidence of birth defects or low birth weight despite the use of doses higher than those used clinically. However, animal studies are not necessarily good indicators of how a drug will behave in humans.

Breast-feeding: There are no adequate reports or well-controlled studies in nursing women. It is unknown whether urokinase enters human breast milk. One-time urokinase use is unlikely to pose a clinically significant risk to a breast-feeding newborn.

Potential drug interactions: Interaction between the following medications and urokinase has the potential to impact the effect of one or more of the drugs. In some instances the interaction can be dangerous or life-threatening and must be avoided: drugs that alter platelet function (e.g., aspirin, indomethacin, phenylbutazone), heparin.

What the FDA says about use in pregnancy: Category B (see Appendix).

What the available evidence suggests about breast-feeding safety: Likely safe.

The bottom line for you:

- Urokinase should be used during pregnancy and while breast-feeding only for the treatment of life-threatening disease.

URSODIOL

Brand names: Actigall, Ursacol, Ursodamor

Drug classes: Gallstone solubilizer; Gastrointestinal

Indications (what it is used for): Dissolve or prevent gallstones, primary biliary cirrhosis (inflamed bile ducts of the liver), primary sclerosing cholangitis (scarring and hardening of the bile ducts), nonalcoholic fatty hepatitis.

How it works: Decreases cholesterol synthesis, secretion, and absorption.

Contraindications (reasons you shouldn't take it): Hypersensitivity to drug or class, hypersensitivity to bile acids, unremitting cholecystitis (continuous inflammation of the gallbladder), acute cholangitis, biliary obstruction, gallstone pancreatitis, biliary-GI fistula, calcified/radiopaque/radiolucent gallstones.

Possible side effects and warnings: Can cause nausea, vomiting, heartburn, abdominal pain, diarrhea, constipation, dizziness, hair loss, low white blood cell count, and cold symptoms.

How it can affect pregnant women: Ursodiol (ursodeoxycholic acid) is a naturally occurring bile acid. Small series of treated patients suggest that it can be effective for the treatment of cholestasis of pregnancy (a severe, itchy rash due to the backup of bile in the liver, most commonly occurs in the third trimester). Cholestasis of pregnancy is associated with increasing illness and even, on occasion, the death of the fetus if it is not delivered in time. After delivery the greatest risk to the mother is hemorrhage. The cause of cholestasis of pregnancy is not clear. A decrease in bile acids does not necessarily improve the disease, and planned early delivery remains the prudent medical choice. One small study concluded that combining ursodiol with S-adenosyl-L-methionine improved maternal responses to ursodiol. There is a case report of a woman with primary biliary cirrhosis treated throughout pregnancy. Ursodiol was effective in relieving her symptoms, although preterm cesarean delivery was required.

How it can affect a developing embryo or fetus: There are no adequate reports or well-controlled studies in human fetuses. Ursodiol apparently does not cross the human placenta.

Breast-feeding: Ursodiol does not enter human breast milk.

Potential drug interactions: Interaction between the following medications and ursodiol has the potential to impact the effect of one or more of the drugs. In some instances the interaction can be dangerous or life-threatening and must be avoided: bile acid–sequestering agents (e.g., cholestyramine, colestipol), aluminum-based antacids, clofibrate, estrogens, oral contraceptives, perhaps other lipid-lowering drugs.

What the FDA says about use in pregnancy: Category B (see Appendix).

What the available evidence suggests about breast-feeding safety: Safe.

The bottom line for you:

- Ursodiol is a first-line medication for the treatment of intrahepatic cholestasis of pregnancy. However, delivery remains the definitive treatment.
- Ursodiol is safe for use while breast-feeding.

VALACYCLOVIR

Brand name: Valtrex
Drug class: Antiviral
Indications (what it is used for): Genital herpes, herpes zoster.
How it works: Stops viral replication.
Contraindications (reasons you shouldn't take it): Hypersensitivity to drug or class, immune compromise.
Possible side effects and warnings: Can cause kidney failure, painful menstruation, nausea, vomiting, headache, dizziness, joint pain, depression, facial swelling, high blood pressure, rapid heart rate, rapid swelling of the layers of the skin, rash, confusion, hallucinations, aplastic anemia, low platelet and/or white blood cell count, anemia, and erythema multiforme (skin disorder). Should be used with caution in women with kidney dysfunction.
How it can affect pregnant women: Valacyclovir is effective and well tolerated for herpes virus suppression for up to 10 years of continuous use. A woman can pass herpes to her newborn in the birth canal if she has an active infection. Herpes affects 1 in 15,000 newborns. The vast majority of infected infants are born to women who are having their first herpes infection during pregnancy. Although there

are no adequate reports or well-controlled studies of valacyclovir in pregnant women, it is used extensively for the listed indications during pregnancy. When taken to prevent an outbreak at 36 weeks or later, acyclovir (the active portion of valacyclovir) reduces both the risk of a herpes outbreak in the mother and the chance she will have a positive cervical culture at delivery, which would necessitate a cesarean delivery. Newborn infection, which occurs when the baby comes in contact with the herpes virus in the birth canal, is dramatically reduced by preventative therapy.
How it can affect a developing embryo or fetus: There are no adequate reports or well-controlled studies in human fetuses. Valacyclovir crosses the human placenta. Maternal oral administration of valacyclovir leads to levels in both mother and fetus high enough to treat infection with either herpes or cytomegalovirus (CMV). However, it is unknown whether treatment of fetal CMV actually improves the newborn's outcome as it does with herpes. Studies conducted since the drug was introduced (1996) suggest that valacyclovir does not increase the risk for birth defects. Rodent studies are reassuring, revealing no evidence of birth defects or low birth weight despite the use of doses higher than those used clinically. However, animal studies are not necessarily good indicators of how a drug will behave in humans.
Breast-feeding: Valacyclovir is converted to acyclovir, which enters human breast milk. However, the amount of acyclovir in breast milk is clinically insignificant.
Potential drug interactions: No clinically relevant interactions identified.
What the FDA says about use in pregnancy: Category B (see Appendix).
What the available evidence suggests about breast-feeding safety: Safe.
The bottom line for you:

- Valacyclovir is a first-choice medication for the treatment of genital herpes and herpes zoster during pregnancy and while breast-feeding.

● Herpes prevention treatment at 36 weeks reduces the risk of an outbreak in the mother and, as a result, the need for cesarean delivery.

VALPROATE

Brand names: Depacon, Epival
Drug class: Anticonvulsant
Indications (what it is used for): Seizures.
How it works: Unknown.
Contraindications (reasons you shouldn't take it): Hypersensitivity to drug or class, liver disease or dysfunction.
Possible side effects and warnings: Can cause potentially fatal liver toxicity, pancreatitis, bone marrow suppression, aplastic anemia, low platelet count, bleeding, low sodium level, high ammonia level, erythema multiforme and Stevens-Johnson syndrome (both skin disorders), nausea, vomiting, appetite and weight changes, heartburn, abdominal pain, diarrhea, weakness, sleepiness, tremor, hair loss, rash, peripheral edema, red or purple spots caused by broken capillaries, blurred vision, involuntary eye movement, ringing in the ears, syndrome of inappropriate antidiuretic hormone secretion (excess release of a hypothalamus produced hormone stored in the pituitary gland that decreases urination), psychosis, and respiratory disorders. Should be used with caution in women with kidney dysfunction, bone marrow suppression, bleeding tendencies, or congenital metabolic disorders, or who are taking other anticonvulsants.
How it can affect pregnant women: Women on medication for a seizure disorder should (when possible) plan their pregnancies, discuss the optimal medication with their neurologist, and begin appropriate supplemental folate therapy before conception (4 mg per day) to minimize the risk of birth defects. The risks of birth defects associated with antiseizure medications must be weighed against the risks of continued seizures to both the mother and fetus. Women who become pregnant during treatment should not stop treatment on their own but

rather meet quickly with their doctor before making a decision.

Valproate is modified valproic acid. There are no adequate reports or well-controlled studies of valproate in pregnant women. There is, however, a long clinical experience with valproate that shows that it is effective in preventing seizures during pregnancy but does have fetal risks (see below). It does not alter the effectiveness of hormonal contraception.
How it can affect a developing embryo or fetus: Valproate is rapidly and actively transported across the human placenta and concentrated in the fetus. Valproate is a recognized cause of birth defects in humans. The fetal effects of valproate include abnormal facial features coupled with a group of birth defects especially involving the central nervous system function, where it increases the risk of spina bifida (an opening in the spine) by about 4 times. The risk is further increased if a pregnant woman has a low level of folate in her blood. Valproate is more likely than carbamazepine to cause birth defects, and the combination of valproate and lamotrigine is even more likely to cause a defect. The higher the dose, the greater the likelihood. A daily dose of valproate more than 1,000 mg is associated with an 8 times increase in risk. Ten percent of newborns with defects due to valproate die in infancy, and a quarter of the survivors have developmental deficits or mental retardation. Affected fetuses may have an abnormal ultrasound at 12 weeks (showing an increased thickness at the back of the neck). A fetal medicine specialist should evaluate the pregnancies of all women who become pregnant while taking valproate.

As for most psychotropic drugs, if this medication is needed, the use of one medication and the lowest effective quantity given in divided doses to minimize the medication peaks in the mother can theoretically reduce the risks to a fetus. In one study, fetuses exposed to more than one anticonvulsant had significantly lower IQs than those exposed to only one drug. In fact, using more than one drug increased the negative effect on IQ more than using high doses of only one drug. Compared with carbamazepine on its own, valproate alone is associated with significantly lower mental and motor developmental scores.

Breast-feeding: Valproate enters human breast milk, but the newborn concentration is low.

Potential drug interactions: New interactions with valproate are constantly being reported. It is important that your doctor and pharmacist know all medications (prescription and over-the-counter) you are taking. So far, we know that interaction between valproate and the following medications has the potential to impact the affect of one or more of the drugs. In some instances, the interaction can be dangerous or life-threatening and must be avoided: drugs that affect the level of expression of liver enzymes, particularly those that elevate levels of glucuronosyltransferases (e.g., carbamazepine, phenobarbital, primidone, phenytoin); aspirin; felbamate; rifampin; amitriptyline; nortriptyline; clonazepam; diazepam; ethosuximide; lamotrigine; barbiturates; zidovudine.

What the FDA says about use in pregnancy: Category D (see Appendix).

What the available evidence suggests about breast-feeding safety: Safe.

The bottom line for you:

- Valproate is a recognized human teratogen (substance that can cause birth defects). The risk of a defect is increased in pregnant women who have a folate deficiency and may be reduced by pre-pregnancy treatment of 4 mg of folate per day.
- Valproate should be used during pregnancy only if the benefit to the woman justifies the potential risk to the embryo or fetus.
- When valproate treatment cannot be avoided in the first trimester, the medication should be used alone if possible, and the lowest effective dose should be prescribed in divided doses to minimize the peaks of medication in the mother's system and possibly reduce the associated risks.
- Women who become pregnant while taking valproate should not discontinue the medication on

their own but should speak immediately with their health-care provider about the best course of action to take for their health and that of their embryo or fetus.

- Valproate is safe for use while breast-feeding.

VALPROIC ACID
Brand names: Depakene, Myproic acid
Drug classes: Anticonvulsant; Bipolar agent; Migraine agent
Indications (what it is used for): Seizures, mania, prevention of migraine.
How it works: Unknown.
Contraindications (reasons you shouldn't take it): Hypersensitivity to drug or class, liver disease or dysfunction.
Possible side effects and warnings: Can cause potentially fatal liver toxicity, pancreatitis, bone marrow suppression, aplastic anemia, low platelet count, bleeding, low sodium level, high ammonia level, erythema multiforme and Stevens-Johnson syndrome (both skin disorders), nausea, vomiting, appetite and weight changes, heartburn, abdominal pain, diarrhea, weakness, sleepiness, tremor, hair loss, rash, swelling of the hands and feet, red or purple spots caused by broken capillaries, blurred vision, involuntary eye movement, ringing in the ears, syndrome of inappropriate antidiuretic hormone secretion (excess release of a hypothalamus produced hormone stored in the pituitary gland that decreases urination), psychosis, and respiratory disorders. Should be used with caution in women with kidney dysfunction, bone marrow suppression, bleeding tendencies, or congenital metabolic disorders, or who are taking other anticonvulsants.
How it can affect pregnant women: Women on medication for a seizure disorder should (when possible) plan their pregnancies, discuss the optimal medication with their neurologist, and begin appropriate supplemental folate therapy before conception (4 mg per day) to minimize the risk of birth defects. The risks of birth defects associated with

antiseizure medications must be weighed against the risks of continued seizures to both the mother and fetus. Women who become pregnant during treatment should not stop treatment on their own but rather meet quickly with their doctor before making a decision.

How it can affect a developing embryo or fetus: Valproic acid is rapidly and actively transported across the human placenta and concentrated in the fetus. Valproic acid is a recognized cause of birth defects in humans. The fetal effects of valproic acid include abnormal facial features, coupled with a group of birth defects especially involving the central nervous system function where it increases the risk of spina bifida (an opening in the spine) by about 4 times. The risk is further increased if a pregnant woman has a low level of folate in her blood. Valproic acid is more likely than carbamazepine to cause birth defects, and the combination of valproate (which is a modified form of valproic acid) and lamotrigine is even more likely to cause a defect. The higher the dose, the greater the likelihood. Ten percent of newborns with defects due to valproic acid die in infancy, and a quarter of the survivors have developmental deficits or mental retardation. Affected fetuses may have an abnormal ultrasound at 12 weeks (showing an increased thickness on the back of the neck). A fetal medicine specialist should evaluate the pregnancies of all women who become pregnant while taking valproic acid.

As for most psychotropic drugs, the use of one medication and the lowest effective quantity given in divided doses to minimize the medication peaks can theoretically reduce the risks. In one study, fetuses exposed to more than one anticonvulsant had significantly lower IQs than those exposed to only one drug. In fact, using more than one drug increased the negative effect on IQ more than using high doses of only one drug. Compared with carbamazepine on its own, valproic acid alone is associated with significantly lower mental and motor developmental scores.

Breast-feeding: Valproic acid enters human breast milk, but the newborn concentration is low.

Potential drug interactions: New interactions with valproic acid are constantly being reported. It is important that your doctor and pharmacist know all medications (prescription and over-the-counter) you are taking. So far, we know that interaction between valproic acid and the following medications has the potential to impact the affect of one or more of the drugs. In some instances, their interaction can be dangerous or life-threatening and must be avoided: drugs that affect the level of expression of liver enzymes, particularly those that elevate levels of glucuronosyltransferases (e.g. carbamazepine, phenobarbital, primidone, phenytoin); aspirin; felbamate; rifampin; amitriptyline; nortriptyline, clonazepam; diazepam; ethosuximide; lamotrigine; barbiturates; zidovudine.

What the FDA says about use in pregnancy: Category D (see Appendix).

What the available evidence suggests about breast-feeding safety: Safe.

The bottom line for you:

- Valproic acid is a recognized human teratogen (substance that can cause birth defects). The risk of a defect is increased in pregnant women who have a folate deficiency and may be reduced by prepregnancy treatment of 4 mg of folate per day.

- Valproic acid should be used during pregnancy only if the benefit to the woman justifies the potential risk to the embryo or fetus.

- If valproic acid treatment cannot be avoided in the first trimester, the medication should be used alone if possible, and the lowest effective dose should be prescribed in divided doses to minimize the peaks in the mother's system and possibly reduce the associated risks.

- Women who become pregnant while taking valproic acid should not discontinue the medication on their own but should speak immediately with their health-care provider about the best course of action to take for their health and that of their embryo or fetus.

- Valproic acid is safe for use while breast-feeding.

VANCOMYCIN

Brand names: Balcorin, Edicin, Ledervan, Lyphocin, Vancocin, Vancoled, Vancor

Drug classes: Antibiotic; Glycopeptide

Indications (what it is used for): Bacterial infection, prevention of bacterial endocarditis (infection of the heart valve).

How it works: Kills bacteria by interfering with protein synthesis.

Contraindications (reasons you shouldn't take it): Hypersensitivity to drug or class.

Possible side effects and warnings: Can cause Stevens-Johnson syndrome and toxic epidermal necrolysis (both rare but serious skin disorders), low platelet and/or white blood cell count, kidney toxicity, ringing in the ears, ear toxicity, chills, fever, nausea, superinfection, hives, rash, "red man" syndrome (flushing and/or a red rash on the face, neck, and upper torso), and blood clots. Should be used with caution in women with liver or kidney dysfunction or hearing loss, or who are taking drugs that are toxic to the kidneys.

How it can affect pregnant women: Vancomycin is most commonly used for the treatment of MRSA (methicillin-resistant *Staphylococcus aureus*) infection, a superbug that is becoming increasingly more common because of the inappropriate widespread use of antibiotics. There are no adequate reports or well-controlled studies of vancomycin in pregnant women. In one series of patients studied, adverse events were common, suggesting that the drug should be given slower than usual. It is used as a second-line agent for the treatment of postpartum uterine infection and as a first-line agent and alternative to metronidazole for the treatment of *C. difficile* diarrhea. Other applications during pregnancy include *Listeria* infection and bacterial endocarditis in IV drug users.

How it can affect a developing embryo or fetus: There are no adequate reports or well-controlled studies in human fetuses. Vancomycin crosses the human placenta, achieving concentrations that exceed the level required to kill group B streptococcus (an infection a mother can pass to her newborn that requires preventative treatment). Rodent studies are reassuring, revealing no evidence of birth defects or low birth weight despite the use of doses higher than those used clinically. However, animal studies are not necessarily good indicators of how a drug will behave in humans.

Breast-feeding: There are no adequate reports or well-controlled studies in nursing women. Vancomycin enters human breast milk but how much is unclear. Considering that little vancomycin is absorbed out of the gut after swallowing, it is unlikely that a breast-fed newborn would achieve a clinically relevant level no matter how much he or she swallowed.

Potential drug interactions: Interaction between the following medications and vancomycin has the potential to impact the effect of one or more of the drugs. In some instances the interaction can be dangerous or life-threatening and must be avoided: other drugs that are potentially toxic to the nervous system or the kidneys (e.g., aminoglycosides, amphotericin B, bacitracin, cisplatin, colistin, polymyxin B, viomycin).

What the FDA says about use in pregnancy: Category B (see Appendix).

What the available evidence suggests about breast-feeding safety: Safe.

The bottom line for you:

- Vancomycin should be used during pregnancy only if the benefit to the woman justifies the potential risk to the embryo or newborn. It should probably be reserved for antibiotic-resistant bacterial infections.
- Vancomycin is safe for use while breast-feeding.

VARICELLA VACCINE

Brand name: Varivax

Drug class: Vaccine

Indications (what it is used for): Prevention of varicella (chickenpox).

How it works: Prevents symptomatic disease by stimulating immunity.

Contraindications (reasons you shouldn't take it): Hypersensitivity to drug or class; various blood disorders; leukemia, lymphomas, or other malignancies affecting the bone marrow or lymphatic systems; immune suppression or compromise (acquired or congenital); fever; active tuberculosis.

Possible side effects and warnings: Can cause fever, injection site reactions, blisters, upper and lower respiratory illness, headache, fatigue, cough, muscle pain, disturbed sleep, nausea, vomiting, lethargy, diarrhea, stiff neck, irritability/nervousness, swollen lymph nodes, chills, eye complaints, abdominal pain, loss of appetite, joint pain, ear infection, itching, other rashes, constipation, and allergic reactions. Should be used with caution in women with acute lymphocytic leukemia that is in remission.

How it can affect pregnant women: Varicella (chickenpox) is a cause of significant maternal and fetal sickness and death around the world. However, 70% of women in North America who do not remember having childhood varicella are actually immune. It is wise for women of reproductive age who are planning to become pregnant to be tested for immunity and then be vaccinated, if necessary, prior to conception. It is estimated that doing so would prevent half the cases of newborns born with varicella.

There are no adequate reports or well-controlled studies of varicella vaccine in pregnant women. Varicella vaccine is a live, modified vaccine, and live vaccines are usually contraindicated (not recommended) during pregnancy because fetal infection can occur.

How it can affect a developing embryo or fetus: There are no adequate reports or well-controlled studies in human fetuses. It is unknown whether the attenuated virus in the varicella vaccine crosses the placenta. The natural, unmodified virus (if a pregnant woman were to contract varicella) does cross the placenta and causes birth defects in humans. The areas affected by varicella include central (brain and spine) and peripheral nerves. The frequency of birth defects from varicella is low because fetuses exposed to the virus between 16 and 38 weeks are unlikely to develop defects. Inadvertent immunization during pregnancy is not associated with birth defects and is not an indication for pregnancy termination. A voluntary Pregnancy Registry established by the manufacturer (Merck) recorded 981 women inadvertently vaccinated during the first trimester between 1995 and 2005, whose pregnancy outcomes were known. There was no evidence of fetal varicella disease and the birth defect rate was a normal 3.7%. Fetal exposure to varicella vaccine does not necessarily provide lifelong immunity.

Breast-feeding: There is no published data with varicella vaccine in nursing women. According to one study by the manufacturer, the modified virus is not excreted into human breast milk and none of the infants who have been studied developed antibodies to varicella. In contrast, infection with the natural, unmodified virus (if a nursing woman contracted chickenpox) is associated with the excretion of virus into human breast milk, which can cause newborn infection.

Potential drug interactions: No clinically relevant interactions identified.

What the FDA says about use in pregnancy: Category C (see Appendix).

What the available evidence suggests about breast-feeding safety: Likely safe.

The bottom line for you:

- Varicella (chicken pox) during pregnancy can cause severe maternal or fetal illness and death.
- Varicella vaccine consists of a live virus and should not be used during pregnancy.
- Women should be checked for immunity to varicella prior to conception and get vaccinated if necessary.

- Pregnant women who have not been vaccinated for varicella probably should be tested during pregnancy and, if negative, vaccinated after delivery.
- Accidental immunization during pregnancy is not associated with fetal disease.
- Breast-feeding is likely safe after vaccination.

VARICELLA-ZOSTER IMMUNE GLOBULIN

Brand names: Varitect, VZIG
Drug class: Immune globulin
Indications (what it is used for): Prevention of varicella (chickenpox).
How it works: Prevents infection after a known exposure by providing the antibodies that neutralize the varicella virus.
Contraindications (reasons you shouldn't take it): Hypersensitivity to drug or class, severe low platelet count if given intramuscularly (VZIG).
Possible side effects and warnings: Can cause redness or swelling at the injection site, constipation, weakness, headache, rash, difficulty breathing/shortness of breath, and rapid swelling of the layers of the skin.
How it can affect pregnant women: Varicella is a cause of significant maternal and fetal sickness and death around the world. However, 70% of women in North America who do not remember having childhood varicella are actually immune. It is wise for women of reproductive age who are planning to become pregnant to be tested for immunity and, if necessary, be vaccinated prior to conception. It is estimated that doing so would prevent half the cases of newborns born with varicella. Varicella pneumonia is the most serious maternal complication of varicella during pregnancy. Smokers and women with more than 100 "poxes" are at particular high risk of developing varicella pneumonia. There are no adequate reports or well-controlled studies of varicella-zoster immune globulin in pregnant women. There is no evidence that its administration

to a susceptible pregnant woman prevents maternal infection; rather, the goal is to lessen the severity of her disease. Varicella-zoster immune globulin administered within 24 hours of exposure to the virus may reduce the severity of maternal disease and is typically coupled with a course of acyclovir to inhibit replication of the virus.
How it can affect a developing embryo or fetus: Varicella travels through the bloodstream to the placenta, where it can infect the fetus and cause disease and birth defects. There are no adequate reports or well-controlled studies of varicella-zoster immune globulin in human fetuses. It is likely that it crosses the human placenta, but it is unknown whether such transfer conveys a level of immunity to the fetus. Newborns are more likely to have a severe case of varicella if the mother's symptoms appear 5 days prior to delivery or within 2 days after delivery. Newborns of women who develop varicella 7 days before or up to 28 days after delivery should be given varicella-zoster immune globulin to decrease the severity of illness. Studies of newborns suggest that the combination of immune globulin and acyclovir is more effective than either one alone.
Breast-feeding: There are no adequate reports or well-controlled studies in nursing women. It is unknown whether varicella-zoster immune globulin enters human breast milk. Other IgG immunoglobulins do, and breast-feeding is encouraged as a potential way to provide immunity to a newborn.
Potential drug interactions: Varicella-zoster immune globulin may reduce the response to live vaccines.
What the FDA says about use in pregnancy: No assigned category (see Appendix).
What the available evidence suggests about breast-feeding safety: Safe.
The bottom line for you:
- Varicella (chickenpox) during pregnancy can cause severe maternal or fetal illness and death.
- Varicella-zoster immune globulin is safe for use during pregnancy and while breast-feeding.

- Susceptible women and their fetuses or newborns may benefit from varicella-zoster immune globulin and acyclovir given within 24 to 48 hours after exposure to the virus.

VECURONIUM

Brand names: Musculax, Norcuron

Drug classes: Anesthetic, adjunct; Neuromuscular blocker, nondepolarizing; Skeletal muscle relaxant

Indications (what it is used for): To create paralysis usually during surgery.

How it works: Blocks nerve impulse transmission by motor nerves.

Contraindications (reasons you shouldn't take it): Hypersensitivity to drug or class, bronchogenic carcinoma (lung cancer).

Possible side effects and warnings: Can cause irregular, rapid, or slow heart rate; low blood pressure; bronchospasm; and flushing. Should be used with caution in women with liver dysfunction or who have low blood volume.

How it can affect pregnant women: Vecuronium prevents the transmission of a nerve impulse needed for muscle contraction. There are no adequate reports or well-controlled studies of vecuronium in pregnant women. It is popular during cesarean delivery performed under general anesthesia.

How it can affect a developing embryo or fetus: There are no adequate reports or well-controlled studies in human fetuses. A very limited amount of vecuronium crosses the human placenta. It is also given directly to the fetus as an alternative to pancuronium during fetal surgical procedures. In contrast to pancuronium, vecuronium has no effect on fetal heart rate. This is an advantage for many procedures, but it is a potential drawback when used with fetal intravascular transfusion performed for Rh disease. Rodent birth defect studies have not been performed.

Breast-feeding: There is no published data in nursing women. It is unknown whether vecuronium enters human breast milk. Considering the one-time use before delivery, it is unlikely to pose a clinically significant risk to a breast-feeding newborn.

Potential drug interactions: Interaction between the following medications and vecuronium has the potential to impact the effect of one or more of the drugs. In some instances the interaction can be dangerous or life-threatening and must be avoided: succinylcholine, other nondepolarizing neuromuscular blocking agents (e.g., gallamine, metocurine, pancuronium, d-tubocurarine), other competitive muscle relaxants, certain antibiotics (e.g., aminoglycosides [dihydrostreptomycin, gentamicin, kanamycin, neomycin, streptomycin], bacitracin, colistin, colistimethate, polymyxin B, tetracyclines), quinidine, magnesium sulfate.

What the FDA says about use in pregnancy: Category C (see Appendix).

What the available evidence suggests about breast-feeding safety: Safe.

The bottom line for you:

- Vecuronium is a useful aid to general anesthesia during pregnancy for delivery and when given to the fetus directly for fetal surgical procedures.
- Vecuronium use for a surgical procedure will not affect breast-feeding.

VENLAFAXINE

Brand names: Effexor, Trewilor

Drug class: Antidepressant, miscellaneous

Indications (what it is used for): Depression.

How it works: Blocks the nerve uptake of various neurotransmitters to alter mood.

Contraindications (reasons you shouldn't take it): Hypersensitivity to drug or class, monoamine oxidase inhibitor (MAOI) use within 14 days.

Possible side effects and warnings: Can cause seizures, headache, nausea, vomiting, diarrhea, sleepiness, loss of appetite, weight loss, constipation, anxiety, blurred vision, dizziness, dry mouth, sleeplessness, high blood pressure, and sweating. Should be used with caution in women with liver or kidney dysfunction, seizures, or history of mania, or who have serious thoughts of suicide.

How it can affect pregnant women: Depression is common during and after pregnancy but often goes unrecognized and untreated. Depression can be made worse by pregnancy or delivery, and suicide is a not uncommon cause of maternal death. Pregnancy is not a reason to discontinue antidepressant drugs if the medication is effective and needed. A woman being treated for depression who becomes pregnant should not discontinue medication abruptly on her own but rather discuss her treatment and condition with her medical provider. Pregnancy may increase the dose needed to be effective, and women with a history of depression have a higher rate of recurrence after delivery.

There are no adequate reports or well-controlled studies of venlafaxine in pregnant women. Blood levels appear to decline between the first to third trimesters, suggesting that the dose will need adjustment to continue to be effective. Venlafaxine may be effective for the treatment of other conditions during pregnancy, including obsessive-compulsive disorder, panic disorder, eating disorders, substance abuse, headaches, hot flashes, and chronic pain. SNRIs as a group have been associated with an increased risk of high blood pressure during pregnancy and preeclampsia (high blood pressure and protein in the urine during pregnancy plus the complications associated with it).

How it can affect a developing embryo or fetus: There are no adequate reports or well-controlled studies in human fetuses. Venlafaxine and its active metabolites (products that it is broken down into in the body) cross the human placenta, reaching the same level in the fetus as in the mother. Studies report no increase in birth defects. There are reports that newborns of women who took venlafaxine during pregnancy had temporary behavioral symptoms that resolved shortly after birth. Rodent studies are generally reassuring, revealing no evidence of birth defects despite the use of doses higher than those used clinically. Low birth weight did occur in some animal studies. However, animal studies are not necessarily good indicators of how a drug will behave in humans.

Breast-feeding: A small amount of the maternal dose of venlafaxine is excreted into breast milk; however, measurable levels of the drug were found in half the breast-fed newborns studied. As a result, breast-fed babies should be monitored closely for any adverse effects.

Potential drug interactions: Interaction between the following medications and venlafaxine has the potential to impact the effect of one or more of the drugs. In some instances the interaction can be dangerous or life-threatening and must be avoided: cimetidine, haloperidol, CYP2D6 inhibitors.

What the FDA says about use in pregnancy: Category C (see Appendix).

What the available evidence suggests about breast-feeding safety: Possibly safe.

The bottom line for you:

- Pregnancy is not a reason to discontinue medication for depression if it is both needed and effective.
- Venlafaxine may be used during pregnancy and while breast-feeding if the mother is receiving benefit from the medication. Nursing infants should be monitored for excessive sedation.
- As for most psychotropic drugs, using only one medication at the lowest effective quantity given in divided doses to minimize the medication peaks in the mother's system may reduce any risks to the embryo or fetus.

VERAPAMIL

Brand names: Calan, Calan SR, Cardiabeltin, Covera-HS, Isoptin, Isoptin SR, Verelan, Verpal

Drug classes: Antiarrhythmic, class IV; Antihypertensive; Calcium channel blocker

Indications (what it is used for): Angina, high blood pressure, heart rate abnormalities, migraine prevention.

How it works: Blocks or slows muscle contraction by inhibiting the flow of calcium into the muscle cell.

Contraindications (reasons you shouldn't take it): Hypersensitivity to drug or class, severe low blood pressure, cardiogenic shock, severe left-sided heart failure, abnormal heart rate rhythms.

Possible side effects and warnings: Can cause congestive heart failure, severe low blood pressure, irregular or severe slow heart rate, constipation, dizziness, nausea, headache, swelling, and fatigue. Should be used with caution in women with a slow heart rate, congestive heart failure, liver or kidney dysfunction, muscular dystrophy (a serious muscle-wasting disease), myasthenia gravis (an autoimmune disease causing muscle weakness), or gastroesophageal reflux disease (GERD).

How it can affect pregnant women: In addition to the indications listed above, verapamil is used for the treatment of bipolar disorder and to slow pre-term labor. There are no adequate reports or well-controlled studies of verapamil in pregnant women. Nor are there any randomized or case-controlled studies of verapamil as the primary drug to slow preterm labor, and the practice of combining it with a beta-blocker has been appropriately abandoned as unproved. Isolated case reports describe the successful use of verapamil to treat certain types of a rapid heart rate during pregnancy. There are also reports of its use to treat preeclampsia (high blood pressure and protein in the urine during pregnancy and complications associated with it), although there is no indication that it offers advantages over other more commonly used blood-pressure-lowering medications. Recently, a relationship between oral erythromycin and sudden cardiac death was reported in patients also receiving strong CYP3A inhibitors (e.g., verapamil, diltiazem, nitroimidazole, antifungal agents, troleandomycin). Pregnant women are often prescribed erythromycin following preterm premature rupture of the membranes (PPROM, water breaking before 37 weeks), so it is important to know if a woman is taking verapamil during pregnancy.

How it can affect a developing embryo or fetus: There are no adequate reports or well-controlled studies in human fetuses. Verapamil readily crosses the human placenta, reaching a level in the fetus that is about 70% of the maternal level. Verapamil has been given during pregnancy to treat a dangerously high fetal heart rate, but it is unclear how effective this approach is. However, direct administration to the fetus by injection has been done successfully. Rodent studies are generally reassuring, revealing no birth defects despite the use of doses higher than those used clinically; miscarriage and low birth weight did occur. However, animal studies are not necessarily good indicators of how a drug will behave in humans.

Breast-feeding: There are no adequate reports or well-controlled studies in nursing women. The amount of verapamil excreted into human breast milk is clinically insignificant.

Potential drug interactions: Interaction between the following medications and verapamil has the potential to impact the effect of one or more of the drugs. In some instances the interaction can be dangerous or life-threatening and must be avoided: CYP3A4 inhibitors (e.g., erythromycin, ritonavir), CYP3A4 inducers (e.g., rifampin), beta-adrenergic blockers, metoprolol, propranolol, atenolol, digoxin, oral antihypertensive agents (blood-pressure-lowering medications; e.g., ACE inhibitors, beta-blockers, diuretics, vasodilators), flecainide, lithium, carbamazepine, phenobarbital, cyclosporine, theophylline. May increase blood alcohol concentrations and prolong its effects.

What the FDA says about use in pregnancy: Category C (see Appendix).

What the available evidence suggests about breast-feeding safety: Safe.

The bottom line for you:

- There are alternative medications with which there is more experience.
- Verapamil should be used during pregnancy only if clearly indicated.

- Oral erythromycin should be avoided in women receiving verapamil. Ampicillin plus sulbactam is the preferred treatment for women who are taking verapamil and have PPROM.
- Verapamil is safe for use while breast-feeding.

VIDARABINE
Brand name: Vira-A
Drug classes: Antiviral; Ophthalmic
Indications (what it is used for): HSV epithelial keratitis (ulceration of the cornea), keratoconjunctivitis (viral infection of the eye), encephalitis (inflammation of the brain).
How it works: Inactivates the virus by blocking DNA synthesis.
Contraindications (reasons you shouldn't take it): Hypersensitivity to drug or class, sterile trophic ulcers.
Possible side effects and warnings: Can cause tearing, foreign body sensation, burning, light sensitivity, and superficial punctuate keratitis (inflammation of the outer layer of the eye).
How it can affect pregnant women: There is no published data with vidarabine for the above indications during pregnancy. Acyclovir is now used to treat many of the conditions vidarabine was previously used for.
How it can affect a developing embryo or fetus: There are no adequate reports or well-controlled studies in human fetuses. It is unknown whether vidarabine crosses the human placenta. Vidarabine caused birth defects in rodents after intravenous administration, because it appeared to interfere with the transport of important nucleic acid building blocks across the placenta. However, it is unlikely that the maternal systemic concentration will reach a clinically relevant level if the medicine is applied topically. Vidarabine is used for newborn treatment.
Breast-feeding: There is no published data in nursing women. It is unknown whether vidarabine enters human breast milk. Topical use is unlikely to pose a clinically significant risk to a breast-feeding newborn.
Potential drug interactions: No clinically relevant interactions identified.
What the FDA says about use in pregnancy: Category C (see Appendix).
What the available evidence suggests about breast-feeding safety: Likely safe (topical); unknown (IV use).
Bottom line for you:
- Vidarabine should be used during pregnancy and breast-feeding only if the benefit to the woman justifies the potential risk to the embryo, fetus, or newborn.

VINCRISTINE
Brand names: Citomid, Oncovin, Vincasar PFS, Vincrex
Drug class: Antineoplastic, antimitotic
Indications (what it is used for): Trophoblastic disease (tumors in the uterus), Hodgkin's disease (a type of cancer of the lymphatic system), leukemia, non-Hodgkin's lymphoma (cancer of the lymphoid tissue), neuroblastoma (a type of cancer in nerve tissue), rhabdomyosarcoma (cancer of muscles that are attached to bones), Wilms' tumor (a type of cancer of the kidney).
How it works: Blocks cell replication.
Contraindications (reasons you shouldn't take it): Hypersensitivity to drug or class, new bacterial infection, bowel obstruction or paralysis, demyelinating Charcot-Marie-Tooth disease (muscle weakness and loss of sensation in various body parts).
Possible side effects and warnings: Can cause bone marrow suppression, peripheral nerve damage, bowel paralysis, intestinal breakdown, central nerve palsy, seizures, bronchospasm, heart attack, syndrome of inappropriate antidiuretic hormone secretion (excess release of a hypothalamus produced hormone stored in the pituitary gland that decreases urination), infertility, hair loss, nausea, vomiting,

loss of appetite, constipation, diarrhea, fatigue, tingling, dizziness, involuntary eye movement, blood clots, lack of gross-muscle control, blood pressure changes, weakness, and electrolyte abnormalities. Should be used with caution in women with bone marrow suppression, neuromuscular disease, pulmonary disease, liver dysfunction, or CYP3A4 interactions, or who are taking drugs that are toxic to the nervous system.

How it can affect pregnant women: There are no adequate reports or well-controlled studies of vincristine in pregnant women. The literature consists of isolated case reports and series of women typically treated during pregnancy for leukemia or lymphoma.

How it can affect a developing embryo or fetus: There are no adequate reports or well-controlled studies in human fetuses. It is unknown whether vincristine crosses the human placenta. Most fetuses that have been exposed are delivered without apparent adverse effects. Vincristine did cause miscarriage or birth defects in rodents, and in a small study, had the same effect in primates. However, animal studies are not necessarily good indicators of how a drug will behave in humans. Fetuses who are exposed to vincristine should be evaluated by a skilled perinatologist for any possible adverse effects.

Breast-feeding: There is no published data in nursing women. It is unknown whether vincristine enters human breast milk.

Potential drug interactions: Vincristine may reduce phenytoin blood levels and increase seizure activity.

What the FDA says about use in pregnancy: Category D (see Appendix).

What the available evidence suggests about breast-feeding safety: Unknown.

The bottom line for you:
- Vincristine should be used during pregnancy and while breast-feeding only when required to treat life-threatening maternal disease.
- Exposure to vincristine in the uterus appears for the most part to be well tolerated and is not an

indication for pregnancy termination, although it does necessitate a thorough exam by a skilled perinatologist.

VITAMIN A, see BETA-CAROTENE
VITAMIN B$_1$, see THIAMINE
VITAMIN B$_5$, see PANTOTHENIC ACID
VITAMIN B$_6$, see PYRIDOXINE
VITAMIN C, see ASCORBIC ACID
VITAMIN D, see CALCIFEDIOL, ERGO-CALCIFEROL
VITAMIN K$_1$, see PHYTONADIONE

WARFARIN

Brand names: Coumadin, Jantoven
Drug classes: Anticoagulant; Thrombolytic
Indications (what it is used for): Anticoagulation, therapeutic and prevention.
How it works: Blocks vitamin K, which is required for the production of several key clotting factors.
Contraindications (reasons you shouldn't take it): Hypersensitivity to drug or class, active bleeding, recent surgery, low platelet count, vitamin K deficiency, use of other anticlotting drugs, recent lumbar puncture, congenital clotting defect.
Possible side effects and warnings: Can cause bleeding, skin necrosis, rash, diarrhea, nausea, abdominal pain, and liver or skin inflammation. Should be used with caution in women who have had recent surgery or who have infection, heparin-induced low platelet count, protein C or S deficiency, liver dysfunction, high blood pressure, or congestive heart failure.
How it can affect pregnant women: Pregnant women are at greater risk for blood clots during pregnancy, because estrogen increases the blood's ability to clot in arteries and veins. There are no adequate reports or well-controlled studies of warfarin in pregnant women. It is most likely that a woman who had a prior blood clot more than a year before her pregnancy and does not have a clotting disorder does not require treatment during her pregnancy. However, women with a clot within the pre-

vious year or who have a clotting disorder require preventative treatment during pregnancy. Women who experience a blood clot during a current pregnancy should remain on anticoagulant medication until at least 6 weeks after delivery.

Warfarin is typically not used during pregnancy unless the mother has an artificial heart valve because of an increased risk of bleeding (as many as 1 out of 5 women being treated with warfarin during pregnancy will have a bleeding complication) and a risk for fetal birth defects (see "How it can affect a developing embryo or fetus" below). A daily dose of warfarin greater than 5 mg is associated with a greater risk of adverse pregnancy outcomes.

Women without an artificial heart valve already taking warfarin and planning a pregnancy should consult with a perinatologist or a hematologist and switch, if possible, to a heparinoid medication prior to conception. If a pregnant woman's condition requires warfarin, it should be replaced with heparin at 36 weeks to decrease the risk to the fetus during birth and then resumed after delivery. Both epidural and spinal anesthesia are contraindicated (should not be used) in women being treated with warfarin because of the risk of puncture-associated bleeding.

Women with an autoimmune disorder associated with blood clots (antiphospholipid syndrome) or who have suffered a prior blood clot should probably be anticoagulated for the rest of their lives. However, there is no consensus on the optimal approach for women with obstetric manifestations of antiphospholipid syndrome (recurrent miscarriage, intrauterine fetal death, low birth weight, preterm birth). Some experts recommend aspirin plus heparin; others consider aspirin alone useful for women with recurrent early miscarriage only.

Women with a mechanical artificial heart valve require special mention. The risk of blood clots in these women if they are not treated with anticoagulants is very high, and heparin does not work as well as warfarin. Miscarriage rates are as high as 37% when warfarin is taken in the first trimester. Some experts therefore recommend heparin anticoagula-

tion during the first trimester and again 4 weeks prior to delivery, with warfarin being used in the intervening time.

How it can affect a developing embryo or fetus: Warfarin is a known teratogen (substance that can cause birth defects). Although there are no adequate reports or well-controlled studies in human fetuses, exposure from 6 to 10 weeks of pregnancy is associated with damage to the embryo; thereafter, exposure is associated with damage to the fetus. Doctors describe the possible defects caused by warfarin as fetal warfarin syndrome, which includes failure of the nasal septum to develop, small eyes, underdeveloped limbs, low birth weight, heart defects, scoliosis [abnormal curving of the spine], deafness, and mental retardation. Warfarin can also cause central nervous system defects including incomplete brain development.

Although damage to the embryo is due to vitamin K deficiency (warfarin blocks the synthesis of vitamin K), the fetal damage results from numerous small hemorrhages that occur as a result of anticoagulation in the fetus. In a large series of women treated throughout pregnancy for a mechanical heart valve, the overall incidence of fetal warfarin syndrome was 5.6%. The pregnancy loss rate was 32%, and the stillbirth rate was 10% of pregnancies that made it to 20 weeks' gestation. School-age children who were exposed to warfarin while in the uterus had an increased frequency of an IQ below 80 (normal range above 90).

Breast-feeding: Warfarin does not enter human breast milk and is compatible with breast-feeding.

Potential drug interactions: An extremely large number of drugs, homeopathic herbs, and diseases alter the effect of warfarin. It is important that your doctor and pharmacist know of all drugs (prescription and over the counter) you are taking. The following list includes drugs more commonly used or diseases encountered during pregnancy that can alter the degree of anticoagulation produced by a dose of warfarin. *Drugs:* 5-lipoxygenase inhibitors, adrenergic stimulants (central), analgesics, inhalation anesthetics, antiandrogens, antiarrhythmics, anti-coagulants, anticonvulsants, antidepressants, anti-malarial agents, antineoplastics, antiparasitics/antimicrobials, antiplatelet drugs, antithyroid drugs, beta-adrenergic blockers, cholelitholytic agents, oral hypoglycemic agents, diuretics, systemic fungal medications, gastric acidity and peptic ulcer agents, GIs (prokinetic agents and ulcerative colitis agents), gout treatment agents, hepatotoxic drugs, hypergly-cemic agents, hypertensive emergency agents, hyp-notics, leukotriene receptor antagonists, monoamine oxidase inhibitors (MAOIs), prolonged use of narcot-ics, nonsteroidal anti-inflammatory drugs (NSAIDs), pyschostimulants, pyrazolones, salicylates, selective serotonin reuptake inhibitors (SSRIs), corticoste-roids, anabolic steroids (17-alkyl testosterone deriva-tives), thrombolytics, thyroid drugs, tuberculosis agents, uricosuric agents, vaccines, vitamins, hypo-lipidemics, bile acid–binding resins, fibric acid de-rivatives, HMG-CoA reductase inhibitors, aspirin. *Diseases:* cancer, collagen vascular disease, conges-tive heart failure, diarrhea, elevated temperature, hy-perthyroidism, poor nutritional state, vitamin K deficiency, infectious hepatitis, jaundice.

What the FDA says about use in pregnancy: Cat-egory X (see Appendix).

What the available evidence suggests about breast-feeding safety: Safe.

The bottom line for you:

- Warfarin may cause birth defects following ex-posure anytime in pregnancy. A daily dose that is greater than 5 mg creates the highest risk. It should be used during pregnancy only if the ma-ternal benefit justifies the potential risk to the embryo or fetus. If required, it should be re-placed with heparin at 36 weeks and resumed after delivery.
- It is probably best to substitute heparin (thera-peutic levels) for warfarin, especially during the first trimester in women with a mechanical heart valve.
- Warfarin is safe for use while breast-feeding.

ZAFIRLUKAST

Brand name: Accolate

Drug classes: Antiasthmatic; Leukotriene antago-nist

Indications (what it is used for): Asthma preven-tion.

How it works: Leukotriene D4 and E4 receptor antagonist.

Contraindications (reasons you shouldn't take it): Hypersensitivity to drug or class, acute asthma.

Possible side effects and warnings: Can cause blood vessel inflammation, headache, runny nose, nausea and vomiting, diarrhea, pain, weakness, ab-dominal pain, dizziness, muscle ache, fever, back pain, liver dysfunction, and heartburn. Should be used with caution in women with liver dysfunction or who are tapering off steroid treatment.

How it can affect pregnant women: Asthma is a common disease in life and in pregnancy. Approxi-mately one-third of pregnant women with asthma get worse during pregnancy, one-third get better, and one-third remain clinically unchanged. When asthma is well controlled it does not affect preg-nancy outcome, but poorly controlled asthma may increase the risk of preterm birth (before 37 weeks) or low birth weight. Inhaled corticosteroids are con-sidered the preventative medication of choice for pregnant women with persistent asthma unless their condition is well controlled by cromolyn or nedo-cromil. Budesonide and beclomethasone are consid-ered the first-line treatments.

Certain medications used during labor and deliv-ery have the potential to worsen asthma, including nonselective beta-blockers, some prostaglandins (used to induce labor), and ergonovine (used to con-trol blood loss after delivery).

There is limited published data with zafirlukast during pregnancy. Leukotriene receptor antagonists are probably safe during pregnancy but should be limited to special circumstances where they are viewed essential for asthma control.

How it can affect a developing embryo or fetus: There are no adequate reports or well-controlled

studies in human fetuses. It is unknown whether zafirlukast crosses the human placenta. In one report, the outcomes among 96 women who took a leukotriene receptor antagonist (LTRA) (montelukast or zafirlukast) were compared with women who exclusively took short-acting beta-agonists and women without asthma. LTRA use was not associated with an increased risk of pregnancy loss, gestational diabetes, preeclampsia, low maternal weight gain, preterm delivery, low Apgar scores (a measure of how well the newborn adjusts to life outside the womb), or decreased birth length and head circumference. The rate of major birth defects in the LTRA group was 5.95%, which was higher than the women who did not have asthma but not different from the group with asthma who were treated with beta-agonists. Further, the defects observed in the LTRA group did not follow a consistent pattern (which means it is difficult to say that the medication caused the defects). Overall, the available studies suggest that LTRAs are not a major human teratogen (substance that can cause birth defects). Rodent and primate studies are reassuring, revealing no evidence of birth defects or low birth weight despite the use of doses higher than those used clinically (except in cases of doses high enough to cause maternal toxicity). However, animal studies are not necessarily good indicators of how a drug will behave in humans.

Breast-feeding: There is no published data in nursing women. Zafirlukast is excreted into human breast milk in low concentrations.

Potential drug interactions: Interaction between the following medications and zafirlukast has the potential to impact the effect of one or more of the drugs. In some instances the interaction can be dangerous or life-threatening and must be avoided: warfarin, erythromycin, theophylline, aspirin.

What the FDA says about use in pregnancy: Category B (see Appendix).

What the available evidence suggests about breast-feeding safety: Likely safe.

The bottom line for you:

- There are other medications for the treatment of asthma with which there is more experience.
- Zafirlukast and other leukotriene receptor antagonists are probably safe during pregnancy but should be reserved for situations where they are essential for asthma control.
- Zafirlukast is probably safe for use while breast-feeding.

ZALCITABINE

Brand names: DDC, ddC, Dideoxycytidine, Hivid
Drug classes: Antiviral; NRTI (nucleoside reverse transcriptase inhibitor)
Indications (what it is used for): Advanced HIV infection.
How it works: Prevents the virus from using the cell machinery to replicate.
Contraindications (reasons you shouldn't take it): Hypersensitivity to drug or class.
Possible side effects and warnings: Can cause seizures, a buildup of lactic acid in the blood, low platelet and/or low white blood cell count, anemia, high eosinophil (a type of white blood cell) count, peripheral nerve damage, liver dysfunction, fatigue, nausea, vomiting, abdominal pain, diarrhea, constipation, rash, itching, hives, oral lesions, depression, headache, fever, cough, and runny nose. Should be used with caution in women with liver or kidney dysfunction, peripheral nerve damage, congestive heart failure, or a history of pancreatitis.
How it can affect pregnant women: Treating HIV during pregnancy significantly reduces the risk of a mother transmitting the virus to her child. There are no adequate reports or well-controlled studies of zalcitabine in pregnant women. Triple therapy (lamivudine, nevirapine, zidovudine) remains the standard treatment for HIV infection during pregnancy. Zalcitabine is a second choice if the woman does not respond to zidovudine.
How it can affect a developing embryo or fetus: There are no adequate reports or well-controlled

studies in human fetuses. It is unknown whether zalcitabine crosses the human placenta; it does cross the primate placenta. Rodent studies showed an increase in birth defects when doses 1,000 times the maximum recommended clinical dose were used. However, animal studies are not necessarily good indicators of how a drug will behave in humans.

Breast-feeding: There are no adequate reports or well-controlled studies in nursing women. It is unknown whether zalcitabine enters human breast milk. If infant formula is available, breast-feeding is not recommended when a mother is HIV positive because HIV can be transmitted to the newborn in the breast milk.

Potential drug interactions: Interaction between the following medications and zalcitabine has the potential to impact the effect of one or more of the drugs. In some instances the interaction can be dangerous or life-threatening and must be avoided: lamivudine, drugs that have the potential to cause peripheral neuropathy (e.g., antiretroviral nucleoside analogues, chloramphenicol, cisplatin, dapsone, disulfiram, ethionamide, glutethimide, gold, hydralazine, iodoquinol, isoniazid, metronidazole, nitrofurantoin, phenytoin, ribavirin, vincristine), drugs that have the potential to cause pancreatitis (e.g., pentamidine), amphotericin, foscarnet, aminoglycosides, probenecid, cimetidine. Absorption is moderately reduced when zalcitabine is given with magnesium- and/or aluminum-containing antacids.

What the FDA says about use in pregnancy: Category C (see Appendix).

What the available evidence suggests about breast-feeding safety: Not safe.

The bottom line for you:

- Combination therapy with zidovudine, lamivudine, and nevirapine significantly reduces the risk of a mother transmitting HIV to her child and remains the standard of care for management of HIV infection during pregnancy.
- Zalcitabine is an alternative reverse transcriptase inhibitor in patients unresponsive to zidovudine.

- If infant formula is available, breast-feeding is not recommended when a mother is HIV positive because HIV can be transmitted to the newborn in the breast milk.
- Women who are taking antiretroviral medication during pregnancy are encouraged to register with the Antiretroviral Pregnancy Registry (1-800-258-4263) to help increase the information available about taking these medications during pregnancy. The registry can also be a source of information for women considering, or undergoing, antiretroviral treatment during pregnancy.

ZALEPLON

Brand name: Sonata

Drug classes: Anxiolytic; Hypnotic

Indications (what it is used for): Short-term treatment of insomnia.

How it works: Interacts with the GABA/benzodiazepine receptor complex to trigger the onset of sleep.

Contraindications (reasons you shouldn't take it): Hypersensitivity to drug or class.

Possible side effects and warnings: Can cause dependency, drowsiness, amnesia, tingling, abnormal vision, dizziness, headache, hangover, and confusion. Should be used with caution in women with liver dysfunction or lung disease, or who have a history of substance abuse.

How it can affect pregnant women: There is no published data with zaleplon during pregnancy.

How it can affect a developing embryo or fetus: There are no adequate reports or well-controlled studies in human fetuses. It is unknown whether zaleplon crosses the human placenta.

Breast-feeding: The small quantities of zaleplon that are excreted into human breast milk are clinically irrelevant.

Potential drug interactions: Interaction between the following medications and zaleplon has the potential to impact the effect of one or more of the drugs. In some instances the interaction can be dangerous or life-threatening and must be avoided: ethanol (alcohol), imipramine, thioridazine, cimetidine.

What the FDA says about use in pregnancy: Category C (see Appendix).

What the available evidence suggests about breast-feeding safety: Safe.

The bottom line for you:

- There are alternative agents with which there is more experience during pregnancy.
- Zaleplon is safe for use while breast-feeding.

ZANAMIVIR

Brand name: Relenza

Drug class: Antiviral

Indications (what it is used for): Uncomplicated influenza.

How it works: Blocks the influenza enzyme neuraminidase that is critical for the virus to replicate.

Contraindications (reasons you shouldn't take it): Hypersensitivity to drug or class, chronic obstructive pulmonary disease (COPD), asthma, inability to use inhaler.

Possible side effects and warnings: Can cause bronchospasm, nausea, dizziness, headache, bronchitis, cough, nasal symptoms, and ear/nose/throat infection.

How it can affect pregnant women: There is no published data with zanamivir during pregnancy. Pregnant women are at increased risk of complications from flu, including pneumonia and death, placing the health of their fetuses at similar risk. The CDC states that pregnancy is not a reason to avoid using zanamivir, as the benefits of the medication outweigh the risks. However, vaccination prior to influenza season is recommended for all pregnant women who can safely take the vaccine.

How it can affect a developing embryo or fetus: There are no adequate reports or well-controlled studies in human fetuses. It is unknown whether zanamivir crosses the human placenta. The CDC

states that pregnancy is not a reason not to take zanamivir because the benefits outweigh the risks. Zanamivir does cross the rodent placenta. Rodent studies are for the most part reassuring, with only minor skeletal abnormalities noted in one strain of rat when the dose exceeded 1,000 times the maximum recommended clinical dose. However, animal studies are not necessarily good indicators of how a drug will behave in humans.

Breast-feeding: There is no published data in nursing women. It is unknown whether zanamivir enters human breast milk.

Potential drug interactions: No clinically relevant interactions identified.

What the FDA says about use in pregnancy: Category C (see Appendix).

What the available evidence suggests about breast-feeding safety: Unknown.

The bottom line for you:

- Zanamivir is considered safe and effective for use during pregnancy and while breast-feeding.
- Unless there is a contraindication (reason a woman should not receive the vaccination), all pregnant women should receive the influenza vaccine.

ZIDOVUDINE

Brand names: Aviral, AZT, Retrovir, Retrovis

Drug classes: Antiviral; NRTI (nucleoside reverse transcriptase inhibitor)

Indications (what it is used for): HIV infection.

How it works: Prevents the virus from using the cell machinery to replicate.

Contraindications (reasons you shouldn't take it): Hypersensitivity to drug or class, severe bone marrow suppression.

Possible side effects and warnings: Can cause bone marrow suppression, anemia, low platelet count, seizures, pancreatitis, muscle damage, buildup of lactic acid in the blood, liver toxicity, nausea, vomiting, abdominal pain, diarrhea, headache, weakness, rash, fever, loss of appetite, somnolence, muscle ache,

522 | The Complete Guide to Medications During Pregnancy and Breast-feeding

malaise, heartburn, profuse sweating, shortness of breath, taste changes, pigmented nails, and tingling. Should be used with caution in women with liver or kidney dysfunction.

How it can affect pregnant women: Treating HIV during pregnancy significantly reduces the risk of a mother transmitting the virus to her child. Combination therapy (lamivudine, nevirapine, zidovudine) remains the standard treatment during pregnancy due to its high efficacy. Ideally, infected women remain on the drug cocktail throughout pregnancy, reaching a point where the virus is no longer detectable in their blood. At that time, the risk of transmitting the infection to their children is minimal.

Zidovudine administration during labor reduces the chance of the mother passing the virus to her child by nearly 70%. When zidovudine is combined with other antiretroviral drugs (protease inhibitors), the effectiveness is almost 90%. The addition of nevirapine to the standard IV zidovudine labor regimen further reduces HIV transmission to the newborn in women who did not receive antiretroviral therapy during pregnancy. The addition of (additional) nevirapine is not beneficial when the woman has been taking triple therapy (lamivudine, nevirapine, zidovudine) throughout pregnancy. It is possible in developed countries to lower the transmission rate from mother to child to below 4% using combinations of available medications. The newborn infection rate in women with detectable levels of virus in their bloodstream is lowered by elective cesarean section before labor begins. Women should be monitored closely for liver toxicity after zidovudine is started.

How it can affect a developing embryo or fetus: Zidovudine and its major metabolites (products that the drug is broken down to in the body) rapidly cross the human placenta, achieving levels in the fetus that are the same as those in the mother. Maternal antiretroviral drug therapy during pregnancy and labor, followed by 6 weeks of zidovudine treatment in the newborn, significantly reduces the risk of the newborn acquiring the infection during deliv-

ery. Additional antiretroviral drugs may be needed in some high-risk newborns. Elective cesarean section prior to the onset of labor also reduces the rate of newborn infection if there is a detectable level of virus in the mother's blood.

Breast-feeding: There is no published data in nursing women. It is unknown whether zidovudine enters human breast milk. If infant formula is available, breast-feeding is not recommended when a mother is HIV positive because HIV can be transmitted to the newborn in the breast milk.

Potential drug interactions: Interaction between the following medications and zidovudine has the potential to impact the effect of one or more of the drugs. In some instances the interaction can be dangerous or life-threatening and must be avoided: stavudine; doxorubicin; some nucleoside analogues affecting DNA replication, such as ribavirin; ganciclovir; interferon alfa; other bone marrow–suppressing medications.

What the FDA says about use in pregnancy: Category C (see Appendix).

What the available evidence suggests about breast-feeding safety: Not safe.

The bottom line for you:

- Triple therapy consisting of zidovudine, lamivudine, and nevirapine significantly lowers the amount of virus in the mother's bloodstream and in doing so reduces the risk of HIV transmission to her child. This therapy should be standard in all women identified to have HIV infection.

- Women with a detectable level of virus at the time of delivery (or unknown status) should receive a short course of zidovudine or a single dose of nevirapine during labor to reduce mother–child transmission of HIV.

- If infant formula is available, breast-feeding is not recommended when a mother is HIV positive because HIV can be transmitted to the newborn in the breast milk.

- Women taking antiretroviral drugs during pregnancy are encouraged to register with the Antiretroviral Pregnancy Registry (1-800-258-4263) to help increase the available information about the use of antiretroviral medication during pregnancy. The registry can also be a source of information for women considering, or undergoing, antiretroviral treatment during pregnancy.

ZOLMITRIPTAN

Brand names: Zomig, Zomigoro

Drug classes: Migraine agent; Serotonin receptor agonist

Indications (what it is used for): Migraine headache.

How it works: Selectively activates a serotonin receptor, which causes blood vessels in the head to constrict and relieves the headache.

Contraindications (reasons you shouldn't take it): Hypersensitivity to drug or class, coronary artery disease, coronary vasospasm, history of heart attack, uncontrolled high blood pressure, basilar migraine, hemiplegic migraine; use of a 5-HT1 agonist within 24 hours, a monoamine oxidase inhibitor (MAOI) within 14 days, or an ergot compound within 24 hours.

Possible side effects and warnings: Can cause acute heart attack, irregular heart rate, angina, brain hemorrhage, stroke, severe high blood pressure, peripheral vascular or bowel ischemia, weakness, nausea, vomiting, dizziness, chest pain, neck and jaw tightness, sleepiness, sweating, palpitations, and muscle ache. Should be used with caution in women with risk factors for heart disease or who have liver dysfunction, severe kidney disease, or peripheral or cerebrovascular disease (reduced blood flow to the limbs or brain).

How it can affect pregnant women: Fifty to 90% of women who suffer migraines experience improvement during pregnancy, mainly during the second and third trimesters. A higher percentage of women who have menstrual migraine experience this improvement compared to women with other types of migraines. There is no published data with zolmitriptan during pregnancy. Triptans, as a group, may be associated with preterm birth and are best avoided at the extremes of prematurity (before 28 weeks) until more data is available.

How it can affect a developing embryo or fetus: There are no adequate reports or well-controlled studies in human fetuses. It is unknown whether zolmitriptan crosses the human placenta. Rodent studies reported miscarriage and skeletal abnormalities when doses more than 500 times the maximum recommended clinical dose were used. However, animal studies are not necessarily good indicators of how a drug will behave in humans.

Breast-feeding: There is no published data in nursing women. It is unknown whether zolmitriptan enters human breast milk. However, considering the nature of treatment, one-time or occasional zolmitriptan use is unlikely to pose a clinically significant risk to a breast-feeding baby.

Potential drug interactions: Interaction between the following medications and zolmitriptan has the potential to impact the effect of one or more of the drugs. In some instances the interaction can be dangerous or life-threatening and must be avoided: ergotamine-containing or ergot-type medications (e.g., dihydroergotamine, methysergide), monoamine oxidase inhibitors (MAOIs), cimetidine, selective serotonin reuptake inhibitors (SSRIs; e.g., fluoxetine, fluvoxamine, paroxetine, sertraline); 5-HT1 agonists.

What the FDA says about use in pregnancy: Category C (see Appendix).

What the available evidence suggests about breast-feeding safety: Likely safe.

The bottom line for you:

- There are alternative medications with which there is more experience during pregnancy. If they fail, zolmitriptan is likely safe for use.

- Triptans, as a group, may be associated with preterm birth and are best avoided at the extremes of prematurity (before 28 weeks) until more data is available.

- Limited zolmitriptan is likely safe to use while breast-feeding.

ZOLPIDEM

Brand name: Ambien

Drug classes: Anxiolytic; Hypnotic

Indications (what it is used for): Short-term treatment of insomnia.

How it works: Interacts with GABA/benzodiazepine receptor complex to trigger the onset of sleep.

Contraindications (reasons you shouldn't take it): Hypersensitivity to drug or class.

Possible side effects and warnings: Can cause lack of gross-muscle control, hallucinations, headache, drowsiness, tiredness, depression, dizziness, cold-like symptoms, sinusitis, sore throat, dry mouth, nausea, heartburn, diarrhea, constipation, palpitations, and joint/back/muscle pain. Should be used with caution in women with depression or substance abuse, or who have impaired breathing.

How it can affect pregnant women: There are no adequate reports or well-controlled studies of zolpidem in pregnant women. However, it has been widely used during pregnancy.

How it can affect a developing embryo or fetus: There are no adequate reports or well-controlled studies in human fetuses. Zolpidem crosses the human placenta, reaching levels in the fetus that are similar to those in the mother. Rodent studies are reassuring, revealing no evidence of birth defects or low birth weight despite the use of doses higher than those used clinically. Prenatal exposure to zolpidem did not affect behavioral stress reactivity in adult male rats. However, animal studies are not necessarily good indicators of how a drug will behave in humans.

Breast-feeding: The quantity of zolpidem excreted into human breast milk is likely clinically insignificant with occasional use.

Potential drug interactions: Interaction between the following medications and zolpidem has the potential to impact the effect of one or more of the drugs. In some instances the interaction can be dangerous or life-threatening and must be avoided: ethanol (alcohol), fluoxetine, sertraline, any drug that depresses the central nervous system, rifampin, flumazenil.

What the FDA says about use in pregnancy: Category C (see Appendix).

What the available evidence suggests about breast-feeding safety: Likely safe.

The bottom line for you:

- Behavioral modification including avoidance of caffeine and a dark quiet room should be used first to promote sleep.
- Zolpidem is likely safe for occasional use during pregnancy and while breast-feeding.

Acknowledgments

This has been a long-term endeavor. I would like to thank my spouse, Carol, for her patience, support and, when needed, kindness. This book is the direct descendant of a text I first wrote with my good friend and colleague, Dr. Catalin Buhimschi. I want to recognize his efforts and along with those of our textbook publisher, Elsevier, who graciously approved of my vision for a patient version. Having a vision is one thing, but producing a readable book for the patient is another. It simply would not have been possible without my writing partner, Kate Rope, who has tutored me nonstop on communication.

I want to recognize you, the purchaser and mother to be, as you struggle through the fog of information and misinformation overload to decide the best course for you and your child. Our goal is to aid your journey.

Lastly, I need to thank the following people whose activities were crucial. Danielle Svetcov at Levine Greenberg for becoming our agent and for providing an active voice for the book. Nichole Argyres, our editor at St. Martin's, whose deft hand always improved. Laura Chasen at St. Martin's, who kept us on task and, finally, St. Martin's Press for seeing the need for information that could not be fit into a snappy little brochure or a one-line Internet search. Thank you all.
—Carl P. Weiner, M.D.

I want to profusely thank the first person who made me believe that I could safely take care of myself and my babies, the unflappable Chad Klauser, M.D., who brought my first daughter into this world, was one of the first people to meet my second daughter, and always answered (and still does) my panicked e-mails promptly. Thank you, Chad. Like pregnant and breast-feeding women the world over, I owe Carl Weiner, M.D., (and also his colleague, Catalin Buhimschi, M.D.) a debt of gratitude for seeking answers to questions that most leave unanswered. Assembling the information women and doctors need to make the best choices possible was a monumental task, and I am grateful to Carl for undertaking it and for trusting me to help him translate it.

My soulmate, David, earns my gratitude daily, but here I want to thank him for living up to vow number 8 and supporting me through this entire time-consuming endeavor. Likewise, I am grateful daily that I get to share this world with my wonderful, thoughtful, joyful girls, A and H, and I must thank them for providing me with enough material for a career in pregnancy and parenting health journalism. I promise to share any royalties.

A not-so-small village took care of those girls while I worked on this book, for which I am so appreciative. You know who you are, but the lion's share of the work was done by Bill and Priscilla Rope, Deborah Gilmartin, and Heather Torriero. Thank you for the peace and quiet. And thank you, DD, for helping me find another kind of peace that made this book possible.

Others who deserve thanks for helping this book reach your local bookstore include: Lewis Buzbee, for helping me find my first agent; Danielle Svetcov at Levine Greenberg, for being that agent and working so hard for us; St. Martin's Press, for recognizing the overwhelming need for this book; Nichole Argyres, our editor, for believing in us and working with us to make the text exactly what we wanted; Laura Chasen, for all of her upbeat and prompt organizational help.

And I want to acknowledge moms and dads everywhere who work so hard every day to take care of themselves and their kids. It is no easy task, but it is a privilege.

—Kate Rope

FDA Pregnancy Risk Categories and Percentage of Drugs in Each

Category A Controlled studies in women fail to demonstrate a risk to the fetus in the first trimester (and there is no evidence of a risk in later trimesters), and the possibility of fetal harm appears remote.

Category B Either animal-reproduction studies have not demonstrated a fetal risk but there are no controlled studies in pregnant women, or animal-reproduction studies have shown an adverse effect (other than a decrease in fertility) that was not confirmed in controlled studies in women in the first trimester (and there is no evidence of a risk in later trimesters).

Category C Either study in animals has revealed adverse effects on the fetus (teratogenic or embryocidal or other) and there are no controlled studies in women, or studies in women and animals are not available. Drugs should be given only if the potential benefit justifies the potential risk to the fetus.

Category D There is positive evidence of human fetal risk, but the benefits from use in pregnant women may be acceptable despite the risk (e.g., if the drug is needed in a life-threatening situation or for a serious disease for which safer drugs cannot be used or are ineffective).

Category X Studies in animals or human beings have demonstrated fetal abnormalities, or there is evidence of fetal risk based on human experience or both, and the risk of the use of the drug in pregnant women clearly outweighs any possible benefit. The drug is contraindicated in women who are or may become pregnant.

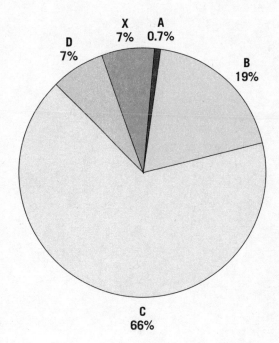

Index

---

selective estrogen receptor modulator (SERM),
    tamoxifen, 472–73
selective serotonin reuptake inhibitor (SSRI)
    citalopram, 104–5
    escitalopram, 175–76
    fluoxetine, 199–200
    paroxetine, 380–81
    sertraline, 454–55
selenium sulfide topical, 453
Selsun. *See* selenium sulfide topical
semisynthetic human insulin, 245–46
senna, 453–54
Senna-Gen. *See* senna
Senokot. *See* senna
Sensorcaine. *See* bupivacaine
sepsis. *See* antiseptic
Septra DS/SS/IV. *See* trimethoprim-sulfamethoxazole
Seranase. *See* haloperidol
Serax. *See* oxazepam
Serevent. *See* salmeterol, inhaled
SERM. *See* selective estrogen receptor modulator
Seromycin. *See* cycloserine
Seroquel. *See* quetiapine
serotonin receptor agonist
    almotriptan, 24–25
    eletriptan, 166–67
    naratriptan, 338–39
    ondansetron, 365–66
    rizatriptan, 445–46
    sumatriptan, 470–71
    tegaserod, 474–75
    zolmitriptan, 523–24
serotonin receptor antagonist
    alosetron, 25–26
    dolasetron mesylate, 159
    granisetron hydrochloride, 218
Serpalan. *See* reserpine
Serpasil. *See* reserpine
Serpatabs. *See* reserpine
Serpate. *See* reserpine
Serpivite. *See* reserpine
sertraline, 454–55
sevoflurane, 455–56
Sevorane. *See* sevoflurane
sibutramine, 456–57
Sideril. *See* trazodone
sildenafil, 457
Silvadene. *See* silver sulfadiazine topical

Silvazine. *See* silver sulfadiazine topical
silver nitrate, 457–58
silver sulfadiazine topical, 458
simethicone, 458–59
Simulect. *See* basiliximab
simvastatin, 459–60
Sinequan. *See* doxepin
Sinomin. *See* sulfamethoxazole
sirolimus, 460–61
skeletal muscle relaxant, vecuronium,
    512
Socotrine. *See* aloe vera
sodium ferric gluconate, 461
Soma. *See* carisoprodol
Somac. *See* pantoprazole
Sonata. *See* zaleplon
Sorine. *See* sotalol
sotalol, 461–62
Sparine. *See* promazine
spasms. *See* antispasmodic
Spectazole. *See* econazole nitrate
spectinomycin, 462–63
spectrum of outcomes, 7
SSD. *See* silver sulfadiazine topical
SSRI. *See* selective serotonin reuptake inhibitor
St. John's wort, 463–64
Stadol. *See* butorphanol
Staphcillin. *See* methicillin
Starlex. *See* nateglinide
statin
    atorvastatin, 42–43
    lovastatin, 285–86
Statobex. *See* phendimetrazine
Stelazine. *See* trifluoperazine
Stilphostrol. *See* diethylstilbestrol
stimulant
    CNS
        amphetamine-dextroamphetamine, 34
        caffeine, 65
        caffeine plus ergotamine, 65–66
        dexmethylphenidate, 135–36
        dextroamphetamine, 136
        diethylpropion, 144–45
        mazindol, 288–89
        methamphetamine, 306–7
        methylphenidate, 316–17
        modafinil, 329–30
        nicotine, 348